W9-BXY-992

INFINITE ELVIS

AN ANNOTATED BIBLIOGRAPHY

MARY HANCOCK HINDS

Library of Congress Cataloging-in-Publication Data
Hinds, Mary Hancock.
    Infinite Elvis : an annotated bibliography / by Mary Hancock Hinds.
        p. cm.
    Includes bibliographical references and index.
    ISBN 1-55652-410-2
    1. Presley, Elvis, 1935–1977—Bibliography. I. Title.
ML 134.5.P73 H56 200
016.78242166'092—dc21

                                                              00-043063

Cover photo courtesy of Elvis Presley Enterprises, Inc.
Cover and interior design by Rattray Design.

Published by A Cappella Books,
an imprint of Chicago Review Press, Incorporated
814 North Franklin Street
Chicago, IL 60610
ISBN 1-55652-410-2
Printed in the United States of America
5 4 3 2 1

To the greater glory of God.
In memory of Ross Katsuro Keikikamalu Miho, Honolulu, Hawaii, (1967–1986).
In celebration of Jocelyn Gabriele Yarbrough and Sasha Ivanov Wilkinson.
A portion of the profits from this book will be donated to the Elvis Presley Charitable Foundation for the Presley Place transitional housing village.

About This Book

IN ALL THINGS created by man, perfection is unattainable. Especially counting and organizing Elvis literature. Thus, *Infinite Elvis* is not billed as Definitive! Complete! or All That Anyone Will Ever Need! Such an accounting is impossible. Elvis titles, like their subject, are everywhere—and just as difficult to pin down. Pick a metaphor—gathering spilled mercury, herding cats, counting angels on the head of a pin—and you have defined the problem of rounding up all Elvis titles and making them stay put.

Prior to *Infinite Elvis*, no one knew how many books, periodicals, plays, articles, and academic documents had been produced about the man—or of their vast number and varied topics. And, with its publication, we still do not know for sure because Elvis literature is so multitudinous and pervasive.

So what can *Infinite Elvis* offer? A complete-as-possible collection of titles exhaustively gleaned during a concentrated two-year period, using sources ranging from the Library of Congress to eBay on-line auctions to Hollywood Boulevard bookstores—compiled to give the reader enough information to search for more.[1]

Confirming that titles existed was a major challenge during this trek. Many of the Elvis authors self-publish or use small publishers, which results in limited press runs and circulation. Others have republished their Elvis books numerous times, often changing only the title. Adding to this is the lazy scholarship of some Elvis authors whose bibliographies contain misinformation, misspellings, and titles that read "Elvis" but have nothing to do with Mr. Presley. Therefore, every title in *Infinite Elvis* has been verified as to existence, contents, and publication information. Those that were not are listed in Part VI, chapter 48, "Unverified Titles."

This verification was accomplished through a number of methods. For a title to be included in *Infinite Elvis*, it must have been: 1) catalogued in a public, national, or academic library; 2) in a private collection; 3) listed in a credible database such as the OCLC[2]; 4) verified by its author or seller; or, 5) held in the hands of the compiler.

---

[1] Because of the volume of material, articles that were not about Elvis per se (i.e., reviews of his records or of books about him) were omitted. The articles that appear in this book are those that were considered most useful to readers and relevant to the demonstration of Elvis's importance in our culture.

[2] OCLC (Online Computer Library Center, Inc.) is a nonprofit research organization whose on-line bibliographic database WorldCat, the world's largest and most comprehensive, links more than 30,000 libraries in 65 countries.

The purpose of this collecting and confirming was not to be the first with the longest list. Instead, it was to erect a solid launching pad from which scholars, librarians, the media, Elvis fans, and curious readers could soar into their own realms of Elvis interest.

So use and enjoy this book as you travel to the many areas of the Elvis literature world. And don't forget to write home with news of what you find along the way.

☆   ☆   ☆   ☆

To the best of the compiler's knowledge, the information in this book is current as of January 2000. Additional titles and information will be added to future editions.

And, as the editorial deadline for this book was met, even more Elvis titles were spewing forth with a reproductive fervor matched only by *Fantasia*'s multiplying brooms.

Contents

Prologue

The Importance of the Elvis Literature

Taking Elvis seriously is difficult to do. The orgiastic media coverage of the 1997 twentieth anniversary of his death—several thousand print stories alone according to Nexis—underscores this challenge. With headlines such as the *Los Angeles Times* "A Hunka, Hunka Elvisosity" and bizarre mainstream TV in which *CBS News* Bill Geist earnestly asked Elvis scholar Marjorie Wilkinson, "Is Elvis alive?"—how can the man ever be considered anything other than a weird pop anomaly?

But when Elvis literature numbers more than 1,700 verified titles—and major universities are offering thoughtful courses and academic conferences relating to him—it is time to dust off the phrase "paradigm shift."

Overall, Elvis literature demonstrates that he is one of the important catalysts of the radical cultural, historical, and societal transformations of the second half of the twentieth century: civil rights, women's liberation, the sexual revolution, the changing context of religion, the end of American regionalism, and, of course, the dominance of rock 'n' roll music over all other genres. Even his death is authoritatively cited as the event that made the mainstream media's ferocious fascination with celebrity respectable. (Neal and Janice Gregory, *When Elvis Died.*)

Indeed, a close study of Elvis literature teaches us not only about the man but also about our history and ourselves.

The first Elvis literature coincided with his meteoric rise to fame in 1956. Some was publicity hype. But in it were the first hints of Elvis's eventual significance.

In 1958 Ruth Pearl Granetz of the University of Chicago wrote her M.A. thesis, "The Symbolic Significance of the Elvis Presley Phenomenon to Teen-Age Females: A Study in Hero Worship Through the Media of Popular Singers and Song." Since then, at least 35 other thesis and dissertation writers have used Elvis to expand upon disciplines ranging from architecture to race relations to religion.

The feminine response chronicled in Granetz's paper was the precursor of the freedoms and rights that women would demand and gain in the coming decades. Elvis was arousing them to the possibilities.

Psychologist Peter Whitmer Ph.D. describes Elvis as "a totemic object to guide the way" for "women to express pure emotion and assert their rights of their gender. . . . The impact of his music would feed the flames, creating a worldwide conflagration of feminist social expression. The women's liberation movement, with sexuality as its heartbeat, is a direct beneficiary of Elvis Presley and still breathes life into his image today." (*The Inner Elvis: A Psychological Biography of Elvis Aaron Presley.*)

Firsthand evidence of this is found in the photographs of Alfred Wertheimer (*Elvis '56: In the Beginning*, Macmillan, 1979) and Jay B. Leviton (*Elvis Close-Up*, Simon and Schuster, 1988). These images palpably capture the remarkable emotional release and disregard for inhibition expressed by Elvis's fans during his 1950s concerts. The photographs still tingle the spine of the 1990s viewer.

In the struggle for racial equality and civil rights, Elvis was a lightning rod. He was discovered by Sun Records legendary founder, Sam Phillips, who was looking for a white singer who naturally sounded—not as a mimic—like a black artist. (Bill E. Burk, *Early Elvis: The Sun Years.*) Thus, the 1950s music that Elvis recorded for Phillips had an "African American sound" that was enthusiastically and predominantly embraced by Caucasian teenagers.

Eldridge Cleaver, writing in *Soul on Ice*, described Elvis as "sowing new seeds of a new rhythm and style in the white souls of white America whose inner hunger and need was no longer satisfied with the white shoes and whiter songs of Pat Boone. . . . [Elvis and others] dared to do in the light of day what America had long been doing in the sneak thief anonymity of night—consorted on a human level with the blacks" (pp. 194–195).

With Elvis's songs and style, the barriers between the races began to experience structural tremors. It was difficult to maintain racial separatist attitudes when so-called "black music and rhythm" stirred your white teenage soul and hormones.

The stirring of these souls and hormones created a volatile mixture. The feelings and drives that had been bottled up for centuries by religious and societal stricture were ready to blow. Elvis's music—with its not-so-subtle rhythms and innuendo, coupled with the freedom that women felt to display their rawest emotions in his presence—popped the cork.

The result: "white bodies that would become aroused by the sexualities riding the back of black rhythms—sexualities that would possess them as though they were its personal devotees," according to Jon Michael Spencer, professor of American studies and music at the University of Richmond. ("Elvis Presley and the White Acquiescence of Black Rhythms," Chadwick, *In Search of Elvis.*)

It took the media a while to completely absorb the impact of Elvis. In fact, it would not occur until he was gone. Early media coverage of Elvis in the 1950s focused on his "questionable" on-stage behavior, impact on teens, music and motion pictures, and U.S. Army service. Many thoughtful periodicals such as *Harper's* and *The New Republic* printed articles that sought to make sense of the Elvis phenomena. However, by the 1960s and 1970s, the reporting was primarily outside of the mainstream, sinking into gossip, sneering, and show business hype.

But something happened to mainstream media on August 16, 1977, the day Elvis died. When the sun came up the next morning, the legitimate press's undying and rampant love affair with celebrity had been born. For the first time, NBC and ABC news programs led with a show business celebrity's death. The tragic death of Princess Diana and the consuming media coverage that followed are the descendants of that hot August day.

The death of Elvis was not the demise of his role as societal vanguard. Those managing his estate would add to Elvis's impact on our culture. The financial world remains in awe of the resuscitation of Elvis's rapidly dwindling estate into an expanding empire worth millions. It stands as a casebook study for current and future CEOs.

Postmortem Elvis has made legal history as well. Pioneering a new area of trademark law, Elvis Presley Enterprises, Inc. (EPE, Inc.)—which manages his estate—has successfully lobbied for legislation and sought court decisions that now allow heirs of the famous to inherit the rights to the celebrity's name, image, and likeness. (Trademark law expert David Wall studies this in depth in his soon-to-be published *Policing the Soul of Elvis*.)

Then there is religion. Through the unparalleled enthusiasm and long-standing devotion of Elvis's fans, are we witnessing the birth of a new religious movement? Noted British author and award-winning BBC religion journalist Ted Harrison has written provocatively about this transmutation: "Perhaps [Elvis] reaches through to the eternal spirit in all of us, which yearns for truth, meaning, and purpose in a cruel, incomprehensible, and uncomprehending world. The worship, adoration, and the perpetuation of the memory of Elvis today closely resembles a religious cult. Indeed, what is now the Elvis cult could be nothing less than a religion in embryo." (*Elvis People: The Cult of the King*.)

The international range of the Elvis religious writings offers clues to his worldwide pervasiveness—and to the significant role he played in post–World War II globalization. Many of the earliest titles about Elvis were European publications such as *Die Tonende Story: Elvis Presley* (De Vecchi, Germany, 1959); *Boken on Elvis Presley* (Bruce, Sweden, 1958); or *Elvis Presley* (Portugal, 1959). They demonstrate the extent to which Elvis was creating a One World for teenagers—and inculcating them with American culture in the process.

Along with Elvis's music, teenagers worldwide gobbled up these publications—and American ideals and beliefs as well. Internationally recognized author Salman Rushdi recalls how he was affected in this manner by Elvis during his teenage years in 1950s Bombay ("Fresh Air," National Public Radio, April 22, 1999). East German Carsten Kaaz credits his youthful exposure to Elvis as an inspiration for his escape over the Berlin Wall (*In the Shadow of the Wall*).

The early Elvis publications causing this disparate and dramatic worldwide reaction were primarily biographies. As to be expected, the biographies are everywhere—and have been since 1956. The best of them give intimate peeks into midtwentieth-century American history. Elvis's life (1935–1977) reflected his times—some of the most life-changing decades in our history. The good Elvis biographies offer a front window view of these years—from the poverty of the Depression South through the unprecedented upward mobility for the poor in the 1940s and 1950s—when welfare, families, and public housing worked—to the drug-and-divorce devastation of the 1970s.

These biographies, along with the rest of the Elvis literature, demonstrate the importance and impact of the man. In rock music historian and critic Greil Marcus's seminal study of Elvis's significance, *Dead Elvis: A Chronicle of a Cultural Obsession*, he observes, "the enormity of his impact on culture, on millions of people, was never really clear when he was alive; it was mostly hidden. When he died, the event was a kind of explosion that went off silently in the minds and hearts; out of that explosion came many fragments, edging slowly into the light, taking shape, changing shape again and again as the years went on."

Elvis literature picks up these fragments of his importance—at all phases of their metamorphoses—and provides them with a context, clarity, and a crucible. As one's exposure to these fragments expands through the Elvis literature, it becomes difficult *not* to take Elvis seriously.

☆   ☆   ☆   ☆

History of the Elvis Literature

Elvis literature is a genre—and industry—without precedent. More than 1,700 titles have been written about him, ranging from books to dissertations to speeches in the Congressional Record. In the process, this genre—and Elvis—have become a unique and significant part of American culture.

The Elvis book numbers alone—1,000-plus English and foreign language titles—place this literary output in league with that of other historical figures. Those for Presidents Dwight D. Eisenhower (985),[1] John F. Kennedy (3,536), and others who changed the course of history such as the Reverend Dr. Martin Luther King (2,083), demonstrate this. When the Elvis book titles are compared against those of his fellow entertainers Frank Sinatra (195) and the Beatles (882), Elvis remains the king.

But unlike the title output about these famous people, the Elvis literature's path to maturity has had a distinct evolution. Beginning with limited fanzine baby steps in the 1950s, it weathered its wild teenage years of sightings, death controversy, and tattler tell-alls to become sensible and serious in its 1990s middle age. With the 1999 publication of Peter Guralnick's final volume of his Elvis biography, *Careless Love*—hailed by *The New York Times Book Review* (Jan 1999) as "among the most ambitious and crucial biographical undertakings devoted to a major American figure of the second half of the twentieth century"—the Elvis literature can look forward to an old age of gravitas and respect.

But it has taken a while to achieve this. During Elvis's career in the simpler, naïve times of the 1950s and 1960s, the literature was a match. Limited in depth, scope, and output, it consisted of fan magazines, along with a few biographies, filmographies, and photograph books, published in the United States, England, Germany, and Scandinavia.

But on August 16, 1977, that changed. Elvis died, and the literary floodgates opened.

In the next 20 days, the few Elvis books already on the market were rushed into additional print runs numbering into hundreds of thousands.[2] At first, this burst of entrepreneurship is easily attributed to the open pocketbooks of Elvis's mourning fans, as well as the normal curiosity that arises after someone famous dies. But something else was happening.

This publication explosion dovetailed with the intense and unprecedented worldwide media attention given to Elvis's death. The combination was historic. The mainstream media's

---

[1] Numbers for those other than Elvis are from a Jan 30, 1999, search of the OCLC WorldCat database.

[2] As reported in the Sept 5, 1977, *Publishers Weekly* issue in which Trade News Editor Robert Dahlin wrote about the phenomenon: "The Unique Appeal of Elvis Presley's Music Now Carries Over to Books About Him," (p. 5):
Dell Purse Book, *Elvis: The Life and Loves of the Country Boy Who Became King of Rock 'n' Roll*—1 million.
Harbinson, *The Illustrated Elvis*—500,000 (40,000 were already in print).
Hopkins, *Elvis*—480,000 (600,000 were already in print).
Mann, Retitling of *Elvis and the Colonel* to *The Private Elvis*—600,000.
Parish, *The Elvis Presley Scrapbook*—200,000 (90,000 were already in print).
West, *Elvis, What Happened?*—published on Aug 1, 1977, 3.35 million were in print by Sept 5, 1977.

love affair with celebrity was born the day Elvis died. The same can be said for our voracious appetite for books about celebrity lives.

Prior to Elvis's death in 1977, the literature about him was almost exclusively targeted at fans and their interests. The only time that readers outside of the Elvis world paid major attention was the publication of Jerry Hopkins's 1971 biography, *Elvis*. Beyond that (and a few others in the 1950s to be mentioned later in this text), the writing level and subjects of the Elvis literature understandably aroused little non-fan interest. That would not occur until the 1990s.

But literature written about Elvis before he died should not be dismissed. At the beginning of his national prominence, 1956–1957, serious writers in serious publications were attracted by the hysteria he was creating. The resulting articles were the first of their kind for a celebrity—appearing everywhere from *Harper's* to *The New Yorker* to London's *Sunday Times*.

After that initial intellectual examination, the Elvis literature settled down to publicity hype and fan publications. This, with two exceptions, would continue until the 1971 publication of Hopkins's *Elvis*.

In 1960, after Elvis had completed the most publicized military service in history, a civilian journalist published *Operation Elvis*—a light-hearted but authoritative description of how the United States Army prepared for and handled its most famous draftee.

One other publication in the pre-Hopkins years stands out for its professional writing and historical value: *Elvis Presley Speaks!* (1956), by Memphis (TN) *Press-Scimitar* reporter Robert Johnson. It is a well-researched biography based on interviews with a wide range of Elvis's family, friends, neighbors, teachers, and more. Through these first-person reports, Johnson gives readers a unique view of the American working poor from the Depression to the national prosperity of the mid-1950s.

After the success of Hopkins's book, a few others ventured forth, most notably rock music historian and critic Greil Marcus. The chapter "Elvis: Presliad" in his 1975 benchmark *Mystery Train* is one of the best analyses of Elvis and his impact.

However, *Mystery Train* was the exception during this period. The other 1970s authors confined themselves to photograph books and flattering biographies. Movie fan magazine writer Mae Mann published rewrites of her Elvis articles in *Elvis and the Colonel* (1975). Three photograph books appeared in 1975: Paul Lichter's *Elvis in Hollywood*, James Robert Parish's *The Elvis Presley Scrapbook*, and W. A. Harbinson's *Elvis Presley: An Illustrated Biography*, which, although riddled with inaccuracies, would be reprinted seven times between 1976 and 1988, under various titles.

The next year, 1976, another photograph book was published based on Elvis's films and biography: Steven and Boris Zmijewsky's *The Films and Career of Elvis Presley*. It also included commentary on Elvis's influences. Just before Elvis's death in 1977, British fan club president Todd Slaughter published the biography *Elvis Presley*.

An interesting segment of the pre-death Elvis literature emerged in the early 1970s. This was a period of revolutionary change in American education. Traditional curriculum subjects and methodology were being displaced by an emphasis on current topics and trends. For the first time, American students were learning to read through books about then-popular celebrities rather than past presidents and other historical figures. Elvis was a natural favorite with this period's educational writers.

Elvis first appeared in a textbook in 1971. *Meet Elvis Presley* by Favius Friedman was a reading comprehension book for high school students that would be reissued in 1973 and after his death in 1977. Others followed, including articles in educational journals detailing teaching methods involving Elvis. (However, the first "Elvis as teaching tool" article was published in 1956 by teacher Al Hurwitz.)

But it would not be until the aftermath of Elvis's death and the subsequent explosion of Elvis literature that serious writers began to show interest. Jerry Hopkins, joining the increasing ranks of those who were fascinated by the circumstances of Elvis's death, published *Elvis: The Final Years* in 1980. Neal and Janice Gregory's seminal analysis of Elvis's effect on modern journalism, *When Elvis Died*, also appeared in 1980. David Marsh produced *Elvis*, a superb examination of the entertainer's life and influence, in 1982. And Albert Goldman's infamous and obsessively vulgar *Elvis* slithered onto the market in 1981.

The first wide-ranging scrutiny of Elvis's impact was written during this time. In the fall of 1979, the University of Southern Mississippi's scholarly journal *Southern Quarterly* was devoted to an examination of Elvis. Consisting of essays reflecting Elvis's diverse influence, the authors ranged from eminent academics to ordinary Elvis fans. It was simultaneously published in book format by Jac Tharpe (*Elvis: Images and Fancies*), and remains one of the most important studies of Elvis.

Immediately after Elvis's death, the Elvis photograph books—a traditional staple of the Elvis literature—began flooding the market, as did a tsunami of publications by those who knew Elvis. The first of these, *My Life with Elvis* by his secretary Becky Yancey, was released in October 1977—two months after his death. It quickly garnered worldwide popularity through translation into Japanese, French, and Norwegian. Yancey's success was followed by a multitude of Elvis friends, relatives, employees, neighbors, fans, coworkers, fellow musicians and actors—with an output that continues unabated today.

Many of these memoirs are invaluable not only to the study of Elvis but also to that of our national culture and history. The sheer number of non-celebrity, non-professional authors provides unprecedented access to the lives and fantasies of ordinary people in the last half of the twentieth century.

The best personal observation of Elvis and his complexities is *Elvis and Me* (1985)—the memoirs of Priscilla Presley, Elvis's former wife and the architect of the astounding success of Elvis Presley Enterprises, Inc. In addition to its unmatched perspective of Elvis, Presley's book provides a rare open window on the dramatically changing roles, behaviors, and mores of young women in the 1950s and 1960s.

In the 1980s, the red-hot fascination with how—and if—Elvis died began its curious life. Initiated by prolific "Elvis is alive" author Gail Brewer-Giorgio (*Orion, Is Elvis Alive?*, et al.), it was fueled by such media as Geraldo Rivera and the *National Enquirer*.

Readers were tantalized by these "sightings," and by the "faked death" books and articles written by everyone from an army buddy (Hatcher, *Elvis, Is That You?*) to former Los Angeles County Medical Examiner Thomas Noguchi (*Coroner at Large*). Like the Elvis literature, this peculiar output would achieve maturity in the 1990s when distinguished scholars R. Serge Denisoff and George Plasketes mantled it with academic validity in *True Disbelievers: The Elvis Contagion*.

In the 1990s, the Elvis literature began arcing toward its yet-unreached apex with thoughtful publications by Peter Guralnick (*Last Train to Memphis, Careless Love*), Greil

Marcus (*Dead Elvis*), Peter Whitmer (*The Inner Elvis*), as well as social and historical observers such as Susan Doll (*Understanding Elvis*) and Gilbert Rodman (*Elvis After Elvis*). Others, especially Bill E. Burk (the *Early Elvis* trilogy) and Sue Wiegert (*Elvis: Precious Memories*), contributed well-written and researched first-person accounts of experiences with Elvis.

In the 1990s, Elvis literature has expanded to provide additional and ample proof of Elvis's influence on our society. Elvis books, dissertations, and articles have appeared in categories ranging from philately to religion to race relations. With at least 17 titles issued in 1999, the Elvis literature industry continues to grow. And with it, so does our understanding of ourselves and our culture.

☆   ☆   ☆   ☆

Did Elvis Presley Read These Books?

This predictable question has an unexpected answer. Elvis Presley was a lifelong, avid reader. In elementary school, he had a well-documented passion for superhero comic books. In middle school, library cards show that his taste (or perhaps assignments) ran the gamut from biographies (President Andrew Jackson) to English fairy tales. In high school, he discovered author/adventurer Richard Halliburton (*Royal Road to Romance*). As an adult, he amassed a personal library of 1,000 books,[3] which leaned toward titles relating to religion, philosophy, spirituality, and metaphysics.

But curiously, no one close to him in the 1960s and 1970s can recall Elvis reading more than one of the books written about him. Elvis's close friend of 14 years Larry Geller, with whom Elvis liked to discuss books and ideas, is familiar with Elvis's personal library as he provided Elvis with many of its titles. Geller remembers that Elvis read some of Jerry Hopkins's book *Elvis: A Biography* and liked what it said. But that was about it.

But what about the devastating "tell-all" *Elvis, What Happened?*, written by his friends and former bodyguards Red and Sonny West and Dave Hebler? The book that, according to legend, pushed Elvis into deep despair in the weeks preceding his death? According to Elvis's close friend Marty Lacker, the only book he can remember the entertainer having read was this devastating tell-all.[4] But Geller believes that Elvis never read it: "Elvis did not read the bodyguards' book. I spoke to him at Graceland a few hours before he died, he mentioned the book and said he would not read it! . . . Elvis was adamant about not reading it, and I'm certain he didn't."[5]

Later that day, after Elvis's body had been taken from the house, his father Vernon Presley asked Geller to pack up Elvis's personal library. "That afternoon, Vernon asked Joe [Esposito], Al Strada, and me to go upstairs to Elvis's bedroom, bathroom, etc., and . . . pack all

---

[3] According to Elvis's friend and fellow bibliophile Larry Geller with whom Elvis consulted for titles. (Interview, July 1998.)

[4] Correspondence with Lacker, March 1999.

[5] Correspondence with Geller, May 1999.

his books . . . I looked around and observed for the very last time all those rooms, and put away all books that Vernon did not want the media or anyone else to get wind of. . . . The bodyguard book was not there. If it had been, I would have seen it."

Other than Geller's and Lacker's comments, there is no record of Elvis reading any book written about him. So, instead of a simple answer, we are led to another question: Why wasn't Elvis interested in what others had to write about him? That answer is for yet another book about Elvis Presley.

THE MAN

PART I

CHAPTER 1
Biographies

WITH MORE THAN two million copies[1] of Elvis biographies tumbling off the presses even before he died, it is no wonder that many readers want to run like the dickens at the sight of them. But those who flee are missing something of great value.

Elvis Presley biographies are the heart of the Elvis literature—for fans and for historians. As they explore the far-reaching corners of Elvis's life, their detailed documentation of time and place does far more than tell the tale of a celebrity's life. Through them, we are able to view a larger picture of who we were and are as a people and a nation.

Few historical figures have had a more documented life[2]—and it is this near-obsessive authentication that benefits scholars from a wide range of fields. What was day-to-day life like in the rural Depression-era South? What happened to rural people who moved to urban centers in the years immediately following World War II? What was celebrity life like in the 1960s and 1970s when our culture's moral structure was still fairly sturdy? The Elvis biographies answer these questions and more.

The first biographies were assembled for fan consumption. But as awareness of Elvis's importance and influence matured, so did the books about his life. A new, and perhaps final, plateau has been reached with the two-volume work of Peter Guralnick, *Last Train to Memphis* (1994) and *Careless Love* (1998). Mr. Guralnick's exhaustive research, coupled with his access to the archives of Elvis Presley Enterprises, Inc., gives his books valid claim to the title "definitive."

The first book-length Elvis biography was *Elvis Presley Speaks!*, written for fans and printed as a 68-page magazine in 1956. Its author, Robert Johnson, a reporter for the *Memphis Press-Scimitar* newspaper, based his story on RCA publicity handouts and interviews with Elvis's friends, relatives, and former schoolmates and neighbors.

Fifteen years passed before another researched biography appeared. In 1971—after much first-hand interviewing that involved "traveling 7,000 miles researching all memorabilia and interviewing all the people involved with Elvis's life"—Jerry Hopkins published the bestselling *Elvis* (book jacket notes).

---

[1]According to the Sept 5, 1977, issue of *Publishers Weekly*—and these were just the English language biographies.

[2]In addition to the more than 100 biographies, several day-by-day books of Elvis's life have been published. (*See* Guralnick in this chapter and the Cotten, Pierce, and/or Worth entries in The Man/Reference.)

Unfortunately, Mr. Hopkins's odyssey did not produce entirely accurate results. His book has several critical deficiencies, including incorrect facts that have been repeated by other writers to whom original research is apparently an unknown concept. In addition to an incorrect time for Elvis's birth, Mr. Hopkins appears to have fathered the countless repetitions of the incorrect version of the first guitar purchase (that the guitar was purchased in lieu of a bicycle; according to the salesman, Mr. Bobo, young Elvis had wanted a rifle[3])—as well as the incorrect version of Elvis's first public appearance.[4] Mr. Hopkins's book also lacks chapter notes, sources, and an index. Most of what followed Mr. Hopkins's book—and before the Guralnick volumes—were too many cut-and-paste Elvis biographies that broke no new ground and repeated material from Hopkins's book. Among the exceptions are: Pat Broeske and Peter Harry Brown's *Down at the End of Lonely Street*, Bill E. Burk's *Early Elvis* trilogy, Elaine Dundy's *Elvis and Gladys*, Dave Marsh's *Elvis*, and Peter Whitmer's *The Inner Elvis*.

One well-known Elvis biographer, not in the above list, requires mention: Albert Goldman, author of the infamous *Elvis* and *Elvis: The Last 24 Hours*, both of which paint a salacious and false portrait of the entertainer. Despite their brisk sales, the value of Goldman's books is limited: they are essential exercises in the pathology of deeply rooted anger, compiled with an inferiority complex—as those problems relate to Goldman, not Elvis.

Fortunately, Goldman's output is a lonely aberration. The remainder of the Elvis biographies are respectful and—most important—provide invaluable insights into American history while they illuminate slices of Elvis's life. Their lesson is that multipronged explorations of an individual's life give broader understanding to a period of history as well. Along with the publishers, the study of American history is richer for these books.

☆   ☆   ☆   ☆

☆ Adair, Joseph

Adair is a contributing writer to rock music magazines.

The Immortal Elvis Presley, 1935–1977. Stamford, CT: Longmeadow Press, 1992. 96 pp. ISBN: 0681415193.

Brief text with 75 previously published black and white photographs. This book was translated into French. (*See* Foreign Language Titles/French.)

Source: Cleveland (OH) Public Library

☆ Adler, David

The Life and Cuisine of Elvis Presley. New York: Crown Trade Paperbacks, 1993. 160 pp. ISBN: 0517880245. London: Smith and Gryphon, 1995. 160 pp. ISBN: none.

---

[3]Mr. Bobo's notarized letter, dated 1980, on display at Booth Hardware Store, Tupelo, Mississippi.

[4]In Elvis's first public appearance as a singer—at the Mississippi-Alabama Fair and Dairy Show in 1945—he won fifth place—not second as far too many authors have written. This has been verified by Robert Johnson in his 1956 biography *Elvis Presley Speaks!* and in scrupulous investigative journalism by Bill E. Burk. (See *Early Elvis: The Tupelo Years* earlier in this chapter.) The confusion appears to have been started by Jerry Hopkins in his 1971 biography *Elvis*, in which he states that Elvis won second prize. Far too many authors since then have relied on Hopkins error, rather than researching the facts on their own. Those instances are noted in the annotated entries in this section.

Elvis's life story told through the foods he ate. Adler examines Elvis's diet at every stage of the entertainer's life, concluding that Elvis's dietary inadequacies were the cause of his death. Interviews with Elvis's relatives, friends, and employees. More than 70 recipes, but the recipe for peanut butter and banana sandwiches is incorrect[5]. A discussion of food service at Graceland. Black and white photographs; credited.

Source: Library of Congress TX715.2.S68 A34 1993

☆ Baumgold, Julie

"Midnight in the Garden of Good and Elvis." *Esquire* (Mar 1995): 92–102.

A biographical article with interviews with Elvis's friends Marian Cocke, Joe Esposito, George Klein, and Richard Davis. Commentary from Elvis Presley Enterprises, Inc., CEO Jack Soden about Elvis as a religious icon.

☆ "Biography of Elvis Presley." *Young Lovers.* Vol. 1, No. 18. New York: Charlton Publications, 1957. 32 pp. [U.S.]: Avalon Communications, 1999.

An article, two pages in length, in a 1950s-romance comic book. Cover blurb reads, "The Real Elvis Presley Story."

Source: eBay auction item #81019471

☆ Black, Jim

Elvis on the Road to Stardom, 1955–1956. London: W. H. Allen, 1988. 159 pp. ISBN: 1852270160 (hdk.). ISBN: 18522706667 (pbk.).

The story of Elvis Presley's life in the year preceding his rise to national attention. Eight pages of black and white and color photographs.

Source: The British Library YC.1991.b.5761

☆ Bobo, L. Peyton, editor and publisher

Elvis: King of Rock 'n' Roll. Millport, AL: Millport Publishing Company, 1977. 46 pp.

A memorial tabloid published by the staff of *The Gazette* newspaper (Millport, Alabama). Ten articles about Elvis Presley's life and death. Five of them are memoirs from Elvis's Uncle Vester; his stepmother, Dee Presley; a personal friend, Barbara J. Bobo; clothier Bernard Lansky; and a fan, Debbie LeFleur. Black and white photographs of Elvis's life and career and his funeral; captioned.

Source: Compiler's collection

☆ Bonner, Michael

"The Write Stuff." *Melody Maker* (Dec 24, 1994): 8–9.

---

[5]According to Elvis's cook, Mary Jenkins (*Memories Beyond Graceland Gates*), the bread must be toasted first. (*See* The Man/Memoirs and Memories.)

Elvis Presley's handwriting is analyzed using graphoanalysis, revealing that he wanted to be noticed.

☆ Brayton, John Anderson

Brayton is a professional genealogist.

"A Foray into the Piedmont 'Non-Plantation South.'" *Notable Kin*, Vol. 2. Ed. Gary Boyd Roberts. Santa Clarita, CA: Published in cooperation with the New England Historic Genealogical Society, Boston, MA, by Carl Boyer, 3rd, 1998–1999. ISBN: 0936124202.

An exploration of the Presley line, including Elvis Presley's relationship to former President Jimmy Carter. Brayton concludes that Elvis is probably Carter's sixth cousin once removed.

Source: Library of Congress CS47.R63 1998

☆ Brock, Van K.

"Images of Elvis, the South and America." Ed. Jac L. Tharpe. *Elvis: Images and Fancies*. Jackson, MS: University Press of Mississippi, 1979. Pp. 87–122. ISBN: none.

Brock explains how Elvis Presley was shaped and insulated by "his [personal] contradictions, the contradictions of his religious teaching and the contradictions of and schisms in the mind of his society." Footnotes with biographical references.

Source: Tharpe, Jac L., Ph.D., editor. Elvis: Images and Fancies.

☆ Brown, Peter Harry, and Pat Broeske

Broeske and Brown, as a writing team, authored *Howard Hughes: The Untold Story* (Dutton/Signet). Peter Brown is an entertainment journalist who has written 10 other books. Pat Broeske is a former entertainment reporter for the *Los Angeles Times*.

Down at the End of Lonely Street: The Life and Death of Elvis Presley. New York: Dutton, 1997. 524 pp. ISBN: 0525942467.

A well-documented focus on some of the mysteries of Elvis Presley's life. Concludes through clinical and document analysis that Elvis died of a heart attack. Bibliographical references. Black and white photographs; captioned and credited. Biographical chronology chart. Filmography. List of television appearances. Source notes. One of the best bibliographies in the Elvis literature (pp. 487–505). Index. This book was translated into German. (*See* Foreign Language Titles/German.)

☆ Buckle, Phillip

All Elvis: An Unofficial Biography of the "King of Discs." UK: Daily Mirror Newspapers Ltd., 1962. ISBN: none.

Mostly black and white photographs with minimal text. Contains some errors (i.e., Elvis's twin brother is called Aaron; he died after about two months and Elvis took his name; Elvis's parents are incorrectly described as orphans).

Source: Collection of David Neale, Belgium
www.geocities.com/SunsetStrip/8200/books.html

☆ Burk, Bill E.

Bill E. Burk reported on Elvis for the *Memphis Press-Scimitar* newspaper from 1956 to the singer's death in 1977. During that time, Burk developed a friendly relationship with Elvis and wrote more than 400 articles about him. Mr. Burk is the founding publisher of *Bill E. Burk's Elvis World* magazine—the longest running commercial Elvis publication. He is the author of 12 Elvis books. (*See* The Man/Elvis in the Army, Photographs; and Foreign Language Titles/Swedish.) He has served as an Elvis consultant for print and electronic media around the world and has contributed to 13 Elvis books.

Bill E. Burk's *Early Elvis* Trilogy

This trio of books about specific periods in the life of Elvis Presley is among the most valuable of the biographies. Mr. Burk's thorough research produced new information from firsthand sources, as well as clarifying several major misconceptions about Elvis, including Elvis's prizewinning first public performance and the purchase of his first guitar. Mr. Burk lets the interviewees tell the story. Therefore, most material is written in the interviewees' first-person perspective.

Early Elvis: The Humes Years. Memphis, TN: Red Oak Press, 1990. 141 pp. ISBN: 0962560405.

Seventeen interviews with individuals who knew Elvis Presley while he was a student at Humes High School. They include Elvis's football coach, close friends, classmates, girlfriends, and gospel quartet leader James Blackwood who reminisces about Elvis's desire to become a gospel quartet singer. Seventeen pages of previously unseen black and white candid and portrait photographs from Elvis's high school days; no captions; all from author's collection. No index. This book is the first of Burk's *Early Elvis* trilogy.

Source: Library of Congress ML420.P96 B8 1990
OCLC 21966568

———.

Early Elvis: The Tupelo Years. Memphis, TN: Propwash Publishing, 1994. 218 pp. ISBN: 1879207508.

The second book in the *Early Elvis* trilogy, exploring Elvis Presley's childhood in Tupelo, Mississippi. Twenty-one interviews with relatives, friends, and townspeople who knew Elvis and his parents. Burk uncovers the facts about the award won by Elvis at his first public singing performance and the correct details of how Elvis got his first guitar. Thirty-two black and white candid photographs of Elvis's life, family, and friends in Tupelo; from author's collection. All photographs are captioned. Bibliography (p. 213). Index.

Source: Library of Congress ML420.P96 B86 1994
OCLC 31066123

————.

Early Elvis: The Sun Years. Memphis, TN: Propwash Publishing, 1997. 222 pp.
   ISBN: 1879207516.

The final book in the *Early Elvis* trilogy—an in-depth examination of the early years of
Elvis Presley's career, 1954–1956, when he was under contract to Sun Records in Memphis, Tennessee. Interviews with people who knew and worked with him during those
years, including Sam Phillips (who discovered Elvis) and Scotty Moore (Elvis's first guitarist). Sixteen pages of rare black and white candid photographs of Elvis and his family,
friends, fans, and coworkers. No index.

Source: Library of Congress ML420.P96 B8 1997

————.

Elvis at 60! January 8, 1995: The Official Elvis Birthday Souvenir. An *Elvis World*
   Special Bonus Edition. Jan 1995. 20 pp. ISBN: none.

A publication of Bill E. Burk's *Elvis World* magazine in which Burk presents the speculations of Elvis Presley authors, friends, and family as to what the entertainer would be
doing had he lived to be 60 years old. Twelve black and white previously unseen photographs; captioned and credited.

Source: Library of Congress ML420.P96 E

————.

*Elvis: A 30-Year Chronicle: Columns, Articles, Stories, and Features Exactly as Origi-
   nally Reported 1954–1983.* Tempe, AZ: Osborne Enterprises, 1985. 351 pp.
   ISBN: 0932117023.

Clippings from the *Memphis Press-Scimitar* covering Elvis's life and career from July 1954
until the newspaper folded in 1983. Almost all were written by Burk. Thirty-two pages of
black and white photographs; captioned and credited.
   This book was reprinted in 1993, with additional material, as *Elvis Memories: Between
the Pages.* (*See* following listing.)

*Source: Memphis/Shelby County (TN) Public Library and Information Center
OCLC 13353223*

————.

Elvis Memories: Between the Pages. Memphis, TN: Propwash Publishing, 1993. 416
   pp. ISBN: 187920715X.

Revised and expanded reprint of *Elvis: A 30-Year Chronicle.* Includes new photographs;
captioned and credited.

*Source: Library of Congress ML420.P96 B
OCLC 27449828*

☆ Buskin, Richard

Elvis: Memories and Memorabilia. London: Salamander Books Ltd., 1995. ISBN: none. [U.S.]: Crescent Books, 1995. 96 pp. ISBN: 051714322.

Brief text with more than 100 color photographs of Elvis memorabilia, movie stills, as well as black and white and color photographs of Elvis at various points in his career. Photographs are captioned and credited. Buskin is a British freelance journalist specializing in popular music, film, and television.

Source: Compiler's collection

☆ Celsi, Theresa

Elvis. Kansas City, MO: Ariel Books/Andrews and McMeel, 1993. 80 pp. ISBN: 0836230450.

A small-size ($3\frac{1}{4}'' \times 3\frac{3}{4}''$) book that repeats the inaccurate "second prize" story. List of 11 movies and theatre productions inspired by Elvis. Sixteen black and white photos (from Pictorial Press).

Source: Compiler's collection

☆ Charlesworth, Chris

Elvis Presley: The Whole Story. Greatest Hits and Pics series. London: Telstar Records, Ltd., 1987. 48 pp. ISBN: 1870759052.

Brief text with previously seen photographs. Repeats the inaccurate "second prize" story. Color and black and white photographs; few are captioned and credited.

Source: Compiler's collection

☆ Clayson, Alan, and Spencer Leigh, editors

Aspects of Elvis: Tryin' to Get to You. London: Sidgwick and Jackson, 1994. 346 pp. ISBN: 0283062177.

Thirty-six essays and fictional works about Elvis Presley, most by British authors. Genealogical chart of the Presley family, showing that Elvis's family came to America from Wales. Thirty photographs of Elvis art, as well as of Elvis with his family and fans and former Alabama Governors George and Lurline Wallace; captioned, but not credited. Discography: "The Complete Discography of Official Elvis Presley Recordings, 1953–1957," by Elvis discographer Peter Doggett, ([291]–335). (*See* Doggett listing in The Music, The Movies/Discography.) Bibliography ([288]–290). Index.

Source: Library of Congress ML420.P96 A9 1994
OCLC 31782316

☆ Clayton, Rose, and Dick Heard

Clayton was a correspondent for *Rolling Stone* and *Billboard* magazines. Heard covered Memphis and Nashville (Tennessee) for the television program *Entertainment Tonight*.

Elvis Up Close: In the Words of Those Who Knew Him Best. Atlanta: Turner Publishing, 1994. 405 pp. ISBN: 15703360588.

Commentary on Elvis's life from approximately 150 of his family members and friends. Brief biographical background on each speaker. Black and white photographs; captioned and credited. Index.

While all quotes are credited, none are footnoted or cited. In the "Acknowledgments" section, authors state that quotes are from interviews and their "seventeen-year collections of interviews with those who knew [Elvis]." They note that some of the quotes have been "edited for clarity" and some have been "combined."

Source: Library of Congress ML420.P96 H53 1994
Dewey Decimal 782.42166'092-dc20 [B]

☆ Cotten, Lee

Lee Cotten is the author of seven Elvis books.

Elvis: His Life History. Sacramento, CA: self-published, 1981. ISBN: none.

A biography limited to 200 copies.

Source: Cotten, Lee, Did Elvis Sing in Your Hometown? (1995), p. ii

———.

The Elvis Catalog: Memorabilia, Icons, and Collectibles Celebrating the King of Rock 'n' Roll. Garden City, NJ: Doubleday, 1987. 255 pp. ISBN: 0385237057 (hdk.). ISBN: 0385237049 (pbk.).

A biography that also features photographs and information on Elvis sites and merchandise as they relate to the phases of his life and career. Chapter on merchandise produced after Elvis's death (up to 1987). More than 400 black and white and color photographs of Elvis merchandise items and of residences in which he lived prior to Graceland. This book was authorized by Elvis Presley Enterprises, Inc., whose staff members assisted in its preparation.

☆ Davis, Julie

Elvis. New York: Lorelei Publishing Co., 1977. 90 pp. ISBN: none.

A pamphlet published immediately after Elvis Presley's death.

Source: The Margaret Herrick Library, Academy of Motion Picture Arts and Sciences

☆ DeWitt, Howard A.

Howard A. DeWitt has taught the history of rock and roll for nearly 20 years in California colleges. He has published books on the Beatles and Van Morrison.

Elvis, The Sun Years: The Story of Elvis Presley in the Fifties. Rock and Roll Reference, #36. Ann Arbor, MI: Popular Culture, Ink, 1991; 1993. 500 pp. (1991). 362 pp. (1993). ISBN: 1560750200 (same for both editions).

Focuses on Elvis's life in 1954–1956, at the beginning of his career. Source list. Six appendices that include Elvis's concerts and reviews, 1952–1955 (pp. 292–300); Elvis's "Sun Sessions and Other Early Recordings" (pp. 303–306); and "Musicians Influencing Elvis's Sun Years" (pp. 311–330). Bibliographic essay (pp. 331–340). Index.

Source: Library of Congress ML420.P96 D49 1933
Dewey Decimal 782.42164/092 B 20
OCLC 24755966 (1991)

☆ Dillon-Malone, Aubrey

The Rise and Fall and Rise of Elvis. Dublin, Ireland: Leopold Publishing, 1997. 165 pp. ISBN: 0952686546.

In addition to text, 32 pages of black and white photographs.

Source: Whittaker's Books in Print, Vol. 4: 9836 (1998)

☆ Doll, Susan M., Ph.D.

Susan Doll, Ph.D., teaches film courses at Chicago-area colleges and is the author of seven books about Elvis Presley and one about Marilyn Monroe. (*See* The Man/Reference and The Academics/Dissertations and Theses.)

Elvis: The Early Years: Portrait of a Young Rebel. New York: Signet/NAL, 1990. 128 pp. ISBN: 0451169298.

Emphasizes Elvis's discovery and early career when he toured the country music circuit. Also features an exploration of his impact on the entertainment industry in 1956, when he became a national figure. A discussion of his films (pp. 82–101). Sixteen pages of black and white and color photographs; captioned and credited.

Source: OCLC 22689289

———.

Elvis: Portrait of the King. Lincolnwood, IL: Publications International, Ltd., 1995. 239 pp. ISBN: 0451823060.

A reprint of *Elvis: Rock 'n' Roll Legend* (1994). (*See* following listing.)

Source: OCLC 32903597

———.

Elvis: Rock 'n' Roll Legend. Lincolnwood, IL: Publications International, Ltd., 1994. 239 pp. ISBN: 0785308717.

An exploration of each phase of Elvis Presley's career and the key events of his personal life. "His professional nicknames and personas are considered and examined to better understand how America responded to the phenomenon that was—and is—Elvis" (p. 11).

Four hundred sepia and color photographs; captioned and credited. Chapter on Elvis memorabilia and films and television movies in which Elvis is a character.

Source: OCLC 31704592

————.

Elvis: A Tribute to His Life. Lincolnwood, IL: Publications International, Ltd., 1989. 256 pp. ISBN: 0881766658. New York: Beekman House/distributed by Crown Pub., 1989. 256 pp. ISBN: 051702005X. London: Omnibus, 1989, 1990. 256 pp. ISBN: 0711921695.

An exploration of Elvis as a legend, with chapters on his postmortem impact and popularity. Bibliographic essay. Index. Black and white and color photographs; captioned and credited. This book was translated into French. (*See* Foreign Language Titles/French.)

Source: Library of Congress ML420.P96 D64 1989
Dewey Decimal 78242166/092 B 20
OCLC 21297340 9 (1989 Publications International); 22939582 (1989 Beekman House); 24740543 (1989, 1990 Omnibus)

————.

Understanding Elvis: Southern Roots vs. Star Image. Garland Studies in American Popular History and Culture series. New York: Garland Publishing, 1998. 219 pp. ISBN: 0815331649.

A study of the complex connection between Elvis Presley's career and his Southern roots—how that identity affected each stage of Elvis's career. Dr. Doll posits that Elvis's career can be divided into three phases, each of which is signified by a specific image. The evolution from one career phase to another was instigated by a specific event and represented a deliberate calculation on the part of Elvis's manager, Colonel Parker, to attract a wider audience. Eight photographs. Bibliography. Index. (*See* The Academics/Dissertations and Theses.)

Source: OCLC 39887142

☆ *Elvis Aaron[6] Presley's Astrological Horoscope and Psychological Profile: Jan 8, 1935–Aug 16, 1977.* Elvis Collectable Ltd. Ed. Southfield, MI: Lifestyles International, 1994. 48 pp. ISBN: 7447084908.

A biography of Elvis Presley based upon his astrological horoscope. His natal chart is reproduced, as well as charts for the major events in his life. (*See also* Jerry Williams listing later in this section.)

Source: Library of Congress BF1728.P74 E48 1994

---

[6]Throughout the Elvis literature, Elvis Presley's middle name is written as either "Aron" or "Aaron." Elvis Presley Enterprises, Inc., has designated the official spelling as "Aaron" because that is the spelling chosen by his father for Elvis's headstone. Elvis was named after his father, Vernon Elvis Presley, and a close family friend, Aaron Kennedy. "Aron" was the spelling chosen by the Presleys at Elvis's birth, and that is the spelling he used for most of his life. In the 1970s Elvis sought to change his middle name to the biblical spelling "Aaron." Knowing Elvis's plans for his middle name, Vernon chose the "Aaron" spelling for the headstone. (Elvis Presley Enterprises, Inc., at www.elvis-presley.com.)

☆ *Elvis (An Unauthorized Biography)*. [n.p.]: [n.p.], [n.d.]. [44] pp. ISBN: none.

An anonymously written biography of Elvis Presley, presumably published while he was alive (the present verb tense is used and there is no mention of his death). Only clue as to date of publication is in this sentence from the text: "Priscilla is currently dating Mike Stone, a Hawaiian-born karate expert and teacher and she is co-owner of a Beverly Hills boutique, Bis & Beau" (p. 41).

Black and white photographs of Elvis in concert during the 1970s and motion picture stills; none are captioned or credited.

Source: Compiler's collection

☆ "Elvis 1935–1977." *View*, Tupelo, MS (Aug 20, 1977). 55 pp.

A newspaper tabloid insert from Elvis Presley's hometown newspaper in Tupelo, Mississippi, published four days after his death. A collection of stories and pictures from his life there and memoir anecdotes from those who knew him.

Source: Compiler's collection

☆ *Elvis Presley: A* Photoplay *Tribute*. New York: Cadrant Enterprises, Inc., 1977. 128 pp. ISBN: none.

Hardcover bound edition of the souvenir magazine *Elvis Presley: A Photoplay Tribute*. The cover is white with gold print: "Elvis Aron Presley January 8, 1935, August 16, 1977." (*See* The Rest/Souvenir Magazines.)

Source: eBay auction item #52011549

☆ "Elvis Presley, Elvis Presley." Section 11. *The Waco Citizen*, Waco, TX (Sept 16, 1977).

A newspaper tabloid section about Elvis Presley's life. Memories of Waco citizens who had experiences with Elvis when he was stationed at nearby Fort Hood, Texas, including his good friend, Eddie Fadal. Black and white candid photographs.

Source: Compiler's collection

☆ "Elvis's Other Avocation." *American Libraries* (Jan 1983): 17.

Brief article about Elvis's volunteer library service while he was a student at Humes High School. Black and white photograph of Elvis and his fellow volunteers.

☆ *Elvis: The Life and Loves of the Country Boy Who Became King of Rock 'n' Roll*. Dell Purse Book 2286-49. New York: Dell Publishing Co., Inc., 1977. 64 pp. ISBN: 7100900049.

A small (3½″ × 5¼″) pamphlet with 47 black and white photographs; some captioned, none credited. This book was published immediately after Elvis died, with a print run of 1,000,000 copies.

Source: Compiler's collection

☆ Frew, Timothy W.

Elvis: His Life and Music. New York: Friedman/Fairfax Publishers, Inc., 1994. 176 pp. ISBN: 1567991203. New York: Barnes & Noble, 1997. 176 pp. ISBN: 0760704899. *Elvis's Golden Records.* New York: RCA Records, 1994. Four sound discs. ISBN: 1567991203 (same as for book). Music No: PCD1-5196; RCA Records. PCD1-5197; RCA Records. 2765-2-R; RCA Records. 1297-2-R; RCA Records. *Elvis CD and Sessions Notes.* Andrew G. Hager, text. Alfred Wertheimer, photographs. New York: Michael Friedman Publishing Group, 1994. 16 pp. ISBN: none.

[Note: The book and CD were also issued in 1994 as a "Numbered Limited Edition." New York: Friedman/Fairfax, 1994. 176 pp. book, 16-page *Elvis CD and Sessions Notes*, and four CDs. ISBN: 1567991114.]

A biography with 200 black and white and color photographs; captioned and credited. Discography (pp. 166–171). Filmography (pp. 138–161). Translated into French. (*See* Foreign Language Titles/French.) Comes with four digitally mastered CDs featuring 48 Elvis recordings from the 1950s and 1960s; CD titles: *Elvis's Golden Records* Vol. I, Vol. II, Vol. III, Vol. IV. Volume I was originally released in 1958; Volume II in 1959; Volume III in 1963; Volume IV in 1968. Also included is a 16-page recording session journal, *Elvis CD and Sessions Notes*, written by Andrew G. Hager with photographs by Alfred Wertheimer.

Source: Library of Congress ML420.P96 F74 1994
Dewey Decimal 782.42166/092 B 20
OCLC 3270286 (1994 book); 37933113 (1997 book); 36020680 (set); 32437675 (CD recordings)

☆ Fulcher, Richard Carlton

The Presley Saga: A Family History. A revised edition. Brentwood, TN: Fulcher Publishing Company, 1978. ISBN: none.

A self-published genealogy of the Presley family in America, with specific focus on Elvis and his lineage. Index.

———.

Presley Family History: Pressly, Pressley, Presley Family in America. Brentwood, TN: Fulcher Publishing Company, 1994. 213 pp. ISBN: none.

A revised and updated edition of *The Presley Saga*.

Source: Memphis/Shelby County (TN) Public Library and Information Center
OCLC 4159585 (1978); 32022122 (1994)

☆ Gehman, Richard

Elvis Presley—Hero or Heel? Louisville, KY: Whitestone Publications, [1957]. 88 pp. ISBN: none.

An early biography of Elvis Presley that examines his impact and phenomena. Includes quotes from other entertainers and journalists. Black and white photographs; candids and stills. Repeats "guitar instead of bicycle" story. No citations, sources, or notes. Insert of a "life size" color portrait of Elvis.

Source: The Mississippi Valley Collection, The University of Memphis (TN)

☆ Gibson, Robert, and Sid Shaw

Gibson was a political correspondent for the *Daily Express* (UK). Shaw is the managing director of Elvisly Yours, "a worldwide fan club and Europe's biggest supplier of Presleyanna" (book jacket cover).

Elvis: A King Forever. London: Elvisly Yours Ltd., 1970; 1979. 185 pp. ISBN: 1869941004. Poole, Dorset, UK: Blandford Press, 1985. 176 pp. ISBN: 0713716673. London: Elvisly Yours Ltd., 1987 (pbk). ISBN: none. New York: McGraw-Hill Paperback, 1987. 176 pp. ISBN: 007056518X.

Introductory essay on the impact of Elvis Presley. Biography text is accompanied by "Elvis Diary" margin notes, which highlight important dates in Elvis's life. Uncited Elvis quotes. Black and white and color photographs of Elvis and of Elvis memorabilia.

Source: The British Library X.431/13798 (1985)
Library of Congress ML420.P96 G5 1985, 1987
Dewey Decimal 785.4.00924 (B)
OCLC 21013896 (1970; 1979); 14001909 (1985)

☆ Goldman, Albert

Goldman also wrote a biography of American satirist Lenny Bruce and was a music critic for *Life* and *Esquire* magazines. Longtime Elvis friend and "Memphis Mafia" member Lamar Fike provided writing assistance for Goldman. Fike is listed as one of the book's copyright holders.

Elvis. "A Kevin Eggers Book." New York: McGraw-Hill/Avon, 1981. 598 pp. ISBN: 0070236577. Ringwood, Victoria, CN: Allen Lane, 1981. 598 pp. ISBN: 0713914742. New York: Avon, 1982. 714 pp. ISBN: none. Harmondsworth [n.p.]; New York: Penguin Books, 1982; 1991. 727 pp. ISBN: 0140059652.

The infamous biography that achieved widespread attention for its negative presentation of Elvis. Twenty-four previously published black and white photographs; captioned and credited. No footnotes, chapter notes, or sources. Index. This book was translated into Dutch, Finnish, French, Icelandic, Japanese, and Swedish. (*See* Foreign Language Titles.)

———.

Elvis: The Last 24 Hours. New York: St. Martin's Paperbacks, 1991. 192 pp. ISBN: 0312925417. United Kingdom: Pan Books; Pan in association with Sidgwick and Jackson, 1991. 192 pp. ISBN: 0330321722.

A chronology of the last day of Elvis's life, with an emphasis on his physical and mental condition. List of the drugs prescribed to Elvis by his Memphis, Tennessee, physician, George C. Nichopolous, M.D. Eight black and white photographs of individuals who played a role in Elvis's last day; captioned and credited. An approximate floor plan of Graceland's second level, drawn by architect Andrew Bennett of New York. (Mr. Bennett was not allowed access to Graceland or to architectural blueprints of the house for this drawing.) No footnotes, chapter notes, or sources. Index. This book was translated into Dutch and German. (*See* Foreign Language Titles/Dutch, German.)

Elvis's stepbrother David Stanley assisted Goldman with this book. Stanley was at Graceland on the day that Elvis died.

☆ **Gray, Michael, and Roger Osborne**

Gray has also written about Bob Dylan and Frank Zappa.

Elvis's America. **London: Swanston Publishing Limited, 1996. ISBN: none.**

A biography of Elvis Presley organized in a geographical format. First section (pp. 10–25) examines Southern music before Elvis began his career. Maps for each section highlight locations of major and minor events in Elvis's life. Repeats the inaccurate "second prize" and "guitar/bicycle" stories, and misdates the latter as occurring in August 1946. Other factual errors, such as placing a fairgrounds in Long Beach, California's Recreation Park (p. 119) and citing an unverifiable book as a quote source (From "Elvis in Memphis," p. 132).

Color and black and white photographs; captioned and credited. Quotes attributed to Elvis; none cited or sourced. List of Elvis's live appearances from July 17, 1954, through June 1977 (pp. 178–183). Bibliography (p. 184). Index.

This book was re-released in 1996 as *The Elvis Atlas: A Journey Through Elvis Presley's America.(See* following entry.)

Source: The British Library

————.

The Elvis Atlas: A Journey Through Elvis Presley's America. **New York: Henry Holt & Co., 1996. 192 pp. ISBN: 0805041591.**

Originally published as *Elvis's America.*

Source: Library of Congress ML420.P96 G72 1996
Dewey Decimal 782.42166'092-dc20

☆ **Grove, Martin A.**

Martin Grove is a celebrity biographer.

The King Is Dead: Elvis Presley. **New York: Manor Books, 1977. 252 pp. ISBN: 0532191625. New York: Manor Books, 1978. 256 pp. ISBN: 053219196X.**

Published immediately after the death of Elvis Presley. A short biography that includes interviews with a variety of individuals who interacted with him. No citations for quotes. Eleven color photo publicity stills from various Elvis films. List of 53 Elvis albums including tracks found on each. List of each of Elvis's films, including cast list, plot summary, and quoted reviews for each.

Source: Compiler's collection (1977)
OCLC 3512164 (1977); 225358 (1978)

☆ Guralnick, Peter

Peter Guralnick is a noted historian and critic who has written extensively about American music and musicians in books and periodicals, as well as liner notes for Elvis Presley RCA/BMG Music recording releases. The first volume of his Elvis biography, *Last Train to Memphis*, was labeled "the definitive Elvis biography" (*Kirkus Reviews*, July 1, 1994). The second volume, *Careless Love*, was pronounced "not simply the finest rock-and-roll biography ever written. It must be ranked among the most ambitious and crucial biographical undertakings yet devoted to a major American figure of the second half of the 20th century," (*The New York Times Book Review*, Jan 3, 1999).

Last Train to Memphis: The Rise of Elvis Presley. Boston: Little, Brown and Company, 1994. 560 pp. ISBN: 0316332208. Boston: Back Bay, 1995. 560 pp. ISBN: 0316332259X. London: Little, Brown and Company, 1994. ISBN: 03136910201. London: Abacus, 1995. 578 pp. ISBN: 0349107815X.

The first volume of a two-part biography of Elvis Presley, this book covers the entertainer's life from 1935 through 1957. Footnotes, chapter notes, and sources. Index. Bibliography (pp. 532–542) of reference works, periodicals, clippings, collections, picture books, and memorabilia, as well as more than 200 Elvis and Elvis-related books. "A Brief Discographical Note." Twenty-four black and white photographs; captioned and credited. Maps of Elvis sites in Memphis. Listed by Elvis Presley Enterprises, Inc., as suggested reading.

This book has been translated into Czech, Finnish, Italian, Japanese, and Spanish. (*See* Foreign Language Titles.)

Unabridged audio recordings of *Last Train To Memphis*. Read by J. Charles (18 hours). Grand Haven, MI: Brilliance Corp., 1995. ISBN: 1561006246.

Read by Christopher Lane (24 hours). Newport Beach, CA: Books On Tape, 1995.

Source: OCLC 32936862.

Abridged audio recordings of *Last Train To Memphis*. Read by J. Charles (180 minutes). Grand Haven, MI: Brilliance Corp., 1995. ISBN: 1561004170. New York: Time Warner Audio Books, 1994. ISBN: 1570422060.

"Advance Reader's Edition" (uncorrected advance proofs bound for reviewing purposes). Boston: Little, Brown and Company, 1994. 488 pp.

Source: OCLC 31748755.

———.

Careless Love: The Unmaking of Elvis Presley. Boston: Little, Brown and Company, 1999. 767 pp. ISBN: 0316332224. London: Little, Brown and Company, 1999. 768 pp. ISBN: 0316644021.

The second and concluding volume of Guralnick's biography of Elvis Presley, covering the entertainer's life from 1958 through 1977. Twenty-eight black and white photographs. Footnotes, chapter notes, and sources. Bibliography (pp. 730–742). Index. This book has been translated into Spanish. (*See* Foreign Language Titles/Spanish.)

Unabridged audio recordings of *Careless Love*. 18 cassettes–28 hours. Grand Haven, MI: Brilliance Corp., 1998. ISBN: 1567406157.

Abridged audio recordings of *Careless Love*. (6 cassettes). Grand Haven, MI: Brilliance Corp., 1998. ISBN: 1567400868. (2 cassettes). Grand Haven, MI: Brilliance Corp., 1998. ISBN: 1567408087.

☆ Guralnick, Peter, and Ernst Jorgensen

Elvis Day by Day. **New York: Ballantine Books, 1999. 391 pp. ISBN: 0345420896.**

A chronology of Elvis Presley's life and record releases by the authors of three definitive Elvis books: Peter Guralnick (two-part biography, *Last Train to Memphis* and *Careless Love*) and Ernst Jorgensen (discography, *Elvis Presley: A Life in Music; The Complete Recording Sessions*). The authors were granted unprecedented access to the archives of Elvis Presley Enterprises, Inc. Thus, this book contains a number of previously unseen photographs, as well as new authenticated information about Elvis's life and recordings.

☆ Hamblett, Charles

Elvis: The Swinging Kid. **Surrey, England: May Fair Books, 1962. 159 pp. ISBN: none.**

A serious biography in comic book format that concludes with the filming of *Blue Hawaii* in 1961. Eight pages of black and white photographs from Elvis's army tour in Germany and from the set of *Follow That Dream*.

Source: OCLC 20738792

☆ Hanna, David

Elvis: Lonely Star at the Top. **New York: Leisure Books, 1977. 233 pp. ISBN: 0843905328.**

Written immediately after the death of Elvis Presley. Repeats inaccurate "second prize" story, and incorrectly states that Elvis's first guitar was purchased by mail order for $12.50. Sixteen black and white photographs; none credited. This book was translated into German. (*See* Foreign Language Titles/German.)

Source: Library of Congress ML420.P96 H 36

☆ Hazen, Cindy, and Mike Freeman

The authors live in Memphis where they operate the Memphis Explorations touring company. They have authored two travel guides to Elvis sites in Memphis. (*See* The Phenomena/Travel Guides.)

The Best of Elvis: Recollections of a Great Humanitarian. Memphis: Memphis Explorations, 1992. 185 pp. ISBN: 0963227408. New York: Pinnacle Books/Windsor Publishing Corp., 1994. 205 pp. ISBN: 0786000260.

The story of Elvis Presley's immense legacy of charity support and kindness to strangers, family, and friends. Anecdotes about his generosity to those in need, as well as his financial support of the U.S.S. *Arizona* Memorial in Hawaii and the sale of his yacht, formerly owned by President Franklin Delano Roosevelt, for the benefit of St. Jude's Children's Research Hospital. Twenty-one leaves of black and white photographs, most from private collections; captioned and credited. Brief bibliography of books, magazines, and videos (pp. 201–205 in 1994 edition).

Source: The Library of Congress ML420.P96 H5 1992/1994
Dewey Decimal 782.42166/092 B 20

☆ Hicks, Carol Johnson, and Nancy Painter Thorn

Presley Family History. [U.S.]: [n.p.], 1993. 248 pp. ISBN: none.

A genealogy of the Presley family in the United States.

Source: OCLC 39222667

☆ "Hillbilly on a Pedestal." *Newsweek* (May 14, 1956): 82.

A brief description of the impact of Elvis Presley on teenaged girls and an assessment of his first Las Vegas appearance ("Elvis was somewhat like a jug of corn liquor at a champagne party"). Quotes from Elvis about his future goals. (Note: Rather than present an accurate picture of Elvis Presley, this article is an attempt to sneer at an individual who is socially and regionally different from the writer and *Newsweek* editors.) This is one of the first mainstream newsmagazine articles about Elvis.

☆ Hopkins, Jerry

Hopkins's research notes and resource documents for this book are archived in the Mississippi Valley Collection at the University of Memphis.

Elvis: A Biography. New York: Simon and Schuster, 1971. 448 pp. ISBN: 671209736. New York: Warner Paperback Library, 1972. 448 pp. ISBN: 0446689386. London: Open Gate, 1972. 448 pp. ISBN: 0333135179. London: Abacus, 1974. 365 pp. ISBN: 0349117179 (pbk.). New York: Warner Books, 1975. 446 pp. ISBN: 0446816655.

The first researched book-length biography of Elvis Presley. It was written during Elvis's lifetime, concluding with 1970, when Elvis was 35 years old. (Hopkins wrote about the remaining years of Elvis's life in *Elvis: The Final Years*, 1980.) No footnotes, chapter notes, or index. Acknowledgments; list of interviewees. Incorrect time of birth for Elvis, as well as "guitar/bicycle" purchase and "second place" story.

Elvis's astrological chart, with an analysis by astrologer Antonia Lamb. Discography (pp. [429]–444) with a chronology of Elvis's records (including label numbers) through December 31, 1970. List also has highest position reached in *Billboard*'s "Hot 100" for each record and which records received "gold" status from the Recording Industry Association of America (RIAA), as of 1970. Filmography with a chronology of Elvis's films according to release date.

(In Abacus 1974 edition: discography, pp. 345–361; filmography, pp. 362–363.)

This book was translated into French and Japanese. (*See* Foreign Language Titles/French, Japanese.) Before publication, the book was serialized in *Look* magazine (May 4 and 18, 1971 issues.) *The Elvis Presley Story*, a 13-hour radio documentary series in 1975, was based upon this book.

Elvis is dedicated to rock and roll musician Jim Morrison of the Doors who suggested that Hopkins write this book. When Elvis died in 1977, there were 600,000 copies of this book in print. The day after he died, Warner Books received orders for 180,000 copies and orders averaging 100,000 in the days following. Three weeks after Elvis died, there were 1.2 million copies of this book—in its seventh printing—in print. (*Publishers Weekly*, Sept 5, 1977, p. 5.)

Source: The British Library X.439/2781 (Open Gate 1972);
X.439/3372 (1974)
Library of Congress ML420.P96 H72
Dewey Decimal 784.5/4/00924 B
OCLC 196593 (1971); 2581836 (Warner 1972); 11063187 (Open Gate 1972);
16248661 (1974)

———.

Hopkins's notes and resource documents for this book are in The Mississippi Valley Collection, the University of Memphis.

Elvis: The Final Years. New York: St. Martin's Press, 1980. 258 pp. ISBN: 0312243847. London: W. H. Allen, 1980. 258 pp. ISBN: none. New York: Playboy Paperbacks, 1981. 304 pp. ISBN: 0872168581. Berkley, NY: Berkley Books, 1981. 304 pp. ISBN: 0425064611. London: Star, 1981. 258 pp. ISBN: 0352308591. Berkley, NY: Berkley Books, 1983. 304 pp. ISBN: 042509880X. Berkley, NY: Berkley Books, 1985. 304 pp. ISBN: 0425089991. Also published as *Elvis: The Final Years: A Biography*, London: Omnibus Press, 1981, 258 pp. ISBN: 17951703.

A chronology of Elvis's life from December 19, 1970, until his death in August 1977. Eleven black and white photographs of Elvis during this period and four of post-Elvis Graceland. The epilogue chronicles the Presley phenomena in the three years following his death. No footnotes, chapter notes, or index. The acknowledgments include a list of interviewees.

Source: Library of Congress ML420.P96 H69 (1980)
Dewey Decimal 784.5'4'00924 [B] (1980)
OCLC 62250242 (1980); 7627868 (Playboy 1981); 10131100 (Berkley 1981);
16539867 (Star 1981); 19450872 (Berkley 1983); 14348953 (Berkley 1985)

———.

"The Hidden Life of Elvis Presley." *Look* (May 4, 1971): 33–38, 43–48. (May 18, 1971): 41–44V.

A two-part biographical series about Elvis Presley adapted from the as-yet-unpublished book *Elvis: A Biography* by Hopkins (published later that year). In the first article, Hopkins incorrectly states Elvis's time of birth and repeats the incorrect "second prize" and "guitar instead of a bicycle" stories.

☆ Husky, Rich

"World Famous Entertainer Presented Coveted Award." *State College Herald* (Arkansas State University). State University, AR. Nov 4, 1960. (Reprinted in the Oct 18, 1994, edition of the Tau Kappa Epislon Fraternity's official magazine.)

The story of Elvis Presley's initiation into the Beta Psi Chapter of Tau Kappa Epsilon fraternity at Arkansas State University in the fall of 1960.

Source: Tau Kappa Epsilon Fraternity, Office of the Grand Chapter, 8645 Founders Road, Indianapolis, IN 46268-1393

☆ Hutchins, Chris, and Peter Thompson

Elvis Meets the Beatles: The Untold Story of Their Tangled Lives. London: Smith Gryphon Limited, 1994. 248 pp. ISBN: 1856850838.

An examination of the influences, impact, and interaction of Elvis Presley and the Beatles, using their only meeting—at Elvis Presley's Los Angeles residence in August 1965—as the focal event. Other chapters detail Elvis's experiences with Truman Capote, Tom Jones, Frank Sinatra, and Raquel Welch. Hutchins recounts his own meeting with Colonel Parker in 1993 ("At the Colonel's Secret Shrine," pp. 232–248). Sixteen pages of black and white photographs of Elvis Presley and the Beatles and their friends and relatives; captioned and credited. No chapter notes, footnotes, or sources. No index. This book was translated into Finnish and Japanese. (*See* Foreign Language Titles/Finnish, Japanese.)

Source: The British Library YC.1995.b.5767
The New York Public Library JNE 95-94
Dewey Decimal 782.42166092 (1996)

———.

Elvis and Lennon: The Untold Story of Their Deadly Feud. London: Smith Gryphon Limited, 1996. 272 pp. ISBN: 1856851060.

A reprint of *Elvis Meets the Beatles.* (*See* preceding listing.)

Source: The British Library YK.1996.a.2682
Dewey Decimal 781.660992 20

☆ James, Anthony

James was a fan magazine reporter in America and England.

Presley: Entertainer of the Century. New York: Belmont Tower Books, 1977. 224 pp. ISBN: 0505512394. Cammeray, N.S.W.: Horwitz, 1978. 244 pp. ISBN: 0725505583.

Emphasis on the controversy surrounding Elvis's death. Quotes from individuals and media sources are not cited. Sixteen previously seen black and white photographs; none credited.

Source: OCLC 34694596 (1977); 27551105 (1978)

☆ Johnson, Derek

Elvis: The Legend Lives On. Starblitz series. London: Dennis Oneshots, 1988. ISBN: none.

Source: The British Library YM.1990.b.140

———.

Elvis: The Early Years. Hits series, No. 8. London: Dennis Oneshots, 1989. [32] pp. ISBN: none.

Source: Trinity College Library (Dublin, Ireland) PX-84-663

☆ Johnson, Robert

Elvis Presley Speaks! New York: Rave Publishing Corporation, 1956. 68 pp. ISBN: none.

Thought to be the first biography of Elvis Presley. Formatted as a souvenir magazine. Title page description of contents: "told for the first time—Elvis's full, intimate story, in his own words and those of his close friend, Robert Johnson." Seven chapters, comprising a chronological biography, in which Elvis is quoted extensively about his life up until early 1956. Black and white candid photographs. Johnson was a reporter for the *Memphis Press-Scimitar.*

Source: University of Memphis Special Collections
OCLC 9842182

☆ Jones, Peter

Elvis. London: Octopus Books Limited, 1976. 88 pp. ISBN: 0706405501. Seacaucus, NJ: Chartwell, 1977.

First published before Elvis's death, this book tells his life story up to 1975. The 1977 reissue was updated to include Elvis's death. The author emphasizes Elvis's musical influences and interactions through comparisons and analysis. Discusses Elvis's financial concerns as of 1975. In the first edition, the author speculates on Elvis's future. Black and white and color photographs from Elvis's career. A Chinese translation was made of this book in 1977. (*See* Foreign Language Titles/Chinese.)

Source: Library of Congress ML420.P96 J6

☆ *The King.* 20 pp. 1997.

A biographical pamphlet accompanying the Official Elvis Presley 20th Anniversary Limited Edition Commemorative Proof Set (a silver coin memorializing the twentieth anniversary of Elvis's death).

Source: eBay auction item #55195906

☆ Kirkland, K. D.

Kirkland is a collector of Elvis recordings.

Elvis. New York: The Mallard Press, 1988; 1991. London: Bison Books, 1988; 1990. 111 pp. ISBN: 0792452100 (Mallard 1988, 1991); ISBN: 0861244990 (Bison, 1988, 1990). Stamford, CT: Longmeadow, 1988. 111 pp. ISBN: 0681005750.

Introduction by former Elvis Presley girlfriend Sandy Martindale. Six chapters spanning Elvis's life, career, and aftermath of his death. Index. Black and white and color photographs; captioned and acknowledged. This book was translated into French. (*See* Foreign Language Titles/French).

Source: The Margaret Herrick Library, Academy of Motion Picture Arts and Sciences OCLC 22454980 (Mallard 1988); 20682284 and 18943586 (Bison 1988, 1990); 30925783 (Longmeadow 1988)

☆ Lawrence, Greer

Elvis: King of Rock and Roll. New York: Smithmark Publishers, 1997. 48 pp. ISBN: 0765194287. New York: Todtri Productions, 1997. [46] pp. ISBN: 1577170210.

Brief (100 words) synopses of various events throughout Elvis's life. Brief essays on Elvis collectibles, Elvis impersonators, and the Vigil Night ceremony held annually on August 15 at the Graceland mansion in Memphis. Quotes by and about Elvis; none sourced. Black and white and color photographs of Elvis; credited, some captioned.

Source: OCLC 40659207 (Todtri Productions)

☆ Leigh, Spencer

Presley Nation. [UK]: Albert Hand, 1963. 24 pp. ISBN: none.

An early, brief biography that was periodically updated and reissued between 1974 and 1975.

Source: Library of Congress xML420.P96

☆ Mann, May

May Mann was a Hollywood entertainment columnist and fan magazine reporter.

Elvis and the Colonel. New York: Drake Publishers, 1975. 273 pp. ISBN: 0847310043. New York: Pocket Books, 1976. 294 pp. ISBN: 0671807242.

A biography of Elvis Presley that consists of the author's previously published fan magazine articles and interviews with the entertainer. Seventeen black and white photographs, eight of which are of Elvis and the author; captioned and credited. In August 1977, immediately after the death of Elvis Presley, this book was expanded and reprinted under the title *The Private Elvis*. (*See* following listing.)

Source: Library of Congress ML420.P96 M3
Dewey Decimal 784.092/4 B

————.

The Private Elvis. New York: Pocket Books, 1977. 294 pp. ISBN: 0671818848.

A 600,000-copy reissue of *Elvis and the Colonel* published less than a month after Elvis's death. Updated by political columnist Molly Ivins[7] to include the *New York Times* obituary and never-before-published black and white photographs.

Source: OCLC 3332657

————.

Elvis, Why Don't They Leave You Alone? A Signet book. New York: New American Library, 1982. 214 pp. ISBN: 0451118774.

Using her personal conversations with Elvis, Mann tells the story of "the last three years of Elvis's untold personal life, his death, and also after his death." Black and white photographs of the author with Elvis.

Source: The Margaret Herrick Library, Academy of Motion Picture Arts and Sciences
OCLC 9006160

☆ Mann, Richard

Elvis. Van Nuys, CA: Bible Voice, Inc. 1977. 186 pp. ISBN: 089728027X.

The story of Elvis's life told as a morality tale: "This book set out to explore a man. . . . Not just a look at Elvis, but also at ourselves. As a reminder. Also, encouragement. And a warning . . . the 'special destiny' Elvis felt and never found. But still available to you and me" (pp. 181, 184). Sixteen black and white photographs from Elvis's adult life; captioned but not credited. Bibliography (eight entries). This book was translated into Spanish. (*See* Foreign Language Titles/Spanish.)

Source: Compiler's collection
OCLC 6271379

---

[7]Molly Ivins wrote the *Times* obituary. A decade later, in the October 1987 issue of the *Progressive*, she described Elvis's mourning fans as carrying "on like banshees" and attacking "you like furies if you happened to observe that the poor man had died a fat drug addict." Ivins is a partisan liberal columnist who frequently excoriates in print those she sees as being less than sensitive. She did not respond to requests for information about her involvement in this rapid postmortem reissue and retitling of Mann's book.

☆ Marsh, Dave

Rock music critic Dave Marsh writes for *Rolling Stone* magazine.

Elvis. Art direction by Bea Feitler. "A Rolling Stone Press Book." New York: Times
Books, 1982. 245 pp. ISBN: 081290947X. London: Elm Tree, 1982. 245 pp.
ISBN: 0241109027. New York: Warner Books, 1983. 245 pp. ISBN:
0446372196. New York: Arlington House/Distributed by Crown Publishers,
1986. 245 pp. ISBN: 0517605201. New York: Thunder's Mouth Press; Distributed by Publishers Group West, 1992; 1997. 248 pp. ISBN: 1560251182. London: Omnibus, 1992. 245 pp. ISBN: 0711932220. New York: Smithmark,
1997. 272 pp. ISBN: 0765194953.

A widely acclaimed biography in which Dave Marsh "confronts the myths about Elvis's
music, analyzing his gripping mixture of gospel, country, and rock" (book jacket notes).
Introduction explores the impact of Elvis. A new introduction was added to the 1992 edition. Filmography (p. 241). Discography (pp. 239–241). Annotated bibliography (p.
241). "Hundreds [of black and white photographs] from every stage of Elvis's career
accompany the text, showing in pictures how the King's life played out in his songs"
(inside back cover). All photographs are credited and captioned. This book was translated
into Japanese. (*See* Foreign Language Titles/Japanese.)

☆ Matthews, Rupert

Matthews has written more than 100 books on a wide range of subjects.

Elvis. New York: Grammercy Books, 1998. 112 pp. ISBN: 0517160536.

An oversize, coffee-table biography of Elvis Presley. Anecdotes from Elvis fans about
meeting Elvis. Chapter on the Elvis postmortem phenomena. No notes, sources, or citations. Black and white and color photographs from Todd Slaughter of the Official Elvis
Presley Fan Club of Great Britain. Captioned photographs. Index.

Source: OCLC 39926505

☆ Mosher, Ann, editor

Elvis Presley: His Complete Life Story in Words with More Than 100 Pictures. New
York: Bartholomew House, 1956. 64 pp. ISBN: none.

Early biography in magazine format. Contents: "Elvis Presley's Complete Life Story—
School Days—Elvis and His Cars—On the Record—The Guitar That Made a Star—
House That Fame Built—Good Citizen—He Calls Backstage—Home—Triple
Dynamo—From Memphis to TV—Fervid Fans—The Boundless Future." Uncited quotes
from Vernon and Gladys Presley about Elvis's childhood. Black and white candid photographs from his childhood through early 1956; captioned but not sourced. (Photographs of two of Elvis's high school woodworking projects, pp. 8–9.)

Source: Library of Congress ML420 P96 E4
OCLC 8564703

☆ *Movieland.* (Oct 1956–Mar 1958). *Movieland and TV Time.* (Sept 1958–Dec 1960).

Thirty-eight articles about Elvis Presley, published in the first decade of his career.

Source: The Margaret Herrick Library, Academy of Motion Picture Arts and Sciences

☆ Nelson, Pete

King! When Elvis Rocked the World. London: Proteus Books Limited, 1985. New York: Proteus Publishing Company, Inc., 1985. 112 pp. ISBN: 0862762065 (hdk.). ISBN: 0862762057 (pbk.).

A third-person narrative biography of Elvis Presley during the years from 1954 through 1958. Author states that he uses dialogue for which he "cannot vouch for the accuracy of every word." Black and white photographs. Appendix I: Sam Phillips biography and the creation of Sun Records. Appendix II: Elvis Presley discography, 1954–1958, with catalogue number and release date for all singles, EPs, and LPs. Filmography for Elvis's four films during this period, each with producer, director, and date of release. Brief chronology of Elvis's life during this period.

Source: Los Angeles Public Library 789.14 P934 Ne
The British Library X.431/13750

☆ *The 1953 Senior Herald.* Port Townsend, WA: Osborne Enterprises, 1988. 112 pp. ISBN: 0932117090.

A reproduction of Elvis Presley's senior year high school yearbook. (He was a member of the 1953 graduating class of Humes High School in Memphis.)

Source: Collection of Jerry Osborne, Port Townsend, WA

☆ O'Grady, John, and Nolan Davis

"Sexual Spadework." *O'Grady: The Life and Times of Hollywood's No. 1 Private Eye.* Los Angeles: J. P. Tarcher, [1974]. ISBN: 0874770289. Pp. 166–170.

The story of a paternity lawsuit filed against Elvis Presley—a case that garnered headlines—as told by the private investigator who was hired to investigate the claim. O'Grady remained friends with Elvis after this case was completed. (The lawsuit failed.)

Source: Library of Congress HV8083.035 A36 1974

☆ Peters, Richard

Elvis: The Golden Anniversary Tribute: Fifty Fabulous Years in Words and Pictures, 1935–1985. London: Pop Universal, 1984. 128 pp. ISBN: 0285626612. Salem, NH: Salem House, 1985. 128 pp. ISBN: 0881620823.

Elvis Presley stories and photographs from the files of *Elvis Monthly*, the longest running Elvis fan club magazine. Includes an Elvis first-person essay based on interviews given by the entertainer between 1956 and 1976. Introductory essay on the Memphis into which the Presley family moved in 1948. A chronology of Elvis's life and career from 1935 through 1985. Interviews with Sam Phillips, Chet Atkins, and Kathy Westmoreland. Memories of Peter Dacre, the first British author to interview Elvis. An A-to-Z listing of all songs recorded by Elvis Presley and their availability as of book's publication date. No citations or sources given for quotes.

Source: Library of Congress ML420.P96 P47 1984
OCLC 12517392 (1984)

☆ *Photoplay.* (Nov 1956–Feb 1979).

Ninety-nine articles about Elvis Presley appearing in *Photoplay* magazine.

Source: The Margaret Herrick Library, Academy of Motion Pictures Arts and Sciences

☆ *A Pocket Guide to the Life and Times of Elvis Presley, 1935–1977.* Chattanooga, TN: Creative History, 1992. 52 pp. ISBN: none.

A small-size format with brief text.

Source: Library of Congress ML420.P96 P62 1992
OCLC 29361060

☆ Pratt, Linda Ray

"Elvis, or the Ironies of Southern Identity." Ed. Jac L. Tharpe. *Elvis: Images and Fancies.* Jackson, MS: University Press of Mississippi, 1979. Pp. 40–51

Pratt explains how the South produced Elvis Presley, and explores why Southerners revere him. This essay is considered one of the important writings about the influences in Elvis's life—in this case his "Southerness," and what that means to his impact and legend. Elvis's racial ambiguity is explored.

Source: Tharpe, Jac L. Ph.D., editor. Elvis: Images and Fancies.

☆ Purcell, Charles

Elvis: The Legend Lives Forever. Australia: Federal Publishing Co.

An overview of the life and career of Elvis in magazine format. Comes with the CD *Platinum: A Life in Music.*

Source: David Neale, "Elvis in Print" www.geocities.com/SunsetStrip/8200/books.html

☆ Roberts, Dave

Elvis Presley. CD Books series. London: Orion Books, 1994. 120 pp. ISBN: 185797588x. [U.S]: Music Book Services Paperback, 1995. 120 pp. ISBN: 1858680581.

Brief text with previously seen color and black and white photographs. Photographs are captioned and credited. Discography (pp. 110–116). Biographical chronology (p. 117). Index. This book was translated into Dutch, German, and Portuguese. (*See* Foreign Language Titles.)

Source: The New York Public Library JNB 95-2 (1994)
The British Library YK.1996.a.16385 (1994)
Dewey Decimal 782.42166092

☆ Ryan, Thomas C.

"Rock 'n' Roll Battle: Boone v. Presley." *Collier's* (Oct 26, 1956): 109–111.

A thoughtful comparison between the two top teenage idols of the time: Pat Boone and Elvis Presley.

☆ Slaughter, Todd

Elvis Presley. [UK]: Mandabrook Ltd., 1977. 128 pp. ISBN: 0427004179.

Written shortly after Elvis Presley's death by the president of the Official Elvis Presley Fan Club of Great Britain. In the Conclusion (pp.114–117), Slaughter writes from a fan's point of view about how Elvis was withheld from his fans by his management—and how that is continuing after his death. Appendices: "Elvis Record Sales Achievement" (pp. 118–119); "Elvis's British Fan Club" (pp. 119–120); "Elvis Presley's Recording History" (pp. 120–126).

Source: The Mississippi Valley Collection, The University of Memphis (TN)
OCLC 7717538

☆ Staten, Vince

The Real Elvis: Good Old Boy. Dayton, OH: Media Ventures, 1978. 150 pp. ISBN: 0896450082.

Elvis's life through 1957. Black and white photographs; credited. Interviews with Elvis's boyhood friends, including his high school sweetheart Dixie Locke. Photographs include Elvis's girlfriends from that period, (i.e., Billie Mae Smith of Kingsport, Tennessee). Copy of Elvis's 1951 report card from Humes High School. Financial details of the Presley family's life in Memphis before 1955. No chapter notes, citations, or bibliography. In the text the author notes names of those interviewed for this book.

Source: Memphis/Shelby County (TN) Public Library and Information Center
Library of Congress ML420.P96 S7

☆ Stern, Jane, and Michael Stern

Elvis World. New York: Alfred Knopf, 1987. 196 pp. ISBN: 0394556194. London: Bloomsbury, 1987. ISBN: 0747500142. [Markham, Ont.]: Viking, 1987. 196 pp. ISBN: 0670818836. New York: Perennial Library, 1990. 196 pp. ISBN: 0060972904. London: Bloomsbury, 1991. 256 pp. ISBN: 0747511802 (hdk.). ISBN: 0747512000 (pbk.).

A biography and an evaluation of the impact of Elvis through brief essays, interviews, and photographs. Includes sections on Elvis literature, fans, motion pictures, memorabilia, and geographic locations associated with Elvis. Color and black and white photographs. Repeats the inaccurate "second prize" story. Incorrect recipe for Elvis's peanut butter and banana sandwiches. Annotated bibliography. Photo credits. This book was translated into French and Swedish. (*See* Foreign Language Titles/French, Swedish.)

☆ Stevens, P. D.

King Elvis: A View from the Stands. Calgary, Alberta, Canada: Perry Graphics, 1977. 140 pp. ISBN: none.

Discography (pp. 107–128). Bibliography. Index.

Source: University of California
OCLC 31662179

☆ Tatham, Dick

Elvis. Story of Rock Special series. London: Pheobus Publishing Company, 1976. 64 pp. Sydney, Australia: Books for Pleasure, 1976. 96 pp. ISBN: 0727100106 (same for both editions).

Written during Elvis Presley's lifetime. Four chapters, including one on his military service. Details of Elvis's feud with singer Tom Jones. Written with the assistance of the Official Elvis Presley Fan Club of Great Britain. This book has been translated into Dutch, Italian, and Swedish. (*See* Foreign Language Titles/Dutch, Italian, Swedish.)

Source: Dewey Decimal 784.092 B
OCLC 28438365

☆ Taylor, John Alvarez

Elvis: The King Lives. New York: Gallery Books, 1990. 111 pp. ISBN: 0831727500.

Brief text, photographs, and index.

Source: The British Library LB.31.c.3140
OCLC 2299009

———.

Forever Elvis. New York: Smithmark, 1992; 1994. 64 pp. ISBN: 0831734698 (same for both editions).

Minimal text with previously seen photographs and motion picture stills. Index. This book was translated into Danish, Dutch, and French. (*See* Foreign Language Titles/Danish, Dutch, French.)

Source: Los Angeles Public Library
OCLC 25820271 (1992); 31759164 (1994)

☆ Taylor, Robyn

Elvis Presley: Not Just The King of Rock and Roll! 1997.

Two essays exploring Elvis's place in the Universal Plan. Both are based on astrology. In "Who Killed The King," Ms. Taylor discusses the planetary influences on Elvis's death. In "Elvis Birth—Even The King Never Knew!," the author discusses Elvis's correct birth time using an astrological chart as erected by expert Dane Rudhyar and conversations with Elvis's close friend and spiritual counselor Larry Geller.

Source: www.robyn.on.net/elvis/index_.html

☆ "Teeners' Hero." *Time* (May 14, 1956): 53–54.

An introduction to Elvis Presley for mainstream readers. Discusses fans' reactions, his musical career, and his first appearance in Las Vegas at the New Frontier Hotel. This is one of the first mainstream newsmagazine articles about Elvis.

☆ Thompson, Patricia, and Connie Gerber

Elvis: Walking in His Footsteps. [U.S.]: Towrey Press, 1980. Unpaged. ISBN: none.

A self-published biography of Elvis using fictional, author-written "news stories" from fictitious newspapers such as the *Tupelo News* to trace the life of Elvis Presley. Maps of Tupelo, Mississippi (Elvis's birthplace), and Memphis, Tennessee, with designations of Elvis-related locations. Untitled poem attributed to Elvis and dated 1975. Memorial poem to Elvis, "Epitaph," attributed to Vernon Presley.

Source: Compiler's collection

☆ Tobler, John, and Richard Wootton

Elvis: The Legend and the Music. London: The Hamlyn Publishing Group Ltd., 1983. 192 pp. ISBN: 0517391503.

Biography (pp. 6–163), with chapter on Elvis Presley's postmortem popularity. Hit singles and albums discography with information on U.S. and U.K. chart positions (pp. 182–183). Filmography of Elvis's motion pictures with producer, director, release date, some cast members, and the name of Elvis's characters (pp. 184–188). Bibliography (18 books). Black and white and color photographs mostly from the collection of the Official Elvis Presley Fan Club of Great Britain. Index.

Source: Library of Congress ML420.P96 T65 1983
Dewey Decimal 784.5/4/00924 B 19

A Tribute to Elvis. Surrey (UK): Inahart Limited, [n.d.]. 24 pp. ISBN: none.

Source: OCLC 20732846

☆ Wallraf, Rainer, and Heinz Plehn

Elvis Presley: An Illustrated Biography. Translated by Judith Waldman. London: Omnibus Press, 1978. ISBN: 0860016137.

An English translation of the German-language Elvis Presley biography *Elvis Presley: Eine Biographie.* (*See* Foreign Language Titles/German).

Source: The British Library LB.31.b.8281

☆ Watts, J. Dan, editor

Elvis: A Tribute to the Life and the Career of Elvis Presley. Lubbock, TX: C. F. Boone, 1977. 81 pp. ISBN: none.

Brief text that includes a reproduction of his will. Essays by Elvis's back-up singer and friend J. D. Sumner: "The Elvis No One Knew . . ." and "What It Was Like at a Concert." Black and white photographs.

Source: The Margaret Herrick Library, Academy of Motion Picture Arts and Sciences OCLC 8509510

☆ Whitmer, Peter, Ph.D.

Whitmer has a practice in Princeton, New Jersey. He has written about other contemporary American culture figures, including Hunter Thompson, and contributes regularly to psychological journals and mainstream newspapers and magazines.

The Inner Elvis: A Psychological Biography of Elvis Aaron Presley. New York: Hyperion Press, 1996. 480 pp. ISBN: 0786861029. New York: Hyperion Press/Adult Paperback Trade, 1997. 496 pp. ISBN: 0786882484.

A clinical psychologist's biographical study of Elvis, proposing that his status as a "twinless twin" was the defining characteristic in his life. (Elvis's twin brother, Jesse Garon, was stillborn.) Chapter notes with bibliographic references. Black and white photographs from the Maria Columbus Collection. Index.

☆ Wiegert, Sue

Wiegert is a Los Angeles–based writer who was friends with Elvis Presley from 1967 until his death in 1977. Since 1964, she has been president of the Blue Hawaiians for Elvis fan club and editor of the widely read *Blue Hawaiians,* a quarterly newsletter about Elvis.

Elvis Is Forever. Los Angeles, CA: self-published, [1975]. Unpaged. ISBN: none.

A compilation of 1950s articles about and interviews with Elvis Presley, relating to his life and career before he was inducted into the army in March 1958. The articles are arranged to demonstrate how his career grew between 1955 and 1958.

Source: Collection of Sue Wiegert, Los Angeles, CA

☆ Williams, Jerry

Elvis Presley: His Astrobiography (Your Authentic Elvis Presley Horoscope). [n.d.]: [n.p.], 1978. ISBN: none.

A brief look at Elvis Presley's life and career through his natal chart. Explanations of planetary aspects on the day of his death. Incorrect birth date for Priscilla Presley. (*See also Elvis Aaron Presley's Astrological Horoscope and Psychological Profile* in this chapter.)

Source: Compiler's collection

See Also:

In The Man/Elvis in Quotes:

Elvis Answers Back.
Farren, Mick, compiler, and Pearce Marchbank, editor, *Elvis in His Own Words.*

In The Man/Graceland:

Elliott, Lawrence, "Where Elvis Lives."
Gillette, Jane Brown, "Elvis Lives."

In The Man/The Impact of Elvis:

Halberstam, David, "Thirty-One." *The Fifties.*
Hammontree, Patsy Guy, *Elvis Presley: A Bio-Bibliography.*
Scott, Vernon, "Elvis, Ten Million Dollars Later."

In The Man/Memoirs and Memories:

Curtin, Jim, *Elvis: Unknown Stories Behind the Legend.*
Geller, Larry, and Joel Spector, with Patricia Romanowski, *"If I Can Dream": Elvis's Own Story.*
Rooks, Nancy, and Mae Gutter, *The Maid, The Man, and His Fans: Elvis is The Man,* (Part One: "The Man: Elvis and Memphis—A Dual Destiny").
Wiegert, Sue, *Elvis's Golden Decade.*

In The Man/Reference:

Cotten, Lee, *All Shook Up: Elvis Day by Day, 1954–1977.*
Petersen, Brian, *The Atomic Powered Singer.*

In The Music, The Movies/Discography:

Carr, Roy, and Mick Farren, *Elvis Presley: The Illustrated Record.*

In The Music, The Movies/Elvis's Influence on Music:

Davis, Francis, "Chuck and Elvis, Hands-On Preservationists, and Soul in the Biblical Sense."
Matthew-Walker, Robert, *Elvis Presley: A Study in Music.*

In The Music, The Movies/Filmography:

Danielson, Sarah Parker, *Elvis: Man and Myth.*

In The Phenomena/Collecting Elvis (Memorabilia):

Templeton, Steve, *Elvis!: An Illustrated Guide to New and Vintage Collectibles.*

In The Phenomena/Cookbooks:

Wolf-Cohen, Elizabeth, *The I Love Elvis Cookbook.*

In The Phenomena/The Law:

Singer, Richard, editor, *Elvis: The Inventory of the Estate of Elvis Presley.*

In The Phenomena/Literary Recreation and Moveable Books:

The Elvis Coloring Book: A Pictorial Life History of the King of Rock 'n' Roll.

In The Phenomena/Psychic Elvis Experiences:

Daniel, Richard, *The Elvis-UFO Connection.*

In The Phenomena/Race:

Pearlman, Jill, and Wayne White, *Elvis for Beginners.*

In The Phenomena/Religion:

Stearn, Jess, *Elvis's Spiritual Journey.*
Stearn, Jess, with Larry Geller, *Elvis's Search for God.*

In Foreign Language Titles/French:

Pouzenc, Jean-Marie, *Elvis à Paris.*

In Foreign Language Titles/Spanish:

El Hombre Senaldado—Historia de Elvis Presley.

In The Rest/Deceptive Titles:

Caldwell, N. V., Jr., *Before Elvis.* (History of Tupelo before Elvis became famous: 1930s–1950.)

In The Rest/Souvenir Magazines:

The Amazing Elvis Presley.
Personality Parade *Elvis: The Legend Lives On.* (Elvis's Lost Brother and His Family.)

Juvenile Biographies

☆ Busnar, Gene

"The First Rock 'n' Roll Star: Elvis Presley." *The Superstars of Rock: Their Lives and Their Music.* New York: J. Messner, 1980. 223 pp. ISBN: none.

A chapter about Elvis Presley in a biographical compilation of rock stars. High school–level readers.

Source: The New York Public Library Sc D 81-309

☆ Daily, Robert

Elvis Presley: The King of Rock 'n' Roll. Impact Biography series. New York: F. Watts, 1996. 144 pp. ISBN: 0531158217.

Written for readers in grades 5 and up, this book attempts to address Elvis's posthumous popularity. Quotes by and about Elvis are sourced but not cited. Twenty-nine black and white photographs (most seen elsewhere); captioned and credited. Discography with six annotated titles. List of Elvis's movies and documentaries. Selected bibliography with 12 titles. Index.

Source: The New York Public Library MNE 98-249

☆ Gentry, Tony

Elvis Presley. Pop Culture Legends series. New York: Chelsea House, 1994. 128 pp. ISBN: 079102329x (hdk.). ISBN: 790123540 (pbk.).

For grades 10 through 12. Includes a discography highlighting the "important phases of Elvis Presley's career," chronology, bibliography, index, and photograph credits. Black and white photographs.

☆ Hardinge, Melissa

Elvis Presley. The Died Too Young series. London: Parragon Books, 1995. 74 pp. ISBN: 075250164X. Philadelphia, PA: Chelsea House Publishers, 1998. 48 pp. ISBN: 0791046303.

For young readers. Chapters on Sun Records founder, Sam Phillips, Colonel Parker, and the accusations of Elvis "corrupting the nation's youth." Black and white photographs.

☆ Harms, Valerie

Tryin' to Get to You: The Story of Elvis Presley. New York: Atheneum/SMI, 1979. 175 pp. ISBN: 0689307268.

For high school–level readers. Using docu-novel format, the story is told through fictional first-person quotes from Elvis and Gladys Presley; no citations or sources. Ten black and white photographs previously seen.

Source: Library of Congress ML3930.P73 H4
Dewey Decimal 784/.092/4 B 92

☆ Krohn, Katherine E.

Elvis Presley: The King. Minneapolis, MN: Lerner Publications Company, 1994. 64 pp. ISBN: 0822528770 (hdk.). ISBN: 0822596547 (pbk.).

For readers in grades 4 through 9. Six chapters examine Elvis's childhood, musical career, films, family life, and his posthumous popularity. First-person statements attributed to

Elvis, but none are cited or sourced. Black and white photographs; captioned and credited.

Source: Library of Congress ML3930.P73 K76

☆ Love, Robert

When this book was published, Robert Love was a senior editor at *Rolling Stone* magazine.

Elvis Presley. Impact Biography series. New York: Franklin Watts, 1986. 125 pp. ISBN: 0531102394.

For high school students. Introduction discusses the impact of Elvis Presley. Suggested reading and film lists. Twenty-five black and white photographs; captioned and credited. Index.

Source: Library of Congress ML3930.P73 L7

☆ Lowen, Nancy

Elvis. Profiles in Music series. Vero Beach, FL: Rourke Enterprises, 1989. 111 pp. ISBN: 0865926069.

For high school students. Examines Elvis's life from birth to death in six chapters. Contains uncited first-person quotes attributed to Elvis's mother, Gladys Presley. Black and white photographs; captioned and credited. Glossary. Index. Suggested "Listening Choices" listing of 16 Elvis songs, 9 albums, and all films.

Source: Library of Congress ML3931.P73
OCLC 19625266

☆ McBratney, Sam

"Presley, Elvis Aron." *Bibliography of Discographies.* Vol. 3: *Popular Music.* New York; London: R. R. Bowker Company, 1983. ISBN: 0835216837 (v. 3). Pp. 130–131.

A biography series for young people (no grade level given), in which one volume explores the life of Elvis Presley. Other volumes cover Prince Charles and Muhammad Ali.

Source: Trinity College Library, Dublin, IR PB 35-350 PB 35- 353; Set 6

☆ Noble, Isobel

Louis, Elvis, and Ludwig. The New Macmillan Reading Program; Series R. A Solo book; Level 35. New York: Macmillan, 1975. 31 pp. ISBN: none.

A reader for students in sixth grade (ages 11–12). Brief biographies of three musical superstars: Louis Armstrong, Elvis Presley, and Ludwig van Beethoven. Color photographs of Elvis with various guitars.

Source: Dewey Decimal 428.4
OCLC 22515155

☆ Rubel, David

Elvis Presley: The Rise of Rock and Roll. New Directions series. Brookfield, CT: The Millbrook Press, 1991. 96 pp. ISBN: 1878841181 (hdk.). 1994, ISBN: 1562948296 (pbk.). [U.S.]: Demco Media, 1994. ISBN: 0606026290 (pbk.).

For high school students. Relates Elvis's life to the rise of rock and roll music and the social changes of the 1950s and 1960s. Rubel explores the birth of rock and roll through Elvis's fusion of black rhythm and blues and white country music. Information based on secondhand sources. Photographs; captioned and credited. Quotes credited (*Elvis: A Biography* by Jerry Hopkins). Chronology of important events in Elvis's life. Notes. Bibliography (four Elvis books, eight rock and roll books). Index.

Source: Library of Congress ML3930.P73 R8 1991
Dewey Decimal 782.42166 Presley

☆ Sonifer, Polly

Elvis Presley. Legends That Never Die series. Mankato, MN: Capstone Press, 1989. ISBN: 156065080X.

For high school students.

Source: Library of Congress ML420.P96 S66 1989
Dewey Decimal 782.42166/092 B 20
OCLC 20530360

☆ Taylor, Paula

Elvis Presley. Rock 'n' Pop Stars series. Mankato, MN: Creative Education, 1975. 31 pp. ISBN: 0871913941.

For grades 4 through 9, "stressing [Elvis Presley's] rise to fame as a singer." Color renderings of scenes from Elvis's life.

Source: Library of Congress ML3930.P3 T4

☆ Tobler, John and Richard Wootton

Elvis: The Legend and the Music. London: The Hamlyn Publishing Group, 1983. 192 pp. ISBN: 0517391503.

A biography and reference book, with color and black/white photographs from the collection of the Official Elvis Presley Fan Club of Great Britain. Chapter on Elvis's post-mortum popularity. Brief bibliography, filmography, and discography. Index.

Source: Library of Congress ML420.P96 T

☆ Woog, Adam

The Importance of Elvis Presley. "The Importance of" Biography series. San Diego: Lucent Books, 1997. 112 pp. ISBN: 1560060840.

An account of the life of Elvis Presely and his contribution to popular music written for high school students. Bibliographic references (pp. 103–107). Quotes on Elvis's impact by fellow entertainers and friends; uncited. Footnotes. Index. Black and white photographs previously seen; captioned and credited.

Source: Library of Congress NK3930,P73 W65 1997
Dewey Decimal 782.42166/092 B 20

☆ Wootton, Richard

Mr. Wootton is the co-author of *Elvis Presley: The Legend and the Music*, with John Tobler. (*See* listing in this section.)

Elvis Presley: King of Rock and Roll. Twentieth Century People series. London: Hodder and Stoughton Ltd., 1982. 128 pp. ISBN: 0340269545.

For high school students. Final chapter explores his posthumous impact. Index. Black and white photographs, mostly candids; captioned and credited. Author acknowledges the printed sources for the material used in writing this book. This book was translated into Norwegian. (*See* Foreign Language Titles/Norwegian.)

Source: The British Library X.435/891
Dewey Decimal 784.092

———.

Elvis! New York: Random House, 1985. 127 pp. ISBN: 0394970462 (lib. bdg.). ISBN: 0394870468 (pbk.).

A reprint of *Elvis Presley: King of Rock and Roll.* (*See* preceeding listing.) First American edition.

Source: Library of Congress ML3930.P73 W66
OCLC 11133680

See Also:

The Academics/Educational Literature

Photo-Biographies

☆ Allen, William, David Gibbon, and Nicola Dent, editors

William Allen is "one of the many pseudonyms for the writer W. A. Harbinson" (book jacket notes). His first biography about Elvis was written in 1975 and reprinted seven times under various titles. (*See* Harbinson listing later in this section.)

Elvis. New York: Smithmark Publishing, Inc., 1992; 1994.192 pp. ISBN: 08313727551. 20th Anniversary edition published by CLB International, Wayne, NJ, 1997. 192 pp. ISBN: 1858336694. 20th Anniversary edition also published by Ken Fin Books, Collingwood, Victoria, Connecticut, 1997. 192 pp. ISBN: 1875973826.

Sourced quotes by and about Elvis; uncited. Bibliography with 18 titles (pp. 179–183). List of Elvis's films and documentaries with synopses (pp. 185–187). A discography of what the author refers to as "the most important albums" (pp. 189–191). Text by William Allen. Color and black and white photographs. The 1992 edition of this book was translated into Dutch and German. (*See* Foreign Language Titles/Dutch, German.)

Source: OCLC 32058733 (1992 and 1994); 37541809 (1997 CLB International); 38832689 (1997 Ken Fin Books)

☆ Cahill, Marie

Forever Elvis. London: Bison Group, 1991. 64 pp. ISBN: 0861248201.

An oversized photo-biography of Elvis Presley's life. Photographs credited; most have been previously seen. Index.

Source: Dewey Decimal 791.43028092

———.

Elvis. North Dighton, MA: J. G. Press, Inc., 1994. 64 pp. ISBN: 1572150327.

The American publication of *Forever Elvis*. (*See* preceding listing.)

Source: Book City Collectibles, Hollywood, CA

☆ Covey, Maureen

Elvis for the Record: The Story of Elvis Presley in Words and Pictures. Compiled by Todd Slaughter and Michael Wells. Cheshire, England: Stafford Pemberton Publishers, 1982.

Color and black and white photographs. Information about Elvis's motion picture career.

Source: Hammontree, Elvis Presley: A Bio-Bibliography, *p. 223.*

☆ Curtin, Jim

The Unseen Elvis: Candids of the King from the Collection of Jim Curtin. "A Bullfinch Press Book." Boston: Little, Brown, 1992. 207 pp. ISBN: 082121912X (hdk.). ISBN: 0821220659 (pbk.). London: Victor Gollancz, 1992. ISBN: 0575053674.

More than 400 previously unpublished black and white and color photographs of Elvis Presley. Covers Elvis's life and career from the 1950s through 1977. Overview biographical essay for each section.

☆ Doll, Susan M., Ph.D.

Dr. Doll is the author of seven books about Elvis Presley.

Elvis: King of Rock 'n' Roll. Lincolnwood, IL: Publications International, 1994. 239 pp. ISBN: 0785308717.

Nearly 400 color and black and white photographs. All photographs credited. This book was reissued in 1995 as *Elvis Presley: Portrait of the King*.

Source: OCLC 0785308717

☆ Frew, Tim

Elvis: A Life in Pictures. A Life in Pictures series. New York: MetroBooks, 1997. 96 pp. ISBN: 1567994377.

Includes a chapter on his death and funeral. "More than 125" (per book cover) black and white and color photographs; captioned and credited. Discography. List of Elvis's films, their studios, and release years. Bibliography (10 items).

☆ Giuliano, Geoffrey, Brenda Giuliano, and Deborah Lynn Black

The Illustrated Elvis Presley. London: Sunburst Books, 1994. 96 pp. ISBN: 1857780361. Edison, NJ: Chartwell Books, 1994. 96 pp. ISBN: 0785800018. Reprinted in 1995 with same ISBN.

Previously seen photographs; not all credited. Some photographs are from the archives of the Official Elvis Presley Fan Club of Great Britain. No footnotes, chapter notes, or sources. No index.

Source: The British Library LB.31.b.11740 m

☆ Glade, Emory

Elvis: A Golden Tribute. Special 50th Birthday Edition. Wauwatosa, WI: Robus Books, [c1984]. [63] pp. ISBN: 0881883476.

Includes photographs of Graceland in the 1970s, before Elvis's death. Also a section on his daughter, Lisa Marie. Photographs are credited to well-known paparazzi photographer Ron Galella.

Source: Cleveland (OH) Public Library ML420.P96 G6 1984
Dewey Decimal 784.5/4/00924 19

☆ Harbinson, W. A.

Elvis Presley: An Illustrated Biography. London: Joseph, 1975. 160 pp. ISBN: 0718114698. New York: Ace Books, 1975. Unpaged. ISBN: 0441365175.

"Over 400" black and white photographs (per book cover). Photograph sources listed in acknowledgments but none are specifically credited. Not all photographs are captioned. In 1976 the book was published in French under the title *Elvis Presley*. (*See* Foreign Language Titles/French.)

Source: Bowling Green State University Library ML420.P96 H4 (Joseph)
OCLC 2543309 (Joseph); 188072 (Ace Books)

☆ Hirshberg, Charles

Elvis: A Celebration in Pictures. Warner Books, 1995. 126 pp. ISBN: 0446520209.

A photographic and text timeline of Elvis's life, based on the January 1995 Collector's Edition of *Life* magazine on Elvis Presley: "Elvis on His 60th Birthday." (*See* The Rest/Souvenir Magazines.) Interviews with Elvis's friends and co-musicians and a quiz on the reader's knowledge of Elvis. Photographs are credited.

Source: Library of Congress ML88.P76 H57 1995

☆ Lichter, Paul

Paul Lichter has published 20 photograph books on Elvis Presley—the first in 1975, the most recent in 2000. A number of his books have been issued as reprints. (*See* The Man/Photographs; The Music, The Movies/Filmography; and Scott and Waldman listings in this section.)

Most of the photographs for these books are from Paul Lichter's Elvis Photo Archives, which owns the rights to 40,000 Elvis photographs. Since 1970, Lichter has operated an Elvis recordings and memorabilia mail order business, The Elvis Unique Record Club. Lichter and the club were the subject of an interview in *Crawdaddy* (Nov 1977), "What Price Glory? Peddling the Relics of Royalty" by Fred Schruers. (*See* The Phenomena/Collecting Elvis.)

Behind Closed Doors. Huntingdon Valley, PA: Jesse Books, 1987. 116 pp. ISBN: none. *Behind Closed Doors*; 10th Anniversary Limited Numbered Edition. Huntingdon Valley, PA: Jesse Books, 1987. 116 pp. ISBN: 0961602740.

A compilation of essays and black and white photographs of Elvis, grouped thematically (i.e., army, childhood, with Priscilla and Lisa, Elvis cars). Essays by author on each theme. Narrative essay of Elvis's visit with President Richard Nixon in 1970. Essay by Colonel Parker, "My Boy," praising Elvis's singing and acting skills. No captions or attribution for photos.

Source: Library of Congress ML420.P96 L5 1987
OCLC 17678619 or 16678249;
24536863 (10th Anniversary Edition)

———.

The Boy Who Dared to Rock: The Definitive Elvis. Garden City, NJ: Dolphin Books/Doubleday and Co., 1978. 304 pp. ISBN: 0385126360. London: Sphere Books Limited, 1980; 1981. 304 pp. ISBN: none. New York: Galahad Books, 1978; 1982. 304 pp. ISBN: 0883656221.

An examination of Elvis Presley's life and career: his biography, concerts, recording sessions, discography (pp. 201–298), and his films (pp. 299–300). "Almost 700 black and white photos and 16 pages in full color" (back cover).

This book was written while Elvis was alive but was published after he died. According to *Publishers Weekly* (Sept 5, 1977: 5), the publication was held until a postmortem epilogue could be added. In the 1982 edition, the title was changed to *The Definitive Elvis: The Boy Who Loved to Rock.*

Source: Library of Congress ML420.P96 L52
OCLC 3380558 (Dolphin Books); 8814020 (Galahad Books);
20740256 (Sphere Books Limited)

———.

The Candid Elvis. Huntingdon Valley, PA: Memphis Flash Enterprises, 1977. [20] pp. ISBN: none.

A book of color and black and white candid photographs, covering Elvis's life in the 1950s, 1960s, and 1970s. Subjects include Elvis's wedding, his home in California, Elvis riding horses, Elvis in a Nashville recording studio, and Elvis with his parents. Author states that only 999 copies of this book were printed.

Source: OCLC 7718509

———.

Elvis Magic Moments. Apache Junction, AZ: Jesse Books, 1994. 176 pp. ISBN: 0961602775.

According to author Lichter, this book was produced with the cooperation of Graceland and Elvis Presley Enterprises, Inc.

Source: Lichter: Elvis Unique Record Club, 10933 E. Elmwood Street, Apache Junction, AZ 85220

———.

Elvis: Portrait of a Legend. Huntingdon Valley, PA: Memphis Flash, 1976. [20] pp. ISBN: none.

Twenty-eight black and white candid photographs—captioned—of Elvis Presley's career and personal life. Includes a photograph of Elvis with entertainer Jackie Wilson. No text other than captions. In 1977, this book was reissued as *Elvis: Portrait of a Legend.* Memorial Collectors Edition.

Source: The Margaret Herrick Library, Academy of Motion Picture Arts and Sciences (1977 edition)
OCLC 7718438 (1976 edition)

———.

Elvis: Rebel Heart. Apache Junction, AZ: Jesse Books, 1992. 200 pp. ISBN: 0961602767.

Text and color and black and white photographs of Elvis Presley from the 1950s through the 1970s, cited by date and place. No captions or credits. A photographic chronology of Elvis's life. Text features "never-before-told" anecdotes from Elvis's family and friends.

Source: Paul Lichter

————.

Millennium Elvis. Apache Junction, AZ: Jesse Books, 2000.

One volume, advertised as "two books in one," which offers photographs of Elvis "behind the scenes at home, on the road, on the set." Also includes what Lichter calls "The Last Photo Session," which "comes from Elvis's personal photo collection." The second set of photographs in the book are from Elvis concerts.

Source: Paul Lichter

————.

Paul Lichter's Elvis: Memories Are Forever. Huntingdon Valley, PA: Memphis Flash, 1978. 100 pp. ISBN: none. Music No: JL-12645, Memphis Flash.

This book comes with a 33⅓-rpm mono, containing the same excerpts from interviews, press conferences, and radio and television appearances as printed in the book. Sound recording issued under the same title.[8] According to Lichter, this package was produced for Crane-Norris TV Marketing and was sold exclusively on television.

Source: Bowling Green State University Library ML420.P96 L55 OCLC 27808145 (book); 10844110 (recording)

☆ *The Life and Death of Elvis Presley*. Harrison House/Barre Publishers, 1977. Unpaged. ISBN: none.

One hundred and fifty-five black and white and color photographs. No author attribution for text.

Source: National Museum of American History, Washington, D.C. ML420.P96 H 3 OCLC 4074361

☆ Morgan, Todd, with Laura Kath (text); Jeffrey Golick, editor

Todd Morgan is Director of Creative Resources at Elvis Presely Enterprises, Inc.

Elvis: His Life in Pictures. New York: Artabras Publishers/Abbeville Publishing Group, 1997. 144 pp. ISBN: 0896600823. New York: A Tiny Folio/Abbeville Press Publishers, 1997. 288 pp. ISBN: 0789201577.

This book, which was published in two different sizes,[9] chronicles Elvis's life and career through photographs from the Elvis Presley Enterprises, Inc., Archives. Photographs vary

---

[8]Companion sound recording housed in the Bowling Green State University Sound Recordings Archives. Call number: 12/33 Memphis Flash JL-12645.

in selection and placement between the two editions. Photographs include Elvis's posses-sions, a room-by-room photographic tour of Graceland, concert jumpsuits, the "Lisa Marie" airplane, and Elvis's vehicles. Section of color photographs of Elvis memorabilia from the Elvis Presley Enterprises, Inc. (EPE), archives. Photographs not owned by EPE are credited.

Brief (21 entries) chronology of Elvis's life. Discography listing of Elvis's full-length albums with dates and *Billboard* chart peak position. Filmography. Index. This book was translated into French. (*See* Foreign Language Titles/French.)

Source: Library of Congress ML420.P96 E356 1997 (same for each edition)
Dewey Decimal 782.42166092 (same for each edition)

☆ Mundy, Julie

At the time of this book's publication, Mundy was president/executive director of the Official Elvis Presley Fan Club of Great Britain and the Commonwealth (OEPFC).

The Official Elvis Presley Fan Club Commemorative Album, 1935–1977. London: Virgin Books, 1997. 223 pp. ISBN: 1852276290.

Three hundred captioned black and white photographs of Elvis in the recording stu-dio, film sets, and with his family, friends, and fans. Photographs are from the collec-tion of the Official Elvis Presley Fan Club of Great Britain and the Commonwealth (OEPFC).

Source: The British Library LB.31.b.14531
Library of Congress ML420.P96 M86 1997
Dewey Decimal 782.42166092

☆ Parish, James Robert

The Elvis Presley Scrapbook. New York: Ballantine Books, 1975. 185 pp. ISBN: 0345247272. New York: Ballantine Books, 1977. 218 pp. ISBN: 0345275942.

First issued two years before Elvis's death. Photographs of memorabilia. Discography (pp. 167–185). Filmography (pp. 197–213). Black and white photographs; captioned and credited. This book was translated into Japanese. (*See* Foreign Language Titles/Japanese.)

When Elvis died in 1977, there were 90,000 copies of this book in print. Within a month, Ballantine Books released 200,000 more (*Publishers Weekly*, Sept 5, 1977, p. 5). Later in 1977, after these were sold, Parish updated and reissued the book with informa-tion on Elvis's death.

Source: Library of Congress ML420.P96 P25 1975;
ML420.P96 P25 1977
Dewey Decimal 784l.092/4 B

---

[9]The Artabras edition measures 305 × 229 mm. The Tiny Folio edition measures 115 × 105 mm. The Artabras edi-tion has 180 photographs; 100 in color. The Tiny Folio edition has 240 photographs; 160 in color.

☆ Ridge, Millie

The Elvis Album. New York: Gallery Books, 1991. 304 pp. ISBN: 0831727497. London: Grange, 1991. 304 pp. ISBN: 1856270084. London: Greenwich Editions, 1998. 306 pp. ISBN: 1856485064. London: PRC, 1999. 306 pp. ISBN same as 1998 edition.

A "pictorial celebration" of the life of Elvis Presley, accompanied by text. Cover claims "660 dazzling photographs" in color and black and white; credited and captioned. Index. This book was translated into French. (*See* Foreign Language Titles/French.)

Source: Los Angeles County Public Library 784.5400924 (1991)
OCLC 40644790 (1998, 1999)

☆ Rijff, Ger J.

Faces and Stages. Amsterdam, Holland: Ger Rijff/Tutti Frutti, 1986. 120 pp. ISBN: none.

This book was translated into Japanese. (*See* Foreign Language Titles/Japanese.)

Source: University of Southern California Cinema/TV Library ML400.G47 1986
OCLC 20708571

☆ Scott, S. K.

Elvis: The Legend Lives On. Edited by Paul Lichter. [n.p.]: King Publishing Co., 1977. 248 pp. ISBN: none.

Nineteen sections of Elvis photographs, black and white and color. Each section begins with brief explanation of photographs. Of interest: candid color photographs of Elvis's last concert. Photographs are not captioned or individually credited. List of five individuals who are thanked for unspecified photographs.

Source: University of Mississippi Archives ML420.P96 E49
OCLC 3959969

The Story of Elvis in Pictures. [U.S.]: [n.p.], [n.d.]. 30 pp.

Booklet with black and white photographs (printed in purple ink) of Elvis through 1963; most previously seen.

Source: Compiler's collection

☆ Waldman, Carl, Jim Donovan, and Paul Lichter

Elvis Immortal: A Celebration of the King. [U.S.]: Legends Press, 1997. 244 pp. ISBN: 0966369807.

More than 300 black and white and color photographs from the collection of Paul Lichter. Foreword by Lichter. Introduction by entertainer Glen Campbell, who writes about his friendship with Elvis. Discography (pp. 232–242). Filmography (p. 243).

The book comes with a CD, *Elvis: Memories Are Forever*, which has interviews and conversations with Elvis's friends and fans. Lichter produced the CD. Book and CD come in a black case with the words "Elvis Immortal" embossed on the front. Each book is numbered and is accompanied by a set of collectors' postage stamps from Tanzania featuring Elvis.

Source: Library of Congress ML420.P96 W27 1997
OCLC 40444733

See Also:

In The Man/Memoirs and Memories:

Ringel, Judy, "Elvis 1955–1956."

In The Man/Photographs:

The Last Vacation.
Shaver, Sean, *The Elvis Book*, Vol. 1 (1935–1967). The Elvis Book series.

In The Rest/Souvenir Magazines:

Elvis on His 60th Birthday: A Celebration in Pictures

Addenda
1965—Where's Elvis?

By the mid-1960s the Elvis Presley who had almost literally set the world on fire in the mid-1950s was barely a glowing ember. Sure, he was appearing in films and selling records, but this artistic output bore greater resemblance to Perry Como's "Hot Diggety, Dog Diggety" and Annette Funicello's *Beach Blanket Bingo* than the edgy, libido stirrings of "Jailhouse Rock" (song and film).

The media took notice. In 1965 writers began to search for the Elvis who made the girls scream, not Hollywood studio revenues rise. This investigation would continue until that December night in 1968, when Elvis appeared on the NBC-TV special *Elvis* in black leather (not Sheik of Araby caftan), surrounded by five casually dressed men (not a harem of scantily clad women), and once again set the world aflame.

These media inquiries produced valuable assessments of Elvis's persona, talents, and impact during this pivotal time in his career.

☆   ☆   ☆   ☆

☆ Booth, Stanley

"**Hound Dog to the Manor Born.**" *Esquire* (Feb 1968): 106–108. (*See* The Man/Major Articles.)

This oft-referenced article contrasts Elvis Presley's 1950s music origins with his status and persona in the 1960s. (When Booth wrote this article, it had been eight years since Elvis had appeared in a live or televised concert. Ten months later, on December 3,1968, Elvis would return to public performing with the airing of the NBC/Singer Company "Elvis" television special.)[10]

☆ Hopper, Hedda

"Peter Pan in Blue Suede Shoes." *Los Angeles Times* (Jan 31, 1965): 1, 10.

An update on Elvis Presley's life and career, with an emphasis on how he spent his time in Hollywood. Comments from Norman Taurog, who had just directed Elvis in their fifth film together, *Tickle Me*.

☆ Jennings, C. Robert

"There'll Always Be an Elvis." *Saturday Evening Post* (Sept 1965): 76–79.

A biography with an emphasis on the current status of Elvis Presley's life and career.

☆ Lewis, Joseph

"Elvis Presley Lives . . . and His 'Come Touch Me' Appeal Seems to Be Inex-haustible." *Cosmopolitan* (Nov 1968): 92–95.

An interview with Elvis Presley and his coworkers on the Cottonwood, Arizona, set of *Stay Away, Joe*. The article explores the type of entertainer and individual Elvis has become since 1956.

☆ "Rock 'n' Roll: Forever Elvis." *Time* (May 7, 1965): 61.

A survey of Elvis's life and career as he turned 30 years of age. Quote from Elvis about his "longing to be someone."

Articles in Scandal Magazines, 1956–1960

"How Elvis Presley Got 'That Way.'" *The Lowdown* (Jan 1956).

Speculation on the origins of Elvis Presley's on-stage gyrations.

"Elvis Presley: The Lowdown on Mr. Rock and Roll." *Top Secret* (Nov 1956).

Elvis talks about his failed performance in Las Vegas.

"Girls! Beware of Elvis's Doll-Point Pen." *Confidential* (Jan 1957).

Articles on Texas fans of Elvis Presley who encouraged their idol to autograph their chests.

"A Girl Confesses: 'My Night with Elvis Presley.'" *Confidential* (May 1957).

[10]This article is reprinted in *The Complete Elvis* (Torgoff, 1982; *see* The Man/Reference) and in *The Elvis Reader* (Quain, 1992; *see* The Man/The Impact of Elvis).

"How Elvis Stole Sinatra's Sexy Squaw." *Top Secret* (Dec 1960).

Elvis's relationship with Juliet Prowse.

"Elvis Presley: Pied Piper of Sex." *Suppressed Annual: The Best of Suppressed.* (No date).

Sources: *Compiler's Collection (Top Secret, Nov 1956)*
Library of Congress (Confidential)
Cranor, Rosalind, Elvis Collectibles, *p. 241. (The Lowdown, Top Secret, and Suppressed Annual)*

Elvis and the Martial Arts

From 1959 until his death, Elvis Presley had a passion for martial arts. He achieved two eighth-degree black belts, one in tae kwon do and another in kendo, took "Tiger" as his karate name, and planned to put together a competition karate team—even having his jumpsuit designer Bill Belew create a logo and uniforms. In the 1970s Elvis became enthusiastically involved in the funding, scripting, and production of a karate documentary, which was never completed.

☆   ☆   ☆   ☆

☆ "About Karate." *Elvis Word for Word.* Ed. Jerry Osborne. Port Townsend, WA: Osborne Publishing Enterprises, 1999. Pp. 230–231.

Transcript of Elvis's 1974 discourse on the history of karate and of his participation in the sport.

Source: Jerry Osborne

☆ Carman, Wayne

Elvis's Karate Legend. [TN]: Legacy Entertainment, Inc., 1998. 184 pp. ISBN: 096653705.

Elvis Presley's former karate training partner tells of the entertainer's interest and competence in the sport. Elvis karate anecdotes from his friends and employees Ed Parker, Kang Rhee, Sam Thompson, Red West, and Kathy Westmoreland. Photographs of Elvis involved in karate activities.

Source: www.bransonbroadcast.com/elvis/elvismain.html

☆ Corcoran, John

"Elvis: The Man and the Martial Artist, Part II." *Inside Kung Fu* (Dec 1977): 14–21.

Part II of "the first in-depth and accurate journalistic record" of Elvis Presley's karate career. (*See* Shively listing later in this section for Part I.)

Source: Compiler's collection

☆ "Don't Step on His Blue Suede Shoes: Elvis's Impact on Karate." *International Fighter* (Oct 1987).

☆ Parker, Ed

"The Elvis Presley I Knew." *Official Karate* (Apr 1978): [4 pp.].

Elvis's karate instructor Ed Parker writes of his experiences with Elvis.

Source: Compiler's collection

☆ Shively, Rick

"Elvis: The Man and the Martial Artist, Part I." *Inside Kung Fu* (Nov 1977): 22–25,41.

"The first in-depth and accurate journalistic record" of Elvis Presley's karate career. Black and white photographs. (*See* Corcoran listing earlier in this section for Part II.)

Source: Compiler's collection

See Also:

In The Man/Memoirs and Memories:

Parker, Edmund, *Inside Elvis.*

Elvis's Boats and Cars

☆ Montz, Gerard

"Elvis: The King of Car Collecting." *Elvis International* (Spring 1999): 12–15.

A survey of the cars purchased by Elvis Presley, with accompanying color and black and white photographs of some of the vehicles (photographs from Elvis Enterprises, Inc.). This issue comes with a pullout 1999 calendar with the photographs from the article.

Source: Compiler's collection

☆ Owens, John

"The Elvis-Craft: The King Is Dead. So Is His Boat." *Boating* (Mar 1990): 22–28.

A history of Elvis Presley's boats. Title refers to a 1963 18-foot Chris-Craft Cavalier, the *Hound Dog*, which at the time of this article was deteriorating in the backyard of Elvis friend and memorabilia seller Jimmy Velvet. (Velvet is incorrectly identified in the article as recording the 1960's hit records "Blue Velvet" and "Mission Bell.")

☆ Presley, Elvis

"Rock 'n' Roll 'n' Drag." *Rod Builder and Customizer* (Sept 1956).

An article, by-lined by Elvis, about his love of cars.

Source: Cranor, Rosalind, Elvis Collectibles, *p. 267.*

Elvis's Lauderdale Courts Residence

The Lauderdale Courts articles show how deeply Elvis has penetrated our national conscious-ness. Why else would readers of the prestigious *The New York Times* be interested in the child-hood home of a pop music entertainer? Who can name the buildings in which the Beatles grew up? This Lauderdale Courts fascination has not been seen before in American journalism.

During the years before he became famous, Elvis Presley and his family lived at a num-ber of addresses. For most of Elvis's high school years, the Presley family's home was apart-ment 328 in the 185 Winchester Street building of Lauderdale Courts—a 400-plus unit, low-income public housing complex in Memphis. According to Elvis biographer Peter Gural-nick, Elvis's years at Lauderdale Courts were "seminal" because Lauderdale "opened up worlds for him." (*See* Yellin listing in this section.)

Presently, the Lauderdale Courts units are mostly unoccupied and scheduled for demo-lition. Despite this, the building where the Presley family once lived remains a mecca for Elvis fans.

☆   ☆   ☆   ☆

☆ Castro, Peter, and Jane Sanderson

"Elvis's Place." *People Weekly* (Jan 8, 1996): 61–62.

An interview with Annette Neal, the resident of apartment 328 in Lauderdale Courts, and Jesse Lee Denson, who was friends with Elvis when he lived there. They talk about life then and now in the housing complex.

☆ "A King's Beginnings." *Economist* (Mar 22, 1997): 35.

The controversy over the proposed demolition of Lauderdale Courts. Examination of fans' efforts to save the building in which the Presley family lived.

☆ Yellin, Emily

"Elvis's Other Home: Unenshrined and All but Uninhabitable." *The New York Times* (Oct 25, 1995): A14.

A story on the condition of Lauderdale Courts in 1995. Interview with the current resi-dent of apartment 328, Annette Neal, who talks about her experiences with Elvis's fans who visit her.

Biographies of Others
Gladys Love Smith Presley

"She was the sunshine of our home."[11]

Elvis Presley enjoyed an exceptionally close relationship with his mother, Gladys. He was her and Vernon Presley's only surviving child. His twin brother, Jesse Garon, had been still-born, and the Presleys had no other children. Elvis was the center of Gladys's world, and her doting attention had a strong, mostly positive influence on his life.

Gladys was born in rural Mississippi in 1912 to Robert Lee Smith and Octavia ("Doll") Mansell Smith, one of eight children. Her parents were low-income working class, so she spent much of her childhood laboring in the fields and other people's homes to help support her family.

Thus, as a young girl, Gladys developed strong work and family ethics that she would carry throughout her life and pass on to Elvis. As an adult, she was always employed, holding a variety of factory and service jobs until Elvis brought affluence to the household. Even after moving into Graceland, she preferred to do the housework and laundry as well as cook for her husband and son.

Her hard-work childhood had left little time for education. She had not graduated from high school, but she was determined that Elvis would—and would also become a polite, religious, hard-working gentleman. Elvis succeeded in meeting her expectations.

Gladys and Vernon married in 1933, when she was 21 and he was 17. Two years later, Elvis was born. Vernon and Gladys were part of two closely intertwined families: Vernon's brother Vester married Gladys's sister Clettes. When Vernon and Gladys moved to Memphis in 1948, many of the family members followed.

Gladys was never comfortable with Elvis's fame. Post-1955 candid photographs of her almost universally reflect this uncertainty and fear. In fact, there are few pictures during this period that show her smiling. Briefly, however, she can be seen beaming with enthusiasm and pride as an extra in the Grand Theater audience scene in Elvis's second film, *Loving You*.

Gladys died of a heart attack in August 1958 while Elvis was stationed at Fort Hood, Texas. The photographs of him in the aftermath are painful to view, so clearly do they show his deep grief. Her body was first buried in Forest Hills Cemetery in Memphis. After Elvis died, it was moved to the Meditation Garden at Graceland.

☆   ☆   ☆   ☆

☆ Dundy, Elaine

British author Elaine Dundy lived in Elvis's hometown, Tupelo, Mississippi, while researching this book.

Elvis and Gladys. New York: Macmillan, 1985. 350 pp. ISBN: 0025539108. London: Weidenfeld & Nicolson, 1985. 288 pp. ISBN: 029778210X. New York: Dell, 1986. 350 pp. ISBN: 0440122716. New York: St. Martin's Press, 1991. 350 pp. ISBN: 031206344X. [UK]: Pimlico, 1995. 368 pp. ISBN: none.

A biography of Elvis Presley and Gladys, his mother, focusing on their relationship. This is the first book to detail her exceptional impact upon Elvis. Includes Gladys's genealogical

[11]From Gladys Presley's headstone, which reads in full: "Gladys Smith Presley, April 25, 1912–August 14, 1958. Beloved wife of Vernon Presley and mother of Elvis Presley. She was the sunshine of our home."

and early histories, and explores Elvis's life up to his mother's death in 1958.

Black and white photographs of Gladys Presley's ancestors, Presley family friends and relatives, Elvis's childhood, and his early career. Elvis's family tree. No footnotes. Bibliography (pp. 335–337) of Elvis books, topic-related books, and archival sources. Index.

In 1986, this book was reissued in London as a paperback, *Elvis and Gladys: The Genesis of the King.* (*See* next listing.)

————.

Elvis and Gladys: The Genesis of the King. London: Futura, 1986. 362 pp. ISBN: 0708830870.

Originally published as *Elvis and Gladys* (1985) by Weidenfeld and Nicholson, London. (*See* preceding listing.)

Source: OCLC 15221264

☆ Miles, William T.

"Elvis's Mother's Friends Recall Sweetness, Beauty, Humility." *Tupelo* (May–June 1965): 7–8, 20–23, 26–27.

Interviews with longtime Tupelo, Mississippi, friends of Gladys Presley, commenting on her life and on Elvis.

Source: The Mississippi Valley Collection, The University of Memphis (TN)

☆ Pett, Saul

"Does His Mama Think He's Vulgar?" *Associated Press* (July, 22, 1956).

Gladys Presley comments on her son's career.

Priscilla Beaulieu Presley

Elvis Presley's wife, Priscilla, was born in 1945, six months before her navy pilot father, James Wagner, would die in combat. Her mother remarried an air force officer, Joseph Beaulieu, and Priscilla had a childhood not unlike that of other military children.

In 1959 her stepfather was assigned to Germany, near where Elvis Presley was stationed. It was there that the two met and fell in love. When Elvis mustered out of the army in 1960 and returned to Graceland, Priscilla remained with her family.

The two stayed in touch, and Priscilla moved to Memphis in 1963 to complete high school. After graduation, she remained there.

Elvis proposed to Priscilla on Christmas Eve 1966, and they were married the following May. In February of 1968, she gave birth to Elvis's only child, Lisa Marie Presley. They divorced in 1973 and remained friends until his death.

After Elvis's death, Priscilla became an actress, holding a regular part on the popular prime-time drama *Dallas*. She had lead roles in the *Naked Gun* movies and most recently on ABC's *Spin City* series.

With the death of Vernon Presley in 1979 and Elvis's grandmother Minnie Mae Presley in 1980, Lisa Marie became his sole heir and Priscilla Presley became the estate's executor. In an effort to save her daughter's inheritance, Priscilla managed an astonishing financial feat: the resuscitation of the estate's dwindling assets into the multimillion-dollar enterprise that exists today. In 1982 she opened the Graceland mansion for public tours. She has since aggressively pursued trademark status for Elvis's name, likeness, and image, along with expanding the estate's business interests to include a shopping complex, hotel, and theme restaurant.

In addition to her financial success with Elvis Presley Enterprises, Inc., Priscilla Presley has developed and marketed her signature perfumes and has written the bestselling book, *Elvis and Me*, which was translated into 14 languages and made into a television miniseries.

Today, she continues overseeing Elvis Presley Enterprises, Inc., and its expansion. She lives in Southern California with writer-director Marco Garibaldi and their son, Navarone.

☆   ☆   ☆   ☆

☆ Andrews, Suzanne

"Making Elvis Pay." *Working Woman* (Sept 1993): 52–53V.

A story examining how Priscilla Presley "spent the last decade quietly building a multimillion-dollar business," Elvis Presley Enterprises, Inc. The article explores the various business interests managed by Ms. Presley.

Source: Library of Congress HQ1101.W78

☆ Battelle, Phyllis

"Priscilla Presley: Her Struggle to Raise Elvis's Daughter." *Ladies Home Journal* (Feb 1984): 26–30, 158–161.

An interview with Priscilla Presley, who discusses her parenting of Lisa Marie Presley, who was 16 years old at the time of this publication.

☆ Davidson, Bill

"Priscilla Presley: The Second Time Around." *McCall's* (Apr 1988): 56–63.

In this interview, given soon after the birth of her son, Navarone, Priscilla Presley discusses her new motherhood, her relationship with Navarone's father, and her daughter, Lisa Marie.

☆ De Vries, Hilary

"The New Priscilla Presley." *McCall's* (Jan 1992): 78–81, 122.

Priscilla Presley relates how she emerged from the shadow of Elvis Presley.

☆ Edwards, Michael

Edwards is the actor/model with whom Priscilla Presley lived from 1978 to 1985.

Priscilla, Elvis and Me: In the Shadow of The King. New York: St. Martin's Press, 1988. 279 pp. ISBN: 0312022689.

In his memoirs, Edwards observes the metamorphosis of Priscilla into a businesswoman and actress and her involvement in Scientology. Thirty-two black and white photographs, most candid; captioned and credited.

☆ Finstad, Suzanne

Child Bride: The Untold Story of Priscilla Beaulieu Presley. New York: Harmony Books, 1997. 388 pp. ISBN: 0517705850. [U.S.]: Berkeley Boulevard Books, 1998. 464 pp. ISBN: 07183100750 (pbk).

An unauthorized biography of Priscilla Presley, focusing on unproven and salacious allegations made by Grant Currie, a friend of Elvis Presley during his military service in Germany. Finstad, an attorney, attempts to psychoanalyze Priscilla Presley and members of her family. Secondary sources cited within the text. Source list, including official documents. Bibliographic references (pp. [371]–381). Index.

Priscilla Presley did not cooperate with or participate in the researching or writing of this book. Grant Currie previously attempted to sell this story to publishers in the 1970s (Torgoff, *The Complete Elvis,* p. 18). In 1964 he wrote a story for *Photoplay* magazine in which he provided questionable information about Priscilla and Elvis's relationship. (*See* The Man/Memoirs and Memories.)

Source: Library of Congress PN2287.P715 E56 1997
Dewey Decimal 791.45/028/092 b 21

☆ Fiore, Mary

"Priscilla Presley: Bringing Up Elvis's Daughter." *Ladies Home Journal* (June 1974): 58–60.

An interview with Priscilla Presley—three years before Elvis's death—in which she discusses her life as a single mother. At the time, Lisa Marie Presley was six years old.

☆ Gordon, Meryl

"Priscilla Presley Today." *McCall's* (Oct 1994): 122–129.

Priscilla Presley reviews her continuing connection with Elvis Presley.

☆ Grant, James

"Priscilla Presley: Never Better than Now." *McCall's* (July 1989): 12–20.

Priscilla Presley discusses her efforts to establish her own identity since her divorce from Elvis Presley in 1973.

☆ Latham, Caroline

Latham is the co-author of *E Is for Elvis*. (*See* The Man/Reference.)

Priscilla and Elvis: The Priscilla Presley Story. New York: New American Library, 1985. 189 pp. ISBN: 0451144198. New York: Signet Books, 1985.

An unauthorized biography of Priscilla Presley, from 1959, the beginning of her relationship with Elvis, through 1985. No source citations or listings, although quotes are attributed to individuals such as Dee Presley, Elvis's stepmother; Rick Stanley, Elvis's stepbrother; and Ed Hookstratton, Elvis's lawyer. Brief bibliography (includes 13 articles and profiles of Priscilla Presley). Thirteen black and white photographs of Priscilla Presley, all credited to AP/Wide World Photos.

Source: Library of Congress PN2287.P715

☆ Presley, Priscilla, as told to Lois Armstrong

"A Mother's Plea; 'When Will It All End?' Elvis's ex shouts down rumors about his only child: 'Lisa Marie and I are not feuding.'" *People Weekly* (Sept 8, 1986): 90–91V.

Priscilla Presley talks about her relationship with Lisa Marie—who was 18 years old at the time—and answers rumors about the two of them.

☆ "Priscilla Presley Finds a Vocation—and Michael Landon Some Frustration—on Location." *People* (Nov 8, 1982): 49–50V.

Interview with Priscilla Presley on the set of her first movie, *Comeback* (which aired on NBC in February of 1983). She speaks about the challenges of making her first film and of building a relationship with her daughter, Lisa Marie.

☆ Scott, Vernon

Scott wrote a thoughtful article in 1963 about Elvis Presley's talent, impact, and future. (*See* The Man/The Impact of Elvis.)

"A Frank Talk with Priscilla Presley." *Good Housekeeping* (Nov 1994): 135, 235.

Priscilla Presley discusses her life with Elvis; her daughter, Lisa Marie; and her daughter's marriage to Michael Jackson.

☆ Sessums, Kevin

"Viva Priscilla." *Vanity Fair* (July 1991): 102, 123–124.

A profile of Priscilla Presley that focuses on her life after Elvis, including her business successes and private life.

See Also:

In The Man/Memoirs and Memories:

Currie, Grant, "Elvis Secretly Engaged."
Presley, Priscilla, *Elvis and Me*

In The Man/Photographs:

Hannaford, Jim, "Elvis: Golden Ride on the Mystery Train," Vol. II. (Includes letter from Vernon Presley relating to rumors of Elvis and Priscilla's engagement.)

In The Rest/Souvenir Magazines:

The Only Woman Elvis Ever Loved: Priscilla, Her Story.

Colonel Thomas Andrew Parker (né Andreas Cornelius van Kuijk)

Colonel Parker became a show business legend through his brilliant—some say ruthless—management of Elvis Presley's career. He first signed Elvis to a contract in 1955, and the arrangement lasted until the entertainer's death in 1977. After Elvis died, a Tennessee court ruled that Parker's management fee of 50 percent of Elvis's earnings was exorbitant and legally forbade any claim on Elvis's estate by the Colonel.

Colonel Parker received his military-sounding title when he was designated an honorary colonel of the state of Louisiana—a political gift from a friend who was then governor of the state; it had nothing to do with military service. He was born in Breda, Holland, and illegally entered the United States as a young man. In the early 1930s he enlisted in the U.S. Army, but he never applied for American citizenship. He changed his name to Tom Parker after leaving the army in 1932 and fabricated a new life history that he maintained until his death. He worked as a carnival promoter, eventually becoming manager for country western stars Hank Snow and Eddie Arnold before signing Elvis. Parker died in 1998.

☆   ☆   ☆   ☆

☆ *Elvis and Colonel Tom Parker: The Partnership Behind the Legend.* Memphis: Elvis Presley Enterprises, Inc., 1994. 32 pp. ISBN: none.

This pamphlet was produced by The Colonel Parker Tribute Committee of Elvis Presley Enterprises, Inc. (EPE), as part of its 1994, year-long commemoration of Colonel Parker's 85th birthday. Chapters with text and color and black and white photographs of Elvis's two-decade relationship with the Colonel. Many of the photographs are from the Colonel's personal Elvis collection. Stories of Elvis's major role in creating the USS *Arizona* Memorial in Hawaii, and Elvis's donation to charity of President Franklin Delano Roosevelt's yacht, USS *Potomac* (which Elvis owned). Two poems about Elvis by the Colonel.

Source: Compiler's collection

☆ Flippo, Chet

"Elvis's Manager, Col. Tom Parker, Dies." *Billboard* (Feb 1, 1997): 18, 68.

☆ Guralnick, Peter

"The Man Behind the Throne." *Rolling Stone* (Mar 20, 1997): 26.

☆ Hopkins, Jerry

"Fame and Fortune: The Life and Times of Colonel Tom Parker." *Rolling Stone* (Sept 22, 1977): 44–47.

A biographical article written by Elvis biographer Jerry Hopkins. (*See* listings earlier in this chapter.) The article quotes Elvis's film directors Norman Taurog and Don Siegel. This article appeared in the acclaimed collection of memorial essays published in the September 22, 1977, issue of *Rolling Stone*. (*See* The Man/Major Articles.)

☆ "Impresarios: The Man Who Sold Parsley." *Time* (May 16, 1960): 61–62.

A profile of Colonel Parker, focusing on his management of—and financial success for—Elvis Presley. This article contains many of the untruths that the Colonel claimed as events of his life: that his parents worked in a traveling carnival and died when he was a child; that he worked for his uncle's Great Parker Pony Circus after he was orphaned; and that he had his own pony-and-monkey act as a teenager.

☆ O'Neal, Sean

O'Neal collects Elvis memorabilia and is the author of *Elvis Inc.* (*See* The Phenomena/Business and Finance.)

My Boy Elvis: The Colonel Tom Parker Story. New York: Barricade Books, Inc., 1998. 343 pp. ISBN: 1569801274.

The first posthumous biography of Colonel Tom Parker, published five months after his death. Unsubstantiated claims with no supporting footnotes, chapter notes, citations, or sources. Eight pages of black and white photographs; captioned but not credited. Appendices include Colonel Parker's will, his promotional plan for *Spinout*, and "A Concert Contract Used by Colonel Parker in 1956." Bibliography relating to Elvis, as well as rock and roll music (pp. 335–336). Index of names.

O'Neal says that he "interviewed hundreds of individuals" for this book but refused to identify them because he claims they were "afraid of [retaliation from] Elvis Presley Enterprises, Inc."[12] Colonel Parker's photograph does not appear on the dust jacket. Instead, the photograph is of Elvis with an unidentified man at the Houston (TX) Astrodome, taken March 1, 1970, during the Houston Livestock Show and Rodeo. O'Neal says that his editor at Barricade Books selected the erroneous photograph but was "in a rush to release the book" and did not show him the cover design until after publication. He says that his editor mistook the unnamed man for Colonel Parker and that a new dust jacket would be issued with a photograph of Elvis and the Colonel.[13] (That has not occurred.)

Source: Library of Congress ML429.P33 O54 1998
Dewey Decimal 782.42166'092-dc21 [B]

☆ Sandler, Adam

"Lost and Found." *Variety* (Apr 16, 1993): 91.

A profile of Colonel Parker in the "Where are they now?" section of *Variety*.

[12]Speech by O'Neal, Aug 13, 1998, Memphis, Tennessee.

[13]Ibid.

☆ Tannenbaum, Rob

"Rock and Roll to Colonel Tom." *Village Voice* (Feb 4, 1997): 62.

☆ Vellenga, Dirk, with Mick Farren

At the time of publication, Mr. Vellenga was a journalist in Breda, Holland, specializing in rock music.

Elvis and the Colonel. New York: Delacorte Press, 1988. 278 pp. ISBN: 0385295219.

A Dutch investigative reporter's well-researched biography with detailed information about Colonel Parker's childhood and early life. The first book to accurately publish the full story of the Colonel's Dutch origins. Reveals Colonel Parker's control of Elvis's life, career, and finances. Black and white photographs of the Colonel as a child and with family members in the Netherlands, as well as throughout his career with Elvis; captioned and credited. Elvis discography as it relates to the Colonel and listing of live appearances (pp. 185–273). No chapter notes, citations, or sources. "Acknowledgments" lists those interviewed in America and in the Netherlands. Index. This book was translated into Dutch, Colonel Parker's native language. (*See* Foreign Language Titles/Dutch.)

Source: Library of Congress ML429.P33V4 1988
Dewey Decimal 784.5'4'00924 [B]

☆ Whitney, Dwight

"The Indomitable Snowman Who Built Himself—and Elvis Too." *TV Guide* (Nov 30, 1968).

Memorial profiles of Colonel Tom Parker (written after his death in January 1998).

See Also:

In The Man/Biographies:

Doll, Susan M., Ph.D., *Understanding Elvis: Southern Roots vs. Star Image.*
Hutchins, Chris, and Peter Thompson, *Elvis Meets the Beatles: The Untold Story of Their Tangled Lives.*

In The Man/Memoirs and Memories:

Crumbaker, Marge, and Gabe Tucker, *Up and Down with Elvis Presley.*

In The Music, The Movies/Filmography:

McLafferty, Gerry, *Elvis Presley in Hollywood: Celluloid Sell-Out.* (An analysis of Colonel Parker's role in shaping Elvis's film career.)

In The Phenomena/Business and Finance:

Saunders, Laura, "Sell Me Tender."

CHAPTER 2
Death, Conspiracy, Sightings

EDGAR CAYCEE, NOSTRADAMUS, and Harry Houdini spent their lifetimes trying to prove what Elvis inadvertently demonstrated when he died—there is indeed life after death.

Few demises have so captivated the world's attention and curiosity as Elvis Presley's—or had such wide-reaching impact. Seldom has there been such speculation over a cause of death—or so much suspicion that a person, whose body was viewed by thousands, might still be alive. And rarely has a death so altered a culture.

Before Elvis died in 1977, most broadcast and print news outlets gave only moderate attention to an entertainment celebrity's accidents or dying. Compare that with 1998, when media preoccupation with the show business famous reached the level where news network CNN broke into its regular programming to cover actor Tommy Lee Jones's fall from a horse.

This consuming interest in the antics and woes of the rich, famous, and irrelevant began on August 17, 1977—the morning after Elvis died. When the sun rose on that day, the world witnessed the birth of our media's fascination with celebrity. According to Neal and Janice Gregory (*When Elvis Died*, p. 36), "Never before had so many newspapers led their front pages with a report that someone other than a head of state had died." The night before, two of the three major network news programs (NBC and ABC) had carried his death as the top story—a first for any entertainer.

But it is not his cultural "contribution" that has fueled the literature about Elvis's death. Rather, it is the questions about the circumstances of his demise—and the fixation on whether he remains alive. His body was autopsied by competent authorities, his corpse lay in state where thousands viewed it up close, and he was buried in plain sight. Yet, Elvis ranks right up there with Area 51 and *The X-Files* when it comes to theories, conspiracies, and questions about how, when, and if he died—or still lives.

It was a book that started it all. Author Gail Brewer-Giorgio—with the help of television gadfly Geraldo Rivera and the *National Enquirer*—was the first to ignite the fascination. Others who were on the scene of Elvis's death, such as security guard Dick Grob, also weighed in with their opinions, as have death and culture experts from the Los Angeles County Medical Examiner Dr. Thomas Noguchi to academics R. Serge Denisoff of Bowling Green State University and George Plasketes of Auburn University. It seems that few authors—and readers—are willing to let him rest in peace.

By not allowing Elvis the man to die—literally and figuratively—the literature about Elvis's death has given life to Elvis the legend. Thus, this body of Elvis literature is the birth mother for one of the truest measurements of his posthumous fame (and life): the universally recognized bumper sticker that reads, "Elvis Lives!"

☆   ☆   ☆   ☆

☆ Bangs, Lester

"Where Were You When Elvis Died?" *Village Voice* (Aug 29, 1977). (Reprinted in *Psychotic Reactions and Carburetor Dung*. Ed. Greil Marcus. New York: Vintage, 1988. ISBN: 06797240456. Pp. 212–216.)

Considered one of the classic Elvis Presley memorial essays because of its insightful exploration of Elvis as our society's last unifying force.

☆ Booth, Stanley

"The King Is Dead! Hang the Doctor!" *The Complete Elvis*. Ed. Martin Torgoff. New York: Delilah Books, 1982. Pp. 70–85.

An examination of Elvis Presley's health and prescription drug issues from the point of view of his physician, Dr. George Nichopoulos ("Dr. Nick"). It also examines the legal problems and media attention that overwhelmed Nichopoulos as he was blamed for Elvis's death. This article is noted for its unique exploration of how and why Elvis died, and for its use of Nichopoulos's situation as a metaphor for the 1970s.

☆ Breo, Dennis

"Elvis Presley." *Extraordinary Care*. Chicago: Chicago Review Press, 1986. ISBN: 0914091956. Pp. 46–62.

The author, a medical journalist, examines the death of Elvis Presley through interviews with Elvis's personal physician, Dr. George C. Nichopoulos, and medical examiner Dr. Jerry T. Francisco who performed the autopsy. This chapter is based on two articles that Breo previously wrote for *American Medical News* (Dec 12, 1979, and Nov 12, 1981).

☆ Brewer-Giorgio, Gail

Brewer-Giorgio is believed to be the first to suggest publicly that Elvis Presley staged his death and is still alive. After she published her novel *Orion: The Living Superstar of Song* (in which the Elvis-like protagonist pretends to die) in 1979, Brewer-Giorgio received a telephone call from a stranger who sounded like Elvis and referred to himself as "Orion." She also received items in the mail that convinced her that Elvis was still alive. (*See* The Phenomena/Fiction.)

These experiences led her to publish *Is Elvis Alive?* This book, which was accompanied by a cassette tape of what was purported to be a post-1977 telephone call from Elvis, quickly became a bestseller and was published in four foreign languages. As a result, Brewer-Giorgio appeared on national television programs ranging from Larry King to Oprah Winfrey to Geraldo Rivera.

In 1990 Brewer-Giorgio published *The Elvis Files: Was His Death Faked?* and wrote the documentary *The Elvis Files*, both of which reiterate her premise that Elvis is alive. In 1991 she co-wrote and produced a television docudrama on her writings (*Elvis: Dead or Alive*). Brewer-Giorgio is an entertainment executive in Georgia.

Is Elvis Alive? The Most Incredible Elvis Presley Story Ever Told. New York: Tudor
    Publishing Company, 1988. 219 pp. ISBN: 0944276318.

A compilation of evidence as proof that Elvis is still alive. The book comes with a 60-minute audiocassette, *The Elvis Tape* (New York: Tudor Publishing Co., 1988), of a telephone call that Elvis allegedly made to Brewer-Giorgio. It was published, with translations of the accompanying audiocassette tape, in Spanish and French. It was translated into Czech and Japanese without the tape. (*See* Foreign Language Titles/Czech, French, Japanese, Spanish.)

————.

The Elvis Files: Was His Death Faked? New York: Shapolsky Publishers; Toronto, Ont,
    Canada: McGraw-Hill Ryerson; Lancaster, England: Impala Books, 1990. 275
    pp. ISBN: 1561710008. New York: S.P.I./Shapolsky Publishing, Inc. 1994. 275
    pp. ISBN: 1561713767. New York: S.P.I. Books, 1997. 288 pp. ISBN:
    1561713767.

Brewer-Giorgio presents evidence from a 10-year investigation in support of her belief that Elvis Presley remains alive and in hiding. Bibliography. This book is accompanied by a 26-minute audiocassette, *The Elvis Files: The Incredible Elvis Presley Tape*. This tape is from a telephone call allegedly made by Elvis to Brewer-Giorgio on October 10, 1988.

A 55-minute video, *The Elvis Files*, was based on this book and examines the theories and evidence found in this book. ([n.p.]: Fox Hills Video, 1990. ISBN: 1558738142.) In 1991, this book served as the basis for a television special, *The Elvis Files*. That program is available on video. (New York: Goodtimes Home Video, 1991. Music No: 9228; Goodtimes Home Video.)

————.

Elvis Undercover: Is He Alive and Coming Back? [U.S.]: Bright Books, Inc., 1999.
    240 pp. ISBN: 1880092492.

New evidence and what Brewer describes as previously secret documents that support the theory that Elvis Presley was an undercover agent for the United States government—and, because of that, is still alive today.

Source: Compiler's collection

☆ Chanzes, Steven C.

Elvis . . . 1935–? Where Are You? Wilton Manor, FL: Direct Products, Inc., 1981. ISBN: none.

This book asks the question: Is Elvis alive? The answer is divided into two parts: an analysis of the circumstances of his death and a fictitious scenario of how Elvis may have faked his death (the substitute body of a terminally ill Elvis look-alike). Chanzes co-produced the album *Sivle Sings Again—Do You Know Who I Am?* The singer, Sivle Nora ("Elvis Aron" spelled backward), claimed to be Elvis.

In August 1982 a book by Al Jeffries with almost the same title (*Elvis—Alive? 1935–? Where Are You?*) was published by Eternal American Productions of Wilton Manor, Florida. That same month, the *Globe* tabloid newspaper carried an article about the book.

Source: Memphis/Shelby County (TN) Public Library and Information Center

☆ Cohen, Daniel

"The Ghost of Elvis." *The Ghost of Elvis, and Other Celebrity Spirits.* New York: G.P. Putnam's Sons, 1994. ISBN: 0399226117. Pp. 3–14.

Anecdotes of four Elvis posthumous sightings, including the oft-referenced one near Kalamazoo, Michigan.

☆ Cuza-Malé, Belkis

Elvis—The Unquiet Grave: Or the True Story of Jon Burrows. Translated by Ileana Fuentes and David Miller. Miami Lakes, FL: E. Press, 1994. 235 pp. ISBN: 0-913827-10-X.

The English-language translation of *Elvis—La Tumba sin Sosiego: O la Verdadera Historia de Jon Burrows.* (*See* Foreign Language Titles/Spanish.) A diary of the author's efforts to hook up with Jon Burrows—the identity that some think was assumed by Elvis Presley after August 16, 1977. She reports finding him in Fort Worth, Texas, and that he agreed to tell her his story. Black and white photographs of the man she claims to be Jon Burrows. "Documents" section includes handwriting comparisons between Elvis and Jon Burrows.

Source: Compiler's collection

☆ Denisoff, R. Serge, and George Plasketes

Denisoff and Plasketes are both university professors. Plasketes is the author of *Images of Elvis Presley in American Culture, 1977–1997.* (*See* The Man/The Impact of Elvis.)

True Disbelivers: The Elvis Contagion. New Brunswick, NJ: Transaction Publishers, 1995. 307 pp. ISBN: 1560001860.

An analysis of various accounts of Elvis Presley's death and transfiguration. The authors examine the works of writers who believe that Elvis is alive, as well as the record industry that profits from this belief. Eleven pages of black and white photographs; captioned but not credited. Bibliography (pp. 287–300). Index.

Source: Library of Congress ML420.P96 D46 1995

☆ Eicher, Peter

The Elvis Sightings. **New York: Avon Books, 1993. 209 pp. ISBN: 0380772051.**

Eyewitness accounts of 25 post-1977 Elvis sightings to conclude that the entertainer is alive. Eight black and white photographs of scenes surrounding Elvis's funeral, and two alleged sighting photographs previously published in the U.S. tabloid, the *Weekly World News*; credited and captioned. No notes or index.

☆ Felsenthal, Edward

"Is Elvis Dead? If So, What Killed Him? Verdict Is Due Today. (Memphis Dentist V. Smith Objects to Medical Examiner J. T. Francisco's Autopsy Verdicts.)" *Wall Street Journal* (Sept 29, 1994): A1+.

Abstract: "Officials are expected to release a report today on whether Tennessee's Shelby County medical examiner Jerry T. Francisco covered up the true cause of singer Elvis Presley's death."

☆ Flippo, Chet

"Funeral in Memphis: Love Me Tender." *Rolling Stone* (Sept 22, 1977): 38–39.

Noted rock and roll writer reports on Elvis Presley's last day, his death, and the immediate aftermath.

☆ Gregory, Neal, and Janice Gregory

Janice Gregory is a nationally recognized expert on Social Security, pensions, and employee benefits. Gregory, a former journalist, now heads a public relations firm in Washington, D.C.

When Elvis Died. **Washington, D.C.: Communications Press, 1980. 292 pp. ISBN: 0894610325. New York: Washington Square Press, 1980. 304 pp. ISBN: 088687663X. New York: Pharos Books, 1992. 304 pp. ISBN: 088687663.**

The first scholarly study to examine the unprecedented worldwide reaction to Elvis's death—in the media and in the culture. Selected newspaper editorials memorializing Elvis. List of Elvis Presley's film and network appearances. Bibliography (pp. 260–281). Index, sources, and notes.

The Gregorys added an epilogue to the 1992 edition that discusses the impact and ramifications of Elvis's death since 1980 (pp. 214–231). This second edition was translated into Thai. (*See* Foreign Language Titles/Thai.) The first edition was recorded on cassette by Recordings for the Blind (Library of Congress no: NNRB (TH0157 [04]).

☆ Hatcher, Harley

Mr. Hatcher was a record producer in Los Angeles at the time of publication.

Elvis Disguised: A Remarkable Personal Experience. Beverly Hills, CA: C.M.I., 1980. 237 pp. ISBN: 0936790008.

First-person account of the author's attempts to prove that a fellow serviceman named John Crowe, whom he met at Ft. Monmouth, New Jersey, in July 1958, was Elvis Presley. Chapter on the analytical methodology used to determine the authenticity of John Crow/Elvis Presley's handwriting samples and voice. Eleven black and white photographs of Ft. Monmouth and of Elvis in Army uniforms; credited and captioned. News clippings relating to Elvis's army career; some not cited.

This book was republished the same year as *Elvis, Is That You? A Remarkable Personal Experience* with the same ISBN. The publishers of the reprint have the same mailing address as that of the publishers of *Elvis Disguised.*

Source: Library of Congress ML420.P96 H44 1980
OCLC 15549627

———.

Elvis, Is That You? A Remarkable Personal Experience. Beverly Hills, CA: Great American Books, 1980. 239 pp. ISBN: 093679008.

The republished edition of *Elvis Disguised: A Remarkable Personal Experience* with the same ISBN. This edition has an epilogue and a reproduction of a "farewell message" allegedly written to Hatcher by Elvis Presley.

Source: OCLC 8999820

☆ "Help Us Find Elvis's Clone." *Official UFO* (May 1978): 12–19, 51–53.

A story—published nine months after Elvis Presley's death—of an Elvis clone's escape from the institution in which it had been created. Black and white photographs of the alleged clone and of Elvis Presley.

Source: Compiler's collection

☆ Holton, Robert, and Lisa Burrell

The King Is Dead. [CA]: Katco Literary Group, 1998. 175 pp. ISBN: 0964648458.

An attempt to cash in on the death of Elvis Presley—22 years after he died. Based on the diary of the funeral home director who handled the arrangements for Elvis's funeral: "never-before-published accounts of Elvis's autopsy, embalming, and burial."

Source: www.amazon.com.html

☆ Hubbell, Sue

"Our Far-Flung Correspondents: The Vicksburg Ghost." *The New Yorker* (Sept 25, 1989): 106–117.

The author's trip to Vicksburg, Michigan, to investigate a reported posthumous sighting of Elvis Presley.

☆ Jeffries, Al

Elvis—Alive? 1935–? Where Are You? Wilton Manor, FL: Eternal American Productions, 1982. ISBN: none.

See Chanzes listing earlier in this chapter.

Source: Brewer-Giorgio, Gail, The Elvis Files, *p. 125.*

☆ Kennedy, Caroline

"Graceland: A Family Mourns." *Rolling Stone* (Sept 22, 1977): 40.

The daughter of President John F. Kennedy writes an eyewitness report on the atmosphere surrounding the funeral of Elvis Presley. (Kennedy was interning at *Rolling Stone* at the time of Elvis's death.)

☆ King, Christine

"The Death of a King: Elvis Presley (1935–1977)." *The Changing Face of Death: Historical Accounts of Death and Disposal.* Eds. Glynnys Howarth and Peter Jupp. Basingstoke. [UK]: Macmillan, 1997. 202 pp. ISBN: 0333638638 (UK). ISBN: 0312164033 (U.S.).

Observations about Elvis Presley's funeral in a collection of essays about mourning customs and funeral rites.

☆ Klein, Joe

"Tupelo: From a Jack to a King." *Rolling Stone* (Sept 22, 1977): 41.

A report on the memorial service held for Elvis Presley in his birthplace, Tupelo, Mississippi.

☆ Lazar, Jerry

"Front Page Blues: From Snap Shots to Cheap Shots. Watching the Media Covering the King." *Crawdaddy* (Nov 1977): 37–39.

The first assessment of the news coverage of Elvis Presley's death and funeral.

☆ Marcus, Greil

"Blue Hawaii: Elvis Spirit and Flesh." *Rolling Stone* (Sept 22, 1977): 56–57.

Marcus is one of America's leading rock music historians and critics.

Greil Marcus reveals his thoughts upon learning of Elvis Presley's death—the tragedy that Elvis had become before his death and what he meant to the world afterward.

☆ Noguchi, Thomas T., M.D.

"The Elvis Presley Case." *Coroner at Large, Thomas Noguchi, M.D.* New York: Simon and Schuster, 1985. ISBN: 0671544624.

Former Los Angeles County Medical Examiner Dr. Thomas Noguchi presents his theory on the cause of Elvis Presley's death. He recalls being called by Memphis medical examiner Dr. Francisco for advice on "how to handle the situation." Noguchi confirms the Memphis coroner's cause-of-death findings, adding, "the combination of prescription drugs he ingested in such quantities that it caused the fatally irregular heartbeat in the first place." (This chapter was excerpted in *Good Housekeeping* [Nov 1985]: 228–230.)

☆ Parker, John

Elvis: The Secret Files. London: Anaya Publishers Ltd., 1993. 272 pp. ISBN: 1854700391.

Parker suggests that "Elvis was the innocent victim in one of the largest FBI criminal investigations of the 1970s." The author states that "on the day [Elvis] died, evidence from himself and his father was to have been presented to a Federal Grand Jury [sic] in a fraud case at the heart of a much wider investigation involving billions of dollars of phoney bonds and key Mafia families." The author's evidence comes from previously unpublished papers, testimony from Elvis's companions, and the personal files of J. Edgar Hoover, the late director of the Federal Bureau of Investigation.
   This book was reissued in 1994 as *Elvis: Murdered by the Mob.*

Source: Library of Congress ML420.P96 P29 1993
Dewey Decimal 782.42166/092 B 20
The British Library YK.1994.b.5215

———.

Elvis: Murdered by the Mob. London: Arrow, 1994. 278 pp. ISBN: 0099319713.

A reissue of Parker's 1993 book, *Elvis: The Secret Files.*
Source: The British Library YK.1994.a.8253
Dewey Decimal 781.66092 20

☆ The Presley Commission

Elvis: Alive or Dead? Moneta, VA: The Presley Commission, [1995]. 200 pp. ISBN: none.

According to the head of The Presley Commission, Phil Aitcheson, his ad hoc organization met, independent of a convening authority, in 1992 to "test theories of [Elvis's] reported death." The Commission, comprised of students and Elvis fans, then spent the next two and one half years compiling documents and data to prove that Elvis hoaxed his death. Their findings are printed in this book. Included are the entertainer's medical history and numerical calculations surrounding his death date and name. Reproduction of documents and photographs.

Source: Publisher's address: P.O. Box 602, Moneta, VA 24121-0602

☆ Presley, Elvis

"Last will and testament of Elvis A. Presley: filed August 22, 1977." 13 leaves.

Notes from OCLC entry: "Filed in the Probate Court of Shelby County, Tennessee."

Source: OCLC 7991316

☆ Smith, Major (USAF Retired) Bill

At the time of publication, Major Smith had been in the music business in Fort Worth, Texas, for more than 30 years.

Memphis Mystery (Requiem for Elvis). Fort Worth, TX: LeCam Publications, 1987. 147 pp. ISBN: none.

An exploration of the possibility that Elvis Presley faked his death and disappeared. The text consists of "a few ideas from the author about what [Elvis's] life would have been, or perhaps is, after 'death'" (cover text). Includes a fictional biography of Elvis's stillborn twin, Jesse Garon.

Source: Collection of Bill and Connie Burk, Memphis, TN
OCLC 39653068

☆ Swaggart, Jimmy

To the point .... Baton Rouge, LA: Jimmy Swaggart Evangelistic Association, [197?]. 32 pp.

Text of "The Death of Elvis Presley," a memorial sermon delivered by televangelist Rev. Jimmy Swaggart. The Rev. Swaggart is the cousin of entertainer and Elvis's friend Jerry Lee Lewis.

Source: The University of California, Santa Barbara

☆ Thompson, Charles C., II, and James P. Cole

Charles C. Thompson is a print and broadcast journalist who has been a producer for ABC's *20/20* newsmagazine and CBS's *60 Minutes.* James P. Cole is a former Memphis journalist.

The Death of Elvis: What Really Happened? New York: Delacorte Press, 1991. 407 pp. ISBN: 0385302282. New York: Dell Paperback, 1992. London: Orion, 1993. ISBN: 0440210488.

The results of a 10-year journalistic investigation into autopsy reports and secret lab files that "expose a massive cover . . . and reveal, for the first time, how—and why—Elvis Presley died." Black and white photos of some of the Elvis friends and medical experts interviewed. Reprints of the Memphis Police Department report on Elvis's death, tables of toxic ranges and drugs present from Elvis's autopsy, and part of a "secret autopsy report" from Baptist Hospital in Memphis. Bibliography. Index. This book was translated into French. (*See* Foreign Language Titles/French.)

☆ Wecht, Cyril, M.D., J.D., with Mark Curriden and Benjamin Wecht

Wecht is a board-certified pathologist specializing in forensic pathology.

"Covering Up for the King: The Death of Elvis Presley." *Cause of Death*. New York: Dutton, 1993. ISBN: 0525936610. Pp. 138–148.

Wecht's story of his experiences as a consultant on the ABC program *20/20*, in which talk show host Geraldo Rivera investigated the circumstances of Elvis Presley's death. Transcript of Wecht's on-camera interview with Rivera. Wecht concluded that Elvis Presley had not died of a heart attack as listed on his death certificate, but of "the combined effect of drugs" (p. 142). Index.

☆ "What Do Americans Believe?" *George* (Dec 1996): 114–117.

The results of a survey taken to determine American beliefs on a range of subjects. Reported findings in this article show that 86 percent of the respondents accept that Elvis Presley is dead.

☆ Williams, Jonathan

It's Only Rock and Roll: In Memoriam: Elvis. Highlands, NC: [Jargon Society], 1979. ISBN: none.

Source: University of California

Articles Memorializing Elvis Immediately After His Death

The following selections represent the best of the memorial writing and reporting that appeared in the weeks and months after Elvis died.

☆ Baker, Jackson

Baker is a distinguished Memphis journalist who, as a boy, lived next to the Presleys on Lamar Avenue. At the time, the Presleys had no telephone, so they used his family's.

"Elvis: End of an Era." *City of Memphis* (Sept 1977): 26–32.

A memorial article in which Baker recounts the last day of Elvis's life and the time immediately following it. This article is noted for the way in which it captures the tone of that 24-hour period and in which it portrays the deep grief and sense of loss felt by mourning fans.

☆ Bradshaw, Jon

"Elvis: A Dossier." *Esquire* (Oct 1977): 96–98. (This article was reprinted in condensed form as "Elvis I. The Man" in *Reader's Digest* [Jan 1978]: 72–75.)

☆ Cocks, Jay

"Last Stop on the Mystery Train." *Time* 110 (Aug 29, 1977): 56–59.

☆ Davies, Russell

"Elvis Presley: He Got Stung." *New Statesman* (Aug 19, 1977): 255.

☆ Marcus, Greil

"Blue Hawaii: Elvis Spirit and Flesh." *Rolling Stone* (Sept 22, 1977): 56–57.

☆ Marsh, Dave

"How Great Thou Art: Elvis in the Promised Land." *Rolling Stone* 248 (Sept 22, 1997): 58.

"The 1950s Are Dead." *Economist* (Aug 20, 1977): 31.

☆ Orth, Maureen

"All Shook Up." *Newsweek* (Aug 29, 1977): 46–49

"The Talk of the Town: Notes and Comment." *The New Yorker* (Aug 29, 1977): 19.

☆ Walton, Samuel

"The Rebel Who Became a Legend." *Saturday Evening Post* (Dec 1977): 56, 83.

Note: a longer list is found in Neal and Janice Gregory's *When Elvis Died.* (*See* listing earlier in this chapter.)

Newspaper Obituaries and Memorials

Note: the most complete listing of editorials relating to Elvis's death can be found in Neal and Janice Gregory's *When Elvis Died* ("Selected Newspaper Editorials," pp. 232–269, 1992 edition).

☆ Borden, Robert

"When Legends Die." *The Milwaukee Bugle* (2–22 Sept 1977).

☆ "Death Captures Crown of Rock and Roll—Elvis Dies After Heart Attack." Memphis: *Commercial Appeal,* 1977. ISBN: none.

A compendium of reportage on the death of Elvis Presley, August 17–21, 1977.

Source: Memphis/Shelby County (TN) public Library and Information Center

☆ "Elvis, 1935–1977." *Tupelo View* (MS) (Aug 20, 1977): 56 pp.

Articles and memories about Elvis Presley from residents of Tupelo, Mississippi—the town where he spent the first 13 years of his life. More than 50 black and white photographs, along with advertisements with personal messages to Elvis.

Source: The Memphis/Shelby County (TN) Public Library and Information Center
OCLC 13650408

☆ *Elvis, 1935–1977.* Sept 28, 1977. 15 pp.

A special supplement accompanying newspapers across America. It contained articles spanning Elvis Presley's life and career, including his funeral. The cover is a full headshot of Elvis, wearing a red, wide-collar shirt. The word "Elvis" is printed across the width of the page, and "1935" is in the lower left-hand corner and "1977" is in the lower right.

Source: Bowling Green State University ML420.P96 E4x
OCLC 3320019; 3419625

☆ *A Lonely Life Ends on Elvis Presley Boulevard.* Memphis, TN: Memphis Press-Scimitar, 1977. 36 pp. ISBN: none.

A compilation of articles about the death of Elvis Presley, published August 17–21, 1977.

Source: Memphis/Shelby County (TN) Public Library and Information Center
OCLC 9318638

☆ *The Stories: August 17–23, 1977.*

A compilation of all the stories related to the death of Elvis Presley that appeared in Memphis's *Commercial Appeal* newspaper, Aug 17–23, 1977. Some black and white photographs from that coverage.

Source: www.gomemphis.com/elvis/stories/index.html

☆ [A tribute to Elvis Presley]. Memphis, TN: Memphis Press-Scimitar [and] Commercial Appeal, 1977. 12 pp.

A special edition co-published by Memphis's two newspapers, containing reprints of stories and pictures relating to Elvis, which were published in these two newspapers during the days following his death. Also on microfilm (one reel, 35 mm, 1979), located at the University of Arkansas, Fayetteville.

Source: OCLC 5722501

See Also:

In The Man/Biographies:

James, Anthony, *Presley: Entertainer of the Century.*
Matthews, Rupert, *Elvis.*
Taylor, Robyn, *Elvis Presley: Not Just the King of Rock and Roll!*

In The Man/Memoirs and Memories:

Cocke, Marian, *I Called Him Babe.*

In The Phenomema/Fans:

Olson, Melissa, and Darrell Crase, "Presleymania: The Elvis Factor."

In The Phenomena/Fiction:

Brewer-Giorgio, Gail, *Orion: The Living Superstar of Song.*
Nicholson, Monte, *The Presley Arrangement.*
Fairytale.
Sammon, Paul L., *The King Is Dead: Tales of Elvis Post Mortem.*

In The Phenomena/Politics:

95th Congress, First Session:
"Blue Suede Shoes"
"Farewell to 'The King'"
95th Congress, Second Session:
"A National Tragedy"

In The Phenomena/Psychic Elvis Experiences:

Panta, Ilona, *Elvis Presley, King of Kings.*

In The Phenomena/The Law

Singer, Richard, *Elvis, The Inventory of the Estate of Elvis Presley*

In Foreign Language Titles/Swedish:

Schoning, Ulf, *Chocken: svenska fans berattar hur de upplevde Elvis dod: en antologi.*

In The Rest/Souvenir Magazines:

The Elvis Cover-Up.

CHAPTER 3
Elvis in the Army

"You mean you actually had to give up two years of your life to serve in the military?"

For centuries, boys have gathered at the feet of their elders and asked, "Grandpa, what was it like in the war?" Today, that traditional inquiry has changed into one of astonishment that young American men were once actually obligated to put their personal pursuits aside in service to their country.

Today's elders would be well advised to answer their incredulous young questioners with stories of Elvis Presley. He was required to enter the U.S. Army in March 1958 at the height of both his career and the Cold War. Unlike so many famous people since, he willingly joined and served as a combat field soldier. Not surprisingly, there are a number of folks who wrote about it.

The resulting books and articles have grown in resource value with the end of universal conscription. More commonly known as "the draft," it was a planned-for (or -around) part of every young American man's life. It was a rite of passage into manhood, an unquestioned duty of citizenship, and an unparalleled exposure to people from different socioeconomic, regional, and racial backgrounds.

Though the draft frequently changed the course of young lives and of our nation, few viewed it as anything other than commonplace, and few thought to record it as it was happening. Fortunately, the Elvis authors did. As a result, perhaps the best information on the day-to-day life of America's peacetime draftees exists within the Elvis literature.

Elvis's army career was a pedestrian one, much like thousands of other young men before and since. He went through basic training ("boot camp") at Fort Chaffee, Arkansas. After advanced training as a tank crewman at Fort Hood, Texas, he was assigned to the 1st Medium Tank Battalion (Patton), 32nd Armor, 3rd Armored Division (Spearhead) at Ray Barracks, Freidberg Kaserne, Germany.

There Elvis was a scout jeep driver with the Reconnaissance Platoon of the Battalion's Headquarters Company. Scout jeeps are used in gathering information on the enemy, and their drivers are considered combat soldiers. Because every member of a reconnaissance platoon is trained to operate in enemy territory, Elvis participated in the same battlefield exercises as did all the soldiers assigned to his unit. By all accounts, he was treated as—and behaved as—every other junior enlisted person.[1]

---

[1] New York photographer Bill Ray recalls that when Elvis first appeared in uniform after his famous G.I. haircut, he refused media requests to take off his G.I. cap. Elvis explained that without it, he would be considered out of uniform. (*People Weekly*, Aug 24, 1998:55.)

73

He received an honorable discharge in March 1960 and left the army with the rank of sergeant, E-4. Elvis's military decorations are the Good Conduct Medal, Sharpshooter badge, Marksman badge, and a 3rd Armored Division Certificate of Achievement for faithful and efficient performance of duty.

Elvis was proud of his military service, but, typically, did not express it. In 1991 when Patsy Andersen and other Elvis Presley Enterprises, Inc., staff members examined the contents of his wallet—which had been kept untouched in a safety deposit box since his death—they found a crumpled newspaper clipping from March 1960. The story—"Elvis Praised in Record"— related the remarks made by U.S. Senator Estes Kefauver, commending Elvis for serving his country. Elvis had carried that clipping for 17 years. (*See* The Phenomena/Politics.)

Other people talked about Elvis's army years besides Senator Kefauver. Men who had experienced military service with him have written most of the literature about Elvis's army life. In doing so, they have given us firsthand information about a past commonality of American culture that shaped generations of young men, and our society as well.

☆   ☆   ☆   ☆

☆ DuBose, Jack

"Me 'n' Elvis 'n' NATO." *American Heritage* (Oct 1991): 32–33.

An anecdote about Elvis Presley's behavior as an enlisted soldier, which underscores the reports that Elvis refused to be treated differently from his fellow GIs. DuBose served with the American armed forces in Germany at the same time as Elvis.

☆ "Elvis and the Frauleins." *Look* (Dec 23, 1958): 113–115.

Mostly black and white photographs of Elvis Presley in army uniform in Germany with fans, military police, and news photographers. Photograph of Elvis with "his first date" in Germany, Margit Buergin. Text describes German fans' reactions (they called him their "rock and roll matador") and how the U.S. Army and the U.S. Department of State were in conflict over whether to assign him to the duties of an ordinary junior enlisted person or to use him as a goodwill ambassador.

☆ *Elvis: Like Any Other Soldier.* Port Townsend, WA: Osborne Productions, 1988. Unpaged. ISBN: 0932117104.

A reproduction of the original 1958 yearbook of the U.S. Army's 2nd Armored Division—the unit with which Elvis did his advanced armored training. Elvis appears in some of the photographs.

Source: OCLC 20960011

☆ Jones, M.Sgt. (U.S. Army–Retired) Ira

Ira Jones is a decorated career soldier who served in World War II and the Korean conflict. He was Elvis's platoon commander from October 1958, when the entertainer arrived in Germany, until May 1959, when Jones left for a new assignment. During that time

Elvis served as Jones's driver. He is well known to Elvis fans and appears frequently at Elvis-related events.

"Has the Army Changed Elvis?" *Family Weekly* (Oct 12, 1959).

M.Sgt. Jones's anecdotes about Elvis's life in the army.

————.

Soldier Boy Elvis. **As told to writer Bill E. Burk. Memphis: Propwash Publishing, 1992. 260 pp. ISBN: 1879207230.**

First-person account of Elvis's army service in Germany as told by his platoon sergeant, covering the time period from October 1958 to May 1959. Thirty-three black and white candid photographs; captioned and credited.

Source: Library of Congress ML420.P96 J63 1992
Dewey Decimal 335/.0092 B 20

☆ Levy, Alan

Levy was a civilian and a reporter in Kentucky for the *Louisville Courier-Journal* at the time he wrote this book.

Operation Elvis. **New York: Holt, 1960. 117 pp. ISBN: none. London: Andre Deutsch Limited, 1960. 117 pp. ISBN: none. UK: World Distributors [Manchester] Ltd., 1962. 149 pp. ISBN: none.**

This book was the first American hardback about Elvis Presley. It details the complex efforts undertaken by the Department of Defense to handle the special problems created by having Elvis as an active duty soldier. Also discusses the campaign by Elvis's fans to keep him out of the army. No photographs. No index.

Source: Memphis/Shelby County (TN) Public Library and Information Center
OCLC 574940 (Holt, 1960); 2510352 (Andre Deutsch, 1960); 7717525 (1962)

☆ *Private Elvis Aaron Presley—Protocol.* **U.S. Army publication. (c. 1958).**

Referenced in *Down at the End of Lonely Street* (Brown, Broeske, 1997—*see* The Man/Biographies) as the publication of "a clandestine Elvis Presley Committee," established by "the Pentagon . . . to monitor the 'enormous cost' and the 'complicated procedures' necessary to turn a rock 'n' roll star into a frontline soldier" (p. 135). According to Brown and Broeske, this booklet has "disappeared from army files." Compiler was unable to locate information about this committee and booklet through the U.S. Army Office of Public Affairs, as well as the United States Army Center of Military History.

☆ Schröer, Andreas, Knorr O. Hentschell

Private Presley: Elvis in Germany—The Missing Years. **160 pp. Weert, [Netherlands]: Uitgeverij B.V., 1993. ISBN: none. London: Boxtree Press, 1993.** *Private Presley: The Missing Years—Elvis in Germany.* **New York: William Morrow/The Merlin Group, 1993. 158 pp. ISBN: 0688046096.**

An in-depth account of Elvis's two years in the army, beginning with his induction in 1958 and concluding with his discharge in 1960. Emphasis is divided between on- and off-duty activities. Introduction by Gordon Stoker, a singer with Elvis's backup group, The Jordanaires. Information about Elvis's relationship with German/Russian actress Vera Tschechowa. "Almost 400" color and black and white photographs, many of which are candids. Photographs of Elvis artifacts from this period, such as books in which he doodled. Bibliography. This book was also published in German. (*See* Foreign Language Titles/German.)

Accompanying this book is the CD: *The Private Presley CD: Elvis Army Interviews and 1954 Live Recordings of Elvis Presley and the Blue Moon Boys.* It contains four press interviews given by Elvis during this time period and seven of his 1954 recordings. (London: Boxtree, 1993. One Sound disc: digital; 4¾". Music No: Boxtree BOX 001.)

Source: New York Public Library—LDC 9434 & JNF 94-101 (CD and London edition of book)
OCLC 28903289 (recording); 30111147 (book)

☆ Taylor, Col. (U.S. Army–Retired) William J., Jr., Ph.D.

Taylor is Senior Vice President at The Center for Strategic and International Studies in Washington, D.C. He has authored 19 books and more than 375 articles relating to national security.

Elvis in the Army: The King of Rock 'n' Roll as Seen by an Officer Who Served with Him. Novato, CA: Presidio Press, 1995. 169 pp. ISBN: 0891415580 (hdk.). Novato, CA: Presidio Press, 1997. 192 pp. ISBN: 0891416277 (pbk.).

An anecdotal memoir of the military officer who served as Elvis Presley's platoon commander during part of the entertainer's tour of duty in Germany. Thirty-two black and white photographs, some not previously published. Review from *Sea Power* (Nov 1995): 41: " . . . interesting reading for military buffs looking for a 'barracks-view' glimpse of military life in the first decade of the Cold War when the draft was in full force and military service was not only a privilege but also . . . an obligation not to be shirked."

☆ "Will the Army Give Elvis Presley the Works?" *The National Police Gazette* (May 1957).

An article in one of America's oldest men's magazines, speculating on whether or not the army would treat Elvis Presley differently from other recruits. It was published nine months before Elvis would enter military service as a draftee.

☆ Yenti, Al

"The Truth About Elvis's Army Junket." *On the QT* (Dec 1959): 12, 58.

Discussion of the army's problems caused by Elvis Presley's presence in Germany. Author writes that it was "the biggest headache that any army ever had" because older Germans, who were the nation's leaders, saw him as disruptive.

See Also:

In The Man/Biographies:

Tatham, Dick, *Elvis*.

In TheMan/Death, Conspiracy, Sightings:

Hatcher, Harley, *Elvis Disguised*.

In The Man/Elvis in Quotes:

"Is This a 'New' Presley?"

In The Man/Memoirs and Memories:

Mansfield, Rex, and Elisabeth Mansfield, *Elvis the Soldier*.

In TheMan/Photographs:

Cortez, Diego, *Private Elvis*.
Elvis Presley in Paris, 1959.

In The Phenomena/Fiction:

Corvino, Nick, *Elvis: The Army Years 1958–1960*.

In The Phenomena/Politics:

Edson, Arthur, "Protests Roll In on Senator Case as Threat to Elvis's Hair Rocks Fans."
86th Congress, Second Session, "Tribute to Elvis Presley."

In Foreign Language Titles/French:

Pouzenc, Jean-Marie, *Elvis à Paris*.

In Foreign Language Titles/German:

Mansfield, Rex, and Elisabeth Mansfield, *Elvis in Deutschland*.

In The Academics/Educational Literature:

Mueller, Jean W., "Rock 'n' Roll Heroes: Letter to President Eisenhower."

In The Rest/Souvenir Magazines:

Elvis in the Army.
Holmes, Robert, *The Three Loves of Elvis Presley: The True Story of the Presley Legend*.

CHAPTER 4
Elvis in Quotes (By and About Elvis Presley)

IN TODAY'S AGE of celebrity, the words of the famous take on an oracular aura. At Harvard's distinguished John F. Kennedy School of Government, students and faculty are treated to the policy musings of pop singer Barbra Streisand, while the august *New York Times* prints sex symbol/movie star Warren Beatty's presentation of himself as a serious presidential contender. Within such a context, the growing number of books about Elvis's comments seems, unbelievably, "normal."

While Elvis quote collection books abound—each "authoritatively" printing his purported insights on subjects ranging from religion to romance—few authors have bothered to verify them. Thus, an accurate accounting of Elvis's comments has been difficult to find. Until recently, the largest number of authenticated Elvis quotes was found in 1950s magazines. This was before Colonel Parker assumed management, and, consequently, the only time that writers had open access to him. (The Colonel tightly controlled interviews—and, if he could get away with it, they came with a price tag.)

These first quote collections were in magazine articles where writers threw softballs at Elvis, such as "Do you have a girlfriend?" (*Elvis Answers Back*). But in fairness to those writers, this is what readers (i.e., fans) wanted to know. (One notable exception is the 1957 interview in *Jet* magazine, in which writer Louie Robinson queried Elvis about race issues. [*See* The Phenomena/Race.])

At the same time, equally simplistic quotes about Elvis appeared in abundance—mostly in fan magazines where fellow celebrities gushed their assessments. And they did not stop talking about him—even after he died.

Until the 1990s, most of the by-and-about Elvis quotes were confined to magazines. But in this decade, a number of authors decided that it would be a rewarding idea to collect by-and-about Elvis quote snippets and publish them in books. Oddly—though perhaps due to this rush to print and profit—almost all of these 1990s quote books lack citations for sources, as well as authentication information such as date and place.[1] So the reader is left to guess as to their accuracy—and veracity. As the 1990s closed, this situation changed. In the last months of the decade, the well-documented *Elvis: Word for Word* was published—a compendium based on scrupulous transcriptions of taped Elvis interviews and concerts. Hopefully, this authentic and authenticated work will inspire others to do the same. Then, who knows? The sagacity of Elvis Presley may, alongside that of Ms. Streisand and Mr. Beatty, inspire and illuminate the halls of higher learning and the pages of higher thought. The rest of us will just be happy with knowing what he really had to say.

☆　　☆　　☆　　☆

Comments by Elvis

☆ Brown, Carlton

"A Craze Called Elvis." *Coronet* (Sept 1956): 153–157.

An interview with Elvis Presley in which he talks about his musical influences and the reactions he is creating. In this article, Elvis's comments are written phonetically in an attempt to capture the sound of Elvis's accent. This stylistic usage is done with respect, unlike the ridiculing incidences of this in the *Time* magazine Elvis articles of that era.

☆ "Editor's Notebook." *Good Housekeeping* (Jan 1978): 4.

Includes the text from a plaque that Elvis gave to his father for Christmas in 1975. In it, Elvis thanks his father for all the contributions he has made to his life.

☆ *Elvis Answers Back.* Lawndale, CA: Sound Publishing Corp., 1956. 34 pp. ISBN: none. Memphis, TN: Elvis Presley Enterprises, Inc., 1997. ISBN: none.

First published in a magazine format in 1956, with a 78-rpm record pressed into the cover (with one of two titles, "Elvis Presley Speaks In-Person" or "The Truth About Me"). The recording was 2 minutes and 10 seconds of a taped 20-minute interview in which Elvis answered questions about himself. Forty-seven black and white photographs.

In 1996 the original tape from which the 78-rpm records had been made was discovered in a recording plant in Santa Monica, California. When the book was republished in 1997, it had annotations about the first edition and recordings as well as the 20-minute interview 78-rpm record ("The Truth About Me") pressed into the front cover. The interview was also included on a picture CD and a 10", 33⅓-rpm gold vinyl record that came with the 1997 edition.

Source: Compiler's collection (1997)

☆ "Elvis Presley Part 3: He Tells How the Little Wiggle Grew." *TV Guide* (Sept 29–Oct 5, 1956).

---

[1]Among the few exceptions are the *Precious Memories* books by Sue Wiegert. (*See* The Man/Memoirs and Memories.)

Elvis describes what it is like to be the object of enthusiastic fans and the target of music and social critics. Colonel Parker is also quoted about these subjects.

☆ Farren, Mick, compiler, and Pearce Marchbank

Mick Farren is a science fiction novelist. Pearce Marchbank is editor of Omnibus Press.

Elvis in His Own Words. **Ed. Pearce Marchbank. London; New York: Omnibus Press, 1977; 1994. 128 pp. ISBN: 0860014878 (1977).**

Fragments of media interviews given by Elvis from the 1950s through his last statement to the press in 1977. None of the quotations are cited or specifically sourced, but the authors provide a list of seven secondary sources from which they took information. No bibliography or acknowledgements. This book consists primarily of black and white photographs; some captioned but none credited.

Source: Compiler's collection (1977)
Library of Congress ML420.P96 A3 1994

☆ Gardner, Hy

" 'Glad You Asked That': Reprint of 1956 Elvis Presley Interview." *Knoxville News Sentinel* **(Nov 29, 1977): Sect 2: 23.**

The transcript from Elvis Presley's July 1, 1956, interview on the *Hy Gardner Calling* television program.

☆ **"Is This a 'New' Presley?"** *Newsweek* **(May 30, 1960): 91.**

Interview given by Elvis Presley on the set of *GI Blues*. He comments on his army service and his future plans.

☆ McKeon, Elizabeth, and Linda Everett, editors and compilers

The Quotable King. **Nashville, TN: Cumberland House, 1997. 192 pp. ISBN: 188895244X.**

A collection of unsubstantiated quotes attributed to Elvis Presley on topics ranging from loneliness to military life to religion. Bibliographical references (pp. 171–172). Previously seen black and white photographs. No footnotes, sources, or citations for the quotes.

☆ Osborne, Jerry

Elvis Word for Word: Everything He Said . . . Exactly as He Said It! **Port Townsend, WA: Jerry Osborne Publishing, 1999. 290 pp. ISBN: 0932117295.**

Transcripts of Elvis interviews, press conferences, and concert comments, in chronological order, from October 1954 to August 1977. Each is dated and sourced as to where the comments were made and where Osborne obtained them. 96 black and white photographs, identified by subject and year. Index.

☆ Poling, James

"Elvis Presley, Go Cat, Go." *Pageant* (July 1956): 6–13.

An early examination of the impact of Elvis Presley on teenage girls and vice versa. Quotes from Elvis about his controversial performance style, his experiences with fans, and other anecdotes of the first year of his career.

Source: New York Public Library

☆ Rovin, Jeff

The World According to Elvis: Quotes from the King. New York: HarperCollins Publishers/HarperPaperbacks, 1992. 140 pp. ISBN: 006100626.

Elvis's comments on a variety of subjects, from acting to zealotry. None of the quotes are cited or placed within a context.

☆ Shearer, Lloyd

"America's Most Controversial Singer Answers His Critics." *Parade* (Sept 30, 1956).

Parade magazine is a newspaper insert periodical that is included in Sunday editions throughout the United States.

See Also:

In The Man/Elvis in the Army:

Schröer, Andreas, O. Hentschell, and M. P. Knorr, *Private Presley: Elvis in Germany—The Missing Years.* (CD)

In The Man/The Impact of Elvis:

Gaillard, Frye, "Race, Rock and Religion."

In The Phenomena/Race:

Robinson, Louie, "The Truth About That Elvis Presley Rumor: 'The Pelvis' Gives His Views on Vicious Anti-Negro Slur."

Comments by Others

☆ Allen, Steve

U.S. News & World Report (Mar 13, 1978): 77.

Negative comments about Elvis Presley made by television comedian Steve Allen. Example: "The fact that someone with so little ability became the most popular singer in history says something significant about our cultural standards."

　　When Elvis appeared on Allen's television program in 1956, he was required, against his wishes, to wear formal evening dress and sing to a dog. On the same show, Allen obliged Elvis, a Cherokee descendent, to participate in a racially insensitive skit in which Native Americans were spoofed.

☆ Choron, Sandra, and Bob Oskam, compilers

Elvis! The Last Word: The 328 Best (and Worst) Things Anyone Ever Said About "The King." Secaucus, NJ: Citadel Press, 1991. 103 pp. ISBN: 0806512806.

Nineteen chapters containing more than 300 quotes about Elvis, covering his life. Quotes are credited, but most are not sourced. Index. Approximately 20 black and white photographs; none credited.

☆ Higgins, Patrick, editor

Before Elvis, There Was Nothing. New York: Carroll & Graff Publishers, Inc., 1994. 127 pp. ISBN: 0786701455.

A book of 53 statements about Elvis made by a range of writers and celebrities (including President Nixon, Imelda Marcos, David Halberstam, and Jackie Gleason). No citations or information that places the quotes in context. 53 black and white photographs; captioned and credited.

☆ Shaw, Sid

Sid Shaw is the proprietor of Elvisly Yours, an Elvis souvenir shop in London.

Elvis in Quotes. UK: Elvisly Yours, 1987. 188 pp. ISBN: 1869941020 (hdk.). ISBN: 1869941039 (pbk.).

Quotes about Elvis Presley from a variety of friends, family, and fellow entertainers. Quotes are identified by speaker but not cited. Previously seen color and black and white photographs. No index.

Source: New York Public Library JNF 89-26
The British Library YM.1987.b.476
OCLC 16684424

☆ Thompson, Peggy, compiler

Viva Las Elvis: Celebrating the King. A Little Red Book series. Vancouver, Canada: Arsenal Pulp Press Ltd., 1995. 92 pp. ISBN: 1551520109.

Quotes about Elvis; no citations or sources. Bibliographic references (pp. 87–88). Discography (pp. 79–86). Index.

Source: OCLC 31286621

See Also:

In The Man/Biographies:

Clayton, Rose, and Dick Heard, *Elvis Up Close: In the Words of Those Who Knew Him Best.*

In the Man/Major Articles:

"A Howling Hillbilly Success."

In the Man/Memoirs and Memories:

Weigert, Sue, *Elvis: Precious Memories*, Vols. I and II.

CHAPTER 5
The Elvis Presley FBI Files

CONTRARY TO POPULAR opinion, files kept by the Federal Bureau of Investigation (FBI) on individual citizens are more for record-keeping purposes than for nefarious reasons. The FBI does maintain documents on people they consider dangerous, such as criminals and subversives. But the majority of the files are for people who hold federal jobs, have been victims in a federal crime, or require employment-related security clearances. Elvis's FBI files are among those of the law-abiders.

This "common man" aspect of Elvis's FBI files is what gives them significance. They provide a rare opportunity not only to examine general FBI file keeping as it existed under Director J. Edgar Hoover but to compare the FBI's record-keeping to facts of a well-known individual's life.

Although Elvis Presley was not personally the subject of an FBI investigation, the FBI maintained records about him. Beginning in 1956, the file contains letters from the public commenting on his performances, newspaper clippings, and documents relating to extortion attempts against Elvis. Included are a 1956 letter to FBI Director Hoover expressing concern about Elvis's adverse effects on American youth and a summary of his famous December 1970 visit with President Richard Nixon.

The Elvis FBI file released to the public is 663 pages long and is not protected by copyright. Thus, it is available to anyone who would like to read, own, or reprint it. Entrepreneurs have sold it in excerpted format in print (*see* Greenwood listing in this chapter) and in its entirety on CD-ROM. (*See The (Elvis) Files* listing in The Man/Reference.) Copies of the 663 pages are available from the FBI, which charges to cover the costs of duplication. The file is also available for downloading from the agency's Web site at www.fbi.gov. Though the public was allowed access to FBI files in 1975, there is no evidence that Elvis ever saw his file—or even knew of its existence. And, given the contents' lack of intrigue, it is doubtful that he would have been interested. For the rest of us, it stands as a source of information about how our government checks up on us.

☆   ☆   ☆   ☆

☆ *Elvis's FBI File*. Washington, D.C.: Elvis File, 1982.

A commercial venture offering brief selections from Elvis Presley's FBI file, including reports from concert venues, attempts to cheat and extort Elvis, and blackmail-threat letters.

Source: Library of Congress ML420.P96 E5 1982
Dewey Decimal 782.42166/092 B 20

☆ Federal Bureau of Investigation, U.S. Department of Justice

Presley, Elvis A., 1956-1977. Washington, D.C.

All 663 pages reproduced from the official FBI file maintained on Elvis A. Presley.

Source: Federal Bureau of Investigation, Washington, D.C.

☆ Greenwood, Earl, and Kathleen Tracy

Greenwood and Tracy are also the co-authors of *The Boy Who Would Be King*. (*See* The Man/Memoirs and Memories.) Greenwood makes the unsupported claim that he is a cousin to Elvis Presley.

Elvis—Top Secret: The Untold Story of Elvis Presley's Secret FBI Files. New York: Signet, 1991. 340 pp. ISBN: 0451173112.

Six anecdotes based upon Elvis's FBI file. An abridged version of the 1956–1972 sections of the file (pp. 177–322). "Last Will and Testament of Elvis Presley" (pp. 327–340). No index.

☆ Johnston, David

"The FBI and the King Both Had Suspicious Minds." *The New York Times* (Aug 17, 1997): Sect. 4: 7.

An overview of the contents of Elvis Presley's FBI file, including Presley's admiring comments about J. Edgar Hoover.

☆ Warden, Robert L.

The Official FBI File on Elvis A. Presley. Chicago, IL: MEM Publishing Company, 1978. 48 pp. ISBN: none.

This book purports to contain "the entire file released by the FBI, with certain deletions provided by law." (It does not.)

Source: Library of Congress

See Also:

The Man/Death, Conspiracy, Sightings.

In The Man/Reference:

The (Elvis) Files.
The Elvis Files Explore His Life.

CHAPTER 6
Graceland

THROUGHOUT HISTORY, the common folk have endowed the dwelling places of mythic individuals—both humans and gods—with a sacred aura that quickly transforms itself into a secular fascination. We study and tour of these sites for what they can tell us, perhaps hoping to absorb some of the famous residents' greatness. The literature about Elvis's home, Graceland, explores this phenomenon.

Elvis Presley purchased the Graceland mansion and its property in March 1957 for $100,000. At that time, the 13.8-acre property held the mansion, a barn, and a smokehouse. Shortly after he moved in, Elvis added the current stone wall along the property's front.

Graceland originated in 1861 as a 500-acre Hereford cattle farm owned by S. E. Toof, then the publisher of the Memphis *Commercial Appeal*. It was named for Mr. Toof's daughter, Grace. In 1939 the owners, Dr. and Mrs. Thomas Moore,[1] built a Southern Colonial mansion on the remaining 13.8 acres of the original farm. The mansion and the acreage assumed the farm's name, Graceland. In the mid-1950s Dr. and Mrs. Moore offered Graceland for sale. Elvis was the buyer.

Elvis's friends and family lived with him in the house and continued to live there after his death. The last resident was Elvis Presley's aunt Delta Biggs, who lived in Graceland from 1967 to her death in 1994. Today, despite a lack of permanent residents, Graceland is still maintained as a functioning home—even though the first floor, gardens, and outbuildings are open for tours all but three days of the year.

When Elvis died, Graceland was the financial savior of his estate. The rapidly dwindling assets were resuscitated when Priscilla Presley—in an effort to save her daughter's inheritance—opened the mansion for paid public tours in 1982.[2] On November 7, 1991, Graceland was

---

[1]Mrs. Moore (Ruth Brown Moore) was a descendent of the Toof family.

[2]The Graceland mansion is maintained by the trust established by Lisa Marie Presley. As such, she is the owner of the house and may use it as her private residence if she chooses. Elvis's will established a trust for Lisa Marie that terminated when she turned 25 years of age. At that time, Lisa Marie signed a trust agreement with Elvis Presley Enterprises, Inc., to continue management of the Graceland property.

listed with the National Register of Historic Places—a distinguished honor[3] involving the documentation and evaluation of a property's significance in American history and culture. According to Carol Shull, chief of registration for the National Register, Graceland was accepted because " . . . the scope and nature of his [Elvis's] influence is an example of the robust popular culture that developed in this country following World War II. Elvis helped define that new culture." (*See* Gillette listing later in this chapter.)

The Graceland literature consists primarily of photograph books, travel articles, and legal documents. But, in the works of Karal Ann Marling, it has assumed much of the same status as Elvis—as a cultural signifier. Marling explores Graceland for what it symbolizes about Elvis and, in a larger context, the Old South.

Graceland holds a special place in our national heart. Celebrated in song,[4] and second only to the White House in numbers of touring sightseers, it is our present day Lourdes or Mt. Olympus—a place signifying greatness, where the magic just might rub off on a mortal visitor.

☆   ☆   ☆   ☆

☆ Balfour, Victoria

"Amazing Graceland." *Life* (Sept 1987): 50–56.

An examination of the 1987 physical and financial status of the Graceland mansion and of the adjoining Elvis Presley Enterprises, Inc., properties. Discusses Elvis Presley's aunt Delta Biggs, who lived in Graceland from 1967 to her death in 1994. Interview with EPE Executive Director Jack Soden. Sidebar about Priscilla Presley's life at Graceland.

☆ Braden, Frank

Elvis's Graceland: The Official Photo Album of Elvis's Home. [n.p.]: Elvis Presley Enterprises, Inc., 1982. 59 pp. ISBN: none.

The first collection of photographs of Graceland's interior and exterior.

Source: OCLC 21941775

☆ Brixey, Ken, and Twyla Dixon

Elvis at Graceland. Memphis, TN: Cypress Press, 1983. [64 pp.]. ISBN: 0961301201.

The first guidebook to Graceland. Biographical text on Elvis is based on interviews with Presley family members and Elvis's close friends. Renowned photographer William Eggle-

---

[3]Among the more than 68,000 listings of the National Register are historic areas in the National Park System, more than 2,200 National Historic Landmarks, and the White House. Listing in the National Register means that the property is of significance to the nation and must be maintained under strict federal historic guidelines. The designation of Graceland was advanced by Jennifer Tucker, who, with the consent of Elvis Presley Enterprises, Inc., completed its nomination as part of her undergraduate degree at Roger Williams College, Rhode Island. (See Gillette listing in this chapter.)

[4]Paul Simon's Grammy-winning album, *Graceland*.

ston's black and white and color pictures of Graceland's interior rooms and exterior property, including the gravesites. Close-up photographs of art and furniture inside of Graceland. One photograph shows the property across the street from Graceland as it appeared in 1983.

Source: Library of Congress ML420.P96 B74 1983

☆ Davidson, J. W., Alfred Hecht, and Herbert A. Whitney

"The Pilgrimage to Graceland." *Pilgrimage in the United States.* **Eds. G. Rinschede and S. Bhardwaj. 1990. Pp. 229–252.**

An examination of what brings visitors (described by the authors as "pilgrims") to Graceland. Exploration of visitors' experiences while touring the home, emphasizing reactions to the mansion's Meditation Garden, where Elvis is buried. Summary in English and German. Bibliography. Map of the Elvis Presley Enterprises, Inc., properties in the Graceland area.

Source: Library of Congress BL619.P5
ATLA Religion Database 1997

☆ Elliott, Lawrence

"Where Elvis Lives." *Reader's Digest* **[U.S. Edition] (Aug 1993): 47–52.** *Reader's Digest* **[Canadian English Edition] (Aug 1993): 99–104.**

An analysis of the reasons visitors come to Graceland: "Why do we come, 670,000 last year alone? Why does Elvis abide in our collective memory?" (p. 48, U.S.). Elliott seeks to answer these questions through a biographical look at Elvis Presley.

Elvis A. Presley Estate and Vicinity. Memphis, TN. **"Certificate date 8-18-1977."**

Cadastral map showing Graceland and surrounding properties with dimensions and owners' names as of 8/18/77. (A cadastral map is one that records property boundaries, subdivision lines, buildings, and related details.) Map on sheet measuring 22 x 28 cm. Scale: 1:4,000.

Source: OCLC 5500956

Elvis A. Presley Estate. Memphis, TN. **"Date drawn: 9-6-1977. File: city 78–1."**

A cadastral map showing property dimensions.

Source: OCLC 5500957

☆ Filler, Martin

"Elvis Presley's Graceland: An American Shrine." *House and Garden* **(Mar 1984): 140–147.**

☆ Fisher, Mark

"It's Only Rock 'n' Roll." *Architecture Design Profile XX*: **46–51.**

An examination of Graceland within the context of its cultural significance. The author makes a comparison/contrast between Graceland and Disneyland and explores the mansion and property as a "celebration of death."

☆ Flippo, Chet

Flippo is a former editor with *Rolling Stone* magazine.

Graceland: The Living Legacy of Elvis Presley. San Francisco: Collins Publishers, 1993; London: Mitchell Beazley, 1993; London: Hamlyn, 1994. 256 pp. ISBN: 0002552507 (Collins Publishers edition).

Written with the endorsement of Elvis Presley Enterprises, Inc. (EPE), an in-depth examination of the rooms and artifacts of Graceland, the Meditation Garden, and the EPE museums, through color photographs and accompanying descriptions. Photographs; captioned and credited.

The text includes a well-researched biographical essay by the author. This essay uses the book by realtor Virginia Grant, who handled the Graceland sale to Elvis, to provide the details of the transaction. (*See* Grant listing in this section.) The essay also describes the rehabilitation of Graceland after Elvis's death. Index. Ephemera. Listing of Elvis Presley's Gold and Platinum albums, singles, and extended play singles, as of 1993. This book was translated into Japanese. (*See* Foreign Language Titles/Japanese.)

☆ Gillette, Jane Brown

"Elvis Lives." *Historic Preservation* (May/June 1992): 46–52, 93–96.

On November 7, 1991, Graceland was placed on the National Register of Historic Places. This article chronicles the nomination and gives an in-depth history of the home during Elvis's lifetime, as well as afterward when it was opened for public tours.

☆ Goodman, Charles

"Priscilla Explains Decision on Graceland." *Memphis Press-Scimitar* (May 4, 1982): 5.

☆ Grant, Virginia

Grant was the realtor who handled the sale of Graceland to Elvis.

How Elvis Bought Graceland: Exactly as It Happened. Memphis, TN: Grant, 1977. 7 leaves. ISBN: none.

A typewritten, first-person, chronological account of the details of the sale of Graceland to Elvis Presley.

Source: Memphis/Shelby County (TN) Public Library and Information Center
OCLC 4312522

☆ Green, Margo Hoven, Dorothy Nelson, and Darlene Clevenger, editors

Graceland. Buchanan, MI: Trio Publishing, 1994. Unpaged. ISBN: None.

A collection of legal documents relating to the Graceland mansion and property from its construction in 1932 to Elvis's death in 1977. A brief overview essay on the history of the Graceland property. Newspaper clippings providing background information on Dr. and Mrs. Thomas Moore, who built the Graceland mansion in 1939. Documents include subdivision map, sales agreements, deeding and probate documents, and a copy of Elvis's will. Black and white candid photographs of the interior before Elvis lived in the house, from the collection of a descendent of the original owners.

Source: Library of Congress ML420.P96 G7 1994
OCLC 34080261

☆ Kath, Laura, and Todd Morgan

Laura Kath was formerly employed by EPE. Todd Morgan is the Director of Creative Resources for EPE.

Elvis Presley's Graceland: The Official Guidebook. Memphis: Graceland Division/Elvis Presley Enterprises, Inc., 1993; 1996. 62 pp. (1993). 71 pp. (1996). ISBN: 1569330182 (both editions).

Short biography of Elvis's life, with photographs from the Elvis Presley Enterprises, Inc. (EPE), archives. Color photographs and descriptions of the rooms in Graceland that are open for public view. Color photographs of the mansion grounds and outbuildings, as well as the EPE museums and gift shops, with accompanying descriptions. Aerial color photograph of the complex and surrounding area. The 1996 edition is an updated and expanded revision of the 1993 edition.

Source: OCLC 36071251 (1993); 39873630 (1996)

☆ Lyons, David

"Totally Hip Graceland." *World Traveler* (June 1996): 46–50, 52–54.

A detailed description of a travel writer's experiences on the Graceland mansion tour.

☆ Marcus, Greil

Greil Marcus is a leading rock music historian.

"William Eggleston's View of Graceland: The Absence of Elvis." *Artforum 22* (Mar 1984): 70–72.

In this article Marcus examines the Eggleston Graceland portfolio photographs for what they tell us about Elvis Presley. Comparisons are made with the images and messages of photographs of the Depression-era sharecroppers taken by Walker Evans. This article is also included in Marcus's *Dead Elvis.* (*See* The Man/The Impact of Elvis.)

☆ Marling, Karal Ann

Marling is a university professor.

"Elvis Presley's Graceland, or the Aesthetic of Rock 'n' Roll Heaven." *American Art* (Fall 1993): 72–105.

The author believes that Elvis Presley's deep attachment to Graceland makes it central to any understanding of him. In this article she examines Graceland's history, analyzes its various decorating phases, and considers the significance of the changes made after Elvis's death when Graceland was opened to the public. Bibliography. Photographs from William Eggleston's Graceland portfolio.

———.

Graceland: Going Home with Elvis. Cambridge, MA: Harvard University Press, 1996. 258 pp. ISBN: 0674358899.

An analysis of the meaning of home to Americans through an examination of Elvis and the places in which he lived. Focuses primarily on Graceland, relating the changing interior to the changes in Elvis's life. No photographs. Chapter notes with bibliographic references.

Source: Library of Congress

☆ *Memphis and Shelby County [TN] Office of Planning and Development Graceland Area Study.* Memphis: The Office, 1979.

A study of the Graceland estate and its value as a tourist attraction. Contains illustrations and maps.

Source: OCLC 5436657

☆ Mid-South Title Company

☆ Presley, Priscilla Beaulieu

Elvis Presley's Graceland. Plainfield, NJ: The Congress Video Group,1985. 1 video-cassette (60) minutes; ½" VHS format.

Priscilla Presley guides viewers through the rooms at Graceland. Sound and color.

Source: OCLC 14510686

☆ *Virtual Graceland.* CD-ROM. Santa Monica, CA: Elvis Presley Enterprises, Inc., 1996. ISBN: 1888491167.

"Your personal tour of Elvis's life and home" (title from disc label). An interactive computerized tour of the Graceland mansion and other sites associated with Elvis Presley's life.

Source: OCLC 36418804

See Also:

In The Man/Biographies:

Clayton, Rose, and Dick Heard, *Elvis Up Close: In the Words of Those Who Knew Him Best.*

In The Man/Memoirs and Memories:

Erwin, Sara, *Over the Fence: A Neighbor's Memories of Elvis.*

In The Phenomena/Fans:

Arthur, Caroline, "Going to Graceland."
Davidson, James W., "Graceland: More than a Hit Song—A Twentieth Century Mecca."
Wright, Daniel, *Dear Elvis: Graffiti from Graceland.*

In The Phenomena/Politics:

H. J. Res. 589.

In The Phenomena/Travel Guides:

Rada, Joe, "Viva Elvis."

In The Academics/Dissertations and Theses:

Davidson, James William, *The Pilgrimage to Elvis Presley's Graceland: A Study of the Meanings of Place.*

CHAPTER 7
The Impact of Elvis

FEW AMERICANS ALIVE today fail to understand the phrase "Elvis is everywhere." Why? Because he is. And that three-word phrase gives the simplest and the most complex explanation to his enduring and ingrained presence. He has impacted our culture that deeply and that thoroughly.

The examination of Elvis Presley's impact began in the 1950s at the same time as his national fame. Then, much of it focused on the unequaled female hysteria generated by his voice and his appearance. Thoughtful social observers in respected publications such as *The New Republic, Harper's*, and *The Sunday Times* in London wrote with wonderment, if not concern, over this stunning emotional reaction. Psychologists leapt in to explain and reassure. (*See* McManus and Reiser listings in this chapter.) Not since the Salem Witch trials in seventeenth-century Massachusetts had America experienced such a fervent, society-affecting phenomenon among teenaged girls. (*See* Granetz listing in The Academics/Dissertations and Theses.)

It was clear in the 1950s that Elvis was affecting our culture. But, with the exception of rock music writer and historian Greil Marcus's 1975 landmark essay "Elvis: Presliad" (*Mystery Train*), few scholars and writers paid much attention as the nation careened through the raucous and riotous 1960s and 1970s. (*See* Marcus listing in this chapter.)

The nation's attention would be most notably grabbed in 1979—two years after Elvis died. Jac L. Tharpe of the University of Southern Mississippi edited the Fall 1979 issue of *The Southern Quarterly: A Journal of the Arts in the South*, which showcased some of the finest academic and analytic observations of Elvis ever written—then or now.[1] (*See* The Academics/Elvis as an Academic Pursuit.)

Two other 1979 publications joined Tharpe to set in motion the great Elvis impact deliberations that have occupied the 1990s. African American minister The Rev. Martin R. Long wrote *God's Works Through Elvis* (1979), describing how Elvis's music helped blend cultures

---

[1] That same year, these articles were published in an anthology edited by Tharpe, entitled *Elvis: Images and Fancies*.

in the South. (*See* The Phenomena/Race.) In Great Britain classical composer and music writer Robert Matthew-Walker described Elvis's musical impact in *Elvis Presley: A Study in Music*. (*See* The Music, The Movies/Elvis's Influence on Music.)

In 1981 Neal and Janice Gregory published their milestone *When Elvis Died*, firmly establishing his death as the birth of our culture's fascination with celebrity. (*See* The Man/Death, Conspiracy, Sightings.) And in 1985 Patsy Hammontree[2] wrote *Elvis: A Bio-Bibliography*, the first study of Elvis's life and impact through the literature written about him.

But it would not be until the 1990s that the Elvis impact literature would catch fire. Fittingly, the first—and considered the most important—was "Presliad" author Greil Marcus's *Dead Elvis: A Chronicle of a Cultural Obsession* (1991). Other thoughtful writers would follow Marcus's lead: Susan Doll, Patsy Hammontree, George Plasketes, and Gilbert Rodman. (*See* listings later in this chapter.)

The titles examining and evaluating Elvis's influence and impact continue unabated. In the process, these explorations firmly cement him into the role of historical and cultural signifier and establish Elvis as a guide for our own journey of national self-discovery—while he still makes the girls scream.

☆　　☆　　☆　　☆

Observations from the 1950s

☆ Baxter, James and Annette

Dr. James Baxter was a professor of psychiatry at Cornell University (NY). Dr. Annette Baxter was a teacher at Barnard College (NY).

"The Man in the Blue Suede Shoes." *Harper's* (Jan 1958): 45–47.

One of the first thoughtful assessments of Elvis Presley's impact, written after he had been world famous for a year-and-a-half. The authors observe: "Ol' Elvis Presley may be a better musician than most people dare to admit—and he might be offering the kids a commodity their parents can't recognize."

☆ **"Beware Elvis Presley."** *America* (June 23, 1956): 294–295.

A Roman Catholic Church magazine article that quotes negative newspaper reviews about Elvis Presley's early performances and dismisses Elvis as a vulgarian.

☆ Bryant, Arthur

"Our Notebook." *The Illustrated London News* (Feb 9, 1957): 210.

A British observer examines how Elvis Presley reflects the American passion for being "oneself, to be uninhibited, and to rejoice in it." Bryant extensively quotes poet Walt

---

[2]In 1979 Patsy Hammontree, a professor of English at the University of Tennessee, taught what is considered to be the first accredited university-level course on Elvis: "Cultural Phenomenon of Elvis Presley: The Making of a Folk Hero."

Whitman in support of his view of Elvis and concludes that "if we are not careful we may find to our astonishment and dismay that even an Elvis Presley and the uncritical worship he engenders can prove the last and unconscious warning milepost of that age-long cycle before a Stalin or a Hitler."

☆ Condon, Eddie

"What Is an Elvis Presley?" *Cosmopolitan* (Dec 1956): 54–61.

Famous jazz musician and music columnist Eddie Condon analyzes the musical background and moral implications of Elvis Presley for 1950s parents. Condon quotes Steve Allen, on whose show Elvis appeared and was required to sing to a dog, as saying "He's a mild-mannered country kid. Not too bright, perhaps, but sincere. In fact, he's sort of likeable." Black and white photographs of Elvis backstage and performing; captioned.[3]

☆ Cooper, Susan

"Mr. Presley Finds the Rock of Gold." *The Sunday Times* (London) (Jan 27, 1957): 12.

A British writer's examination of Elvis Presley's influence on teenagers in the 1950s.

☆ *Drew Pearson's Washington Merry-Go-Round* [no. 1]. Dir. William Neel. 1994.

Drew Pearson, a nationally syndicated columnist and television commentator, discusses the life, career, and impact of Elvis Presley on his television program *Drew Pearson's Washington Merry-Go-Round*, circa 1957. He comments on the social significance of rock music, including the controversy around Elvis's on-stage body movements. (41 minutes; Elvis's story is part one of this two-part tape.)

Source: American University Library LIB Media Services VHS

☆ McManus, Margaret

"Presley No Serious Peril, Noted Psychologist Feels." *Washington Star* [DC] (Sept 30, 1956).

An interview with a professor of psychology about the possibility of emotional and psychological damage to Elvis's teenaged fans. The interview was conducted shortly after Elvis Presley's famous appearance on *The Ed Sullivan Show*.

☆ Pleasants, Henry

"Elvis Presley." *The Great American Popular Singers*. New York: Simon and Schuster, 1974. ISBN: 671216813. Pp. 263–279.

One of the earliest and best analyses of Elvis Presley's musical style and impact. In this chapter, published during Elvis's lifetime, noted musicologist Henry Pleasants analyzes

[3]When this article appeared, *Cosmopolitan* magazine was not the soft-porn, sex-obsessed periodical that it is today. Rather, it showcased thoughtful observations by respected writers.

Elvis Presley as a musician, as well as his effect on American music and his place in music history. Unsourced direct quotes attributed to Elvis and his friends

☆ Reiser, Martin

"A Note on the Analysis of the 'Elvis Presley' Phenomenon." *The American Imago* 15 (Spring 1958): 97–100.

A "psychoanalytic speculation" of the adolescent adulation of "the notion 'Elvis Presley.'" The author concludes "the figure, 'Elvis Presley,' forms a half-way station" that "allows for satisfaction of suppressed infantile impulses" and is also "the body reality through which object love is found." References from psychology journals and texts. *The American Imago* was "a Psychoanalytic Journal for the Arts and Sciences."

Source: Library of Congress BF173.A2 A 55

☆ Salisbury, Harrison

"Presley Records a Craze in Soviet." *The New York Times* (1957).

An article on the growing popularity of Elvis Presley among young people in the Soviet Union during the 1950s. He tells of the Elvis-inspired *stilyagi* (Soviet "zoot-suited" young people). (*See* also Lee Hockstader listing in The Phenomena/Fans.)

☆ Weales, Gerald

"Movies: The Crazy, Mixed-Up Kids Take Over." *The Reporter* (Dec 13, 1956): 40–41.

Written shortly after the premier of *Love Me Tender*, this is a thoughtful examination of the "new film heroes"—Marlon Brando, James Dean, and Elvis Presley—in light of what they represent and what they say about the young people of the 1950s.

Source: Library of Congress D839. R385

☆ **"What a Twisted Scale of Values!"** *The Christian Century* (May 25, 1960): 630.

An editorial in a Roman Catholic Church magazine decrying the amount of money paid to Elvis Presley for a recent television performance ($125,000)—"more money than the yearly salary of the President of the United States." The author also warns that continuing to reward the kind of behavior exhibited on-stage by Elvis will ruin our society.

Source: Library of Congress BR1. C45

☆ Wolfe, Charles, Ph.D.

Wolfe is a professor of English at Middle Tennessee State University and an important American musicologist.

"Presley and the Gospel Tradition." *Elvis: Images and Fancies.* Ed. Jac Tharpe. Jackson, MS: University Press of Mississippi, 1979. ISBN: none. Pp. 135–150.

Wolfe is the first scholar to study Elvis Presley's gospel root and how he, in turn, influenced gospel music. Sources.

Observations 1960–1977

☆ Carsch, Henry

"The Protestant Ethic and the Popular Idol in America: A Case Study." *Social Compass* 15.1 (1968): 45–69.

The author applies the life and circumstances of Elvis Presley to a set of attributes ascribed to traditional American folk heroes. Tables of survey results among Elvis fans. Notes. Bibliography.

Source: Library of Congress BL60. S6

☆ "1955: The Beginning of Our Own Time." *South Atlantic Quarterly* 73.4 (1974): 428–444.

Written while Elvis Presley was alive, the author considers the problem of dating American cultural periods and tests his theories by dating the beginning of the 1970s with the year 1955. Three people—Elvis Presley, Allen Ginsberg, and Le Corbusier—are examined for their cultural works, which were "destined to ring in a new era." Notes. Biographical references.

Source: Library of Congress AP2. S75

☆ Scott, Vernon

"Elvis: Ten Million Dollars Later." *McCall's* (Feb 1963): 90, 124–126, 128.

A serious appraisal of Elvis Presley's talent, impact, and future as an entertainer in 1963. At the time of this article Elvis was not performing in public, instead spending his professional energies on recording and making low-quality films. Scott interviewed motion picture director Norman Taurog, who would direct a total of nine Elvis films. Scott provides a detailed description of one of the football games that Elvis and his friends played regularly in a Los Angeles–area park.

☆ Sharnik, John

"The War of the Generations." *House and Garden* (Oct 1956): 40–41.

The author thoughtfully examines the reactions to Elvis Presley in the context of generational differences. He predicts that Elvis will drift away from national attention as he ages and will eventually reappear as a middle-aged host of a weekly *The Elvis Presley Show*, where "as a kind of middle-aged statesman, he speaks for his generation in the defense against whatever new musical menace has arisen among its baffling young." (In this article Sharnik also discusses a gender connection between Marilyn Monroe and Elvis Presley.)

Posthumous Observations

☆ Armstrong, Karen

"Elvis Presley and American Culture." *Suomen Antropologi* 18.1 (Jan 1993): 10–19.

The author theorizes that Elvis Presley—as an image and an icon—is also a methodology through which cultures can examine themselves. Armstrong uses her birthplace, Cecil County, Maryland, as the location for her observations. Abstract from article: "In his lifetime, Elvis moved from being a cultural marker for the middle class (the young, rebellious Elvis) to becoming a cultural marker for the middle-aged working class. The romantic image of Elvis links him to problematic gender relations as well."

Source: Library of Congress WMLC. 93/2535

☆ Bayles, Martha

Martha Bayles is a music historian and critic.

"Will the Real Elvis Please Stand Up?" *The Wall Street Journal* (Aug 15, 1997): A16.

Bayles comments on Elvis's musical and culture legacies.

☆ Carlson, Thomas C.

"Ad Hoc Rock: Elvis and the Aesthetics of Postmodernism." *Studies in Popular Culture* XVI.2 (Apr 1994): 40–50.

The author examines postmodernism through the filter of Presley's life, career, and impact. Notes. "Works Cited."

☆ Colman, Stuart

"Elvis Presley—Once a King." *They Kept On Rockin': The Giants of Rock 'n' Roll.* Poole, Dorset (UK): Blandford Press, 1982. 160 pp. ISBN: 0713712171. Pp. 122–127.

A highly regarded essay on Elvis Presley's influence on rock and roll.

Source: Library of Congress ML3543.C64 1982

☆ Doll, Susan M., Ph.D.

Susan Doll, Ph.D., has written seven books about Elvis.

Elvis: Rock 'n' Roll Legend. Lincolnwood, IL: Publications International, 1994. 239 pp. ISBN: 0785308717.

An exploration of the impact of Elvis. This book examines "each phase of Elvis Presley's career as well as the key events of his personal life. His professional nicknames and personas are examined to better understand how America responded [to Elvis]" (p. 11). Approximately 100 color and sepia-tone photographs; credited.

Source: Library of Congress ML420.P96 D65 1994
Dewey Decimal 782.42166/092 B 20
OCLC 31704592

☆ Egerton, John

"Elvis Lives! The Stuff That Myths Are Made Of." *The Progressive* (March 1979):
20–23.

The author attempts to explain—in 1979—Elvis Presley's meteoric rise and "the perpetual motion of his memory." Among others, he interviews novelist and historian Shelby Foote. On pages 22–23, he discusses Elvis's place in the Civil Rights Movement.

☆ Estes, Clarissa Pinkola, Ph.D.

"Elvis Presley: F'ama and the Cultus of the Dying God." *The Soul of Popular Culture.* Ed. Mary Lynn Kittelson. Chicago: Open Court, 1998. ISBN: 0812693639. Pp. 19–50.

The feminist author of *Women Who Run With Wolves* uses Elvis Presley as the subject for her "catalog of the psychological conditions and steps required to lead a soul, symbolically or otherwise, into becoming the sacrificial victim at the center of what I came to term 'the cultus of the dying God' . . . where the king is not meant to live a long life, but rather is meant to revivify the culture, and then be lost to an early demise" (pp. 19–20).

Source: Library of Congress BF 175.4.C84568 1998

☆ Gaillard, Frye

"Potshots at Elvis." *Race, Rock and Religion: Profiles from a Southern Journalist.* Charlotte, NC: East Woods Press, 1982. ISBN: 0914788590. Pp. 71–76.

Gaillard, a respected Southern journalist who covered Elvis Presley's death and funeral, "attempts to affirm [Elvis's] importance in American culture, exploring the diverse elements that comprise his appeal—including his radical fusion of white and black musical sounds" (p. 71). Gaillard quotes Elvis on the roots of his music and his complaints about being singled out for his "wiggle."

Source: Library of Congress F2116.2.G34 1982

☆ Guralnick, Peter

"Elvis: Entertainer of the Century." *TV Guide* (Jan 1, 2000): 14–17.

Premier Elvis biographer Guralnick succinctly and brilliantly defines Elvis's impact upon our culture. (Note: Without changing the content, the publishers of *TV Guide* printed two editions of this issue—each with a different cover photograph of Elvis. Each cover reads, "One of two collector's covers this week!")

☆ Halberstam, David

Halberstam is a distinguished historian and journalist.

"Thirty-One." *The Fifties*. New York: Villard Books, 1993. ISBN: 0679415599. Pp. 456–469.

Halberstam's observations on the impact of Elvis Presley upon our culture.

☆ Hammontree, Patsy Guy, Ph.D.

Hammontree is a professor of English at the University of Tennessee. Previous to this publication, she had written about Elvis for *The Journal of Country Music* and the *Southern Quarterly*.

Elvis Presley: A Bio-Bibliography. Popular Culture Bio-Bibliographies series. Westport, CT: Greenwood Press, 1985. 301 pp. ISBN: 0313228671.

An evaluation of Elvis Presley's contributions to music and popular culture. Biographic, impact, and bibliographic essays with notes and citations. Bibliographic essay (pp. 191–223) categorizes and assesses the cycles of Elvis publishing genres. Bibliography of books and periodical and newspaper articles (pp. 223–231). Chronology of Elvis's life (pp. 233–239). Filmography and an essay with assessments of representative movies (pp. 240–260). Discography essay and Sun and RCA singles and LP album listings up to 1985 (pp. 261–292). Index. List of individuals interviewed.

☆ Hiltbrand, David

"The Greatest Ever? Forget Springsteen, Jackson and Madonna. Elvis Is Still King!" *TV Guide* (Jan 21, 1989): 4–11.

The influence of rock stars, particularly Elvis Presley, on the television medium.

☆ Hoffman, Abbie

"Too Soon the Hero." *Crawdaddy* (Nov 1977): 39–41.

Former 1960s anti-war activist Abbie Hoffman (who, inexplicably, is described as *Crawdaddy*'s travel editor) discusses how Elvis Presley's counter-culture revolutionary impact in the 1950s did not carry over to the 1960s; how Elvis and the 1950s were made for each other, just as Elvis and the 1960s were not.

☆ Kanchanawan, Nitaya, Ph.D.

Kanchanawan translated the Thai language edition of *When Elvis Died* by Neal and Janice Gregory. (*See* Foreign Language Titles/Thai.)

"Elvis, Thailand, and I." Ed. Jac L. Tharpe. *Elvis: Images and Fancies*. Jackson, MS: University Press of Mississippi, 1979. ISBN: none. Pp. 162–168.

Kanchanawan describes how she and her fellow Thais became Elvis fans in the 1950s— even though most had never been to the United States. She explores Elvis's international

THE IMPACT OF ELVIS 103

impact, particularly in her Buddhist country: "Elvis was special in that when you talked about Elvis you never realized that he was an American or a Christian or that he spoke English—he was just Elvis."

Source: Tharpe, Jac L., Ph.D., editor, Elvis: Images and Fancies.

☆ Katz, Jon

"Why Elvis Matters." Wired (Apr 1995): 100–105.

An examination of Elvis Presley's role in leading young people to fight for the right to their own culture. The author notes that "Elvis presided over the birth of a new means of expression, thus dealing a blow to the system."

Source: ProQuest Periodical Abstract 02321036.

☆ King, Christine

"His Truth Goes Marching On: Elvis Presley and the Pilgrimage to Graceland." Pilgrimage in Popular Culture. Eds. Ian Reader and Tony Walter. London: The Macmillan Press, Ltd., 1993. ISBN: none. Pp. 92–104.

An examination of the pilgrimage aspect of Elvis Week held each August in Memphis by Elvis Presley Enterprises, Inc. A brief biography focusing on how Elvis Presley has been "canonized by popular acclaim." List of references (eight items).

Source: Library of Congress CB430.P43 1993

☆ Kroll, Jack

"The Heartbreak Kid." Newsweek (Aug 29, 1977): 48–49.

An assessment of Elvis Presley's impact on our culture, written the week after he died.

☆ Marcus, Greil

Greil Marcus is a leading rock and roll critic and historian and an early editor at Rolling Stone magazine. Marcus's essay "Elvis: Presliad," is one of the most important pieces of writing about Elvis. (See The Man/Major Articles.)

Dead Elvis: A Chronicle of a Cultural Obsession. New York: Doubleday, 1991. ISBN: 0385417187. 233 pp. New York: Anchor Books, 1992. ISBN: 0385417195. 233 pp. New York: Viking, 1992. ISBN: 0670838462. 233 pp. London: Penguin, 1992. 233 pp. ISBN: 0670838462. Cambridge, MA; London: Harvard University Press, 1999. 288 pp. ISBN: 0674194225.

This highly acclaimed and oft-referenced book is one of the classic studies of Elvis Presley and his place in American culture. Examination of the themes of freedom, responsibility, authority, sex, repression, youth, age, tradition, novelty, guilt, and redemption as they have been expressed through Elvis as cultural icon. Color and black and white reproductions of original artwork related to Elvis. (In the Harvard reprint edition, all reproductions are in black and white.) Biographical references (pp. 207–212). Citations. Index. This book was translated into German and Japanese. (*See* Foreign Language Titles/German, Japanese.)

————.

R U Elvis? Berkeley, CA: Black Oak Books/Okeanos Press, 1991. One broadside; 38 x 26 cm.

Selections from Marcus's book *Dead Elvis*. From OCLC Notes: "This is a gift from Black Oak Books, Berkeley, on the occasion of a reading by the author."

Source: Brown University
OCLC 27712657

☆ Marling, Karal Ann

Marling is a well-known popular culture writer.

"When Elvis Cut His Hair: The Meaning of Mobility." *As Seen on TV: The Visual Culture of Everyday Life in the 1950s.* Cambridge, MA: Harvard University Press, 1994. ISBN: 0674048822. Pp. 165–311.

The author uses Elvis's flamboyant hairstyles and clothes during the 1950s as a metaphor for that period's changing social views: "Elvis's regal dandyism was the most extreme example of a new male fascination with color and finery. . . . Elvis's outlandish get-ups represent feelings of personal liberation and pleasure in a visual language already understood by the culture at large."

Source: Library of Congress E169.02.M 3534 1994

☆ Nash, Alanna

In 1977 Nash was a journalist who reported on Elvis's death and funeral. She is the author of *Elvis Aaron Presley: Revelations from the Memphis Mafia.* (*See* The Man/Memoirs and Memories.)

"Elvis: Why the King Still Matters." *Stereo Review* (Sept 1997): 86–88.

Nash examines the groundbreaking aspects of the entertainer's career and why he remains so popular today.

☆ Plasketes, George M.

Images of Elvis Presley in American Culture, 1977–1997: The Mystery Terrain. New York: Haworth Press, 1997. 304 pp. ISBN: 1560238615.

A thoughtful examination of the broad scope of Elvis Presley's influences and pervasiveness in American culture. Bibliographic references. Discography of songs about Elvis. Filmography and videography of movies that relate to Elvis. Index.

☆ Quain, Kevin

The Elvis Reader: Texts and Sources on the King of Rock 'n' Roll. New York: St. Martin's Press, 1992. 334 pp. ISBN: 0312069669.

Twenty-nine essays, articles, and manuscript excerpts, described on the flyleaf as a "collection of the very best writing on Elvis—from critical inquiry to musical scholarship. . . ." Writings span 1956 through the 1980s. Authors include Priscilla Presley, Charles Wolfe, Lester Bangs, and Stanley Booth. Articles from *The New Republic* (1956), *Time* (1977), *Newsweek* (1977), and *Harper's* (1958). Reference section (pp. 308–343) with lists identifying the people close to Elvis, locations associated with Elvis. Bibliography (pp. 340–342). Index.

☆ Rodman, Gilbert B.

Elvis After Elvis: The Posthumous Career of a Living Legend. London; New York: Routledge, 1996. 231 pp. ISBN: 0415110025 (hdk). ISBN: 0415110033 (pbk).

A scrutiny of Elvis's posthumous popularity, written to "shed light on the myths by which American culture survives." Presents several theories for the enduring and ubiquitous presence of Elvis as a cultural icon. Demonstrates how "Elvis has become inseparable from many of the defining myths of U.S. culture." Thirty-one black and white plates; captioned and credited. Chapter Notes. Bibliography (pp. 211–226), listing of printed materials, sound recordings, and films, videos, and television broadcasts. Index. This book was based upon Rodman's dissertation. (*See* The Academics/Dissertations and Theses.)

☆ Roy, Samuel

Roy is an American entertainment journalist.

Elvis: Prophet of Power. Brookine, MA: Branden Publishing Company, 1985. 195 pp. ISBN: 0828318980.

The author states that "the purpose of this book is to offer a greater understanding of the forces that helped shape his talent—by understanding the man, we can better understand his multifaceted musical genius" (p. 4). Nine black and white photographs of Elvis performing in 1970s concerts; none captioned or credited. No notes. Bibliography (25 titles). List of Elvis's friends who were interviewed for this book. Index.

Source: Memphis/Shelby County (TN) Public Library and Information Center
Library of Congress ML420.P96 R7 1985
OCLC 11574800

☆ Scherman, Rowland, photographer, and Mark Pollard, editor

Elvis Is Everywhere. New York: Clarkson Potter/Publishers, 1991. [79] pp. ISBN: 0517586053.

A collection of black and white photographs of Elvis images (signs, artwork, references) grouped to demonstrate his pervasiveness in our society.

Source: Library of Congress ML88.P76 S33 1991

☆ Shales, Tom

Shales is a Pulitzer Prize–winning television critic and historian. He writes for *The Washington Post.*

"Down at the End of Lonely Street." *Legends: Remembering America's Greatest Stars.* New York: Random House, 1989. 207 pp. ISBN: 0394575210. Pp. 150–157.

Shales comments on Elvis's pre- and posthumous impact on television and, by extension, society.

☆ Shapiro, Joseph P.

"The King Is Dead, but His Rich Legacy Still Grows." *U. S. News & World Report* (Aug 24, 1987): 56.

An examination of Elvis Presley's financial, musical, and racial legacies in the city of Memphis.

☆ Silberman, Neil Asher

Silberman is an archaeologist.

"Elvis: The Myth Lives On." *Archaeology* 43 (July/Aug 1990): 80.

The author theorizes that a study of Elvis Presley's posthumous impact provides a social dimension that is lacking in archaeological studies of ancient cults. He believes that Elvis's position in contemporary American culture allows "a fleeting reflection of hero-worship of antiquity."[4]

☆ Stromberg, Peter

"Elvis Alive?: The Ideology of American Consumerism." *Journal of Popular Culture* 24 (Winter 1990): 11–19.

An examination of the author's thesis that "the reason Elvis lives [posthumously] has to do with what Elvis stands for, what sort of symbol he is in a popular ideology . . . it turns out to be a rather revealing exercise in the study of contemporary American popular culture to analyze why Elvis lives beyond the grave." Notes. "Works Cited."

☆ Stuller, Jay

"Legends That Will Not Die." *The Saturday Evening Post* (July/Aug 1985): 42–50.

Examines individuals who have been elevated into legendary status—and why celebrities are the elevated ones instead of great physicians and scientists. Elvis Presley is among those studied.

☆ Tosches, Nick

"Elvis in Death." *Goldmine.* No. 92. (Jan 1984).

One of the best observations on the mystery of the Elvis phenomenon and our culture's obsession with the man. Translated into German. (*See* Foreign Language Titles/German.) Also reprinted in Quain, *The Elvis Reader.* (*See* entry earlier in this section.)

---

[4]A subsequent letter to the editor of *Archaeology* concerning this article demonstrates the difficulties that Elvis academics have with sneering colleagues. ["No Place for Elvis," Nov/Dec 1990:10.]

☆ Wilson, Charles Reagan, Ph.D.

Reagan is the director of the Center for the Study of Southern Culture at the University of Mississippi.

"The Iconography of Elvis." *Judgement and Grace in Dixie: Southern Faiths from Faulkner to Elvis.* Athens (GA); London: University of Georgia Press, 1995. ISBN: 0820317535. Pp. 129–38.

The classic examination of Elvis Presley as a contemporary icon: " . . . pop icons still embody heroic models for human behavior and represent a striving for transcendence from the everyday world. The Elvis Icon reflects his Time, Place, and People." Notes. Biographical references. This chapter was originally published in the journal *Rejoice* I (Summer 1988).

Addenda

☆ Ostler, Scott

"Coincidence? We Think Not! The Babe and Elvis Died on the Same Day—and the Eerie Parallels Only Begin There." *Sports Illustrated* (Aug 18, 1997): 80.

A comparison of the cultural icons—Babe Ruth and Elvis Presely—including such similarities as a signature wink and a rise from poverty to iconic fame.

☆ "Sport of the King." *Sports Illustrated* (Feb 18, 1991): 12.

A 1991 list of the 16 horses then registered with The Jockey Club who had names related to Elvis Presley or Elvis's songs.

See Also:

In Appendix II Major Articles:

Crawdaddy (Nov 1977).

In The Man/Biographies:

Clayson, Alan, and Spencer Leigh, *Aspects of Elvis: Tryin' to Get to You.*
Doll, Susan, *Elvis: A Tribute to His Life.*
"Don't Step on His Blue Suede Shoes; Elvis's Impact on Karate." *International Fighter.*
Gehman, Richard, *Elvis Presley—Hero or Heel?*
Gibson, Robert, and Sid Shaw, *Elvis: A King Forever.*
Hammontree, Patsy Guy, *Elvis Presley: A Bio-Bibliography.*
Hutchins, Chris, and Peter Thompson, *Elvis Meets the Beatles: The Untold Story of Their Tangled Lives.*
Jones, Peter, "Gold Disc," pp. 82–84, *Elvis.*
Stern, Jane, and Michael Stern, *Elvis World.*
Woog, Adam, *The Importance of Elvis Presley.*
Wootton, Richard, *Elvis Presley: King of Rock and Roll.*

In The Man/Death, Conspiracy, Sightings:

Bangs, Lester, "Where Were You When Elvis Died?"
Gregory, Neal and Janice, *When Elvis Died.*
Lazar, Jerry, "Front Page Blues: From Snap Shots to Cheap Shots: Watching the Media Covering the King."

In The Man/Elvis in Quotes:

"Elvis Presley Part 3: He Tells How the Little Wiggle Grew."
Poling, James, "Elvis Presley, Go Cat, Go." *Pageant.*

In The Man/Graceland:

Davidson, J. W., Alfred Hecht, and Herbert A. Whitney, "The Pilgrimage to Graceland."
Marcus, Greil, "William Eggleston's View of Graceland: The Absence of Elvis."

In The Man/Major Articles:

Pleasants, Henry, "Elvis Presley."

In The Man/Photographs:

Cortez, Diego, *Private Elvis.*
"Elvis—A Different Kind of Idol." *Life.*

In The Man/Reference:

Farren, Mick, *The Hitchhiker's Guide to Elvis.* (Introductory essay.)

In The Music, The Movies/Concerts and Television Appearances:

Chapter section: Significant Reviews of Elvis's Post-1950s Live Performances.

In The Music, The Movies/Discography:

Carr, Roy, and Mick Farren, *Elvis: The Illustrated Record.*
Jahn, Mike, "The 1940s and the 1950s: Gonna Raise a Holler."
Plasketes, George M., "The King Is Gone but Not Forgotten: Songs Responding to the Life, Death, and Myth of Elvis Presley in the 1980s."

In The Music, The Movies/Elvis's Influence on Music

"The Elvis Effect."

In The Music, The Movies/Filmography:

Rai, Amit, "An American Raj in Filmistan: Images of Elvis in Indian Films." (An example of the universality of Elvis Presley.)

In The Phenomena/Fans:

McManus, Margaret, "Presley No Serious Peril, Noted Psychologist Feels."
Ward, Robert, "Down at the End of Lonely Street."
Woodward, Helen Beale, "The Smitten Female: From Lord Byron to Elvis Presley Certain Males Have Affected Women as Locoweed Does a Heifer."

In The Phenomena/Fiction:

Sloan, Kay, and Constance Pierce, editors, *Elvis Rising: Stories on the King.* (Introduction essay.)

In The Phenomena/Gender:

Poiter, Uta G., "Rock 'n' Roll, Female Sexuality, and the Cold War Battle over German Identities."

In The Phenomena/Politics:

Plasketes, George, "From Post Office to Oval Office: Idolatry and Ideology in the 1992 Presleydential Elections."

In The Phenomena/Race:

Fager, Charles E., "Swinging Singles."
Long, Martin R., The Reverend, *God's Works Through Elvis.*

In The Phenomena/Religion:

Cooper, Richard, "Did the Devil Send Elvis Presley?"
King, Christine, "His Truth Goes Marching On: Elvis Presley and the Pilgrimage to Graceland."
Sieveking, Paul, "Forteana."

In The Academics/Elvis as an Academic Pursuit:

Firth, Simon, "The Academic Elvis."
Stewart, Doug, "Now Playing in Academe: the King of Rock 'n' Roll."

In The Academics/Dissertations and Theses:

Aparin, Julia, "He Never Got Above His Raising: An Ethnographic Study of a Working Class Response to Elvis Presley."
Bertrand, Michael Thomas, "The King of Rock as Hillbilly Cat: The National Response to a Southern Regional Performer."
Bertrand, Michael Thomas, "Southern Youth in Dissent: Rock 'n' Roll, Race, and Elvis Presley, 1945–1960."
DiPrima, Liza, "Elvis and Them: Reactions to Elvis Presley, 1954–1958."

Doll, Susan M., "Elvis Presley: All Shook Up. The Effect of Ideology and Subculture on Star Image."
Granetz, Ruth Pearl, "The Symbolic Significance of the Elvis Presley Phenomenon to Teen-Age Females: A Study in Hero Worship Through the Media of Popular Singers and Songs."
Johnson, Brigitte E., "Elvis Presley, The Symbol of an Age."
Rodman, Gilbert, "Elvis After Elvis: The Posthumous Career of a Living Legend."
Wireman, J. D., "Textual Elvis."

In Foreign Language Titles/French:

Monin, Emmanuel-Yves, *Le Message d'Elvis Presley: Un Heros Civilisateur.*

In The Rest/Elvis Impersonators:

Spigel, Lynn, "Communicating with the Dead: Elvis as Medium."

CHAPTER 8
Major Articles

These are the articles that succeeded, as did Elvis, in shaking it up. And their impact continues to rattle and roll. Each illuminates some aspect of Elvis to the point of palpable glare. So, prepare for flashes of brilliance and insight.

☆ Baker, Jackson

Baker is a distinguished Memphis journalist who, as a boy, lived next to the Presleys on Lamar Avenue. At the time, the Presleys had no telephone, so they used the Baker family's.

"Elvis: End of an Era." *City of Memphis* (Sept 1977): 26–32.

A memorial article in which Baker recounts the last day of Elvis's life and the time immediately following it. This article is noted for the way in which it captures the tone of that 24-hour period and portrays the deep grief and sense of loss felt by mourning fans.

☆ Bangs, Lester

"Where Were You When Elvis Died?" *Village Voice* (Aug 29, 1977). (Reprinted in *Psychotic Reactions and Carburetor Dung*. Ed. Greil Marcus. New York: Vintage, 1988. ISBN: 06797240456. Pp. 212–216.)

Considered one of the classic Elvis Presley memorial essays because of its insightful exploration of Elvis as our society's last unifying force.

☆ Blount, Roy Jr.

"Elvis!" (From "Golden Anniversary Collector's Issue: 50 Who Made a Difference, A Celebration of 50 American Originals.") *Esquire* (Dec 1983): 172–176.

This article is considered one of the definitive explorations of Elvis Presley's impact and contributions. Blount, known for his humorous assessments of the sports world, seriously examines Elvis Presley's lasting endurance as an American icon.

☆ Booth, Stanley

"Hound Dog to the Manor Born." *Esquire* (Feb 1968): 106–108.

This oft-referenced article contrasts Elvis Presley's 1950s music origins with his status and persona in the 1960s. (When Booth wrote this article, it had been eight years since Elvis had appeared in a live or televised concert. Ten months later, on December 3,1968, Elvis would return to public performing with the airing of the NBC/Singer Company *Elvis* television special.)

Note: This article is reprinted in *The Complete Elvis* (*see* Torgoff listing in The Man/Reference) and *The Elvis Reader* (*see* Quain listing in The Man/The Impact of Elvis).

———.

"The King Is Dead! Hang the Doctor!" *The Complete Elvis*. Ed. Martin Torgoff. New York: Delilah Books, 1982. Pp. 70–85.

An examination of Elvis Presley's health and prescription drug issues from the point of view of his physician, Dr. George Nichopoulos ("Dr. Nick"). It also examines Nichopoulos's legal problems and media attention that overwhelmed him as he was blamed for Elvis's death. This article is noted for its unique exploration of how and why Elvis died, and for its use of Nichopoulos's situation as a metaphor for the 1970s. Note: This article is reprinted in *The Elvis Reader*. (*See* Quain listing in The Man/The Impact of Elvis.)

☆ Brock, Van K.

"Images of Elvis, the South and America." Ed. Jac L. Tharpe. *Elvis: Images and Fancies*. Jackson, MS: University Press of Mississippi, 1979. Pp. 87–122.

"Hillbilly on a Pedestal." *Newsweek* (May 14, 1956): 82.

A brief description of the impact of Elvis Presley on teenaged girls and an assessment of his first Las Vegas appearance ("Elvis was somewhat like a jug of corn liquor at a champagne party"). Quotes from Elvis about his future goals. (Note: Rather than present an accurate picture of Elvis Presley, this article is an attempt to sneer at an individual who is socially and regionally different from the writer and *Newsweek* editors.) This is one of the first mainstream newsmagazine articles about Elvis.

☆ **"A Howling Hillbilly Success."** *Life* (Apr 30, 1956): 64.

Two black and white photographs of the audience while Elvis Presley performed in Amarillo, Texas, and in a Nashville recording studio. One paragraph on fans' reactions. Quote from Elvis about these reactions. This is the first mainstream media magazine article about Elvis.

☆ Marcus, Greil

"Elvis: Presliad." *Mystery Train: Images of America in Rock 'n' Roll Music*. New York: E. P. Dutton, 1975; 1976 (pbk); 1982; 1990; 1997. ISBN: 0525484078 (1982). Pp. 141–209.

The first serious examination of Elvis Presley's place in American society, this essay places the entertainer as a pivotal figure in American music: the person who bridged the gap between the blues musicians of the past and the rockers of the current time. It also looks at the American myths and cultural forces that brought Elvis as an icon into existence.

The uniqueness and importance of this essay lie in part with the time it was written—mid-1970, when Elvis was no longer cutting edge and had yet to obtain his posthumous historical status. The timing offers a rare opportunity to read an assessment of Elvis while he was still alive and in a phase of his career that was dramatically different from the 1950s. This essay was also published in Greek as a book. (*See* Foreign Language Titles/Greek.)

Mystery Train is considered a classic in American music literature. It is a discussion of six risk takers in rock and roll who shaped that music.

☆ Pleasants, Henry

Pleasants is a noted musicologist.

"Elvis Presley." *The Great American Popular Singers*. New York: Simon and Schuster, 1974. ISBN: 671216813. Pp. 263–279.

One of the earliest and best analyses of Elvis Presley's musical style and impact. In this chapter, published during Elvis's lifetime, Pleasants analyzes Elvis as a musician, as well as his effect on American music and his place in music history. Unsourced direct quotes attributed to Elvis and his friends.

☆ Pratt, Linda Ray

"Elvis, or the Ironies of Southern Identity." Ed. Jac L. Tharpe. *Elvis Images and Fancies*. Jackson, MS: University Press of Mississippi, 1979. Pp. 40–51.

Pratt explains how the South produced Elvis Presley, and explores why Southerners revere him. This essay is considered one of the important writings about the influences in Elvis's life—in this case, his "Southerness" and what that means to his impact and legend. Elvis's racial ambiguity is explored.

☆ Presley, Vernon, as told to Nancy Anderson

"Elvis." *Good Housekeeping* (Jan 1978): 80–81, 156–161.

The only major interview given by Elvis Presley's father, Vernon, this article was published five months after Elvis's death. In it, Vernon Presley talks about his memories of his son.

☆ Sharnik, John

"The War of the Generations." *House and Garden* (Oct 1956): 40–41.

The author thoughtfully examines the reactions to Elvis Presley in the context of generational differences. He predicts that Elvis will drift away from national attention as he ages and will eventually reappear as the middle-aged host of a weekly *The Elvis Presley*

Show, where "as a kind of middle-aged statesman, he speaks for his generation in the defense against whatever new musical menace has arisen among its baffling young." (In this article Sharnik also discusses a gender connection between Marilyn Monroe and Elvis Presley.)

☆ "Teeners' Hero." *Time* (May 14, 1956): 53–54.

An introduction to Elvis Presley for mainstream readers. Discusses fans' reactions, his musical career, and first appearance in Las Vegas at the New Frontier Hotel. This is one of the first mainstream newsmagazine articles about Elvis.

☆ Wilson, Charles Reagan, Ph.D.

Reagan is the Director of the Center for the Study of Southern Culture at the University of Mississippi.

"The Iconography of Elvis." *Judgement and Grace in Dixie: Southern Faiths from Faulkner to Elvis*. Athens (GA); London: University of Georgia Press, 1995. ISBN: 0820317535. Pp. 129–38.

The classic examination of Elvis Presley as a contemporary icon: " . . . pop icons still embody heroic models for human behavior and represent a striving for transcendence from the everyday world. The Elvis Icon reflects his Time, Place, and People." Notes. Biographical references. This chapter was originally published in the journal *Rejoice I* (Summer 1988).

☆ Wolfe, Charles, Ph.D.

A leading American musicologist, Wolfe is a professor of English at Middle Tennessee State University.

"Presley and the Gospel Tradition." Ed. Jac L. Tharpe. *Elvis: Images and Fancies*. Jackson, MS: University Press of Mississippi, 1979. Pp. 135–150.

Wolfe is the first scholar to study Elvis Presley's gospel roots and how he, in turn, influenced gospel music. Sources.

CHAPTER 9
Memoirs and Memories

EVEN WITH THE briefest perusal of the Elvis literature, it appears that almost everyone knew Elvis—and then wrote about it. The memoirs by Elvis Presley's family and friends could be among the largest number ever published about one person. Well over 100 have been released, from slick hard covers of major publishers to copied pages from the author's typewriter, with writers ranging from Priscilla Presley to the director of Elvis's funeral.

As with all memoirs, they are written through the dual prisms of personal perspective and agenda. And as with all memoir subjects, a few fall into the category of "met Elvis once, wrote a book." Despite these drawbacks, most of the titles are noteworthy for the dizzying array of viewpoints and information about America during Elvis's lifetime.

The books written by Elvis's fans are an example. He was extraordinarily friendly and patient with his fans, sitting for long periods to sign autographs, wandering down to Graceland's front gate to chat, and inviting them to accompany him to the movies. Elvis's bond with his fans is one that few celebrities have enjoyed. This special comradeship produced an unusual aspect of the memoir genre: fan reminiscences. More than 20 of these life-as-an-Elvis-fan memories have been published. Their importance is unparalleled. Few times in history has such access been available to the private thoughts and daily activities of young women.

As is to be expected, a number of Elvis's relatives have written about their lives with him, with his stepbrothers, the Stanleys, being the most prolific. But among the most useful memoirs are those written by Elvis's employees: his secretary, cooks, fellow musicians, and his aides (the so-called "Memphis Mafia"). These are everyday people who write about their lives in such textbook detail that this part of the Elvis literature is unsurpassed in its information about family structure and societal expectations of the last half of the twentieth century.

Three of these employees' books were written by Elvis's African American cooks, Mary Jenkins and Nancy Rooks. Another cook, Alvena Roy, wrote an essay for Elizabeth McKeon's cookbook *Elvis in Hollywood*. Their stories not only give first-hand descriptions of the mid-twentieth-century Southern diet, they also provide unfiltered glimpses of the delicate dance of Southern race relations during that period. These ladies had warm relationships with Elvis, who in turn treated them with the same respect and concern that most Southern white children are taught to give to blacks. Their memoirs demonstrate the often close and mutually considerate relationships that have long existed between white Southerner employers and their minority employees. In short, these books blow away a number of the stereotypes about white Southerners in general, and Elvis and his background in particular.

Not all of the memoirs are lovingly crafted reminiscences. In the most infamous—the image-shattering *Elvis, What Happened?* (1977)—three of Elvis's recently fired employees became the first to pull back the carefully woven image curtain that had always surrounded Elvis, relating sordid tales of less-than-appropriate and unhealthy behavior.

But negative or not, the Elvis memoirs are a front-row seat to the major surges in the tide of American life from the 1930s onward. From them, we learn the realities of rural poverty in the Depression South, of the poor's quest for a better life in the booming post-war cities, of life in public housing when that meant "up and out," not "down and out." They detail day-to-day life in the cultural explosions of the 1960s and 1970s. And, overall, they offer unmatched views of ordinary people reacting to extraordinary circumstances as life in the last half of the twentieth century roared upward and onward.

☆   ☆   ☆   ☆

Memoirs

☆ Cajiao, Trevor

Cajiao writes for *Elvis: The Man and His Music*, and he has co-authored Elvis books with Ger Rijff.

Talking Elvis: In-Depth Interviews with Musicians, Songwriters, and Friends. Amsterdam: Elvis: The Man and His Music/Tutti Frutti Productions, 1998. 239 pp. ISBN: none.

Twenty-seven in-depth interviews with musicians, songwriters, producers, co-stars, and friends, compiled from unpublished material and articles in *Elvis: The Man and His Music* and *Now Dig This* magazines.

Source: Loose Ends Gift Shop, Memphis
www.arbook.com

☆ Curtin, Jim

Curtin is the author of six Elvis photograph books.

Elvis: Unknown Stories Behind the Legend, Vol. 1. Nashville, TN: Celebrity Books, 1998. 400 pp. ISBN: 1580291023.

Collection of 500 anecdotes, uncredited and unsourced, about the life and career of Elvis Presley. Includes 35 photographs from Curtin's collection. Introduction by Will Hutchins, Elvis's co-star in *Spinout* and *Clambake*. No notes, bibliography, or index.

Note: In this volume Curtin announces that Volume 2 is "coming soon" and that its ISBN is 1580291031.

Source: Library of Congress ML420.P96 C93 1998
Dewey Decimal 782.42166/092
OCLC 39210098 and 39841433

☆ "Elvis Presley Part 2: The Folks He Left Behind Him." *TV Guide* (Sept 22–28, 1956): 17–19.

Comments about Elvis Presley from his girlfriend Barbara Hearn, bosses at his pre-fame jobs, Sun Records producer Sam Phillips, Memphis disc jockey Dewey Phillips, teachers Mrs. J. C. Grimes and Miss Mildred Scrivener, and high school friend and Memphis Mafia member Red West. Also Guy Lansky of Lansky Brothers Clothing in Memphis, where Elvis purchased clothing.

☆ Gregory, James

The Elvis Presley Story. New York: Hillman Books, 1960. 160 pp. ISBN: none. UK: Thorpe & Porter, 1960. ISBN: none. London: May Fair Books, 1961. ISBN: none.

One of the first books about Elvis, this is a paperback consisting of articles that had previously appeared in *Movieland Magazine, Movieland,* and *TV Time Magazine,* April 1957–February 1960. Introduction by Dick Clark. Articles include "Elvis Personally Answers His Critics" by Memphis journalist Bob Johnson; "What It's Like to Date Elvis" by Hollywood columnist Army Archard; "The Day Elvis Made Me Cry" by Elvis's girlfriend Anita Wood. Also, 32 pages of black and white publicity photographs; none credited, few captioned. Discography, "A Complete List of Elvis Presley's RCA Recordings," with titles and record numbers.

Source: OCLC 6260008 (Hillman, 1960)

☆ Haining, Peter, editor

Elvis in Private. London: Hale, 1987. 256 pp. ISBN: 0709029713. New York: St. Martin's Press, 1987. 175 pp. ISBN: 031290920. A Lythway Book series. Bath, U.K.: Chivers. 1989. [240] pp. (large print). ISBN: 074510908X.

Includes 29 chapters of interviews and previously published memoirs by a range of Elvis Presley's relatives, friends, and fellow musicians. They include Priscilla Presley, Scotty Moore, Roy Orbison, Johnny Burnette, Vester Presley, and Ann-Margaret. No citations, sources, or chapter notes. Sixteen pages of black and white photographs; captioned and credited. Appendix I: Chronology of Elvis Presley's life (pp.167–175). Appendix II: Abbreviated Presley genealogy chart (two leaves). No index.

☆ Herbst, Peter, and Dave Marsh, editors

"Echoes of Love: Elvis's Friends Remember." *Rolling Stone* (Sept 22, 1977): 48–53.

Elvis's friends, from a range of backgrounds, share brief anecdotes and comment on how Elvis affected their lives.

☆ Slayman, Evelyn, compiler

Wings of Compassion. Cerritos, CA: Elvis Presley TLC Fan Club, 1999. ISBN: 0967368707.

Brief anecdotes and commentary from people who knew Elvis, from his fans, and from his fellow entertainers. Wire service and media quotes, cited.

Source: Publisher's address: P.O. Box 3598, Cerritos, CA 90703-3598

☆ Wiegert, Sue, with contributions by Elvis friends and Elvis fans

Elvis: Precious Memories, Vol. 1 (first of two vols.; *see* next listing for Vol. 2). Los Angeles, CA: self-published, 1987. 100 pp. ISBN: none.

Wiegert's remembrances of Elvis in concert, on filming locations, and in Memphis. Wiegert, a fan since the 1950s, includes the recollections of celebrities who knew Elvis. She sent questionnaires to a variety of show business people (i.e., Army Archerd, Hank Snow, Danny Thomas, Paul Anka, Dick Sargent, Victor French, Billy Barty, Ed Asner, and Dick Clark). She reprints their replies in the formats in which she received them.

Source: New York Public Library JNK 91-3
OCLC 22243372

———.

Elvis: Precious Memories, Vol. 2. Los Angeles, CA: self-published, 1989. 124 pp. ISBN: none.

The second volume of Wiegert's collection of Elvis Presley memories from fans, his fellow celebrities, and those of her own. Memories include that of actress Celeste Yarnall who was with Elvis when he learned of the death of The Rev. Dr. Martin Luther King, Jr. Introductory essay by author (pp. 3–30), in which Wiegert relates her experiences with Elvis. Black and white candid photographs; credited.

Source: OCLC 31025065

☆ Wolmuth, Roger

"The King of Rock Keeps on Rollin'." *People Weekly* (Aug 17, 1987): 85–92.

Memories of people who were involved in Elvis's life: Sam Phillips, Wink Martindale, Hank Snow, photographer William Speer, "Heartbreak Hotel" composer Mae Boren Axton, clothing store owner Bernard Lansky, Hollywood car customizer George Barris, composers Jerry Leiber and Mike Stoller, fellow singers J. D. Sumner and Joe Moscheo, and romantic interests Sandy Ferra Martindale and Sheila Ryan Caan.

See Also:

In The Man/Biographies:

Bobo, L. Peyton, *Elvis: King of Rock 'n' Roll.*

Burk, Bill E., *Early Elvis Trilogy.*
Clayton, Rose, and Dick Heard, *Elvis Up Close: In the Words of Those Who Knew Him Best.*
"Elvis 1935-1977," *View.*
"Elvis Presley, Elvis Presley," *The Waco Citizen.*

In The Phenomena/Cookbooks:

McKeon, Elizabeth, *Elvis in Hollywood* (introductory essay by Alvena Ray).

In The Rest/Souvenir Magazines:

Elvis: A Saint or Sinner?

Employees

☆ Crumbaker, Marge, and Gabe Tucker

Tucker, a musician and publicist who worked sporadically for the Colonel for almost 30 years, handled business matters for the Colonel in the 1950s.

Up and Down with Elvis Presley. New York: G. P. Putnam's Sons, 1981. 256 pp. ISBN: 039912571X. [U.S.]: New English Library. ISBN: 0450054926.

An examination of the relationship between Colonel Parker and Elvis, this memoir covers the business details of that period of Elvis's career when Tucker was involved. Salacious and unproven stories about Elvis's personal behavior. Mostly black and white photographs from Tucker's personal collection; captioned and credited. No index.

☆ Gee, Denise

"A Kingly Kitchen." *Southern Living* (Oct 1995).

Interview with Elvis Presley's cook Mary Jenkins about her employer's favorite foods. Among Jenkins's comments: "I never saw him even once eat a jelly doughnut."

☆ Jenkins, Mary, as told to Beth Pease

During Jenkins tenure at Graceland, Elvis gave her seven cars and a house. She appeared in the 1981 movie *This Is Elvis.* As a teenager, Pease was among those who regularly stood at Graceland's gate to see Elvis.

Elvis, the Way I Knew Him. Memphis: Riverpark Publishers, 1984. 99 pp. ISBN: none.

The memories of Elvis's cook Mary Jenkins who worked at Graceland from 1963 to 1977. Includes three recipes for "some of Elvis's favorites": homemade vegetable soup, southern cornbread, and macaroni salad. No index. Twenty-four black and white candid photographs; credited.

Source: Compiler's collection

————.

Memories Beyond Graceland Gates. Buena Park, CA: West Coast Book Publishers, 1989. 128 pp. ISBN: none.

Jenkins's memoirs of her time with Elvis Presley. Thirty-three of Elvis's favorite recipes, including correct instructions for making the famous peanut butter and banana sandwich. More than 100 color and black and white photographs; many of them candids from Jenkins's personal collection.

Source: Compiler's collection

☆ Parker, Edmund K.

Parker was Elvis's bodyguard and kempo karate instructor in the 1970s.

Inside Elvis. Orange, CA: Rampart House, 1978. 198 pp. ISBN: 0897730003.

Parker relates his experiences working for Elvis. He discusses Elvis's drug use and his spiritual and occult interests. Black and white photographs and line drawings of Elvis and the author.

Source: Library of Congress ML420.P96 P28

☆ Rooks, Nancy, and Mae Gutter

Rooks worked as a cook for Elvis from 1966 to 1977 and was on duty when Elvis died. In 1980 she and Elvis's uncle Vester Presley co-authored a cookbook, *The Presley Family Cookbook. (See* The Phenomena/Cookbooks.) Gutter became an Elvis fan after the entertainer's death. Her perspective is unique as she is the only African American fan to write about Elvis.

The Maid, The Man, and His Fans: Elvis Is The Man. New York: Vantage Press, 1984. 51 pp. ISBN: 533060532.

The memoirs of Rooks and Gutter. The first section, "The Man: Elvis and Memphis—A Dual Destiny," traces the development and intertwining of the entertainer and the city. Chapter notes with sources. The second, "The Fans," relates how Gutter became a fan after Elvis's death. She relates how she was affected by visits to Graceland and Elvis's birthplace in Tupelo, Mississippi. The third section is Rooks's recollections of her life at Graceland. Three black and white portraits: Elvis, Rooks, and Gutter.

Source: Library of Congress ML420.P96 R66 1984

☆ Thompson, Sam

Thompson is an attorney and General Sessions judge for Shelby County, Tennessee. He was Elvis Presley's bodyguard in the 1970s and the brother of Elvis's girlfriend Linda Thompson.

Elvis on Tour: The Last Year. Memphis, TN: Still Brook Publishing Company, 1992. 40 pp. ISBN "applied for."

Thomas's memoirs include a seven-page essay on his experiences with Elvis and documents from Elvis's tours #5–#9 in 1976. (The documents relate to the logistics and costs of the tours, including rooming lists for the entourage and fuel costs for the airplane.) Thirteen black and white candid photographs of Thompson and Elvis.

Source: OCLC 27180290

☆ Yancey, Becky, and Cliff Linedecker

Yancey worked as Elvis's secretary from 1962 to 1975.

My Life with Elvis: The Fond Memories of a Fan Who Became Elvis's Private Secretary. New York: St. Martin's Press, 1977; London: W. H. Allen, 1977. 360 pp. ISBN: 0312558341 (hdk.). New York: Warner Books, 1977, 1979. ISBN: none.

Published two months after Elvis Presley's death, this was the first of the memoir books. Yancey writes about Elvis's home life and her life with him, including numerous anecdotes about fans and fellow employees. Footnotes in each chapter. No index. Twenty-nine pages of black and white photographs; captioned, some credited

My Life with Elvis was translated into French, Japanese, and Norwegian. (*See* those chapters in Foreign Language Titles.) It was a Doubleday Book Club alternate and was excerpted in the *National Enquirer.*

Fans

☆ Apsley, Brenda

Memories of the King. Manchester, UK: Albert Hand Publications Ltd., 1978. 32 pp. ISBN: none.

A British fan memorializes Elvis Presley and shares her memories.

Source: OCLC 20738478

☆ Boswell, Mary Curbo

Elvis and Us in the 60's. Memphis, TN: Pyramid Education, Inc., 1997. 22 pp. ISBN: none.

Boswell, a teenage fan who lived in Memphis during the 1960s and was invited to parties at Graceland, shares her memories of those experiences.

Source: Pyramid Education, Inc., Memphis, TN

☆ Canada, Lena

To Elvis, with Love. New York: Everest House, 1978. 178 pp. Pickering, Ontario, Canada: Beaverbooks, 1978. 178 pp. ISBN: 0896960099. New York: Scholastic Book Service, 1979. 190 pp. ISBN: 0590057790.

The story of a correspondence between Elvis Presley and a young handicapped Swede named Karen. Abandoned by her mother and suffering from cerebral palsy, Karen was living in a Swedish state home for disabled children. When she had retreated into a self-imposed isolation, Lena Canada, her therapist, encouraged Karen to write to Elvis. After the correspondence began, Karen's attitude greatly improved. Karen and Elvis maintained this pen pal relationship until her death in 1975.

In 1980 a motion picture was made of this story: *Touched by Love*. (VHS #60307 by Columbia TriStar Home Video, [Burbank, CA]. 95 minutes. ISBN: 0800133129.) Its script is listed in The Phenomena/Dramas and Musicals About Elvis as *To Elvis with Love*.

Source: Library of Congress ML420.P96 C3 1979 (book)
OCLC 7079803 (book); 11181828 (video)

☆ Cogan-Bradley, Arlene, with Rose Clayton

Clayton is the co-author of *Elvis Up Close*. (*See* The Man/Biographies.)

The Other Side of Elvis: Five Short Stories from the Personal Life of Elvis Presley.
(Special Preview Edition). [n.p.]: Arlene Cogan-Bradley, [n.d.], 1992. 26 pp.
ISBN: none.

A pamphlet previewing the as-yet-unpublished book *The Other Side of Elvis*. (As of 2000, the book had not been released.) Five anecdotes, occurring between 1957 and 1962, involving Elvis and the author.

Source: Compiler's Collection

☆ Coogan, Arlene, with Charles Goodman

Elvis, This One's for You. Memphis, TN: Castle Books, 1985. 276 pp. ISBN:
0916693058.

The memoirs of four Elvis Presley fans who followed him in his early years. Black and white candid photographs.

Source: Compiler's collection

☆ Deen, Jeannie

"A Young Girl's Fancy." Ed. Jac L. Tharpe. *Elvis: Images and Fancies*. Jackson, MS:
University Press of Mississippi, 1979. ISBN: none. Pp. 169–179.

An Elvis Presley fan since 1956, Deen discusses her experiences with and reactions to events in Elvis's life and career. This essay is valuable as a source of first-hand reports of a fan's reactions to well-known events in Elvis's adult life.

☆ Goodge, Betty Tuttle

Goodge is an Elvis Presley fan who formed one of the entertainer's first fan clubs in the 1950s: The Elvis Presley Teddy Bears.

We're So Grateful That You Did It Your Way. A Hearthstone Book. New York: Carlton
Press, Inc. 40 pp. ISBN: 080621483X.

The memoirs of Goodge who met Elvis on several occasions and attended his concerts. Black and white photographs from the author's collection. The second part of the book relates the author's experiences with an Elvis tribute artist.

Source: Library of Congress ML420.P96 G68
Memphis/Shelby (TN) County Public Library and Information Center

☆ Hill, Wanda June

We Remember, Elvis. Palos Verdes, CA: Morgan Press, 1978. 139 pp. ISBN: 0894300288.

Reminiscences of Elvis fan Wanda Hill, as well as the memories and poems of 14 other fans. Sixteen pages of black and white photographs from the author's collection.

Source: Los Angeles Public Library 789.14 P934 Hi
OCLC 4315939

———.

Elvis, We Remember, 1978, and *Elvis: Face to Face,* 1985. Lone Starr Productions, 1985. ISBN: 0962141305.

Source: www.amazon.com

☆ Johnson, Marilyn

"Missing Elvis." *Life* (Aug 1997): 31–32.

The author discusses her life as an Elvis Presley fan and how Elvis has become a target of mockery.

☆ Keenan, Frances

Keenan became an Elvis fan when she saw him in a 1955 concert. After that, she attended 70 Elvis concerts.

Having Fun with Elvis in Las Vegas. Special Preview Limited Edition. [U.S.]: self-published, 1994. 28 pp. ISBN: none.

A promotional pamphlet for an as-yet-unpublished book by the same name. (Excerpts from this pamphlet were repeated in Keenan's book, *Elvis, You're Unforgettable* [1997].) This pamphlet contains four of the author's experiences with Elvis. Black and white photographs from the author's collection.

Source: Collection of Bill and Connie Burk, Memphis, TN

———.

Elvis, You're Unforgettable: Memoirs from a Fan. Tampa Bay, FL: Axelrod Publishing, 1997. 381 pp. ISBN: 0936417536.

Keenan relates her experiences as an Elvis Presley fan, including meeting him on numerous occasions and attending his concerts. Bibliographical references (pp. 378–379).

Source: New York Public Library B Presley K
Dewey Decimal 782.42166 P934xke

☆ Keith, Don Lee

"Heartbreak Hotel." *New Orleans Magazine* (Aug 1992): 99.

The story of a teenage girl's evolution as an Elvis Presley fan in the 1950s.

☆ Lewis, Donna, with Craig A. Slanker

Hurry Home, Elvis: Donna Lewis' Diaries. Vol. 1, 1962–1966. Busted Burd Productions, 1996. 226 pp. ISBN: 0965508633.

Hurry Home, Elvis: Donna Lewis' Diaries. Vol. 2, 1967–1968. Busted Burd Productions, 1997. 305 pp. ISBN: 0965508625.

One of the most thorough documentations of life as an Elvis fan, this is a remarkable diary of a teenage Memphis fan's almost day-to-day Elvis activities in the 1960s, with the entries printed exactly as she wrote them. In addition to a detailed account of middle-class family and teenage life in the 1960s, Lewis provides the best descriptions of Elvis's fans' deep devotion to him, as well as ample evidence of his interest in, concern for, and tolerance of them.

During the 1960s and 1970s, the author and her family lived near Elvis Presley's Graceland mansion. She was one of the regulars at the Graceland gate, even quitting high school to devote more time to being an Elvis fan. Her father worked at Graceland and at Elvis's Circle G, and the family was frequently invited to accompany Elvis to private movie showings in Memphis. The Lewis family were guests at Elvis and Priscilla's Graceland wedding reception. (A thank-you note from Priscilla for their gift is reproduced.) Color and black and white candid photographs from the Lewis family's collection.

Lewis plans to publish two additional volumes in this series: *Hurry Home, Elvis: Donna Lewis' Diaries.* Vol. 3, 1969–1970 and *Hurry Home, Elvis: Donna Lewis' Diaries.* Vol. 4, 1971-1977.

Source: Publisher's address: P.O. Box 429293, Cincinnati, OH 45242
Publisher's e-mail: Buzzburd@aol.com

☆ McLemore, P. K., editor and compiler

Letters to Elvis: Real Letters Written by His Faithful Fans. New York: St. Martin's Griffin, 1997. 124 pp. ISBN: 031216906X.

The author contacted "thousands of fans," asking them to send him old and new fan letters that they had written to Elvis, before and after his death. In this book, McLemore reprints 47 of those letters.

☆ McRae, Gay

"Notes of a Fan-atic." Ed. Jac L. Tharpe. *Elvis: Images and Fancies*. Jackson, MS: University Press of Mississippi, 1979. ISBN: none. Pp. 173–179.

As part of Tharpe's groundbreaking anthology of Elvis Presley's impact, Elvis fan Gay McRae thoughtfully writes about what inspired her to become a loyal Elvis fan. She relates her fan experiences, beginning with her response to his September 9, 1956, appearance on *The Ed Sullivan Show*.

☆ Olmetti, Bob, and Sue McCasland, editors

Elvis Now—Ours Forever. San Jose, CA: Bob Olmetti and Sue McCasland, 1977; 1984. 150 pp. ISBN: none.

A collection of 50 Elvis Presley fans' stories and personal experiences with him. Fans' and editors' black and white candid photographs of Elvis; captioned.

Source: Elvis Presley Enterprises, Inc., Archives

☆ Page, Betty, with Rechey Davidson, editor

I Got Ya, Elvis, I Got Ya. Memphis, TN: Pages Publishing Inc., 1977. 72 pp. ISBN: none.

Page moved to Memphis in 1975 and became one of the "Gate Fans," (fans who congregated daily at the main Graceland gate). This is the story of her attempts to meet Elvis. Sixteen pages of black and white photographs from the author's collection.

Source: Memphis/Shelby County (TN) Public Library and Information Center

☆ Scott, Liz

"Elvis in New Orleans." *New Orleans* (Aug 1991): 73–75.

Fan memories of meeting Elvis Presley in 1958, while he was in New Orleans performing in concert and filming *King Creole*.

☆ Starsen, Melle

"A Gift from Elvis." *Ladies' Home Journal* (Aug 1990): 18–22.

The author's memories of meeting Elvis Presley in 1967 while he was filming *Staying Away Joe* in Arizona. She explains how Elvis's comments during that meeting made a positive change in her relationship with her mother (the "gift" of the title).

☆ Wheeler, Kay, and William A. Harbinson

As a teenage girl, Wheeler formed one of the first Elvis Presley fan clubs. Harbinson is the author of *Elvis: An Illustrated Biography*. (*See* The Man/Biographies.)

Growing Up with the Memphis Flash. Amsterdam, Netherlands: Tutti Frutti Productions. 223 pp. ISBN: none.

Wheeler's autobiography and Elvis memories. Stories of Elvis's early years as a performer give insight into the background from which he and his earliest fans came. Childhood photographs of Wheeler juxtaposed against those of Elvis at the same age. Black and white candids of Wheeler and Elvis.

Source: Michael Ochs Archives, Venice, CA
Publisher's address: Tutti Frutti Productions, Box 16758, 1001 RG Amsterdam, The Netherlands

☆ Wiegert, Sue

Weigert is a Los Angeles–based writer. Since 1964, she has been the president of the Blue Hawaiians for Elvis fan club, and she is the editor of the widely read *Blue Hawaiians*, a quarterly Elvis Presley newsletter. She frequently acts as an Elvis consultant to authors and the media, including Elvis biographer Peter Guralnick.

Elvis—For the Good Times. Los Angeles, CA: self-published, 1978. 178 pp. ISBN: none.

The memoirs of an Elvis Presley fan who was his friend for the last 10 years of his life. During that time, Wiegert followed Elvis to Memphis, Los Angeles, motion picture sets, and concerts.

Source: OCLC 25461609
Publisher's address: P.O. Box 69834, Los Angeles, CA 90069

———.

Elvis's Golden Decade. Los Angeles. 46 pp. ISBN: none.

Elvis Presley's career up to 1966, with Wiegert's first-hand observations of the filming of *Blue Hawaii* and *Paradise, Hawaiian Style*. Six pages of black and white candids from author's collection.

Source: Sue Wiegert

———.

Elvis Is Forever. Los Angeles: Sue Wiegert and the Blue Hawaiians for Elvis, 1975. 48 leaves. ISBN: none.

Wiegert's self-published memories of seeing and interacting with Elvis in the 1960s and 1970s. Written while Elvis was still alive. Six pages of black and white photographs; captioned. Essay on what to expect from Elvis in the next 21 years.

Source: Compiler's Collection

See Also:

In The Man/Biographies:

Slaughter, Todd, *Elvis Presley.*

In The Man/The Impact of Elvis:

Kanchanawan, Nitaya, "Elvis, Thailand, and I."

In The Man/Photographs:

Lichter, Paul, Carl Waldman, and Jim Donovan, *Elvis Immortal: A Celebration of the King.*

In The Man/Reference:

Hand, Albert, *Elvis Special.*

In The Phenomena/Fans:

Wright, Daniel, *Dear Elvis: Graffiti from Graceland.*

In The Phenomena/Psychic Elvis Experiences:

Thornton, Mary Ann, *Even Elvis.*

In Foreign Language Titles/Swedish:

Schoning, Ulf, *Chocken: svenska fans berattar hur de upplevde Elvis dod: en antologi.*

In The Rest/Souvenir Magazines:

Photoplay Presents a Tribute to Elvis Presley. 4th Anniversary Memorial Edition, 1981. *Elvis Diary*, 1979.

Fellow Entertainment Professionals

☆ "Amazing Graceland." *Life* (Sept 1987): 45–46, 50–56.

Elvis memories and commentary from entertainers Carl Perkins, Robert Plant, Joan Jett, The Beastie Boys, Roy Orbison, and Ron Wood.

☆ Axton, Mae Boren

Elvis Presley. Tampa: Rinaldi Printing Company, [1978]. 20 pp. ISBN: none.

The memoirs of a publicist who worked with Elvis Presley in the 1950s and who co-wrote Elvis's signature 1956 hit, "Heartbreak Hotel." In 1955 she began promoting and organizing the publicity for Elvis's appearances. Axton wrote these remembrances shortly after Elvis died.

Source: The Mississippi Valley Collection, The University of Memphis (TN)
OCLC 7717893 (Note: the OCLC listing has an incorrect date for this publication [1955].)

————.

Mae Axton tells how she met Elvis Presley and wrote "Heartbreak Hotel." One sound reel tape. 1977. From a "Voices in the Wind" broadcast on National Public Radio, Sept 6, 1977.

Axton talks about getting Elvis his first million seller, "Heartbreak Hotel." One sound reel tape. 1979.

A second "Voices in the Wind with Ms. Axton" was broadcast on National Public Radio, Sept 25, 1979.

Source: OCLC 27880836 (1977); 28154788 (1979)

☆ Dawson, Walter

"Interview with Sam Phillips." *Memphis Press-Scimitar* (Aug 20, 1977). "Elvis Presley Part 1: The People Who Know Say He Does Have Talent." *TV Guide* (Sept 8–14, 1956): 5–7.

An assessment of Elvis Presley and his talent by co-workers. Observations from actress Cynthia Baxter, who was cast opposite Elvis in his Hal Wallis screen test. Also from movie star Esther Williams, and Charlotte Clary, the Paramount Studios dramatic coach.

☆ Fontana, D. J.

D. J. Fontana was Elvis Presley's original drummer. He toured and recorded with Elvis from 1955 until the late 1960s. Fontana continues to perform and record, and makes frequent appearances at Elvis-related concerts and events.

***D. J. Fontana Remembers Elvis.* [U.S.]: Curtis Wood Publications, 1981. [40] pp. ISBN: none. Reissued in 1983.**

An $8\frac{1}{2}'' \times 11''$ pamphlet of black and white photographs and copies of letters, cards, and telegrams relating to Elvis Presley (from Fontana's collection). Introduction by Fontana, recalling his history with Elvis. Photographs are captioned but not credited. They include candids of Elvis, the author, and fellow musicians Bill Black and Scotty Moore. Also a candid of Elvis with President and Mrs. Jimmy Carter.

According to Fontana, only a few of these magazine-format books were printed, and "the fellow who printed them took most of them and left town."[1] This book was reissued in 1983 in its same format and text under the copyright of "Marshall Sehorn, Jerry Wilson, and Arthur Trankos Trustee." Curtis Wood holds the copyright for the 1981 edition.

Source: The Margaret Herrick Library, Academy of Motion Picture Arts and Sciences
OCLC 20713386 (1983)

[1]Conversation with compiler, Memphis, Tennessee, August 1997.

☆ Goodman, Charles

"Jordanaires Share Memories of Beautiful Years with Elvis." *Memphis Press-Scimitar* (Aug 15, 1978).

The members of Elvis Presley's first back-up singing group talk about Elvis's early years with RCA.

☆ Hill, Ed, as told to Don Hill

Where Is Elvis? Atlanta, GA: Cross Roads Books, 1979. 128 pp. ISBN: 0899890113.

A long-time member of The Stamps gospel quartet, which backed Elvis Presley in concert and on recordings, tells his memories of touring with Elvis, including anecdotes about Elvis's "spiritual side." Title refers to whether or not Elvis is in heaven or hell.

Source: University of Georgia Library ML420.P96 H550 1979

☆ Lennon, John

Ze King and I. [n.p.], [n.d.]. ISBN: none.

John Lennon's first-person account of the evening that he and the other Beatles spent with Elvis Presley on August 27, 1965.

Source: www.elvispresleyonline.com/html/ze_king_and_i.html

☆ Logan, Horace, with Bill Sloan

"The Shy Kid from Memphis." *Elvis, Hank, and Me: Making Musical History of the Louisiana Hayride.* New York: St. Martin's Press, 1998. ISBN: 0312185731. Pp. 1–8.

Memoirs of *Louisiana Hayride* director Horace Logan. Elvis Presley began performing almost weekly on the show's radio broadcast, beginning in October 1954.[2] Logan discusses the audience reactions to Elvis and the change in Elvis's managers when he was appearing on the *Hayride*. Seven black and white photographs of Elvis during the period he performed on the *Hayride*; captioned and credited. A reproduction of Elvis's first *Hayride* contract. Index.

☆ Montefiore, Simon Sebag

"Mother Delores." *The New Republic* (Oct 4, 1993): 9, 12.

An interview with Mother Dolores, Mother Superior of the Abbey of Regina Laudis in Bethlehem, Connecticut, who was known as Delores Hart when she co-starred with Elvis Presley in *Loving You* (1957) and *King Creole* (1958). She discusses the false but persistent rumor that she and Elvis had a child.

[2]The *Louisiana Hayride* was a mid-century country music radio program, considered to be the "Junior Grand Ole Opry." It was also televised in the mid-1950s, and on its March 5, 1955, broadcast, Elvis made his TV debut.

————.

"A cloistered life." *Psychology Today* (Nov 1993): 24–27+.

A rewrite of Montefiore's October 1993 *The New Republic* profile of Mother Dolores (Elvis's co-star Delores Hart).

☆ Ozment, Lloyd, and Walter Bruce

Ozment was a *Louisiana Hayride* performer and friend of Elvis in the 1950s.

Elvis Presley: The Fifties. Shreveport, LA: Bruce Treasure Corporation, 1995. 100 pp. ISBN: 070652797.

The story of Ozment and his friendship with Elvis Presley in the 1950s. The second part of this book discusses alleged "Elvis relics" (" . . . coins, jewelry, and artifacts that were associated with Elvis"), unearthed at a Shreveport, Louisiana, lake where Elvis spent time in the 1950s. Black and white candids of Elvis and Ozment in the 1950s and of the discovered Elvis objects.

Source: Publisher's address: P.O. Box 7172, Shreveport, LA 71137

☆ Pall, Gloria

Pall is the actress who played the stripper in *Jailhouse Rock*.

'Twas the Night I Met Elvis. North Hollywood, CA: Showgirl Press, [1990]. ISBN: none.

Anecdotes from the filming of *Jailhouse Rock*. Part of the scene in which Pall appears is the famous shot where Elvis peers between her legs as she dances on a bar counter. Black and white photos, candids and stills of Pall and Elvis during the filming.

In the September 1996 issue of *Elvis The Man and His Music*, writer Trevor Cajiao interviewed Pall about her experiences with Elvis in Las Vegas and on the set of the film (pp. 10–15).

Source: www.gloriapall.com
Publisher's address: Showgirl Press, 12828 Victory Blvd. #163, North Hollywood, CA 91606

☆ Palmer, Robert

"Big Boss Man: Working with the King." *Rolling Stone* (Sept 22, 1977): 54–55.

Speaking with the writer right after Elvis's death, D. J. Fontana and J. D. Sumner recount their experiences with Elvis. This article appeared in the acclaimed Elvis memorial edition of *Rolling Stone*.

☆ Scheuer, Philip K.

"Elvis Matches Dean's Skill Doin' What Comes Naturally." *Los Angeles Times* (Nov 4, 1956): Part V: 2.

David Weisbart, the director of Elvis Presley's first film, *Love Me Tender*, discusses Elvis as an actor and in comparison with James Dean. (Weisbart directed Dean in *Rebel Without a Cause*.)

☆ Stoker, Gordon

"14 Very Good Years." *The Akron* (OH) *Beacon Journal* (May 3, 1991): D2.

A longtime member of The Stamps quartet recalls recording and touring with Elvis.

☆ Tio, Maria Mercedes

"Otis Blackwell: The Power Behind Elvis." *Essence* (May 1978): 16.

A profile of the composer of "All Shook Up," "Don't Be Cruel," and "Return to Sender." Blackwell discusses the financial arrangements involving his songs that Elvis recorded.

☆ Weiss, Allan

"Elvis Presley: Rock Music Phenomenon." *Close-Ups: Intimate Profiles of Movie Stars by Their Co-Stars, Directors, Screenwriters, and Friends.* Ed. Danny Peary. New York: Workman Pub., 1978. ISBN: 0894800442. Pp. 83–86.

Weiss wrote the screenplays for six of Elvis Presley's films. In this chapter, he comments on Elvis as an actor, his on-set behavior, and the problems and pleasures of working with him.

Source: Library of Congress PN 2285. C55 1978

☆ Westmoreland, Kathy, with William G. Quinn

Westmoreland joined Elvis as a featured female vocalist in 1970. She appeared with Elvis in more than 1,000 concerts during the last seven years of his life

Elvis and Kathy. Glendale, CA: Glendale House Pub., 1987. 312 pp. ISBN: none.

Westmoreland's memoirs of Elvis and the concerts in the 1970s.

Source: The Margaret Herrick Library, Academy of Motion Picture Arts and Sciences

See Also:

In The Rest/Souvenir Magazines:

Elvis Lives On! 1992.

In The Rest/Unverified Titles:

Matthews, Neal, *Elvis: A Golden Tribute.*

☆ Scotty Moore

Elvis Presley's original guitarist, who along with bassist Bill Black helped Elvis Presley discover his sound and style. In 1954 Sun Records producer Sam Phillips asked Memphis guitarist Moore to work with Elvis Presley in an effort to develop Elvis's unique sound. Moore remained with Elvis through the 1950s, playing on all of his tours and television appearances and on all of Elvis's Sun Records and early RCA recordings. He left Elvis in the 1960s and returned to appear with him on the 1968 "Comeback Special" television show. Moore has had a long career in performing and record producing. He continues to make regular appearances at Elvis-related events. In March 2000, he was inducted into the Rock and Roll Hall of Fame.

☆   ☆   ☆   ☆

☆ Dougherty, Steve

"Present at the Creation." *People Weekly* (Oct 13, 1997): 30.

An interview with Scotty Moore in which he discusses his relationship with Elvis and his pioneering role in rock and roll.

"Elvis and Scotty: Tales from the Heartbreak Hotel." *Guitar Player* (July 1997).

Interview with Moore about his musical career.

☆ Moore, Scotty, with James Dickerson

That's Alright, Elvis: The Untold Story of Elvis's First Guitarist and Manager, Scotty Moore. New York: Schirmer Books; London: Prentice Hall International, 1997. 271 pp. ISBN: 0028645995.

Moore's memoirs, including 65 black and white photographs; captioned and credited. Notes. Bibliography. Discography of Scotty Moore's recordings with Elvis. Index.

J. D. Sumner

Gospel quartet legend J. D. Sumner, with his group The Stamps, backed Elvis Presley on recordings and in concerts from 1972–1977. Sumner met high school student Elvis in the early 1950s, when he allowed Elvis to sneak in the back of Memphis's Ellis Auditorium to watch the gospel shows. Sumner's gospel singing career spanned half a century. He and The Stamps continued to perform at Elvis-related events until his death in 1999.

☆   ☆   ☆   ☆

☆ Palmer, Robert

"Big Boss Man: Working with the King." *Rolling Stone* (Sept 22, 1977): 54–55.

J.D.'s commentary on Elvis, made in the immediate aftermath of Elvis's death.

☆ Sumner, J. D., with Bob Terrell

Elvis: His Love for Gospel Music and J. D. Sumner. Nashville, TN: WCI Publishing, 1991. 104 pp. ISBN: 187889403X.

Sumner's memoirs. (Note: in 1971 Sumner and Terrell published *J. D. Sumner: Gospel Music Is My Life*. During this time period, Sumner was performing with Elvis. That book, located in the Library of Congress, did not discuss Elvis.)

Source: New York Public Library JND 92-85

☆ Terrell, Bob

The Life and Times of J. D. Sumner, the World's Lowest Bass Singer. Nashville: J. D. Sumner, Publisher, 1994. ISBN: none.

Sumner writes about his friendship with Elvis, and he addresses questions about Elvis's alleged drug abuse and sightings. Fourteen candid black and white photographs of Sumner with Elvis; captioned but not credited.

Source: www.jdsumnerandthestamps.com

See Also:

In The Man/Biographies:

Peters, Richard, *Elvis: The Golden Anniversary Tribute: Fifty Fabulous Years in Words and Pictures, 1935-1985.* (Chet Atkins, Sam Phillips, Kathy Westmoreland.)
Waldman, Carl, and Jim Donovan, *Elvis Immortal: A Celebration of the King.* (Glenn Campbell.)
Walls, J. Dan, editor, *Elvis: A Tribute to the Life and the Career of Elvis Presley.* (J. D. Sumner.)

In The Man/Elvis in Quotes:

Allen, Steve, *U.S. News & World Report.*

In The Man/The Impact of Elvis:

Condon, Eddie, "What Is an Elvis Presley?" (Steve Allen quotes.)

In The Man/Memoirs and Memories:

Wiegert, Sue, with contributions by Elvis friends and Elvis fans. *Elvis: Precious Memories,* Vols. 1 and 2.

In The Rest/Souvenir Magazines:

Hit Parader Presents the Immortal Elvis, 1978. (Memories of Felton Jarvis.)
The Life and Death of Elvis Presley, 1977. (Cher, Pat Boone, Carl Wilson, Frank Sinatra, and Roy Orbison.)

Friends

☆ Cocke, Marian J.

Cocke has retired from nursing and appears frequently at Elvis fan club events. She regularly conducts charity fund-raising in Elvis's memory.

I Called Him Babe: Elvis Presley's Nurse Remembers. **20th Century Reminiscence Series.** Memphis, TN: Memphis State University Press, 1979. 160 pp. ISBN: 0878700536.

The memoirs of Elvis Presley's nurse and friend. Cocke met Elvis when he was hospitalized in January 1975 at Memphis's Baptist Memorial Hospital where she was assigned to be his nurse. She recalls Elvis's kindness and generosity during the last two years of his life and discusses his medical problems and death. Fourteen black and white photographs from Cocke's collection; credited.

Source: Library of Congress ML420.P96 C6
Dewey Decimal 784.5/4/00924

☆ Currie, Grant

In 1964 Currie ran an advertisement in *Photoplay* magazine for his memoirs (*Elvis and Priscilla*)—a book that remains unpublished (Torgoff, *The Complete Elvis*, p. 18). He assisted with the writing of *Child Bride* (1997), in which implausible and tasteless assertions are made about the circumstances under which Elvis and Priscilla met. (*See* Finstad listing in The Man/Biographies.)

☆ "Elvis Secretly Engaged." *Photoplay* (Jan 1964): 28, 78–80.

Currie—who claims that he introduced Priscilla Beaulieu to Elvis Presley in 1959, when he and Elvis were stationed with the army in Germany—tells his version of how that happened and how he continued to foster the relationship after Elvis returned to the States.

☆ Fadal, Edward W.

Elvis . . . Precious Memories. Waco, TX: The Waco Citizen, 1980. [24] pp.

Memories and photographs (black and white) of Elvis Presley's friend Eddie Fadal. (Elvis and Fadal met in Waco, Texas, in 1958, while Elvis was in advanced army training at nearby Ft. Hood.) Also contains an article by then–Baylor University Head Coach Grant Teaff, decrying the cult atmosphere that had arisen around Elvis since his death: "Cultist Movement Is Wrong."

Source: Compiler's collection

☆ Jolkovsky, Binyamin L.

"Elvis: His Favorite Meal Was Peanut Butter and Bacon on Challah." *New York* (Aug 25, 1997): 21.

The memories of Jeannette Fruchter about her Memphis neighbor and friend Elvis Presley. In 1953 the Presley family became the Fruchter's downstairs neighbors at 462 Alabama Avenue. Elvis served as the family's shabbes goy (a Gentile who performs acts that are forbidden to Jews on the Sabbath, such as lighting a stove or turning on an electrical switch). She also comments on Elvis's relationship with his mother, Gladys.

☆ Mansfield, Rex, and Elisabeth Mansfield

Rex Mansfield served in the U.S. Army with Elvis, from basic training though their service in Germany. The two were good friends. Elisabeth Mansfield was Elvis's private secretary in Germany.

Elvis the Soldier. Translated by authors. Graceland Book series #2. Bamburg, West Germany: Collectors Service GmbH, 1983. 163 pp. ISBN: 3922932010.

English translation of Elvis in Deutschland. (*See* Foreign Language Titles/German.) The two authors, friends of Elvis, detail their experiences with him in the United States and during Elvis's military service. (Mr. Mansfield served with Elvis, and his wife was Elvis's secretary in Germany.) Color and black and white photographs of Elvis, Graceland, and military locations and individuals associated with him during this time; many are candid shots taken by the authors and other Elvis friends. Photographs are different in each version of the book. Two question and author answer sections. The book comes with a 33⅓, 8″ sound disc of a 1960 interview Elvis gave to the Armed Forces Network (AFN).

Source: New York Public Library JND 88-60 (book)
LS8X 18 Rodgers and Hammerstein Archives (sound disc)

See Also:

In The Man/Biographies:

Baumgold, Julie, "Midnight in the Garden of Good and Elvis." (Marian Cocke.)
Staten, Vince, *The Real Elvis: Good Old Boy.*

The Memphis Mafia

From the beginning of his career, Elvis Presley surrounded himself with a growing number of young men who were friends, associates, and employees. They traveled and socialized with him, performed a variety of work as employees, and, in some instances, lived at Graceland. In the early 1960s Elvis and his entourage were in Las Vegas. They arrived in front of the Riviera Hotel in two long black limousines. Elvis and about 10 men got out, all wearing black mohair suits and sunglasses. Someone on the sidewalk shouted, "Who are they, the Mafia?" The next day, the event was mentioned in the *Las Vegas Sun.* From then on the media always referred to Elvis's entourage as the Memphis Mafia.[3]

Because there were so many young men coming in and out of Elvis's life, it is difficult to develop a specific membership roster. There were 8 original members, though the number sometimes ranged as high as 13.[4] They included his closest friends and relatives, such as Joe Esposito; Lamar Fike; Alan Fortas; Richard Davis; Marty Lacker; Billy, Gene, and Junior Smith; and Sonny and Red West.

☆   ☆   ☆   ☆

☆ *Elvis: An Audio Scrapbook.* Audiocassette. Simon & Schuster Audioworks series. New York: Simon & Schuster Audio, 1994. ISBN: 0671894854. Music No: 89485-4.

Elvis Presley friend George Klein hosts a collection of interviews and material from radio archives, including Elvis, Priscilla Presley, Colonel Tom Parker, and Scotty Moore. Marion

[3]The Memphis Mafia Homepage: www.memphismafia.com
[4]Ibid.

Keisker of Sun Records was present at Elvis's first recording session and gives an eyewitness account of that event. A sound cassette, 60 minutes in length: analog, stereo, Dolby processed.

Source: Alexandria (VA) Public Library AUDIO B Presley Pre
OCLC 31195943

☆ Esposito, Joe, and Elena Oumano

After Elvis's death, Esposito managed road tours for recording artists John Denver, Michael Jackson, Wayne Newton, Karen Carpenter, and the BeeGees. He frequently appears at Elvis events and has co-produced a book of Elvis photographs called *Elvis . . . Intimate & Rare*. (*See* The Man/Photographs.)

Good Rockin' Tonight: Twenty Years on the Road and on the Town with Elvis. New
    York: Simon and Schuster, 1994. 268 pp. ISBN: 0671795074. New York: Avon
    Books, 1996. ISBN: 0380726947.

The memoir of Joe Esposito, who was a close aide and friend to Elvis from 1960 until Elvis's death in 1977. After meeting Elvis in the army, he became Elvis's road manager. Esposito served as one of two best men at Elvis's wedding to Priscilla Beaulieu. He appeared in several of Elvis's films.
    Sixteen pages of Esposito's candid black and white photographs; captioned. No index or chapter notes. This book was translated into Czech and Icelandic. (*See* Foreign Language Titles/Czech, Icelandic.)

☆ Fong-Torres, Ben

"Broken Heart for Sale: Elvis's Bodyguards Talk About 'What Happened.'" *Rolling
    Stone* (Sept 22, 1977): 42–43.

Red and Sonny West talk about their experiences with Elvis and their negative book, *Elvis, What Happened?*, which had been released several weeks before Elvis died.

☆ Fortas, Alan

Alan Fortas, nephew of U.S. Supreme Court Justice Abe Fortas, was with Elvis Presley from 1958 to 1969. He served as manager of Elvis's Circle G Ranch and as bodyguard and travel arrangement manager.

*Elvis—from Memphis to Hollywood: Memories from My Twelve Years with Elvis
    Presley*. Ann Arbor, MI: Popular Culture Ink, 1992. 322 pp. ISBN:
    156075026X.

Fortas relates anecdotes about the Memphis Mafia lifestyle on the road, in Hollywood, and at Graceland. Candid black and white photographs from the author's collection; captioned. Included is a photograph of Elvis's high school report card. Index.

Source: Library of Congress ML420.P96 F67 1992
OCLC 30402048

☆ Geller, Larry, and Joel Spector, with Patricia Romanowski

Geller is a lifelong religious scholar who is also professionally involved in cosmetology and nutrition. He met Elvis in 1964. Elvis had heard of Geller's skill as a hair stylist and arranged an appointment with him. During that first meeting, the two men developed a deep, lasting friendship based upon their mutual interest in philosophical discussion and studies. They remained close until Elvis's death. Geller has co-authored three other books about Elvis's interest in religion and spirituality. (*See* Stearn listings in The Phenomena/Religion and in this section.) He frequently speaks at Elvis-related events.

If I Can Dream: Elvis's Own Story. New York: Simon and Schuster, 1989. 331 pp.
   ISBN: 0671659227. New York: Simon & Schuster, 1989. [Book Club Edition].
   331 pp. ISBN: none. London: Century, 1989. 331 pp. ISBN: 0712630082. London: Arrow, 1990. 331 pp. ISBN: 0099686309. New York: Avon, 1990. 346 pp.
   ISBN: 038710420.

The memoirs of one of Elvis Presley's closest confidants in the 1960s and 1970s. Geller ignited Elvis's passion for the study of religions and spirituality, providing him with several hundred books on these subjects.[5] The two men had frequent and lengthy discussions about religious and spiritual topics. This book is based upon Geller's diaries of these conversations. The text contains many quotes attributed to Elvis concerning his thoughts and beliefs about religion and his place in the universe.

   Black and white candid photographs from Geller's personal collection. A bibliography of Elvis's favorite readings on religion and spirituality (pp. 325–328). Astrological charts for Elvis and Priscilla Presley. No index. This book has been translated into Czech, Danish, Dutch, German, and Swedish. (*See* those chapters in Foreign Language Titles.)

☆ Hodge, Charlie, with Charles Goodman

Me 'n' Elvis. Memphis, TN: Castle Books, 1988. 204 pp. ISBN: none.

The memoirs of Charlie Hodge, who was Elvis Presley's friend and employee. A professional musician, who first met Elvis in 1956, Hodge served with Elvis in the army and worked for him from 1960 until the entertainer's death in 1977. Hodge appeared in Elvis's films and accompanied him on guitar during concerts and recording sessions.

   Twenty-five black and white candid photographs; captioned, but not cited. No index, chapter notes, or citations.

Source: Library of Congress ML420.P96 H64 1984

☆ Lacker, Marty, Patsy Lacker, and Leslie S. Smith

Marty Lacker was a classmate of Elvis's at Humes High School in Memphis, Tennesse, and continued a friendship and work association until Elvis's death in 1977. He was one of two best men at Elvis's marriage to Priscilla Beaulieu. He worked for Elvis as Chief Personal Aide full-time from 1961–1968 and then handled special projects for him until 1977.

---

[5]Elvis had a personal library of nearly 1,000 books, 300 of which he carried with him at all times according to Geller (p. 325). There are many published photographs of Elvis carrying books, particularly when entering or exiting airplanes.

Elvis: Portrait of a Friend. Memphis, TN: Wimmer Brothers Books, 1979. 316 pp. ISBN: 0918544297.

A three-part memoir by longtime Elvis friends Marty Lacker and his wife, Patsy. In the book's first section, "Portrait of a Friend," Marty Lacker discusses his 20-year friendship with Elvis. As a member of the Memphis Mafia, he traveled with Elvis for concerts and filming, served as his accountant, and lived on the grounds of Graceland with his family. Patsy Lacker provides the perspective of a Memphis Mafia spouse in the second part, "Wife Was a Four Letter Word." The third part, "A View from the Outside," by magazine editor and publisher Leslie S. Smith, explores Elvis's alleged prescription drug abuse. Black and white photographs; captioned and credited. No index or notes.

Source: Library of Congress ML420.P96 L3

☆ Nash, Alanna, with Billy Smith, Marty Lacker, and Lamar Fike

Billy Smith, Elvis's maternal first cousin, was very close to him from childhood until the entertainer's death. He worked full-time for Elvis and lived on the Graceland grounds with his wife, Jo. Lamar Fike met Elvis in 1957 and worked for him until 1977, except for a period of time in the 1960s, when he managed the career of singer Brenda Lee. Nash wrote the widely circulated newspaper insert *Elvis: 1935-1977*, which appeared in newspapers throughout America immediately following Elvis's death.

Elvis Aaron Presley: Revelations from the Memphis Mafia. New York: HarperCollins, 1995. 792 pp. ISBN: 0060176199. New York: Harper Mass Market Paperbacks, 1996. 947 pp. ISBN: 006109336x.

An oral biography of Elvis Presley by three members of the Memphis Mafia. Each man comments upon Elvis's childhood, adult life, and death aftermath in an effort to find an answer as to why someone with such phenomenal success would spiral into destruction. "Aftermath" chapter discusses events after Elvis's death. Sixteen pages of black and white photographs of Elvis and his friends and family; captioned and credited. Index. This book was translated into Japanese. (*See* Foreign Language Titles/Japanese.)

☆ Stearn, Jess, and Larry Geller

The Truth About Elvis. New York: Jove Publications, Inc., 1980. 287 pp. ISBN: 0515051543. Cammeray [N.S.W.]: Horwitz, 1981. 286 pp. ISBN: 0725511044.

Geller's observations and memories about Elvis Presley and his relationships, his interests in spirituality and metaphysics, and his strong belief that he was an earthly messenger sent by God. Told in first-person anecdotal format with direct quotes from Elvis, this book is based upon Geller's 13-year friendship with the entertainer.

☆ West, Red, Sonny West, and Dave Hebler, as told to Steve Dunleavy

Sonny and Red West attended high school with Elvis. Elvis employed them since the 1950s. Hebler worked for Elvis since 1972. Red West has a long career in show business writing songs for Pat Boone and Ricky Nelson and appearing in television dramas and commercials and motion pictures. Sonny West is a former disc jockey and lives in Tennessee. Dave Hebler met Elvis in 1972 while he was running a karate school in Memphis.

Elvis, What Happened? **New York: Ballantine Books, 1977. 332 pp. ISBN: 0345272153.**

The infamous book, written by three of Elvis Presley's bodyguards and published just before his death, alleges drug use, womanizing, and out-of-control behavior by Elvis. This was the first time that these accusations had been made in public. According to the authors, this book was to be "a desperate effort to communicate to Elvis one last time. 'He will read and he will get hopping mad at us because he will know that every word is the truth,' said Sonny West, ' . . . but maybe, just maybe, it will do some good.'" (Page [1] of book.) Fifteen black and white photographs; some credited, all captioned. No index or notes.

The Wests and Hebler were fired by Elvis's father, Vernon Presley, in July 1976. They began writing this book after their dismissal. This book was published on August 1, 1977, just 16 days before Elvis would die. In *Elvis: The Final Years* (p. 233), Elvis biographer Jerry Hopkins writes that news of the book devastated Elvis. According to Elvis's close friend Larry Geller—with whom he discussed the book a few hours before his death—Elvis never read it.[6] This book was translated into French, German, and Hungarian. (*See* those chapters in Foreign Language Titles.) Immediately following Elvis's death, Ballantine printed an additional 3.35 million copies (*Publishers Weekly*, Aug 29, 1977 and Sept 5, 1977).

See Also:

In The Man/Biographies:

Baumgold, Julie, "Midnight in the Garden of Good and Elvis." (Joe Esposito, George Klein, and Richard Davis.)

In The Man/Photographs:

Shaver, Sean, and Hal Noland, *The Life of Elvis Presley. With intimate memories of Charlie Hodge, Dick Grob, and Billy Smith.*

In The Phenomena/Religion:

Stearn, Jess, *Elvis's Spiritual Journey.* (Larry Geller.)
Stearn, Jess, with Larry Geller, *Elvis's Search for God.*

In The Rest/Unverified Titles:

Fortas, Alan, *My Friend Elvis.*

---

[6]Correspondence, May 1999.

Priscilla Beaulieu Presley

☆ Baker, Jackson

Baker is a respected Memphis journalist. In 1977 he wrote an important memorial article about Elvis. (*See* The Man/Death, Conspiracy, Sightings.)

"Who Was This Woman? Who Was This Girl?" *Memphis* (July/Aug 1998): 36–42, 47–48.

A profile of Priscilla Presley in which she discusses how Elvis has affected her life. She comments on their daughter Lisa Marie's marriage to Michael Jackson. She makes a strong case for Elvis as a role model for today's young people.

☆ **"Living in a TV Twilight."** *Life* (Sept 1987): 46.

Priscilla Presley reminisces about her experiences while living at Graceland.

☆ Presley, Priscilla, with Sandra Harmon

Elvis and Me. New York: G. P. Putnam's Sons, 1985. 320 pp. ISBN: 0399129847. New York: G. P. Putnam's Sons/Book Club edition, 1985. 214 pp. ISBN: none. London: Century, 1985. 320 pp. ISBN: 0712611312. London: Arrow, 1986. 320 pp. ISBN: 0099470004 (pbk.). New York: Berkley, 1986. 320pp. ISBN: 0425091031.

Priscilla Presley's story of her life with Elvis Presley. Three eight-page sections of black and white photographs; captioned and credited. Index. This book was translated into Czech, Danish, Dutch, Finnish, French, German, Icelandic, Italian, Japanese, Norwegian, Spanish, and Swedish. (*See* those chapters in Foreign Language Titles.) A large print edition of this book was issued in 1986. (*Elvis and Me.* Thorndike, ME: Thorndike Press, 1986. 380 pp. ISBN: 0896212926.)

A three-hour television mini-series was based on this book. It was released on video in 1988, under the title *Elvis and Me* (Los Angeles, CA: New World Video, C60101). The video was rereleased under the same name in 1990 (Torrance, CA: R&G Video LP, ISBN: 1560681462); and again in 1995 by the same company (ISBN: 1560688939).

The Literacy Volunteers of New York City issued *Selected from Elvis and Me*—with selections from the original for adult literacy programs. (*See* The Academics/Educational Literature.)

☆ Sheevey, Sandra

"My Life With and Without Elvis Presley." *Ladies Home Journal* (Aug 1973): 82, 137+.

Priscilla Presley's first interview after her divorce from Elvis. She discusses their courtship, marriage, and breakup, as well as her post-divorce life and plans. She talks about considering the "Religion of Science" (Scientology) as the basis of Lisa Marie's religious foundation.

See Also:

The Man/Biographies

Relatives

☆ Davis, Dottie Presley, as told to Kevin Cox

Elvis's Cousin, Wonderful Wayman and Little Sis. 1992.

The autobiography of the daughter of Wayman Presley [whose relationship to Elvis the compiler was unable to ascertain]. Three pages about her visit to Graceland, as well as a memory of seeing Elvis in concert.

Source: eBay auction item #112591238

☆ Early, Donna Presley, and Edie Hand, with Lynn Edge

Early spent her summers at Graceland. Her mother, Nasval Pritchett, was Vernon Presley's sister. (*See* Pritchett listing in this section.) Hand spent time as a teenager and a young adult at Graceland.

Elvis: Precious Memories. Birmingham, Alabama: The Best of Times, Inc., 1997. 311 pp. ISBN: 1886049106.

Elvis Presley's first cousin, Donna Presley Early, and another cousin, Edie Hand, reveal the Presley family's perspectives of Elvis and discuss the family's speculations about Elvis's death.

Source: Library of Congress ML420.P96 E27 1996

☆ Goodin, Vera Jane

Elvis and Bobbie: Memories of Linda Jackson. Branson, MO: Limited Star Editions, 1994. 36 pp. ISBN: none.

A proposal for a book and motion picture about Elvis Presley and his cousin Bobbie Mann, who was the daughter of Elvis's maternal aunt Lillian Smith Mann. [Compiler was unable to find evidence that such a book had been published or movie produced and released.]

Source: Elvis Presley Enterprises, Inc.

☆ Greenwood, Earl, and Kathleen Tracy

The Boy Who Would Be King: An Intimate Portrait of Elvis Presley by His Cousin. New York: Dutton, 1990. 310 pp. ISBN: 0525249028. New York: Signet, 1990. 347 pp. ISBN: 0451170393. London: Signet, 1992. 358 pp. ISBN: 045117403.

Memories of life with Elvis Presley from a man who says that he is Elvis's second cousin. No footnotes, chapter notes, or sources. No index. Thirty-two pages of black and white photographs; captioned and credited. This book was also released in audio-tape format.

The dust jacket states that Greenwood was "a second cousin to the late Elvis Presley, was with Elvis in a personal and professional capacity—serving as his press agent for a time—throughout Presley's career." This is not supported by Elvis's longtime friend Marty Lacker.[7] Lacker says that Greenwood was a fan club president in the 1950s who stood at the Graceland gate with other fans, hoping to see Elvis. Lacker states, " . . . every once in awhile [he] was allowed up to the house with a group of other people, but he was no close confidant of Elvis and was absolutely not related to Elvis." He adds, "He was not [Elvis's] p.r. person. He had a one-page newsletter for his fan club, but that all ended in the very early sixties, and he was not allowed around anymore."[8]

☆ Hand, Edie

"Reflections of Elvis." *Southern Living* **(Aug 1997): 204.**

Hand, a first cousin to Elvis Presley, recounts Elvis's special acts of kindness to her.

☆ Loyd, Harold

Loyd, Elvis's first cousin, grew up with him in Tupelo and Memphis. He worked as a guard at Graceland's front gate. After Elvis's death in 1977, Loyd recorded a tribute record for the Memphis label, Modern Age Enterprises. It was entitled "A Prayer for Elvis."

Elvis Presley's Graceland Gates. **Franklin, TN: Jimmy Velvet Publications, 1987. 127 pp. ISBN: none.**

This is a reissue of Loyd's 1978 book, *The Graceland Gates*. Additional candid color and black and white photographs with this acknowledgement: "Photos by Jimmy Velvet and Elvis fans everywhere." None are captioned. No notes or index.

The book's publisher, Jimmy Velvet, is well known to Elvis's fans. In the endnotes, Velvet is incorrectly identified as having recorded several hit records, including "Blue Velvet" (recorded by Bobby Vinton), "Mission Bell" (recorded by Donnie Brooks), and "Teen Angel" (recorded by Mark Dinning). In the 1980s Velvet operated four Elvis Presley Museums, containing items donated by Elvis's friends and relatives. In the 1990s he auctioned off a number of these items. (*See* Butterfield & Butterfield listing in The Phenomena/Collecting Elvis.)

Source: Compiler's collection

☆ Loyd, Harold, with George Baugh

The Graceland Gates. **Memphis: Modern Age Enterprises, 1978. 128 pp. ISBN: none.**

This is a memoir of anecdotes involving both Elvis Presley and his fans. Loyd tells stories of Elvis's romantic interests, his pets, and his pranks on Graceland's grounds. Anecdotes are

[7]Correspondence, Nov 22, 1997.

[8]Correspondence, Oct 10, 1997.

also related about Elvis's fans and their behavior at Graceland's gates and surrounding wall. Includes 110 black and white photographs from Loyd's personal collection; captioned.

In 1987 this book was reissued under the title *Elvis Presley's Graceland Gates*. (*See* preceding listing.)

Source: Library of Congress ML420.P96 L7

✩ Presley, Dee Stanley
(See *The Stanleys section in this chapter.*)

✩ Presley, Vernon, as told to Nancy Anderson

"Elvis." *Good Housekeeping* (Jan 1978): 80–81, 156–161.

The only major interview given by Elvis Presley's father, Vernon. This was published five months after Elvis's death. In it, Presley talks about his memories of his son.

✩ Presley, Vester, with Deda Bonura

Vester Presley co-authored a cookbook with Graceland cook Nancy Rooks. (*See* The Phenomena/Cookbooks.) He died in 1997.

A Presley Speaks. Memphis: Wimmer Brothers Books, 1978. 150 pp. ISBN: 0918544106.

The memoirs of Elvis's uncle Vester Presley, who worked for more than 20 years as a guard at Graceland's gates. His remembrances include Presley family history. Includes a section called "Facts You May Not Know About Elvis Aaron Presley." Record discography. Filmography. Color and black and white candid photographs; captioned but not credited.[9]

Source: Numbered edition with scarf: Bluff Park Books, Long Beach, CA.
Unnumbered edition: Library of Congress ML420.P96 P7
Dewey Decimal 784/.092/4 B

✩ Pritchett, Nasval Lorene Presley

One Flower While I Live: Elvis as I Remember Him. Memphis: Shelby House, 1987. 154 pp. ISBN: 0942179056.

The Reverend Nasval Lorene Presley Pritchett is Elvis's paternal aunt. Her memoirs are a 23-chapter typewritten manuscript detailing the author's and Elvis's lives and relatives. Fifty-four black and white candids from the author's personal collection; each captioned.

Source: Library of Congress ML420.P96 P73 1987

✩ Smith, Gene

Smith lived in Memphis with his wife, Louise, working as a truck driver until his death in 1999.

---

[9]This book was also issued in a 15,000-copy numbered, library-bound edition, which came packaged in a blue and gold box, accompanied by a white polyester scarf with a facsimile of Elvis Presley's signature stamped on it. This edition was published in June 1978 with the ISBN 0918544114.

Elvis's Man Friday. Nashville, TN: Light of Day Publishing, 1994. 292 pp. ISBN: 0964256606.

This is the memoir of Gene Smith, Elvis Presley's maternal first cousin, who was his closest playmate in childhood and as a teenager. Smith was a member of the Memphis Mafia and worked for Elvis from 1956 until the late 1960s. The anecdotes in this book focus on Elvis's childhood, teenage years, and motion picture career.

Introduction by Peter Nazareth, Ph.D., of the University of Iowa, who is credited with teaching one of the first for-credit course on Elvis Presley. Sixteen pages of candid black and white photographs of the author and Elvis together as children, teens, and as adults; and of various members of author's family. Photographs are from the collection of Smith and his sister, Laverne Smith.

Source: Library of Congress ML420.P96 S55 1994

The Stanleys

Elvis Presley's stepmother, Dee, and his three stepbrothers are among the most ubiquitous of the Elvis memoir authors, producing eight books between them, as well as giving numerous interviews in print and on air and appearing in Elvis videos. In 1996 David Stanley promoted an Elvis fan cruise on which he, as Elvis's stepbrother, would be the featured attraction.

Dee Stanley met Elvis's father, Vernon Presley, while she and her army husband were living in Friedberg, Germany, near where Elvis was stationed. A few months after Elvis returned to the United States in 1960, she and Vernon were married. The new Mrs. Presley brought her three young sons, Billy, David, and Ricky, to live with them at Graceland. The Stanley brothers grew up there and worked for Elvis from their teenage years until his death in 1977.

Today, David Stanley is an entrepreneur and Rick Stanley is an ordained Baptist minister. Dee and Vernon Presley separated in 1974 and divorced in 1977.

☆   ☆   ☆   ☆

☆ Presley, Dee, Bill Stanley, David Stanley, and Rick Stanley, with Martin Torgoff

Elvis: We Love You Tender. "A Delilah and Mike Franklin Book" series. New York: Delacorte Press, 1980. 395 pp. ISBN: 0440023238. London: New English Library, 1980. 426 pp. ISBN: 0450048152. Delacorte Press/Book Club Edition, 1980. 321 pp. ISBN: none. New York: Dell Publishing Company, 1981. 490 pp. ISBN: 0440123232.

The story of Dee Presley's and her sons' life with Elvis. Delacorte Press and Dell editions have 16 leaves of black and white photographs from the authors' collections; New English Library and Delacorte Press Book Club editions have 32. Index.[10]

---

[10]In *The Complete Elvis*, co-author Martin Torgoff provides a narrative of his preparation for and writing of the book and how his editors significantly altered the text (pp. 19–38). (*See* The Man/Reference.)

————.

Elvis—"We love you tender." Distributed by the Los Angeles Times Syndicate, [1980]. 36 pp.

Excerpts from *Elvis: We Love You Tender* by Dee Presley and her sons Billy, David, and Rick Stanley printed as a newspaper insert. Black and white photographs from the Presley/Stanley book; captioned.

Source: Compiler's collection.

☆ Stanley, Billy, with George Erickson

Elvis, My Brother. New York: St. Martin's Press, 1989. ISBN: 0312925700 (pbk.)

Elvis Presley's youngest stepbrother writes about his life at Graceland and the influence Elvis had on him.

Source: Library of Congress ML420.P9656 1989

☆ Stanley, David, with David Wimbish

Life with Elvis. Old Tappan, NJ: Fleming H. Revell Company, 1986. 223 pp. ISBN: 0800714903.

From book jacket: " . . . Dave tells his own story to set the record straight."

Source: Library of Congress ML420.P96 S62 1986
Dewey Decimal 784'5'00924

☆ Stanley, David, with Mark Bego

Raised on Rock: The Autobiography of Elvis Presley's Step-Brother. Edinburgh, Scotland: Mainstream Publishing Projects, Ltd., 1996. 189 pp. ISBN: 185158852.

Elvis's stepbrother David Stanley writes of his life with the entertainer. This is also the story of Stanley's "struggle to come to terms with the legacy of drugs and deception which Elvis bequeathed to him" (book jacket notes). Sixteen pages of photographs; some from the author's collection. Bibliography/Source List (six books). No index. Stanley has also written an Elvis reference book. (*See* The Man/Reference.)

Source: Dewey Decimal 782.421660922
OCLC 36408769

☆ Stanley, Rick

"Remembering the King." *People Weekly* (Aug 21, 1989): 32–39.

Elvis Presley's stepbrother Rick Stanley discusses his life with Elvis.

☆ Stanley, Rick, with Michael K. Haynes

The Touch of Two Kings: Growing Up at Graceland. [U.S.]: LT2K, 1986. 186 pp. ISBN: 09142770020.

The memoirs of Elvis Presley's stepbrother Rick Stanley. Seven pages of black and white candids of the author and Elvis and of Stanley's life after Elvis's death; captioned, not credited.

Source: Compiler's collection

☆ Stanley, Rick, with Paul Harold

Caught in a Trap: Elvis Presley's Tragic Lifelong Search for Love. Dallas, TX: Word
   Publishing, 1992. 232 pp. ISBN: 0849909791. [UK]: Milton Keynes, 1993. 232
   pp. ISBN: 0850095867.

Rick Stanley wrote this book to "address the why questions that continue to swirl around the paradox that was, and to some extent is, Elvis." He attempts to answer questions in the manner in which "[Elvis] answered for himself," such as "What's the secret of happiness? Where do I find meaning and purpose in my life?" Question and answer section (pp. 159–204), in which Rev. Stanley provides answers to the questions that he is most frequently asked about Elvis. No photographs. No index or notes.

Source: Library of Congress ML420.P96 S64
Cambridge University Library UK M557.d.95.778

See Also:

In TheMan/Elvis in Quotes:

"Editor's Notebook."

Romantic Interests

☆ Bova, Joyce, as told to William Conrad Nowels

Joyce Bova was a career employee of the United States House of Representatives' Committee on Armed Services. She is now retired.

*Don't Ask Forever: My Love Affair with Elvis: A Washington Woman's Secret Years with
   Elvis Presley.* New York: Kensington Books, 1994. 386 pp. ISBN: 0821746162.

The story of a young woman's three-year relationship with Elvis Presley. Joyce Bova met Elvis while on vacation in Las Vegas in 1969, during a time when he was separated from his wife, Priscilla. In 1994 excerpts of this book appeared in *Ladies' Home Journal* and the supermarket tabloid *Star.* Black and white candid photographs of Elvis's family and friends and of Elvis with Bova; credited and captioned.

☆ Daroff, Elizabeth

"Elvis." *McCall's* (July 1980): 97–98, 141–144.

The memoirs of Linda Thompson, Elvis Presley's romantic interest between 1972 and 1976. During that time, Thompson lived at Graceland and in a nearby home, purchased for her by Elvis. Thompson has not written a book about her life with Elvis. This article is the most in-depth view of that relationship.

☆ de Barbin, Lucy, and Dary Matera

Are You Lonesome Tonight? The Untold Story of Elvis Presley's One True Love and the Child He Never Knew. New York: Villard Books, 1987. 296 pp. ISBN: 0394558421. (hdk). New York: Charter Books, 1987, 1988. ISBN: 0099569302. (pbk).

The memoirs of a woman who maintains that she gave birth to Elvis Presley's child. De Barbin makes the questionable claim that she met Elvis in the fall of 1953, when they both performed at the home of Louisiana ex-governor James Noe. (Note: in the fall of 1953, Elvis was operating a drill press at Precision Tool in Memphis and had only performed in public at his high school's talent show.) De Barbin says that they became lovers then, remaining so until his death in 1977. She maintains that she gave birth to Elvis Presley's daughter, Desiree, in August 1958, lying about paternity on the birth certificate to hide the child's existence from Elvis.[11]

Black and white archival photographs of Elvis, along with candids of the author and her children; credited and captioned. Reproduction of Desiree Presley's birth certificate. Short bibliography. This book was translated into Dutch, French, and Japanese. (*See* those chapters in Foreign Language Titles.)

☆ Dougherty, Steve, and Linda Marx

"Elvis Prom Date Remembers a Shy Guy in Blue Suede Shoes." *People Weekly* (July 17, 1989): 99–100.

Elvis Presley's senior prom date, Regis Wilson Vaughn, recalls her friendship with him. Black and white photographs from the prom.

☆ Juanico, June

Elvis: In the Twilight of Memory. New York: Arcade, 1997. 320 pp. ISBN: 1559703938. London: Warner, 1998. 332 pp. ISBN: 0751519472. [U.S.]: Ulverscroft Large Print Books, 1998. ISBN: 0708989799.

The memoirs of an Elvis Presley romantic interest during the 1955–1956 period, just as he was on the brink of fame. Juanico ended her relationship with Elvis in early 1957. Sixteen pages of previously unseen photographs from the author's collection. Introduction by Elvis biographer Peter Guralnick.

☆ "Love Him Tender." *People Weekly* (18 Aug 1997): 80–86.

June Juanico Taranto, Linda Thompson, and Ginger Alden discuss their romances with Elvis Presley.

☆ Martindale, Sandy

Martindale, now the wife of television personality Wink Martindale, recounts her romance with Elvis in the 1960s when she was a teenager.

[11]In March 1998 *Newsday* newspaper's syndicated columnist Liz Smith reported that the child Desiree uses the last name "Presley de Rodriguez and lives in Southern California." Smith also wrote, "CBS is now planning a four-hour mini-series of Lucy's original book . . . ."

Elvis: His Life. [n.p.]: Bookthrift, 1988. ISBN: 0791701891.

Source: Sandy Martindale, Memphis, TN, Aug 1997

☆ Murphy, Mary

"Cybil Shepherd: A Passion for Pillow Talk." *TV Guide* (Apr 20, 1996): 18–24.

Actress Cybil Shepherd discusses her romantic relationship with Elvis Presley.

☆ Storm, Tempest

"The Lady Is a Vamp." *Cosmopolitan* (March 1988): 152–155.

Notorious striptease artist Tempest Storm writes about her brief 1957 romance with Elvis Presley. She also recounts this experience in her book *Tempest Storm: The Lady Is a Vamp* (Atlanta: Peachtree, 1987). Storm also claims a romantic liaison with President John F. Kennedy.

☆ Wiegert, Sue

Elvis Is Forever. Los Angeles: Sue Wiegert and the Blue Hawaiians for Elvis, 1975. 48 leaves. ISBN: none.

Three chapters of Judy Powell Spreckels's memories of her romance with Elvis in the 1950s (pp. 2–7). Spreckels, an heir to a sugar fortune, dated Elvis in 1958.

Source: Compiler's collection

See Also:

In The Man/Biographies:

Kirkland, K. D., *Elvis.* (Introduction by Sandy Martindale.)
Staten, Vince, *The Real Elvis: Good Old Boy.* (Dixie Locke, Elvis's first serious girlfriend.)

Others

☆ Archer, Jules

"I Had Dinner with Elvis." *Reminisce* (March/April 1995): 27.

The memories of a reporter who interviewed Elvis Presley during his first day on the set of *Love Me Tender.* Archer relates how he and the film's crew and cast expected a "sneering, arrogant delinquent" and were very surprised by Elvis's polite and friendly demeanor.

Source: Compiler's collection

☆ Burk, Bill E.

Bill Burk is the founding publisher of *Bill E. Burk's Elvis World* magazine, which is the longest running commercial Elvis publication, and also the author of 12 Elvis books. (*See*

The Man/Biographies, Elvis in the Army, Reference and The Music, The Movies/Concert and Television Appearances.)

Elvis Through My Eyes. Memphis, TN: Burk Enterprises, 1987. 196 pp. ISBN: 0942179005. Memphis, TN: Propwash Publishing, 1996. 200 pp. ISBN: 1879207168.

As a writer and columnist for the *Memphis Press-Scimitar*, Burk reported on Elvis Presley for 20 years. This is the story of Burk's experiences during that time. Sixteen pages of "rarely seen" black and white candid photographs of Elvis; captioned and credited. This book was translated into Swedish in 1992 and titled *Elvis: Tidernas Story.* (*See* Foreign Language Titles/Swedish.)

Source: Library of Congress ML420.P96 B88 1996
Dewey Decimal 782.42166/092 B 21

☆ Erwin, Sara

Over the Fence: A Neighbor's Memories of Elvis. Memphis: The King's Press, 1997. Limited Edition, 20th Anniversary. 70 pp. ISBN: 0965926508.

Sara Erwin grew up—and still lives—in a home that abuts the Graceland property. She maintained an acquaintanceship with Elvis from the time of his purchase of Graceland in 1957 until his death in 1977. This is her story of interactions with Elvis, how he related to his neighbors, what Graceland activities she observed from her backyard, and what happened to the neighborhood in the immediate aftermath of his death. Seventeen black and white candids of Elvis from the author's collection and those of her friends. Copy of a letter written by Elvis to a fan in 1960.

Source: Memphis/Shelby County (TN) Public Library and Information Center
Publisher address: The King's Press, 2519 Summer Avenue, Memphis, TN 38112
OCLC 38433018

☆ Ringel, Judy

"Elvis 1955–1956." *Memphis* (July/Aug 1986): 60–76.

An interview with prize-winning amateur photographer Robert Dye of Memphis, who, between August 1955 and September 1956, extensively photographed Elvis Presely in concert and with fans and friends. Fourteen of Dye's black and white photographs, each captioned with his memories of the event.

☆ Shaver, Sean

Elvis in Focus. Kansas City, MO: Timur Publishing Inc., 1992. 303 pp. ISBN: 090282637.

Shaver's memoirs of his career as an Elvis photographer. Includes author's black and white and color photos of Elvis, on stage and backstage at various concerts throughout his career.

Source: Collection of Sarah Wilkinson, Cambridge, Massachusetts

See Also:

In The Man/Biographies:

Grove, Martin A., *The King Is Dead*: Elvis Presley.
Hirshberg, Charles, *Elvis: A Celebration in Pictures*.
Lichter, Paul, *Behind Closed Doors*. (Colonel Parker.)

In The Man/Elvis in the Army:

DuBose, Jack, "Me 'n' Elvis 'n' NATO." *American Heritage*.
Taylor, William J., Jr., Ph.D., *Elvis in the Army: The King of Rock 'n' Roll as Seen by an Officer Who Served with Him*.

In The Man/Graceland:

Balfour, Victoria, "Amazing Graceland." (Jack Soden, CEO of EPE)

In The Man/Reference:

Currotto, William F., *From a Humble House to Fame; From Tupelo, MS, to Memphis, TN: An Elvis Presley Scrapbook*. (Singer Brenda Lee, an August 16, 1977, ambulance driver, and a high school friend.)

In The Music, The Movies/Concerts and Television Appearances:

Shaver, Sean, *Elvis: Photographing the King*.

CHAPTER 10
Photographs

"THE PHOTOGRAPH BOOKS *are* Elvis; the rest are *about* Elvis."[1] Elvis Presley photograph books are a not-so-secret passion of many Elvis fans. Take an Elvis photo book into your bedroom, turn down the lights, put on "Love Me Tender," and the years, pounds, and heartaches melt away. It is the late 1950s again—a time when romance and fantasy were a possibility easily within the grasp of every teenager. The world was safe, the future was secure, and girls gave their hearts—not their bodies—to their beaux.

And when the lights go on again, it's back to the arthritis meds and remembering your brother who died in Vietnam. But young, vital Elvis and his time still live—in the Elvis photograph books.

The Elvis photo books are a sure ticket to the happier past. And, thus, they are by far the most popular, as amply demonstrated by sales and sheer number published. In fact, the most prolific Elvis authors—Paul Lichter (20 books), Ger Rijff (18), Joe Tunzi (16)—produce only photograph books.

Prior to Elvis's death, Lichter was the only one publishing Elvis photograph books. This was in large part due to the tight control maintained by Colonel Tom Parker over photographers' access to Elvis. (Lichter circumvented this by publishing candid photographs taken by fans and independent professional photographers.)

After Elvis's death in August 1977, the appetite for Elvis photographs soared. With it, so did Elvis photograph book publishing continues unabated today.

Of these many books, the photographs of Alfred Wertheimer stand out (*Elvis '56*). In 1956, the year that Elvis exploded across America, Wertheimer was assigned by RCA Records to photograph Elvis. He traveled with Elvis for several months and was the last professional photographer to have such unfettered access. In addition to the unparalleled documentation of Elvis in the benchmark year of his career, Wertheimer's photographs are important for what they show us about 1950s American life. For example, Wertheimer's picture of two African American teenagers seeking Elvis's autograph ("Sign My Book"), speaks volumes about Elvis's contribution to the twentieth century's changing racial attitudes.

---

[1] Elvis publishing authority Jerry Osborne, explaining the photograph books' popularity, Aug 14, 1998.

Other notable photograph books were compiled by photojournalists who covered Elvis. (*See* John Reggero, Jim Reid, and Guy Sterling listings in this chapter.) But the most charming of the genre have to be the collections of candids taken by fans. (*See* Shapiro listing in this chapter.)

For fans, the Elvis photograph books keep him—and their youth—alive. For the rest of the world, they are a unique treasure trove of an America where the sun shone on a world of limitless possibilities.

☆   ☆   ☆   ☆

☆ Carbini, Mario, editor

A Big Hunk O' Elvis. **Roma: Elvis Times, 1970. ISBN: none.**

Black and white photographs of Elvis Presley from the 1950s and 1960s. No text.

Source: eBay auction item #94757452

☆ Clark, Alan

Elvis Presley (Number One). **64 pp. ISBN: none.**

"Includes many rare photographs, interviews, etc."

Source: www.arbooks.com/elvisp.html

———.

Elvis Presley Memories. **West Covina, CA: Leap Frog Productions, 1982. ISBN: none.**

Source: Guralnick, Last Train to Memphis, *p. 541.*

———.

The Elvis Presley Photo Album. **West Covina, CA: Alan Clark Productions, 1981. ISBN: none.**

Source: Guralnick, Last Train to Memphis, *p. 541*

☆ Cortez, Diego, editor

Private Elvis. **Stuttgart, Germany: FEY Verlags GmbH, 1978. 198 pp. ISBN: 3883611018.**

Photographs of Elvis Presley during an evening at a Munich, Germany, nightclub in 1959. Text in German and English. (*See* Foreign Language Titles/German.)

Source: Compiler's collection

☆ Curtin, Jim

Curtin has been collecting Elvis memorabilia for more than 35 years, including 25,000 photographs of Elvis. He is the author of six Elvis photograph books with pictures from his collection.

Christmas with Elvis. Nashville, TN: Celebrity Books, 1999. ISBN: 158029104X.

Four hundred photographs of Elvis Presley at Christmas and of Elvis-related Christmas collectibles. Elvis Christmas remembrance essays. Photographs are from Curtin's collection.

Source: OCLC 39739607

———.

Elvis and the Stars: From the Collection of Jim Curtin. Wayne, PA: Morgin Press, Inc., 1993. 144 pp. ISBN: 0963097628.

Author's collection of black and white photographs of Elvis and celebrities from the 1950s though the 1970s. Most are publicity stills or candids taken on the sets of Elvis's television appearances and motion pictures. List of the 179 celebrities featured in the photographs.

Source: Library of Congress ML88.P76 E43 1993

———.

The Elvis Scrapbook. A Citadel Press Book. Seacacus, NJ: Carol Publishing Group, 1994. ISBN: 0806515317.

According to the author, this book was pulled from publication and has not been released.

Source: Jim Curtin

☆ Early, Donna Presley, and Edie Hand, with Susie Pritchett

Donna Presley Early is Elvis's first cousin. She is the daughter of Elvis's aunt Nash Presley Pritchett. (*See* Pritchett listing in the The Man/Memoirs and Memories.) As a teenager and young adult, Early spent time at Graceland.

Precious Family Memories of Elvis. [U.S.]: self-published, 1997. 64 pp. ISBN: 0965700801.

Features 53 black and white photos of Elvis and other family members, from the authors' collection. Photographs span Elvis's life, career, and death and are accompanied by relevant Bible verses.

Source: Memphis/Shelby County (TN) Public Library and Information Center

☆ "Elvis: The Colonel's King." *Memphis* (July/Aug 1992): 46–55.

Never-before-seen black and white candid photographs from the personal collection of Colonel Tom Parker.

☆ "Elvis—A Different Kind of Idol." *Life* (Aug 27, 1956): 101, 106–109.

Some of the best photographs of the intense passions and devotion that Elvis inspired in his fans: screaming and clutching at his clothes, picking blades of grass on his front lawn, as well as the religious controversy stirred by Elvis. Brief text relates to Elvis's impact on teenage girls and the "indecency controversy" surrounding 1956 Jacksonville, Florida, concerts. Photographers include the legendary Alfred Wertheimer.

☆ *Elvis Presley in Paris, 1959*. Paris: Panam Productions, 1986. [48] pp. ISBN: none.

Black and white photographs from Elvis's 1959 vacation in Paris, while he was serving in the army. No text. Photographs are not captioned or credited.

Source: The University of Mississippi
OCLC 27878157

☆ *Elvis Presley—1935-1977: A Tribute to the King*. "Elvis Goodbye." Wednesbury, West Midlands, UK: Bavie Publications, 1977. 5 Vols. [35] leaves. ISBN: none.

Five volumes, unpaged, consisting primarily of black and white photographs. The 1975 photographs are credited to J. Rock Caile; the ones from 1966–1967, to John Herman. The remaining photographs are by others and have been reproduced elsewhere. Between one and five poems in each volume, copyrighted by A. R. Naphray. (*See* Naphray listing in The Phenomena/Poetry.)

Source: New York Public Library JNF 83-95
Trinity College Library, Dublin, Ireland: PX-10-873.
OCLC 4466337

Note: The British Library has each volume catalogued separately, as follows: Vol. I–X. 435/610, Vol. II–X.435/613, Vol. III–X.435/604, Vol. IV–X.435/611, Vol.V–X.435.612.

☆ *Elvis Presley: The Rebel Years: Photographed During the Fantastic Years of the King of Rock 'n' Roll, 1954-1960*. Schirmer's Visual Library. New York: W. W. Norton and Company, Inc., 1994. 120 pp. ISBN: 0393316254.

English translation of *Elvis Presley: Tutti Frutti Oder Die Allgemeine Erektion der Herzne: Photographen aus den Wunderbaren Jahren des Konigs des Rock 'n' Roll 1954-1960*, (1990). (*See* Foreign Language Titles/German.)
   Primarily photographs of Elvis during 1954–1960. Sixty-four duotone and color photographs; credited and captioned. Introductory essay, "Where Were You When Elvis Died?" by Lester Bangs, first appeared in the *Village Voice* (Aug 28, 1977). Brief chronology of Elvis's life. Discography (1954–1960). Filmography with plots, stars, and discussion of songs from the films *Love Me Tender* (1956), *Loving You* (1957), *Jailhouse Rock* (1957), and *King Creole* (1958). Bibliography listing 13 Elvis titles.

Source: New York Public Library JME 98-482
OCLC 37160780

☆ *Elvis: Sixteen Glossy Photos*. Montrose, CO: Thurston Moore Country, Ltd., 1978. Unpaged. ISBN: none.

Small, previously seen portrait photographs of Elvis Presley throughout his career. Spiral-bound booklet, measuring $4\frac{1}{2}'' \times 3\frac{1}{4}''$.

Source: Compiler's collection.

☆ *Elvis Still Lives.* Australia: Stag Publishing Co., 1977. 52 pp.

Brief text and 72 photographs of Elvis Presley. Photographs and text credited to Cinema International Corporation.

Source: eBay auction item #127133902

☆ Eriksson, Sven-Ake

Elvis Presley: Today, Tomorrow and Forever. 20th Anniversary 1977–1997. [n.p.]: [n.p.], [n.d.]. Unpaged. ISBN: none.

Black and white photographs (mostly movie and publicity stills), accompanied by a fictional letter from Elvis explaining his career and style, dated 1969. Reproduction of Elvis's handwritten and signed copy of a passage from *The Infinite Way,* on Las Vegas Hilton stationery.

Source: Compiler's collection

☆ Esposito, Joe, and Darwin Lamm

Esposito was a friend and aide to Elvis from 1960 until Elvis's death in 1977. Lamm is the publisher and editor of *Elvis International* magazine, formerly known as *Elvis International Forum.*

Elvis . . . Intimate and Rare: Memories and photos from the personal collection of Joe Esposito. Thousand Oaks, CA: Elvis International Forum Books, 1997. 100 pp. ISBN: none.

Memories and photographs of Elvis Presley from the personal collection of Elvis's longtime friend Joe Esposito. Approximately 400 photographs, including those taken during the *Elvis: Aloha from Hawaii* television special, as well as karate practices and concerts in Las Vegas. Index.

Source: OCLC 37759425

☆ Fox, Sharon R.

Fox has been an Elvis Presley fan since the 1950s. She is the compiler of *Elvis: His Real Life in the 60s. (See* The Man/Reference.) She co-authored *The Elvis Album. (See* DeNight listing in The Man/Reference.)

Elvis: He Touched My Life! A Selection from the Photo Collection of Sharon R. Fox. Chicago: self-published, 1978. Unpaged. ISBN: none.

Full-page black and white photographs of Elvis Presley. Four from the author's collection, the remainder from previously seen sources.

Source: The Michael Ochs Archives, Venice, CA

☆ Hannaford, Jim

For more than 15 years, Hannaford has been one of the leading dealers in Elvis Presley memorabilia. He has an extensive collection of Elvis photographs and works closely with other Elvis photograph book producers.

"Elvis: Golden Ride on the Mystery Train," Vol. I. Alva, OK: Jim Hannaford Publications, 1986. 96 pp. ISBN: none.

Black and white candid and still photographs of Elvis Presley from Hannaford's collection. Most are captioned. Essay on Elvis's impact. (Listings for Volumes II and III follow.)

Source: Collection of Bill and Connie Burk, Memphis, TN

———.

"Elvis: Golden Ride on the Mystery Train," Vol. II. Alva, OK: Jim Hannaford Productions, 1991. 80 pp. ISBN: none.

In addition to photographs, this book contains essays and memories about Elvis Presley, written by Hannaford. Topics include fan clubs, Colonel Parker, Elvis memorabilia, and Elvis Week memories. Others written by fans telling how they met Elvis. Black and white candid photographs; captioned and credited.

Source: Compiler's collection

———.

"Elvis: Golden Ride on the Mystery Train," Vol. III. Alva, OK: Jim Hannaford Productions, 1994. 80 pp. ISBN: none.

A collection of Hannaford's memories of Elvis Weeks and Elvis's Las Vegas concerts, as well as reproduced ads and letters relating to Elvis, and black and white candid photographs; captioned and credited.

Source: Compiler's collection

☆ Israel, Marvin

Israel was art director of *Seventeen* and *Harper's Bazaar* magazines and mentor to noted photographers Diane Arbus and Richard Avedon.

Elvis Presley/1956. New York: Harry N. Abrams, Inc., 1998. 96 pp. ISBN: 0810908999.

A collection of 61 photographs taken in 1956 by the author, showing Elvis Presley in Dayton, Ohio; at home on Audubon Drive; and in New York City for the premiere of *Love Me Tender.* With the exception of two photographs that appeared in *Seventeen* magazine, these "never before published" pictures were discovered after Israel's death in 1984.

☆ Kricun, Morrie E., and Virginia M. Kricun

Elvis 1956 Reflections. Wayne, PA: Morgin Press, 1991, 1992. 182 pp. ISBN: 0963097601.

"Over 100" black and white photographs and news and magazine article reprints focusing on Elvis in 1956. The photographs are from an August 18, 1956, photo shoot of Elvis in the Hollywood Knickerbocker Hotel. According to the authors, "a few" of the photographs had been previously published in *Elvis Answers Back*. (*See* The Man/Elvis in Quotes.)

Discography of titles (with record numbers) both recorded and released by Elvis in 1956. Concert and performance listings for 1956. Brief bibliography. Lists of songs, cast, and production crew for *Love Me Tender*, the only Elvis film in 1956. Annotated chronology of 1956 newspaper and periodical articles about Elvis.

Source: Library of Congress ML88.P76 K7 1992

☆ *The Last Vacation.* Memphis, TN: Graceland Associates, 1978. 12 pp. ISBN: none.

An 8½″ × 11″ booklet with photographs and narratives of Elvis Presley's last vacation taken in Hawaii, March 1977.

Source: Elvis Presley Enterprises, Inc., Archives

☆ *The Legend of Elvis.* Goodlettsville, TN: Southern Post Card Company of America, 1989. Unpaged. ISBN: none.

Brief folio of black and white and color photographs spanning Elvis Presley's performing career, from the archives of Elvis Presley Enterprises, Inc. No text.

Source: Compiler's collection

☆ Presley, Dee

The Elvis Family Photo Album. [U.S.]: [Jimmy Velvet], 1998. [50] pp.

A book of photographs from the personal collection of Elvis Presley's stepmother, Dee Presley, who was married to Elvis's father, Vernon, from 1960–1977. The book is covered in velvet and tied with a gold cord so that it resembles a photograph album. Originally announced in 1997 as *Dee Presley's Family Album*.

Source: eBay auction item #253945581

☆ Reid, Jim

Reid photographed Elvis extensively during his 28 years as a staff photographer for the *Memphis Press-Scimitar*.

Fond Memories of Elvis: 1954–1977, Twenty-Three Years of Photos, Vol. I. Memphis, TN: James R. Reid, 1980. 42 pp. ISBN: none. Reprinted in 1989, 1990. Revised and reprinted in 1992 and 1994. 52 pp. ISBN: none. *Fond Memories of Elvis: 1954–1977, Twenty-Three Years of Photos*, Vol. II. Memphis, TN: James R. Reid, 1991. Unpaged. ISBN: none.

Former Memphis newspaper photographer's black and white pictures of Elvis Presley, from the 1950s through Elvis's funeral in 1977. Photographs are captioned. Volume II contains additional photographs from Reid's collection, as well as a copy of Elvis's birth certificate and the earliest known photograph of Elvis.

Source: Memphis/Shelby County (TN) Public Library and Information Center
Library of Congress 784.540092 P934 XRE
OCLC NO 18111878 (1980)

☆ Rijff, Ger, and Jan van Gestel

Fire in the Sun. Amsterdam: Tutti Frutti, 1991. 144 pp. ISBN: 1561820369. Wilmington, DE: Atomium Books, Inc., 1991. ISBN: 1561820369.

Photographs (credited) from Elvis's 1950s performances and recording sessions, his 1956 Las Vegas appearance, and his army years. Text by Jan van Gestel, who explores the feelings evoked by Elvis.

Source: Michael Ochs Archives, Venice, CA (Tutti Frutti)
Barnesandnoble.com (Atomium)

☆ Rijff, Ger, Alfred Wertheimer, and Jan van Gestel

Elvis Presley: Songs of Innocence. Amsterdam, The Netherlands: Tutti Frutti, 1995. 113 pp.

Alfred Werteimer's sepia-toned photographs of Elvis Presley at the RCA recording studios in July 1956. Essay on Wertheimer's perspective of the photo shoot. Text about the sessions by Jan van Gestel.

Source: Collection of Connie and Bill Burk, Memphis, TN

☆ Shapiro, Angela, and Jerome Shapiro, editors

Candidly Elvis. [n.p.]: Anje Publishing Co., Inc., 1978. Unpaged. ISBN: none.

Compilation of candid color photographs from the 1970s, taken by Elvis Presley fans. Few captions; none credited. "Tombstone Eulogy" poem by Vernon Presley is on the back cover. Reproductions of Elvis's high school diploma and of his and Priscilla Presley's marriage certificate. This book was also published with a burgundy leather cover.

Source: Michael Ochs Archives, Venice, CA

☆ Shaver, Sean, and Hal Noland

As a freelance photographer, Sean Shaver shot Elvis at concerts and public appearances from 1967 to 1977. During this time, he estimates that he took 75,000–80,000 pictures. Charlie Hodge was a longtime Elvis friend. Dick Grob worked as a security guard for Elvis in the 1970s. Billy Smith is Elvis's first cousin on his mother's side and was close to Elvis all of his life.

The Life of Elvis Presley. With Intimate Memories of Charlie Hodge, Dick Grob, and Billy Smith. New York: Time Publishing, Inc., 1979. 300 pp. ISBN: 0960282602.

"Over 300" color and black and white candid photographs of Elvis on stage and interacting with fans, from the early 1950s until his death. The 1950s photographs are attributed to Alfred Wertheimer. (*See* listing later in this chapter.) Biographical essay concentrates upon Elvis's touring years. Hodge, Grob, and Smith comment on Elvis's romances, his childhood, his health, how he relaxed, why he stopped wearing capes, his sense of humor, and life at Graceland. Discography (pp. 286–293).

Source: Library of Congress ML420.P96 S5
Dewey Decimal 784/.092/ 4 B
OCLC 5749806

✩ Shaw, Sid, compiler

Shaw is the editor of *Elvisly Yours* monthly magazine.

Rare Elvis: Volume One; The Very Best of "Elvisly Yours." London: Elvisly Yours Ltd., 1990. 96 pp. ISBN: 1869941047.

A collection of "all the best photographs, stories, and fun taken from 10 years of *Elvisly Yours* magazine" (from back cover). 73 black and white, full-page candids and motion picture stills from the *Elvisly Yours* files. No captions. Stories, word games, letters, and poems about Elvis.

Source: Dewey Decimal 782.42166092
OCLC 26355751

✩ *Studio B Blues—Elvis.* [U.S.]: Straight to the Moon Publications, 1998. 112 pp. ISBN: none.

More than 100 previously unpublished black and white photographs from the recording session for "I Want You, I Need You, I Love You," April 14, 1956, in Nashville, Tennessee. Additional black and white photographs from 1956, as well as press clippings.

Source: www.arbooks.com

✩ *The Unseen Elvis: Candids of the King from the Collection of Jim Curtin.* "A Bullfinch Press Book." Boston: Little, Brown, 1992. 207 pp. ISBN: 082121912X (hdk.). ISBN: 0821220659 (pbk.). London: Victor Gollancz, 1992. ISBN: 0575053674.

More than 400 previously unpublished black and white and color photographs of Elvis Presley. Covers Elvis's life and career from the 1950s through 1977. Overview biographical essay for each section.

✩ Wertheimer, Alfred, and Gregory Martinelli

Elvis '56: In the Beginning. New York: Macmillan, 1979, 1994; Stanmore, New South Wales: Cassell Australia, 1979. ISBN: none. London: Cassell, 1979. ISBN: none. London: Plexus, 1989. ISBN: none. London: Pimlico, 1994. ISBN: none.

This book was translated into German. (*See* Foreign Language Titles/German.)

Elvis Presley Picture Postcard Books

☆ *Elvis Presley: Book of 30 Postcards.* Wigston, Leicester England: Magna Books, 1992. Unpaged. ISBN: 1854223240.

Source: OCLC 40928482

☆ *Elvis: 20 Classic Picture Postcards.* London: Bloomsbury Books, 1994. Unpaged. ISBN: 185471420.

Twenty black and white postcard film and public relations stills.

Source: Collection of Bill and Connie Burk, Memphis, TN

☆ Marriott, John

Elvis Presley: Classic Postcard Collection. London: Pyramid, 1990. Unpaged. ISBN: 1855100576.

Source: Cambridge University Library (UK) B1990.1087

Elvis Presley Poster Books

These are books containing large photographs of Elvis Presley, which can be removed and used as posters.

☆ *Elvis Poster Book: A Book of 20 Tear-Out Posters.* 20 leaves. 1987. ISBN: none.

An 11½" × 17" book of 20 full-color, tear-out posters of Elvis Presley.

Source: eBay auction item #29105649

☆ *Elvis Presley Poster Book, New Series.* [22] leaves. New York: Prime Press/Nostalgia Press, 1977. ISBN: 0878970517.

A 16½" × 12" book of full-page color posters of Elvis Presley. No text.

Source: Bowling Green State University (OH) Library (ovsz) ML420.P96 E467
OCLC 3163706

☆ *Elvis Presley Poster Book*, Vols. 1 and 2. New York: Prime Press, 1977. ISBN: 0878970509 (Vol. 1). ISBN: 0517532972 (Vol. 2).

Full-page color posters of Elvis Presley.

Source: Bowling Green State University (OH) Library (Vol. 1) (ovsz) ML420.P96 E4669
(Vol. 1)
OCLC 3613726 (Vol. 1) (Vol. 2)

☆ *Elvis Tear-Out Photo Book.* London: Oliver Books, 1993. [40] pp. ISBN: 1870049837.

Twenty 9″ × 11½″ color and black and white photographs of Elvis Presley in performance or in publicity stills; none credited. Brief chronological notes on the highlights of Elvis's life and career.

Source: New York Public Library MWES (Presley, E.) 97-10173
OCLC 37511306

Photographs of Concert and Television Appearances

☆ Brown, Christopher

As a teenager, Brown attended and photographed 29 Elvis Presley concerts. These two books are a compilation of Brown's photographs.

Elvis in Concert. Ajax, Ontario, Canada: C. Brown, 1993. 249 pp. ISBN: none.

A show-by-show photographic review of Elvis Presley's concert tours from June 24, 1974, through June 25, 1977. These include the 1976 New Year's Eve concert (Pontiac, Michigan) and the 1977 concert (Ann Arbor, Michigan), where segments of Elvis's *Moody Blue* LP were recorded. All photographs are captioned and were taken by Brown, unless otherwise credited.

Source: Publisher: C. Brown, 50 Dominy Drive, Ajax, Ontario, Canada, L1T 3B9

————.

On Tour with Elvis. Ajax, Ontario, Canada: C. Brown, 1991. 225 pp. ISBN: 0969550200.

Photographs from Elvis Presley's May 30 through June 10, 1975, concert tour. Text describes Brown's experiences while attending these concerts. Included are reproductions of ticket stubs, newspaper reviews (cited), and venue seating plans for each of the concerts. With the exception of the photographs accompanying newspaper reviews and ads, all others were taken by the author and are sourced as to date and location.

Source: OCLC 26853144

☆ Burk, Bill E.

Bill Burk covered Elvis for the *Memphis Press-Scimitar* from 1956 to 1977. He has written 12 books about Elvis.

Elvis in Canada. Memphis, TN: Propwash Publishing, 1996. 66 pp. ISBN: 1879207249.

Photographs and the story of Elvis Presley's only concerts outside of the United States—in 1957 in Toronto and Ottawa, Canada. "More than 60 extremely rare photographs"; captioned and credited. Bibliography. No index.

Source: Memphis/Shelby County (TN) Public Library and Information Center
OCLC 35689514

☆ Cross, Ricky, and Charles Wittkopp

Elvis in Tidewater. [U.S.]: [n.p.], 1982. 32 pp. ISBN: none.

A compendium of photographs and eye-witness accounts of Elvis's seven appearances in the Tidewater area of Virginia, 1955–1976.

Source: eBay auction item #248658723

☆ de Wit, Simon

Auld Lang Syne: Elvis's Legendary New Year's Eve Show in Pittsburgh, PA, 1976. Elvis Presley: The Live Series, Vol. I. Rotterdam, NL: Simon de Wit Productions, 1995. [87] pp. ISBN: 9075534019.

Black and white photographs of Elvis Presley's New Year's Eve 1976 concert in Pittsburgh, Pennsylvania—which fans consider to be his last great performance. Photographs are captioned but not credited. One page of text relating to the concert. Brief essay by Elvis's friend and security guard Sam Thompson, recalling his memories of that night.

————.

King of Vegas. Rotterdam, The Netherlands: Simon de Wit Publications, [n.d.]. 90 pp. ISBN: none.

A self-published, detailed account of Elvis Presley's July 1969 to December 1976 performances in Las Vegas. Transcripts of press conferences related to some of the performances. Black and white candid photographs of Elvis on stage and with fans.

Source (for both de Wit books): Publisher's address: Box 3170, 300 3AD Rotterdam, The Netherlands

☆ *Elvis: Adios, the Final Performance.* Luxembourg: Eternal Flame Productions, 1993. 63 pp. ISBN: none.

Photographs and text about Elvis Presley's final concert, June 26, 1977, in Indianapolis, Indiana. Text is from Jerry Hopkins's *Elvis: The Final Years.* Photographs by Elvis photographers David Reynolds, Bob Heis, Len Leech, Terry Hartman, and Sean Shaver.

Source: Elvis Presley Enterprises, Inc.

☆ *Elvis: A Pictorial Tribute; The Last Tour.* [U.S.]: Star Fleet Productions, Inc., 1977.

An eight-panel foldout with an Elvis poster on one side and, on the other, color photographs from Elvis's June 21, 1977, concert in Rapid City, South Dakota. Commentary from Elvis's stepbrother David Stanley.

Source: Compiler's collection

☆ *Elvis in Canada.* Lennoxville, Quebec, Canada: Live Productions, [n.d.]. 22 pp. ISBN: none.

Includes 22 black and white candid photographs of Elvis Presley, performing at concerts in Ottawa and Vancouver, Canada, in 1957. Photographs are undated and not credited or captioned.

Source: OCLC 20738826
Publisher's address: Live Productions, PO Box 127, Lennoxville, Quebec, Canada, JIM IZ4

☆ *Elvis Now.* Livonia, MI: [Strictly Elvis], [n.d.]. [20] pp. ISBN: none.

A pamphlet of black and white photographs of Elvis Presley in concert during the 1970s. Text consists of an unsigned introduction, indicating that "this is an extra from *Strictly Elvis* magazine" (inside front cover). Photographs are non-specifically credited.

Source: Compiler's collection
Strictly Elvis address (as printed in publication): 35244 Parkdale, Livonia, MI 48150

☆ *Elvis on TV.* [n.p.]: [n.p.], [n.d.]. 31 pp. ISBN: none.

Text and black and white photographs relating to Elvis Presley's appearances on television, from the *Louisiana Hayride* in 1955 to the *Aloha from Hawaii* special in 1973.

Source: Compiler's collection

☆ *Elvis World Presents a Tenth Anniversary Tribute to Elvis at Madison Square Garden . . . : A Souvenir Scrapbook.* Bound Brook, N.J.: Elvis World,[2] 1982. 56 pp.

A collection of photographs from Elvis Presley's Madison Square Garden concerts in New York City, June 1972.

Source: OCLC 28753061

☆ Heffernan, Bill

The First Year: 1954–1955. [n.p.]: [n.p.], [n.d.]. 6 leaves. ISBN: none.

A six-page pamphlet of 1954–1956 black and white publicity stills of Elvis Presley, his original bassist, Bill Black, and his original guitarist, Scotty Moore. Black and white reproductions of Elvis's concert posters from that period. Reproduction of contract between Scotty Moore and Elvis, naming Moore as Elvis's manager.

Source: Compiler's collection

☆ Leviton, Jay B., and Ger J. Rijff

Leviton is a photographer whose work has appeared in major news magazines. When the photographs in this book were taken, he was on assignment for *Collier's* magazine. Publication of *Collier's* ceased before the pictures could be run.

---

[2]*Elvis World* magazine appeared briefly in the early 1980s. It is not to be confused with *Bill E. Burk's Elvis World* magazine, which has been publishing since 1985.

Elvis Close-Up: Rare, Intimate, Unpublished Photographs of Elvis Presley in 1956. A Fireside Book. New York: Simon & Schuster, 1988. 35 pp. ISBN: 0671669559. London: Century, 1989. 135 pp. ISBN: 0712629394.

Originally printed as *Florida Close-Up.* (*See* Rijff listing later in this section.) Also printed in Dutch. (*See* Foreign Language Titles/Dutch.)

☆ Lichter, Paul

Paul Lichter has published 20 photograph books on Elvis Presley; the first in 1975, the most recent in 2000.

Elvis, All My Best. Huntingdon Valley, PA: Jesse Books, 1989. 232 pp. ISBN: 0961602759. 1998. ISBN: 0961602791.

Photographs of Elvis Presley in concert in Las Vegas during the 1970s. Text of comments made by Elvis during some of these concerts. According to Lichter, most of these photographs are appearing in print for the first time.

Source: OCLC 20065809 (1989)

———.

Elvis from the City of Brotherly Love to the Big Apple. Apache Junction, AZ: Jesse Books, 2000. ISBN: none.

Photographs from Elvis concerts in Philadelphia and New York City. Forward by Elvis's longtime announcer, Al Dvorin.

Source: Paul Lichter

———.

Elvis Memories: A Love Story. Golden Anniversary Edition (1st edition). Huntingdon Valley, PA: Jesse Books, 1985. [300] pp. ISBN: none.

A photo and essay perspective of Elvis's 1970s concerts. Full-page color and black and white photographs of Elvis performing in jumpsuits. Names given for each jumpsuit, as well as the date and location of each photograph. Comes with 1985 Elvis poster calendar that notes key events in his life, and six color photographs of Elvis in the Eagle jumpsuit. Bound in white leather.

Source: Library of Congress ML88.P76 L5 1985
OCLC 13394401

———.

Elvis, Thank You Very Much. Apache Junction, AZ: Jesse Books, 1998. 144 pp. ISBN: 0961602791.

Color and black and white photographs of Elvis Presley in concert, 1970–1973. Text is "Elvis's own words." Introduction by Jonathon Taurog, Elvis's friend and the son of Norman Taurog, who directed nine of Elvis's motion pictures.

Source: OCLC 41931988

————.

E.P. in Concert. 1997.

Color photographs of Elvis performing in what the author states is "every jumpsuit that Elvis ever wore." This is a limited number collector's edition.

Source: Paul Lichter

————.

The Elvis Presley Memorial Book of Days. [U.S.]: [National Media Marketing], 1978. [13] leaves. Size: 19" × 36."

A 1978 calendar with 13 detachable posters of photographs of Elvis Presley performing in concerts. Brief Elvis history notes for each day.

Source: Compiler's collection

☆ Prince, James D.

The Day Elvis Came to Town. Lexington, NC: Southern Heritage Publishing, 1995. ISBN: none.

Photographs, newspaper clippings, and anecdotes relating to a March 21, 1956, Elvis concert in Lexington, North Carolina. Black and white photographs from author's collection; captioned.

Source: Collection of Bill and Connie Burk, Memphis, TN

☆ Reggero, John

Reggero was a photojournalist whose work has appeared in *Life*, *Us*, *Photoplay*, and *Country Music* magazines.

Elvis in Concert. New York: Delta Special/Lorelei, 1979. Unpaged. ISBN: 0440022193.

The author's photographs from Elvis Presley's June 21, 1977, concert in Rapid City, South Dakota. Concert photographs show Elvis in "The Gypsy Jumpsuit." Introduction by Elvis's stepbrother David Stanley, describing his duties on that day and during the concert.

Source: Library of Congress ML420.P96 R4

☆ Rijff, Ger

Ger Rijff is a prolific Elvis author, compiling and producing 18 Elvis photograph books. A longtime Elvis fan, Rijff served as president of the Dutch Elvis Presley fan club from 1977 to 1984.

Elvis: The Cool King. Amsterdam, The Netherlands: Tutti Frutti, 1989. ISBN: none.

Photo essay of three of Elvis's 1956 concerts in Florida. Photographs by St. Petersburg, Florida, photographer Bob Moreland. Text by Jan van Gestel.

Source: Publication information page, The Cool King.

————.

The Cool King. Wilmington, DE: Atomium Books, 1990. 104 pp. ISBN: 1561820105.

First U.S. edition of *Elvis: The Cool King.*

Source: Dewey Decimal 781.42166092 20
OCLC 23865226

————.

Florida Close-Up. Amsterdam, The Netherlands: Tutti Frutti, 1987. 135 pp. ISBN: none.

The original version of *Elvis Close-Up: Rare, Intimate, Unpublished Photographs of Elvis Presley in 1956.* (*See* Leviton listing in this section and in Foreign Language Titles/Dutch.) More than 120 of American photographer Jay B. Leviton's black and white photographs of Elvis Presley taken before, during, and immediately after his August 8, 1956 concert appearance in Jacksonville, Florida. Includes a photo essay about Elvis and fan Andrea June Stevens, who won *Hitparader* magazine's "Win a Date with Elvis" contest.

Source: Library of Congress ML88.P76 R5 1988
Dewey Decimal 779.978454
OCLC 20708653

☆ Rijff, Ger, Jean Paul Commandeur, and Trevor Cajiao

Shock, Rattle and Roll: Elvis Photographed During the Milton Berle Show: *From the Michael Ochs Archives.* London: Blandford, 1997. 93 pp. ISBN: 0713726903.

Black and white candids of Elvis rehearsing and performing for *The Milton Berle Show* in 1956. Narrative text by Trevor Cajiao.

Source: Library of Congress ML88.P76S58 1997

☆ Rijff, Ger, Linda Jones, and Peter Haan

Steamrolling over Texas. The Netherlands: It's Elvis Time Productions. 1997. ISBN: none.

Black and white and color photographs of Elvis's concerts in Texas during 1969 and the 1970s. Essay by Elvis's back-up singer Kathy Westmoreland with anecdotes about one of the concerts (March 3, 1974).

Source: Loose Ends, Memphis, TN

☆ Rijff, Ger, and Andrew Solt

Sixty Million TV Viewers Can't Be Wrong! Amsterdam, The Netherlands: Tutti Frutti Productions, 1994. 120 pp. ISBN: none.

Black and white photographs from Elvis's performances on *The Ed Sullivan Show.*

Source: Loose Ends, Memphis, TN

☆ Saso, Katsuo, editor

"This Is Elvis" Presents Elvis Presley's Hawaii Special Photo Album. Tokyo, Japan: "This Is Elvis," 1985. 83 pp. ISBN: none.

Black and white candid photographs from Elvis Presley's 1973 *Aloha Special* televised performance in Hawaii, airport arrival, and press conference.

Source: Elvis Presley Enterprises, Inc.

☆ Schittler, Peter, and Thomas Schreiber

San Bernardino. Austria: Bringin' It Back, 1997. 90 pp. ISBN: none

More than 100 photographs of Elvis Presley during two San Bernardino, California, concerts: November 12, 1972, and May 10, 1974. Photographs are credited to fan Mickey Pfleger. (Bringin' It Back is an Austrian fan club.)

Source: Collection of Bill and Connie Burk, Memphis, TN

————.

Unchained Melody. English translation by Gerti Emanthinger. Bringin' It Back Special Edition #2. Vienna, Austria: Bringin' It Back, 1994. 55 pp. ISBN: 3901418016.

A "pictorial concert-review" of Elvis Presley's February 17, 1977, concert in Savannah, Georgia. Text in both German and English. "Many never-before-seen photos" taken by *Savannah Morning News* press photographer Bob Morris. Song list from the concert.

Source: Collection of Bill and Connie Burk, Memphis, TN

☆ Shaver, Sean

As a freelance photographer, Sean Shaver covered Elvis at concerts and public appearances, as well as candidly, on a full-time basis from 1967 to 1977. (Between 1955 and 1967, he photographed him on six occasions.) During this time, Shaver estimates that he took 75,000–80,000 pictures. He is the author of 13 books containing his Elvis photographs.

————.

The Elvis Book, Vol. 1 (1935–1967). The Elvis Book Series. Kansas City, MO: Timur Publishing., [1980]. ISBN: none.

Black and white and color photographs of Elvis Presley's life and concert performances through 1967. Print run of this book was 999 copies.

The Elvis Book, Vol. 2 (1968–1973). The Elvis Book Series. Kansas City, MO: Timur Publishing, 1983. 336 pp. ISBN: 0960282645.

Color photographs of Elvis performing on stage, 1968–1973. Print run of this book was 999 copies.

The Elvis Book, Vol. 3 (1974–1977). The Elvis Book Series. Kansas City, MO: Timur Publishing, 1987. 327 pp. ISBN: 0960282645.

Photographs of Elvis's life from 1974–1977, in text and photographs. Print run of this book was 999 copies.

The Elvis Book, Vol. 4 *The Candid Elvis*. The Elvis Book Series. Kansas City, MO: Timur Publishing, 1991. 176 pp. ISBN: 060282653.

Candid photographs of Elvis Presley from the author's collection.

Source for the series: Sean Shaver

Elvis: Photographing the King. Kansas City, MO: Timur Publishing, 1981. 256 pp. ISBN: 096028267X.

Approximately 100 color and black and white photographs of Elvis Presley in his concert jumpsuits, taken during performances and backstage. First person narrative essay about the author's work in photographing Elvis. Anecdotes from Elvis's friends. Captions for each photograph.

Source: Library of Congress ML88.P76 S5 1981
OCLC NO 10999107

————.

Elvis's Portrait Portfolio. Kansas City, MO: Timur Publishing, 1983. 304 pp. ISBN: 0960282611.

A black and white photograph portfolio of Elvis Presley in concert from 1954 to 1977. None of the pre-1967 photographs are credited. Each photograph captioned; some dated by year. Two foldout 8½″ × 14″ photographs of Elvis on stage.

Source: Library of Congress ML88.P76 S55 1983
OCLC NO 11316147

————.

Elvis Presley: A Pictorial Portfolio.

According to Shaver, this book is erroneously listed in the OCLC as one of his titles.

Source: OCLC 7717843

————.

Elvis Presley: Softly . . . I Must Leave You . . . The Last Few Months! Kansas City, MO: Timur Pub., 1977. [16] pp. ISBN: none.

Full-page, color photographs from Elvis's last tour of 1976 (to Cleveland and Minneapolis) and 1977 tours. Includes Elvis's last concert, June 26, 1977, in Indianapolis, Indiana. Also includes 30 small photographs of Elvis in his jumpsuits and with fans.

Source: The Mississippi Valley Collection, University of Memphis (TN)
OCLC NO: 7717843 (This book is mistakenly titled Elvis Presley: a pictorial book in the OCLC entry.)

————.

Elvis . . . Through My Lens. Kansas City, MO: Timur Pub., 1974. [16] pp. ISBN: none.

Photographs of Elvis Presley in concert in 1974.

Source: OCLC 7717872

☆ Sterling, Guy, and Wayne Deel

At the time of publication, Guy Sterling was a reporter for the Roanoke [VA] *The World News*. Currently, he is a reporter for the Newark [NJ] *The Star-Ledger*. Wayne Deel is an award-winning news photographer who took many of the photographs that appear in this book.

Elvis in Roanoke. Roanoke, VA: Leisure Publishing, 1977. 46 pp. ISBN: none.

A text and black and white photo history of Elvis's appearances in Roanoke, Virginia. Chapters on each concert appearance (1955, 1972, 1974, 1976) and the 1960 train station stop made by Elvis on his way home from Germany. Interviews with Roanoke fans, officials, and concert promoters. Story about the August 24, 1977, memorial concert held in place of the Elvis Presley concert that had been scheduled for that date.

Source: Compiler's collection
OCLC 7717939

☆ Tunzi, Joseph A.

Tunzi has published 18 Elvis Presley photograph books. His books feature introductory essays from individuals who worked with Elvis.

Aloha '73. Chicago: J.A.T. Productions, 1999. ISBN: none.

An updated edition of *Elvis '73, Hawaiian Spirit* with new photographs and text. (*See* listing in this section.)

Source: Joseph A. Tunzi

———.

Elvis: Aloha via Satellite. Chicago: J.A.T. Productions, 1998. ISBN: none.

The second edition of *Elvis '73, Hawaiian Spirit*, published on the twenty-fifth anniversary of Elvis Presley's 1973 Hawaii-based television special. Candids of Elvis on stage and with fans. Includes the BMG CD, *Elvis: Aloha via Satellite* (DPC 12214), with tracks from the special.

Source: Collection of Bill and Connie Burk, Memphis, TN

———.

Elvis, Encore Performance: Rare, Unpublished Photographs of Elvis Presley in 1972. Chicago: J.A.T. Productions, 1990. 103 pp. ISBN: 0962008311.

A black and white photographic essay of a 1972 Elvis Presley concert in Chicago, Illinois. Introduction by Joan Deary, the RCA Records executive in charge of the Elvis catalogue until her retirement in 1987.

Source: Library of Congress ML88.P76 T8 1990
Dewey Decimal 782/42166/092 20
OCLC 22208363

———.

Elvis, Encore Performance II: In the Garden. Chicago: J.A.T. Productions, 1993. 97 pp. ISBN: 0962008346.

A black and white photographic essay of Elvis Presley's June 6, 1972, concert in New York's Madison Square Garden. Transcript of the pre-concert press conference. Text from *The New York Times* articles about the concert.

Introduction by Glen D. Hardin, a pianist and musical arranger for Elvis.

Source: Library of Congress ML88.P76 T82 1993.
OCLC 27898285

———.

Elvis, Encore Performance III: Back to Chicago—1977. Chicago: J.A.T. Productions, 1999. ISBN: none.

Steve Yach's photographs from the 1977 Elvis Presley concert in Chicago.

Source: Tom Sanocki, Chicago, IL

————.

Elvis, Highway 51 South, Memphis, Tennessee: Featuring the June 10, 1975, and the July 5, 1976, concerts at the Mid-South Coliseum. Chicago: J.A.T. Productions, 1995. 119 pp. ISBN: 0962008389.

A photo essay about two of Elvis Presley's Memphis concerts in 1975 and 1976. Reviews of these concerts from the Memphis *Commercial Appeal.* Black and white photographs by Ken Ross, a photographer for the *Memphis Press-Scimitar* for 25 years, during which he covered Elvis Presley. Introduction by former Elvis drummer Ronnie Tutt.

Source: Library of Congress ML8.P76 E44 1995
Dewey Decimal 782.42166/092 20
OCLC 32432353

————.

Elvis '70: Bringing Him Back! Chicago: J.A.T. Productions, 1994. 102 pp. ISBN: 0962008362.

Reviews and black and white photographs of Elvis Presley concert appearances in 1970, from the *Houston Post, Houston Chronicle, Detroit News,* and *Los Angeles Herald Examiner.* Photographs are captioned and credited. Introduction by David Briggs, who played piano and keyboard accompaniment for Elvis.

Source: Library of Congress ML88.P76 T785 1994
Dewey Decimal 782.42166/092 20
OCLC 30972647

————.

Elvis '74, Enter the Dragon. Chicago: J.A.T. Productions, 1996. 101 pp. ISBN: 1888464003.

Black and white photographs of Elvis Presley in his dragon-themed concert jumpsuit. Foreword by Bill Belew, the designer of Elvis's concert jumpsuits and capes, as well as his personal wardrobe.

Source: Library of Congress ML88.P96 E4 1996
Dewey Decimal 782.42166/092 B 21
OCLC 37770562

————.

Elvis '73, Hawaiian Spirit. Chicago: J.A.T. Productions, 1992. 103 pp. ISBN: 0962008338.

A photographic journal of Elvis Presley's April 1973 television special, *Elvis: Aloha from Hawaii,* which was beamed by satellite from Hawaii to 36 countries. Press concert transcripts, including a question and answer period with Elvis at the concert announcement in

September 1972. Black and white and color photographs of the concert's press conferences, rehearsals, and the performance, plus candids of Elvis with his fans. Photographs from the NBC Television Network and Reiko Yukawa of Hawaii.

Source: Library of Congress ML88.P76 T79 1992
Dewey Decimal 782.42166/092 20
OCLC 26723610

————.

J.A.T. Publishing Presents Tiger Man, Elvis '68. Chicago: J.A.T. Productions, 1997. 124 pp. ISBN: 188846402X.

Photographs and text (including production notes and schedules) relating to preparations, rehearsal, and taping of the NBC-TV/Singer Company's *Elvis* program, which aired on December 3, 1968. Introduction by the show's producer, Steve Binder.

Source: Library of Congress ML88.P96 T89 1997
OCLC 39485221

————.

Elvis '69, The Return. Chicago: J.A.T. Productions, 1991. 106 pp. ISBN: 096200832X.

A photo essay about Elvis's return to concert touring in July of 1969. Introduction by Bruce Banke, former Director of Publicity/Public Relations of the Las Vegas, Nevada, Hilton Hotel, and a close friend of Elvis's manager, Colonel Tom Parker. Black and white photographs of the concert's press conference, as well as Elvis performing on stage at the Hilton.

Source: Library of Congress ML88.P76 T78 1991
Dewey Decimal 782.42166/092 20
OCLC 23255878

————.

Elvis, Standing Room Only, 1970–1975. Chicago: J.A.T. Productions, 1994. 150 pp. ISBN: 092008370.

Photographs and interviews with Elvis Presley from selected concerts, 1970–1975. Concert logistics lists. Black and white and color candid photographs. Introduction by James Burton, a former guitar player for Elvis.

Source: Library of Congress ML88.P76 T85 1994
Dewey Decimal 782.42166/092 20
OCLC 31815548

————.

Photographs and Memories. Chicago: J.A.T. Productions, 1998. 111 pp. ISBN: 1888464038.

More than 100 previously unpublished photographs—candids and posed—of Elvis, from the 1950s through the early 1970s. A performance photograph section and a color photograph section. Text includes memoirs of people associated with Elvis. Introduction by Ray Walker from Elvis's backup group, The Jordanaires.

Source: Library of Congress ML88.P76 T895 1998
Dewey Decimal 782.42166/092 B 21
OCLC 39539174

Concert Tour Souvenir Photo Albums/Folios

Souvenir booklets have long been a staple of live performances, from Broadway stage shows to outdoor arena concerts. They are usually sold only at the performance and consist of photographs and brief text. The Elvis Presley concert booklets (first called "souvenir photo albums" and later "souvenir folios") faithfully trace his concert career—with publication in the 1950s and again in the 1970s, when Elvis returned to live performing after a decade hiatus.

Six of these albums/folios were sold in the 1950s, each relating to a tour of which Elvis was the star or was on the billing. There is only one for the 1960s as he did not perform live until 1969. In the 1970s, the Elvis concert photo folios were issued annually until his death. There were seven of them, consisting of 10–20 pages of photographs of Elvis and advertisements for future Elvis concerts.[3] The two Elvis Presley Enterprises, Inc., concerts in the 1990s—"Elvis the Tribute" (1995) and "Elvis in Concert '97" (1997)—had accompanying souvenir folios.

☆   ☆   ☆   ☆

(In chronological order)

☆ *The Hank Snow Show Souvenir Photo Album.* 1955.

Elvis, Scotty Moore, and Bill Black were on this tour. Elvis had a full-page publicity photograph and a brief biography in this album. Hank Snow is on the cover.

Source: Cotten, Lee, The Elvis Catalog, p. 18.

☆ *Elvis, the Rockin' Rebel: Live in '55 Concert Photo Booklet.* 1955.

Includes 16 pages of black and white photographs of Elvis. (Note: Although this title is listed in the OCLC database, it is unclear as to whether or not its date of publication and/or title are accurate. The compiler has been unable to locate a copy of this booklet or further information about it.)

---

[3]Because these are for the most part identical, each contained previously seen photographs and no information about the singers, musicians, and venues of the concerts—they are not listed here.

Source: OCLC 7717904

☆ *Elvis Presley Souvenir Picture Album.* Jan–Apr 1956.

Subtitle: "Country music's 'Mr. Rhythm' sensational new RCA Victor singing star." Elvis head-shot photograph on the cover and on three pages. Photos of other stars who were on this tour.

Source: Cotten, Lee, The Elvis Catalog, *p. 37.*

Souvenir Photo Albun (sic): Elvis Presley (Mr. Dynamite) RCA Victor Artist. ("All material prepared by ELVIS PRESLEY'S Advertising and Promotion Dept.") [U.S.]: [n.p.], 1956. 12 pp.

Believed to be the first tour booklet devoted solely to Elvis. On the front cover, the word "Album" is misspelled as "Albun." From front cover: "Dynamic Star of Television, Records, Radio and Movies"; "The Nation's Only Atomic Powered Singer." Black and white photographs taken in 1955 and 1956 of Elvis on stage, making personal appearances, with fans, and at home with his parents in the Audubon Drive house in Memphis.

Source: The University of Mississippi Archives
OCLC 12546932

Elvis Presley: Souvenir Photo Album. 12 pp. Nov 1956.

Includes 13 black and white, 8″ x 10″ publicity portraits of Elvis. Reprint of Elvis's 1956 film and recording resume. Front and back covers are full-color publicity headshots of Elvis from his first film, *Love Me Tender.*

Source: Library of Congress ML 420 P96

Elvis Presley Photo Folio. 1957.

The final concert tour booklet of the 1950s. Cover has a blue-tinted publicity head shot from *Jailhouse Rock.* This had two printings: in the second, the original back cover, which advertised *Jailhouse Rock,* was changed to promote the *Elvis Golden Records* album which was issued in 1958. This folio was also sold by mail.

Source: Cotten, Lee. All Shook Up: Elvis Day by Day, *1954–1977.*

Elvis the Tribute. [28] pp. Oct 1995.

Mostly photographs of the entertainers who performed at this event, including Chet Atkins, Tony Bennett, Jerry Lee Lewis, Iggy Pop, and Carl Perkins.

Source: Compiler's collection

Elvis in Concert '97. 18 pp. Aug 16, 1997.

Black and white and color photographs of Elvis in concert in the 1950s and 1970s.

Source: Compiler's collection

See Also:

In The Man/Memoirs and Memories:

Shaver, Sean, *Elvis in Focus.*

In The Music, The Movies/Concerts and Television Appearances:

Bailye, I. R., *Elvis: The T.V. Years.*

In The Music, The Movies/Discography:

Elvis '56.

In The Music, The Movies/Filmography:

Rijff, Ger, Jan van Gestel, and Lloyd Shearer, *Elvis Presley: Memphis Lonesome.*

CHAPTER 11
Reference

LITERATURE CONTAINING Elvis Presley facts and trivia began appearing in print almost as soon as he did. Fans hungered for the most microscopic details of his life, and as the years progressed, this voracious appetite expanded to include the minutest aspects of his films, concerts, and recordings. (*See* The Music, The Movies/Discography, Filmography.) As Elvis interest increased posthumously, this appetite spread beyond his fans, reaching the worlds of media, academia, and popular culture.

Unfortunately, as the reference literature expanded, its accuracy did not. Many authors have used misinformation gathered and promulgated by others without verification. In addition, the sheer volume of facts has caused errors to be overlooked. The result has been everything from incorrect house addresses to misidentification of Elvis's family and friends to misleading versions of his life's events. For example, many reference authors still cite the story of Elvis's first guitar as a purchase made in lieu of a bicycle. This despite the prominent display of the salesman's notarized letter detailing the purchase, in the Tupelo (Mississippi) Booth Hardware Store. On exhibit since 1980, the letter clearly states that the then 11-year-old Elvis had his heart set on a rifle.

Most notable among the erroneous Elvis reference books is Patricia Jobe Pierce's *The Ultimate Elvis*, of which on-line Elvis book reviewer David Neale bemoaned, "Has there ever been a more mistake-ridden book about Elvis?"[1] A number of other authors—either through ignorance or laziness—have used Pierce's information rather than researching first-hand, resulting in publishing embarrassments such as Greenwood Press's *The Printed Elvis* by Steven Opdyke. (*See* The Phenomena/Bibliographies.)

However, problems such as these should now be a thing of the past with the publication of Elvis biographer Peter Guralnick and Elvis musicologist Ernst Jorgensen's *Elvis Day by Day*. This book was created after extensive research, as well as unprecedented access to the archives of Elvis Presley Enterprises, Inc. It stands as the single most accurate and informative reference book about Elvis.

As a body, the reference books provide both a destination and a beginning for the exploration of Elvis and the world in which he lived. Just double-check the facts.

---

[1]www.geocities.com/SunsetStrip/8200/books.html

☆　　☆　　☆　　☆

☆ Aros, Andrew A.

At the time of publication, Andrew Aros was a librarian at the Rosemead (CA) Public Library.

Elvis: His Films and Recordings. **Diamond Bar, CA: Applause Publications, 1980. ISBN: 0932352014.**

A three-part reference work: 1) a discography of Elvis's albums through 1979; 2) a selective (27-title) bibliography annotating the author's selection of "major written works about Elvis" through 1979; 3) a filmography of all the Elvis motion pictures. Index. (Bibliography includes two titles unrelated to Elvis Presley, both by Maria Gripe. *See* The Rest/Deceptive Titles.)

Source: Memphis/Shelby County (TN) Public Library and Information Center

☆ Barlow, Roy, David Cardwell, and Albert Hand, compilers

The Elvis Presley Encyclopaedia: Bringing You Everything You Wish to Know About Elvis, in Concise Chronological Order. **Heanor, Derbyshire, UK: Albert Hand Publications, 1964, 1966. 52 pp. ISBN: none.**

An A-to-Z listing of all things Elvisian. Updated in 1966. The text includes the author's personal evaluations of Elvis, his movies, and his recordings.

OCLC 30245292 (1st Edition, 1964); 30271429 (2nd Edition, 1964)
Compiler's Collection (3rd Edition, 1966)

☆ Burk, Bill E.

Bill Burk covered Elvis for the *Memphis Press-Scimitar* from 1956 through 1977.

Elvis: Images of a Legend. **Memphis, TN: Propwash Publishing, 1990. 52 pp. ISBN: 1879207001.**

A collection of rare candid Elvis Presley photographs and Elvis documents, ranging from his first publicity photograph through his concerts and his 1958–1960 years in Germany and Paris. Also includes reproductions of three Elvis autographs, a handwritten letter from Elvis, and a valentine card given by Elvis to 1950s girlfriend Anita Wood. Essays by Memphis Mafia member Lamar Fike (Elvis's trip to Paris), and Kang Rhee (Elvis's karate instructor). Elvis trivia section. Quotes by Elvis section. All photographs are captioned and credited.

Source: Library of Congress ML420.P96 B9 1990
Dewey Decimal 782.42166/092 20

☆ Coffey, Frank

Frank Coffey co-authored Elvis's stepbrother David Stanley's book, *Elvis Encyclopedia.* (*See* Stanley listing in this section.)

Complete Idiot's Guide to Elvis. The Complete Idiot's Guide series. New York: Alpha Books, 1997. 348 pp. ISBN: 0028618734.

An encyclopedia of Elvis Presley information, written in an abbreviated, humorous style. Released to coincide with the twentieth anniversary of Elvis's death. Repeats the inaccurate "second prize" and the "guitar/bicycle" stories. Full-color eight-page photo insert. Index.

☆ Cotten, Lee

Lee Cotten is the author of seven Elvis books.

All Shook Up: Elvis Day by Day, 1954–1977. Rock and Roll Reference series, #13. Ann Arbor, MI: Pierian Press, 1985. 580 pp. ISBN: 0876501722. Ann Arbor, MI: Popular Culture Ink, 1993. ISBN: 1560750332. Ann Arbor, MI: Popular Culture, Ink, 1998. ISBN: 1506750464.

A chronology (updated in 1998) covering the life of Elvis Presley from his birth in 1935 to his death in 1977. (The years 1935–1953 are covered in one chapter.) Introductory biographical essay. Pressley/Presley family tree. Appendices including the Sun Records sessions, a chronological list of Elvis's appearances, 1954–1977, and lists of Elvis's recordings' appearances on *Billboard* and *Variety* charts. A discussion of Elvis's place in the Memphis music scene prior to July 1954. Bibliography (pp. 545–547). Index.

The 1998 update incorporates information found in Cotten's *Did Elvis Sing in Your Hometown?* and *Did Elvis Sing in Your Hometown Too?* (*See* The Music, The Movies/Concerts and Television Appearances.) There are additional details on Elvis's recording sessions and alternate takes, and the CD bootleg recordings of Elvis's live concerts.

Source: Library of Congress ML420.P96 C67x 1985
Dewey Decimal 784.5/4/00924 B 19 (1985)
OCLC 12737300 (1985); 28706985 (1993)

☆ Currotto, William F.

From a Humble House to Fame; From Tupelo, MS, to Memphis, TN: An Elvis Presley Scrapbook. Memphis, TN: W. F. Currotto, 1995. 54 pp. ISBN: none.

A collection of reproduced newspaper and magazine articles on the life of Elvis Presley, ranging from 1960 (Elvis's return from military service) to posthumous memories of a variety of individuals (singer Brenda Lee and one of the medics who responded on August 16, 1977).

Source: Memphis/Shelby County (TN) Public Library and Information Center
OCLC 31944510
Publisher's address: 4150 Brunswick Road, Memphis, TN 38133

☆ Curtin, Jim

Elvis, the Early Years: A 2001 Fact Odyssey. 2001 Fact Odyssey series. [U.S.]: Celebrity Books, 1999. 300 pp. ISBN: 1580291066.

The first of a planned series of what Curtin describes as "the ultimate reference book on the King of Rock 'n' Roll." Facts and trivia—some previously unpublished—and many heretofore unseen photographs.

Source: Jim Curtin
www.angelfire.com

☆ Doll, Susan M., Ph.D.

Best of Elvis. Lincolnwood, IL: Publications International, 1996. 216 pp. ISBN: 0785319824.

A resource book that categorizes Elvis's career, life, and impact into 38 "Best" lists, which detail the best of Elvis on any given subject. Subjects range from the expected (Best Movies, Best Albums) to the serious (Best Books About Elvis) to the unusual (Best Elvis-Related Records) to the humorous (Best Elvis Bumper Stickers). "Best Quotes About Elvis" and "Best Quotes by Elvis" are cited. Color and black and white photographs; credited. Index.

Source: Library of Congress ML420.P96 D63 1996
OCLC 36085232

☆ *Elvis Album*. New York: Beekman House, 1991. 319 pp. ISBN: 0517060906. 1997. ISBN: 0785323872.

A biography of Elvis Presley in scrapbook format, consisting of black and white and color photographs, as well as newspaper articles from the collections of Bill DeNight, Sharon Fox, and Ger Rijff. Photographs are captioned and credited. Newspaper articles are dated and sourced. Elvis-related media, and recording listings, 1977–1991.

Source: OCLC 24270468

☆ *The Elvis Album*. Sydney, AU: Weldon Publishing, 1991. 239 pp. ISBN: 1863021728.

Primarily newspaper and magazine articles relating to Elvis Presley's life and later, 1938–1989. "Many [articles] reprinted for the first time" (book jacket notes.) Reprinted articles include the news story of the 1938 trial of Elvis's father, Vernon Presley, and the obituary for Elvis's paternal grandfather, Jesse Presley. An article on the memories of Elvis's teachers. All articles credited. Color and black and white photographs; credited and captioned. Bibliography. Index.

Source: New York Public Library JNF 93-201

☆ "Elvis by the Numbers." *The Guardian* (London) (July 19, 1997): T2.

"Twenty-Nine Interesting Things" about Elvis Presley.

☆ *The (Elvis) Files*. CD-ROM. Phoenix, AZ: Sky Creative Media Group, 1998.

An interactive CD-ROM containing the 663 pages of the FBI file on Elvis Presley. Also includes a discography of "every recording Elvis ever made"; a bibliography of "153 current and in-print books—plus videos and CDs" about Elvis; and a "detailed biography of Elvis in timeline form with expandable full-color photographs."

Source: Publisher's address: 2432 West Peoria Avenue, Suite 1262, Phoenix, AZ 85029

☆ *The Elvis Files Explore His Life*. Phoenix, AZ: Sky Creative Media Group, 1996. Computer laser optical disc, 4¾″ plus user's insert.

A detailed biography of Elvis Presley, complete filmography of Elvis's feature-length movies, and access to Elvis's "complete and uncut" FBI files.

Source: OCLC 39752226

☆ *Elvis Presley Album*. Lincolnwood, IL: Publications International, Ltd., 1997. 92 pp. ISBN: 078532190-X. London: Signet, 1999. ISBN: 0454199235.

Copies of newspaper clippings and black and white and color photographs spanning Elvis's career from July 1954 to the period immediately following his death in 1977. Black and white and color photographs; captioned and credited. Many newspaper articles are not cited or sourced.

Source: Library of Congress ML420.P96 E385 1997
Dewey Decimal 782.42166/092 B 21

☆ *Elvis Presley Encyclopedia, Collectors Edition*. Globe Mini Magazine #364. New York: Globe, 1981. 65 pp. ISBN: none.

A 5″ × 3¼″ compendium of facts about Elvis Presley, arranged in alphabetical order.

Source: Compiler's collection

☆ *Elvis Presley Fact Finder: A Ready Reference Guide of Facts and Information*. [n.p.]: [n.p.], 1978. 10 pp. ISBN: none.

A book of facts about Elvis Presley with a paper wheel attached to the cover. When the wheel is activated, the user may select fact categories such as "height/weight" and receive an answer. Color photographs of Elvis during concerts.

Source: eBay auction item #65863323

☆ Elvis Presley: File of clippings and miscellanea. 1 portfolio. Undated.

Note from OCLC entry: "Collected at Michigan State University Library in the Russell B. Nye Popular Culture Collection's Popular Culture Vertical File (PCVF)."

Source: OCLC 25055291

☆ Farren, Mick

The Hitchhiker's Guide to Elvis. Burlington, Ontario, Canada: Collector's Guide Publishing, 1994. 176 pp. ISBN: 0969573650.

An A-to-Z encyclopedia of more than 340 entries of primarily obscure people, places, and things associated with Elvis Presley (i.e., the military officer who administered Elvis's U.S. Army induction intelligence test). Most descriptions are subjective, not fact-based. Introductory essay examines Elvis's impact and his fans' continuing devotion to him. Ninety black and white photographs; none credited. Cover artwork is an artist's rendering of Elvis in prayer, with a doughnut halo, surrounded by images of Jesus and the Virgin Mary. In addition to reflecting Farren's religious bigotry, the cover art also mirrors his contempt for Elvis and Elvis fans as demonstrated in the book's text.

Source: Compiler's collection

☆ Foerster, Trey

Elvis Just for You: A Special Goldmine *Anthology.* Iola, WI: Krause Publications, 1987. 128 pp. ISBN: none.

Twenty-three articles about Elvis Presley previously printed in *Goldmine* magazine. Topics covered: Elvis's early career, his Sun Years, his records, and his films.

Source: Compiler's collection

☆ Fontana, Jesse

Wise Men Say: An Incomparable Collection of Little-Known Facts About Elvis. New York: Avon Books, 1999. 186 pp. ISBN: 038079599X.

Source: OCLC 41955703

☆ Fox, Sharon R., editor

Sharon Fox has been an Elvis fan since the 1950s. She is the compiler of *Elvis, He Touched My Life! (see* The Man/Photographs) and co-author of *Elvis Album (see* listing in this chapter).

Elvis, His Real Life in the 60's: My Personal Scrapbook. Chicago: self-published, 1989. 80 pp. ISBN: none.

A fan's collection of Elvis's clippings, magazine covers, and concert advertisements, spanning 1960–1969.

Source: Compiler's collection
Publisher's address: 5742 West Giddings Street, Chicago, IL 60630

☆ Frew, Timothy

Elvis. A Friedman Group book. New York: Grange Books, 1992. 176 pp. ISBN: 1856271889. New York: The Mallard Press, 1992. 176 pp. ISBN: 0792457544.

A reference book about Elvis Presley. Biography (pp. 8–125), including black and white photographs; captioned and credited. Chapter of color photographs of memorabilia; credited but not captioned. List of Elvis's television appearances. Filmography lists (pp.

138–161). Fan club mailing list as of 1994. List of Elvis's million-selling singles. "The Elvis Reading List" (31 items). Index. In 1992 this book was also published in Australia as *Elvis Companion*. (*See* the following listing.)

———.

Elvis Companion. Balwyn, Australia: The Five Mile Press Pty. Ltd., 1992. 176 pp. ISBN: 0867884142.

The Australian edition of *Elvis*. (*See* preceding listing.)

Source: New York Public Library JNF 93-132
OCLC 27593211

☆ Haining, Peter, editor

The Elvis Presley Scrapbooks, 1955–1965. London: Robert Hale, 1991. 192 pp. ISBN: 0709043473.

A collection of press clippings covering the first 10 years of Elvis's career. Mostly from British sources, with some from the United States and other countries.

Source: Library of Congress ML420.P96 E43 1991x
The British Library YC.1991.b.6307
OCLC 24792506

☆ Hand, Albert, compiler

Hand was one of the earliest Elvis fans to write about his idol. From 1959 until his [Hand's] passing in the 1970s, Hand produced a number of Elvis titles, mostly in conjunction with his fan club and his magazine, *Elvis Monthly*. Hand was president of the Official Elvis Presley Fan Club of Great Britain and the Commonwealth, as well as founder of the International Elvis Presley Appreciation Society.

The A to Z of Elvis Presley. Heanor, Derbyshire, England: Albert Hand Publications Ltd., 1976. 186 pp. ISBN: none.

A reference book compiled during Elvis Presley's lifetime by Elvis expert Albert Hand. Photographs.

Source: OCLC 41041999

———.

A Century of Elvis. Heanor, Derbyshire: A. Hand, 1959. 40 pp. ISBN: none.

The first Elvis publication in Great Britain. Contents: "The power of Elvis"; "Meet Mr. Violent Anti-Presley"; "The Man of Many Voices"; "Silencing the Critics"; "A Century of Elvis" (a discography); "The League of Elvis" (a British fan competition); "Elvis as an Actor"; "The Best of Elvis"; "The Future of Elvis." four black and white publicity photographs.

Title of book refers to the one hundredth Elvis Presley song released in Great Britain. The book went through three impressions in 1959: April 21, May 14, and September 1. Each had a different foreword.

Source: Library of Congress xML420.P96
OCLC 30246706

———.

Elvis Pocket Handbook. UK: Albert Hand, 1961. 64 pp. ISBN: none.

This book features a list of Elvis's English record releases, reviews of his first five films, details of each of Elvis's recorded songs (as of 1961), and "A Page of Elvis Facts." Thirty-two pages of photographs from Elvis's sixth film, *Flaming Star.* A full-color poster of Elvis.

Source: OCLC 30225840

———.

The Elvis They Dig. Heanor, Derbyshire, GB: A. Hand, 1959. 35 pp. ISBN: none.

Articles by British and American Elvis Presley fans, submitted in response to the editor's invitation in *A Century of Elvis* (1959). Fan letters and poetry. Five black and white publicity still photographs from Decca Record, Ltd.

Source: Library of Congress XML420.P96
OCLC 20702431

———.

Elvis Special. Manchester, UK: World Distributors, [annually 1962–1978?]. [Pagination ranges between 100–130 pp.]. [Separate ISBN for each issue.]

An annual yearbook published by *Elvis Monthly* magazine, containing articles, short stories, and poems by Elvis fans and experts; facts about Elvis's life and career including photographs, quotes, reviews, and filmography and discography lists.

Source: Bodleian Library, University of Oxford, UK
OCLC 7715176 (for all editions)

———.

Meet Elvis. 1962. 48 pp. ISBN: none.

The first of the *Elvis Special* yearbooks. Softcover.

Source: OCLC 20738745

☆ Johnson, Bill and Moneen

The Elvis Presley News Diary. Nashville, TN: Pyramid Media, 1981. 230 pp. ISBN: none.

Reproduced news articles, with accompanying photographs, from a variety of Tennessee newspapers, from August 1977 through July 1981.

Source: Elvis Presley Enterprises, Inc.

☆ Lannahann, Margaret

Elvis the Legend. Kansas City, MO: Ariel Books/Andrews McMeel Publishing, 1998. 128 pp. ISBN: 0836252446.

A miniature book ($2^1/2'' \times 1^3/4''$) with chapters on quotes about Elvis by celebrities (none cited or sourced), and facts about Elvis (repeats the false "guitar instead of a bicycle" anecdote). Forty-seven photographs, color and black and white; all are attributed.

☆ Latham, Caroline, and Jeannie Sakol

E Is for Elvis: An A-to-Z Illustrated Guide to the King of Rock and Roll. New York: NAL Books, 1990. 301 pp. ISBN: 045300732-5. New York: Plume, 1991.

An alphabetized encyclopedia of persons, places, and things associated with Elvis. Short bibliography. Thirty-seven black and white photographs, credited.

Source: The Margaret Herrick Library, Academy of Motion Picture Arts and Sciences

☆ Linedecker, Cliff

All You Wanted to Know About Elvis. Globe Mini Mag series. Boca Raton, FL: Globe Communications Corp., 1989. 64 pp. ISBN: none.

A miniature-size format pamphlet that briefly covers events, persons, and details in Elvis Presley's life. Chapter on paternity suits against Elvis.

Source: OCLC 40928527

☆ Loper, Karen

The Elvis Clippings. Houston, TX: "The Elvis Clippings," [n.d.]. 222 pp. ISBN: none.

A compilation of clippings about Elvis Presley's career.

Source: Elvis Presley Enterprises, Inc.

☆ Nash, Bruce M., and Allan Zullo, with John McGran

Bruce Nash has also authored *Amazing but True Dog Tales, Freebies for Cat Lovers,* and *The Golf Nut's Book of Amazing Feats and Records.*

Amazing but True Elvis Facts. Kansas City, MO: Andrews and McMeel, 1995. 147 pp. ISBN: 0836270282.

A trivia book with unsubstantiated facts and anecdotes about Elvis Presley. Unsourced quotes attributed to Elvis. No chapter notes, sources, citations, or index.

Source: OCLC 31710071

☆ Petersen, Brian

Petersen is an air traffic controller in Sweden. He is currently at work on a second book, which will cover Elvis's life and career from January 1957 forward.

The Atomic Powered Singer. Morrum, Sweden: Brian Petersen, 1994. 240 pp. ISBN: none.

An in-depth reference guide to Elvis Presley's life and career in 1956, with a chapter devoted to each month of that year. Advertisements for 1956 concerts and 1956 press clippings relating to Elvis's personal and professional lives. Song lists for appearances with transcript of master of ceremonies' comments. More than 200 black and white photographs. Foreword by RCA producer and Elvis music expert Ernst Jorgensen. Information includes 40 previously unknown Elvis concerts in 1956.

Source: Elvis Presley Enterprises, Inc.
Publisher's address: Brian Petersen, Nygardsvagen 13, 375 34 Morrum, Sweden

☆ Pierce, Patricia Jobe

Pierce is described as a public speaker, fine arts appraiser, freelance writer, and the director of the Pierce Galleries, Inc.

The Ultimate Elvis: Elvis Presley Day by Day. New York: Simon and Schuster, 1994, 1997. 560 pp. ISBN: 067187022X (1994 edition). New York: Scribner's, 1995. ISBN: 0684803283 and 0671853430.

Bill Burk—author of 12 Elvis books, publisher of the longest-running commercial Elvis magazine, and a former Memphis journalist who covered Elvis's entire career—says of this book, "Without a doubt, the Patricia Jobe Pierce *Ultimate Elvis* was the worst-researched book on ANY subject, not just Elvis."[2] Burk refused to sell the book through his magazine because of the large number of errors he found in the first 100 pages. Indeed, Pierce misidentifies Burk as a high school friend (pp. 54, 61) and also makes a mistake about Elvis's first bassist, Bill Black (p. 61). She incorrectly credits Burk as a source of information several times (pp. 54, 64, 285) and misspells his name as "Burke" throughout.

This book is divided into four sections relating to Elvis's life, his posthumous chronology (as of 1994), movie data, Elvis's friends and family, Elvis memorabilia, and discography (as of 1994). Some addresses for Elvis's homes are incorrect. Quotations by and about Elvis are not cited. Bibliography incorrectly lists the Maria Gripe book *Elvis and His Friends*, which has nothing to do with Elvis. (*See* The Rest/Deceptive Titles.) No footnotes or citations. Index.

In the acknowledgments, Pierce thanks President and Mrs. Bill Clinton as among those "who have had the patience and discernment to see the long-term project through to the end" (p. 7).

☆ Rijff, Ger

Rijff served as president of the Dutch Elvis Presley fan club from 1977 to 1984. He is the compiler and editor of 18 books of Elvis photographs.

[2]Correspondence, Nov 5, 1997.

Elvis Presley: Long Lonely Highway. Amsterdam, The Netherlands: Tutti Frutti, 1985. 184 pp. ISBN: none.

Newspaper clippings, concert advertisements, and candid photographs relating to Elvis in the 1950s. Reprinted the same in the United States under the title *Long Lonely Highway: A 1950s Elvis Scrapbook*, with new front material and indexes. (*See* following listing.)

Source: OCLC 18111772

————.

Long Lonely Highway: A 1950s Elvis Scrapbook. Rock and Roll Remembrances series #8. Ann Arbor, MI: Pierian Press, 1985, 1987. 200 pp. ISBN: 0876502370.

Reprint of *Elvis Presley: Long Lonely Highway* with new front matter and indexes. Introduction on how the book was created. Foreword essay by Lee Cotten, "Elvis in the Fifties: A Look Back." Newspaper clippings, concert advertisements, and candid fan and concert photographs relating to Elvis in the 1950s. "Index to People, Places, and Things." "Index to Dates."

Source: Michael Ochs Archives, Venice, CA
OCLC 17204497 (1985); 18256811 (1987)

☆ Rijff, Ger, and Poul Madsen

Elvis Presley: Echoes of the Past. Voorschoten, The Netherlands: "Blue Suede Shoes" Productions, 1976. Unpaged. ISBN: none.

A collection of fan magazine articles and accompanying photographs of Elvis, dated 1956 and 1957. None are attributed or cited.

Source: Michael Ochs Archives, Venice, CA

☆ Sauers, Wendy, compiler

Elvis Presley, A Complete Reference: Biography, Chronology, Concerts List, Filmography, Discography, Vital Documents, Bibliography. Jefferson, NC, and London: McFarland and Company, Inc., 1984. 194 pp. ISBN: 0899501109.

Two-page biography that repeats the inaccurate "second prize" and "guitar/bicycle" stories. Chronology, including concerts from 1969–1977 (pp. 11–36). Filmography with cast, crew, and songs for each film (pp. 37–53). Discography (pp. 53–121). Memorabilia chapter with copies of Elvis's birth and death certificates and his will. Index.

The bibliography of books and periodical articles (pp. 141–179) contains misspellings of authors' names and includes Marie Gripe's book, which has nothing to do with Elvis Presley. (*See* The Rest/Deceptive Titles.)

Source: Library of Congress ML420.P96 S28 1984
Dewey Decimal 784.5/4/00924

☆ Saville, Ted, compiler

International Elvis Presley Appreciation Society Handbook. Heanor, Derbyshire, England: The Society, 1967, 1970. 72 pp. (1967).

A pamphlet encyclopedia of facts about Elvis Presley, which is intended as a handbook for new members of the International Elvis Presley Appreciation Society of Derbyshire, England.

Source: The Mississippi Valley Collection, Memphis State University, TN
Bodleian Library, University of Oxford, UK

☆ Stanley, David, with Frank Coffey

David Stanley grew up at Graceland and was later employed by Elvis. His mother was married to Vernon Presley from 1960 to 1977. He has written two books about his life with Elvis and co-authored a book about Elvis with his brothers and mother. (*See* The Man/Memoirs and Memories.)

Elvis Encyclopedia: The Complete and Definitive Reference Book. Santa Monica, CA: General Publishing, Inc., 1994. 287 pp. ISBN: 1881649245. [London]: Virgin, 1995. 287 pp. ISBN: 1852278723. Santa Monica, CA: General Publishing, Inc., 1997. 250 pp. ISBN: 1574406X.

A biographical chronology of Elvis's life by his stepbrother David Stanley, interspersed with commentary from Stanley, his mother, Dee (Mrs. Vernon) Presley, and Memphis Mafia member Lamar Fike—who also contributes a personal memoir introductory essay. Brief biographies of 50 of Elvis's friends. Synopses and production information for Elvis's motion pictures. An annotated anthology of Elvis's commercially released recordings, including recording industry records held by Elvis, as of 1995. Two hundred and fifty color and black and white photographs; credited. Index.

Inaccuracies in several places, including addresses of Elvis's homes, repeating the "second prize" and "guitar/bicycle" stories, and misidentifying Elvis's employee Dick Grob as a United States Air Force Academy graduate and a fighter pilot. In 1995 David Stanley was sued for copyright violation over use of a photograph that is labeled "the last known picture of Elvis," p. 149 (*Dayton* [OH] *News*, Dec 8, 1995: 1A).

Source: OCLC 30625123 (General Publishing, Inc., 1994); 35136200 (Virgin)

☆ Thompson, Susan, and Armand Eisen

Elvis: A Tribute to the King. Kansas City, MO: Ariel Books/Andrews McMeel, 1998. 127 pp. ISBN: 0836252349.

A "CD book" (name relates to circular shape of book, which resembles a compact disc). Brief biography. Unsourced and uncited quotes by Elvis. Black and white and color photographs; credited.

☆ Tobler, John, and Graham Bates

The A–Z of Elvis. [U.S.]: Mason's Music, 1982. ISBN: none.

A reference guide to the basic facts about the films, song titles, people, and places in Elvis Presley's life. Tobler has authored other books about rock entertainers.

Source: Compiler's collection

☆ Torgoff, Martin, editor

Torgoff is the co-author of *Elvis: We Love You Tender*, the memoirs of Elvis's stepmother and stepbrothers, the Stanleys.

The Complete Elvis. New York: G. P. Putnam's Sons/Delilah Books, 1982. ISBN: 0933328206. London: Virgin, 1982. 256 pp. ISBN: none. New York: Putnam's Publishing Group, 1984. ISBN: 0671067176.

This book is a collection of original and reprinted articles and stories about Elvis and a compendium of Elvis facts. Included are Stanley Booth's article "Hound Dog to the Manor Born" and Lester Bangs's short story "Graceland Uber Alles." Author's essay, "After the Flood: Elvis and His Literary Legacy," discusses Elvis authors and their works. Three essays by Elvis fans. An alphabetized listing of brief descriptions of Elvis's life, music, films, books, people, places, and friends. Color and black and white photographs, both portraits and candids, most not identified or dated. A bibliography of more than 150 titles and articles, including entries for two books by Maria Gripe which have nothing to do with Elvis. (*See* The Rest/Deceptive Titles.) No index.

☆ *The Voice of Rock 'n' Roll: Elvis in the Times of Ultimate Cool.* Rotterdam, The Netherlands: It's Elvis Time, 1993. 104 pp. ISBN: none.

"Over 100" photographs, as well as newspaper clippings, of Elvis Presley from the 1954–1957 period of his career. A selection of recording sheets.

Source: Now Dig This, 69 Quarry Lane, South Shield, Tyne and Wear NE34 7NW, UK

☆ West, Joe

Elvis: His Most Intimate Secrets. Globe Mini Mag series #250. Boca Raton, FL: Globe Communications, 1993. 64 pp. ISBN: 8995506876.

A small (3½" × 5¼") paperback that offers uncited anecdotes of Elvis sightings, his family and friends, his pets, his films, secret lovers and possible children, and Colonel Tom Parker. An "Update" section on Lisa Marie Presley's activities as an adult.

Source: Compiler's Collection
Publisher's address: Globe Communications Corp., 5401 N.W. Broken Sound Boulevard, Boca Raton, FL 33487

☆ Whistler, John A.

At the time of publication, John Whistler was on the staff of the Memphis/Shelby County (TN) Public Library in Memphis, Tennessee.

Elvis Presley: Reference Guide and Discography. Metuchen, NJ: Scarecrow Press, 1981. 258 pp. ISBN: 081081434X.

A reference book that includes the first professionally compiled bibliography of the Elvis literature. Citations include references to reviews of the books. Chapters of periodical and newspaper articles bibliographies. Biographical chronology (pp. 233–239). Filmography (pp. 240–260). Discography (pp. 261–292). Index.

Source: Library of Congress ML134.5.P73 W5
Dewey Decimal 016.7845/0092/4 B 19

☆ Worth, Fred L., and Steve D. Tamerius

Worth is the author of numerous books, including *The Complete Unabridged Super Trivia Encyclopedia*. At the time of publication, Tamerius was a writer for the television game show *Jeopardy*.

All About Elvis. New York: Bantam Books, 1981. 414 pp. ISBN: 0553141295.

A reference book listing "every single release, Extended Play album, and Long Playing album associated with Elvis" (as of 1980). "Mini biography." "Chronology of the Life of Elvis Presley." Alphabetical listing of songs, places, and people associated with Elvis. Bibliography (pp. 411–414). In August 1987, this book was named by *USA Today* newspaper as one of the five best books about Elvis.

———.

Elvis: His Life from A to Z. Chicago: Contemporary Books, Inc., 1988. 618 pp.
ISBN: 0809245280. London: Corgi, 1989. 618 pp. ISBN: 0552993794 (pbk.).
Chicago: Contemporary Books, Inc., 1990. 618 pp. ISBN: 0809240831 (pbk.).
New York: Wings Books, 1992. 618 pp. ISBN: 0517066343.

The most widely used Elvis encyclopedia, with "more than 2,000 categories and 10,000 facts, figures, and never-before-published details" (book jacket notes). Chronology of Elvis's life. More than 250 black and white photographs and document reproductions. Genealogical charts for Elvis's maternal and paternal families of origin. Discography (as of 1992) of Elvis's recordings, as well as bootleg, novelty, and tribute albums. Filmography of Elvis's films, with cast lists, song titles, events that occurred during filming, and trivia. Lists of Elvis's radio and television appearances and concert tour schedules. Lists of films and TV specials about Elvis.

Anecdotes in "The Man" section are not sourced or cited. Quotation section identifies speakers but does not provide citations and contexts. Repeats the inaccurate "bicycle/guitar story."

See Also:

In The Man/Biographies:

Guralnick, Peter, and Ernst Jorgensen, *Elvis Day by Day*.

In Foreign Language Titles/Italian:

Ruggeri, Paolo, *Elvis Presley: Vita, Canzoni, Dischi e Film*.

THE MUSIC, THE MOVIES

PART II

CHAPTER 12
Concerts and Television Appearances

Elvis Presley appeared in hundreds of concert performances—from Memphis's Overton Park Shell on July 30, 1954 (immediately after the release of his first record), to the Indianapolis Market Square Arena on June 26, 1977. These concerts were the foundation of Elvis's legend as a playful, personable, and extraordinarily versatile entertainer. Through them, Elvis received his true lifeblood—personal and physical connection with his fans.

But it was on television where the world first met Elvis Presley, and that was where the world would witness his phoenix-like rise from the muck of his regrettable 1960s movies. His first appearance on national television came early in 1956—*Jimmy and Tommy Dorsey's Stage Show* on CBS. That debut was quickly followed by five more bookings with the Dorseys and six on other programs hosted by Steve Allen, Milton Berle, Hy Gardner, and Ed Sullivan.

His next appearance on TV would be just as dramatic, but it would not occur until 12 years later. On December 3, 1968, TV viewers held their collective breath as heretofore closeted Elvis—who had not performed live since 1961—nervously took the stage on the NBC-TV presentation of the Singer sewing machine company's *Elvis*.[1] At the end of his first song, there was an atmospheric change as that breath was exhaled. Elvis was back.

The concert and television reference books lovingly and obsessively detail these events though enumerative lists, trivia, anecdotes, and photographs. But their rightful importance comes from the window they provide. It is the concert photograph books that afford a unique documentation of societal change. The birth of women's liberation is recorded on the emotionally contorted faces of Elvis's young female audiences who are in the process of tearing down the ancient rules of feminine deportment. The future of civil rights is glimpsed as Elvis fans of all races blend into a sea of cheering, smiling faces as their idol performs.

---

[1] This concert is frequently referred to as "The Comeback Special," or "The '68 Special."

The body of this genre, which includes both photographs and reference books, is a detailed portrait of the birth and maturation of rock and roll. In it, the rapid and radical alterations of attitudes, acceptances, and cultural behaviors of Elvis's era are frozen in time.

☆　　☆　　☆　　☆

☆ Bailye, I. R.

Elvis: The T.V. Years. [UK]: [n.p.], 1986. 334 pp. ISBN: none.

A chronological overview of Elvis Presley's television performances from 1956 to the last televised special (CBS) in 1977. Most of the book's photographs are pictures of television screens that have images of Elvis performing. The book contains dialogue transcripts of some of the programs and transcripts from press conferences related to some of the programs.

Source: Collection of Bill and Connie Burk, Memphis, TN

☆ Cotten, Lee

Lee Cotten is the author of seven Elvis books.

Did Elvis Sing in Your Hometown? Sacramento, CA: High Sierra Books, 1995. 259 pp. ISBN: 0964658801 (hdk.). ISBN: 096465881X (pbk.).

An annotated, chronological listing, 1945–1961, of Elvis Presley's singing performances. City-by-city index.

Source: Library of Congress ML420.P96 C672 1995
Los Angeles Public Library 789.14 P9 34 Cot-1/2
OCLC 32911699

————.

Did Elvis Sing in Your Hometown Too? Sacramento, CA: High Sierra Books, 1997. 321 pp. ISBN: 0964658828 (hdk.). ISBN: 0964658836 (pbk.).

The sequel to *Did Elvis Sing in Your Hometown?*, continuing the annotated chronology of Elvis Presley's singing performances, 1968–1977. Includes the logistics involved in putting on an Elvis concert. Index.

Source: OCLC 37620477

☆ "Elvis Forever!: Twenty Years Later, We Celebrate Presley and His TV Legacy." *TV Guide* 45 (Aug 16, 1997): A15.

An overview of television appearances made by Elvis Presley.

☆ *Elvis's Television Special.* 1968. 32 pp. (4″ × 9″.)

A promotional booklet used to announce the December 3, 1968, NBC-TV special, as well as his December 1, 1968, half-hour Christmas radio show.

Source: Cotten, The Elvis Catalog, p. 164.

☆ Gordon, Robert

The King on the Road: Elvis on Tour, 1954–1977. New York: St. Martin's Press, 1996. 208 pp. ISBN: 0312141467.

A comprehensive examination of Elvis Presley's concert tours from his first in 1954 until his last performance in 1977. One hundred and fifty black and white photographs from Elvis's tours, as well as newspaper clippings and tickets—all from the Elvis Presley Enterprises, Inc., archives.

☆ Gould, Jack

"Elvis Presley: Lack of Responsibility Is Shown by TV in Exploiting Teen-Agers." *The New York Times* (Sept 16, 1956).

An op-ed article, published the week after Elvis Presley's famous appearance on *The Ed Sullivan Show*, excoriates television executives whom he believes are irresponsibly using Elvis's fans to reap profits. Gould also comments on Elvis's role as a rallying point for teenagers when "ours is still a culture in a stage of frantic and tense transition. . . . Quite possibly Presley just happened to move in where society has failed the teenager."

☆ James, Caryn

"TV's Elvis Sightings." *The New York Times,* Weekend Section (July 5, 1996): C1.

An overview of Elvis's early television appearances as shown in the 1996 retrospective exhibit "All Shook Up: Elvis Presley on Television," mounted by the Museum of Television and Radio in New York City.

☆ Lardner, John

"Devitalizing Elvis." *Newsweek* (July 16, 1956): 59.

Observations about Elvis Presley's appearance on *The Steve Allen Show* (1956), describing the experience as an example of the older generation attempting to crush the new. Lardner takes Allen to task for his attempts to "mute and frustrate" Elvis through embarrassing on-stage situations (i.e., "dressing him like a corpse in formal evening dress and requiring him to sing to a dog").

☆ Skar, Stein Erik

Elvis: the Concert Years, 1969–1977. Translation by Elizabeth Watering and Barry Love. Norway: [n.p.], 1997. 270 pp. ISBN: none.

An English-language translation of the Norwegian book of the same name. (*See* Foreign Language Titles/Norwegian.) A reference for Elvis Presley's concert tours from 1969 to 1977. Each concert is accompanied by press reviews, name of the jumpsuit worn by Elvis, attendance numbers, lists of musicians and backup singers, and all songs performed. Final chapter covers statistical material related to Elvis and his career. "Over 200" color and black and white photographs of Elvis performing in these concerts; captioned and credited.

Source: "Elvis in Print" www.geocities.com/SunsetStrip/8200/books.html

Significant Reviews of Elvis's Post-1950s Live Performances

(Listed in chronological order)

☆ Dalton, Dave

"Elvis." *Rolling Stone* #52 (Feb 21, 1970).

Dalton comments on Elvis Presley's return to live performing in August 1969, Las Vegas, Nevada. Considered one of the classic reviews of Elvis in concert.

☆ Landau, John

"In Praise of Elvis Presley." *Rolling Stone* (Jan 1972).

An enthusiastic appraisal of Elvis's performance and musical skills at his November 10, 1971, concert at the Boston Gardens. Reprinted as "All the King's Splendor: A Performance" in the memorial section of *Rolling Stone* (Sept 22, 1977): 84.

☆ Heckman, Don

"Presley, Talents Richly Intact, Shifts Emphasis to Rock/Gospel." *The New York Times* (June 10, 1972).

A positive review of Elvis's first concert in New York City, June 9, 1972, at Madison Square Garden.

☆ Willis, Ellen

"Musical Events: Rock, Etc." *New Yorker* (July 1, 1972): 66.

A moving account of the transformation of a sophisticated journalist from Elvis sneerer to Elvis fan during Elvis Presley's June 1972 Madison Square Garden concert in New York. Willis describes how Elvis was able to touch the emotions of his audiences, young and old—his voice and music moved her to tears.

☆ Kalina, Mike

"Elvis Rings In '77 at the Civic Arena." *Post Gazette* (Pittsburgh, PA) (Jan 1977).

A review of what musicologists and Elvis fans consider to be Elvis's last great concert—New Year's Eve 1976 in Pittsburgh, Pennsylvania.

☆ Rose, Rita

"Elvis Performs in True Presley Style Before 18,000." *The Indianapolis Star* (June 1977).

Elvis's last concert review—from his last concert, June 26, 1977, in Indianapolis, Indiana.

See Also:

In The Man/Biographies:

DeWitt, Howard A., *Elvis: The Sun Years.*
Gray, Michael, and Roger Osborne, *Elvis's America.*
Watts, J. Dan, *Elvis: A Tribute to the Life and the Career of Elvis Presley.* (Essay by J. D. Sumner, "What It Was Like at a Concert.")

In The Man/The Impact of Elvis:

Hiltbrand, David, "The Greatest Ever? Forget Springsteen, Jackson and Madonna. Elvis Is Still King!"
McManus, Margaret, "Presley No Serious Peril, Noted Psychologist Feels." (Commentary on Elvis Presley's appearance on *The Ed Sullivan Show.*)

In The Man/Memoirs and Memories:

Scott, Liz, "Elvis in New Orleans."

The Man/Photographs

In The Man/Reference:

Petersen, Brian, *The Atomic Powered Singer.*

In Foreign Language Titles/German:

Baumann, Peter, Norman Duncan, Peter Schittler, and Herald Trittner *The Burbank Sessions and The Burbank Puzzle.*

In The Academics/Educational Literature:

Scoppa, Bud, "Elvis Is Back (or Is He?)." (Review of a Madison Square Garden concert.)

CHAPTER 13
Discography

CATALOGUING THE RECORDINGS of Elvis Presley is a consuming passion for many authors whose dedication is especially impressive when one considers Elvis's astronomical output—it is so vast that the compiler was unable to locate any source with an accurate count of his recordings and albums.

More than 35 discographies have been published; the first in 1974, the latest in 1999. While some are limited to specific types of Elvis recordings (i.e., the bootlegs, those on CD, or those released in a specific country), all are a testament to Elvis's prodigious contribution to contemporary American music.

With such variety and volume, it is difficult to name any title as "the best" Elvis discography. Elvis Presley Enterprises, Inc. (EPE), suggests the discography books by Jerry Osborne and RCA/BMG record producer Ernst Jorgensen.[1] (*See* Osborne and Jorgensen listings in this chapter.) Bill E. Burk, the leading seller of Elvis books, names Jorgensen's *Elvis Presley: A Life in Music; The Complete Recording Sessions* as the most popular title among his buyers in 1998.

With the continuing release of Elvis CD and cassette sets (RCA issued three between January and June 1999), it appears certain that the creation of these books will keep pace.

☆   ☆   ☆   ☆

☆ Ares, Carlos R.

Viva Elvis! The Ultimate Discography and Record Price Guide from Argentina. Argentina: C. A. Productions, [n.d.]. 120 pp. ISBN: none.

One of the first publications to fully document Elvis Presley's record releases in Argentina. More than 500 photographs of Argentine pressings, including color reproductions of album covers released in Argentina. English and Spanish text. Print run limited to 500 copies.

---

[1]Since the publication of EPE's list in 1997, Osborne has updated his price guide, *Official Price Guide to Elvis Presley Records and Memorabilia 1998*, and Jorgensen has published a new discography, *Elvis Presley: A Life in Music; The Complete Recording Sessions*, 1998.

Source: Carlos Ares
www.elvis.com.ar

————.

Elvis, South-American Style. Buenos Aires, Argentina: Carlos R. Ares/Carlos Ares Productions, 1999. 72 pp. ISBN: applied for.

More than 200 color photographs of "rare South-American Elvis items," including movie memorabilia, publications, press books, and Super 8mm films. Lists of Elvis recordings and CDs released in South America. Price guide.

Source: Carlos Ares
www.elvis.com.ar

☆ Banney, Howard F.

Discography of Elvis Tribute and Novelty Records, 1956–1981. Ann Arbor, MI: Pierian Press, 1987. Rock and Roll Reference series No. 29. 318 pp. ISBN: 0876502389.

A collector's guide to more than 1,000 song recordings that mention Elvis, parody him and his music, or pay him tribute. Approximately 200 black and white reproductions of album covers. Indexes to titles and names.

Source: New York Public Library L 89-1549
OCLC 18073964

☆ Barry, Ron

At the time of publication, Ron Barry was a radio disc jockey with an extensive Elvis record collection.

All American Elvis: The Elvis Presley American Discography. Phillipsburg, NJ: Spectator Service, Maxigraphics, 1976. 255 pp. ISBN: none. (Reissued after Elvis's death as a "Memorial Edition," but publication date is unknown.)

A chronology of Elvis Presley's films and recordings from 1954 to 1976. Black and white reproductions of Elvis's record and album covers. A chapter on collecting Elvis's recordings.

Source: Michael Ochs Archives, Venice, CA

☆ Baumann, Peter

Elvis on CD: 1984–1992. Wien, Austria: P. Baumann, 1992. 383 pp. ISBN: none.

Self-published discography of Elvis's CDs up to 1992. Most CD sleeves are illustrated and details such as country of origin, matrix number, and availability on vinyl. Sixteen pages of photographs. Index.

Source: OCLC 29327890.
Author's address: P. Baumann, P.O. Box 74 A-1095, Wien, Austria

————.

Elvis on CD. Wien, Austria: P. Baumann, 1994. Pp. 382–714 (pages are numbered to coincide with the pagination of *Elvis on CD: 1984–1992*). ISBN: none.

A second volume of the 1992 book of the same title, bringing their total catalogued number to "more than" 1,250 CDs. Contents also include German label variations. Black and white photographs previously seen; not credited. Text in German and English. Index to both volumes.

Source: Peter Baumann

————.

Elvis on Vinyl. Vol. 1. Wien, Austria: P. Baumann, 1995. 140 pp. ISBN: 3901418024.

Detailed information (i.e., matrix/pressing numbers, etc.) about each Elvis single. Black and white illustrations of sleeves and labels. The second volume will cover extended play (EP) albums.

Source: www.arbooks.com/elvisp.html

☆ Carr, Roy, and Mick Farren

Elvis Presley: The Illustrated Record. New York: Harmony Books, 1982; London: Eel Pie Publishing Ltd., 1982. 191 pp. ISBN: 0906008646 (hdk.). ISBN: 0906008549 (pbk.).

A discography/biography of Elvis Presley covering the period of 1954 to his death. The discography includes "every official Elvis release" (as of 1982). Recordings are listed in chronological order accompanied by composer credits, matrix number, catalogue number, date of release, personnel, studio location, date of recording, and a critical commentary. Chapters cover spoken-word records, bootlegs, mail order records, and a U.K. discography. More than 300 color and black and white photographs; credited and captioned.

Source: New York Public Library JNG 82-330
OCLC 12506619

☆ Cotten, Lee, and Howard A. DeWitt

Lee Cotten is the author of seven Elvis books. Howard A. DeWitt, a history professor, has published an Elvis reference book. (*See* The Man/Reference.)

Jailhouse Rock: The Bootleg Records of Elvis, 1970-1983. Rock and Roll Reference series, #8. Ann Arbor, MI: Pierian Press, 1983. 367 pp. ISBN: 0876501587. Ann Arbor, MI: Popular Culture Ink, 1993. 367 pp. ISBN: 1560750340.

A reference guide to the 1970–1983 unauthorized reproductions ("bootlegs") of Elvis Presley's recordings, cassette tapes, Super 8 films, and videotapes and albums about Elvis, as well as unauthorized overseas releases of Elvis's albums. Chronology of Elvis bootlegs. Black and white reproductions of album and record covers. Name and label indices. The text was updated in 1993.

Source: Library of Congress ML156.7 P7C67 1983
Dewey Decimal 789./136454/00924 19
OCLC 10449198 (1983); 32538857 (1993)

☆ Doggett, Peter

Complete Guide to the Music of Elvis Presley. [n.p.]: Omnibus Press, 1994. 128 pp. ISBN: none.

An examination of almost every recorded song in Elvis Presley's catalog.

Source: Dewey Decimal 782.42166

☆ Dowling, Paul

Elvis: The Record Covers of the King. New York: St. Martin's Press, 1994. 160 pp. ISBN: 0312112696.

Color reproductions of 226 Elvis Presley album, EP, and singles covers, from the 1950s through the 1970s. Covers are organized by decades and themes to demonstrate how the marketing of Elvis evolved over the course of his career.

In an annotation to the book's listing in www.amazon.com, Dowling expresses his displeasure with the publisher's edits to his book. He announces the availability of "a special booklet that gives more information about each cover and also lists the current market value." Contact address is www.elvis@gte.net.html.

Source: Library of Congress ML156.7.P7 D69
Dewey Decimal 782.42166"092

———.

Elvis: The Ultimate Album Cover Book. New York: Harry N. Abrams, Inc., 1996. 160 pp. ISBN: 0810932687.

A reissue of *Elvis: The Record Covers of the King.* (*See* preceding listing.)

Source: Library of Congress ML156.7.P7 1996

———.

Worldwide Elvis Record Guide. (Announced but never published.)

In Neal Umphred's *A Touch of Gold,* Dowling ran an advertisement announcing the forthcoming publication of this book with availability in "late 1990." This book was never published. (*See* Umphred listing later in this section.)

Elvis CD and Sessions Notes. Andrew G. Hager, text. Alfred Wertheimer, photographs. New York: Michael Friedman Publishing Group, 1994. 16 pp. ISBN: none.

A recording sessions journal accompanying the book *Elvis: His Life and Music* and its sound discs, *Elvis's Golden Records.* (*See* Frew listing in The Man/Biographies.)

Elvis Presley's the First Noel. New York: Hapercollins Juvenile Books, 1999. 32 pp.
ISBN: 006028126X.

Intended for children ages 4–8, the text of this book is the five verses of the Christmas
carol "The First Noel." The drawings accompanying the text illustrate the verses. Elvis
photo on the back cover. Supplementing the text is a CD of Elvis's 1971 recording of the
first two verses of the carol (BMG Special Products, DPC12148).

Source: www.amazon.com

☆ Escott, Colin, and Martin Hawkins

Twenty Years of Elvis: The Elvis Session File. Maidstone, Kent, England: Martin
Hawkins, 1974. 62 pp. ISBN: none. Sussex, England: Swift Record Distributors,
1977. 62 pp. ISBN: none

The first Elvis Presley discography. A listing of his session dates, albums, singles, EPs,
motion pictures, bootlegs as of 1974. Brief essay about Elvis's musical roots. In 1981 this
book was updated and republished as *Elvis Presley: The Illustrated Discography.* (*See* following listing.)

Source: OCLC 207714449 (1974)
Compiler's collection (1977)

———.

☆ *Elvis Presley: The Illustrated Discography.* London; New York: Omnibus Press,
1981. 96 pp. ISBN: 0860017468.

An updated version of *Twenty Years of Elvis: The Elvis Session File.* (*See* preceding listing.)

Source: Bowling Green State University Library ML156.7.P7 H38
OCLC 9368141

☆ Gray, Michael H.

"Presley, Elvis Aron." *Bibliography of Discographies.* Vol. 3: *Popular Music.* New
York; London: R. R. Bowker Company, 1983. ISBN: 0835216837 (v. 3). Pp.
130–131.

A bibliographic citation listing of 34 books and magazine articles containing Elvis Presley
discographies.

Source: Library of Congress ML156.2.B49 or ML156.4.P6
Dewey Decimal 016.01678991/12

☆ Hampton, Dale

*Elvis for CD Fans Only: The Elvis Presley U.S. Compact Disc Reference and Price
Guide.* Knoxville, TN: RuJak Publication and Dale Hampton, 1993. [183 pp.].
ISBN: none.

Alphabetized list of Elvis Presley compact disc recordings, referencing their value, the songs on them, and production information. Also lists rarities and "lost" CDs. Catalog and matrix numbers.

Source: Library of Congress ML156.7.P7 H36 1993

☆ Jorgensen, Ernst

Jorgensen is a leading Elvis Presley music expert who has been the director of Elvis Presley's catalog at RCA for a numbers of years. He co-authored one of the earliest Elvis discographies, *Elvis Presley Recording Sessions* (1975), and has most recently published one of the most definitive, *Elvis Presley: A Life in Music* (1998). Jorgensen co-produced four Grammy Award–nominated releases of Elvis's recordings for RCA. He is a discography consultant to Elvis Presley Enterprises, Inc.

Elvis Presley: A Life in Music; The Complete Recording Sessions. New York: St. Martin's Press, 1998. 454 pp. ISBN: 0312185723.

Complete data and essays for all of Elvis Presley's recording sessions, 1953–May 1977 (124 entries). Separate discographies for releases before and after Elvis's death, 1954–1977 and 1978–1997. Outtakes chapter. Index. Foreword by Elvis biographer Peter Guralnick.

☆ Jorgensen, Ernst, Eric Rasmussen, and Johnny Mikkelsen

In 1970 the three authors—who were leaders in the Danish Elvis Presley fan club—began collecting facts about Elvis's recordings. This led to the publication of four books on Elvis discography, ranging from 1975 to 1998.

Elvis Presley—Recording Sessions. Stenlose, Denmark: JEE-Production, 1975. 110 pp. ISBN: none.

One of the earliest of the Elvis Presley discography books, written while he was alive. Details and notes for Elvis's recordings from 1954–1974. Title index. Discography.

Source: Michael Ochs Archives, Venice, CA

———.

Elvis Presley Recording Sessions. Stenlose, Denmark: JEE-Production, 1977. 110 pp. ISBN: none. Second edition: same publication information, 114 pp. ISBN: 8798061305.

This book is a revised and extended edition of the authors' earlier work, *Recording Sessions* covering 1954–1974. A chapter was added to cover Elvis's recording sessions during 1975–1977. Black and white reproductions of album covers and record sleeves. Thirteen black and white photographs; one captioned, none credited.

Source: OCLC 39907346 (first edition) 9006411 (second edition)

———.

Elvis Recording Sessions. Baneringen, Denmark: JEE Productions, 1984. 272 pp. ISBN: none.

An updated edition of the 1975 and 1977 *Recording Sessions*. Session information including dates, take numbers, and personnel used. Black and white candids of some sessions. This book was reprinted with additions in 1986 as *Reconsider Baby: The Definitive Elvis Sessionography, 1954–1977*.

Source: OCLC 17556851

————.

Reconsider Baby: The Definitive Elvis Sessionography, 1954–1977. Rock and Roll Reference series, #27. Ann Arbor, MI: Pierian Press, 1986. 308 pp. ISBN: 0876502206.

An expanded reprint of *Elvis Recording Sessions* (1984). Twenty-two chronologically arranged chapters with a list of and commentary for all records issued and recording sessions as of 1984. Discography, including bootlegs (pp. 209–308).

Source: Library of Congress ML156.7.P7 J6 1986
OCLC 16516623

☆ Lichter, Paul

Elvis: A Portrait in Music. Huntingdon Valley, PA: Jesse Books, 1983. 126 pp. ISBN: none.

According to Lichter, this book covers "every Elvis record ever issued" (as of 1983). Chapters for American records, rare records, worldwide box sets, RCA promotional 45 rpms, picture records, bootlegs, and foreign-produced records. Recordings are listed by record number, value as of 1983, release date, and chart ranking. Songs are listed for each album. Foreign-produced LPs are included.

Source: Library of Congress ML156.7.P7 L5 1983
OCLC 11370619

☆ Meijers, Edwin

Off and Back on the Mystery Track. The Netherlands: All Shook Up! Productions, [1995].

Meijers is editor of *The Elvis Magazine* (Holland).

A collection of information on more than 450 songs rumored to have been recorded or performed by Elvis Presley.

Source: Publisher's address: All Shook Up! Productions, Box 2181, 5500 BD Veldhoven, The Netherlands

☆ Osborne, Jerry

Jerry Osborne is one of the leading Elvis memorabilia and recordings experts. His Presleyana series, spanning from 1980 through 1997, is a comprehensive history of collector prices for Elvis recordings. Osborne has written 71 books about music, 14 of which are

Elvis titles. He writes the nationally syndicated column "Mr. Music." Elvis Presley Enterprises, Inc., refers questions relating to Elvis collectibles to Osborne.

Presleyana. First Edition. Osborne and Hamilton's Osborne and Hamilton's Original Record Collectors Price Guide series. Phoenix, AZ: O'Sullivan Woodside and Company, 1980. 273 pp. ISBN: 0890190739.

"A listing of records and their current market values," including singles, LPs, EPs, tapes, promotional records, bootleg and novelty recordings, acetates, and foreign releases (England, Chile, Germany, Eastern-Bloc Countries, and Israel). Introductory overview of the state of Elvis Presley record collecting as of 1980.

Source: Library of Congress ML156.7.P7 O8
Dewey Decimal 789.9/1245/00924 19

———.

Presleyana: Elvis Presley Record Price Guide. Second Edition. Osborne and Hamilton's Original Record Collectors Price Guide series. Phoenix, AZ: O'Sullivan Woodside and Company, 1983. 184 pp. ISBN: 0890190836.

An updated version of the first edition, with "the most useful chapters" of that version "dissected, amended, and highly streamlined within a completely restructured format" (p. 7). All reissues are listed and priced separately, and this also lists the release date of all issues and every known reissue. Photographs of Sun and RCA 78s, and all the reprocessed stereo originals, including the rare "silver tops." A chronological study of Elvis's recording career (pp. 13–30).

Source: Library of Congress ML156.7.P7 O8 1983
OCLC 9758144

———.

Presleyana III: The Elvis Presley Record Price Guide. Port Townsend, WA: Jellyroll Productions, 1992. 216 pp. ISBN: 0932117171.

An updated version of the second edition *Presleyana*. Osborne introduces two consequential modifications in pricing Elvis Presley recordings—separate pricing for all the recordings that make up a package—and precise individual identification of pressings.

Source: Library of Congress ML156.7.P7 O8 1992
OCLC 26997532

———.

Presleyana IV: The Elvis Presley Record Price Guide. "Special 20th Anniversary (1977–1997) Tribute Edition." Port Townsend, WA: Jellyroll Productions, 1997. 342 pp. ISBN: 0932117260.

More than 100 pages of additions and revisions to *Presleyana III*. In this edition Osborne explains how prices are determined, providing a 10-point grading system. Advice on selling to dealers.

Source: OCLC 39983678
Publisher's address: Jellyroll Productions, Box 255, Port Townsend, WA 98368

————.

Rockin' Records: Special Elvis Edition. Port Townsend, WA: Jellyroll Productions, 1986. ISBN: 093211704.

An Elvis recordings price guide.

Source: Jerry Osborne

☆ Peters, Richard

Elvis: The Music Lives On; The Recording Sessions of 1954–1976. London: Pop Universal/Souvenir Press, 1992. 144 pp. ISBN: 0285630997.

A history of Elvis Presley's singing career, with details about his recordings and studio sessions. Approximately 100 black and white photographs of Elvis in recording studios.

Source: The British Library YK.1993.b.11680
The New York Public Library

☆ Petrelle, David

Solid Gold Elvis: The Complete Collectors Manual. Denver, Colorado: Timewind Publishing, 1998. 720 pp. ISBN: none.

According to Petrelle, this book covers, in detail, every issue and every record or cover variation of every U.S. Elvis record pressing, from 1954 to April 1998. Listings of all live performances and radio, TV, and interviews; chart positions of all records and compact discs; every U.S. single, extended play, and album with every reissue and sleeve variation; film soundtrack recordings with every alternate take; listings of more than 500 bootleg compact discs and albums; all reel-to-reel, cassette, 8- and 4-track tapes. More than 1,400 pictures of sleeves and records. This book is self-published.

Petrelle has collected Elvis recordings since 1957. In 1960 he began a handwritten journal covering all the U.S. pressings of Elvis recordings. *Solid Gold Elvis* is the result of his 40-year effort.

Source: Publisher's address: Timewind Publishing, 1699 South Colorado Boulevard, Unit B, Denver, CO, 80222

☆ Plasketes, George M.

Plasketes is the author of *Images of Elvis Presley in American Culture, 1977–1997: The Mystery Terrain. (See* The Man/The Impact of Elvis.)

"The King Is Gone but Not Forgotten: Songs Responding to the Life, Death, and Myth of Elvis Presley in the 1980s." *Studies in Popular Culture* XII.1 (1989): 58–74.

This article examines the more than 200 records about Elvis Presley that were released worldwide in the four-month period following his death—and another 100 that appeared in 1978. Discography (pp. 73–74). Chapter notes.

☆ Rijff, Ger

Ger Rijff has produced 18 books about Elvis Presley.

Return to Sender. **Ann Arbor, MI: Pierian Press, 1988.**

A complete discography of Elvis Presley tribute recordings—soundalikes, novelties, narratives, 1956–1986. Photographs of some covers and sleeves.

Source: Clayson, Allan, and Spencer Leigh, editors. Aspects of Elvis: Tryin' to Get to You.

☆ Robertson, John

According to cover notes, " 'John Robertson' is the pseudonym of a noted UK rock critic." OCLC entry for this book lists "Add'l Name: Charlesworth, Chris."

The Complete Guide to the Music of Elvis Presley. **Series. London: Omnibus Press, 1994. 118 pp. ISBN: 0711935491. Music No: OP47376; Omnibus Press.**

"An album by album, track by track rundown of everything recorded by Elvis during his 22-year career." Song and album chronology and track index. Chapters on Elvis reissues, as well as CD and box set compilations. One hundred uncaptioned black and white and color photographs. In the mid-1990s this book was reissued by Omnibus Press and was packaged for sale with an Elvis-themed tee shirt.

Source: Canterbury (UK) Public Library 781.66 PRE
The Library of Congress ML156.7.P7 R6 1994
OCLC 31637867

☆ Silverton, Pete

Essential Elvis: A Photographic Survey of His Top Fifty Recordings. **London: Chameleon Books, 1997. 127, [1] pp. ISBN: 0233002456.**

Cursory examination of Elvis Presley's 50 top-selling recordings, as well as the top 10 of his currently available albums. Bibliographical references (pp. 127–[128]). Color and black and white photographs seen elsewhere.

Source: The British Library YK.1998.b.3008
OCLC 40195016

☆ Townson, John, Gordon Minto, and George Richardson

Elvis, U.K.: The Ultimate Guide to Elvis Presley's British Record Releases, 1956–1986. **Poole, Dorset, UK: Blandford Press, 1987. 565 pp. ISBN: 0713715634 (pbk.). ISBN: 0713715642 (hdk.).**

A discography reference book with listings and information on Elvis Presley's British-released singles (pp. 33–182), extended play albums (pp. 183–234), long play albums (pp.

235–526), and other Elvis record releases (pp. 527–556). Sections on label features and variations. Black and white reproductions of labels, sleeves, and album covers. Song and interview indices.

Source: Library of Congress ML134. T69 1987
Cambridge (UK) University Library MRR.48.PRE.1

☆ Tunzi, Joseph A.

Elvis Sessions: The Recorded Music of Elvis Aron Presley, 1953–1977. Chicago: J.A.T. Productions, 1993. 345 pp. ISBN: 0962008354.

"This volume is the first to present complete and accurate listings of Elvis's recording data and song titles" (p. xiii). Also includes chart positions and awards. Introduction by Scotty Moore, Elvis's first guitarist. Index of songs and songwriters. Black and white photographs; credited. This book was expanded in 1996 to include bootleg recordings. (*See* following listing.)

Source: Library of Congress ML156.7.P7 T86 1993
Dewey Decimal 016.78242166/092 20
OCLC 29799615

———.

Elvis Sessions II: The Recorded Music of Elvis Aron Presley, 1953–1977. Chicago: J.A.T. Productions, 1996. 415 pp. ISBN: 1888464011.

An updated and expanded reissue of *Elvis Sessions: The Recorded Music of Elvis Aaron Presley, 1953–1977.* Additions include the discography for the documentaries *Elvis: That's the Way It Is* and *Elvis on Tour* plus listings of acetates, private recordings, "essential" bootlegs, and tape legends. Al Pachucki, Elvis's recording engineer and friend, wrote the introduction to this edition. Index.

Source: Library of Congress ML156.7.P7 T86 1996
Dewey Decimal 782.42166/092 21
OCLC 36261232

☆ Umphred, Neal, editor

Elvis Presley: The Complete Elvis Presley U.S. Record Price Guide. 1985–1986 Edition. O'Sullivan Woodside Record Collectors Reference & Price Guide series. Phoenix, AZ: O'Sullivan Woodside, 1985. 173 pp. ISBN: 089019887.

According to Elvis author and music expert Jerry Osborne, this book is an unauthorized reworking of his book *Presleyana: Elvis Presley Record Price Guide* (1983). Osborne pursued legal action against the O'Sullivan Woodside publishing house and Umphred for copyright infringement and was awarded a favorable judgement.[2] The compiler was unable to locate Mr. Umphred for comment.

[2]Information based on interview with Jerry Osborne, Feb 9, 1999, and on copies of legal documents and correspondence relating to this matter as provided by him.

Source: Library of Congress ML156.7.P7 U46 1985
Dewey Decimal 78.9/1245 19
OCLC 13947615

☆ Umphred, Neal, with Linda Jones and Walter Piotrowski

A Touch of Gold: The American Record Collector's Price Guide to Elvis Presley Records & Memorabilia. Saugus, CA: White Dragon Press, 1990. 326 pp. ISBN: none.

A price guide to Elvis Presley's music on singles, albums, tapes, compact discs, counterfeit bootleg records, sheet music, and radio program tapes. Essays on collecting Elvis Presley radio show tapes. Advertisements for Elvis record dealers and collectors.

Source: Library of Congress ML156.7.P7 U4 1991
Dewey Decimal 782.42166/092 20

See Also:

In The Man/Biographies:

Clayson, Alan, and Spencer Leigh, *Aspects of Elvis: Tryin' to Get to You.*
Frew, Tim, *Elvis: His Life and Music.*

In The Phenomena/Collecting Elvis (Memorabilia):

Osborne, Jerry, *The Official Price Guide to Elvis Presley Records and Memorabilia.*

In Foreign Language Titles/Italian:

Elvis Presley: La Storia, Il Mito.

Liner Notes and Record Booklets Accompanying Albums and CDs

Liner Notes

The term "liner notes" refers to pamphlets and folders that are packaged with records and CDs. As the packaging of Elvis Presley's recordings became historically oriented in the late 1980s, liner notes were written by respected musicologists.

Elvis '56. New York: BMG Entertainment, 1996. 26 pp. ISBN: 7863668172.

A hardback book that contains the CD *Elvis '56.* Twenty-two black and white candid photographs of Elvis Presley taken by Alfred Wertheimer in 1956.

☆ Guralnick, Peter

Guralnick is a noted music historian who authored the highly acclaimed two-volume biography of Elvis: *Last Train to Memphis* and *Careless Love.*

Elvis, the King of Rock 'n' Roll: The Complete 50's Masters. New York: BMG Music,

1992. Unpaged. ISBN: none.

Source: Library of Congress M P934 n. 1-5 gde
OCLC 32371326

—————.

Elvis: From Nashville to Memphis. New York: BMG Music, 1993. Unpaged. ISBN: none.

Source: OCLC 32356541

—————.

Platinum: A Life in Music. [U.S.]: RCA, 1997. 47 pp. ISBN: none.

—————.

Sunrise. New York: BMG Music, 1999. Unpaged. ISBN: none.

Source: Compiler's collection

☆ Wolfe, Charles, Ph.D.

Wolfe is a leading expert on American gospel music.

Elvis Presley, Amazing Grace: His Greatest Sacred Performances. RCA, 1994. 31 pp.

See Also:

In Foreign Language Titles/Japanese:

Elvis Presley/Hawaii.

Record Booklets

Some of Elvis Presley's 1970s albums were accompanied by booklets containing photographs, reproductions of press clippings, and advertisements for other Elvis releases. An example is the three-album *A Legendary Performer*, which had a booklet packaged with each record. The booklets had the same titles as the album series they accompanied.

RCA Record Catalogs

Between 1965 and 1973, RCA annually issued catalogs of Elvis Presley recordings and tapes that were available for purchase. They were all titled *Elvis's RCA Victor Records* or *Elvis's Records and Tapes.* These catalogs also contained Elvis's live performance schedules, brief filmographies, and information about Elvis merchandise.

CHAPTER 14

Elvis's Influence on Music

ELVIS PRESLEY IS the most influential musician in the last half of the twentieth century. Period. His revolutionary breakthroughs have had a greater effect on music than anyone else of the time, and possibly the century.

Fellow music legends such as Little Richard and Jerry Lee Lewis credit Elvis with opening the doors for their own fame and fortune. Rock and roll icons such as John Lennon and the Rolling Stones claim Elvis as their inspiration. The authors of the musical influence titles explain why.

☆　　☆　　☆　　☆

☆ Austin, John

"Elvis: A New Love, A New Career." *Pageant* (March 1974): 38–45.

An assessment of Elvis Presley's career as of 1974, with an emphasis on his gospel music.

*Source: New York Public Library *DA (Pageant)*

☆ Clements, Andrew

"The Quiff That Roared." *The Guardian* (UK) (July 18, 1997): T2.

An examination of Elvis Presley's role in the birth of rock and roll: " . . . the single person who kick-started it all, made rock believe in itself, and made its followers convinced of its power."

☆ Davis, Francis

"Chuck and Elvis, Hands-On Preservationists, and Soul in the Biblical Sense." *The History of the Blues.* New York: Hyperion, 1995. ISBN: 0786881240. Pp. 206–229.

An examination of Elvis Presley's role in bringing black music into mainstream American culture. Discography (pp. 259–273). Bibliography (pp. 275–[279]). Index. (Note: *The History of the Blues* is the companion volume to a three-part 1995 Public Broadcasting System (PBS) series of the same name.)

☆ "The Elvis Effect." *Economist* (Aug 15, 1987): 22–23.

On the Tenth anniversary of Elvis Presley's death, August 16, 1987, the author examines the effect that Elvis and his music has had upon American culture.

☆ "He Can't Be . . . but He Is." *Look* (Aug 7, 1956): 82–85.

Text warns that Elvis has "dragged 'big beat' music to new lows in taste." Black and white candid photographs of Elvis and his fans.

☆ Jahn, Mike

"The 1940s and the 1950s: Gonna Raise a Holler." *Rock from Elvis Presley to the Rolling Stones.* New York: Quadrangle/The New York Times Book Company, 1973. ISBN: 0812903145. Pp. 1–89.

Written while Elvis Presley was still alive, this chapter places him in the context of the origins of rock and roll.

☆ Malone, Bill C.

Bill C. Malone is a country music historian and scholar.

"Elvis, Country Music, and the South." Ed. Jac L. Tharpe. *Elvis: Images and Fancies.* Jackson, MS: University Press of Mississippi, 1979. Pp. 123–134.

The author undertakes the first serious discussion of Elvis Presley's country music roots.

Source: Jac L. Tharpe, Ph.D., editor, Elvis: Images and Fancies.

☆ Marsh, Dave

"Elvis: How He Rocked the World." *TV Guide* (Aug 9, 1983): 35–38.

An essay examining Elvis Presley's musical contribution in pioneering a new form of music. The author, a highly regarded rock music writer, suggests that "Elvis will come to be seen as the most revolutionary and important indigenous American singer of the postwar decades."

☆ Matthew-Walker, Robert

Elvis Presley: A Study in Music. Speldhurst, England: Midas Books, 1979. 154 pp. ISBN: 0859361624. Series in Modern Music. London: Omnibus Press, 1983. 154 pp. ISBN: 0711900868.

An analysis of Elvis Presley, with an emphasis on his musical contributions. Brief biography and chronology with errors (i.e., incorrect guitar purchase story; the Presley's move to Tupelo in 1946). Analysis of Elvis's impact on this century's music. Discography. Filmography.

In 1988 this book was reissued in an expanded version as *Heartbreak Hotel: The Life and Music of Elvis Presley. Heartbreak Hotel* was reissued in an expanded version in 1995.

Source: Library of Congress ML420.P96 M35 (1979)
Dewey Decimal 784.5/4/00924 (1979)
OCLC 6330791 (1979); 10033093 (1983)

————.

Heartbreak Hotel: The Life and Music of Elvis Presley. London: Archway, 1988. 264 pp. ISBN: 1853880825. Revised Edition: 1995. 251 pp. ISBN: 2860740553. Chessington, Surrey: Castle Communications, 1995. 251 pp. ISBN: 1860740553.

An expanded edition of the previously published *Elvis Presley: A Study in Music*. New material examines additional recordings by Elvis Presley.

Source: OCLC 18626263 (1988); 35057153 (1995 Archway); 35091430 (1995 Castle Communications)

☆ Middleton, Richard

Richard Middleton is a musicologist.

"All Shook Up? Innovations and Continuity in Elvis Presley's Vocal Style." Ed. Jac L. Tharpe. *Elvis: Images and Fancies*. Jackson, MS: University Press of Mississippi, 1979. Pp. 151–161.

This book discusses Elvis Presley's vocal styles. Music-note graphics to demonstrate the author's conclusions. Footnotes.

Source: Jac L. Tharpe, Ph.D., editor. Elvis: Images and Fancies.

☆ "Music vs. Elvis Presley." *Jazz World* (Mar 1957).

In a article strongly reminiscent of the *Jailhouse Rock* cocktail party scene where sophisticates discuss the superiority of jazz in words usually reserved for opera commentary, a music writer sniffs about Elvis Presley's music: "One can't blame him for riding an unfortunate trend and getting what he can out of it. On the other hand, one can't help getting a certain satisfaction out of the fact that he won't be around for long. He's not music."

☆ Roy, Samuel, and Tom Aspell

Roy is also the author of *Elvis: Prophet of Power. (See* The Man/The Impact of Elvis.)

The Essential Elvis: The Life and Legacy of the King as Revealed Through 112 of His Most Significant Songs. Nashville, TN: Rutledge Hill Press, 1998. 256 pp. ISBN: 1558536930.

An examination of Elvis Presley's effect on popular music through an analysis of 112 songs that the authors believe defined Elvis's career. Interviews with Elvis's friends and family. Foreword by Elvis back-up singer Gordon Stoker of the Jordanaires. Index.

Source: Library of Congress ML420.P96 R72 1998
Dewey Decimal 782.42166/092 21

☆ Sobran, M. J., Jr.

"Heirs of Elvis." *National Review* (Oct 14, 1977): 1185–1186.

A memorial article examining Elvis as the unwitting forefather of both the rock culture and the rock tradition. The influences of Elvis are traced in the music of artists such as Bob Dylan, Joni Mitchell, and Carly Simon.

☆ Starr, Mark

"Rock and Roll Forever." *Newsweek* 122 (July 5, 1993): 48–49.

A discussion of why the popular recording artists from the 1960s—including Elvis Presley—continue to sell hundreds of thousands of records each year even though they are dead.

See Also:

In The Man/The Impact of Elvis:

Bayles, Martha, "Will the Real Elvis Please Stand Up?"
Guralnick, Peter, "Elvis: Entertainer of the Century."

In The Man/Major Articles:

Pleasants, Henry, "Elvis Presley." *The Great American Popular Singers.*
Wolfe, Charles, "Presley and the Gospel Tradition."

In The Academics/Elvis as an Academic Pursuit:

Firth, Simon, "The Academic Elvis."

CHAPTER 15
Filmography

ELVIS PRESLEY'S 31 motion pictures are not his greatest contribution to the world.[1] But the books covering this aspect of his career provide a saving grace as unique sources of information about Hollywood in the 1960s.

The Elvis filmography books range from trivia guides (Bartel, *Reel Elvis! The Ultimate Trivia Guide to the King's Movies*) to serious analysis of his acting career (McLafferty, *Elvis Presley in Hollywood: Celluloid Sell-Out*). In between, the others offer production histories and anecdotes, copies of media reviews, candid on-the-set photographs, plot synopses, interviews with co-workers, and insight into motion picture financial dealings. As a whole, this body of writing furnishes unmatched material about Hollywood filmmaking in the 1950s and 1960s.[2]

Unfortunately, most of Elvis's film career does not match the value of the filmography books. Elvis's first picture, *Love Me Tender* (1957), and the three others he made before entering military service in 1958,[3] are considered to be the best examples of his considerable serious acting talent. The movies released after Elvis's return to civilian life (made between 1960 and 1969) are the plot-wobbly, romantic musicals most often associated with his film career. Their major contribution to the study of the twentieth century is proof that on-screen underpants dropping has not always been a plot staple of the motion picture industry. Fortunately, we have the filmography books.

☆ ☆ ☆ ☆

☆ Bartel, Pauline C.

Pauline Bartel has also written a guide to collecting Elvis memorabilia, *Everything Elvis*. (*See* The Phenomena/Collecting Elvis.)

---

[1] However, his two documentaries (*Elvis: That's the Way It Is*, 1970, and *Elvis on Tour*, 1972) are superb sources of information about Elvis's concerts and tours, as well as the 1970s milieu.

[2] Since 1992, Peter Nazareth, Ph.D., professor of English and African American World Studies at the University of Iowa, has been offering a for-credit, cultural/historical course based on Elvis filmology, entitled "Elvis as Anthology."

[3] Elvis said that it was in *King Creole* that he did his best acting (press conference, Memphis, TN, Feb 25, 1961).

Reel Elvis! The Ultimate Trivia Guide to the King's Movies. Dallas: Taylor Publishing Company, 1994. 185 pp. ISBN: 0878338527.

A review of Elvis's motion picture career, listing anecdotes and details for all his films. Black and white still photographs from the films. Includes a mail-in application for a "Ph.D.D. in Presleyana." Bibliography (pp. 183–184). No index.

Source: Library of Congress ML420.P96 B42 1994
Dewey Decimal 791.43'75-dc20

☆ Bowser, James W., editor

Starring Elvis: Elvis Presley's Greatest Movies. New York: Dell Publishing Company, 1977. 255 pp. ISBN: 0440192417.

Plot summaries of the editor's favorite Elvis Presley films: *Love Me Tender, Loving You, Jailhouse Rock, King Creole, Wild in the Country, Blue Hawaii, Viva Las Vegas, Follow That Dream, Kid Galahad, Girls! Girls! Girls!, Roustabout, Harum Scarum,* and *Charro!* Each summary is accompanied by the names of the producers, directors, writers, and studio.

Source: OCLC 3333738

☆ Braun, Eric

The Elvis Film Encyclopedia. Woodstock, NY: Overlook Press, 1997. 192 pp. ISBN: 0879518146. London: Batsford, 1997. 192 pp. ISBN: 0879518146.

A reference book on Elvis Presley's films, including synopses, credits, music, and background information on each of his 31 films and two documentaries. Brief bibliography.

Source: Library of Congress ML420.P96 B7 1997
OCLC 36961126

☆ Danielson, Sarah Parker

Elvis: Man and Myth. London: Bison Books, 1990. 95 pp. ISBN: 0861246640. New York: Mallard Press, 1990. ISBN: none.

An analysis of Elvis's legend using his motion pictures. Color and black and white photographs. Comes with a color poster of Elvis playing a guitar. This book was translated into French. (*See* Foreign Language Titles/French.)

Source: The British Library LB.31.c2993

☆ Doll, Susan M., Ph.D.

The Films of Elvis Presley. Lincolnwood, IL: Publications International, Ltd., 1991. 95 pp. ISBN: 1561732788.

Overview essay "Elvis on Celluloid" (pp. 4–7) on Elvis Presley's film career. Storyline, Behind the Scenes, cast list, credits, movie stills, and album covers for each of the 33 films and documentaries starring Elvis.

Source: OCLC 26268319

☆ Guttmacher, Peter

Elvis! Elvis! Elvis! The King and His Movies. New York: Metro Books/Friedman/Fairfax, 1997. 128 pp. ISBN: 1567995306.

A filmography with descriptions of and anecdotes from each of Elvis Presley's 31 films and two documentaries. Also includes interviews with some of Elvis's co-stars and excerpts from critics' reviews. "Preslese Slang" chart (p. 53). One hundred and fifty color and black and white photographs; credited. Index. This book is accompanied by a 15-track CD of songs from Elvis's films.

☆ Hampton, Howard

"Elvis Dorado: The True Romance of *Viva Las Vegas.*" *Film Comment* (July–Aug 1994): 44–48.

Elvis's film *Viva Las Vegas* is compared to Christian Slater's *True Romance* as a "visionary artifact" which mirrors "every American fantasy of innocence and lust, flawless beauty and easy money, good times and charmed lives." *Film Comment* is a bimonthly publication of the Film Society of the Lincoln Center in New York City.

Source: Library of Congress PN1993.F438

☆ Lichter, Paul

Paul Lichter has published 20 photograph books on Elvis Presley; the first published in 1975, the most recent in 2000.

Elvis in Hollywood. A Fireside Book. New York: Simon and Schuster, 1975. 188 pp. ISBN: 671221531 (hdk.). ISBN: 67122154X (pbk.). London: Hale, 1975; 1977. 188 pp. ISBN: 0709157339.

The first Elvis filmography. A detailed account of Elvis Presley's film career published when the entertainer was alive. Background essays on Elvis's movies. Color reproductions of movie posters. Lists of songs in each film's album. According to *Publishers Weekly*, this book sold 5,000 copies on August 17, 1977, and 15,000 more were immediately printed (Sept 5, 1977: 5).

☆ McLafferty, Gerry

Elvis Presley in Hollywood: Celluloid Sell-Out. London: Robert Hale Ltd., 1989. 240 pp. ISBN: 0709037279 or 0709037299.

A thoughtful examination of Elvis Presley's acting career. A film-by-film study "to determine the pros and cons of what was, although financially rewarding, a greatly misguided career" (p. 13). An analysis of Colonel Parker's role in shaping Elvis's film career. More than 100 black and white photographs from Elvis's films and life in Hollywood. Filmography.

Source: New York Public Library MWES (Presley, E.) 90-2284
The British Library YC.1989.b.7855
OCLC 19264547
Michael Ochs Archives, Venice, CA

☆ Pond, Steve (text)

Elvis in Hollywood: Photographs from the Making of Love Me Tender." New York: New American Library/A Plume Book, 1990. 108 pp. ISBN: 0451263786. Canada: Penguin Books Canada Limited, 1990. ISBN: none.

100 black and white photographs documenting the filming of Elvis Presley's first film *Love Me Tender* (1956). Overview essay and narratives. Filmography.

Source: Library of Congress ML88.P76E47 1990

☆ Rai, Amit

"An American Raj in Filmistan: Images of Elvis in Indian Films." *Screen.* [London] (Spring 1994): 51–77.

Discusses the image of Elvis Presley in the films of India. By the early 1960s images of Elvis were also familiar to Indian urban youth. Dr. Rai suggests that for these young people, Elvis was a signifier for anti-government protest. He examines the hybrid figure of Elvis/Krishna in the Indian films *College Girl* and *Bluffmaster.*

Source: Library of Congress Microfilm 06985

☆ Rijff, Ger, editor

Inside Jailhouse Rock. [Amsterdam, The Netherlands]: [Tutti Frutti], 1994.

Based on the Jim Hannaford essay of anecdotes from the filming of Elvis's second film, *Jailhouse Rock.* (Jim Hannaford is the editor of three books of Elvis photographs. [*See* The Man/Photographs.]) Black and white photographs from the filming and reproductions of memorabilia associated with it.

Source: Michael Ochs Archives, Venice, CA

☆ Rijff, Ger, Jean Paul Commandeur, and Glen Johnson

Inside King Creole. Amsterdam, The Netherlands: Tutti Frutti Productions, 1999. 104 pp. ISBN: none.

Text by Glen Johnson covers filming of *King Creole* as well as Elvis's motion picture career. Black and white photographs of unused scenes from the movies and candids from the set. Reproductions of script pages, some magazine covers, and cartoons attributed to Elvis's *Loving You* co-star, Delores Hart. Essay on "The Search for 'King Creole' in the New Orleans of Today."

Source: Collection of Bill and Connie Burk, Memphis, TN

☆ Rijff, Ger, Jan van Gestel, and Lloyd Shearer

Elvis Presley: Memphis Lonesome. Amsterdam, The Netherlands: Tutti Frutti Productions, 1988. 120 pp. ISBN: 051757825.

A two-part photo/text book that explores Elvis Presley's career in 1955 and 1956, including the story of Elvis's first film appearance—in Cleveland (Ohio); disc jockey Bill Randle's never-released rock music documentary, *The Pied Piper of Cleveland*, filmed in 1955. Also contains photographs and text relating to an August 1956 Elvis concert in Florida and the filming of *Loving You* in 1957. Photographs include candids of Vernon and Gladys Presley.

Source: Michael Ochs Archives, Venice, CA

☆ Schuster, Hal

Hal Schuster's The Films of Elvis Presley: The Magic Lives On. Las Vegas, NV: Pioneer Books, 1989. Unpaged. ISBN: 1556982232.

An overview and assessment of the motion pictures and documentaries made by Elvis Presley. Filmography. Author commentary on the quality of each film.

Source: Library of Congress ML420.P96 S38 1989
OCLC 20954964

☆ Tunzi, Joseph A.

The First Elvis Video Price and Reference Guide. Chicago: J.A.T. Productions, 1998. 192 pp. ISBN: 89620008303.

An anthology and price guide of American and international Elvis Presley videos through 1987, including CD and laser discs, promotional tapes, and unauthorized tapes.

Source: Library of Congress MLCS 92/00930 (M)
OCLC 19700914

☆ Zmijewsky, Steven, and Boris Zmijewsky

Elvis: The Films and Career of Elvis Presley. Secaucus, NJ: Citadel Press, 1976. 223 pp. ISBN: 0806505117. Reissued in 1983; ISBN: 0806508892.

Biography chapter (pp. 13–100) written before Elvis Presley's death. Brief "Epilogue" chapter added to 1983 reissue, dealing with his death. One chapter for each of Elvis's movies and documentaries. "The Elvis Presley Discography of Million Record Sellers" (pp. 216–224). No index.

Press Books for Elvis's Films and Documentaries

Publicity efforts for each of Elvis Presley's 31 films and two documentaries included a promotional "press book"—formally titled "Merchandising Manual and Press Book." These were sent to theaters at the time of each movie's release. They contained plot synopsis, cast and production information, photographs, scripts for local radio promotion, pre-prepared advertising copy, and photographs of promotional give-away items for the film.

The largest collection of these press books available to researchers is housed at The Margaret Herrick Library, Academy of Motion Picture Arts and Sciences in Beverly Hills, California. Permission to view them must be made in advance. In addition, Elvis press books are frequently sold at eBay auction "All the King's Things." Web site: www.ebay.com/elvis/.

Scripts from Elvis's Films

The Core Collection of the Margaret Herrick Library, Academy of Motion Picture Arts and Sciences in Beverly Hills, California, has the most complete accumulation of scripts from Elvis Presley's films available for public reading. Permission to view them must be obtained in advance.

See Also:

In The Man/Biographies:

Celsi, Theresa, *Elvis*. ("Movies and Theater Productions Based on or Inspired by Elvis's Life or Legend," pp. 72–73.)
Doll, Susan, *Elvis: The Early Years: Portrait of a Young Rebel*.

In The Man/The Impact of Elvis:

Hammontree, Patsy Guy, *Elvis Presley: A Bio-Bibliography*.
Weales, Gerald, "Movies: The Crazy, Mixed-Up Kids Take Over." (*Love Me Tender*)

In The Man/Memoirs and Memories:

Archer, Jules, "I Had Dinner with Elvis." (*Love Me Tender*)
Dawson, Walter, "Elvis Presley Part 1: The People Who Know Say He Does Have Talent."
Pall, Gloria, '*Twas the Night I Met Elvis*.
Scheuer, Philip K., "Elvis Matches Dean's Skill Doin' What Comes Naturally." (Director of *Love Me Tender*)
Scott, Liz, "Elvis in New Orleans." (*King Creole*)
Weiss, Allan, "Elvis Presley: Rock Music Phenomenon."
Wiegert, Sue, *Elvis's Golden Decade*. (*Blue Hawaii*; *Paradise, Hawaiian Style*)

In The Man/Reference:

Aros, Andrew A., *Elvis: His Films and Recordings*.
The Elvis Files Explore His Life.
Whistler, John A., *Elvis Presley: Reference Guide and Discography*.
Worth, Fred L., *Elvis: His Life from A to Z*.

In The Phenomena/Literary Recreation and Moveable Books:

Elvis Goes Hollywood (a children's coloring book).

In Foreign Language Titles/French:

Presley, Elvis, 1935–1977 [clippings]. 1999.

In The Rest/Souvenir Magazines:

Elvis Presley in Hollywood.
The Films of Elvis Presley.
Photoplay Presents a Tribute to the Films of Elvis: 5th Anniversary Memorial Edition.

THE PHENOMENA

PART III

CHAPTER 16
Art

ELVIS AS IMAGE has so pervaded our global culture that a black wig with sideburns, lying in the road alongside a pair of gold-framed sunglasses, means the same thing in Nebraska as it does in Nicaragua. Artists have been drawn to this image—in part because of what Elvis represents and, perhaps, in part because of Elvis's facial similarities to such classical artistic figures as the "Antiochus of Commagene" and Michelangelo's "David." (*See* "The Face Is Familiar" in this chapter.) This fascination has produced a body of work that—in its scope and range—exists as an artistic genre of its own.

But curiously, a complete examination of this art has yet to be written. A few thoughtful commentaries have appeared as periodical articles and catalog essays, and several collections of Elvis art have been published. But this general lack of interest is puzzling when one considers the unwavering captivation that Elvis holds on our shared cultural consciousness.

This dearth cannot be explained by lack of professional artist interest. Andy Warhol used Elvis as a subject for his artistic exploration of popular culture images. The result—the 1964 silk-screen and acrylic *Elvis I* and *Elvis II* of Elvis in cowboy dress pointing a pistol at the viewer—was one of the first clues that Elvis's status had gone beyond the temporal world of entertainment. Thirty years later, one of the Warhol Elvises would hang in the National Gallery of Art in Washington, D.C., while picture postcards of it were sold in the gift shop.

As Elvis evolved from man to myth, others in the art world began to take notice. In 1994 an internationally exhibited show devoted to works featuring Elvis and, separately, Marilyn Monroe, toured America, Japan, and Mexico. The result—108 artists, including Warhol, Edward Ruscha, Robert Arneson, Keith Haring, and Laurens Tan—firmly established Elvis as a legitimate artistic muse. (*See* de Paoli, Geri, editor, *Elvis + Marilyn: 2 x Immortal* in this chapter.)

Elvis is also an object of fascination among the increasingly popular outsider artists, so-called because they are generally viewed as eccentric, not formally trained in art, and living—figuratively, if not literally—"outside" of society. The famous outsider artist Howard Finster of Summerville, Georgia, is one of the most prolific when it comes to Elvis. His works on wood, paper, metal, cloth, and canvas—some of which are owned by the National Gallery of Art and the Library of Congress—are a range of images that fascinate him, especially

Elvis.[1] The Rev. Finster uses his Elvis statues and prints to express his views on religion and spirituality.[2]

Fan artists are a sub-genre of Elvis art. They are mostly amateurs, but their work clearly captures the depth of their affection for Elvis. The annual Elvis Tribute Week Art Show at Graceland (August 10–17) garners more than 100 entries each year. But only one fan artist, a professional, has produced books of her work. (*See* Betty Harper listing in this chapter.)

Another area of Elvis art—the "Elvis on Velvet" genre—remains unexplored by the Elvis literature. In the 1960s mass production artists—particularly those in Northern Mexico—began pumping out assembly line portraitures of famous people, using oils on a black velvet "canvas." The predominant subjects tended toward iconology: at first, subjects appealing to Mexican culture such as Jesus Christ, bullfighters, and figures in traditional Mexican dress. As the appeal and audience of this art grew and spread into the United States, American icons were added: President John F. Kennedy, The Rev. Dr. Martin Luther King . . . and Elvis.[3]

As the popularity of Elvis as artistic muse grows—in velvet and the National Gallery of Art—appropriate Elvis literature on this subject is certain to follow.

☆　　☆　　☆　　☆

☆ **"Delta Axis Contemporary Arts Center Presents: In Search of Elvis."** *Elvis.* **Oxford, MS: The University of Mississippi International Conference on Elvis Presley, 1995. Pp. 14–27.**

Details and black and white and color photographs of exhibits in the 1995 Elvis-related art show at Memphis's Delta Axis Contemporary Arts Center. Artists include Howard Finster, Joni Mabe, Elayne Goodman, and the Reverend Frank Boyle. The show was held in conjunction with The University of Mississippi's First International Conference on Elvis Presley.

Delta Axis had previously mounted an Elvis art exhibit, "Elvis: A Cultural Obsession," in 1993. In 1997 another was mounted in conjunction with the Third International Conference on Elvis Presley, "Elvis 20/20: Past and Future." This exhibit had to remove a number of works when Elvis fans threatened to "take down the building brick by brick" in opposition to Elvis-themed paintings that ridiculed Christian ideology and symbols (*Commercial Appeal*, Aug 11, 1997).

Source: The University of Mississippi

[1] The Rev. Finster related to the compiler that Elvis "died several years before I had the pleasure of meeting him." One day, according to Rev. Finster, he was working in his garden when Elvis appeared. "I said, 'Elvis, how about staying a while?' But Elvis said, 'I'd like to, Howard, but I'm on a tight schedule,' and left." (August 1995, Oxford, MS.)

[2] At the First Annual International Conference on Elvis Presley (The University of Mississippi, 1995), the Rev. Finster spoke of Elvis's influence on him, other artists, and our society. (*See* Chadwick, *In Search of Elvis* in The Academics/Elvis as an Academic Pursuit.)

[3] Before the North American Free Trade Agreement (NAFTA), it was difficult to enforce copyrights in foreign countries. This situation allowed velvet Elvis paintings from Mexico to be readily available in the United States—even across the street from Graceland. Nowadays, travel to Tijuana, Mexico, is required.

☆ de Paoli, Geri, editor

Elvis + Marilyn: 2 x Immortal. New York: Rizzoli International Publications, 1994. 176 pp. ISBN: 0847818829 (hdk). ISBN: 0847818403 (pbk).

The catalog from the traveling art exhibition *Elvis + Marilyn: 2 x Immortal.* This exhibit is the first visual arts examination of the societal, cultural, and religious influences of Marilyn Monroe and Elvis Presley. The book features the work of 108 artists, including Andy Warhol, Edward Ruscha, and Laurens Tan. Color reproductions of each work in the show. Foreword by David Halberstam. Essays on Elvis by a range of authors, musicians, and artists, including Bono of the rock group U2. Chapter notes on the essays. Index.

The exhibition was displayed in Boston, Houston (Texas), Charlotte (North Carolina), Cleveland (Ohio), New York City, Nashville (Tennessee), San Jose (California), Honolulu, and Tokyo. For the Tokyo exhibition, the catalog was translated into Japanese. (*See* Foreign Language Titles/Japanese.)

Source: Library of Congress ML88.P76 E5 1994
Dewey Decimal 306'.0973

☆ Doss, Erika

"The Power of Elvis. (Power of Images in Late Twentieth Century America.)" *American Art* (Summer 1997): 4–7.

A discussion of art that provokes emotional responses among contemporary Americans, specifically works inspired by Elvis Presley. Elvis artists Joni Mabe (*see* The Phenomena/ Collecting Elvis) and Elayne Goodman are featured.

"The Face Is Familiar." *Look* (Dec 11, 1956): 130.

Black and white photographs and text that demonstrate Elvis Presley's physical relationship with the *Discobolus* by Myron (Fifth Century B.C., Greece) and Michelangelo's *David.*

☆ Harper, Betty

Harper is an Elvis fan and professional artist who is widely known for her portraits of entertainment celebrities. During her career, she has created more than 10,000 drawings of Elvis, documenting every stage of his life.

Elvis: Newly Discovered Drawings of Elvis Presley. New York: Bantam Books, 1979. [95] pp. ISBN: 055301241X.

Reproductions of 70 drawings of Elvis Presley by artist Betty Harper. One foldout drawing of Elvis's lips in various poses. This book was also published in German. (*See* Foreign Language Titles/German.)

Source: Library of Congress ML88.P76 H37 19
OCLC 6399807; 16613244

————.

The Magic of Elvis Through the Art of Betty Harper. Oak Hickory, TN: Marketing Alliance, Inc., 1985. Unpaged. ISBN: none.

Forty-eight of Harper's charcoal graphic illustrations of Elvis, as well as poems she has written about Elvis.

Source: Compiler's collection
Publisher's address: 3323 Old Hickory Road., Old Hickory, TN 37138

————.

Suddenly and Gently: Visions of Elvis Through the Art of Betty Harper. New York: St. Martin's Press, 1987. [41] pp. ISBN: 0312007078.

Reproductions of 65 charcoal and pen-and-ink drawings of Elvis. Some are accompanied by her poems. Foreword by Elvis author Bill E. Burk.

Source: Library of Congress ML88.P76 H39
Dewey Decimal 741.973
OCLC 15224292

☆ Panter, Gary

Invasion of the Elvis Zombies. Raw One-Shot series, #44. New York: Raw Books and Graphics, 1984. [32] pp. ISBN: 0915043017.

Pen-and-ink drawings relating to Elvis Presley by a celebrated punk artist. Accompanied by a 33⅓-rpm 6″ flex-disc recorded by the author entitled *Precambrian Bath*. This book was also released in Spanish. (*See* Foreign Language Titles/Spanish.)

Source: Library of Congress NC1429.I35 I57
New York Public Library PARSP N7433.4.P36 A4 1984 (English)

☆ Taylor, Roger G., compiler

Elvis in Art. London: Elm Tree Books/Hamish Hamilton Ltd., 1987. ISBN: none. New York: St. Martin's Press, 1987. ISBN: 0312013817.

Reproductions of 100 paintings and drawings of Elvis Presley created by British artists in the 1980s. Artwork is accompanied by unsourced quotes that are attributed to Elvis's friends, family members, and admirers.

Source: Library of Congress ML88.P76 E45 1987
Dewey Decimal 757.3/0973 19

See Also:

In The Man/The Impact of Elvis:

Marcus, Greil, *Dead Elvis: A Chronicle of a Cultural Obsession*. (Book's illustrations are primarily reproductions of Elvis-themed artwork by a variety of artists.)

In The Music, The Movies/Discography:

Dowling, Paul, *Elvis: The Ultimate Album Cover Book.*
Dowling, Paul, *Elvis Presley: The Record Covers of the King.*

In The Phenomena/Collecting Elvis (Memorabilia):

Mabe, Joni, *Everything Elvis.*

CHAPTER 17
Bibliographies

UNTIL NOW, SERIOUS interest in cataloging the Elvis literature was confined to a brief period in the 1980s. In 1981 Memphis librarian John Whistler compiled the first Elvis bibliography (128 titles)[1] for his reference book, *Elvis Presley Reference Guide and Discography*. (*See* The Man/Reference.) In 1982 author Martin Torgoff wrote the first bibliographic essay on the Elvis literature. (*See* listing in this chapter.) In 1985 Dr. Patsy Guy Hammontree wound up this period with a thoughtful bibliographical essay discussing the Elvis titles' history and impact through the mid-1980s. (*See* The Man/The Impact of Elvis.)

Two attempts were made in the 1990s to tuck all the titles under one set of covers. In the mid-1990s, Elvis bibliophile Maria Columbus compiled a manuscript titled *Elvis in Print*. As of 2000, it remains unreleased, even though it occasionally appears in bibliographic references as a published item. In 1999 Greenwood Press published one of the most unscholarly Elvis books ever printed: *The Printed Elvis* by Steven Opdyke. The book covered only 400 titles and Opdyke lists books that are unrelated to Elvis (i.e., Gripe's *Elvis and His Friends* and *Elvis and His Secret* [pp. 141-142]; Everez's *Shooting Elvis* [p. 47]). In a few instances, he misidentifies book types such as classifying Marino's fictional *The Day Elvis Came to Town* and Leigh's middle school textbook *Elvis Presley* [p.53] as personal memoirs [p.53].

As the flow of Elvis books proceeds unabated, the need for a correct and complete listing grows as well. Hopefully, *Infinite Elvis* is a step in that direction.

☆   ☆   ☆   ☆

☆ Baker, Robert D.

"In Search of Elvis." *Wilson Library Bulletin* 69 (May 1995): 39-41.

An overview of the Elvis material available for researchers and readers in the Memphis/Shelby County (TN) Public Library and Information Center. Anecdotes about working with researchers who use the Elvis materials.

---

[1]The total number of titles in Whistler's listing is less than 128 as he made separate entries for each edition of the same book (i.e., Yancey, *My Life with Elvis,* has four entries).

The Memphis/Shelby Country Library maintains a collection of archived materials in its Memphis Room. Most of the Library's Elvis holdings are located there. Advance permission is required before examination of these materials can be made.

☆ Dahlin, Robert

"The Unique Appeal of Elvis Presley's Music Now Carries Over to Books About Him." *Publishers Weekly* (Sept 5, 1977): 5.

Published three weeks after the death of Elvis Presley, this article discusses the astonishing number of Elvis books that had been reissued in that brief time frame. Print runs for specific books are given.

☆ Opdyke, Steven

The Printed Elvis: The Complete Guide to Books About the King. Westport, CT: Greenwood Press, 1999. 320 pp. ISBN: 0313308152.

Contains references to only 400 titles, some of which have nothing to do with Elvis. Written in narrative format with limited information for each book. Incorrect descriptions and facts for some of the titles. (*See* essay at beginning of this chapter.) Essays on Elvis's success, Elvis and African Americans, and Colonel Parker. Guide to collecting Elvis books (which inexplicably profiles Elvis eccentric Paul MacLeod who does not collect Elvis books).[2] Incomplete chronology of Elvis titles. Source notes. Indices.

☆ Terreo, John

A Bibliography of Holdings Concerning Elvis Aron Presley in the Mississippi Valley Collection. Memphis, TN: Memphis State University, 1983. ISBN: none.

A catalog of the Elvis Presley items in the Mississippi Valley Collection of the John William Brister Library at the University of Memphis (formerly known as Memphis State University). Researchers wishing to view this collection must apply in writing for permission.

Source: The Mississippi Valley Collection, The University of Memphis (TN)
OCLC 9874195

☆ Torgoff, Martin

"After the Flood: Elvis and His Literary Legacy." *The Complete Elvis.* Ed. Martin Torgoff. New York: Delilah Books, 1982. ISBN: 0933328281. Pp. 19-38.

An overview of the Elvis titles and literary genres. Torgoff focuses on the books he believes to be worthwhile and those that he believes are not. Torgoff also writes of the Elvis fans' skepticism about these books.

Source: Torgoff, Martin, editor, The Complete Elvis.

---

[2]MacLeod and his son are personal friends of the *Infinite Elvis* compiler. (*See* Chadwick, *In Search of Elvis*, p. 178.) MacLeod, who charges for interviews, reports that he did not speak with Opdyke.

☆ Tucker, Stephen R., Ph.D.

"Visions of Elvis: Changing Perceptions in National Magazines, 1956-1965." Ed. Jac L. Tharpe. *Elvis: Images and Fancies*. Jackson, MS: University Press of Mississippi, 1979. Pp. 27-39.

The author, a scholar from Tulane University, traces magazine media responses to Elvis from the beginning of his career through 1965. Tucker explores how acceptance of Elvis by the American middle class changed radically during the 1956 through 1965 period. Footnotes with biographical references.

Source: Tharpe, Jac L., Ph.D., editor, Elvis: Images and Fancies.

See Also:

In The Man/Biographies:

Gray, Michael H., "Presley, Elvis Aron," *Bibliography of Discographies.*

In The Man/The Impact of Elvis:

Hammontree, Patsy Guy, *Elvis Presley: A Bio-Bibliography.*

In The Man/Photographs:

Kricun, Morrie E., and Virginia M. Kricun, *Elvis 1956 Reflections.*

In The Man/Reference:

The (Elvis) Files.
Sauers, Wendy, *Elvis Presley, A Complete Reference: Biography, Chronology, Concerts List, Filmography, Discography, Vital Documents, Bibliography.*
Whistler, John A., *Elvis Presley: Reference Guide and Discography.*

In The Academics/Dissertations and Theses:

Wireman, J. D., "Textual Elvis."

CHAPTER 18
Business and Finance

THE BUSINESS AND financial area of the Elvis Presley literature is an unmined cache of information that, when revealed, will divulge amazing stories of commercial acumen and entrepreneurship. It has remained untouched, in large part, because of the varying degrees of privacy with which Elvis's father, Vernon, and Elvis's manager, Colonel Tom Parker, surrounded the entertainer's financial records. Though others have published information about Colonel Parker's dealings—most notably in 1981, when the estate was ordered by the Probate Court to sue Parker for improper management—the facts of his financial management remain untold. (*See* The Phenomena/The Law.)

The management of Elvis's estate, Elvis Presley Enterprises, Inc. (EPE), continues to maintain Colonel Parker's veil of financial privacy.[1] The EPE Board of Directors, which includes Priscilla Presley, administers Elvis's estate in trust for Lisa Marie Presley, his daughter and sole surviving beneficiary. Thus, information about the EPE financial undertakings is appropriately maintained only between Lisa Marie Presley and the Board of Directors.

EPE's accomplishments have been remarkable, if nothing short of historical. Priscilla Presley, as executor for the estate and acting in that capacity, and Jack Soden, Chief Executive Officer of EPE, have taken a dwindling, debt-ridden inheritance and created a booming multimillion-dollar concern with enterprises that include one of the nation's top tourist attractions, licensed merchandise, a hotel, the first of a planned series of Elvis-themed restaurants (E.P.'s Memphis), and more. When Soden writes his story, it will be mandatory reading at schools of business.

Only one author has attempted to examine the financial dealings of EPE, Sean O'Neal, in his *Elvis Inc.: The Fall and Rise of the Presley Empire.* Unfortunately, it is flawed by unsubstantiated data and speculation, as well as a lack of footnotes, citations, chapter notes, and list of sources. Fortunately, a researcher in this area can gain authenticated details from periodical articles. (*See* listings in this chapter.) But the book of this remarkable business and financial story remains to be written.

[1]Elvis Presley Enterprises, Inc., was established in 1956 to market Elvis-related merchandise.

☆   ☆   ☆   ☆

☆ Baker, Jackson

"Jack Soden: The Keeper of the Kingdom." *Memphis* (July/Aug 1992): 22–32, 45, 56–58.

Story of how Jack Soden, CEO of Elvis Presley Enterprises, Inc., worked with Priscilla Presley to build Elvis's estate to its current secure and growing status.

☆ Bosquet, Jean

"He's a 'Man' Now—and an Industry." Four-part series. New York: *Journal-American* (June 12–16, 1960).

☆ "Elvis Presley Died in 1977. Guess How Much He Will Earn This Year?" *Forbes* (Oct 3, 1988).

☆ "Enterprise: Presley Spells Profit." *Newsweek* (Feb 18, 1957): 84–85.

One of the earliest serious assessments of Elvis Presley's expanding profitability beyond his recordings and films. The article, written just a year after his first national appearance,[2] examines the numbers of Elvis souvenirs that had been produced and their profits. Interview with Henry G. Saperstein who oversaw the licensing and sales of Elvis souvenirs. Quote from Saperstein about Elvis's reaction to these souvenirs.

☆ Feinberg, Andrew

"Elvis's Graceland: The Attraction That Sells Itself." *Adweek's Marketing Week* (July 10, 1989): 17.

Interview with Todd Morgan (then–communications manager for EPE, now Director of Creative Resources) about EPE's future marketing plans.

☆ "The Great Elvis Presley Industry." *Look* (Nov 13, 1956): 98–107.

The first article to examine in detail the commercialization of Elvis Presley. Focuses on the efforts of Colonel Parker and Elvis merchandising manager Hank Saperstein. Discussion of the 1956 output and earnings of the operation.

☆ "If He Isn't Dead, He Owes an Awful Lot of Back Tax." *Economist* (Aug 16, 1997): 48.

An exploration of why Elvis Presley is still generating income 20 years after his death. According to the article, "Memphis, Tennessee, reckons Elvis is responsible for most of the tourist industry's $1.8 billion annual revenues and 37,000 jobs."

☆ Meeks, Flemming

"Elvis Lives." *Forbes* (Aug 21, 1989): 104.

[2] *Jimmy and Tommy Dorsey's Stage Show* on Jan 28, 1956.

An assessment of Elvis Presley Enterprises, Inc.'s, financial status as of 1989. Brief biography on and comments by Jack Soden, EPE's CEO.

☆ O'Neal, Sean

O'Neal collects Elvis memorabilia. He is the author of *My Boy Elvis*. (*See* The Man/Biographies.)

Elvis Inc.: The Fall and Rise of the Presley Empire. Rocklin, CA: Prima Publishing, 1996. 242 pp. ISBN: 0761503986. Prima Publishing, 1997. 256 pp. ISBN: 076151127X.

An assumptive financial history of the estate of Elvis Presley and its trustee, Elvis Presley Enterprises, Inc. (EPE), which makes unsupported and sensational claims such as "a portion of the revenue from EPE does go to the Church of Scientology in the form of donations" (p. 185). No notes, citations, or sources. Eight pages of black and white photographs; captioned but not specifically credited. Bibliography (pp. 229–230). Index.

☆ Owen, Elizabeth

"The King's Ransom: Elvis Presley Lives On as a Billion-Dollar Business." *Life* (Aug 1984): 76–84.

☆ Saunders, Laura

"Sell Me Tender." *Forbes* (Feb 13, 1984): 42–43.

Interview with Joe Rascoff, an Elvis Presley Enterprises, Inc., accountant who was handling the marketing and expansion plans. Rascoff comments on the current activities of the estate as well as future plans. This article is accompanied by an overview of Colonel Tom Parker's financial involvement with Elvis and with the trustees of Elvis's estate.

☆ Schwartz, Tony

"The Spoils of Elvis." *Newsweek* (Jan 30, 1978): 58.

This article discusses the growth of the Elvis Presley memorabilia market since his death six months earlier. Emphasis on how entrepreneurs with no connection to Elvis Presley's estate are planning to capitalize on the market.

☆ "Sellvis." *Economist* 327 (Apr 10, 1993): 66.

Discussion of the manner in which "the management of Elvis Presley's estate and fortune has turned Graceland into a financial gold mine" (ProQuest Periodical Abstracts 01498846.)

☆ "Taking Care of (the King's) Business." *People Weekly* (Mar 1, 1993): 70.

An overview of the history and financial status of the Elvis Presley estate.

☆ Westenberger, Theo

"The King's Ransom." *Life* (Aug 1984): 79–82.

A profile of the financial status of Elvis Presley Enterprises, Inc., as of 1984, with discussion of future expansion and investment plans. Overview of current and future status of Elvis recordings and videos, as of 1984.

See Also:

In The Man/Biographies:

Andrews, Suzanne, "Making Elvis Pay."

In The Man/Graceland:

Balfour, Victoria, "Amazing Graceland."
Gillette, Jane Brown, "Elvis Lives."

In The Man/The Impact of Elvis:

Shapiro, Joseph P., "The King Is Dead, but His Rich Legacy Still Grows."

In The Man/Memoirs and Memories:

Crumbaker, Marge, and Gabe Tucker, *Up and Down with Elvis Presley.*
Thompson, Sam, *Elvis on Tour the Last Year.*
Tio, Maria Mercedes, "Otis Blackwell: The Power Behind Elvis."

In The Music, The Movies/Discography:

Dowling, Paul, *Elvis: The Record Covers of the King.*

In The Phenomena/Collecting Elvis (Memorabilia):

Tai, Pauline, "Collectibles: Elvis's Great Career Move."

In The Phenomena/Fans:

Arthur, Caroline, "Going to Graceland."

In The Phenomena/The Law:

Gwynne, S. C., "Love Me Legal Tender."

CHAPTER 19
Collecting Elvis (Memorabilia)

THE COLLECTING OF Elvis Presley memorabilia[1] began its wild ride on the wave of amassing mania that roared through the economically flush 1980s. It has remained atop the crest as the collecting passion soars through the 1990s.

In the process, a separate collecting industry has grown up around Elvis. The prestigious auction house Butterfield and Butterfield has held three highly profitable Elvis Presley memorabilia sales. (*See* Butterfield listing in this chapter.) The on-line auction wunderkind eBay.com has a separate Elvis auction homepage, "All The King's Things,"[2] as well as internationally recognized Elvis memorabilia expert Robin Rosaaen on staff. (*See* listing in this chapter.)

As this passion has grown, so have its prices.[3] Elvis memorabilia price guides have kept pace. (*See* Cranor, Osborne, and Templeton listings in this chapter.) But although Lee Cotten produced a comprehensive book on this subject in 1987, a current history of Elvis collectibles has yet to be written. (*See* Cotten listing in this chapter.)

Other books about Elvis collections range from the practical to the fanciful. Pauline Bartel, Rosalind Cranor, Jerry Osborne, and Steve Templeton have written how-to guides for developing, acquiring, and caring for an Elvis memorabilia collection. At the other end of the spectrum is Georgia artist and Elvis fan Joni Mabe's *Everything Elvis*—a glorious photographic survey of her internationally exhibited collection of Elvisian memorabilia and art.

One surprising void in these collecting guides is any title relating specifically to Elvis books and magazines. Imagine! A segment of the Elvis world that still needs exploring! While Cranor, Cotten, Osborne, and Templeton give descriptions and prices of selected

---

[1] Elvis collectibles range from items he owned to those produced after his death. Thus, they include everything from a signed library card from his junior high school days to the No. 1 Elvis Christmas ornament produced by the Carlton Company in 1995.

[2] www.ebay.com/elvis/.

[3] Elvis Presley Enterprises, Inc., refers Elvis collectibles valuation queries to Jerry Osborne of Port Townsend, Washington, and has his latest Elvis memorabilia price guide on the EPE Suggested Elvis Reading list. (*See* Osborne listing below, as well as Osborne's web site: www.jerryosborne.com.

titles, there is no book comprehensively covering this sector of Elvis collecting. Somebody get busy!

☆　　☆　　☆　　☆

☆ *All the King's Things: The Ultimate Elvis Memorabilia Book.* San Francisco: Bluewood Books, 1993. 32 pp. ISBN: 0912517042.

Color photographs of and text about the 40,000-piece collection of Elvis memorabilia and photograph authority Robin Rosaaen. Rosaaen has been collecting Elvis memorabilia for the past three decades and is widely recognized as an expert in the field.

Source: Library of Congress ML420.P96 A69 1993

☆ Bartel, Pauline

Everything Elvis. Dallas, TX: Taylor Publishing Company, 1995. 172 pp. ISBN: 0878338780.

A guide to collecting Elvis memorabilia with chapters on developing, acquiring, and caring for a collection. Overview of Elvis collectibles. Resources for locating Elvis collectibles. Bibliography related to Elvis memorabilia (pp. 171–172). No index.

Bartel has also published an Elvis filmography. (*See* The Music,The Movies/Filmography.)

Source: Library of Congress ML420.P96 B417 1995

☆ Canady, Barbara

Elvis Memorabilia: Catalog and Price Guide. Hampton, VA: B and B Enterprises, 1981. 80 pp. ISBN: none.

A 1981 survey of Elvis collectibles and their value. Photographs.

Source: OCLC 11031550

☆ Cotten, Lee

Lee Cotten is the author of seven Elvis books.

The Elvis Catalog: Memorabilia, Icons, and Collectibles Celebrating the King of Rock 'n' Roll. "A Dolphin Book." Garden City, NY: Doubleday, 1987. 255 pp. ISBN: 0385237057 (hdk.), ISBN: 0385237049 (pbk.).

A reference and historical guide to Elvis Presley memorabilia that organizes its text in a biographical format. A directory of memorabilia manufacturers licensed by Elvis Presley Enterprises, Inc., as of 1987. Black and white and color photographs and poster and record cover reproductions; captioned and credited. Cover note: "Authorized by Elvis Presley Enterprises."

☆ Cranor, Rosalind

Elvis Collectibles. Paducah, KY: Collector Books, 1982. 366 pp. ISBN: 0891452052. Paperback edition, 1983. ISBN: same.

Elvis Collectibles. Revised 2nd Edition. Johnson City, TN: Overmountain Press, 1987. 400 pp. ISBN: 0932807224.

The 1982 edition was the first comprehensive guide to Elvis Presley collectibles—excluding recordings. Chapters cover novelty items, RCA collectibles, postcards, sheet music, photographs, Las Vegas and concert items, publications, and motion picture collectibles. The revised second edition has updated price valuations and the addition of foreign Elvis memorabilia. Contributing editors for both editions: Steve Templeton and Ted Young.

Source: OCLC 8883701 (1982)
Library of Congress ML420.P96 C7 1983; ML420.P96 C7 1987

☆ Cranor, Rosalind, and Steve Templeton

Updated Price Guide to Elvis Collectibles. Johnson City, TN: Overmountain Press, 1992. [48] pp. ISBN: 093280781X.

A supplement containing updated prices for *Elvis Collectibles*, 1987.

Source: OCLC 33048832

☆ Cranor, Rosalind, with Steve Templeton and Ted Young

Elvis Collectibles. 3rd Edition. Johnson City, TN: Overmountain Press, 1994. ISBN: 1570720134.

Same photographs and text as the 1987 *Elvis Collectibles* (Revised 2nd Edition). Updated price valuations. Recommended by Elvis Presley Enterprises, Inc.

Source: OCLC 31618907 (1994)

☆ "Elvis: Fifty Years After His Birth, His Fans Still Love Him Tender." *Collectibles Illustrated.* (Jan/Feb 1985).

[Elvis trading card sets.] Collect. *Jan 1993.*

The premier issue of trading card price guide *Collect* magazine, devoted to the history and pricing of Elvis Presley trading card sets.

☆ Guttman, Monika

"To Collectors, the King's Alive." *U.S. News & World Report* (Aug 8, 1994): 78–80.

Examines the high prices of Elvis collectibles and discusses the types of Elvis collectibles that sell well and the factors that influence their value.

☆ Mabe, Joni

The Elvis Room: An Installation. [Athens, GA]: [The University of Georgia], 1983. 1 vol. ISBN: none.

Mabe's M.F.A. project at The University of Georgia—a room filled with Elvis objects.

Source: OCLC 13728813

————.

Everything Elvis. New York: Thunder's Mouth Press, 1996. 136 pp. ISBN: 1560251077. [London]: Pavilion Books Ltd., 199 pp. ISBN: 1857937627. New York: Thunder's Mouth Press, 1998. 140 pp. ISBN: 1560251786.

Approximately 125 color photographs of Mabe's Elvis memorabilia collection and her Elvis artwork, exhibited internationally as the "Traveling Panoramic Encyclopedia of Everything Elvis." The collection consists of a variety of items, from lamps and bedspreads to paintings and a possible Elvis toenail. Reproductions of Mabe's Elvis-themed collages.

☆ Osborne, Jerry

Osborne has written 71 books about music, including 14 about Elvis memorabilia and recordings. Elvis Presley Enterprises, Inc., refers Elvis collectibles questions to him.

The Official Price Guide to Elvis Presley Records and Memorabilia. 1st Edition. New York: House of Collectibles, 1994. 430 pp. ISBN: 0876379390.

Introduction offering advice and information on collecting, pricing, grading, and selling Elvis recordings and memorabilia. Chapters covering prices and details of more than 6,000 Elvis 8-track tapes, compact discs, long play albums, extended plays, RCA labels, Elvis inner sleeves, acetates, titles for all singles and all flip-side singles, and Elvis memorabilia. "Elvis Music Chronology." Buyers and sellers directory. Black and white and color reproductions of sleeves, album covers, and record labels. Movie memorabilia editor: Steve Templeton.

————.

Official Price Guide to Elvis Presley Records and Memorabilia. 2nd Edition. New York: House of Collectibles/Ballantine Publishing Group, 1998. 539 pp. ISBN: 0676601413.

An updated edition of Osborne's *The Official Price Guide to Elvis Presley Records and Memorabilia.* (*See* preceding listing.) Also lists Elvis CDs.

☆ Osborne, Jerry, with Perry Cox and Joe Lindsay

Cox and Lindsay are the co-authors of *The Beatles Price and Reference Guide.* At the time of publication Lindsay was a record and memorabilia dealer in Memphis, Tennessee.

The Official Price Guide to Memorabilia of Elvis Presley and the Beatles. Official Price Guide series. New York: House of Collectibles, 1988. 432 pp. ISBN: 0876370806.

Valuations, as of 1988, of collectibles and records relating to Elvis Presley and to the Beatles. Introductory overview on collecting records and autographs (pp. 1–19). Discographies. Videographies. (OCLC has also listed this book as an annual serial publication, Vol. 1 [OCLC 19364794].)

☆ Peers, Alexandria

"Elvis Relics Fetch Big Bids at Vegas Sale." *Wall Street Journal* (June 20, 1994), Eastern Ed.: C1+.

A report on the first major Elvis memorabilia auction, held at Butterfield and Butterfield in June 1994. (*See* Auction Catalogs in this chapter.)

☆ Putnam, Stan P.

Momento, Souvenir, Keepsake, Collector's Kit of the Life and Music of Elvis Presley. 1987. ISBN: 0944047092.

Source: www.amazon.com

————.

New Found Facts and Memorabilia of Elvis Presley. ISBN: 0944047076.

Source: www.amazon.com

☆ Rodger, William

"The Beat Goes On." *Hobbies: The Magazine for Collectors* (Feb 1980): 100, 104.

An article examining Elvis Presley autographs from a collector's perspective and assessing their current and future values.

☆ Schruers, Fred

"What Price Glory? Peddling the Relics of Royalty." *Crawdaddy* (Nov 1977): 35–36.

A feature article on the selling of Elvis records and memorabilia, focusing on salesman and Elvis author Paul Lichter. (*See* The Man/Biographies; The Man/Photographs; The Music, The Movies/Filmography.) Author analyzes the psyche of both seller and purchaser/collector.

☆ Tai, Pauline

"Collectibles: Elvis's Great Career Move." *Money* (Aug 1987): 30–31.

Discussion of the lucrative business of Elvis collectibles and of Elvis's postmortem prosperity in a magazine aimed at sophisticated consumers and investors.

☆ Templeton, Steve

Templeton has been researching and collecting Elvis memorabilia for more than 20 years. He is co-author (with Rosalind Cranor) of *Elvis Collectibles* and *The Best of Elvis Collectibles.*

Elvis! An Illustrated Guide to New and Vintage Collectibles. Philadelphia, PA: Courage Books, 1996. 128 pp. ISBN: 1561387118. London: Apple Press, 1996. 128 pp. ISBN: 1850766533.

A chronicle of Elvis Presley's life through more than 500 collectibles. Advice on collecting Elvis Presley memorabilia (in categories such as Elvis in Las Vegas, his motion pictures, publications), as well as valuations and availability of collectibles. Color and black and white photographs. Suggested purchasing sources (p. 125). Discography (p. 127). Filmography (p. 126). Index.

Source: OCLC 34380192 (Courage Books)
Cambridge University Library (UK) MR557.a.95.35 (Apple Press)

☆ Templeton, Steve, with Rosalind Cranor, Ted Young, and John Diesso

The Best of Elvis Collectibles. Johnson City, TN: Overmountain Press, 1992. 115 pp. ISBN: 0932807771.

Recommended by Elvis Presley Enterprises, Inc. (Recordings are not covered in this book.)

Source: OCLC 27129875

See Also:

In The Man/Biographies:

Buskin, Richard, *Elvis Memories and Memorabilia.*
Cotten, Lee, *The Elvis Catalog: Memorabilia, Icons, and Collectibles Celebrating the King of Rock 'n' Roll.*

In The Man/Reference:

Farren, Mick, *The Hitchhiker's Guide to Elvis.*

In The Music, The Movies/Filmography:

Press Books for Elvis Presley's Films and Documentaries.

In The Phenomena/Business and Finance:

Schwartz, Tony, "The Spoils of Elvis."

In The Rest/Souvenir Magazines:

The Love of Elvis.
A Tribute to Elvis: 20th Anniversary Special.

Auction Catalogs

W. and F. C. Bonham and Sons, Limited

Elvis Is Back! Via Satellite. The Paul Lichter Collection and Other Important Properties. Sale 27,312. (Catalog for the Aug 30, 1997, sale, London, UK, and Berlin, GE.)

Source: Compiler's collection

☆ Butterfield and Butterfield, Auctioneers Corporation Catalogs

Elvis Presley Memorabilia. Sale 6279. (Catalog for Oct 6 and 7, 1995, sale, Los Angeles and Las Vegas.)

The Elvis Presley Museum Collection. Vol. B40, Sale 6074 B. (Catalog for the June 18–19, 1994, sale, Las Vegas and San Francisco.)

The Elvis Presley Museum Collection. Sale 6529. (Catalog for the Nov 3, 1996, sale, Los Angeles.)

☆ Guernsey's

Elvis Presley: The Official Auction Featuring Items from the Archives of Graceland. (Catalog for the Oct 8–10, 1999, sale, Las Vegas.)

Source for all auction catalogs:
Collection of Marjorie Wilkinson, Mill Valley, CA

☆ Don B. Smith Auction Co., Inc. and Empire Auctioneers

. . . *The Personal Property Formerly Owned by Elvis and Priscilla Presley: Their Former Home at 1174 Hillcrest Road, Beverly Hills, California.* (Catalog for the Sept 30, 1980, sale, Hollywood [CA] Palladium.)

Source: Compiler's collection

CHAPTER 20
Comic Books

COMIC BOOKS ABOUT Elvis Presley reflect their times. Thus, Elvis's first appearance in this genre was in a 1957 romance comic book/story magazine, *Young Lovers*. (*See* The Man/ Biographies.) This was a text-only article simply titled "Biography of Elvis Presley." The cover cartoon was of a young woman gazing lovingly at a photograph of Elvis. It fit perfectly with the delightfully naïve 1950s when teenage girls believed that "one day my prince will come"—and he might be Elvis.

By the 1990s Elvis comics had changed. In this decade, when chronological grown-ups sought to delay their behavioral maturity, adult consumer comics became popular. Thus, most of the Elvis-related ones were serious biographies—though a few appeared to be in competition to see who could garner more attention and a more outré reputation through pathetically crude and outrageous text and drawings.

The most unusual of these post-1990 comic books unabashedly uses Elvis to attract believers to the Libertarian political philosophies through an Elvisian rewrite of the Ayn Rand classic *Atlas Shrugged*. (*See* McCray listing in this chapter.)

As comic books have morphed their way out of childhood into serious art and literature, their treatment of Elvis has followed. In this manner, the Elvis comics serve as yet another touchstone for the progress of our culture.

☆   ☆   ☆   ☆

☆ *Archie's Girls Betty and Veronica.* 1959.

A one-page biography of Elvis in the popular *Archie* series comic books.

Source: eBay auction item #110557455

☆ *Elvis: His Life and Afterlife.* #1. [U.S.]: Jam Press, Aug 1992.

A biography of Elvis that also explores the possibility that he still lives.

Source: eBay auction item #190334967

☆ *Elvis Presley.* Personality Classics #3; Limited Trading Card Edition. Northport, NY: Personality Comics, Inc., May 1992. [20] pp. ISBN: none.

A brief cartoon biography of Elvis Presley's life and career. Limited edition of 2,000; each copy is numbered. Four cartoon trading cards relating to Elvis Presley accompany this comic.

Source: Compiler's collection

☆ Honeycutt, Mike, and Steve Willis

Zzzzzz Elvis! New Wave comics. Seattle, WA: Starhead Comix, 1985. 8 pp. ISBN: none.

Source: OCLC 297312243

☆ McCray, Patrick

Elvis Shrugged Graphic Novel. San Diego, CA: Revolutionary Comics, 1993. 109 pp. ISBN: none.

An Elvis-themed cartoon satire of Ayn Rand's novel *Atlas Shrugged.* This book was originally published in a three-part comic book–format series, *Elvis Shrugged: The Most Shocking Epic Ever.* (*See* following entry.)

Source: OCLC 40516681

———.

Elvis Shrugged: The Most Shocking Epic Ever. 3 vols. San Diego: Revolutionary Comics, Feb 1991 (Vol. 1); Aug 1992 (Vol. 2); Apr 1993 (Vol. 3). ISBN: none.

A three-part serialization of *Elvis Shrugged Graphic Novel.*

Source: Compiler's collection

☆ McCray, Patrick, and Herb Shapiro

The Elvis Presley Experience. 7 issues. San Diego, CA: Revolutionary Comics, 1992–1994. ISBN: none.

A fictionalized biography of Elvis Presley in comic book format, released in seven issues. Back cover, Issue 1 synopsis: "A linear journey through the soul of the King as observed by Elvis himself in eternity." Issues 1–6 are fantasized accounts of real events in his life. Issue 7 is an imaginary story in which Elvis returns from the dead to become President of the United States.

Source: OCLC 31521005
Publisher's address: 9528 Miramar Road, #278, San Diego, CA 92126

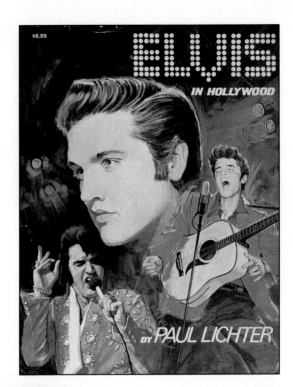

Prolific Elvis author Paul Lichter's 1975 compilation of Elvis's films. (*See* The Music, The Movies/ Filmography)

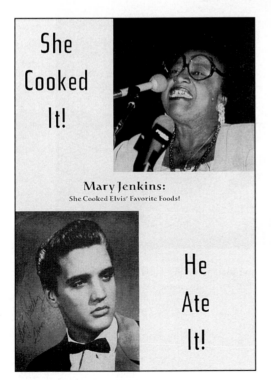

A pamphlet of recipes and memories from Elvis's cook Mary Jenkins.

Elvis Presley for America's Libraries

READ

Elvis posthumously encourages literacy and reading for the American Library Association. (From the collection of Elvis Presley Enterprises, Inc.)

Elvis's original drummer, D. J. Fontana, who was with him before and after he became famous, shares his photos and a brief memory. (*See* The Man/Memoirs)

Elvis reads a movie script with his pet chimpanzee Scatter. (From the collection of Elvis Presley Enterprises, Inc.)

The novel by Gail Brewer-Giorgio that started the "Elvis is alive" phenomenon. (*See* The Phenomena/Elvis Fiction)

A reproduction of the original 1958 yearbook of the U.S. Army's 2nd Armored Division—the unit with which Elvis did his advanced armored training. Elvis appears in some of the photographs. (*See* The Man/Elvis in the Army)

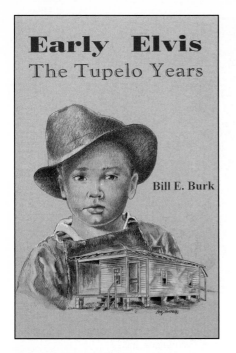

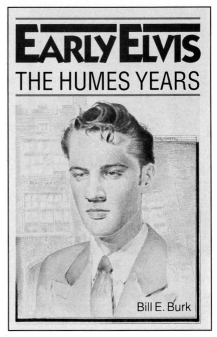

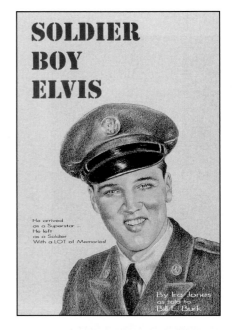

A trilogy from distinguished Elvis author Bill E. Burk, covering Elvis's childhood, teen years, and beginnings as a singer; and Elvis memories from MSgt. Ira Jones (USA-ret.), who was Elvis's platoon sergeant during the entertainer's Army service. (*See* The Man/Elvis in the Army) Mr. Burk reported on Elvis from 1956 to 1977 for the *Memphis Press-Scimitar* newspaper. (*See* The Man/Biographies chapter) (Cover art by Betty Harper. *See* The Phenomena/Art)

The first photograph collection of Graceland's interior and exterior. (*See* The Man/Graceland)

The official guidebook. (*See* The Man/Graceland)

Elvis in his famous gold lamé suit from the 1950s, holding an issue of *TV News*. (From the collection of Robin Rosaaen)

Produced by Elvis Presley Enterprises, Inc., in honor of the Colonel's 85th birthday. (*See* The Man/Biographies)

Poetic homage to Elvis, written by long-time fan Kathy Bei. (*See* The Phenomena/Poetry)

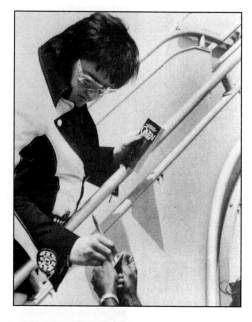

Elvis poet, humorist, and entertainer Sybil Marie Presley describes her fellow fans in verse. (*See* The Phenomena/Poetry)

Elvis boards his airplane, the *Lisa Marie*, in the 1970s, with his personal copy of *The Omen*—a novel about the birth of an anti-Christ. (From the collection of Robin Rosaaen)

Elvis reviews a movie magazine. (From the collection of Robin Rosaaen)

An example of the many books published and cherished by Elvis's fans. Sharon Fox, a fan since the 1950s, put together a collection of her Elvis clippings and photos to share. (*See* The Man/Photographs)

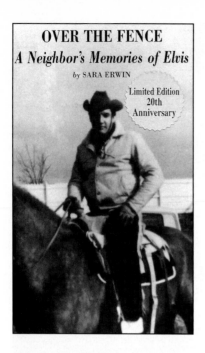

Elvis's neighbor Sara Erwin shares her Elvis memories. (*See* The Man/Memoirs)

Among the rarest of Elvis books. Published anonymously in English in 1985. (*See* The Phenomena/Fiction)

The memoirs of Elvis's uncle Vester Presley, beloved by fans, who was a fixture at Graceland's gates for more than 20 years. (*See* The Man/Memoirs and Memories)

☆ Michael, Douglas

The Elvis Mandible. New York: Piranha Press/DC Comics, 1990. [48] pp. ISBN: 1563890089.

A fictional tale of havoc wrought among a series of individuals who each take possession of what is thought to be Elvis's supernaturally empowered mandible.

Source: OCLC 21741307

☆ Quinn, Keith, with J. K. Stephen and Garrett Berner

Elvis, "The Unauthorized Biography." Music Comics series #4. Melville, NY: Personality Comics, 1992. 23 pp.

Source: OCLC 31055142

☆ Vodicka, David, editor and publisher

The Unauthorized Biography of Elvis: The True Story of His Public and Private Lives. Fox Comics Legends series #2. East Doncaster, Victoria, Australia: Fox Comics/Fantagraphics Books, 1992. 24 pp. ISBN: none.

A serious, respectful biography of Elvis Presley, with cartoon illustrations. Recommended biographies for further reading.

Source: Compiler's collection

See Also:

In The Man/Biographies:

"Biography of Elvis Presley." *Young Lovers* #18.
Hamblett, Charles, *Elvis, the Swinging Kid.*

In The Rest/Deceptive Titles:

Young Romance.

CHAPTER 21
Cookbooks

ELVIS HAD STRONG food preferences, and foods are strongly associated with him—thus creating another celebrity first. What edibles evoke an image of Frank Sinatra or Cher—or even Abraham Lincoln? If a food category "answer" on the *Jeopardy!* television game show is "Peanut butter and banana sandwiches," how many would fail to respond correctly?

Beyond this curious food identification with Elvis lies a small but valuable section of the Elvis literature. Part of the intense documentation of Elvis Presley's life includes the foods that he and his family preferred—and, by extension, those of people like them throughout the mid-twentieth-century South. Consequently, the best of the Elvis cookbooks provide rare, intimate views of the cuisine and eating habits of a significant population during an equally significant period.

The most historically useful Elvis cookbooks are those written by his relatives and those by his cooks—Mary Jenkins, Nancy Rooks, and Alvena Roy—along with Elvis's uncle Vester Presley and his cousins Donna Presley Early and Edie Hand. They provide difficult-to-find Southern recipes as well as first-hand information on the food and dining preferences of Elvis and his family.

But the majority of the Elvis cookbooks have been written by authors with no eyewitness knowledge of Elvis's and his family's tastes—as underscored by the fact that almost none of them has the correct recipe for the famous peanut butter and banana sandwich (which requires that the bread be toasted before frying[1]). Notably, one stands out for its unique approach. David Adler's *The Life and Cuisine of Elvis Presley* creates a new literary genre—a biography as told through the foods eaten by the subject. (*See* The Man/Biographies.)

Taken as a whole, these cookbooks provide a glimpse through the rapidly closing window of regional American foods. As the comforting sameness of Denny's and Burger King proliferates across the nation, these books stand as a reminder of the once diverse American diet.

---

[1] According to Elvis's cook Mary Jenkins in *Memories Beyond Graceland Gates,* p.109.

☆ ☆ ☆ ☆

☆ Butler, Brenda Arlene, compiler

Are You Hungry Tonight? Elvis's Favorite Recipes. New York: Grammercy Books, 1992. 64 pp. ISBN: 051708242X.

Introductory essay on Elvis's favorite foods and recipes. Fifty-five of "Elvis's favorite recipes," though none are cited or sourced. Interpretation of the original recipe for Elvis and Priscilla Presley's wedding cake. Black and white and color stills of Elvis, previously seen; all credited. Elvis memorabilia expert Robin Rosaaen served as consultant to this book.

☆ Early, Donna Presley, and Edie Hand

Donna Early is Elvis's first cousin. Hand is also an Elvis cousin.

The Presley Family and Friends Cookbook. Nashville, TN: Cumberland House, 1998. 288 pp. ISBN: 188895275X.

Elvis's cousin Donna Early writes a memoir of life at Graceland with an emphasis on the cuisine and dining rituals. Nearly 300 recipes for Elvis's favorite foods, along with those from Elvis fan clubs and Presley family and friends. "More than 100" black and white and color candid photographs of Elvis, his family, and his friends, with accompanying anecdotes and captions. Photographs are not credited. Recipes included are from Elvis's cook Mary Jenkins and his aunt Nasval Presley Pritchett (Early's mother). Index of recipe titles.

☆ McKeon, Elizabeth

McKeon is co-author of *The Quotable King.* (*See* The Man/Elvis in Quotes.)

Elvis in Hollywood: Recipes Fit for a King. Nashville, TN: Rutledge Hill Press, 1994. 237 pp. ISBN: 155653301X.

More than 250 recipes; some from the late Alvena Roy who cooked for Elvis in Los Angeles and at Graceland. In the introduction, Roy recalls the menu details of Elvis and Priscilla Presley's wedding dinner party, as well as Christmas dinner and a "midnight supper" for Elvis and the Beatles in 1965. Roy began working as a cook for Elvis Presley in May 1963, primarily in his California homes. She prepared his meals on the set of *Stay Away Joe* in Sedona, Arizona, and also cooked for him at Graceland. When she retired in her native Southern California, Elvis purchased a home for her.

Includes 100 photographs from the collections of Elvis fans. Anecdotes from Elvis's Hollywood friends and co-workers (none sourced). Introduction by entertainer Wayne Newton. Brief memoir essay by Roy. Brief filmography. Index.

☆ McKeon, Elizabeth, Ralph Gevirtz, and Julie Bandy

Fit for a King: The Elvis Presley Cookbook. Nashville: Rutledge Hill Press, 1992. 240 pp. ISBN: 1558531963. New York: Grammercy Books, 1998. 240 pp. ISBN: 0517189178.

More than 300 recipes. Lists of items kept in Elvis's pantry and suggested menus created from "those dishes that Elvis especially enjoyed." Seventy black and white candid photographs. Brief food anecdotes and quotes relating to Elvis's life and career; none cited or sourced. Index.

☆ Rooks, Nancy, and Vester Presley

Nancy Rooks worked as a maid and cook at Graceland from May 1967 until her retirement in the 1980s. Vester Presley was Elvis's paternal uncle, who was married to Elvis's mother's sister, Clettes. Vester Presley worked as a guard at Graceland for more than 23 years. He died in 1998.

The Presley Family Cookbook. Memphis, TN: Wimmer Brothers Books, 1980. 188 pp. ISBN: 0918544505.

Written by one of Elvis's cooks and his uncle with recipes for dishes that were commonly eaten in the mid-twentieth-century South. They are Rooks's recipes—exactly as used when she prepared them for Elvis. She includes commentary on Elvis's food favorites and dining preferences. Black and white photographs of Rooks preparing food. Index.

Source: Compiler's collection

☆ Wolf-Cohen, Elizabeth

The I Love Elvis Cookbook. [U.S.]: Courage Books/Running Press Book Publishers, 1998. 80 pp. ISBN: 0762402768.

A biographical cookbook with 50 recipes tracing Elvis Presley's life and culinary tastes. Incorrect recipe for the Fried Peanut Butter and Banana sandwich. More than 100 color photographs, mostly of food and Elvis memorabilia. Photographs are credited. Recipe title index. This book was translated into Finnish. (*See* Foreign Language Titles/Finnish.)

Source: Library of Congress

See Also:

In The Man/Biographies:

Adler, David, *The Life and Cuisine of Elvis Presley.*

In The Man/Memoirs and Memories:

Jenkins, Mary, *Memories Beyond Graceland Gates.*

CHAPTER 22
Dramas and Musicals About Elvis

DRAMAS AND MUSICALS about Elvis Presley demonstrate our culture's fascination with him as a springboard for creativity. In the Elvis fiction, he is a character or a leitmotif. In the Elvis dramas and musicals, he becomes a framework from which fantasy, magic, and myth are spun.

The first Elvis drama appears to be a 1978 children's play entitled *Operation Elvis*, in which a boy pretends to be Elvis until he learns to be secure with his own identity. (*See* Taylor listing in this chapter.) In 1979 the television film *To Elvis with Love* aired, based on a memoir of the same name by Lena Canada. (*See* The Man/Memoirs and Memories.) But as with so much of the Elvis literature, the growth of Elvis in theatrical productions would not occur until the 1980s.

Elvis was richly represented by a range of productions in this decade—from a 1983 drama that uses a recurrent Elvis theme in a story of marital misery (Kureishi, *The King and Me*) to a 1989 multimedia musical extravaganza (Rabinowitz's *Elvis: A Musical Celebration*).

In the 1990s Elvis-inspired theatrical productions have expanded to include ballets (*see* Nahat and Petronio listings in this chapter) and concert productions (Paul Dolden's *The Elvis Cantata*). Also, there has been a growth of Elvis influences on the motion picture screen—everything from the Flying Elvii in *Honeymoon in Vegas* to the 1988 feature-length romance *Heartbreak Hotel*.

Elvis—who longed to be taken seriously by the theatrical world—has finally achieved that dream.[1]

☆   ☆   ☆   ☆

☆ Bleasdale, Alan

Are You Lonesome Tonight? London: Faber and Faber, Ltd., 1985. 95 pp. ISBN: 0571137326.

A musical drama that examines the status of a cultural hero by counterpointing the last days of Elvis Presley's life with his early career as "the white boy who sang like a Negro" (back cover). Prologue, two acts, fourteen characters. Features 14 songs previously recorded by Elvis. This play was awarded the Standard Drama Award in 1985 for "Best Musical" (Great Britain).[2]

Source: Library of Congress PR6052.L397 A89 1985
Dewey Decimal 822/.914 19
Compiler's collection (album)

☆ Dolden, Paul, composer

The Elvis Cantata. 1995.

A post-modernist musical, celebrating the life of Elvis Presley. Maximalist composer Paul Dolden transformed original Elvis recordings through 400 electro-acoustically layered tracks. The musical was performed at St. Andrew's–Wesley Church in Vancouver, Canada, on September 24, 1994.

Source: Gasparini, Leonard "The Elvis Cantata". Review of The Elvis Cantata. Performing Arts in Canada (Spring 1995): 35.

☆ *Elvis Lives!* 1977.

A Broadway show starring Elvis Presley impersonator Larry Seth. It won the Evening Standard Award for Best Musical in 1977. (Award winners for 1976 and 1978 were, respectively, *A Chorus Line* and *Annie*.)

Source: Worth and Tamerius, p. 54.

☆ *Elvis Mania.* 1984.

A musical featuring songs made famous by Elvis Presley. The show consisted of three concert-style sets representing the 1950s, the 1960s, and the 1970s decades of Elvis's career.

---

[1]The purpose of this chapter is to demonstrate the diversity of theatrical productions about Elvis (musicals, ballets, plays) that have been written and performed. In some instances, the compiler was unable to find complete publication information, especially for the ballets and musical productions. Thus, the reader should refer to the source listings for these entries.

[2]Original London cast album, with Martin Shaw and Simon Bowman, is available on First Night Records; Exallshow Ltd.; Music Number: OCR CD6027. OCLC: 36197841.

The musical was performed at the Off-On-Broadway Theater in New York City in September 1984, starring Elvis impersonator Johnny Seaton.

Source: Pareles, Jon, "Theater: 'Elvismania,' Presley Years." Review of Elvis Mania. *New York Times (Sept 5, 1994).*
O'Haire, Patricia, "'Elvis Mania' A Near Miss." Review of Elvis Mania. *Daily News (New York City) (Sept 6, 1984).*

☆ Jensen, Uwe Jens, and Hansgeorg Koch

Elvis and John: Zwei Bilder aud dem Kunstlerleben. **Wien, AS: Agens Werk Geyer+Rei SSER, 1987. 164 pp. ISBN: none.**

Two biographical musicals. The first, written in English, is about Elvis Presley (pp. 5–37). The other, written in German, is about John Lennon of the Beatles (pp. 39–80). The remainder of the book consists of a biographical timeline of each man, as well as comparative quotes by and about them (unsourced), reprints of magazine and newspaper clippings, reproductions of album covers, and black and white photographs; none credited. Bibliography.

This play was performed at the Burgtheater in Vienna, Austria, on October 7, 1986. English-language translation of title: "Elvis and John: Two Portraits from the Life of an Artist."

Source: Die Deutsche Bibliothek
New York Public Library JFC 91-1267
OCLC 23533762

☆ Kureishi, Hanif

Outskirts; The King and Me; Tomorrow-Today! **In** *Playscript 102.* **London: J. Calder; New York: Riverrun Press, 1983. 88 pp. ISBN: 0714539716.**

The King and Me (pp. 27–43) "examines the strain of married life of a [British] couple who fill their empty existence with Elvis adoration" (back cover). Elvis fascination is used as a plot device to move the couple toward a fulfilling relationship. The play was first performed at the Soho Poly Theatre in London on January 7, 1980.

Source: Library of Congress PR6061.U68 O9 1983

☆ Lowe, Malcom

Miracle in Memphis: A Musical in Two Acts. **French's Musical Library. New York: S. French, 1996. 84 pp. ISBN: 35362920.**

A musical drama based upon the life of Elvis Presley.

Source: Library of Congress ML50.L827 M57 1996
Dewey Decimal 782.1/4/0268 21

☆ Mueller, Lavonne, editor

Mueller is a published playwright, textbook author, and Elvis fan.

Elvis Monologues. Portsmouth, NH: Heinemann, 1998. 164 pp. ISBN: 0435070444.

Includes 35 Elvis-themed monologues by a variety of writers.

Source: Library of Congress PS627.P74 E45 1997
Dewey Decimal 812'.04508351 21

☆ Nahat, Dennis, concept, choreographer, artistic director

Nahat is a lifelong Elvis fan, first seeing him in concert in 1956. He has created more than 70 ballets for the Cleveland and San Jose Ballet Company and is head of both professional schools of ballet in those cities.

Blue Suede Shoes. 1996.

A ballet production set to the music of Elvis Presley, highlighting his life and influence from his high school days in the early 1950s to his posthumous fame. First performed by the Cleveland San Jose Ballet Company at the State Theatre, Playhouse Square Center, Cleveland, Ohio, on May 29, 1996.

Source: South Bay Performances (Santa Clara, CA), (April–May 1997).

☆ Petronio, Stephen

The King Is Dead. 1995.

A post-modern ballet in which the vibrant life of Elvis Presley in the 1950s is contrasted against the decadency of the 1990s. Elvis is a metaphor for the disintegration of the world of "sex, drugs, and rock and roll" into AIDS, selfishness, and death. First performed at the Joyce Theater in New York City in spring 1995.

Source: Langland, Paul, "Sex, Death, and Elvis: Thoughts on Stephen Petronio's The King Is Dead." Contact Quarterly (Northhampton, MA) (Winter/Spring 1996): 35–37.

☆ Rabinowitz, Robin

Elvis: An American Musical. 1988.

A multimedia stage show about the life and music of Elvis Presley, which was revised in 1989 as *Elvis: A Musical Celebration.* (*See* following listing.)

———.

Elvis: A Musical Celebration. 1989.

The revised production of *Elvis: An American Musical,* performed in association with Elvis Presley Enterprises, Inc. (EPE). Done in three parts, each with a different actor playing

Elvis. It was first performed at the Las Vegas Hilton in July of 1989. (Performance program has Elvis facts and black and white and color photographs covering Elvis's life and career.)

Source: "Night Club Reviews—Elvis." Review of Elvis: A Musical Celebration *by Robin Rabinowitz.* Variety *(Aug 2, 1989): 74.*

☆ Rankin, Robert

Armageddon: The Musical. London: Bloomsbury Publishing Ltd., 1990. 239 pp. ISBN: 0747505152.

In the year 2050, Elvis Presley, through time travel from 1958, has landed in the twenty-first century. The plot revolves around the 153rd Dalai Lama's fear that Elvis wants to kill him.

Source: New York Public Library JFE 91-3940

☆ Schaufuss, Peter

The King. (Reviewed in *Dancing Times*, London, May 1999, pp. 719, 721.)

A choreographic work, based on the life of Elvis Presley, which premiered in Holstebro, Denmark, on February 24, 1999.

Source: OCLC 41895100

☆ Taylor, C. P.

C. P. (Cecil Philip) Taylor wrote more than 50 plays for children and adults before his death in 1981.

Operation Elvis. Live Theatre: Three Plays. Iron Press Drama Editions. North Shields, England: Iron Press, 1981. ISBN: 0906228085. Pp. 6–33.

Written for 10- and 11-year-olds, *Operation Elvis* is about a boy who confuses fantasy with reality—pretending that he is Elvis Presley until he develops a relationship with a mentally handicapped child who helps him gain an awareness of his true self. *Operation Elvis* was written in 1978 and was first performed in January of that year in Newcastle, England.

Source: Dewey Decimal 822.914 19
Cambridge University Library (UK) 1993.8.1356

———.

Operation Elvis. Live Theatre: Four Plays for Young People. Theatrescript (Second Series) No. 12. London: Methuen, 1983. ISBN: O41351790X. Pp. 6–32.

Second publication of *Operation Elvis.* (*See* preceding listing.)

Source: Dewey Decimal 822.914 19
Cambridge University Library (UK) 1983.8.2653

☆ *To Elvis with Love.* [U.S.]: Dove, Inc., 1979. 106 pp. ISBN: none.

The television script for the television film based on *To Elvis, with Love* by Lena Canada. (*See* The Man/Memoirs and Memories.) Handwritten title on cover: *Touched by Love.*

Source: OCLC 18510580

☆ Tredinnick, Miles

It's Now or Never! London: Warner Chappell Plays, 1991. 98 pp. ISBN: 0856761486.

Listed under subject title "Elvis Presley" in *Play's Index* (New York: The H. W. Wilson Company, 1993, p. 315).

Source: The British Library YK.1993.1.2564
OCLC 26356729

☆ Williams, Tennessee

Orpheus Descending, 1957. New York: Dramatists Play Service, 1959. 83pp. ISBN: none.

A play by one of America's most distinguished playwrights, based upon the wild scenes created by Elvis Presley during his personal appearances, with a story reminiscent of Greek mythological musician Orpheus whose musical powers tamed wild animals and charmed humans, but who died at the hands of women who ripped him apart. In Williams's play, a small-town Tennessee young man becomes a famous guitarist who is destroyed by idolatry and corruption. Williams wanted Elvis to star in *Orpheus Rising* but was turned down by Colonel Parker.[3] This play was later made into a movie starring Marlon Brando, *The Fugitive Kind* (1960).

Source: Library of Congress PS 3545.I536507 1959

See Also:

In The Man/Biographies:

Celsi, Theresa, *Elvis.* ("Movies and Theater Productions Based on or Inspired by Elvis's Life or Legend," pp. 72–73.)

In Foreign Language Titles/Dutch:

Garon Presley; Taking Care of Business in a Flash: Dead Brother Part 1.

---

[3] "All Things Considered," National Public Radio, 28 May 1999.

In Foreign Language Titles/French:

Valletti, Serge, *Saint Elvis; suivi de, Carton plein: theatre.*

In The Rest/Elvis Impersonators:

MacLeod, Joan, *Toronto, Mississippi.*
Willard, Fred, *Elvis and Juliet.*

CHAPTER 23
Fans

ELVIS FANS, LIKE their idol, are everywhere. Scratch the surface ever so slightly and they pop up in the most unlikely of circumstances—from distinguished scholars at the Library of Congress to secretaries in Macedonia. Wear an "I love Elvis" pin or place an Elvis decal on your car, and you are constantly hailed by strangers with smiles who want to tell you that they or their mother are Elvis fans too.

Only the fans' ardor and enthusiasm for Elvis match this pervasiveness. More than 500 fan clubs worldwide are registered with Elvis Presley Enterprises, Inc. And these are not people who just gather to listen to records. According to *The Chronicle of Philanthropy* (*see* Demko listing in this chapter), Elvis fans raised at least $1.1 million for charity between 1986 and 1996 through bake sales, raffles, and sales of handmade crafts. AIDS clinics, police departments, and hospital children's wards are annually inundated by teddy bears— purchased or handmade by Elvis fans in commemoration of his fondness for these toys. Animal shelters are kept awash in pet food coupons from Elvis's fans. The list goes on.

But sadly, these same generous Elvis fans face some of the worst discrimination that can be dished out by the bigots of America. Elvis fans are right up there with Christians as being societally approved targets for derision and intolerance. Elvis fans with Ph.D.s and Phi Beta Kappa keys face the same sneering contempt as do those with high school diplomas and trailer park addresses. And even sadder, there are Elvis authors who promulgate this. (*See* Doss listing in this chapter.)

Fortunately, thoughtful authors have recognized Elvis fandom for what it truly is: a universal family who happily and enthusiastically celebrates Elvis through friendships, fun, and helping those in need. (*See* Hammontree and Joyrich listings in this chapter.) It is one of the few groups where friendships are formed between such ordinarily disparate people as legal professionals and Wal-Mart cashiers. And it is one of the few communities where the door is always open. The only requirement for entry is shared Elvis enthusiasm.

☆　　☆　　☆　　☆

☆ "Ain't Nothin' but a Hairdo." *Life* (Mar 25, 1957): 55–57.

The impact of Elvis Presley as demonstrated by 1,000 girls in Grand Rapids, Michigan, who each had her hair styled into an imitation of Elvis Presley's. Black and white photographs.

☆ Arthur, Caroline

"Going to Graceland." *American Demographics* 11 (May 1989): 47–48.

A statistical examination of Graceland's visitors, as well as the fund-raising among Elvis's fans for the Med Foundation of Memphis's Baptist Memorial Hospital (site of the Elvis Presley Memorial Trauma Center—the third largest in America).

☆ Ashbaugh, Dick

"Elvis Presley." *This Week* (weekly magazine of the *Washington Star* [DC] newspaper) (Mar 3, 1957): [2 pp.].

The experiences of a journalist who took his teenaged daughter with him when he was assigned to interview Elvis Presley after a concert. Ashbaugh describes the teenage audience's reaction to Elvis, as well as his own.

Source: Martin Luther King Memorial Library, District of Columbia Washington Star files.

☆ Bragg, Rick

"The King Is Long Dead, but Long Live the King." *The New York Times* (Aug 16, 1997): A6.

An overview of Elvis Presley fans who attended Elvis Week in Memphis on the twentieth anniversary of Elvis's death. Interviewees discuss what Elvis means to them.

☆ Davidson, James W.

"Graceland: More Than a Hit Song—A Twentieth Century Mecca." *Studies in Popular Culture* 10.1 (1987): 51–62.

The author investigates the concept of pilgrimage in contemporary culture through interviews with seven Elvis Presley fans during Elvis Week 1984: "By examining their perceptions of the late singer, we begin to understand why visiting Graceland is truly a pilgrimage rather than a nostalgic or frivolous act." References ("Works Cited").

☆ Deen, Jeannie

"A Young Girl's Fancy." Ed. Jac L.Tharpe. *Elvis: Images and Fancies*. Jackson, MS: University Press of Mississippi, 1979. Pp. 169–172.

The memories of an Elvis fan that trace her enchantment with him in 1956 to her disappointment in him in 1976—a journey that mirrored so many other fans' emotional experiences with Elvis.

Source: Tharpe, Jac L., Ph.D., editor, Elvis: Images and Fancies.

☆ Demko, Paul

"Elvis Lives! (in Philanthropy)." *The Chronicle of Philanthropy* (May 2, 1996): 39–30.

In a magazine that reports on the world of non-profit organizations, an article about charity fund-raising and donations by Elvis Presley's fans. "More than 500 Elvis Presley fan clubs have . . . raised at least $1.1 million for charity in the past 10 years, according to estimates by officials at Graceland." Identification of the charities to which fans donate, including the amounts given. Interviews with fans involved in fundraising in Elvis's name.

☆ Doss, Erika Lee, Ph.D.

Elvis Culture: Fans, Faith, and Image. CultureAmerica series. Lawrence, KS: University Press of Kansas, 1999. 304 pp. ISBN: 0700609482.

An example of the narrow-mindedness and stereotyping that Elvis fans endure. From a few examples, fans are painted as racists, with Elvis appearing to be a white supremist icon. Elvis Presley Enterprises, Inc. is also targeted for alleged hypocritical practices against fans. Chapter notes. Index.

Source: Library of Congress ML420.P96 D68 1999
Dewey Decimal 782.42166/092 B 21

☆ Gilbert, Eugene

"Elvis Fans 'Infantile,' Says Gilbert Survey." *Washington Star* (Mar 23, 1958).

The results of a 1958 survey conducted by a professional research organization (Gilbert Youth Research Co.), which, "using the knowledge and tools developed by the social scientists and applying them on a larger scale through the survey technique, sought the whys and the wherefores of Elvis worship." The survey team randomly selected 100 teenagers and questioned them about their hobbies, interests, extracurricular activities, scholastic achievements, and future plans. From this collected data, the researchers found a "definite pattern" that gave "an outline sketch of the typical Presley fan," which found that Elvis's fans were "C"-average students who tended not to join clubs or other groups and had no future plans. The Elvis fans in this study were compared to those of Pat Boone and Frank Sinatra.

When the results of this survey were published in the *Washington Star*, a companion article ran in which Washington, D.C.–area teenagers responded to the findings. (*See* Gorska entry following.)

Source: Martin Luther King Memorial Library, District of Columbia Washington Star *files.*

☆ Gorska, Fifi

"Teen-Agers Reply: 'Hideous,' 'Not Right,' Say Presley Fans." *Washington Star* (Mar 23, 1958).

Washington D.C.–area teenaged Elvis Presley fans—black and white, male and female—react defensively to the published results of an Elvis fan survey that concluded they were "infantile" and their idol was "a symbol of destruction." (*See* Gilbert listing earlier in this chapter.)

Source: Martin Luther King Memorial Library, District of Columbia Washington Star files.

☆ "Gracelandtoo, Holly Springs, Miss." *People Weekly* (Aug 5, 1996): 80.

A visit with Paul MacLeod, "the world's number one Elvis fan," whose home in northern Mississippi is an Elvis Presley museum, open for touring 24 hours a day, 7 days a week. MacLeod's home/museum, "Gracelandtoo," has been featured extensively in print and electronic media stories worldwide.

☆ Hammontree, Patsy G., Ph.D.

"Audience Amplitude: The Cultural Phenomenon of Elvis Presley." Ed. Jac L. Tharpe. *Elvis: Images and Fancies.* Jackson, MS: University Press of Mississippi, 1979. Pp. 52–60.

Hammontree profiles "the Elvis Presley fan" through assessments, commentary, and anecdotes about fan behavior. She concludes that the universality of his appeal has resulted in a "worldwide community and worldwide communion" of Elvis fans.

Source: Tharpe, Jac L., Ph.D., editor, Elvis: Images and Fancies.

☆ Hinerman, Stephen

"'I'll Be Here with You': Fans, Fantasy, and the Figure of Elvis." Ed. Lisa Lewis. *The Adoring Audience: Fan Culture and Popular Media.* London; New York: Routledge, 1992. Pp. 107–134.

An examination of fans' daydreams about Elvis Presley for the purpose of studying the cultural causes of the need to fantasize about a celebrity.

Source: Library of Congress HM291.A343 1992

☆ Hockstader, Lee

"Elvis Lives at Moscow Tribute." *The Washington Post* (Aug 17, 1993): A11.

An overview of Elvis Presley's Russians fans, before and after the collapse of the Soviet Union. Focuses on the founders of Moscow's Elvis fan club. Discussion includes Elvis's popularity in Russia in the 1950s when entrepreneurial bootleggers copied his recordings onto used hospital X-ray plates and sold them for use on record players. (*See also Harrison Salisbury listing in* The Man/The Impact of Elvis.)

☆ "A Howling Hillbilly Success." *Life* (Apr 30, 1956): 68.

Two black and white photographs of the audience while Elvis Presley performed in Amarillo, Texas, and in a Nashville recording studio. One paragraph on fans' reactions. Quote from Elvis about these reactions. This is the first mainstream media magazine article about Elvis.

☆ Joyrich, Lynne

"Elvisophilia: Knowledge, Pleasure, and the Cult of Elvis." *Differences: A Journal of Feminist Cultural Studies* 5.1 (1993): 73–91.

The author expands the concept of addiction by studying fans' devotion to Elvis Presley. She concludes that it is a positive, open-ended form of addiction, celebrating "the connection between knowledge and sexuality, curiosity, and pleasure." Notes. "Works Cited."

Source: Library of Congress HQ1101.D54

☆ Kaaz, Carsten, with Michael Riemann

In the Shadow of the Wall. Memphis, TN: Guild Bindery Press, 1994. ISBN: 1557930236.

A German fan, who grew up in East Berlin, relates how his interest in Elvis—including attempts to start a fan club—were treated by the East German government. He credits Elvis Presley as his inspiration to attempt a successful escape over the Berlin Wall. (Kaaz was the last person to escape before the Wall fell in 1989.)

Source: Compiler's collection

☆ Martin, Peter, editor

The Hound Dog Elvis Yearbook. Tiburon, CA: Collectors Features, 1960; 1963; 1972; 1977. [98] pp. ISBN: none.

A series of yearbooks (1977 edition is a reprinting of 1960). Mostly articles by and about fans, expressing their feelings and memories about Elvis. Biographical articles which quote Elvis (unsourced). Black and white photographs; most captioned and most previously seen.

Source: Compiler's collection

☆ Nixon, Anne

Elvis: Ten Years After. [UK]: Heanor Record Centre Ltd., 1987. ISBN: none.

A British fan's look at Elvis, 10 years after his death.

Source: David Neale, "Elvis in Print."
www.geocities.com/SunsetStrip/8200/books.html

☆ Olson, Melissa, and Darrell Crase

"Presleymania: The Elvis Factor." *Death Studies* 14.3 (May–June 1990): 277–282.

A psychological interpretation of Elvis fan reactions to his death and their continued interest after he died. Demographic portrait of "loyal fans" (p. 281). Notes and references.

☆ Reedijk, C.

Elvis Fans: Graceland's Pilgrims: An Ethnographic Study. 1984. (No publishing information available.)

Source: Olson, Melissa, and Darrell Crase, "Presleymania: The Elvis Factor," Death Studies 14.3 (1990): 281.

☆ Slaughter, Todd

Forever Elvis: The Memorial Tour to Memphis. Manchester, England: World Publishing, 1980. 48 pp. ISBN: none.

A record of a trip to Memphis made by members of Elvis Presley's UK fan club.

Source: Advanced Book Exchange, Inc., June 1998. www.abe.com

☆ Ward, Robert

"Down at the End of Lonely Street." *Crawdaddy* (Nov 1977): 29–34.

One of the few essays to capture the larger reasons behind the devotion that so many Elvis fans hold for Elvis Presley: Elvis connected with us in our adolescent confusion and remains strongly tied to an era in which life was perceived as full of endless possibilities.

Ward writes of the impact Elvis Presley had on him as a 12-year-old in 1956, when he was seeking relief in rock and roll music from the angst of adolescence. He reflects on his own reactions to Elvis's death and its larger societal impact.

☆ Woodward, Helen Beale

"The Smitten Female: From Lord Byron to Elvis Presley Certain Males Have Affected Women as Locoweed Does a Heifer." *Mademoiselle* (July 1957): 64, 104.

Elvis Presley is used to examine why women are so wildly affected by distant "demigods." Others mentioned are Franz Liszt, Prince Edward of Wales, Frank Sinatra, Rudolph Valentino, and Lord Byron. Anecdotes of fan frenzy caused by these gentlemen, which reflect the reactions to Elvis.

☆ Wright, Daniel

Dear Elvis: Graffiti from Graceland. Memphis, TN: Mustang Publishing Co., 1996. 96 pp. ISBN: 0914457756.

A collection of nearly 400 messages written by fans and visitors on the front wall of the Graceland property. Photographs of the messages. Two brief essays: "The Graceland Experience," which discusses the practice of writing on the Graceland wall (pp. 36–40); and "Graceland Trivia" (pp. 62–64).

Source: New York Public Library JND 97-40

Articles About Elvis Fans in *American Demographics*

Just who are Elvis's fans? In 1991 Bob Lunn, president of Direct Image Concepts in Texas, was hired to find out. The producers of a videotape about Elvis asked Lunn to assist them with a direct-market campaign. He accumulated a mailing list of 7,000 fan club members and used the addresses and zip-code data to develop a demographic profile of Elvis fans. Lunn did geocoding to get block group data in areas heavily populated with Elvis fans. He matched these data to the Claritas Corporation's 40 PRIZM clusters, which characterized the demographic and lifestyle characteristics of every U.S. household.

American Demographics magazine further analyzed the data to identify counties with a high proportion of householders who fit the Elvis fan profile developed by Lunn. The magazine used this information for two articles: one in 1993, and another in 1998.

According to a senior systems analyst at a highly regarded Virginia research firm[1] (who is also an Elvis fan), using the addresses of fan clubs assumes a false Elvis fan homogeneity, which, in all likelihood, will not accurately reflect Elvis fan diversity. This is supported by a newspaper reporter in Alaska who found that highly ranked Kotzebue, Alaska, is "a collection of ten small Inuit and Eskimo villages, with no roads to speak of" (*American Demographics*, Jan 1998, p. 19).

☆ "Where Elvis Lives." *American Demographics* (Aug 1993): 64.

A demographic profile of Elvis fans, accompanied by a map depicting U.S. counties with high and low concentrations of Elvis fans. Also included are age, education level, and racial makeup of fans.

☆ "Elvis Lives Again." *American Demographics* (Jan 1998): 18–19.

Using their own and Lunn's data, staff at *American Demographics* created a new Elvis fan–related map that they claim demonstrates the "propensity of households to purchase Elvis memorabilia by U.S. county, ranked by quintile, 1990." The accompanying article repeats information from the 1993 article, lists the items that "Elvis lovers buy," and provides update of Lunn's Elvis fan data experiences since the 1993.

See Also:

In The Man/Biographies:

Slaughter, Todd, *Elvis Presley*.

In The Man/Elvis in Quotes:

Poling, James, "Elvis Presley, Go Cat, Go."

In The Man/The Impact of Elvis:

Carsch, Henry, "The Protestant Ethic and the Popular Idol in America: A Case Study."
Condon, Eddie, "What Is an Elvis Presley?"
Cooper, Susan, "Mr. Presley Finds the Rock of Gold."
Kanchanawan, Nitaya, "Elvis, Thailand, and I."

---

[1]This individual requested not to be identified. However, notes from the author's interview are available for inspection.

King, Christine, "His Truth Goes Marching On: Elvis Presley and the Pilgrimage to Graceland."
McManus, Margaret, "Presley No Serious Peril, Noted Psychologist Feels."
Reiser, Martin, "A Note on the Analysis of the 'Elvis Presley' Phenomenon."

In The Man/Memoirs and Memories:

Fans section
"A Howling Hillbilly Success."

In The Man/Reference:

Saville, Ted, *International Elvis Presley Appreciation Society Handbook.*

In The Music, The Movies/Concerts and Television Appearances:

Gould, Jack, "Elvis Presley: Lack of Responsibility Is Shown by TV in Exploiting Teen-Agers."

In The Music, The Movies/Elvis's Influence on Music:

"He Can't Be . . . but He Is."

In The Phenomena/Gender:

Poiger, Uta G., "Rock 'n' Roll, Female Sexuality, and the Cold War Battle over German Identities."

In The Phenomena/The Law:

Kaye, Jeff, "Presley Estate May Sue to Stop Episode of *Designing Women.*"

In The Phenomena/Politics:

Edson, Arthur, "Protests Roll In on Senator Case as Threat to Elvis's Hair Rocks Fans."

In The Phenomena/Religion:

Harrison, Ted, *Elvis People: The Cult of the King.*
Morris, Valarie Ziegler, "Love Me Tender: Incarnational Theology and Elvis."
Rosenbaum, Ron, "Among the Believers."

In The Academics/Educational Literature:

Mueller, Jean W., "Rock 'n' Roll Heroes: Letter to President Eisenhower."
(Fans concerned about Elvis in the Army.)

In Foreign Language Titles/Swedish:

Eriksson, Sven-Ake, *Elvis International Tribute Week, '92, August 8–16.*

CHAPTER 24
Fiction

FICTION IS WHERE Elvis Presley's ascent from flesh-and-blood human to timeless, pervasive fantasy is most evident. Here the Elvisian archetype is developed to its brightest clarity: Elvis as a signifier of romance—Elvis as a sense of time and place—Elvis as a figure of mystery—Elvis as a symbol of playfulness.

Thus, the Elvis fiction is not limited to imaginary stories about the man—rather it is a body that uses his cultural image as a subject, character, plot device, theme, and/or to snag the reader's attention. It is in this fiction that Elvis achieves his deepest personal connection with the world. It is here that he becomes universally personalized—an image upon which anyone, anywhere can fashion dreams, desires, fantasies, and fun.

Interestingly, it is non-Elvis fans who most eagerly embrace this genre. Elvis fiction simply does not sell to his admirers, according to leading Elvis bookseller, Bill E. Burk.[1] Elvis fans maintain a strong connection to their idol through his music, his photographs, his films, and the words of those who knew him and are happy to talk about it.

Non-Elvis fans enthusiastically write and purchase this literature for precisely the reason that the fans do not. While Elvis remains a flesh-and-blood man to his fans, he is a universal signifier of time, place, and emotion to non-fans. In this way, they are just as connected to Elvis as those who buy his records and attend Elvis Week in Memphis.

Because the Elvis literature produced before his death was aimed at consumers who experienced him as a human being, there was no such thing then as Elvis Fiction. In 1976 the curious Elvisian fable *The Minstrel* was self-published, but it had been written as a gift to Elvis, not as a salable tale. (*See* Benson listing in this chapter.) Little other fiction appeared until after his death. It was then that his ascent to mythological status began—and the fictional literature about him began to appear.

The first posthumous fiction was an interesting exercise in which the author created fan letters to Elvis in an attempt to reflect the sentiments of Elvis fans. (*See* Adler listing in this chapter.)

[1]Interview, Aug 12, 1997, Memphis, Tennessee.

As the Elvis fiction output grew, an unprecedented literary transformation took place—fiction became non-fiction. Here, in the fiction books, the possibility that Elvis might still be alive first surfaced. Jazzman's science-fiction *Elvis, Come Back!* (1978) first told of technologies that kept Elvis alive. Then, fed by novels such as Brewer-Giorgio's *Orion* (1979), the anonymously written *Fairytale* (1985), and Nicholson's The Presley Arrangement (1987), readers looked past the fantasy, hoping, then believing it to be true. Non-fiction books supporting this conviction quickly appeared. (*See* The Man/Death, Conspiracy, Sightings.) And Elvis took his place in urban mythology alongside spiders in the beehive hairdo and toasted rats in the Kentucky Fried Chicken bucket.

In spite of this innovative range of Elvis imagination, fans remain unenthused about this genre. Fortunately, few novelists have heeded, and the Elvis fiction output continues at a delightfully dizzying rate.

☆   ☆   ☆   ☆

☆ Adler, Bill

Bill Adler's Love Letters to Elvis. New York: Grosset and Dunlap, 1978. Unpaged. ISBN: 0448147173 (hdk.). ISBN: 0448147173 (pbk.).

Fictional letters written by the author to reflect the sentiments of Elvis's fans. Sixteen black and white photographs, none credited or captioned. Adler has authored other fictional "letters to" books, focusing on such subjects as the Beatles and the New York Mets baseball team.

Source: Library of Congress ML 420.P96A65

☆ Arthur, Gene, and Gail Brewer-Giorgio

Orion. Atlanta, GA: Golden Eagle Publishing Company, 1978. ISBN: none.

An early edition of *Orion.* (*See* Brewer-Giorgio listing following in this chapter.)

Source: Gail Brewer-Giorgio

☆ Baty, Keith, and Robert Graham

Elvis: The Fotonovel. New York: Dell Publishing Company, 1983. ISBN: 0440021952. [n.p.]: Dufour Editions, 1997. 222 pp. ISBN: 1899344195. *Elvis—The Novel.* London: Granada Publishing Ltd., 1984. ISBN: 0586061622. London: Do-Not-Press, 1997. 222 pp. ISBN: 1899344195.

A humorous fantasy of Elvis Presley's life in which he records with the Beatles, hosts his own opera show on television, and "takes care of" Colonel Parker on national television. The 1997 edition is "updated and revised." Bibliographical references (p. [221]–222). This book was translated into German. (*See* Foreign Language Titles/German.)

Source: The British Library H.98/325 (1997)
The Collection of Richard Palmer, Wakefield, West Yorkshire, England (1984)
OCLC 41067785

☆ Benson, Bernard

The Minstrel. With comments by Dick Grob and Charlie Hodge. Memphis, TN: Minstrel Publishing, 1976. Unpaged. ISBN: none. New York: G. P. Putnam's Sons, 1977. ISBN: 399122508. (1977 edition published simultaneously in Canada by Longman Canada Limited, Toronto.)

An allegory demonstrating how music reverses "man's invasion of nature." Elvis appears as a reincarnated minstrel in a fictional kingdom. Commentary by Elvis employee Dick Grob and Elvis friend Charlie Hodge. Benson wrote this as an unpublished personal gift to Elvis in honor of the entertainer's forty-second birthday, January 8, 1977. The first publicly available edition (Minstrel Publishing, Memphis, Tennessee, 1976) was signed, numbered, bound in white leather, accompanied by a peacock feather, and delivered to the purchaser by a chauffeur in a white Cadillac (this according to the 1977 press release by Media Marketing, Inc., Newark, Delaware).

Source: Compiler's collection

☆ Bourgeau, Art

The Elvis Murders: Will the Real Elvis Please Stand Up? A Charter Book. New York: Berkley Publishing Group/Charter Mystery, 1985. 214 pp. ISBN: 0441204317.

A murder mystery in which an Elvis impersonator wins a contest that allows him to live like Elvis for a year, in a home just like Graceland and going out on concert tours. His friends become his "Memphis Mafia." The plot revolves around the deaths of those close to him.

Source: Bowling Green State University Pop Culture Library PS3552.O833 E6 OCLC 12159443

☆ Brewer, Steve

Lonely Street. New York: Pocket Books, 1994. 213 pp. ISBN: 0671747347.

Publisher synopsis, "Albuquerque [New Mexico] private eye Bubba Mabry is hired by a gold-swathed man named Buddy to work security for the King—a back-from-the-dead, low-profile Elvis—and becomes the sole suspect in two murders."

Source: Cleveland (OH) Public Library OCLC 30502750

☆ Brewer-Giorgio, Gail

Orion: The Living Superstar of Song. Atlanta, GA: Capricorn, 1979. 271 pp. ISBN: none. New York: Pocket Books, 1981. 353 pp. ISBN: 0671415034. (Reissued as *Orion.* New York: Tudor Publishing, 1989. 353 pp. ISBN: 0944276393.)

A novel based on Elvis Presley's life, with the protagonist, Orion, serving as the Elvis figure. The story ends with Orion, overwhelmed by his celebrity, faking his death so he can live an "ordinary" life in disguise.

Marin [CA] Independent Journal writer Jeff Prugh reports that after publication, Brewer-Giorgio received a "mysterious" telephone call from a male voice that sounded like Elvis's (Aug 17, 1997: B7). When she asked his name, the response was "Orion." Later she received in the mail a gold ring inscribed "Orion." In 1987 she received an audiotape, allegedly of Elvis Presley in a post–August 16, 1977, telephone conversation. These events led her to write a second book, *The Most Incredible Elvis Presley Story Ever Told* (1988), in which she questions whether or not Elvis died in 1977. (*See* The Man/Death, Conspiracy, Sightings.)

Source: OCLC 15875699 (1979); 8030394 (1981); 19245417 (1989)

☆ Charters, Samuel Barclay

Elvis Presley Calls His Mother After The Ed Sullivan Show: *A Novel.* **Minneapolis, MN: Coffee House Press, 1992. ISBN: 0918273986.**

The "transcript" of a fictional 1956 telephone conversation in which Elvis calls his mother to relay his astonishment over all that has happened to him—and what he hopes will come in the future.

Source: Library of Congress PN3553.H327E 45 1992

☆ Childress, Mark

Tender: A Novel. **New York: Harmony Books, 1990. 566pp. ISBN: 0517576031. Audio version: New York: Random House Audio Books, Random House Audio Publications, 1990. 2 sound cassettes (ca. 3 hours). ISBN: 0679401261. Read by author. Narrated by Robert O'Keefe.**

The story of Leroy Kirby, a poor boy from Tupelo, Mississippi, who moves to Memphis to become the most famous rock and roll singer in the world. The plot closely follows Elvis's life, ending when the protagonist enters military service.

Source: Library of Congress PS3553.H486 T46 1990

☆ Church, Solomon (Louie Ludwig), B.T., D.R., MSh., editor

"Solomon Church" is a nom-de-plume for Louie Ludwig.

The Gospel of Elvis: Containing the Testament and Apocrypha Including All the Greater Themes of the King. **Arlington, TX: The Summit Publishing Group, 1995. 179 pp. ISBN: 1565301870.**

An allegorical story of Elvis's life, written to explore "our near religious worship of pop icons" (book jacket notes). Plot borrows from the Bible, and Elvis is presented as a messiah, though not in a religious connotation. Footnotes for biographical and historical clarification. Bibliography of mostly religious titles.

Source: Compiler's collection

☆ Corvino, Nick

Elvis: The Army Years 1958–1960. **Nashville, TN: Green Valley Record Store, Inc., [n.d.]. 93 pp. ISBN: none.**

A fictionalized re-creation of Elvis Presley's experiences during his army service.

Source: Compiler's collection

☆ DeMarco, Gordon

Elvis in Aspic. Portland, OR: West Coast Crime, 1994. 224 pp. ISBN: 1883303117.

A suspense-thriller novel in which the protagonist, a tabloid journalist, seeks to find out whether or not the CIA killed Elvis Presley. The plot revolves around the protagonist's suspicions that Elvis had been told of a CIA plot to assassinate President Jimmy Carter.

Source: Library of Congress PS3554.R44
OCLC 29999445

☆ Duff, Gerald

That's All Right, Mama: The Unauthorized Life of Elvis's Twin. Dallas, TX:
  Baskerville Publishers, 1995. 278 pp. ISBN: 1880909332.

A plot based upon the question: what if Elvis's twin, Jesse, had lived? In this story, Jesse's existence was kept secret. From birth, he was relegated to serving as a lifelong stand-in for Elvis. This is the story of his life.

Source: Library of Congress PS3554.U3177 T48 1995

☆ *Fairytale.* (UK): [n.p.], [c1985]. Pagination unknown. ISBN: none.

The story of rock and roll star Aaron Wade who plans to fake his death, but then dies, mysteriously and for real. The story has a "to-be-continued" denouement, which fueled the interest of those who believe that Elvis Presley is still alive. Though published in the United Kingdom, the story's copyright is held by a German company, Bringes ans Licht. Pages are typewritten. The book was available for purchase through the Heanor Record Center Limited, 41/47 Derby Road, Heanor, Derbyshire, England. This novel is cited by Elvis death-conspiracy author Gail Brewer-Giorgio in *The Elvis Files* (1990, p. 71) to support her theory that Elvis is still alive. (*See* The Man/Death, Conspiracy, Sightings.)

Source: Collection of Richard Palmer, Wakefield, West Yorkshire, England
Brewer-Giorgio, The Elvis Files *(1990)*

☆ Fox, Les, and Sue Fox

Return to Sender: The Secret Son of Elvis Presley. Tequesta, FL: West Highland Publishing Company, 1996. 339 pp. ISBN: 0964698609.

A high school student, living with whom he thinks are his biological parents, inherits four million dollars from an anonymous source. This is the story of his quest to uncover the origins of the inheritance—Elvis Presley, who, before his death, had established a legal framework that would allow this young man, his biological son, to have a "perfect life; free from the poverty of Tupelo, Mississippi, and the heartbreak of fame and fortune."

Source: Library of Congress PS 3356.O69R48 1996
Dewey Decimal 813'54 QB195-20392

☆ Hallum, Boen, editor

Elvis the King. Columbus, OH: Boen Hallum, 1987. 76 pp. ISBN: 0960885404.

A self-published collection of fictional first-person narratives from real-life people such as Gladys Presley, Sam Phillips, and Ed Sullivan, expressing feelings and thoughts about Elvis Presley.

Source: Memphis/Shelby County (TN) Public Library and Information Center
OCLC 15726213
Publisher's address: 4977 Lockbourne Road, Columbus, OH 43207

☆ Hines, Barry

Elvis over England. London: Michael Joseph Ltd., 1998. 224 pp. ISBN: 718141180.

After a fight with his wife, 55-year-old Eddie spends all his redundancy (retirement) money on an aging Cadillac, dons his old Teddy Boy suit, and starts on a pilgrimage to Prestwich Airport in Scotland where Elvis once briefly touched down. Throughout his journey, Elvis is everywhere.

Source: Dewey Decimal 823.914

☆ Hope, Christopher

Me, the Moon, and Elvis Presley. London: Macmillan, 1997. 263 pp. ISBN: 333722035 (pbk.). ISBN: 0333595793 (hdk.). London: Picador, 1999. 256 pp. ISBN: 0330354736.

A political satire set in a remote South African township, describing how various citizens' lives have changed from the 1950s to the mid-1990s. The music of Elvis Presley is introduced to the town in the 1950s, and by 1995 he is a local hero. The novel's climax revolves around the town's Elvis impersonator contest.

Source: Library of Congress PR9369.3.H65 M4 1997
OCLC 40754622 (1999)

☆ Jaffe, Paul

Clothed in Light. Grass Valley, CA: Elvis Presley Online, 2000. ISBN: 096721310X.

Told through Elvis first-person—as a returned soul—of his death and reflects on his life and mythology.

Source: Paul Jaffe and www.elvispresleyonline.com

☆ Jazzman, Sheila

Elvis, Come Back! Los Angeles: Western Elite Press, 1978. 177 pp. ISBN: none.

A science-fiction tale of Elvis being brought back to life through technologies known as "revitalization" (the act of restoring something or someone to life) and "latency" (an alteration of metabolism with the potential of being returned to life).

Source: Compiler's collection

☆ Kalpakian, Laura

Graced Land. New York: Grove Weidenfeld, 1992. 264 pp. ISBN: 0802114741.

The story of single mother, Elvis fan, and welfare recipient Joyce Jackson's survival and success, as she carries on "Elvis's work" of generosity and benevolence. The plot tells of her efforts to meet the challenges in her lifestyle and of how she changes the life of her young social worker.

In 1992 the television film *The Woman Who Loved Elvis*, starring Roseanne Arnold, was based on this book. (Teleplay by Rita Mae Brown, Roseanne Arnold, Tom Arnold, Cynthia Gibb, et al. ISBN: 157362294X. Music NO: VM6173 Trimark Home Video.)

Source: Library of Congress PS3561.A4168G7 1992
Dewey Decimal 813'.54–dc20

☆ Karen, Karma

Karma Karen is the pseudonym of a professional photographer.

Love Me Tender: The True Story of Marilyn and The King as Told by Karma Karen. [U.S.]: Readhead Press, 1997. 291 pp. ISBN: 0965722805.

The story of a secret romance between Elvis Presley and Marilyn Monroe. The plot includes links to former President John F. Kennedy and answers to the questions surrounding all of their deaths.

Source: Collection of Bill and Connie Burk, Memphis, TN

☆ Kluge, P. F. (Paul Frederick)

Biggest Elvis. New York: Viking Books, 1996. 341 pp. ISBN: 0670869740.

A mystery/romance novel in which the career of Elvis Presley—through Elvis impersonators representing his professional life's three stages—is used as a metaphor for America's progression from "lean innovator to overblown superpower." (Amazon.com commentary [1996].) The story is told through three Elvis impersonators who work in a seedy bar called Graceland in Olongapo, Philippines, just outside the main gate of the Subic Bay Naval Base.

Source: Library of Congress PS3561.L77 B5 1996

☆ Levinson, Robert S.

The Elvis and Marilyn Affair. A Tom Doherty Associates Book. New York: Tor/Forge, 1999. 304 pp. ISBN: 0312869681.

Fictional love letters between Marilyn Monroe and Elvis Presley are the premise for this murder mystery involving the threatened exposure of a secret 1956 affair between the pair.

Source: OCLC 413246991

☆ Maughon, Robert Mickey, M.D.

Elvis Is Alive. Kodak, TN: Cinnamon Moon, 1997. 254 pp. ISBN: 0965036626.

Dr. Robert St. John, a Memphis, Tennessee, coroner, is ordered by the state to exhume the Elvis Presley gravesite at Graceland. What he discovers leads him to an Elvis impersonator in Paris who says he is Elvis Presley and that he staged his death in 1977.

Source: OCLC 37514446

☆ Mee, Susie

The Girl Who Loved Elvis. Atlanta, GA: Peachtree Publishers, Ltd., 1993. 215 pp. ISBN: 1561450804.

A coming-of-age story of a young girl who works in a Tennessee mill in the mid-1950s. The story follows her discovery of and enchantment with Elvis Presley. This novel first appeared as a short story in *Redbook*, "Mama Won't Budge."

Source: Library of Congress PS3563.E284 G57 1993

☆ Nicholson, Monte

The Presley Arrangement. New York: Vantage Press, 1987. ISBN: none.

A novel about a dead man who resembled Elvis whose body was briefly and mysteriously exhumed. After the body is returned to his family, they are paid a great sum to remain silent about the affair. Nicholson states, "If it is true that Elvis Presley is alive, my book would be pretty close to the truth." (Brewer-Giorgio, *The Elvis Files*, [1990], [p. 72]. (*See* The Man/Death, Conspiracy, Sightings.) At the time of the novel's publication, Nicholson was a detective with the Los Angeles County Sheriff's Department.

Source: Brewer-Giorgio, The Elvis Files (1990).

☆ Siddons, Anne Rivers

Heartbreak Hotel. New York: Simon and Schuster, 1976. 252 pp. ISBN: 0671223151. Popular Library, 1977. Hampton Falls, NH: Beeler Large Print, 1986 (large print edition). ISBN: 1574900757.

A coming-of-age novel set at an Alabama college in the 1950s, with Elvis Presley's hit recording "Heartbreak Hotel" as a leitmotif. Its lyrics are used as mood-evoking elements. This book was made into a motion picture in 1989, entitled *Heart of Dixie* (a Steve Tisch production; an Orion Pictures release). It is available for viewing at the University of California, Los Angeles, Library.

Source: Library of Congress PZ4.S5682 He
PZ3569.I28 H42 1996 (large print edition)
OCLC 2151096; 36037774 (large print edition)

☆ Slegman, Ann

Return to Sender. Kansas City, MO: Helicon Nine Editions, 1995. ISBN: 1884235107.

The story of an Elvis Presley fan who goes to Graceland for the entertainer's funeral. The immediate aftermath of Elvis's death is used as the background for this novel about family dynamics.

Source: Library of Congress PS3569.L358 R47

☆ Tanner, T. J.

Jack, Tell the World. New York: Vantage Press, 1994. 184 pp. ISBN: 0533106419.

A couple travels to Graceland and is overtaken by the spirit of Elvis Presley.

Source: Collection of Bill and Connie Burk, Memphis, TN

☆ Wall, David S., Ph. D.

Wall is director of the Cyberlaw Research Unit, Department of Law, University of Leeds, England. He is an internationally recognized expert on intellectual property law. (*See* The Phenomena/The Law.)

The Amazing Adventures of Space Elvis **An abridged version of the** *Space Elvis Chronicles.* **Parts 1–8. 1995.**

An eight-episode story of Sevil Selprey, director of the James T. Kirk Centre of Planet Heart (whose mission is to study Planet Earth's leader, King Elvis). Sevil copies the King, and when his project is aborted by a political coup on Planet Heart, he blasts off in "a rather attractive green 'burning love' jump-suit" to find Earth. The episodes detail Elvis's ensuing adventures fighting for justice on Earth under the name of "Space Elvis." *The Space Elvis Chronicles* were subsequently published in *Blipvert* magazine.

Source: http://sunsite.unc.edu/elvis/oldeps.html

☆ Wesseler, Marlis

Elvis Unplugged. [Ottawa] Canada: Oberon Press, 1998. 123 pp. ISBN: 0778010937 (hdk.). ISBN: 0778010945 (pbk.).

A novel about Elvis sightings.

Source: OCLC 40254449

☆ Willis, Barry

The Strange Case of the Lost Elvis Diaries. Memphis, TN: Waynoka Press, 1995. 95 pp. ISBN: 1885197004.

A humorous mystery. "Something funny is going on . . . Reporter Jeff Parrish is hot on the trail of Elvis Presley's legendary lost journals. But are they for real, or is it all a don't-be-cruel hoax?" (*The Strange Case of the Lost Elvis Diaries* on-line homepage.)

Source: Library of Congress PS3573.I456515S77
Dewey Decimal 813/.54 20
http://home.mem.net/~welk/elvisdiaries.html

☆ Womack, Jack

Ambient. New York: Weidenfeld and Nicolson, 1987. 259 pp. ISBN: 1555840825.

A science-fiction novel of the future when gangs rule the streets of New York City. The largest church worships Elvis Presley, and "ambients" (freaks born after a nuclear reactor exploded) are considered sages.

Source: Library of Congress PS3573.0575 A8 1987

—————.

Elvissey. New York: Tor/A Tom Doherty Associates Book, 1993. 319 pp. ISBN: 0312852029. New York: Grove Press, 1997. 319 pp. ISBN: 0802134955.

A science-fiction novel in which a couple travels across time, from 2033 back to 1954, to kidnap Elvis Presley at the beginning of his career. They hope to rescue him from his future tragedies. They succeed and establish him as a demi-god in a decadent urban future. *Elvissey* was the winner of the 1993 Philip K. Dick award for Best Original Paperback.

Source: Library of Congress PS3573.0575 E48 1993/1997
OCLC 35174878 (1997)

☆ Yancey, Bill

Elvis Saves. Princeton, NJ: Xlibris Corporation, 1998. 256 pp. ISBN: 073880085 (hdk.). ISBN: 0738800864 (pbk.).

An unscrupulous marketing director attempts to make profitable the takeover of Graceland by a large entertainment corporation. He hires an Elvis impersonator as part of a major effort to convince the world that Elvis has returned. He is quickly involved in the disappearance of both the impersonator and the body of Elvis Presley.

Source: Publisher's address: Box 2199, Princeton, NJ 085432199

☆ Yeovil, Jack

Comeback Tour: The Sky Belongs to the Stars. Dark Future series. East Sussex [England]; Baltimore, MD: GW Books, 1991. 237 pp. ISBN: 1872372198.

A fantasy thriller in which Elvis Presley remains in the army for 20 years, serving as a counter-terrorist. The plot revolves around his fight to defeat the evil Avatar of the Apocalypse.

Source: OCLC 31302059

Juvenile Fiction

☆ Boyer, Cass

Elvis, My Man. Sydney, Australia: Pan Macmillan, 1994. 158 pp. ISBN: 0330274562.

For teenage readers. No plot information available.

Source: "Presley, Elvis" listing, Australian Books in Print *(1997), p. 812*

☆ *Elvis Jones and the Truckstoppers* series. Pymble, N.S.W., Australia: Harper-Collins, 1998.

These three juvenile novels are listed under the Library of Congress category "Presley, Elvis, 1935–1977—Juvenile Fiction." They are novelizations of an Australian cartoon series titled *Elvis Jones and the Truckstoppers.*

Marker, Steve, and Peter Viska

They Say It's Your Birthday; and You Can't Buy the Playground. 91 pp. ISBN: 0207196575.

Source: Library of Congress A 823.91 M345 J2 1

Monkey Sea, Monkey Do; and It's a Dog's Life. 91 pp. ISBN: 0207196567.

Source: Library of Congress A 823.91 M345 J1 1

Riddle, Tohby

Caught in a Trap: Boggled. 72 pp. ISBN: 0207196591.

Source: Library of Congress A 823.91 R543 J7 1

Greenburg, Dan

Greenburg also authored the novel *Kiss My Firm but Pliant Lips* upon which Elvis Presley's twenty-eighth film, *Live a Little, Love a Little*, was based.

Elvis the Turnip—and Me. The Zack Files series. New York: Grosset and Dunlap, 1998. ISBN: 0448417499.

A story for readers in grades 4–6. "Late one night when 10-year-old Zack hears strains of 'Heartbreak Hotel' coming from the refrigerator, he discovers the possibility that Elvis lives on as a turnip."

☆ Levy, Elizabeth

All Shook Up. Point series. New York: Scholastic, 1986. 172 pp. ISBN: 0590331159.

A story for high school readers. In 1954 a 16-year-old girl in Tennessee becomes romantically involved with a boy named Elvis Presley who is just beginning his career.

Source: Library of Congress PZ7.L5827 A1 1986

☆ Littlesugar, Amy

Shake Rag. New York: Philomel Books, 1998. ISBN: 039923005X.

A historical fiction set during the period in Elvis Presley's life when his family lived in the

Shake Rag section of Tupelo, Mississippi.[2] The plot revolves around Elvis's introduction to the soulful music of the Sanctified Church that traveled to his town. Includes bibliographic references. Illustrations by Floyd Cooper.

Source: Library of Congress PZ7.L7362 Sh 1998
OCLC 36438920

☆ Marino, Jan

The Day Elvis Presley Came to Town. Boston: Little, Brown and Company, 1991. 204 pp. ISBN: 0316546186.

Set in 1964 Georgia, this is a story of personal growth and racial understanding for teenage readers, using Elvis Presley as a plot device.

Source: Library of Congress PZ7.M33884 Day 1991

☆ McRae, John

The Elvis Mystery. Edward Arnold Readers Library series. London: Edward Arnold, 1990. 48 pp. ISBN: 0340526386. London: Edward Arnold, 1990. 48 pp. ISBN: 0175560838X (pbk.).

A Level 2 reader: elementary to lower-intermediate grade students. No plot information available.

Source: The British Library YK.1990.a.6005
Dewey Decimal 428.6
OCLC 20565019

☆ Mooser, Stephen

Elvis's Back, and He's in the Sixth Grade. New York: Bantam Books, 1994. 129 pp. ISBN: 0553481770.

While sixth-grader Eldon Grant is impersonating Elvis Presley in a school program, he gets a shock from his electric guitar and begins acting like the real Elvis. His popularity soars, and then crashes. He learns that people like you for who you are, not who or what you look like. Also includes an Elvis word search puzzle. Written for readers in grades 4–6.

Source: Los Angeles Public Library

☆ Townsend, Tom

Trader Wooly and the Ghost in the Colonel's Jeep. Austin, TX: Eakin Press, 1991. ISBN: 089015807X.

---

[2] The Presleys lived in Shake Rag at 1010 North Green Street during 1948. It was their last home in Tupelo before leaving in September of that year. At that time, Shake Rag was a neighborhood where poor African Americans lived—though there were three rental houses in which Caucasian families traditionally resided. (When the Presleys moved out, Elvis's maternal aunt Lillian Smith Mann Fortenberry moved in with her family.)

A junior high school boy, living with his army nurse mother on a military base in Germany, sees the ghost of Elvis Presley in a jeep and begins a time travel adventure. For grades 6–9.

Source: OCLC 223357198

Short Stories

☆ Bangs, Lester

"Graceland Uber Alles." Ed. Martin Torgoff. *The Complete Elvis.* New York: Delilah Books, 1982. ISBN: 0933328206. Pp. 130-133.

An imaginary meeting in a hotel room between Elvis Presley and Bob Dylan.

Source: Library of Congress ML420.P96 C65 1982

☆ Block, Lawrence

"The Burglar Who Dropped In on Elvis." *Some Days You Get the Bear.* New York: Avon Books, 1994. 302 pp. ISBN: none.

A former burglar is recruited by a national tabloid newspaper to break into Graceland to get photographs of Elvis's bedroom. The burglar has other plans.

☆ Driskell, Leon V.

"The Day That Elvis Presley Died." *Passing Through.* Chapel Hill, NC: Algonquin Books, 1983. ISBN: none. Pp. 106–130.

The events and day of Elvis Presley's death—August 16, 1977—are used as the backdrop for a story of a family coming to terms with itself.

Source: Library of Congress PS 3554.R497 P3

☆ Ebersole, Lucinda, and Richard Peabody, editors

Mondo Elvis: A Collection of Fiction and Poems About the King. New York: St. Martin's Press, 1994. 228 pp. ISBN: 0312105053.

A collection of 30 stories and poems relating to Elvis, 22 of which are reprinted from other sources. Author/poet biographies. Includes the following stories: Nick Cave, "Tupelo"; Cornelius Eady, "Young Elvis"; Rachel Salazar, "Words and Pictures"; Eleanor Earle Crockett, "Elvis Cuts Loose"; Diana Wakoski, "Blue Suede Shoes"; Greil Marcus, "Jungle Music: The All-Time All-Star 1950s Rock 'n' Roll Movie"; Howard Waldrop, "Ike at the Mike"; Janice Eidus, "Elvis, Axl, and Me"; Elizabeth Ash, "Elvis P. and Emma B."; Eri Makino, "Sproing!"; Lynne McMahon, "An Elvis for the Ages"; Pagan Kennedy, "Elvis's Bathroom"; Rafael Alvarez, "The Annuciations"; Ai, "The Resurrection of Elvis Presley"; Michael Wilkerson, "The Elvis Cults"; Brian Gilmore, "Elvis"; and Cathryn Hankla, "Elvis in Perspective."

Also includes Elvis poetry by David Wojahn and excerpts from Elvis novels by Mark Childress, Samuel Charters, Judy Vernon, William McCranor Henderson, Susie Mee, and Laura Kapalkian.

☆ Hill, Sandra, Linda Jones, Sharon Pisacreta, and Amy Elizabeth Saunders

Blue Christmas. New York: Leisure Books/Dorchester Publishing Co., Inc., 1998. 368 pp. ISBN: 0843944471.

A collection of four romance short stories set against the backdrop of Christmas at Graceland. In each story, the spirit of Elvis brings love to a young couple. They are Amy Elizabeth Saunders, "I Can't Help Falling in Love"; Linda Jones, "Always on My Mind"; Sharon Pisacreta, "All Shook Up"; and Sandra Hill, "Fever."

Source: Compiler's Collection

☆ Kaye, Lenny

"If Elvis Had Lived." Ed. Martin Torgoff. *The Complete Elvis*. New York: Delilah Books, 1982. ISBN: 0933328206. Pp. 126–129.

A fantasy of how Elvis Presley redeemed himself following a near-death experience on August 16, 1977.

Source: Library of Congress ML420.P96 C65 1982

☆ Kinsella, W. P.

"Elvis Bound." *Red Wolf, Red Wolf*. Dallas, TX: Southern Methodist University Press, 1987. ISBN: none.

Elvis touches individual lives through the romantic story of a professional baseball player who accepts and uses his wife's devotion to Elvis to strengthen their marriage.

Source: Library of Congress PR9199.3.K443 R43 1990

☆ Meads, Kat

"When Elvis Died." *Born Southern and Restless*. Pittsburgh: Duquesne University Press, 1996. Pp. 105–109.

The death of Elvis Presley is used as a plot device for this story of a woman dealing with her boss.

Source: Library of Congress PS 3563.E172Z47 1996

☆ Petry, Alice Hall

"Who Is Ellie? Oates's 'Where Are You Going, Where Have You Been?'" *Studies in Short Fiction* 25 (Spring 1988): 155–157.

The author examines her theory that Elvis Presley is the basis for the character of Ellie Oscar in Joyce Carol Oates's short story "Where Are You Going, Where Have You Been?"

Source: Library of Congress PN3311.58

☆ Sammon, Paul L., editor

The King Is Dead: Tales of Elvis Post Mortem. New York: Delta, 1994. 380 pp. ISBN: 0385312539.

Short stories and commentary about Elvis.

The short stories include Robert Zasuly, "Burnin' Love"; Lynne Barrett, "Elvis Lives"; Del James, "Backstage"; Chet Williamson, "Double Trouble"; Lawrence Block, "The Burglar Who Dropped In on Elvis"; Joyce Carol Oates, "Elvis Is Dead: Why Are You Alive?"; Lewis Shiner, "The Shoemaker's Tale"; Christopher Fahy, "Want"; J. S. Russell, "Limited Additions"; Joe R. Lansdale, "[Bubba Ho-Tep]"; Michael Reaves, "Elvis Meets Godzilla"; Harlan Ellison, "The Pale Silver Dollar of the Moon Pays Its Way and Makes Change"; D. Beecher Smith II, "Return of the King [A Fantasy]"; Karl Edward Wagner, "Deep in the Depths of the Acme Warehouse"; Janet Berliner Gluckman, "Wooden Heart"; Neal Barrett, Jr., "Donna Rae"; Stephen A. Manzi, "The King and I"; Alan Dean Foster, "Fitting Time"; David Morrell, "Presley 45"; Nancy Holder, "Love Me Tenderized or You Ain't Nothin' but a Hot Dog"; Wayne Allen Sallee, "Elviscera"; Kevin Andrew Murphy, " 'I'm Having Elvis's Baby!' by Miss Janet Carter of Pope County, Arkansas"; Paul M. Sammon, "The Heart of Rock 'n' Roll"; and Victor Koman, "The Eagle Cape."

The cultural commentary includes: Lou Reed, "Damaged Goods"; Greil Marcus, "Someone You Never Forget"; Roger Ebert, "This Is Elvis"; Clive Barker, "Notes on St. Elvis"; Martin Amis, "Elvis: He Did It His Way"; and Neal and Janice Gregory, "When Elvis Died: Epilogue."

Source: Library of Congress PS648.P65 K56 1994
Dewey Decimal 813/.0108351 20

☆ Sloan, Kay, and Constance Pierce, editors

Elvis Rising: Stories on the King. New York: Avon Books, 1993. 262 pp. ISBN: 0380772167.

Includes 16 stories about Elvis. Short stories include: Julie Hecht, "I Want You I Need You I Love You"; T. Coraghessan Boyle, "All Shook Up"; W. P. Kinsella, "Elvis Bound"; Elizabeth Hand, "The Have-Nots"; Kay Sloan, "Presleystroika"; Howard Waldrop, "Ike at the Mike"; Rebecca Hood-Adams, "Said You Was High Class"; Constance Pierce, "Memphis"; Spiro Zavos, "Elvis Is Dead"; Les Roberts, "The Fat Stamp"; Laura Kapalkian, "Starlight Coupe"; Gardner Dozois, et al., "Touring"; Bo Ball, "It's Just One Elvis"; William Hauptman, "Good Rockin' Tonight." Excerpts from novels include: Peter Hedges's *What's Eating Gilbert Grape* and Samuel Charters's *Elvis Presley Calls His Mother After* The Ed Sullivan Show. Introductory essay by the editors, discussing the growing posthumous impact of Elvis Presley. Author biographies.

Source: New York Public Library JND 96-93

☆ Tanaka, Rita Knight

Elvis Fantasies. **Special 20th Anniversary Commemorative Edition.** Los Angeles: Knight Publishing Company, 1997. 60 pp. ISBN: none.

A collection of author's and others' fantasies about Elvis Presley.

Source: Compiler's collection
Publisher's address: Knight Publishing Company, 10550 Rose Avenue, Suite 1, Los Angeles, CA 90034

☆ Taylor, Rich

"One Afternoon with the King; You Meet the Strangest People in Rabbit Hash, Kentucky." *Cycle World* (May 1989): 36.

A motorcycle devotee meets a fellow cyclist who looks like Elvis Presley. The stranger relates how he faked his death after reading an Isak Dinesen story about an opera singer who did the same. (*Cycle World* is a magazine for motorcycle enthusiasts.)

Source: Los Angeles Public Library

☆ Walker, Alice

"Nineteen Fifty-Five." *You Can't Keep a Good Woman Down.* New York: Harcourt Brace Jovanovich, 1981. ISBN: 0151997543. Pp. 3–20.

Told from the point of view of a black woman who wrote and recorded a song that became the signature tune of an Elvis Presley–like entertainer. The story follows the woman's life as she interacts with the entertainer over a 22-year period.

☆ Walker, Lisa

"From 100 Elvis Stories." *New Yorker* (Nov 2, 1987): 38–39.

An allegory about the divisiveness of human nature, using fictional Graceland City and its inhabitants to tell the story. Graceland City was created after its founder met Elvis and is populated by people whose names contain those of Elvis and his family. It is a place where all things are Elvisian and townspeople regularly send their mayor to Washington, D.C., to submit Elvis Constitutional amendments and currency ideas.

See Also:

In The Man/Biographies:

Clayson, Alan, and Spencer Leigh, *Aspects of Elvis: Tryin' to Get to You.*

In The Phenomena/Comic Books:

Elvis Shrugged Graphic Novel.
McCray, Patrick, *The Elvis Presley Experience.*

In Foreign Language Titles/Dutch:

Hart, Kees't, *Land van Genade.*

In Foreign Language Titles/Italian:

Horrakh, Livio, *Heartbreak Hotel/L'Hotel dei Cuori Spazzati.*

In The Rest/Elvis Impersonators:

Gantos, Jack, *Zip Six.*
Henderson, William McCranor, *Stark Raving Elvis.*
Miles, Cassie, *Heartbreak Hotel*
Travis, Jessica, *The Groom Wore Blue Suede Shoes.*

CHAPTER 25
Gender

"ELVIS FAN." What images do those words conjure up? The answer is such a universally ingrained stereotype that there is no need to respond. Elvis is indeed a female phenomenon.

From his first public appearance as an entertainer, Elvis made the girls scream. And it was this hysteria among teenage girls that brought him international attention. Since then, female consumption of him—both psychic and through record, book, magazine, souvenir, and concert ticket purchases—has continued to fuel his popularity. Bottom line: Elvis Presley, like few before him, touched the emotional G Spot of those of us with vaginas—and we and the world are still reeling from that liberating orgasm.

But why?

For one thing, Elvis Presley stimulated the cultural change that forever freed women to express their most primitive feelings in public. Girls and women in his audiences quite simply "lost it"—screaming, writhing, and emoting in great secular delight such as no one had ever seen. Not only did they love doing it, they transported this emotional freedom into every other aspect of their femininity. So much so that it would take a paper-bag-over-the-head denial not to acknowledge Elvis as a father of feminism.

Another reason for this female embrace is that Elvis met the criteria we established for husbands. He was just so cute—in the same physical way that made hearts flutter over historical heartthrobs like Lord Byron. (*See* Paglia listing in this chapter.) And he was good to his mother. (*See* Dundy listing in The Man/Biographies.)

But Frank Sinatra had these qualities—and reactions. How was Elvis different?

The authors in this chapter propose that the basis for his role in feminism, as well as the hypnotic attraction he holds for women, is this: Elvis, with his androgynous looks and flirtatious ways, was as much female as he was male. (*See* Graber, Paglia, and Wise listings in this chapter.)

But here's the peculiar part. Despite this feminization of Elvis, the Elvis literature is masculine territory—even though the Elvis of most male awareness is pro football player Grbac. The largest sections of the Elvis literature—the biographies, discographies, and photograph books—are dominated by, if not totally the dominion of men. Male writers have been the most active in plumbing the depths of Elvis's impact. And the most widely recognized and respected Elvis writers—such as Peter Guralnick and Greil Marcus—are, you guessed it, men.

Reasons for this disconnect range from the primal (male role as bread winner/warrior/competitor) to the pragmatic (traditionally men have authored more books than women have). But it could be that guys are just as fascinated by the Elvis Man/Woman as are the girls. Joel Williamson Ph.D. of the University of North Carolina thoughtfully addressed this in his yet-to-be-published paper delivered at the Second International Conference on Elvis Presley (The University of Mississippi, 1996, "Elvis, Faulkner, and Feminine Spirituality").

But despite the historical gender imbalance in the Elvis literature, female writers are increasingly taking their places in Elvis authordom. With this change—and its emphasis on feminine perspectives and interests—the value of the Elvis titles increases as they open more doors to an understanding of the female psyche. Through this literature, we learn more about what it is to be a woman—and an "Elvis fan."

☆   ☆   ☆   ☆

☆ Graber, Marjorie

"The Transvestite Continuum: Liberace—Valentino—Elvis." *Vested Interests: Cross-Dressing and Cultural Anxiety.* New York HarperPerennial, 1993. ISBN: 0060975245. Pp. 353–374.

The author examines Elvis Presley as the latest manifestation of a continuum (that also includes Valentino and Liberace) in which male sex symbols[1] achieve fame and desirability through their adaptation—or "impersonation"—of female characteristics. She notes that "it is almost as if the word 'impersonator,' in contemporary popular culture, can be modified by either 'female' or 'Elvis'" (p. 372).

Source: Library of Congress HQ 77.G37

☆ Paglia, Camille

[Elvis, gender, and sexuality commentary]. *Sexual Personae: Art and Decadence from Nefertiti to Emily Dickinson.* First Vintage Books Edition. New York: Vintage Books, 1991. ISBN: 0679735798. Pp. 115, 165, 361–364, 453.

America's leading feminist historian and critic comments on Elvis Presley's role in the annals of gender and sexuality.

☆ Poiger, Uta G.

"Rock 'n' Roll, Female Sexuality, and the Cold War Battle over German Identities." *The Journal of Modern History* 68 (Sept 96): 577–616.

The writer examines the rebellious actions of female rock and roll fans in the context of the Cold War struggles between East and West German national behaviors. She maintains that through the meeting of American influences and rock and roll in German life, par-

---

[1] Liberace's homosexuality was not widely known until after his death. Throughout much of his career, he was marketed to women as a romantic figure.

ticularly in young women, one can trace the changing cultural politics of national recon-struction and the German Cold War. (Paraphrased from *Humanities Abstracts* entry.)

☆ Shumway, David R.

"Watching Elvis: The Male Rock Star as Object of the Gaze." Ed. Joel Foreman. *The Other Fifties: Interrogating Midcentury American Icons.* Urbana; Chicago: The University of Illinois Press, 1997. ISBN: none. Pp. 124–143.

The author states "this essay looks at the visual aspects of Elvis Presley's performances as an indication of fractures in the seemingly solid edifice of traditional gender roles." The emergence of Elvis in the 1950s "marked the beginning of a shift in the representation of gender in mass culture." Elvis was presented as a highly sexualized image, and society fol-lowed suit. Notes. "Works Consulted."

☆ Wise, Sue

"From Butch God to Teddy Bear? Some Thoughts on My Relationship with Elvis Presley." *Studies in Sexual Politics* (1986): 13–14, 98–113.

"Past and present experiences of an Elvis Presley fan are discussed, focusing on the appar-ent incompatibility of Elvis and feminism. . . . The need for a feminist analysis of female fans' reactions to the Elvis phenomenon and a critical evaluation of male interpretations of Elvis is stressed. It is suggested that Elvis was a source of liberation rather than oppression for female fans." (*Sociological Abstracts*, 035, 03, 1987). Twenty references.

———.

"Sexing Elvis." *Women's Studies International Forum* 7 (Nov 1, 1984): 13–17.

Elvis Presley fan Wise examines Elvis as a creation of male writers who molded him in their own fantasy image of a sexual folk hero and archetypal macho man. Wise posits that the "emphasis on sex has disguised the existence of differing experiences among Elvis fans," particularly those who experience Elvis as "a mascot, secret friend, or hobby."

She examines how the "total domination of the male-defined sexual image of Elvis, adopted also by feminists, leads to interesting questions about how and why such a one-sided view of reality emerged and how such knowledge survives unquestioned." She explores these questions by analyzing her own personal experiences as an Elvis fan.

Source: Library of Congress HQ1101.W775
OCLC 7590245

See Also:

In The Man/The Impact of Elvis:

Armstrong, Karen, "Elvis Presley and American Culture."
Reiser, Martin, "A Note on the Analysis of the 'Elvis Presley' Phenomenon."
Sharnik, John, "The War of the Generations."

In The Phenomena/Fans:

Ashbaugh, Dick, "Elvis Presley."
Joyrich, Lynne, "Elvisophilia: Knowledge, Pleasure, and the Cult of Elvis."

In The Academics/Dissertations and Theses:

Granetz, Ruth Pearl, "The Symbolic Significance of the Elvis Presley Phenomenon to Teen-Age Females: A Study in Hero Worship Through the Media of Popular Singers and Song."

CHAPTER 26
Humor

POKING FUN AT Elvis Presley is about as fresh and cutting-edge as joking about blondes. But that is no deterrent to the writers and publishers who—inexplicably—believe that these oh-so-witty frat-house thigh-slappers will make them some money.

This body of—one hesitates to use the word "literature"—ranges from the truly offensive, such as Jacobs, *The Two Kings: Jesus Elvis,*[1] to the breathtakingly humorless, such as Kelly, *Herstory: Lisa Marie's Wedding Diary,* to the incredible "why on earth would someone pay $25.00 for *this?*"(the sale price for Norman, *Conversations with Elvis*).

☆   ☆   ☆   ☆

☆ Committee to Elect the King

Elvis for President. New York: Crown Publishers, Inc., 1992. 61 pp. ISBN: 0517592541.

A satirization of the 1992 Clinton-Gore presidential campaign book, *Putting People First,* outlining the reasons that Elvis should be elected President of the United States. Includes policy issues as well as comparisons between Elvis and the three major party candidates in the 1992 presidential election.

Source: Compiler's collection

☆ "Elvis Extravaganza! Elvis Turns 56!" *Inside Out: Detroit's Guide to Going Out.* Southfield, MI: WRIF Radio, Jan 7–13, 1991. 40 pp.

A pamphlet-size magazine containing reprints from tabloids such as the *Sun* and the *Weekly World News.*

Source: Compiler's collection

[1]This is notable as the first mainstream publishing house (Bantam) book dedicated to jokes about Jesus Christ.

☆ Jacobs, A. J.

The Two Kings: Jesus Elvis. New York: Bantam Books, 1994. Unpaged. ISBN: 0553373757.

An attempt—bordering on blasphemy and bigotry—to draw humorous parallels between the lives of Jesus Christ and Elvis Presley. An example: "Jesus is remembered on Palm Sunday in the spring. Elvis went to Palm Springs for the sun." Cartoon drawings.

Source: Library of Congress PN 6231.P695J323

☆ Kelly, Sean, and Chris Kelly

Herstory: Lisa Marie's Wedding Diary. New York: Villard Books, 1996. Unpaged. ISBN: 0679775404.

A fictional diary with commentary on Lisa Marie Presley's relationship with Michael Jackson.

Source: Library of Congress PN6231.P966 K45 1996

☆ Klein, Daniel, and Hans Teensma

Where's Elvis? Documented Sightings Through the Ages. New York: Viking Penguin, 1997. 80 pp. ISBN: 0670876356.

A photographic lampoon of "Elvis sightings." Includes 32 color and black and white photographs of recent historical events into which a likeness of Elvis has been inserted, i.e., the Million Man March in Washington, D.C., the student uprising at Tiananmen Square, a New York marathon.

Source: New York Public Library JMG 98-241

☆ Norman, Cecil Orlando

Conversations with Elvis. [U.S.]: Xlibris Corporation, 1998. 320 pp. ISBN: 0738802190 (hdk.); ISBN: 0738802204 (pbk.).

A sophomoric effort to use Elvis Presley as a literary device so that the author can demonstrate what he believes to be wit. The premise: "suppose you could ask Elvis the most puzzling questions about existence." The discussion that follows is trite as well as disrespectful to Elvis, involving the ridicule of prostitutes and radio talk show host Rush Limbaugh.

Source: www.barnesandnoble.com

☆ van Oudtshoorn, Nic

The Elvis Spotters Guide. Harrogate, N. York, UK: Take That Books, 1992. 96 pp. ISBN: 0951948903.

An attempt to find humor in posthumous Elvis Presley sightings.

Source: Compiler's collection

CHAPTER 27
The Law

IN A MANNER he could not have imagined while alive, Elvis Presley made legal history in death. Through Elvis Presley Enterprises, Inc. (EPE)—which represents the interests of his only surviving beneficiary, Lisa Marie Presley—new areas have been forged in trademark and copyright law. EPE has successfully lobbied for legislation and pursued court decisions that have opened the legal doors for heirs of the famous to inherit the rights to the celebrity's name, image, and likeness.

EPE—which owns the name, image, and likeness of Elvis—vigorously enforces its trademark rights and continues to set legal precedents. Fascinated legal writers have explored this in journals and periodicals ranging from law school reviews to *Advertising Age*.

But little in-depth study has been made of this landmark legal activity, with the exception of character merchandising expert David Wall, Ph.D., of the Department of Law at Leeds University (UK). Wall examines Elvis copyrights/trademarks in legal journal articles and also in his soon-to-be published book *Policing the Soul of Elvis* (Pluto Press, 2000). (*See* listing in this chapter.)

A gossipy, dilettantish attempt was made by Sean O'Neal in *Elvis Inc.: The Fall and Rise of the Presley Empire*. (*See* The Phenomena/Business and Finance.) Unfortunately, O'Neal sought the sensational and presented little if any verified information. Consequently, it falls short of what is needed to understand the legal workings of EPE.

The tenacity with which EPE pursues protection of Elvis's posthumous persona is often misinterpreted to be something other than what it is: an attempt to create order out of the chaos of product and image Elvisness. And, most important, to ensure the respectful preservation of Elvis's person and legacy. While Elvis belongs to the world, the protection of who he was and will remain rests on the shoulders of EPE—a frequently thankless effort.

The legal landmarks made in the name of Elvis Presley are not directly related to him or his talents. But they demonstrate how much his image's pervasiveness and malleability can be credited to EPE. The organization's aggressiveness and creativity in promoting and protecting Elvis is a significant factor in his staying power as a cultural fixture. In few other places is this more clearly evident than in the law.

☆   ☆   ☆   ☆

☆ "All Shook Up: Elvis Estate Irked by Bar Name." *ABA Journal* 83 (Mar 1997): 14.

The outcome of the *Elvis Presley Enterprises, Inc. v. Capece* case is discussed, in which EPE sued the owner of a Houston bar called "The Velvet Elvis" for copyright infringement, unfair competition, and dilution.

☆ Brescia, Matty

"Presley Estate Gains Possession of Costumes from Tom Parker." *Variety* (Nov 3, 1982): 2.

In addition to an Elvis Presley Enterprises, Inc. (EPE), lawsuit against Colonel Parker, this article also discusses litigation by EPE related to the selling of Elvis merchandise by the non-EPE-related souvenir shops across the street from the Graceland mansion.

☆ Diamond, Sidney A.

"A Matter of Survival." *Advertising Age* 52.54 (Dec 28, 1981): 20.

A discussion of the legalities surrounding rights of publicity using the case of *Factors Etc., Inc. v. Pro Arts, Inc.* (1981) as an example of federal court determination of whether or not a firm has the right to use the Presley name and likeness for commercial purposes.

☆ "Elvis Presley." *Amusement Business* (Feb 26, 1996): 10.

☆ "Graceland Under Fire." *People Weekly* (Dec 19, 1994): 35.

Discusses Elvis Presley Enterprises, Inc.'s, cancellation—for copyright infringement—of "Heartbreak Hotel" (an on-screen tour called "Cyber Graceland").

☆ Gross, Joan

"The Right of Publicity Revisited: Reconciling Fame, Fortune, and Constitutional Rights." *Boston University Law Review* 62 (July 1982): 965–1001.

The author examines three cases—one of which is *Estate of Presley v. Russen*—to demonstrate how federal courts are elevating the legal significance of publicity rights to an unprecedented level.

☆ Gwynne, S. C.

"Love Me Legal Tender." *Time* (Aug 4, 1997).

An examination of the legal undertakings, as of 1997, of Elvis Presley Enterprises, Inc.

☆ Kaye, Jeff

"Presley Estate May Sue to Stop Episode of *Designing Women*." *TV Guide* (Nov 19, 1988): A-1.

Abstract: "The estate of Elvis Presley intends to file a lawsuit to halt the broadcast of an episode of CBS's *Designing Women* in which the show's cast visits Graceland. Estate officials believe that the script is degrading to Presley's fans."

☆ Marks, Kevin S.

"An Assessment of the Copyright Model in Right of Publicity Cases." *California Law Review* 70:3 (May 1982): 786–815.

Discusses various cases that have added to the body of right of publicity law. Applies Elvis Presley to the rights of image marketing.

☆ *Reconstructing Elvis. Refereed Working Papers in Law and Popular Culture*, Series Two, Number 2. Manchester (UK): Manchester Institute for Popular Culture, 1995.

A pamphlet that served as the basis for David S. Wall's article in the *International Journal of the Sociology of Law*

Source: *University of Leeds (UK) Law Library Pamphlets Law Library E-81 q WAL*

☆ Singer, Richard, editor

Elvis: The Inventory of the Estate of Elvis Presley. "A Public Record Reprint." Whitestone, NY: Arjay Enterprises, 92 pp. ISBN: 096526419X.

A reprint of the official estate inventory of the property of Elvis Presley. Contains the details of objects and furnishings in each room of the Graceland mansion, including the closets. It enumerates Elvis's airplanes, vehicles, and mobile homes. A copy of the Clerk's Report on Settlement, as well as the Summary of Final Settlement for the period of August 1, 1985–December 11, 1985. Includes information on loans made by Elvis Presley. Index.

Source: *New York Public Library JMF 98-211*

☆ "United Kingdom Registrar of Trademarks Handed Down Decision That Trademark Rights of the Name Elvis and Elvis Presley Belong to Elvis Presley Enterprises. . . ."

The case is noteworthy in that unlike the United States, there is no recognition of rights of publicity in the United Kingdom, only trademark rights. (Abstract.)

☆ Wall, David S., Ph.D.

David S. Wall is director of the Cyberlaw Research Unit, Department of Law, University of Leeds, England. In addition to his work in the fields of criminal justice studies and cybercrimes, he writes about intellectual property law. He is particularly interested in the impact of recent developments in intellectual property law upon the emerging political economy of information capital. This will be the subject of his forthcoming book *Policing the Soul of Elvis*. Wall is also the author of *The Amazing Adventures of Space Elvis*. (*See* The Phenomena/Fiction.)

Reconstructing Elvis. Refereed Working Papers in Law and Popular Culture, Series Two, Number 2. Manchester (UK): Manchester Institute for Popular Culture, 1995.

A pamphlet that served as the basis for David S. Wall's article in the *International Journal of the Sociology of Law.*

Source: *University of Leeds (UK) Law Library Pamphlets Law Library E-81 q WAL*

————.

"Reconstructing the Soul of Elvis: The Social Development and Legal Maintenance of Elvis Presley as Intellectual Property." *International Journal of the Sociology of Law* 24.2 (June 1996): 117–143.

The first scholarly article examining the development of intellectual property law associated with the image of Elvis Presley. The legal protection and action required to police the image of Elvis under U.S. common and state law is discussed.

————.

"Returned to Sender." *New Law Journal* 147 (1997): 405.

————.

"Taking Care of Business: Trademarking the Soul of Elvis." *New Law Journal* 147 (1997): 540–541.

☆ Whitman, Robert, and Thomas J. Dembinski

"A Simplified Approach to Preserving Rights of Publicity on Death for Famous Clients." *Trusts and Estates* 121.4 (Apr 1982): 49–50.

A history of the right of publicity, including the legal filings of Elvis Presley Enterprises, Inc. "Lawsuits engendered by the death of Elvis Presley provide the most searching, if unconclusive, analyses of the right of publicity . . ." (*ABI/Inform Abstract.*)

☆ Zimmerman, Kevin

"No More Monkey Business, Say Protectors of Presley's Name." *Variety* (July 13, 1988): 59.

An interview with Jack Soden, CEO of Elvis Presley Enterprises, Inc., about efforts to stop the unlicensed use of Elvis Presley's name or likeness.

See Also:

In The Man/Death, Conspiracy, Sightings:

Presley, Elvis, "Last will and Testament of Elvis A. Presley: Filed August 22, 1977."

Colonel Tom Parker's Legal Involvement with Elvis Presley's Estate

During his management of Elvis Presley, Colonel Tom Parker's contract guaranteed him half of Elvis's earnings. He maintained this financial situation after Elvis's death in 1977, with claims on Elvis's assets. In May of 1980, the estate of Elvis Presley disputed this arrangement in court action. A probate court in Tennessee appointed Memphis entertainment attorney Blanchard L. Tual as Guardian ad Litem for Elvis's surviving beneficiary, Lisa Marie Presley, in the legal proceedings. Tual investigated the Colonel's financial interests in the estate and found that the Colonel had "violated his duty to Elvis and to the estate" (Worth and Tamerius, *Elvis: His Life from A to Z*, p. 199). A judge then ordered that all payments from Elvis's estate to the Colonel should cease.

In 1983 the Colonel entered into an out-of-court settlement with RCA in which the Colonel received payment for relinquishing his rights to Elvis's recordings.

☆　　☆　　☆　　☆

☆ Clayton, R.

"Colonel Parker Accused of Ripping Off Elvis." *Rolling Stone* (Sept 17, 1977): 8–9.

☆ Tual, Blanchard E.

In the Probate Court of Shelby County [TN] in re: The Estate of Elvis A. Presley, Deceased: Report of the Guardian ad Litem to the Honorable Joseph W. Evans, Judge of Division II of the Probate Court of Shelby County, TN. 1980. Filed Sept 1980, No. A-655, with exhibits. 52 [275] leaves.

Tual's findings that Colonel Parker had "violated his duty to Elvis and to the estate." Commonly known as The Tual Report.

Source: Harvard School of Law Library KFT147.T835x 1981 folio
OCLC 38119798

———.

In the Probate Court of Shelby County [TN] in re: Estate of Elvis A. Presley, Deceased: Guardian ad Litem's Amended Report. Filed July 31, 1981, No. A-655, with exhibits. 50 [34] leaves.

An amendment to The Tual Report.

Source: Harvard School of Law Library KFT147.T835x 1981 folio
OCLC 38119812

See Also:

In this chapter:

Brescia, Matty, "Presley Estate Gains Possession of Costumes from Tom Parker."

CHAPTER 28
Literary Recreation and Moveable Books

HAVING FUN WITH Elvis Presley is not limited to fiction and the theater. Books to test one's Elvis knowledge and books that are "Elvis toys" appeared as early as 1957. In that year Elvis fans could purchase a photographic flipbook that, when activated, sets into motion the "Jailhouse Rock" dance sequence. (*See John's Pocket-Movie Elvis Presley* listing in this chapter.) But it wasn't until the 1980s that "Elvis as literary recreation" became popular.

Since then, these books have poured forth in a profusion of Elvisian gaiety: Elvis coloring books, paper doll books, quiz books, pop-up books, reader-activated musical books, and "find Elvis in the crowded drawing" books.

To the scholar, this genre offers the added dimension of "Elvis as figure of fun" to the cultural fascination with the man. To everyone else, it extends an invitation for an amusing good time.

☆　　☆　　☆　　☆

☆ Bentley, Dawn (text)

Elvis Remembered: A Three-Dimensional Celebration. Kansas City, MO: Pop-Up Press, 1997. Unpaged. ISBN: 1888443456.

A biography of Elvis, told in pop-up book format.

Source: Library of Congress ML420.P96 B49 1997
Dewey Decimal 782.42166/092 B 21

☆ Brown, Hal, editor, and Rick Sales, illustrator

In Search of Elvis: A Fact-Filled Seek-and-Find Adventure. Forth Worth, TX: The Summit Group, 1992. 44 pp. ISBN: 1565300033.

Cartoon game book in which the reader must find a small cartoon figure of Elvis Presley in large, crowded cartoon pictures. A question and answer section covering events of Elvis's life.

Source: Library of Congress ML420.P96 I5 1992
Dewey Decimal 784'.0924

☆ Burt, Rob, and Michael Wells (concept)

Elvis Musical Pop Up. New York: Bonanza Pop-Up Books, 1985, 1986. 4 leaves. ISBN: 0517496348. London: Orbis Publishing Limited, 1985. 4 leaves. ISBN: 0517496348.

A pop-up book. The life of Elvis in five two-page, full-color pop-up spreads—each representing a significant period in Elvis's life. On the last page, music plays. This book was previously published in 1985 as *The Elvis Story*. (*See* Peterkin listing in this chapter.)

Source: Library of Congress ML420.P96 B97 1986
OCLC 12668920

☆ Gelfand, Craig, and Lynn Blocker-Krantz

In Search of the King. "A Perigee Book." New York: Putnam Publishing Group, 1992. [24] pp. ISBN: 0399517383.

Full-page cartoon drawings of various events in Elvis Presley's life, such as filming a movie, performing in Las Vegas, being in the U.S. Army, his Graceland wedding reception. The reader is challenged to find the cartoon drawing of Elvis in each scene.

Source: OCLC 25248177

☆ *Happy Birthday, Elvis*. Buena Park, CA: West Coast Book Publishers, 1988. [2 leaves.] Unpaged. ISBN: none.

A two-page birthday card/chart with trivia from the year 1935.

Source: Elvis Presley Enterprises, Inc.

☆ Holladay, John

Where's Elvis? Los Angeles, CA: Checkerboard Press, 1992. ISBN: 1562882600.

A caricature figure of Elvis Presley is hidden in crowded, two-page cartoon drawings of various events. The reader is challenged to locate it.

Source: Library of Congress PZ7.H70794
OCLC 25245971

☆ *John's Pocket-Movie Elvis Presley*. [U.S.]: Elvis Presley Enterprises, Inc., 1957. Unpaged. ISBN: none.

"Jailhouse Rock" dance sequence from Elvis Presley's film *Jailhouse Rock*. When the pages are flipped rapidly, Elvis appears to be moving.

Source: eBay auction item #30738081

☆ Moore, W. Kent, and David L. Scott

The Elvis Quiz Book: What Do You Know About the King of Rock and Roll? Chicago: Contemporary Books, 1991. 131 pp. ISBN: 0809239558.

A quiz book on Elvis Presley with approximately 1,000 questions, as well as word scrambles, crossword puzzles, and fill-in-the-blanks. Topics cover people, dates, and events relating to Elvis and his music and movies. The authors used *The Boy Who Dared to Rock* by Paul Lichter (*see* The Man/Biographies) and *Elvis: His Life from A to Z* by Fred Worth and Steve Tamerius (*see* The Man/Reference) in developing the questions. Bibliography of eight Elvis-related books. Black and white photographs, previously seen.

Source: Library of Congress ML420.P96 M67

———.

The Ultimate Elvis Trivia Quiz Book. Nashville, TN: Rutledge Hill Press, 1999. 160 pp. ISBN: 1558537481.

A variety of 70 quizzes and more than 25 photographs of Elvis Presley.

Source: OCLC 41388251

☆ Nash, Bruce

The Elvis Presley Quiz Book. New York: Warner Books, 1978. 110 pp. ISBN: 0446898236.

A variety of quizzes and word game puzzles relating to Elvis Presley.

Source: The British Library X.439/8542
OCLC 8231598

☆ Oliver, Chuck

On the Throne with the King: The Ultimate Bathroom Elvis Quiz Book. [U.S.]: Pinnacle Books, 1998. 224 pp. ISBN: 0786005432.

Synopsis from www.amazon.com: "an amazing bathroom quiz book that unloads all the dish, rumors, facts, follies, highs, lows, firsts, and worsts about the king of rock and roll."

Source: www.amazon.com

☆ Peterkin, Mike, and Pete Campbell

The Elvis Story. Rockups series. London: Orbis Publishing, 1985. [8] pp. ISBN: 0856138851.

A musical pop-up book covering Elvis's life and career. It was reissued in 1985 as *Elvis Musical Pop Up* by the same publisher. (*See* Burt listing in this chapter.)

Source: The British Library Cup.936/665
OCLC 13668675

☆ Rosenbaum, Helen

The Elvis Presley Trivia Quiz Book. Signet Books, #451. New York: New American Library, 1978. 154 pp. ISBN: none.

Includes 100 quizzes with 1,001 trivia questions about Elvis Presley.

Source: OCLC 4297427

Elvis Coloring Books

☆ *Elvis the Coloring Book: From Tupelo to Fame.* Florissant, MO: Namar Enterprise, Inc., 1993. [65] pp. ISBN: 1882739019.

Scenes to color from Elvis Presley's life and career. Some are drawn from well-known photographs of Elvis. Includes drawings of some of Elvis's jumpsuits.

Source: Memories of Elvis Gift Shop, Memphis, TN

☆ *The Elvis Coloring Book: A Pictorial Life History of the King of Rock 'n' Roll.* Memphis, TN: Tennessee Manufacturing and Distribution Company, 1983. [24] pp. ISBN: none.

A biography of Elvis Presley for children, in coloring book format.

Source: The University of Mississippi Archives
OCLC 28469109

☆ *The Elvis Coloring Book: Can We Have a Kiss?* 1992. ISBN: none.

Source: eBay auction item #30419219

☆ *Elvis Goes Hollywood.* Florissant, MO: Namar Enterprise Inc., 1993. [34] leaves. ISBN: 1882739000.

Children's coloring book with scenes from Elvis Presley's 33 films and documentaries.

Source: Compiler's collection

☆ *Elvis Presley's Graceland, Memphis, Tennessee, Coloring and Activity Book.* [n.p.]: EPE, [n.d.]. Unpaged. ISBN: none.

Drawings of Graceland's interior rooms and exterior grounds for children to color. Also "Lisa Marie" jet and museum exhibits.

Source: Compiler's collection

☆ *Gwaceland Coloring and Activity Book.* Ashland, OH: Landoll's Inc., 1996. Unpaged. ISBN: none.

Drawings to color and pencil games relating to a story of Bugs Bunny and Elmer Fudd fighting over who gets to stay in "Gwaceland" (which unsurprisingly bears strong similarities to Graceland).

Source: Compiler's collection

Elvis Paper Doll Books

☆ *Elvis "Lover Doll": A Paper Doll Portfolio.* Vol. 1, No. 3. No publication information available.

A paper doll cutout book with outfits (spanning 1956–1962).

Source: eBay auction item #41231934

☆ *Elvis, The Paperdoll Book.* New York: St. Martin's Press, 1982. [38] pp. ISBN: 0312243820/0312243928.

A paper doll cutout book with three Elvis paper dolls, one Priscilla Presley paper doll, 26 cutout outfits for the Elvis figures, and five for the Priscilla figure. Outfits for Elvis span events of his career. Black and white photograph collages of Elvis's career.

Source: Library of Congress ML88.976F6
Dewey Decimal 784.5'4'00924
OCLC 8387728

CHAPTER 29
Philately

THE WORLDWIDE ISSUES of Elvis Presley postage stamps are tangible proof of his global influence—and profitability. At least 34 countries have been releasing these stamps since 1978, ranging from the United States to the remote former Soviet Union republic of Touva (Tuva).

Most of the Elvis stamps are issued by small, often obscure countries seeking to produce government revenue—which may be one reason why Elvis is so ever-present on these stamps: as the advertisers who use the single word "Elvis" to attract buyers know, he sells.

But beyond the profit motive, these stamps—released singly or as part of commemorative sets—demonstrate Elvis's universal status as both a fantasy figure and an historically important individual. Two examples: the Russian Federation member Abchasia's 1995 stamp depicting a reenactment of Leonardo da Vinci's *The Last Supper* with Marilyn Monroe at Christ's place and Elvis as an apostle—and the 1988 Madagascar commemorative stamp set honoring great composers: Bach, Schubert, Bizet, and Elvis. (*See* Woodward listing in this chapter.)

The first Elvis Presley stamp is most likely the one issued by Grenada on the first anniversary of his death, August 1978. Since then, St. Vincent's in the West Indies has been the most prodigious with 25 releases by 1997—followed by Guyana with 13, Madagascar with 15, and the Central African Republic with 15.

Taken as a whole, the Elvis Presley stamps indicate that he is not an icon confined to the United States and other industrialized nations. Elvis truly belongs to the world.

☆   ☆   ☆   ☆

☆ King, R. G., and Floyd Kidd

King is an Elvis stamp collector.

Elvis on Stamps. Vol. I. Greeneville, TN: K&K Publishing, 1996. 100 pp. ISBN: none.

A reference book for Elvis Presley stamps. Information and pictures for stamps featuring Elvis from 12 countries. Each stamp is accompanied by a map of the issuing country, as well as information on the denomination and quantity issued. Color photographs and artwork from Elvis's life, musical career, and movies. This was the first of four planned volumes that would have encompassed a total of 37 countries. That plan was cancelled in March 1999.

In 1998 this book was republished as *Elvis on Stamps: A Pictorial Reference*. Elvis's friend Charlie Hodge was co-publisher with King of this reissue.

Source: R. G. King, c/o Smokey Mountain Publishing Co., 7690 Asheville Highway, Greeneville, TN 37743

———.

Elvis on Stamps: A Pictorial Reference. Greeneville, TN: Smokey Mountain Publishing Co., 1997. 100 pp. ISBN: 0965512320.

A reissue of *Elvis on Stamps*. Vol. I.

Source: R. G. King

☆ Woodward, Josephine

Elvis in the Post. Canterbury, Kent, UK: TCB Publishing, 1997. 103 pp. ISBN: 0953060101.

Full descriptions with black and white illustrations of more than 200 stamps featuring Elvis. Thirty-four nations represented. Each stamp is reproduced in a black and white photograph and is described in detail, including the artist's name, release date, and the stamp's denomination. Geographical details of each issuing country. Section on Elvis First Day Covers for the U.S. stamp. Section on stamps that mention or feature Elvis when the subject is of no relevance to him.

Source: Cambridge University Library, UK A.1997.1284
Publisher: 1 The Oast House, Old Wives Lees, Canterbury, Kent CT4 8 AS, England

The United States Postal Service's Elvis Presley Stamp

On January 8, 1993, Elvis Presley's 58th birthday, the United States Postal Service (USPS) issued a first-class stamp bearing the likeness of Elvis Presley. Previous to this release, the USPS had engaged the nation in a contest to decide which image of Elvis to use: a stylized drawing of Elvis from the 1950s ("the young Elvis") or the 1970s ("the old Elvis"). Postcard ballots were distributed through every post office in the country, and the verdict was roundly for the 1950s picture.

Not surprisingly, the USPS followed up with a barrage of products bearing the stamp's likeness, everything from potholders to beach towels. And, not surprisingly, it became the most popular, bestselling stamp in USPS history.

☆   ☆   ☆   ☆

☆ "Elvis Lives!!" *Direct Marketing* (Nov 1993): 33.

Discussion of the success of the United States Postal Service's direct-mail campaign promoting the Elvis Presley stamp and collectibles.

☆ Fisher, Christy

"*Advertising Age* Marketing 101: Elvis Stamp." *Advertising Age* (July 5, 1993): S23.

A discussion of the groundbreaking promotion of the Elvis stamp.

"Pat Geiger Is Stuck on Elvis and She Wants Him to Be Stuck on Her—or Rather, on Her Mail." *People Weekly* (Aug 29, 1988): 44–45.

Pat Geiger is the Elvis fan who spearheaded the movement to convince the USPS to issue a stamp honoring Elvis. This article reports on her efforts.

☆ Trebay, Guy

"Return to Sender." *Village Voice* (Mar 24, 1992): 19.

Elvis Presley is discussed in relation to the USPS's public survey to decide whether a commemorative stamp should feature a young or old portrait of the singer.

☆ Wattenberg, Daniel

"Will the Real Elvis Please Stand Up?" *Insight* (Mar 23, 1992): 15–16+.

Discussion of whether to depict Elvis Presley as a young man or a middle-aged man on the Elvis stamp.

In the February 6, 1993, Issue of *Stamps*:

Axtell, Denise. "An Insider's Look at the Elvis Stamp," p. 161.

A profile of artist Mark Stutzman who designed the winning Elvis Presley stamp.

Babbitt, John S. "Elvis Sighted All Across the Country," p. 160.

Background on the selection and public reaction to the stamp.

Scannell, Caroline. "Can't Lick Elvis," pp. 149, 169.

Discussion of the first day of stamp issue ceremony and what happened at post offices across the nation.

See Also:

In The Phenomena/Politics:

Plasketes, George, "From Post Office to Oval Office: Idolatry and Ideology in the 1992 Presleydential Elections."

CHAPTER 30
Poetry

"Your monument shall be my gentle verse,
Which eyes not yet created shall o'er read; . . .
You shall still live—such virtue hath my pen
Where breath most breathes,—even in the mouths of men."

(William Shakespeare, Sonnet 81)

POETRY IS ONE of the most enduring and engaging ways in which Elvis Presley exists in our culture. Elvis poems are unique—few historical figures have inspired such volume. And this quantity of Elvis poetry is even more amazing when one considers that most have been written in a time when the poetic art is buried beneath the heaping piles of rhyming joke books. Why?

Many of history's romantic figures have been poetic muses. But unlike the verses about Lord Nelson and Evangeline, the Elvis poetry is a gauge of his prevalence and meaning in our culture.

Professional poets tend to use Elvis as a device rather than as a subject. In their works "Elvis" moves beyond a specific human being to become a powerful mojo, conjuring visions, emotions, and atmospheres. Through these poems, it is very easy to experience a new reality of Elvis—not who he was, but how hearing and seeing his name makes one feel. This is a human transition unmatched in history.

Amateur poets, most of whom are fans, write the most remarkable and charming of the Elvis poems. Most are self-published and reveal deep Elvis-inspired emotions and fantasies. Their poems are indeed the "monuments" of Shakespeare's verse—enduring memorials to Elvis's power. But most important, these untrained poets open the door a bit wider to reveal the mystery of our enduring fascination with Elvis. They bring us close to the answer to the question "Why?"

☆ ☆ ☆ ☆

311

☆ Bei, Catherine

Cathy Bei is an Elvis fan who lives and works in Memphis. As a teenager, she regularly waited outside the Graceland gates to see Elvis.

Language of Love Always and Forever, Elvis. Indian Rocks Beach, FL: Creative Christian Concepts, 1993. 112 pp. ISBN: none.

A self-published book of poetry about Elvis, with pages for the reader to add drawings and poetry.

Source: Compiler's collection
Publisher's address: Creative Christian Concepts, 81 North Gulf Boulevard, Indian Rocks Beach, FL 34635

☆ Charles, Tony, editor, with Gordon Wardman

Return to Sender: An Anthology of Poems for Elvis Presley. Somerton, Somerset, UK: Headlock Press, 1994. 70 pp. ISBN: 1898987033.

Includes 45 poems about Elvis Presley, written by a variety of poets. Poems were selected to "reflect all these different aspects of the Elvis culture: biographical, homage, autobiographical, reflective and ironic" (introductory essay). Citations for poems not written specifically for this book. Biographical notes on contributors.

Source: Library of Congress PR1195.P665 R48 1994
OCLC 34414531

☆ *Elvis's Father and the Colonel Present Always Elvis.* [Las Vegas, NV]: [n.p.], Sept 8, 1978. [20] pp. ISBN: none.

Memorial poem to Elvis written by Elvis's manager Tom Parker and published in the official souvenir program from the dedication of Carl Romanelli's Elvis statue at the Las Vegas Hilton Pavilion.

Source: OCLC 7702977

☆ "A Final Tribute." [Vancouver, BC, Canada]: A & K Productions, 1977. 1 Sheet. ISBN: none.

A poem memorializing Elvis.

Source: OCLC 15895255

☆ Giorgio, Gail B.

Roses to Elvis. [U.S.]: Arctic Corp/2 A Group Inc., 1992. 162 pp. ISBN: none.

An anthology of poems about Elvis Presley written by his fans.

Giorgio is the author of several books that examine the possibility that Elvis Presley hoaxed his death. (*See* The Man/Death, Conspiracy, Sightings.)

Source: Elvis Presley Enterprises, Inc.

☆ Glaze, Paul L.

Glaze attended Humes High School in Memphis at the same time as Elvis Presley. Elvis and Glaze were casual acquaintances during those years.

From the Mind of the Poet Mystic. (n.d.). ISBN: none.

A collection of Glaze's Elvis poetry: "When Elvis Died," "Elvis in R.O.T.C.," "The Mystery Singer," and "Porky's Drive-In."

Source: http://sunsite.unc.edu/elvis/poem.html

☆ Greenfield, Marie

Elvis, Legend of Love (a poetic tribute to the KING). Mountain View, CA: Palos Verdes Book Company/Morgan Pacific Corp., 1980. 95 pp. ISBN: 09863848022.

Includes 67 memorial poems by the author, each paying tribute to Elvis Presley.

Source: OCLC 19737943

☆ Johnson, John, and Alice Johnson

An Anthology of Lyrics to Elvis Aron Presley: Elvis in Retrospect. [Miami, FL]: Jonal Productions, 1978. 20 pp. ISBN: none.

A book of poems about Elvis Presley published a year after his death.

Source: OCLC 37589011

☆ Mank, Chaw

Elvis Presley: Man or Mouse? [n.p.]: [n.p.], 1959. 24 pp. ISBN: none.

A $3\frac{1}{2}'' \times 5\frac{3}{4}''$ booklet consisting of three postcard insert cards, each with a song or poem about Elvis. All songs and poems were written by Mank.

Source: Jerry Osborne, The Official Price Guide to Elvis Presley Records and Memorabilia, *2nd Edition, p. 473. (See* The Phenomena/Collecting Elvis Memorabilia.*)*

☆ Manuszak, Sue

Manuszak is a longtime Elvis fan and is active with the Florida fan club, E.P. Continentals.

And I Love You So: A Collection of Poems. [FL]: Pearls of Rhyme, 1995. Unpaged. ISBN: none.

A collection of 15 poems by Manuszak memorializing Elvis and celebrating Elvis fans.

Source: Compiler's collection

―――――.

"A Christmas Miracle." *Elvis International Forum* (Nov 4, 1992): 3.

An adaptation of Clement C. Moore's poem, " 'Twas the Night Before Christmas," with Elvis Presley taking the role of Santa Claus.

Source: Library of Congress WMLC 93/4708 (Elvis International Forum)

☆ Meyers, M.

Elvis Presley: An Anthology in Memoriam (January 8, 1935–August 16, 1977.) Bristol, IN: Bristol Banner Books, 1994. 58 pp. ISBN: 1879183242.

Source: Library of Congress MLCS 95/4919 (P)
OCLC 32314769

☆ Mullins, Jack

Mullins is a military retiree who knew Elvis when they were both stationed in Germany with the U.S. Army.

The Life and Times of the Man, in Poem. [n.p.]: [n.p.], 1977. Unpaged. ISBN: none.

Self-published book of 16 poems about Elvis, most lamenting his 1977 death. Twenty-two black and white candid photographs; credited but not captioned.

Source: Compiler's collection

☆ Naphray, A. R.

Elvis—Pyromania. (Poems Dedicated to the KING). Wednesbury, West Midlands, UK: Bavie Publications, 1976. ISBN: none.

Poetry paying homage to Elvis Presley. Photographs of Elvis Presley. (*See Elvis Presley— 1935–1977: A Tribute to the King.* "Elvis Goodbye" in The Man/Photographs.)

Source: The British Library X.0435/120
OCLC 16596866
Publisher's address: 2 Engine Lane, Wednesbury, West Midlands, UK

———.

Goodbye. Wednesbury, West Midlands, UK: [Bavie], [1977]. ISBN: none.

Memorial poems about Elvis Presley, written immediately after his death. Black and white photographs by J. Rock Caile and John Herman.

Source: The British Library X.0435/119

☆ Presley, Sybil Marie, and Scarlett Magnolia Parsley

Scarlett Magnolia Parsley is a character created by Sybil Presley. Each Elvis Birthday Celebration and Elvis Week in Memphis, Presley attends events dressed as Scarlett.

You're an Elvis Fan If . . . . Memphis, TN: Lord's-Peace Productions, 26 pp. ISBN: none.

A pamphlet of Elvis-themed poems by fan Sybil Marie Presley.

Source: Compiler's collection
Publisher's address: P.O. Box 771106, Memphis, TN 38117

☆ Watkins, Darlene

Watkins has been an Elvis fan since she saw him on *The Ed Sullivan Show* in 1956.

Elvis, We Love You Tender. Commerce City, CO: Kisco, 1988. 108 pp. ISBN: none.

Includes 25 poems by Watkins about Elvis, his family, and his friends. Color and black and white photographs; most captioned and all credited to Elvis Presley Enterprises, Inc., and "Jimmy Velvet's Museum."

Source: Compiler's collection
Publisher's address: Kisco, 5565 East 52nd Avenue, Suite D-1, Commerce City CO 80022

☆ West, Joan Buchanan

Elvis: His Life and Times in Poetry and Lines. Hicksville, NY: Exposition Press, 1979. 48 pp. ISBN: none.

Includes 44 tribute poems by Elvis fan West, each examining a facet of Elvis Presley's life and impact.

Source: OCLC 5037579

――――.

Elvis: Through the Eyes of Love. Welcome, NC: Wooten Printing Company, 1982. 94 pp. ISBN: none.

Poems to and about Elvis Presley, written by the author.

Source: Elvis Presley Enterprises, Inc.

☆ Wojahn, David

Wojahn is the author of seven books of poetry and is Lilly Professor of Poetry at Indiana University.

Mystery Train. Pittsburgh Poetry Series. Pittsburgh, PA: University of Pittsburgh Press, 1990. 85 pp. ISBN: 0822936372 (hdk.); ISBN: 0822954294 (pbk.).

Poems about Elvis Presley. Titles include "Elvis Moving a Small Cloud: The Desert Near Las Vegas, 1976"; "The Assassination of Robert Goulet as Performed by Elvis Presley: Memphis 1968"; and "Nixon Names Elvis Honorary Federal Narcotics Agent at Oval Office Ceremony: 1973."

Source: Library of Congress PS3573.044M9 1990
Dewey Decimal 811/.54 20

See Also:

In The Man/Memoirs and Memories:

Hill, Wanda June, *We Remember, Elvis.*
Hill, Wanda June, *Elvis: We Remember*, 1978, and *Elvis: Face to Face*, 1985.
Parker, Edmund K., "The Jackals," *Inside Elvis.*

In The Man/Photographs:

Elvis: A Pictorial Tribute: The Last Tour.
Elvis Presley—1935–1977: A Tribute to the King. "Elvis Goodbye."

In The Phenomena/Psychic Elvis Experiences:

Panta, Ilona, "Invisible Love," *Elvis Presley, King of Kings.*

In Foreign Language Titles/Finnish:

Into, Markku, *Elvis, Eli, Elamansayksin.*

In Foreign Language Titles/Portuguese:

Carneiro, Antonio (Baelier), *Elvis Esoterico: parte 1.*
Carneiro, Antonio (Baelier), *Epopaeia Elvis: Canto 1.*
Soares Junior, Jose, *A Morte de Elvis Presley.*

In The Rest/Souvenir Magazines:

Song Hits Magazine's Tribute to Elvis.

In The Rest/Unverified Titles:

Pierson, Jean, *Elvis, the Living Legend: and Other Heartwarming Poems.*

CHAPTER 31
Politics

WAS ELVIS PRESLEY a Democrat or a Republican?

No one seems to know. The Memphis City Registrar of Voters has no record of his political registration. Longtime close Elvis friends Larry Geller and Marty Lacker say Elvis remained apolitical under Colonel Parker's orders.[1] And, no evidence exists that he ever supported a candidate—although a 1956 *Newsweek* article alleged his support for 1956 Democratic presidential candidate Adlai Stevenson. (*See* "Music: Inextinguishable" listing in this chapter.)

But the mystery of his political affiliation gains some clarity when his bi-partisan relationships with two presidents are examined. Quite simply, he, like many Americans, considered the man, not the politics.

Elvis's most famous political association was with Richard Nixon. In 1970 Elvis went to the White House, unannounced and uninvited, and requested a meeting with President Nixon. He wanted to offer his assistance in the "war on drugs." That the two met in the Oval Office—seemingly bizarre until one considers that Elvis held President Nixon's strong pro-military, pro–law enforcement, anti-drug, anti-"hippie" sentiments—continues to fascinate Americans. Chronicled in detail by Nixon White House aides Egil Krough and Joe Finlator (*see* listings in this chapter), this meeting also has been the subject of a television motion picture, *Elvis and Nixon* (HBO, 1997). The official White House photographs taken during the meeting are among the items most requested from the National Archives, and one may purchase key chains, magnets, stationery, computer mouse pads and screen savers, postcards, mugs, tee shirts, and plastic dishes with these photographs on them.

Though Richard Nixon and Elvis never became friends, Elvis and Jimmy Carter did. Upon Elvis's death, President Carter issued a statement whose wording indicates that he felt a true loss. (This is the first presidential statement released upon the death of a celebrity.) The strength of their friendship was such that 20 years after Elvis's death, Douglas Brinkley, writing in *The New Yorker*, would examine that relationship. (*See* listing in this chapter.)

---

[1] Lacker says "From the very beginning [1955] Parker told him not to get involved in politics because no matter which side he took on an issue, or which candidate he spoke of, he would end up getting the other side angry at him. Parker wanted him to play it safe and not alienate anyone." (Correspondence, March 1999.)

As Elvis's pervasiveness has expanded further in our 1990s culture, it was inevitable that he would emerge in the political arena. Rock music historian and critic Greil Marcus was the first to bring attention to this phenomenon. (*See* Marcus listing in this section.) During the 1992 campaign, Marcus described how candidates such as Bill Clinton and now–U.S. Senator Russ Feingold (D-WI)[2] were using Elvis as a campaign leitmotif.

Bill Clinton would lay particular claim to Elvis, most likely because it served him in projecting a youthful and hip image, as well as that of a good ole Southern boy, depending upon the audience. During the 1992 campaign, Candidate Clinton played a saxophone rendition of "Heartbreak Hotel" on comedian Arsenio Hall's television program. Media reported that his Secret Service code name was "Elvis" (though an agency spokesman says this is not correct[3]). And President Clinton's 1993 inaugural parade included an Elvis impersonator.

After the 1992 election, the Clintonian-Elvisian symbiosis grew. By 1997 it had become a definable process. That year, *Economist* ran an essay describing how President Clinton had gone from "outside rebel" into the middle of American mainstream by using the Elvisian formula. (*See* "Bill Presley and Elvis Clinton" listing in this chapter.)

The Republicans have been a little slow to catch up with the Democrats' Elvisness. But as the 2000 Presidential Campaign heats up, they are ready—with leading candidate Governor George W. Bush's biographer continually referring to him as "the GOP's Elvis."[4]

But perhaps the truest expression of Elvis's current role in partisan politics comes from longtime political observer Molly Ivins, who wrote in her January 10, 2000, column, "I long since decided that if the candidate doesn't have some Elvis to him, he ain't gonna make it."[5]

So, was Elvis a Democrat or Republican, in spirit if not in fact? As he has ascended from manhood to myth to cultural signifier, this has become an irrelevant question. The importance of Elvis and politics is that it gives us a way of keeping tabs on him and ourselves. Tracking Elvis's role in politics is a means for tracking Elvis's progress in our culture—and vice versa.

☆   ☆   ☆   ☆

☆ **"Bill Presley and Elvis Clinton."** *Economist* (Aug 10, 1996): 24.

This article, which was written with assistance from the *Infinite Elvis* compiler, demonstrates how Bill Clinton patterned his presidential career on Elvis Presley.

☆ Brinkley, Douglas

"Dept. of Missed Opportunities: The White House–Graceland Connection That Might Have Saved Elvis." *The New Yorker* (Aug 18, 1997): "Talk of the Town."

---

[2] In his Senate campaign, Feingold aligned himself with Elvis by using the entertainer's image in political advertising. (*See* Masterson listing in this chapter.)

[3] Interview, March 1999.

[4] Bill Minutaglio (*First Son: George W. Bush and the Bush Family Dynasty*), appearing on "Cross Talk" (MSNBC, December 1, 1999).

[5] *Press-Telegram* (Long Beach, CA), p. 411.

An examination of President Jimmy Carter's admiration of Elvis Presley, including a description of a telephone call between the two, which the former President now believes he could have used to help Elvis with his prescription drug problems.

☆ Edson, Arthur

"Protests Roll In on Senator Case as Threat to Elvis's Hair Rocks Fans." *Washington Star* (AP Newsfeatures) (Feb 14, 1957).

The story of New Jersey Republican Senator Clifford Case's involvement in determining whether or not Elvis Presley would receive a regulation haircut during his required two-year military service. After receiving an inquiry from a constituent, the Senator wrote to army officials. Senator Case's response to his constituent was released to the media, and his office received numerous letters on the subject.

Source: Martin Luther King Memorial Library, District of Columbia, Washington Star files

☆ Finlator, John

"Elvis." *The Drugged Nation: A 'Narc's Story.* New York: Simon and Schuster, 1973. 352 pp. ISBN: 671216120. Pp. 102–105.

An anecdote about Elvis Presley's visit with President Nixon, written by John Finlator, then the head of the United States Bureau of Narcotics and Dangerous Drugs (BNDD). Before Elvis went to the White House, he met with Finlator to offer his assistance and ask for a BNDD badge and credentials. Finlator turned him down. (Later in the day Finlator was summoned to the White House so that President Nixon could present a badge to Elvis.)

Finlator's narrative demonstrates that Elvis's visit to President Nixon was not entirely a spur-of-the-moment idea on Elvis's part. He writes about "feelers" that had been made before the visit and notes that he, Finlator, "had made some moves to try to enlist Presley in the antidrug fight . . . an antidrug movement on his part would certainly help others in the same business to follow his lead" (p.102).

Source: Library of Congress HV 5825.F54

☆ Gregory, Neal, and Janice Gregory, When Elvis Died.

☆ Kirchberg, Connie, and Marc Hendrickx

Marc Hendrickx is the author of the Elvis biography *Muzierk Mens Mythe*. (*See* Foreign Titles/Dutch.) Connie Kirchberg is a freelance writer.

Elvis Presley, Richard Nixon, and the American Dream. Jefferson, NC: McFarland & Company, Inc. Publishers, 1999. [232] pp. ISBN: 0786407166.

An examination of Elvis Presley and Richard Nixon, tracing "the remarkable parallels in their lives." In biographies of both men, the authors "trace their journeys from success . . . to failure and back upward to respectability near the end." Photographs and reproductions of letters. Chapter notes. Bibliography.

☆ Krough, Egil "Bud"

Krough was a member of President Richard Nixon's White House staff in the early 1970s. He currently practices law in Seattle, Washington.

The Day Elvis Met Nixon. Bellevue, WA: Pejama Press, 1994. 61 pp. ISBN: 0964025108.

A detailed narrative of Elvis Presley's visit with President Richard M. Nixon, written by Egil Krough, the White House staff member who was responsible for coordinating the meeting. (Krough was responsible for the President's drug initiatives, so he was placed in charge of arranging and conducting the meeting.)

Included in the book are reproductions of the White House memos in preparation for the meeting and Elvis's handwritten letter to the President requesting the meeting. A color photograph of the President with Elvis. Also, a photograph of Elvis's Bureau of Narcotics and Dangerous Drugs Special Assistant badge issued by the U.S. Department of Justice. Official photographs from the visit; captioned.

Note: The official photographs of Elvis's visit with President Nixon may be ordered from the Nixon Presidential Materials section of the United States National Archives and Records Administration in College Park, Maryland. Other photographic mementos of this visit are available at the Richard M. Nixon Presidential Library in Yorba Linda, California.

Source: Library of Congress ML420.P96 K

☆ Marcus, Greil

Double Trouble: Bill Clinton and Elvis Presley in a land of no alternatives. New York: Henry Holt, 2000. 272 p. ISBN: 080506513x

A collection of Marcus's essays that explore the remarkable kinship between Bill Clinton and Elvis Presley, deonstrating how they both embody the American struggle over purity and corruption, fear and desire.

Source: Library of Congress E886.2M365 2000

———.

"The Elvis Strategy." *The New York Times* (Oct 27, 1992): OP-ED.

Noted music critic and historian Greil Marcus was the first to raise the Bill Clinton–Elvis Presley connection with this article, outlining how the Democrat Party took ownership of Elvis during the 1992 presidential campaign. (Marcus reports that "Elvis Aron Presley" was listed in the 1992 Democrats' national convention literature as the "Entertainment Coordinator.")

☆ Masterson, Peg

"*Advertising Age* Marketing 100: U.S. Sen. Russ Feingold." *Advertising Age* (July 5, 1993): S23.

During U.S. Senate Candidate Russell Feingold's campaign, he ran a television advertisement featuring a tabloid headline reading, "Elvis Endorses Feingold." Feingold won. This article examines this ad within the context of the successful creativity of the Feingold campaign.

☆ "Music: Inextinguishable." *Newsweek* (Aug 27, 1956): 68.

Brief about Elvis Presley with a footnote indicating that Elvis endorsed the Democrats' Presidential Candidate Adlai Stevenson (no reference given).

☆ [The official statement by President Jimmy Carter upon the death of Elvis Presley]. *Compilation of Presidential Documents*, Vol. 15, No. 40: 1815–1816.

This is the first time in presidential history that a statement had been issued upon the death of a celebrity. According to Neal and Janice Gregory (*When Elvis Died*, p. 145), this statement received "large headlines and editorial comment" in foreign countries. They paraphrase a major West German newspaper as stating that "the Carter statement showed the strength of the American democracy, for no German head of state could have commented on a pop singer and remained in office."

☆ Plasketes, George M.

"From Post Office to Oval Office: Idolatry and Ideology in the 1992 Presleydential Elections." *Popular Music and Society* 18.1 (Spring 1994): 19–50.

"In 1992—Elvis 15 A.D. and an election year—the lines between politics, culture, and religion grew increasingly and intensively entangled. The unprecedented and extravagant sequence of events surrounding the issue of the Elvis stamp, which both parallels and intersects with the 1992 presidential process, is examined," (*UMI Abstract*). Notes. Biographical references.

☆ "The President Himself." *When Elvis Died*. Washington, D.C.: Pharos Books, 1992. Pp. 139–145.

The official statement issued by President Jimmy Carter upon the death of Elvis Presley—the first ever issued by a president on the occasion of a celebrity's death—is traced through its preparation. Also, the story of the relationship between the Carters and Elvis Presley, including Elvis's call to President Carter seeking assistance for his friend George Klein who was on trial for mail fraud.

Source: Gregory, Neal, and Janice Gregory, When Elvis Died.

☆ West, Diana

"Against Conservative Cool." *The Weekly Standard* (Aug 5, 1996): 20–24.

In a magazine for Libertarians and conservative Republicans, the author uses Elvis Presley's 1970 meeting with Richard Nixon as the starting point for her examination of the GOP's melding of the bourgeois and rock worlds. From the front cover: "When Nixon met Elvis in 1970, it was in secret. Now, Republicans proclaim their devotion to the culture of rock. What happened?"

See Also:

In The Man/Biographies:

Lichter, Paul, *Behind Closed Doors*. (Nixon visit.)

In The Phenomena/Humor:

The Committee to Elect the King, *Elvis for President*.

Statements and Resolutions Relating to Elvis Presley in the *Congressional Record*

The *Congressional Record* is the official documentation of the proceedings of the United States House of Representatives and the United States Senate. It is published each day that Congress is in session. It contains the transcripts of all remarks made during that day's session, all bills introduced, all votes taken, and extended remarks (those not made during the proceedings but later inserted into that day's *Congressional Record*. These are generally comments or speeches that the Member or Senator had been unable to deliver while the Congress was in session that day).

Comments regarding Elvis Presley in the *Congressional Record* relate to his military service, his death, Graceland, and to House Joint Resolutions (H. J. Res.) honoring him.

☆ 85th Congress, Second Session
Extension of Remarks:

"Divinations, Soothsayings, and Young Mr. Tompkins." U.S. Senator Mike Monroney (D-OK). *Cong. Rec.* (Vol. 104) Jan 9, 1958: A104.

The insertion of a December 29, 1957, *New York Times* column by James Reston. It is a humorous view of American politics and society in which Elvis Presley's draft deferments are used as a metaphor.

☆ 86th Congress, Second Session
Floor Statement:

"Tribute to Elvis Presley." U.S. Senator Estes Kefauver (D-IL). *Cong. Rec.* (Vol. 106, Pt. 4) Mar 5, 1960: 4499.

Remarks made at the time of Elvis Presley's discharge from the U.S. Army, honoring him for his service and patriotism. According to Patsy Andersen of Elvis Presley Enterprises, Inc., for the rest of his life, Elvis carried in his wallet a Memphis *Commercial Appeal* clipping which repeated Sen. Kefauver's statement.

☆ 95th Congress, First Session
Extension of Remarks:

"Blue Suede Shoes." U.S. Representative Patricia Schroeder (D-CO). *Cong. Rec.* (Vol. 123, Pt. 22) Sept 8, 1977: 28340.

A memorial to Elvis Presley. Rep. Schroeder inserted a commentary from the August 29, 1977, issue of *The New Yorker*.

☆ Floor Statement:

"Farewell to 'The King.'" U.S. Senator Howard Baker (D-TN). *Cong. Rec.* (Vol. 123, Pt. 22) Sept 9, 1977: 28435-6.

Memorial speech for Elvis Presley. Insertion of "Elvis Went from Rags to Riches," by William Thomas, [Memphis] *Commercial Appeal* August 17, 1977. Also inserted, "Elvis Presley," *Memphis Press-Scimitar* August 17, 1977.

☆ H. J. Res. 589:

"Authorizes the Secretary of the Treasury to acquire by donation or purchase the Graceland Mansion and its grounds on Elvis Presley Boulevard, Memphis, Tennessee, for the establishment of an 'Elvis Presley National Historic Site.'" Introduced by U.S. Representative Biaggi, (D-NY). *Cong. Rec.* (Vol. 123, Pt. 23) Sept 12, 1977: 289221.

☆ 95th Congress, Second Session
Extension of Remarks:

"A National Tragedy." U.S. Representative Robert K. Dornan (R-CA). *Cong. Rec.* (Vol. 124, Pt. 21) Sept 7, 1978: 28459.

Rep. Dornan's call for a congressional hearing on the growth of prescription drug dependency in America, using Elvis Presley's death as an example. He urged the House Select Committee on Narcotics Abuse and Control to call Dr. E. Eric Muirhead, chief pathologist at Baptist Memorial Hospital in Memphis, to testify on Elvis's death by prescription drugs. Dornan inserted an uncited article about Elvis's death, "Exclusive: Secret Autopsy Report . . . It Contradicts Medical Examiner's Official Findings."

☆ 96th Congress, Second Session
H. J. Res. 488:

"A joint resolution to authorize and request the President to issue a proclamation designating January 8, 1981, as 'Elvis Presley Day.'" Introduced by U.S. Representative Barbara Mikulski (D-MD). *Cong. Rec.* (Vol. 127, Pt. 1) Jan. 29, 1980: 1046.

☆ 97th Congress, First Session
H. J. Res. 296:

"A joint resolution to provide for the designation of January 8, 1992, as 'National Elvis Presley Day.'" Introduced by U.S. Representative Harold Ford, Sr., (D-TN). *Cong. Rec.* (Vol. 127, Pt. 10) June 23, 1981: 133468.

☆ 102nd Congress, Second Session
Floor Statement:

"'Love Me Tender' or 'Hound Dog.'" U.S. Representative James Traficant (D-OH). *Cong. Rec.* (Vol. 138, Pt. 6) Apr 7, 1992: 8218.

A speech made by Rep. Traficant in which he contrasts the public enthusiasm for voting for the Elvis Presley stamp portrait with the apathy of Democrat voters in the primary elections.

☆ H. J. Res. 461:

"A joint resolution designating January 8, 1993, as 'Elvis Presley Day.'" Introduced by U.S. Representative Glenn Anderson (D-CA). *Cong. Rec.* (Vol. 138, Pt. 6) Apr 7, 1992: 8298.

CHAPTER 32
Psychic Elvis Experiences

THE MYSTERIES THAT swirl around the circumstances and realities of Elvis Presley's death are a natural attraction for writers of metaphysical literature. Some tell of visitations from Elvis's spirit or being used as his "channel" to communicate beyond-the-grave messages. Two co-authors earnestly forward the theory that Elvis and his mother Gladys were UFO abductees who returned from capture with documented supernatural powers.

Books of this kind do not appear about other dead celebrities such as John Lennon, Marilyn Monroe, James Dean—despite the hold they maintain on our interest. So why Elvis? Why does he inspire this cosmic depth of personal involvement? What is it about him that transcends perceptible reality? Does the key lie in these psychic experience titles? The truth may indeed be out there.

☆　　☆　　☆　　☆

☆ Blua, Margoz

Herrre's Elvis: Broadcasting from the Stars. Las Vegas, NV: EI/Blua Creations, 1981.
　　84 pp. ISBN: none. LCCN: 85–453.

"Elvis psychic quotes and drawings are being presented to you by clairvoyant Margoz Blua—(her name is Bluma Margaret)—who has been in touch almost daily with Elvis [sic] beautiful spirit ever since his death, August 16, 1977. Her files contain over 5,000 entries all channeled from Elvis Presley" (book jacket notes).

Source: Compiler's collection
Publisher's address: 605 Oakmount Drive #2034, Las Vegas, NV 89109

☆ Cohen, Daniel

"The Ghost of Elvis." *The Ghost of Elvis and Other Celebrity Spirits.* New York: G. P. Putnam's Sons, 1994. ISBN: 0399226117. Pp. 3–14.

For young readers in grades 6–9. Four Elvis posthumous sighting anecdotes, including the famous grocery store sighting near Kalamazoo, Michigan.

Source: Library of Congress BF 1461.C667

☆ Daniel, Richard

"Richard Daniel" is the combined two first names of the individuals who co-authored this book. Both are UFO enthusiasts.

The Elvis-UFO Connection. Woodinville, WA: Castle Rock Enterprises, 1987. 180 pp. ISBN: none.

Author's thesis: Gladys and Elvis Presley were UFO abduction victims. "If we avoid the conventional explanations given concerning patterns of recurring symptoms displayed by UFO victims to his (Elvis's) life experience, a pattern of alien contact with Elvis can be seen." A scholarly presentation using anecdotes from books by Elaine Dundy, Red and Sonny West, Albert Goldman, Dave Marsh, and others as support. Comparison of Gladys's and Elvis's behaviors and life experiences to those of documented UFO abductees. Sources cited in bibliography.

Source: Los Angeles Public Library

☆ Farmer, Paula

Elvis Aaron Presley: His Growth and Development as a Soul Spirit Within the Universe. Thornhill, Ontario, Canada: Prime Books, 1996. ISBN: 1895250145.

This is a spiritual self-help book in which Elvis Presley speaks through channeler Paula Farmer. "From the Soul Plane, Elvis . . . contacts Paula Farmer, a Direct Transfer Channel, to assist him in delivering his story of his spiritual journey with the hope of helping mankind."

The author explains that this is "a true account of Elvis Aaron Presley, in his own words as he came to me from July 1994 to August 1995."

Source: Library of Congress ML420.P96 F37 1996
OCLC 35932532
www.elvisproducts.com/SpritualJourney.htm

☆ Gould, Jay

Elvis 2000: The King Returns! London: Glitter, 1999. 200 pp. ISBN: 1902588029. Library of Congress category "Presley, Elvis,—1935–1977 (Spirit) Prophecies. Spiritualism."

Source: OCLC 41503617

"Help Us Find Elvis's Clone." *Official UFO* 3 (May 1978): 12–19, 51–53.

The story of an Elvis Presley clone that allegedly escaped from the laboratory in which it had been created. A request for readers to join in the search for the clone. Black and white photographs of the alleged clone and of Elvis.

Source: Compiler's collection

☆ Holzer, Hans

Hans Holzer has written extensively on ghosts, paranormal experiences, and metaphysical subjects.

Elvis Presley Speaks. London: New English Library, 1980. ISBN: none. New York: Manor Books, 1980. ISBN: none.

Reports on the Elvis-related séances of American psychic Dorothy Sherry, who claims to have talked to Elvis's spirit in July 1978.

Source: The British Library X.439/121123

————.

Elvis Speaks from The Beyond and Other Celebrity Ghost Stories. New York: Dorset Press, 1993. ISBN: 1566190533. New York: Random House Value Publishing, Inc., 1999. ISBN: 0517207168. Pp. 1–61.

The Elvis Presley chapter relates the metaphysical experiences of psychic Dorothy Sherry in attempting to contact the spirit of Elvis, including automatic handwriting, astral flights, and séance transcripts.

Source: Compiler's collection

☆ Kingston, Kenny, as told to Valerie Porter

"Elvis Presley." *I Still Talk to . . .* New York: Berkley Books, 1994. ISBN: 0425142353. Pp. 55–69.

The author, a famous celebrity psychic, relates his metaphysical experiences with Elvis Presley, before and after the entertainer's death.

Source: Library of Congress 133.9 K55

☆ Moody, Raymond A., Jr., M.D.

Moody, a graduate of the Medical College of Georgia, is author of a number of books and articles exploring death and bereavement, including the bestselling *Life After Life*.

Elvis After Life: Unusual Psychic Experiences Surrounding the Death of a Superstar. Atlanta, GA: Peachtree Publishers, 1987. 158 pp. ISBN: 0934601402.

The author, a noted expert on death and bereavement, explores the profound, worldwide impact of Elvis's death through interviews with individuals who claim psychic posthumous experiences with Elvis. In each of these experiences, Elvis provided comfort and assistance to people in need, frequently influencing the direction of their lives. Moody examines them as a part of the human grief experience. This book was translated into Japanese. (*See* Foreign Language Titles/Japanese.)

Source: Library of Congress ML420.P96 M66 1987
Dewey Decimal 784.5/4/00924 19
OCLC 16172471

☆ Panta, Ilona

Elvis Presley, King of Kings. Hicksville, NY: Exposition Press, 1979. 247 pp. ISBN: 0682492663.

Panta writes that in 1976, she heard voices telling her that Elvis was going to die and that her mission was to let him know of this danger. (At the time Panta was living in Communist-held East Hungary and had never before heard the name "Elvis.") She sent Elvis a warning letter.

After his death in 1977, Panta says that she had a vision of Elvis in his astral body standing beside her: "the appointed woman who will bear the shortly reincarnated new body of Elvis." Later that month, a male voice thought to be Elvis "ordered" her to write this book.

Source: Library of Congress ML420.P96 P23
New York Public Library JND 81-45

☆ Sieveking, Paul

"Forteana." *New Statesman and Society* (June 24, 1994): 47.

The story of a British woman who says that she, her friend, and her three-year-old son have seen the spirit of Elvis Presley in her home.

☆ Swasy, Alecia

"Elvis Is a No-Show but Ben Franklin's in the Air." *Wall Street Journal* (Mar 2, 1993): A16.

The author's experiences at a meeting of the Cincinnati, Ohio, chapter of the Junto Society where a psychic attempted to contact the spirits of Elvis Presley and Benjamin Franklin. (Franklin founded the Junto Society in Philadelphia, Pennsylvania, in 1728 to deal with community problems of garbage collection and fire services.) The spirit of Elvis did not appear.

☆ Thornton, Mary Ann

Thornton is an Elvis fan who first visited Graceland in 1971.

Even Elvis. Harrison, AR: New Leaf Press, 1979. 128 pp. ISBN: 089221063x.

An autobiography in which the author claims that God appointed her to save Elvis. She recounts her attempts to do so.

Source: Memphis/Shelby County (TN) Public Library and Information Center

See also:

In The Man/Biographies:

Elvis Aaron Presley's Astrological Horoscope and Psychological Profile, January 8, 1935–August 16, 1977.
Elvis Presley: His Astrobiography (Your Authentic Elvis Presley Horoscope).
Taylor, Robin, *Elvis Presley: Not Just The King of Rock and Roll!*

CHAPTER 33
Race

CAUCASIAN ELVIS PRESLEY burst upon the national scene via his interpretations of African American music. In the process he overtly and covertly broke down barriers separating the two races. The Elvis and Race literature examines this little recognized chapter in American music and Civil Rights histories.

Despite the stereotyping of his background (working-class white from Deep South Mississippi), there is simply no record of Elvis Presley ever speaking or behaving in a bigoted manner[1]—even before he achieved fame. Early in his career, a rumor spread through African American communities that had Elvis sneering, "The only thing Negroes can do for me is buy my records and shine my shoes." This was quickly put to rest by an associate editor of the venerable African American magazine *Jet* who interviewed Elvis. (*See* Robinson listing in this chapter.)

While some blacks dispute Elvis's title as "king of rock and roll"—even he said that the credit belonged to other entertainers, not him (*see* Robinson listing)—many more, as seen in the literature, respect him for his contributions and behavior.

Taken as a body, the Elvis and Race literature further defines his impact on American culture and history. But, equally as important, it provides the contemporary, racial advocacy-deafened reader with an honest picture of the dignified and thoughtful origins of the Civil Rights Movement and of Elvis's contributions to its success.

☆   ☆   ☆   ☆

☆ **"Bo Didley Still Can't Accept Elvis as 'King.'"** *Jet* (May 8, 1980): 61.

Interview with veteran blues singer Bo Didley in which he claims that Elvis "stole his [Elvis's] act" from African American artists, and, therefore, should not be labeled as "the king of rock 'n' roll." He believes that title should go to others, such as Chuck Berry.

---

[1]On the *Million Dollar Quartet* CD—which is a recording made of an informal jam session during which none of the participants knew they were being recorded—Elvis refers politely and admiringly to African American entertainers Chuck Berry and Jackie Wilson. He uses the term "colored," which is the way respectful whites referred to blacks in that era. Elvis's language in this unguarded setting tells a great deal about his attitude toward those of other races.

☆ Cleaver, Eldridge

Soul on Ice. A Delta Book. New York: Dell Publishing Company, 1968. ISBN: none. Pp. 194–195.

A leading Civil Rights writer and activist discusses Elvis Presley's impact on race relations.

☆ Collier, Aldore

"Elvis Presley's Black Cook Tells of His Other Side in Her New Book." *Jet* (Oct 20, 1986): 58–60.

Mary Jenkins, one of Elvis Presley's longtime cooks at Graceland whom he fondly called "Maywee," offers anecdotes about him in response to "still persistent rumors about his alleged racist remarks about Blacks." (The "new book" in the title refers to Jenkins's *Elvis: The Way I Knew Him.*)

☆ **"Critics Dispute Elvis as King of Rock 'n' Roll."** *Jet* (Aug 31, 1987): 53.

An argument that rock 'n' roll did not begin with Elvis Presley. The writer uses Elvis's comments from a 1957 *Jet* interview to show that Elvis agreed (*see* Robinson listing in this chapter). Also quoted, from other sources, are songwriter Otis Blackwell ("Don't Be Cruel"; "All Shook Up") and entertainer/composer Johnny Otis.

☆ Fager, Charles E.

"Swinging Singles." *The Christian Century* (July 9, 1969): 928–929.

A discussion of songs released in the spring of 1969, including Elvis Presley's "In the Ghetto." Fager expresses surprise that Elvis would record "a message song," as well as approval of Elvis's selection of a song about "Black America's problems. . . . It must be remembered that Mr. Presley speaks to a vast audience that is not reached by other, more strident voices of social comment and criticism." He adds, " 'In the Ghetto' is an important record and its success is a good omen."

Source: Library of Congress Bri.C45

☆ Jacobs, Bruce A.

"Elvis Has Not Left the Building." *Race Manners: Navigating the Minefield Between Black and White Americans*. New York: Arcade Pub., 1999. ISBN: 1559704535. Pp. 80–89.

The next plateau for Elvis Presley's role in race relations: to bring blacks and whites back together in the twenty-first century as he first did in the mid-twentieth century. The author suggests that Elvis was a creation of blacks and whites and, therefore, a unique shared experience between the two races. Embracing Elvis across racial lines, once again, will bring us back together.

Source: Library of Congress E185.615.J297 1999

☆ Long, Martin R., The Reverend

God's Works Through Elvis. Hicksville, NY: Exposition Press, 1979. ISBN: 06824949.

The Reverend Long, an African American minister, writes a memoir of his life as a poor Southerner living under segregation, and demonstrates how he was "finally freed by the blending of cultures that was brought about in large part by the music of Elvis" (book jacket notes). In doing so, The Rev. Long answers the questions: "Why is Elvis Presley our greatest cultural prophet? How did he influence conditions in the New South? How has he affected all our lives?" (Ibid.).

"Born poor and black in the South of cotton fields and segregation, Rev. Long knows well what it was like then and how it changed after Elvis had become the king of rock and roll. He is convinced that Elvis was an instrument of God and part of His plan for us" (Ibid.).

Source: The University of Mississippi ML420.P96 L65 1979

☆ "Musical Genius Ray Charles Says Elvis Copied Musical Style of Blacks: He's Not 'The King.'" *Jet* (July 25, 1994): 56–57.

Legendary musician Ray Charles says that Elvis Presley became famous because he copied African American musicians. He compares the reactions to Elvis with those to Nat King Cole. The article is based upon a televised interview, which Charles gave on the NBC-TV *Now* program.

☆ Pearlman, Jill (text), and Wayne White (illustrations)

Elvis for Beginners. A Writers and Readers Documentary Comic Book. New York, London: Writers and Readers Publishing/Unwin Paperbacks, 1986, 1996. [159 pp.]. ISBN: 0049270117 (UK); ISBN: 0863161103 (U.S.).

Told in a documentary style, with approximately 200 pen-and-ink cartoon drawings, this book traces the roots of rock and roll music and the key events in Elvis's life, with an emphasis on race. Pearlman states, "Elvis was the White Negro of the teen masses." Unfortunately, this book is marred by irresponsible writing such as the uncited attribution of a racial slur to Sam Phillips. No footnotes, sources, or index. "Elvis testimonials" from 10 celebrities and former President Jimmy Carter; none are cited.

Source: Library of Congress ML420.P96
Dewey Decimal 784.500924
OCLC 13670974

☆ Pitts, Leonard, Jr.

"Elvis's Lasting Influence: He Cut Across Racial Divide." *The Herald* (Miami, FL) (Aug 10, 1997) Section I: 1, 41.

A thoughtful examination of Elvis Presley's role in the Civil Rights Movement.

☆ Rheingold, Todd

Dispelling the Myths: An Analysis of American Attitudes and Prejudices. New York: Believe in the Dream Publications, 1993. 173 pp. ISBN: 9994651730.

An exploration and debunking of the belief that Elvis was racist and exploited black entertainers such as Little Richard and Chuck Berry by copying their styles and eclipsing them in the process. Traces Elvis's interactive role with African Americans through black musical legends who were Elvis's friends (B.B. King, James Brown, Rufus Thomas, Jackie Wilson). Also interviewed was band leader Johnny Otis, a Caucasian aligned with 1950s/1960s African American music, who did not view him kindly. The book expands to a larger scrutiny of the situation of early African American rock and roll artists. Citations. Bibliography (55 titles). No index.

Source: Library of Congress ML420.P96 R48 1993

☆ Robinson, Louie

"The Truth About That Elvis Presley Rumor: 'The Pelvis Gives His Views on Vicious Anti-Negro Slur." *Jet* (Aug 1, 1957): 58–61.

An important title in the Elvis and Race genre because of its groundbreaking exploration of the Black/White racial divide as reflected by Elvis Presley. An interview with Elvis and African Americans to disprove the rumor that Elvis said "The only thing Negroes can do for me is buy my records and shine my shoes." Elvis discusses the African American origins and influences on his style. Blacks quoted in the article are Dr. W. A. Zuber of Tupelo, Misssissippi, Elvis's piano accompanist Dudley Brooks, and Otis Blackwell who composed "Don't Be Cruel" and "All Shook Up." Black and white photographs of Elvis with African American entertainers B. B. King, Billy Ward, and Claudia Ivy.

☆ Rodman, Gilbert B., Ph.D.

"A Hero to Most?: Elvis, Myth, and the Politics of Race." *Cultural Studies* (Oct 1994): 457–482.

An exploration of the links between Elvis Presley's posthumous image and our cultural myths of race. Rodman suggests that Elvis is a multi-dimensional figure of both integration and "racist appropriation, of musical miscegenation, and of cultural assimilation" (p. 477). Chapter notes. Bibliography (pp. 481–483).

☆ Welch, Richard

"Rock 'n' Roll and Social Change." *History Today* (Great Britain) (Feb 1990): 32–39.

This article examines how Elvis Presley, Carl Perkins, and Jerry Lee Lewis—by merging black and white musical traditions into rock 'n' roll—fostered an appreciation of African American culture that strengthened the emerging Civil Rights Movement.

"What Negroes Think About Elvis." *Sepia* (Apr 1957).

A pictorial interview article in which African Americans offer opinions about Elvis Presley and his impact.

Source: Library of Congress E185.5.S44

☆ Williams, Hugo

"Freelance." *Times Literary Supplement* [GTLS] (Dec 2, 1994): 16.

White versions (or "covers") of songs originally recorded by blacks are discussed, with an emphasis on Elvis Presley's recording of "One Night"—relating how the words were rewritten to erase references to adultery and venereal disease.

See Also:

In The Man/Biographies:

Pratt, Linda Ray, "Elvis, or the Ironies of Southern Identity."
Rubel, David, *Elvis Presley: The Rise of Rock and Roll.*

In The Man/The Impact of Elvis:

Egerton, John, "Elvis Lives! The Stuff That Myths Are Made Of."
Gaillard, Frye, "Potshots at Elvis." *Race, Rock and Religion: Profiles from a Southern Journalist.*
Shapiro, Joseph P., "The King Is Dead, but His Rich Legacy Still Grows."

In The Man/Memoirs and Memories:

Jenkins, Mary, *Elvis, the Way I Knew Him.*
Rooks, Nancy, and Mae Gutter, *The Maid, The Man, and His Fans.*
Tio, Maria Mercedes, "Otis Blackwell: The Power Behind Elvis Presley."
Wiegert, Sue, *Elvis: Precious Memories*, Vol. 2. (P. 59: co-star Celeste Yarnall describes Elvis's reaction to the assassination of the Rev. Dr. Martin Luther King, Jr.)

In The Music, The Movies/Elvis's Influence on Music:

Davis, Francis, "Chuck and Elvis, Hands-On Preservationists, and Soul in the Biblical Sense."

In the Phenomena/Fans:

Gorska, Fifi, "Teen-Agers Reply: 'Hideous,' 'Not Right,' Say Presley Fans."

In Foreign Language Titles/Dutch:

Scheers, Rob van, *Elvis in Nederland.*

CHAPTER 34

Religion

THIS SMALL SECTION in the Elvis literature investigates a very large question: through the unparalleled enthusiasm and long-standing devotion of Elvis's fans, are we witnessing the emergence of a new religious movement?

Noted British author and award-winning BBC religion journalist Ted Harrison believes so. Harrison was the first to seriously examine this question in his seminal *Elvis People: The Cult of the King* (1992). He was later joined by author John E. Strausbaugh in *E: Reflections on the Birth of the Elvis Faith* (1995). And thoughtful religious journals from the *National Catholic Reporter* to *Christianity and Crisis* have considered this as well.[1]

Elvis Presley would be deeply troubled by his potential deification. He was a profoundly spiritual man for whom religious faith was central from earliest childhood. Raised as a Pentecostal in the Assembly of God church, he attended services regularly during his childhood and youth. Dates with his high school sweetheart Dixie Locke included gospel concerts and church activities. As a teenager, he hoped for a career in music—not pop, but as a gospel quartet member.

As an adult, he continued attending church, though sporadically, and gave generously to secular and religious organizations. As a performer, his jam sessions and performance warm-ups consisted almost entirely of gospel music, and his backup groups were primarily gospel quartets. As a recording artist, his only Grammys would come from his religious music albums. At the moment of death, he was reportedly reading *The Scientific Search for the Face of Jesus.*

---

[1] Titles relating to Elvis Presley's spirituality are found in The Man/Biographies under the Geller and Stern listings. In The Man/Memoirs and Memories, fellow entertainers J. D. Sumner and Ed Hill of The Stamps quartet write about Elvis's passion for gospel music. In The Music, The Movies/Discography, musicologist Charles Wolfe explores Elvis's gospel music roots.

But none of this dissuades questions about the religious parallels of Elvis. As a result, the literature about this phenomenon continues to expand, providing a front row seat to the prenatal stirrings of something that might closely resemble the birth of a new faith.

☆　　☆　　☆　　☆

☆ Beckham, Sue Bridwell

"Death, Resurrection and Transfiguration: The Religious Folklore in Elvis Presley Shrines and Souvenirs." *International Folklore Review* (1987): 88–95.

An examination of the level of religious adoration to which Elvis Presley has risen since his death. Specifically, the author examines the traditional aspects of reverence: relics, pilgrimages, shrines. She concludes that, among Elvis admirers, there is a "confusion between the very mortal and corporeal Elvis and the risen saviour of Christianity" (p. 95). To her credit, the author emphasizes that "one can be certain that any of Elvis's followers would be shocked to be accused of confusing Elvis Presley with a messiah" (p. 94).

　　Footnotes with bibliographic citations. (In footnote 2, the author incorrectly identifies Graceland as being built in 1910.)

Source: Library of Congress GR1.164

☆ Beifuss, Joan Turner

"Elvis: They Still Love Him Tender." *National Catholic Reporter* 18 (Sept 10, 1982): 19.

Author's views on the posthumous adoration of Elvis Presley as an example of personal religious practice and principle. "The folk religion of Elvis Presley speaks to something so deep and widespread in the psyche that orthodox religious leaders who ignore it are failing to see how religion works at a gut level" (p. 19).

☆ Cooper, Richard

"Did the Devil Send Elvis Presley?" *True Strange* 3 (May/June 1957).

"Is the spell that Elvis Presley casts over our teenagers natural, or does he possess some mysterious force?" Article seriously examines Elvis as a messenger from Satan. Seven black and white photographs; captioned.

Source: eBay auction item #32313540

☆ Dobson, James, Ph.D.

Letter from Dr. James Dobson. Boulder, CO: Focus on the Family Ministry, Aug 1997.

One of America's most respected Christian leaders, Dobson, of the Focus on the Family organization, recounts his visit to Graceland and makes observations on the life of Elvis Presley. Seeing Elvis's latter years as spiritually empty because of his rejections of the teachings of Christ, Dobson believes that "if we ignore the Lord and violate His commandments, there will be no meaning for us, either." Endnotes.

Source: Compiler's collection

☆ Ferraiulol, Perucci

"King of Kings? Some Say Elvis." *Christianity Today* (Apr 25, 1994): 44.

A brief examination of attempts to deify Elvis Presley through worship services at Denver, Colorado's, Church of the Risen Elvis and elsewhere.

☆ Forbes, Cheryl

"Elvis." *Christianity Today* (Sept 23, 1977): 32.

Observations on the impact of Elvis Presley by a fan and Christian music singer. Published one month after his death.

☆ "God Spoke to Me." *Elvis Presley: A Photoplay Tribute* (1977): 56–60.

An article describing Elvis Presley's religious experiences at the time of his mother's death in 1958. Told through the first-person, with quotes attributed to Elvis. (*See* The Rest/Souvenir Magazines.)

☆ Godfrey, Cinda

The Elvis–Jesus Mystery: The Shocking Scriptural and Scientific Evidence That Elvis Presley Could Be the Messiah Anticipated Throughout History. New Philadelphia, OH: Revelation Publishing, 1999. 340 pp. ISBN: none.

The author suggests that Elvis Presley could be the Messiah as described in the Bible. Godfrey says she spent 10 years researching the connection between Jesus Christ and Elvis Presley, using scripture, astrology, numerology, and ancient folklore. "Learn why God had to conceal Elvis's true identity—the greatest secret of all ages! See hundreds of clues Elvis left behind to help us discover the truth" (advertising flyer).

Source: Advertisement from publisher
Publisher's address: P.O. Box 1125, New Philadelphia, OH 44663

☆ Grigg, John

"Poor White Fantasy-Figure." *Spectator* (London) (Aug 27, 1977).

A commentary which warns against posthumous idolization of celebrities using the impact of Elvis Presley to support the thesis. After examining Elvis's life and career, Grigg cautions that such worship "is full of menace for civilization and has to be taken seriously as such . . . the worship of pop stars cannot be dismissed as a trifling phenomenon."

☆ Harrison, Ted

Harrison is a religion journalist and the author of nine books on religion and religious figures. He is a regular voice on BBC Radio 4 and is presenter of the ITV Series, *The Human Factor.*

Elvis People: The Cult of the King. London: Fountpaperbacks/HarperCollins Religious, 1992. 188 pp. ISBN: 0006276202.

A BBC Religious Affairs correspondent seriously and thoughtfully investigates the possibility that the fervor of Elvis fans is a classic example of the origins of a new faith. Harrison made a documentary on this subject, which aired on the BBC in 1996, *Elvis and the Presleytarians.*

Source: *Library of Congress BF1311.P73 H37 1992*
Dewey Decimal 781.66092 20
The British Library

☆ Hoggart, Simon

"Elvis of Nazareth." *New Statesman and Society* (July 10, 1992): 24.

Discusses how, 15 years after his death, Elvis Presley has become a religious figure for many people. Examines how Elvis offers spiritual comfort that may not be so easily available in churches. Compares the life of Elvis with that of Jesus Christ.

☆ James, Andrew L. J.

"Perspective: The Church of Elvis." *Christianity and Crisis* (Feb 1, 1993): 4–5.

James uses the satirical Church of Elvis of Portland, Oregon, as a symbol of "religion reduced to mere form, and the current superficial manner in which our culture seeks peace and forgiveness."

Source: *Library of Congress BR1.C6417*

☆ Kelly, Tom

"Elvis II: A Question of Grace." *Christianity and Crisis* (Feb 15, 1993): 28–29.

Written in response to an earlier article in *Christianity and Crisis.* (*See* James listing preceding.) Kelly discusses what made Elvis Presley so special with an emphasis on Elvis's understanding of grace and his role as an agent of grace.

☆ King, Christine

"His Truth Goes Marching On: Elvis Presley and the Pilgrimage to Graceland." *Pilgrimage in Popular Culture.* Eds. Ian Reader and Tony Walter. London: The Macmillan Press, Ltd., 1993. Pp. 92–104. ISBN: none.

An examination of the pilgrimage aspect of the annual Elvis Week held each August in Memphis by Elvis Presley Enterprises, Inc. A brief biography focusing on how Elvis Presley has been "canonized by popular acclaim." List of references (eight items).

Source: *Library of Congress CB430.P43 1993*

☆ Mallay, Jack D., and Warren Vaughn

Elvis: The Missiah? [U.S.]: Tcb Pub. Inc., 1993. 162 pp. ISBN: 1883795001.

Thesis: Elvis was a divine leader whose mission it was to lead mankind into a new millennium. Authors support their premise by examining "a multitude of mysterious incidents in Elvis's life," as well as his fascination with Eastern religions and psychic phenomenon.

Source: Compiler's collection

☆ Marsh, Dave

"How Great Thou Art: Elvis in the Promised Land." *Rolling Stone* (Sept 22, 1977): 58.

In the acclaimed Elvis memorial issue of *Rolling Stone*, noted rock music writer Dave Marsh discusses links between Elvis and religion, and Elvis's role as a spiritual leader.

☆ Morris, Valarie Ziegler

"Love Me Tender: Incarnational Theology and Elvis." *Modern Churchman* 30 (2/1988): 24–27.

A religious educator's examination of Elvis fans' devotion, calling it "the parable of Elvis" and the lessons that it has for Christians.

Source: Library of Congress BX5011.M6

☆ Rosenbaum, Ron

"Among the Believers." *The New York Times Magazine* (Sept 25, 1995): 50+.

The author's experiences during the 1995 Elvis Tribute Week in Memphis. He speculates that the "Elvis Culture" has transcended the familiar contours of a dead celebrity cult and has begun to assume the dimensions of a redemptive faith.

☆ Sieveking, Paul

"Forteana." *New Statesman and Society* (Apr 28, 1995): 55.

A survey of the unusual ways in which people around the world demonstrate reverence towards Elvis Presley. Emphasis on how people continue to be affected by him even though he has been gone since 1977.

☆ Stearn, Jess

Stearn has written about yoga, astrology, and metaphysics.

Elvis's Spiritual Journey. **Norfolk, VA: The Donning Company, 1982. 252 pp. ISBN: 0898651980.**

Based on interviews with Larry Geller, Elvis's close friend and fellow student of religions and spirituality, the author traces Elvis's growing passion for these subjects. Black and white photographs from Geller's personal collection.

Source: Library of Congress ML420.P96 S73 1982
Dewey Decimal 784.5400924 B 19
OCLC 8220342

☆ Stearn, Jess, with Larry Geller

Elvis's Search for God. Murfreesboro, TN: Greenleaf Publications, 1998. 246 pp. ISBN: 1883729076.

The story of Larry Geller's friendship with Elvis during which he guided Elvis in his spiritual quest through discussions, meditations, prayer, and books. Geller was close to Elvis for 13 years and today continues his and Elvis's deep interest in religious scholarship.

Source: OCLC 40622956

☆ Strausbaugh, John E.

E: Reflections on the Birth of the Elvis Faith. New York: Blast Books, 1995. 233 pp. ISBN: 0922233152.

An examination of the religious fervor with which some fans approach their devotion to Elvis Presley. He calls this passion "Elvism" and demonstrates how its manifestations follow the format of more traditional faiths. The author explores parallels to Elvis worship in that of past and present cultures. Fifty black and white photographs. Bibliography (pp. 221–223). No index.

Source: Library of Congress ML420.P96 S87 1995
Dewey Decimal 782.42166 P934

☆ Tucker, Stephen R., Ph.D.

"Pentecostalism and Popular Culture in the South: A Study of Four Musicians." *Journal of Popular Culture* 16 (1982): 68–80.

See Also:

In The Man/Biographies:

Baumgold, Julie, "Midnight in the Garden of Good and Elvis."
Brock, Van K., "Images of Elvis, the South and America."
Mann, Richard, *Elvis.*

In The Man/Death, Conspiracy, Sightings:

Swaggart, Jimmy, *To the Point . . . .*

In The Man/Graceland:

Davidson, J. W., Alfred Hecht, and Herbert A. Whitney, "The Pilgrimage to Graceland."

In The Man/The Impact of Elvis:

Stromberg, Peter, "Elvis Alive?: The Ideology of American Consumerism."

In The Man/Memoirs and Memories:

Fadal, Edward W., *Elvis . . . Precious Memories*. ("Cultist Movement Is Wrong.")
Geller, Larry, and Joel Spector, with Patricia Romanowski, *"If I Can Dream": Elvis's Own Story*.
Stearn, Jess, with Larry Geller, *The Truth About Elvis*.

In The Phenomena/Fiction:

Church, Solomon, (Louie Ludwig), B.T., D.R., MSh., editor *The Gospel of Elvis: Containing the Testament and Apocrypha Including All the Greater Themes of the King*.

In The Phenomena/Psychic Elvis Experiences:

Thornton, Mary Ann, *Even Elvis*.

In The Phenomena/Race:

Long, Martin R., The Reverend, *God's Works Through Elvis*.

In The Academics/Dissertations and Theses:

Daniels, William R., "A Psychological Study of the Quest for Meaning Through Rock 'n' Roll."
Davidson, James William, "The Pilgrimage to Elvis Presley's Graceland: A Study of the Meanings of Place."
Keebler, Mary Alice, "The Persistence of Hagiographic Themes in Modern Culture: Parallels Between Selected Medieval Saints' Lives and the Life of Elvis Presley."

In The Rest/Elvis Impersonators:

Spigel, Lynn, "Communicating with the Dead: Elvis as Medium."

CHAPTER 35

Travel Guides

GUIDES TO ELVIS sites have enjoyed a limited popularity, which is odd when compared to the overall enthusiasm for everything else Elvisian. But this lack of interest does not diminish their fun. These few books serve not only as travel assists and information sources, but also as interesting reading. Their authors frequently move beyond locating and describing historical Elvis sites to those sites that celebrate him in unique ways, such as "roadside museums."

But a caution must be given. Because of the Elvis world's increasingly altered landscape—where buildings are torn down and place names are changed—it is advisable to verify the accuracy of the information in these books. In addition to material becoming outdated, some books simply make mistakes. For example, *Placing Elvis: A Tour Guide to the Kingdom* lists an incorrect house number for the Presleys' Lauderdale Courts apartment, as well as advising visitors to use the wrong entrance. (*See* Urquart listing in this chapter.)

The value of these Elvis travel guides is their demonstration of the breadth of Elvis geography and the continuing, intense interest in the details on his life. No where else in the history of entertainment—or most other fields—do readers have such a choice of books on sites connected to the famous. Something to ponder while exploring the Elvis highways and byways.

☆   ☆   ☆   ☆

☆ Barth, Jack

Roadside Elvis: The Complete State-by-State Travel Guide for Elvis Presley Fans.
   Chicago: Contemporary Books, 1991. 184 pp. ISBN: 0809239817.

A guide to Elvis sites in most of the 50 states, as well as sites in Australia, Canada, and Europe. Black and white photographs of many of the sites; captioned and credited. Map showing states that, as of 1991, have declared January 8 as Elvis Presley Day. Bibliography (14 items). Index.

———.

Travels with Elvis: A Guide Across America to All the Places Where the King Lived, Loved and Laughed. New York: Grammercy Books, 1999. ISBN: 051720309X. Originally published as *Roadside Elvis.* (*See* preceding entry.)

☆ Hazen, Cindy, and Mike Freeman

Cindy Hazen and Mike Freeman also have written about Elvis's charity work. (*See* The Man/Biographies.) The authors operate Memphis Explorations, a touring company that offers guided visits to the locations highlighted in this book.

Memphis Elvis-Style. Winston-Salem, NC: John F. Blair, 1997. 235 pp. ISBN: 089 5871734.

A guidebook to Elvis Presley's Memphis, including where he worshiped, lived, performed, and bought clothes and records. Rare and previously unpublished photographs, as well as interviews with people who knew Elvis. Organized into a chronological format, it is also an informal biography.

Source: Library of Congress ML420.P96 H53 1997

———.

The Whole Elvis Tour: A Pocket Guide to the King's Memphis. Memphis, TN: [n.p.], 1990. ISBN: none.

Source: Hazen, The Best of Elvis, *p. [207].*

☆ Rada, Joe

"Viva Elvis." *Southern Living* (May 1993): 16–20.

Article detailing a tour of the Graceland mansion.

☆ Urquart, Sharon Colette

Placing Elvis: A Tour Guide to the Kingdom. New Orleans, LA: Paper Chase Press, 1994. 112 pp. ISBN: 187906571.

A guide to Elvis Presley sites in Tupelo, Mississippi (his birthplace), and Memphis, Tennessee. Suggested places to stay, shop, and dine in each city. Eight maps show locations for sites mentioned in the text. Brief history of both sides of Elvis's family, the Smiths and the Presleys. Black and white photographs; captioned and credited. List of resource books. Index.

Source: Library of Congress ML420.P96 U77 1994

☆ Winegardner, Mark David

Elvis Presley Boulevard: From Sea to Shining Sea, Almost. Traveler series. New York: The Atlantic Monthly Press, 1987. 223 pp. ISBN: 0871132052.

A Steinbeckian Travels-with-Charley journey across America made by Winegardner in the 1980s. Aside from a chapter on Winegardner's visit to Graceland (pp. 78–99) and another on an Elvis museum, there is little else about Elvis Presley. Winegardner notes throughout the paper about the sites and situations in which he finds Elvis connections. Incorrectly identifies Elvis's backup singer and head of The Stamps quartet, J. D. Sumner, as "the guitar player during Presley's Vegas years." This book was based upon Winegardner's M.F.A. thesis. (*See* The Academics/Dissertations and Theses.)

☆ Yenne, Bill

The Field Guide to Elvis Shrines. Los Angeles, CA: Renaissance Books, 1999. ISBN: 1580630502.

This book is a photographic tour of private and public shrines erected in honor of Elvis Presley. Index.

Source: OCLC 39936759

See Also:

In The Man/Biographies:

Gray, Michael, and Roger Osborne, *The Elvis Atlas: A Journey Through Elvis Presley's America*

In The Phenomena/Fans:

Slaughter, Todd, *Forever Elvis: The Memorial Tour to Memphis.*

THE ACADEMICS

PART IV

CHAPTER 36
Elvis as an Academic Pursuit

IN THE EARLY 1970s the value of Elvis as an academic pursuit was firmly established in public education. (*See* Educational Literature section in this chapter.) But it would not be until after his death that those in higher education would realize Elvis's fertile potential as a subject of study.

Appropriately, The University of Memphis was the first to recognize this. Two years following Elvis's death, the university's Dr. John Bakke organized the first Elvis academic seminar. It featured scholars and journalists in serious discussions of Elvis's life and impact. (*See* *Memphis State University Presents a Seminar* listing in this chapter.) Though contemporary culture scholars at The Universities of Iowa, Mississippi, and Tennessee would offer for-credit college courses on Elvis, it would not be until some 15 years later in the mid-1990s when Elvis would garner international attention as a viable subject for academics.

In 1995 The University of Mississippi offered The First Annual International Conference on Elvis Presley, "In Search of Elvis: Music, Race, Art, Religion." It was your standard higher education gathering with ponderous academic treatises and eyeball rolling as rival scholars leapt to their feet to make a point. But it was also one of the strangest intellectual gatherings on record with presentations by the "World's #1 Elvis Fan," by a long-haul truck driver who was Elvis's cousin, and a well-known rock and roll writer who passed out, reeking of alcohol, in the middle of his talk.[1] (*See* Stewart, Wallace, and Academic Anthologies section in this chapter.)

The next logical evolution of Elvis in higher academia was realized in 1998, when the first Elvisian college textbook was written by Dorothy Leasman of Orange Coast College in Costa Mesa, California. Professor Leasman, an Elvis fan, used Elvis's life and career to illuminate basic principles of sociology. (*See* The Academics/Educational Literature.)

---

[1]In 1996 the university dropped its sponsorship, and the subsequent International Conferences have been held at various venues in Memphis, Tennessee.

It was Gladys Presley's doggedly pursued dream that Elvis graduate from high school. How proud she would be to see how far he has gone in college.

☆   ☆   ☆   ☆

☆ Fernandez, Sandy

"The Iconography of Elvis and Marilyn." (May 4, 1994): A10, A16.

An overview of the 1994 Georgetown University (DC) conference examining how images of Elvis Presley and Marilyn Monroe function in American culture. The conference was titled "Icons of Popular Culture I: Elvis and Marilyn."

☆ Firth, Simon

"The Academic Elvis." Eds. Richard J. King and Helen Taylor. *Dixie Debates: Perspectives on Southern Culture.* New York: New York University, 1996. 99–114.

Firth, a scholar of popular music theory, argues that Elvis Presley is a valid source of academic study because of the differences he made in the history of music and of culture. He examines the study of Elvis and his contributions from musical, sociological, and cultural perspectives.

Source: Library of Congress F215.2.D593 1996

☆ *Memphis State University Presents a Seminar, "Perspectives on Elvis: Life and Times." August 16, 1979.* Memphis, TN: Memphis State University, 1979. [2 pp.].

The program for the first Elvis Presley academic conference, organized by Dr. John Bakke, of the University's Department of Theatre and Communication Arts. Elvis scholars and journalists who had covered him were the speakers. Although there is no published transcript of the proceedings, a videotape was made of all the conference sessions. The tape is available for viewing through the Department of Theater and Communication Arts.

Source: OCLC 38290494

☆ Stewart, Doug

"Now Playing in Academe: The King of Rock 'n' Roll." *Smithsonian* (Nov 1995): 56–66.

An examination of the impact of Elvis Presley as explored at the First Annual International Conference on Elvis Presley: "In Search of Elvis: Music, Race, Religion, Art, Performance." In the article Stewart, who attended the conference, examines the lectures and interviews the Elvis academics and fans in attendance.

☆ Wallace, Amy

"Scholarly Study of Elvis Has Academia All Shook Up." *The Los Angeles Times* (Sept 1995): A36+.

An in-depth exploration of the validity of Elvis Presley as a subject for academic study by an education writer who attended the 1995 International Conference on Elvis Presley at the University of Mississippi.

Academic Anthologies

There are two anthologies of academic writings about Elvis Presley. The first was compiled in 1979 by Jac L. Tharpe, a professor of English at the University of Southern Mississippi. With its broad range of contributors—both academic and fans—it set the standard for serious intellectual explorations of the Elvis phenomenon.

The second was published in 1997. Titled *In Search of Elvis: Music, Race, Art, Religion*, it contains most of the papers presented at the First International Conference on Elvis Presley at the University of Mississippi in 1995.

☆　　☆　　☆　　☆

☆ Chadwick, Vernon, editor

In Search of Elvis: Music, Race, Art, Religion. Boulder, CO: Westview Press, 1997. 294 pp. ISBN: 0813329868 (hdk.); ISBN: 0813329876 (pbk.).

A collection of papers and artwork presented at The First International Conference on Elvis Presley, held August 6–11, 1995, at the University of Mississippi in Oxford, Mississippi. The purpose of the six-day academic conference was to analyze and examine Elvis's impact on the world.

Conference papers reprinted in this book are those by noted scholars Bill Malone Ph.D., Peter Nazareth Ph.D., John Shelton Reed Ph.D., and Stephen Tucker Ph.D.; Elvis discologist Ernst Jorgensen; Elvis authors Neal and Janice Gregory; folk artist Howard Finster; Elvis's cousin Gene Smith; and self-proclaimed "World's Number One Elvis Fan" Paul MacLeod.

Source: Library of Congress ML420.P96 I5 1997

☆ Tharpe, Jac L., Ph.D., editor

Elvis: Images and Fancies. Jackson, MS: University Press of Mississippi, 1979. 179 pp. ISBN: none.

The first collection of academic essays about Elvis Presley, authored by respected scholars from a range of fields, as well as three articles by fans. These essays originally appeared in *The Southern Quarterly: A Journal of the Arts in the South*, Fall 1979.

Source: Library of Congress ML420.P96 E36

CHAPTER 37
Dissertations and Theses

ELVIS PRESLEY HAS interested scholars since he burst onto the scene in the 1950s. This attraction reached new heights in the 1990s, attesting to Elvis's rise in our national consciousness and culture as a figure through which almost all scholarly inquiry can be filtered.

The first of these titles appeared in 1958, as a Master of Arts thesis at the University of Chicago. It was an examination of the astounding feminine response that Elvis was creating. (*See* Granetz listing in this chapter.) Since then, the dissertations and theses have spread to a wide range of fields—including geography, musical composition, folklore, religion, and history.

This expanding academic interest bespeaks a renaissance of the type of intellectual curiosity long thought to have disappeared behind today's rigidly defined structure of what constitutes an intellectual pursuit and what is beneath consideration. So, in the Elvis dissertations, as he did with his music, Elvis is again awakening us to new possibilities.

☆   ☆   ☆   ☆

☆ Aparin, Julia

"He Never Got Above His Raising: An Ethnographic Study of a Working Class Response to Elvis Presley." Dissertation. University of Pennsylvania, 1988. 157 pp. DAI-A 50/01 (July 1989): 179.

This study defines Elvis Presley as the working-class hero of the American dream: "unlike others, he inverts the standard of mobility pattern, thus affirming the dignity and worth of those generally ignored or despised in American society."

Source: ProQuest-Dissertation Abstracts Order No: AAC 8908302

☆ Bertrand, Michael Thomas

"The King of Rock as Hillbilly Cat: The National Response to a Southern Regional Performer, 1954–1958." Thesis (M.A.). University of Southwestern Louisiana, 1988. 451 leaves.

Bibliography (pp. 402–440). Subject: Presley, Elvis—1935–1977; Popular Music.

Source: OCLC 18319616

———.

"Southern Youth in Dissent: Rock 'n' Roll, Race, and Elvis Presley, 1945–1960." Dissertation. Memphis State University, 1995. 397 leaves.

Bibliography (pp. 367–396).

Source: OCLC 32875582

☆ Davidson, James William

The Pilgrimage to Elvis Presley's Graceland: A Study of the Meanings of Place. Thesis (M.A.). Wilfrid Laurier University, 1985. Ottawa, Canada: National Library of Canada, 1986. ISBN: 0315231769.

The writer examines how sites become sanctified places. He uses Elvis Presley's Graceland mansion and the Elvis fans' pilgrimages for his case study.

Source: OCLC 16024477

☆ DiPrima, Liza

"Elvis and Them: Reactions to Elvis Presley, 1954–1958." Honors Thesis (A.B.). Harvard University, 1989. [19] leaves.

Source: OCLC 200838276

☆ Doll, Susan M.

"Elvis Presley: All Shook Up. The Effect of Ideology and Subculture on Star Image." Dissertation. Northwestern University, 1989. 570 pp. DAI-A 51/02 (Aug 1990): 320.

An examination of Elvis Presley's career to explore how the image of a celebrity conveys meaning to an audience. Looks at Elvis's career in three phases, each corresponding to a specific image as constructed and circulated by Elvis and his managers. (This dissertation was published as a book, *Understanding Elvis: Southern Roots vs. Star Image. See* The Man/Biographies.)

Source: ProQuest-Dissertation Abstracts Order No: AAC 9009636
OCLC 31084627 (University Microfilms International, 1990. 6 microfiches); 28648475
(University Microfilms International, 1992. 22 cm.)

☆ Granetz, Ruth Pearl

"The Symbolic Significance of the Elvis Presley Phenomenon to Teen-Age Females: A Study in Hero Worship Through the Media of Popular Singers and Song." Thesis (M.A.). University of Chicago, 1958. 48 leaves. ADD-S 0330.

This is the first thesis or dissertation to be written about Elvis. It explored the meaning of the unprecedented display of emotion by young women over Elvis Presley.

Source: OCLC 22750581

☆ Johnson, Brigitte E.

"Elvis Presley, The Symbol of an Age." Thesis (M.A.). California State University, Fullerton (CA), 1988. 259 pp. MAI 27/02 (Summer 1989): 195.

This study interprets Elvis Presley as a powerful public symbol of American culture in general and of American life in the 1950s—someone who portrayed the American dominant cultural ethos in his person, life, and music.

Source: ProQuest-Dissertation Abstracts Order No: AAC 1335341

☆ Keebler, Mary Alice

"The Persistence of Hagiographic Themes in Modern Culture: Parallels Between Selected Medieval Saints' Lives and the Life of Elvis Presley." Thesis (M.A.). University of Tennessee, Knoxville, 1993. 75 leaves.

Source: OCLC 29665776

☆ Rodman, Gilbert

Elvis After Elvis: The Posthumous Career of a Living Legend. Dissertation. University of Illinois at Urbana-Champaign, 1996. 244 pp. DAI 57/08A (n.d.): 3314. London and New York: Routledge, 1996. 231 pp. ISBN: 0415110025 (hdk.); ISBN: 0415110033 (pbk.).

Explanations for the pervasive and growing presence of Elvis as a cultural icon. This was published in book format as *Elvis After Elvis.* (*See* The Man/The Impact of Elvis.)

Source: First Search Dissertations Database No: AAG0577798

☆ Wireman, J. D.

"Textual Elvis." Thesis (M.A.). University of Wyoming, 1995. 72 leaves.

This paper explores Elvis Presley's impact on literature, with texts examined from three major genres: biography, essay, and short fiction. The author suggests that Elvis's most important contribution to modern culture may be his effect on literature.

Source: OCLC 32538494

CHAPTER 38
Educational Literature

ELVIS PRESLEY'S ABSORPTION into our national psyche began before his death—through our 1970s school curriculum. This was not an orchestrated campaign; in fact, few even realized that it was occurring. But as students across America were tutored in any number of Elvis biography textbooks and readers, the symbiosis was born.

In the early 1970s American public education was making many of its most radical changes ever—from teachers wearing casual clothes in the classroom to innovative curriculum reorganizations. It was during this period that teachers of reading, history, and English moved their young scholars away from a classics-based curriculum—theorizing that young people would be more eager to learn if the object of study was someone they recognized from their lives.

It was this change to vox populi in our nation's classrooms that in part helped imprint Elvis Presley into our national conscience. Through the Elvis textbooks with their quizzes, discussion questions, word games, filmstrips, and read-along cassettes, American students soon knew as much about Elvis's life and career as they did about George Washington's.

The first Elvis textbook was a biography reader published in 1970—*Meet Elvis Presley* by Favius Friedman. (*See* Friedman listing in this chapter.) It was very popular and was reprinted two more times in 1973 and 1977. Others would soon follow, with more appearing in the 1980s and 1990s.

In addition to the biography textbooks, Elvis has been used as a teaching tool in subjects ranging from art to writing to history. Articles in professional educational journals—the first in 1957—demonstrate how Elvis can be the springboard for student interest and creativity. (*See* Hurwitz listing in this chapter.)

Other entertainers such as the Beatles and John Lennon would also be used as subjects of study. But it was Elvis who produced the most texts over the longest period of time. As more and more youngsters answered "Elvis" to the nightly dinner table question "what did you learn in school today?," he became more and more ingrained in our culture.

Note: See The Man/Biographies for juvenile biographies of Elvis that are used in teaching, but not specifically as textbooks.

☆   ☆   ☆   ☆

☆ Alico, Stella H.

Elvis Presley; The Beatles. Pendulum Illustrated Biography Read-Along series. West Haven, CT: Pendulum Press, 1979. 63 pp. ISBN: 0883013649 (activity book); ISBN: 0883013762 (audiovisual); ISBN: 9998184010 (1987 edition).

Educational teaching kit (grades 6–8) that presents, separately, the lives of Elvis Presley and the Beatles in cartoon format with written and recorded text. One filmstrip (71 frames), two sound cassettes, one recording, one answer key, and posters. Student activity book includes vocabulary words, comprehension questions, and discussion topics.

Source: OCLC 6639567 (sound recording, filmstrip, poster, two books, one answer key); 8750667 (one filmstrip, one cassette, one book); 7224822 (sound cassette).

☆ Beggs, Karen, and Peter Beynon

Elvis Presley. [UK]: NEWMAT [for] ALBUSU, 1988. National Institute of Adult Education (England and Wales), Adult Literacy and Basic Skills Unit. 22 pp. ISBN: 871174066.

Elvis biography reading textbook for new adult literates and slow-reading adults.

Source: Bodleian Library, Oxford University, UK

☆ Bowman, Kathleen

On Stage, Elvis Presley. The Entertainers series. Mankato, MN: Children's Press, 1975; Creative Education, 1976, 1978. 46 pp. ISBN: 0871914883 (1976).

A biography of Elvis Presley written for middle school readers.

Source: Library of Congress ML3930.P73 B7

☆ *Elvis Presley.* Illustrated Pocket Classics. West Haven, CT: Academic Industries, Inc., 1984. 55 pp. ISBN: 9997260279 (hdk.). ISBN: 0883017784 (pbk.).

Comic book format, easy reading textbook for grades 6–8; also used for adult literacy education. "Quiz Yourself!" chapter with answer key (pp. 52–[56]). Accompanied by a skill check card and a read-along sound cassette: *Fearon Education Presents! Elvis Presley.* (Belmont, CA: David S. Lake, Pub., 1979; 1989. OCLC: 20908809.)

Source: OCLC 13288232

☆ Friedman, Favius Louis

Meet Elvis Presley. New York: Scholastic Book Services, 1971. 127 pp. ISBN: none.

The first book on Elvis Presley intended for instructional purposes. It was updated in 1973 and again in 1977 with an epilogue covering Elvis's death.

Source: OCLC 718477 (1971); 1885184 (1973); 3642361 (1977)

☆ Harmer, Jeremy

Elvis Presley, King of Rock 'n' Roll. People of Our Time/Longman Structural Readers, Stage 1. Harlow [UK]: Longman Group, 1982. 16 pp. ISBN: 0582798248.

A cartoon biography of Elvis Presley for use as a reading text for beginning level students of English as a Second Language (ESL) programs. Sixty-five cartoon frames with captions.

Source: Library of Congress PE 1128 I2 P46
The British Library X.439/12419 (1981); X.439/13530 (1982)

☆ Hurwitz, Al

At the time this article was published, Hurwitz was a Miami, Florida, high school teacher.

"Elvis Presley and Art." *School Arts* 57 (Sept 1957): 17–20.

This is the first time that Elvis was used as the subject of a professional journal article. Hurwitz writes about his success in using Elvis recordings to inspire creativity in his students. He suggests that using students' interest in Elvis can benefit lessons in all academic disciplines.

Source: Library of Congress N81.S4

☆ "The King of Rock and Roll." *Dynamite* #24 (1976).

A biographical article appearing in a middle school–level reading skills magazine, published for classroom use by Scholastic Magazines, Inc., of Englewood, New Jersey.

☆ Leasman, Dorothy Arnall

Elvis: A Sociological Portrait. Needham Heights, MA: Simon and Schuster Custom Pub., 1998. 139 pp. ISBN: 0536012113.

A textbook for lower-division college courses in sociology. The life and career of Elvis Presley is used to illuminate social institutions and relationships such as marriage and family, social class and mobility, race and ethnic relations, religion, and social change.

Source: Orange Coast College, Costa Mesa, CA

☆ Leigh, Vanora

Elvis Presley. Great Lives series. New York: The Bookwright Press, 1986; East Sussex, England: Wayaland (Publisher's) Limited, 1986. 32 pp. ISBN: 531150735.

A biography of Elvis Presley, including a chapter on his death, written for students aged 10–14. Glossary and list of books to read. Index. In 1988 Narkaling Productions in Perth, Australia, produced a teaching kit to accompany this book. It consists of one read-along sound cassette (41 minutes): *The Elvis Presley.* ISBN: 00850788595.

Source: Book: Library of Congress ML3930.P73 L4
Teaching kit: Dewey Decimal 784.500924

☆ Mueller, Jean W.

"Rock 'n' Roll Heroes: Letter to President Eisenhower." *Social Education* 49 (May 1985): 406–408.

Demonstrates how to use a primary source document to teach secondary students about contemporary history. The document is a letter written to President Dwight D. Eisenhower by three teenagers, concerning the induction of Elvis Presley into the army. Sample class activities are included.

☆ Scoppa, Bud

"Elvis Is Back (or Is He?)." *Senior Scholastic* (Sept 5, 1972): 27–28.

An article for high school reading and English classes written while Elvis was still alive. The author discusses Elvis's changing music styles, focusing on his 1972 appearance in New York City's Madison Square Garden. *Senior Scholastic* is a reading skills and comprehension development weekly periodical that is distributed nationally to teachers of English at the high school level.

☆ *Selected from* Elvis and Me. Writers' Voices series. New York: Signal Hill, 1991. 63 pp. ISBN: 0929631277 (pbk.). New York: Literacy Volunteers of New York City, 1991. 63 pp. ISBN: same.

Selections from Priscilla Presley's memoir, *Elvis and Me,* for adults who are learning to read.

Source: OCLC 33128444 (Signal Hill); 24436616 (Literacy Volunteers of New York City)

See Also:

The Man/Biographies

The Phenomena/Fiction

FOREIGN LANGUAGE TITLES
PART V

CHAPTER 39

Basque, Chinese, Czech, Danish, and Dutch

Basque

☆ Montoia, Xabier

Plastikozko Loreak Erregearentzat. Narratiba series 28. Zarautz, Spain: Susa, 1998. 105 pp. ISBN: 848676680X.

A book about the Graceland mansion.

Source: OCLC 40811736

Chinese

☆ Jones, Peter

Mao wang P'u-li-ssu-lai ti i sheng/Pi-te-chung-ssu chu. Translated by Ts'ai-yun Chang. Taipei, Taiwan: Yuan ch'eng wen hua t'u shu kung ying she, 1977. 194 pp. ISBN: none.

Translation of *Elvis.* Black and white and color photographs. (*See* The Man/Biographies.)

Source: University of Hong Kong ML420.P96 J612
OCLC 34969087

Czech

☆ Brewer-Giorgio, Gail

Zije Elvis? Translated by Vladimir Kintera. Praha (Prague), Czech Republic: Elka Press, Severografie, 1994. 204 pp. ISBN: 8090169406.

Translation of *Is Elvis Alive?* (*See* The Man/Death, Conspiracy, Sightings.) Does not come with sound cassette. Sixteen leaves of photographs.

Source: OCLC: 39603602

☆ Cernocký, Pavel

Legenda Jménem Elvis Aaron Presley: 1935–1977: Prehledný Zivotopis, diskografie, filmografie. Praha (Prague), Czech Republic: ETC Publishing, 1997. 174 pp. ISBN: 808600645X.

A reference book on Elvis Presley.

Source: OCLC 38152786

☆ *Elvis Convention Prague '97: 15. C Ervna 1997 Lucerna Music Bar [Praha].* Praha (Prague), Czech Republic: Fan Club Elvis Presley, 1997. 1 Plakat Jednobareve.

A fan club publication on the twentieth anniversary of the death of Elvis Presley.

Source: Náraodní Knihovna Ceské Republiky (national library of the Czech Republic)

☆ Esposito, Joe, with Elena Oumano

Bozský Elvis: Dvacet let na Zajezdech a Flaméch s Elvisem. Translated by Hana Kucerova. Praha (Prague), Czech Republic: ETC, 1996. 234 pp. ISBN: 8090179258.

Translation of *Good Rockin' Tonight.* (*See* The Man/Memoirs and Memories.)

Source: OCLC 37249884

☆ Geller, Larry, and Joel Spector, with Patricia Romanowski

Elvis Presley: Pravdivý Príbeh o Jeho z Ivote a Smrti. Translated by Jarmila Skodova. Praha (Prague), Czech Republic: Knizní Klub, 1995. 267 pp. ISBN: 8071761036 (Knizní Klub). ISBN: 808579716X (JEVA).

Czech translation of *If I Can Dream: Elvis's Own Story.* (*See* The Man/Memoirs and Memories.)

Source: Náraodní Knihovna Ceské Republiky
OCLC 36613071

☆ Guralnick, Peter

Poslendí Vlak do Memphisu: Cesta Elvise Presleyho ke Slave. Translated by Jiri Hanus. Ceský Klub series. Praha (Prague), Czech Republic: Nakladatelství Josefa Simona, 1996. 597 pp. ISBN: 8085637340.

Translation of *Last Train to Memphis.* (*See* The Man/Biographies.)

Source: OCLC 36882383

☆ Presley, Priscilla Beaulieu

Muj Zivot s Elvisem. Translation by Marie Belikova and Zdenek Ziegler. Spirála Spirála series. Praha (Prague), Czech Republic: Ceskoslovensky Spisovatel, Tiskárny Vimperk, 1992. 245 pp. ISBN: 8020203672 (Broz.).

Muj Zivot s Elvisem. Second edition. Knihovna Moderní Zeny series. Praha (Prague), Czech Republic: Ceský Spisovatel, Tiskárny Vimperk, 1994. 234 pp. ISBN: 8020205063 (vaz.).

Translation of *Elvis and Me.* (*See* The Man/Memoirs and Memories.) Includes 10 pages of black and white photographs in the 1992 edition; 16 in the 1994 edition.

Source: OCLC 39573617 (1992); 36603595 (1994)

☆ Taterová, Milada

Elvis Presley. Praha (Prague), Czech Republic: Supraphon, 1969. 34 pp. ISBN: none.

The first Elvis Presley book to be printed in the Czech language. A biography of Elvis written during his lifetime. Black and white publicity stills and Elvis's wedding photographs; captioned and non-specifically credited. Bibliography of sources (eight items). List of Czech releases of Elvis's recordings (five titles).

Source: Library of Congress ML420.P96 T4
Náraodní Knihovna Ceské Republiky

☆ Tilgner, Wolfgang

Elvis Presley. Translated by Milan Richter. Kamarád series. Bratislava, Czech Republic: Opus, [n.d.]. 215 pp. ISBN: 807093039. Translated by Jirí Pondelícek. Praha (Prague), Czech Republic: Práce, 1991. 289 pp. ISBN: 8020801618.

Translation of *Elvis Presley.* (*See* Foreign Language Titles/German.)

Source: Náraodní Knihovna Ceské Republiky
OCLC 39576165 (1991)

Danish

☆ *Bogen om Elvis Presley.* Copenhagen, Denmark: [n.p.], 1959. 50 pp. ISBN: x527806322(m).

The first Danish-language biography of Elvis Presley.

Source: Det Kongelige Bibliotek (national library of Denmark)

☆ De Mylius, Jørgen

Elvis, Stjernen der Aldrig Slukkes. [n.p.]: [n.p.], 1977.

Source: Entry for Elvis: 1935–1977, *Det Kongelige Bibliotek*

———.

Elvis: 1935–1977. [Copenhagen, Denmark]: Mallings, 1985. 202 pp. ISBN: 8773333026.

A reprint of *Elvis, Stjernen der Aldrig Slukkes.*

Source: Det Kongelige Bibliotek

☆ *Elvis.* Denmark, 1976.

From the front cover: "Elvis' Liv I Tekst og Billender No. 1." A magazine about Elvis Presley, published while he was alive.

Source: Cranor, Rosalind, Elvis Collectibles, *p. 279.*

☆ *Elvis Presley: Hans Liv, Hans Dod.* Frederiksberg, Denmark: MS, 1996. 152 pp. ISBN: 8798632604.

A biography of Elvis Presley, with an exploration of his impact. Photographs; captioned and credited.

Source: Det Kongelige Bibliotek

☆ Geller, Larry, and Joel Spector, with Patricia Romanowski

Elvis' Egen Historie. Translated by Jette Røssell. Hillerød, Denmark: Roth, 399 pp. ISBN: 8789005236.

Translation of *If I Can Dream: Elvis's Own Story.* (*See* The Man/Memoirs and Memories.)

Source: Det Kongelige Bibliotek

☆ Hansen, Mogens

Elvis—Er Ikke Død: et Mindealbum. [Denmark]: SV Press, 1978. 93 pp. ISBN: 8741610997.

Reference book on Elvis Presley. Biography, including "Interview med Elvis Presley" (pp. 31–33). Chapter on Elvis's Danish fan club. Discography (pp. 79–93). Filmography (pp. 53–78). Black and white photographs; captioned but not individually credited.

Source: Det Kongelige Bibliotek
Library of Congress ML420.P96 H38
OCLC 5708964

☆ Korreborg, Leif

A Life Guide: 1935–1977: Elvis Presley. [n.p.]: Leif Korreborg; Randers, Denmark: I samarbejde med The Official Elvis Presley Fan Club of Denmark, 1993. 93 pp. ISBN: x920526127.

A biography of Elvis Presley.

Source: Det Kongelige Bibliotek

☆ Lindboe, Ole

Lindboe is a Danish journalist who has been an Elvis fan since 1959.

Elvis Flammende Stjerne. Denmark: Ultima, 1991. 78 pp. ISBN: 8789614089.

A reference book about Elvis Presley. Biography. Quotes about Elvis, originally in English and translated in Danish. Filmography (pp. 72–73). Bibliography, eight books in English, one in Danish (pp. 74–75). Addresses for three Danish Elvis Presley fan clubs. Black and white photographs from concerts and films; captioned.

Source: Det Kongelige Bibliotek
Collection of Bill and Connie Burk, Memphis, TN

———.

Elvis—Lyden fra Memphis. Denmark: Ultima, 1992. 116 pp. ISBN: 8789614151.

A biography of Elvis Presley.

Source: Det Kongelige Bibliotek

———.

Elvis Scrapbog. Glostrup, Denmark: Ultima, 1993. 96 pp. ISBN: 8789614550.

A biography of Elvis Presley.

Source: Det Kongelige Bibliotek

☆ Pedersen, Stig Ultima

Elvis—Aerlig Talt. Translated by Alice Th. Ulrichsen and Stig Ultima Pedersen. [Greve], Denmark: Ultima, 1992; 1993. 157 pp. ISBN: 8789614194.

First-person review of Elvis Presley's life.

Source: David Neale, Elvis in Print, www.geocities.com/SunsetStrip/8200/books.html

———.

Elvis Liksikon. Translated by Alice Th. Ulrichsen and Stig Ultima Pedersen. Denmark: Ultima, [n.d.]. 182 pp. ISBN: 8789614720.

Source: Det Kongelige Bibiotek

———.

Elvis' Soldaterliv. Glostrup, Denmark: Ultima, 1993. 70 pp. ISBN: 8789614372.

Source: Det Kongelige Bibiotek

———.

Elvis—Taler Ud. Havdrup, Denmark: Ultima, 1990. [20] pp. ISBN: 8798182781.

Source: Det Kongelige Bibiotek

☆ Presley, Priscilla Beaulieu, with Sandra Harmon

Elvis og Mig. Translated by Michael Krefeld. Copenhagen, Denmark: Peter Asschen-feldt, 1986. 205 pp. ISBN: 8773653241. (Peter Asschenfeldt's Bogklub edition, 1986. 205 pp. ISBN: 8773656933.

Translation of *Elvis and Me*. (*See* The Man/Memoirs and Memories.)

Source: Det Kongelige Bibliotek

☆ Taylor, John Alvarez

Elvis—For Evigt. Herning, Denmark: Rostrup, 1993. 64 pp. ISBN: 87882500075.

Translation of *Forever Elvis*. (*See* The Man/Biographies.)

Source: Det Kongelige Bibliotek

☆ Thyboe, Kurt

Elvis—Myten On Manden. [Lynge], Denmark: Bogan, [1977]. [128] pp. ISBN: 8787533073.

A biography of Elvis Presley, published after his death. This book was translated into Norwegian and Swedish. (*See* Foreign Language Titles/Swedish and Norwegian.)

Source: Det Kongelige Bibliotek

Dutch

☆ Allen, William, David Gibbon, and Nicola Dent, editors

Elvis Presley. Translated by Anna Vesting. Lisse, The Netherlands: Rebo Productions, 1992. 191 pp. ISBN: 903660817.

Translation of *Elvis* (1992). (*See* The Man/Biographies.)

Source: Koninklijke Bibliotheek (national library of The Netherlands)

☆ Anthierens, Jef, and Dietrich Schulz-Koehn

Elvis Presley: Analyse van een Fenomeen. Vlaamse Pockets series, 34. Hasselt, Belgium: Heideland, 1961. 110 pp. ISBN: none.

An early Dutch-language biography of Elvis Presley. Includes 31 black and white photographs. Discography up to 1961 (pp. 105–108).

Source: Widener Library, Harvard University, Cambridge, MA 62737
Koninklijke Bibliotheek Albert I/Bibliotheque Royale Albert Ier (national library of Belgium)
OCLC 27115100

☆ *Bach of Elvis: Een Kristelijke Bezinning over de Klankboodschap in Onze Tijd*. Brussels, Belgium: Interdiocesane Kommissie der Opiniemachten Brussel, [1962?]. 32 pp.

English translation of the title: *Bach or Elvis: A Christian Message on the Sound in Our Time.* Produced by the Catholic Television and Radio Centre and the Catholic Film League, both in Brussels, Belgium.

Source: Bibliotheque Royale Albert Ier/Koninklijke Bibliotheek Albert I-879712 KADOC BKDC: KBRB2052

☆ Brem, Bert

Elvis Presley. Belgium: Uitgeverij Heideland, 1961. ISBN: none.

An early Dutch-language biography, emphasizing Elvis Presley's rise to fame. Discussion of Elvis and youth rebellion. Black and white photographs.

Source: David Neale, Elvis in Print, www.geocities.com/SunsetStrip/8200/books.html

☆ Connolly, Ray

Elvis Presley Compleet: tekst en muziek van zijn grootste hits. Translated by Anita van de Ven. Amsterdam, The Netherlands: Loeb, [1985]. 231 pp. ISBN: 9052135544.

Translation of the Elvis Presley songbook, *The Complete Elvis.*

Source: Koninklijke Bibliotheek

☆ de Barbin, Lucy, with Dary Matera

Are You Lonesome Tonight?: een lang bewaard geheim onthuld. Translated by Tom van Beek. Haarlem, The Netherlands: Rostrum, 1987. 302 pp. ISBN: 903280591.

Translation of *Are You Lonesome Tonight?* (*See* The Man/Memoirs and Memories.)

Source: Koninklijke Bibliotheek

☆ De Laet, Danny

De Films van Elvis Presley. De Films van . . . series, #12. [Belgium]: Cinema Magazine; Borgerhout, 1978. 46 pp. ISBN: none.

A filmography of Elvis Presley's motion pictures and documentaries.

Source: Bibliotheque Royale Albert Ier/Koninklijke Bibliotheek Albert I

☆ "Dit is Elvis Presley." Number 10 in *Teenager-Parade* series. Helmond, The Netherlands: Uitgeverij Helmond, 1962, 77 pp. ISBN: none.

An early Dutch-language single-issue magazine about Elvis Presley. Includes 18 pages of photographs.

Source: OCLC 41036269

☆ Ekker, Ernst A.

Elvis in de Wolken. Translated by Hanneke Otter and Gertie Jaquet. Zutphen, The Netherlands: Thieme, 1987. 80 pp. ISBN: 9003900752.

Translation of *Und Elvis in den Wolken.* (*See* Foreign Language Titles/German.)

Source: Koninklijke Bibliotheek

☆ *Elvis: De Lengendarische Rock Koning.* Dordrecht, Belgium: Sari B.V., 1977. 68 pp. ISBN: none.

A biography magazine published after Elvis Presley's death. Black and white photographs.

Source: Compiler's collection
De Hass, Fons, and Katholiek Televisie-en Radiocentrum Brussel and Katholieke Filmliga Brussel

☆ *Elvis: tweemaandelijks tijdschrift/Elvis: mensuel.* Brussels, Belgium: International Elvis Presley Fan Club, 1977–1981. ISBN: none.

A monthly fan club magazine about Elvis Presley published in Belgium. Each issue is bilingual: Dutch and French. Between 1982 and 1985, it was published bi-monthly.

Source: Bibliotheque Royale Albert Ier/Koninklijke Biblioteek Albert I

☆ Farren, Mick, and Pearce Marchbank

Elvis Autobiografisch. Translated by Pieter Cramer. Amsterdam, The Netherlands: Loeb, 1989. 123 pp. ISBN: 9037900895.

Translation of *Elvis in His Own Words.* (*See* The Man/Elvis in Quotes.)

Source: Koninklijke Bibliotheek
OCLC 40908560

☆ *Garon Presley; Taking Care of Business in a Flash: Dead Brother Part 1.* 1995.

A monologue describing the life of Elvis Presley, as related by his stillborn brother Jesse Garon. This monologue was first performed on May 18, 1995, during the "Theater aan de Werf Festival" at the Werftheater in Utrecht, The Netherlands.

Source: www.xs4all.nl/~rragas/elvis.html

☆ Geller, Larry, and Joel Spector, with Patricia Romanowski

Elvis Aron Presley: de mens achter de legende. Translated by Ger Storms. Katwijk aan Zee, The Netherlands: Panta Rhei, 1990. 293 pp. ISBN: 9073207061.

Translation of *If I Can Dream: Elvis's Own Story.* (*See* The Man/Memoirs and Memories.)

Source: Koninklijke Bibliotheek

☆ Goldman, Albert

De Laatste Dagen van The King. Naarden, The Netherlands: Mammoet, 1991. 139 pp. ISBN: 9060107500.

Translation of *Elvis: The Last 24 Hours.* (*See* The Man/Biographies.)

Source: Koninklijke Bibliotheek

————.

Elvis: de schokkende, alles onthullende biografie van een superster. Translated by Lucien Duzee. Alphen aan den Rijn, The Netherlands: Sijthoff, 1982. 543 pp. ISBN: 9021828960.

Translation of *Elvis.* (*See* The Man/Biographies.)

Source: Koninklijke Bibliotheek

☆ Hart, Kees't

Land van Genade. Amsterdam, The Netherlands: Querido's Uitgeverij B.V., 1989. 127 pp. ISBN: 9021465388.

A fictional examination of Elvis Presley and St. Francis of Assisi. From inside jacket cover: the author "presents a new view on the lives of Francis of Assisi and Elvis Presley in order to add weight to his arguments."

Source: New York Public Library JFD 91-9573

☆ Hendrickx, Marc

Elvis A. Presley: Muziek, Mens, Mythe. Antwerpen, Belgium: Coda, 1994. 592 pp. ISBN: 9052321205. Utrecht, Netherlands: QM Publishing, 1998. 592 pp. ISBN: 9052321205 (hdk.). ISBN: 906481807X (second edition).

An encyclopedic, year-by-year biography of Elvis Presley. Second edition was updated to include the years up to 1997. No index. This book was adapted into the Dutch language radio series, *100 x Elvis*, and translated into French. (*See* Foreign Language Titles/French.)

Source: Koninklijke Bibliotheek

☆ *Herinneringen Elvis Presley.* Vaassen, The Netherlands: Uitgeverij "De Denker," 1985. 126 pp. ISBN: none.

A basic biography, with black and white photographs. "Herinneringen" is Dutch for "memories."

Source: Elvis in Print, www.geocities.com/sunsetstrip/8200/books.html
OCLC 41236232

☆ *Het Intieme Foto Album van Elvis.* Weekslad Juepie Special. [Belgium]: [n.p.], 1977. 62 pp.

A souvenir magazine published after Elvis's death. Approximately 100 photos, black and white and color. Discography. From the front cover: "Meer dan 100 nooit eerder gepubliceerde foto's; memorial superposter; beelden uit al zijn films."

Source: eBay auction item #26054608

☆ *Het Verborgen Leven van E.* [Belgium]: N. V. Sparta, [1977].

A special edition of *Joepi*, a Belgian magazine printed in Dutch. A biography of Elvis Presley. Black and white and color photographs.

Source: David Neale, Elvis in Print, www.geocities.com/SunsetStrip/8200/books.html

☆ Kling, Bernd, and Heinz Plehn

Elvis Presley: het Volledige Platenverhaal. Trans. Lodewijk Rijff and Pim Oets. Amsterdam, The Netherlands: Becht, [1980]. 117 pp. ISBN: 9023003268.

Translation of *Elvis Presley: eine Illustrierte Dokumentation.* (*See* Foreign Language Titles/German.)

Source: Koninklijke Bibliotheek

☆ Langbroeck, Hans

The Hillbilly Cat. The Netherlands: [n.p.], 1970; 1981.

Self-published biography of Elvis Presley.

Source: Guralnick, Peter, Careless Love, p. 735 (1970)
www.abebooks.com (1981)

☆ Leviton, Jay B., Jan van Gestel, and Ger Rijff

Elvis Close-Up. [The Netherlands]: Bruna, 1987. 120 pp. ISBN: 119740130X.

Dutch-language edition of *Elvis Close-Up.* (*See* Leviton listing in The Man/Photographs.)

Source: Koninklijke Bibliotheek 4015227

☆ Parker, John

Elvis: de Geheime Dossiers. Translated by Piet Hein. 's-Gravenhage, The Netherlands: BZZToH, 1993. 256 pp. ISBN: 906291890.

Translation of *Elvis: The Secret Files.* (*See* The Man/Death, Conspiracy, Sightings.)

Source: Koninklijke Bibliotheek

☆ Poulsen, Lu

Elvis een Intieme Roman. Antwerpen, Belgium: Tijdschrifgten Uitgevers Maatschappij, 1978. 128 pp. ISBN: none.

A biography, written as a novel, published after Elvis's death.

Source: Compiler's collection

☆ Presley, Priscilla Beaulieu, with Sandra Harmon

Mijn Leven met Elvis. Translated by Tom van Beek. Haarlem, The Netherlands: Rostrum, 1986. 288 pp. ISBN: 903280460X.

Translation of *Elvis and Me.* (*See* The Man/Memoirs and Memories.)

Source: Koninklijke Bibliotheek

☆ Rijff, Lodewijk

De Biografie van een Fenomeen. Dordrecht, Belgium: Sari B.V., [n.d.]. ISBN: 9061981514.

A biography of Elvis Presley. Color and black and white photographs. Discography, including references to unreleased recordings.

Source: David Neale, Elvis in Print, www.geocities.com/SunsetStrip/8200/books.html

☆ Roberts, Dave

Elvis Presley. Translated by Klaske Kamstra and Ireen Niessen. Lisse, The Netherlands: Star Boox, 1996. 119 pp. ISBN: 9056310313.

Translation of *Elvis Presley.* (*See* The Man/Biographies.)

Source: Koninklijke Bibliotheek

☆ Rodger, Mike E.

Remember Elvis: Elvis Presley, zij noemden hem de King. [Zaandam, The Netherlands]: Almere Projects, 1977. 96 pp. ISBN: 9070205017.

A biography published after Elvis Presley's death. Rodger also published a German-language biography about Elvis Presley.

Source: Koninklijke Bibliotheek

☆ Scheers, Rob van

Scheers is a Dutch journalist.

Elvis in Nederland. [Baarn], The Netherlands: De Prom, 1997. 207 pp. ISBN: 9068015559.

An examination of Elvis Presley's impact in The Netherlands. Interviews with Dutch Elvis experts. Chapters on Elvis in sites and art in Tennessee. Chapter on Elvis and African American influence, and one on Elvis's Dutch-born manager, Colonel Parker. Interview with a Dutch Elvis impersonator. Photographs from the collection of Ger Rijff. (*See* The Man/Photographs.)

Source: Koninklijke Bibliotheek
New York Public Library JMD 97-998
OCLC 38241010

☆ Schroer, Andreas, and Knorr Hentschell

Private Presley: Elvis in Duitsland, de verzwegen jaren. Translated by Willem Oorthuizen. Weert, The Netherlands: M & P, 1993. 160 pp. ISBN: 9065907343.

Translation of *Private Presley*. (*See* The Man/Elvis in the Army.)

Source: Koninklijke Bibliotheek

☆ Tas, Henk

Henk Tas: [Elvis Versus God]. Amsterdam, The Netherlands: Galerie Torch, 1989. [24] pp.

Catalog of an exhibition of Tas's Elvis-themed photographs at the Galerie Torch in Amsterdam, March 2–21, 1991.

Source: OCLC 37028286

☆ Tatham, Dick

Elvis Presley. Amsterdam, The Netherlands: Plusproducties, 1977. 63 pp. ISBN: 9063090129.

Translation of *Elvis*. (*See* The Man/Biographies.)

Source: Koninklijke Bibliotheek

☆ Taylor, John Alvarez

Elvis Presley. Eke, The Netherlands: ADC, 1992. 64 pp. ISBN: 9054950102.

Translation of *Forever Elvis*. (*See* The Man/Biographies.)

Source: Koninklijke Bibliotheek

☆ Vellenga, Dirk

Elvis & de Colonel. Weesp, The Netherlands: CenterBoek, 1989. 195 pp. ISBN: 9050870767.

Translation of *Elvis and the Colonel*, a biography of Elvis Presley's manager, Colonel Tom Parker. (*See* The Man/Biographies.)

Source: Koninklijke Bibliotheek
OCLC 41043307

☆ Verbruggen, Peter

Elvis—King of Belgium. Ghent, Belgium: Uitgeverij Scoop, 1999. 240 pp. ISBN: 9053121269.

Elvis's career as experienced and recorded in Belgium. Reproductions of every Belgian Elvis film poster, as well as clippings from the Belgian press. Section on Belgian Elvis record releases. Chapter on Belgian fans. The first 500 copies of this book came with a CD of the same name, containing four Elvis recordings.

Source: Koninklijke Bibliotheek Albert I

☆ Verwerft, Gust

Elvis de Koning die niet kon sterven. Ghent, Belgium: Het Volk, 1977. 102 pp. ISBN: none.

Motion picture studio stills; captioned but not credited.

Source: Koninklijke Bibliotheek
Library of Congress ML420.P96 V5
OCLC 4640244

☆ Wielick, Han

Elvis Presley: koning van de rock 'n' roll. Mimosa-Reeks series, #G-105. Maastricht, The Netherlands: N.V. Leiter-Nypels, 1960. 124 pp. ISBN: none.

An early Dutch-language biography of Elvis Presley. Twelve pages of photographs.

Source: OCLC 41042053

☆ Wilson, Kenneth

Elvis [Presley]. Brussels, Belgium: Archers, 1977. ISBN: none.

A biography of Elvis Presley, published after his death. Because it was published in bilingual Belgium, there is also a French-language version with the same name. (*See* Foreign Language Titles/French.)

Source: Bibliotheque Royale Albert Ier/Koninklijke Bibliotheek Albert I

CHAPTER 40
Finnish and French

Finnish

☆ Bagh, Peter von

Elvis!: Amerikkalaisen Laulajan Elama Ja Kuolema. Helsinki, Finland: Love kustannus, 1977; 1987. 122 pp. ISBN: 951835006X.

A biography of Elvis Presley. Discography (pp. 115–119).

Source: Helsingin Yliopiston Kirjasto (national library of Finland)
OCLC 4437763

☆ *Elvis: Kertomus Aikamme Mielikuvituksellisimmasta Urasta.* [Tampere], Finland: Pecos Bill, 1958. 34 pp. ISBN: none.

The first Finnish-language publication about Elvis Presley.

Source: Helsingin Yliopiston Kirjasto

☆ Goldman, Albert

Elvis. Translated by Seppo Suihkola. Helsinki, Finland: Otava, 1982. 634 pp. ISBN: 9511069272.

Translation of *Elvis.* (*See* The Man/Biographies.)

Source: Helsingin Yliopiston Kirjasto

☆ Guralnick, Peter

Nuori Elvis:Viimeinen Juna Memphisiin. Translated by J. Pekka Makela. Helsinki, Finland: Like, 1997. 500 pp. ISBN: 9516784816.

Translation of *Last Train to Memphis: The Rise of Elvis Presley*. (*See* The Man/Biographies.)

Source: Helsingin Yliopiston Kirjasto

☆ Hutchins, Chris, and Peter Thompson

Elvis vastaan Beatles. Translated by Jukka Jaaskelainen. Jyvaskyla Helsinki, Finland: Gummerus, 1996. 266 pp. ISBN: 9512047233.

Translation of *Elvis Meets the Beatles*. (*See* The Man/Biographies.)

Source: Helsingin Yliopiston Kirjasto

☆ Into, Markku

Elvis, Eli, Elamänsä Yksin. Helsinki, Finland: Tammi, 1991. 73 pp. ISBN: 951309846X.

Finnish-language poetry about Elvis Presley.

Source: The British Library YA.1992.a.19586
OCLC 37571945

Kaikki Rockin Kuninkaasta. [Finland]: Photoplay Magazine, 1977. 130 pp.

Translation of *Elvis Presley: A* Photoplay *Tribute*. (*See* The Rest/Souvenir Magazines.)

Source: http://koti.kolumbus.fi/

☆ Presley, Priscilla Beaulieu, and Sandra Harmon

Elvis Ja Minä. Translated by Anna-Maija Pursiainen. Jyvaskyla Hki, Finland: Gummerus, 1986. 288 pp. ISBN: 9512027577.

Translation of *Elvis and Me*. (*See* The Man/Memoirs and Memories.)

Source: Helsingin Yliopiston Kirjasto

☆ Rekala, Pertti

Elvis Presley: Elämä Ja Musiikki. Helsinki, Finland: Kuslannursosakeyhlio Tammi, 1991. 288 pp. ISBN: 9513097161.

A reference book on Elvis Presley. Biography. Black and white photographs; captioned and credited. Filmography, with a chapter for each of Elvis Presley's motion pictures and documentaries (pp. 181–213). Discography 1956–1990 (pp. 216–270). Bibliography of English-language titles (p. 283). Fan club listings (pp. 284–287). Index.

Source: Collection of Bill and Connie Burk, Memphis, TN
Helsingin Yliopiston Kirjasto

☆ almi, Vexi

Elvis Elää: Romaani. Porvoo, Finland: W. Söderström, 1997. 216 pp. ISBN: 9510222305.

Source: OCLC 39936980

☆ Wolf-Cohen, Elizabeth

I Love Elvis Keittokirja: yli 50 Hittireseptiä. Translated by Hilppa Loikkanen. Helsinki, Finland: Kolibir, 1998. 80 pp. ISBN: 951576999X.

Translation of *The I Love Elvis Cookbook.* (*See* The Phenomena/Cookbooks.)

Source: Helsingin Yliopiston Kirjasto

French

☆ Adair, Joseph

Elvis. Adapted by Pierre Calamel. Les Immortels series. Paris, France: Grund, 1992. 96 pp. ISBN: 2700054407.

Translation of *The Immortal Elvis Presley, 1935–1977.* (*See* The Man/Biographies.)

Source: Bibliotheque Nationale, France (national library of France)

☆ Blachas, Christian

Le Mystère Elvis. Paris, France: M. Lafon, 1997. 257 pp. ISBN: 2840982633.

A biography, with filmography (pp. 236–239), discography (pp. 243–252), and bibliography (pp. 252–253).

Source: Bibliotheque Nationale, France

☆ Brewer-Giorgio, Gail

Elvis Est-il Vivant? Saint-Hubert, Québec, Canada: Éditions Un Monde Different, 1989. 292 pp. ISBN: 2892251451.

Translation of *Is Elvis Alive?,* accompanied by the audiocassette *The Elvis Tape.* (*See* The Man/Death, Conspiracy, Sightings.)

Source: Bibliotheque Nationale du Quebec ML420.P7 B74 1988/ F/ 1989 OCLC 21445097

☆ Danielson, Sarah Parker

Elvis: l'homme, le mythe. Translated by Jean-Jacques Schakmundes. Paris, France: Minerva, 1990. 95 pp. ISBN: 2830701194.

Translation of *Elvis: Man and Myth.* (*See* The Music, The Movies/Filmography.)

Source: Bibliotheque Nationale, France

☆ de Barbin, Lucy, with Dary Matera

Elvis Mon Amour. Translated by Anne-Marie Deschodt. Paris, France: Carrere, 391 pp. ISBN: 2868045472.

Translation of *Are You Lonesome Tonight?* (*See* The Man/Memoirs and Memories.)

Source: Bibliotheque Nationale, France

☆ Delessert, Jacques

Elvis, Mon Ami. Collection "Les Planches." Lausanne, Suisse (Switzerland): Editions Pierre-Marcel Favre, 1983. 449 pp. ISBN: 282890131.

A biography of Elvis Presley written by a French fan. Black and white candid photographs taken by the author; most captioned. Photographs are of the author's visits to Elvis-related sites, candids of Elvis, and pictures of the author with Elvis's relatives and friends. Discography, including bootleg titles, songs about Elvis recorded by other artists, and a chronology of his gold records. Filmography. List of television appearances. Bibliography.

Source: New York Public Library JNE 84-24
Library of Congress ML420.P96 D44
OCLC 10924777

☆ Doll, Susan

Elvis, Homage à Sa Vie. Translated by Julie Damour. Paris, France: Ramsay, 254 pp. ISBN: 285956943X.

Translation of *Elvis: A Tribute to His Life.* (*See* The Man/Biographies.)

Source: Bibliotheque Nationale, France

☆ Dugas, Louise

"Greta, Elvis, Michael et les Autres: essai sur une symbolisation d'époque." L'Université du Québec à Montréal (Canada). 1989.

Source: Bibliotheque Nationale, Quebec MIC/B2362 GEN

☆ Dureau, Christian and Christophe L.

Elvis Presley. Collection "Grand écran" series, #0756-628X. Paris, France: PAC, 1985. ISBN: 285336240/X.

An examination of Elvis Presley's career, with detailed analysis of his films and documentaries. Chapters on each motion picture. Filmography with the French titles of his films (pp. 145–176). Discography (pp. 177–188). Chapters on Elvis's million-selling recordings in the United States and the Elvis albums released by RCA in France. Black and white and color photographs of movie stills. Cinema-related bibliography (p. 189).

Source: Bibliotheque Nationale, France
New York Public Library MWES + (Presley, E.) 86-2404
Library of Congress ML88.P76 D9

☆ Efratas, Pierre

Le King . . . Et Moi. [France]: Lefrancq Literature, 1997. ISBN: 287153470.

A collection of interviews with Elvis Presley, and with famous individuals in Belgium and France who describe how Elvis Presley affected their lives. Several chapters on Elvis's place in history, including a comparison to French singers Edith Piaf and Johnny Halliday. Color and black and white photographs.

Source: Collection of Paul Millot, Bourges, France

☆ *Elvis.* Montreal, Québec, Canada: Presses Sélect, 1977. 120 pp. ISBN: none.

(The OCLC entry for this book indicates that it was translated from English. Compiler has been unable to ascertain which of the many books titled *Elvis* was the original for translation.) A biography published after Elvis Presley's death. Translation from the front cover: "a tribute to the king of rock 'n' roll; more than 40 photos of his life, his loves, and his death."

Source: Bibliotheque Nationale, Québec 20761 CON
OCLC 15845265

☆ *Elvis: mensuel/Elvis: tweemaandelijks tijdschrift.* Brussels, Belgium: International Elvis Presley Fan Club, 1977–1981.

A monthly fan club magazine about Elvis Presley published in Belgium. Each issue is bilingual: Dutch and French. Between 1982 and 1985 it was published bi-monthly.

Source: Bibliotheque Royale Albert Ier/Koninklijke Bibliothek Albert I

☆ *Elvis Presley (Album Souvenir).* [Belgium]: Cine-Revue Editions, [1977].

A biography of Elvis Presley published after his death. Color and black and white photographs.

Source: David Neale, Elvis in Print, www.geocities.com/SunsetStrip/8200/books.html

☆ Flippo, Chet

Graceland: Mémoire Vivante d' Elvis Presley. Translated by Isabelle Le Corre. Paris, France: Bookking International, 1994. 256 pp. ISBN: 2877142353.

Translation of *Graceland: The Living Legacy of Elvis Presley.* (*See* The Man/Graceland.)

Source: Bibliotheque Nationale, France

☆ Frew, Timothy W.

Elvis: Sa Vie, Sa Musique. Translated and adapted by Michel Beauvais. Paris, France: France Loisirs, 1997. 176 pp. ISBN: 274410647X.

Translation of *Elvis: His Life and Music.* (*See* The Man/Biographies.)

Source: Bibliotheque Nationale, France

☆ Goldman, Albert

Elvis: Un Phénomène Américain. Translated by Yvonne Baudry, Frederic Develay, and Michelle Garene. Paris, France: R. Laffont, 1982. 528 pp. ISBN: 2221009142.

Translation of *Elvis.* (*See* The Man/Biographies.)

Source: Bibliotheque Nationale, France

☆ Gordon, Robert

Le King en Concert. Translated by Isabelle St. Martin. Paris, France: Vade Retro, 1996. 208 pp. ISBN: 2909828336.

Translation of *The King on the Road.* (*See* The Music, The Movies/Concerts and Television Appearances.)

Source: Bibliotheque Nationale, France

☆ Goulet, Paul-Henri

Le Roi du Rock. Collection Montréal, Québec, Canada: Les Publications Éclair, 1976. 130 pp. ISBN: none. Montreal, Quebec, Canada: Bert-Hold, 1977. 130 pp. ISBN: none.

A reference book offering a biography (pp. 9–20); filmography (pp. 21–36); chronology of Elvis's life (pp. 37–82); discography (pp. 97–127). List of 15 fan clubs, with addresses, in the United States and Europe. A section of facts about Elvis. Black and white photographs; captioned but not credited.

Source: Library of Congress M420.P96
Dewey Decimal 784.092
OCLC 15846642 (1976); 16063026 (1977)

☆ Harbinson, W. A.

Elvis Presley. Translation by Jean-Dominque Brierre and Armand Vlactamar. Rock and Folk series. Paris, France: Albin Michel, 1976; 1977. 159 pp. ISBN: 222600392.

Translation of *Elvis Presley: An Illustrated Biography.* (*See* The Man/Biographies.) Second edition was issued immediately after Elvis Presley's death.

Source: OCLC 19021356 (1976)

☆ Hendrickx, Marc

Elvis A. Presley, Mystère et Vie d'un Mythe. Antwerp, Belgium: CODA, 1994. 600 pp.

Translation of *Elvis A. Presley: Muziek, Mens, Mythe.* (*See* Foreign Language/Dutch.)

Source: Collection of Paul Milliot, Bourges, France

☆ Henry, Pierre

Elvis: The Rockin' Rebel (The Rock Years). Collection Rock 'n' Roll Memoires, #3. Paris, France: Éditions Horus, 1979. 94 pp. ISBN: 286387019.

A celebration of the life and career of Elvis Presley, written after his death. Written in association with the King's Memorial Club of Paris, France. Discography (pp. 87–90).

Source: Bibliotheque Nationale, France
OCLC 21912123

☆ Hopkins, Jerry

Elvis: Biographie. Translated by Antoine Bodard. Scope series. Paris: Solar; Montreal, Québec, Canada: Presses de la Cité, 1972. 310 pp. ISBN: none.

Translation of *Elvis: A Biography.* (*See* The Man/Biographies.)

Source: Bibliotheque Nationale, Québec ML420.P7 H66 F
OCLC 15836422

☆ Israel, Marvin

Elvis Presley 1956. Translated by Jean-Luc Muller. Paris, France: Ed. De la Martiniere, 1998. Unpaged. ISBN: none.

Translation of *Elvis Presley 1956.* (*See* The Man/Photographs.)

Source: Bibliotheque Nationale, France

☆ Jélot-Blanc, Jean-Jacques

Elvis à Hollywood. Cine-Memoires series, #1. Paris, France: Éditions Horus, 1979. 128 pp. ISBN: 286387010-VI.

The first French-language book about the cinematic career of Elvis Presley. Essays on each of Elvis's motion pictures, his two documentaries, and the 1979 efforts between his father, Vernon, and Hollywood producer Hal Wallis to make a posthumous Elvis film, *Elvis Presley Years*, as well as other proposed Elvis-related cinema projects. Approximately 150 black and white reproductions of French and Belgian posters for Elvis's films, his album covers, and photo stills from his movies; captioned and credited. Filmography (pp. 84–118). Only 3,000 copies of this book were printed.

Source: Library of Congress ML420.P96 J4
Bibliotheque Nationale, France

☆ Jouffa, Francois, with Jacques Barsamain

Elvis Presley Story. Rock Collection, #1. Boulogne, France: Éditions Alain Mathieu, 1978. 127 pp. ISBN: none.

A biography in French, compiled from 13 hours of radio programming that aired throughout Europe (on Europe no. 1) from 1973 to 1977. Includes a chapter entitled "The Final Confession of Elvis" purporting to be Elvis's final one-on-one interview (June 1974). Text is interspersed with transcriptions of statements made by Elvis's friends and family. No citations for these statements. Repeats the inaccurate "second prize" story.

Black and white photographs, some previously unseen; none are credited. A listing of 33 albums with reference numbers (p. 126). Listing of Elvis's 31 films and two documentaries, and eight television appearances (p. 127).

Source: Bibliotheque Nationale, France

☆ Kirkland, K. D.

Elvis. Translated by Philippe Safari. [Paris, France]: Ed. Horus collection, 1997. 79 pp. ISBN: 225804653X.

Translation of *Elvis.* (*See* The Man/Biographies.)

Source: Bibliotheque Nationale, France

☆ Major, André

La Folle d'Elvis: Nouvelles. Montréal, Québec, Canada: Québec/Amérique, 1981. 137 pp. ISBN: 28903780X.

A novella in which the only Elvis Presley plot connection occurs when the protagonist has intercourse with a woman while Elvis recordings are played. There is a drawing of Elvis on the cover of the book. This book was also translated into English. (*See* The Rest/Deceptive Titles.)

Source: Library of Congress

☆ Monin, Emmanuel-Yves

Le Message d'Elvis Presley: Un Heros Civilizateur. [France]: Auto Edition, 1995. 207 pp. ISBN: 291009703x.

An exploration of the thesis that Elvis was the messenger of the Universe and that he changed the world. His songs and film dialogue are examined for messages. A list of "coincidences estranges" ("strange coincidences") is also presented in support of the thesis. Bibliography (pp. 205–206) of French-language Elvis books, originals and translations, and some in English.

Source: Bibliotheque Nationale, France
The University of Mississippi ML420.P96 M65 1995
OCLC 37376518

☆ Morgan, Todd, and Laura Kath (text); Jeffery Golick, editor

Elvis: Images du King. Translated by Dominique Lablanche. Paris, France: Ed. Abbeville, 1997. 287 pp. ISBN: 2879461308.

Translation of *Elvis: His Life in Pictures.* (*See* The Man/Biographies.)

Source: Bibliotheque Nationale, France

☆ Pouzenc, Jean-Marie

Elvis à Paris. Paris, France: La Revue Elvis My Happiness, 1999. 157 pp. ISBN: 2951394209.

Mostly black and white candid photographs from Elvis Presley's June 1959 visit to Paris, while he was serving in the U.S. Army. Photographs are credited but not captioned. Text, in French and English, gives the background and the details of the visit. Brief memoir from Elvis's friend and Casino de Paris dancer, Line Renaud. Reproductions of French media news stories about Elvis, as well as color reproductions of the covers of Elvis's French recording releases. The author, an Elvis fan since 1956, has been president of France's largest Elvis Presley fan club (Elvis My Happiness) for many years.

Source: Compiler's collection

☆ *Presley, Elvis, 1935–1977* [clippings]. 1999.

OCLC abstract: "Includes 1997 articles in French from *Le Monde*, *Le Figaro*, and other French journals about Elvis Presley films shown at the Cinematheque de la danse in Paris."

Source: OCLC 41128206

☆ Presley, Priscilla Beaulieu, avec collaboration de Sandra Harmon

Elvis et Moi. **Translation by Francois Jouffa. Paris, France: France Loisirs, 1986. 297 pp. ISBN: 2724231137. Paris, France: Ramsay, 1986. 297 pp. ISBN: 2859564845. Paris, France: J'ai Lu, 1987. 285 pp. ISBN: 22772221570.**

Translation of *Elvis and Me.* (*See* The Man/Memoirs and Memories.) Includes 32 pages of black and white photographs.

Source: Bibliotheque Nationale, France (all editions)

———.

Elvis Intime. **Translated by Francois Jouffa. Paris, France: Ramsay, 1997. 301 pp. ISBN: 284114304.**

Previously published as *Elvis et Moi.* (*See* preceding listing.)

Source: Bibliotheque Nationale, France

☆ Ridge, Millie

Album Elvis. **Translated by Daniele de Yparraguirre. Geneva, Switzerland; Paris, France: Minerva, 1993. 304 pp. ISBN: 2830701887.**

Translation of *The Elvis Album.* (*See* The Man/Biographies.)

Source: Bibliotheque Nationale, France
OCLC 09330012

☆ Rogale, Jean-Yves

Le Roi Elvis. **Paris, France: Mengès, 1981. 159 pp. ISBN: 2856201318.**

A biography that the author hopes will be the first view of Elvis Presley without the myths that have surrounded him ("Avant-Propos" essay). Includes memories of Elvis's romantic interest Linda Thompson. Elvis's natal astrological chart. A listing, with explanations, of people associated with Elvis during his lifetime. Discography (pp. 139–141). Filmography (pp. 143–154). Bibliography (p. 161). Includes 32 black and white photographs; captioned but not credited.

Source: Library of Congress ML420.P96 R6
Dewey Decimal 784.5/4/00924 B 19
Bibliotheque Nationale, France
OCLC 8218997

☆ Stern, Jane, and Michael Stern

Elvis: Le Monde d'Elvis: Elvis au Pays des Merveilles. French text by Francois Jouffa. Paris, France: Ramsay, 1987. Paris, France: France Loisirs, 1988. 198 pp. ISBN: 2724236823 (1988).

Translation of *Elvis World.* (*See* The Man/Biographies.)

Source: Bibliotheque Nationale, France

☆ Taylor, John Alvarez

Elvis: Pour Toujours. Translated by Caroline Vie. Paris, France: Minerva, 1991. 64 pp. ISBN: 2830701461.

Translation of *Forever Elvis* by John Alvarez Taylor. (*See* The Man/Biographies.)

Source: Bibliotheque Nationale, France

☆ Thompson, Charles C., II, and James P. Cole

Elvis: Ses Derniers Jours: La Vérité. Paris, France: Ed. Lincoln, 1992. 276 pp. ISBN: 2738205674.

Condensed translation of *The Death of Elvis.* (*See* The Man/Death, Conspiracy, Sightings.)

Source: Bibliotheque Nationale, France

☆ Tillinac, Denis

Tillinac is the author of more than 20 books exploring music and pop culture.

Elvis. Paris, France: Quai Voltaire, 1994. 121 pp. ISBN: 287653228X.

An examination of the author's journey to investigate the Southern origins of Elvis Presley's impact, life, and career.

Source: Bibliotheque Nationale, France
Library of Congress ML420.P96 T6
OCLC 32683070

☆ *Tintin,* 40 (Oct 1977).

A comic strip biography of Elvis Presley, beginning with his career in 1956.

Source: David Neale, Elvis in Print, www.geocities.com/SunsetStrip/8200/books.html

☆ Valletti, Serge

Saint Elvis; suivi de, Carton plein: théatre. [Paris, France]: C. Bourgois, 1990. 173 pp. ISBN: 2267008904.

A play, described on the back cover as a "a cross-cut of Elvis Presley's life, the boredom that was truly Elvis."

Source: New York Public Library JFD 91-6182
Library of Congress PQ2682.A434 S3 1990
OCLC 22891385

☆ West, Red, Sonny West, and Dave Hebler as told to Steve Dunleavy

Elvis ou le Roi Dechu. Translated by France-Marie Watkins and Solange Metzger. Paris, France: O. Orban, 1977. 269 pp. ISBN: none.

Translation of *Elvis, What Happened?* (*See* The Man/Memoirs and Memories.)

Source: Bibliotheque Nationale, France

☆ Wilson, Kenneth

Elvis [Presley]. Brussels, Belgium: Archers, 1977. ISBN: none.

A biography of Elvis Presley, published after his death. Because it was published in bilingual Belgium, there is also a Dutch-language version with the same name. (*See* Foreign Language Titles/Dutch.)

Source: Bibliotheque Royale Albert Ier/Koninklijke Bibliotheek Albert I, Belgium

☆ Womack, Jack

L'Elvissee: Roman. Translated by Jean Bonnefoy. Paris, France: Denoel, 1995. 366 pp. ISBN: 2207305554.

Translation of *Elvissey* by Jack Womack. (*See* The Phenomena/Fiction.)

Source: Bibliotheque Nationale, France

☆ Yancey, Becky, and Cliff Linedecker

Ma Vie avec Elvis: Les Souveniers Pleins de Tendresse d'une Fan Qui Devient Secrétaire Personnelle d'Elvis. Montréal, Québec, Canada: Presses Sélect, 1978. 333 pp. ISBN: none.

Translation of *My Life with Elvis.* (*See* The Man/Memoirs and Memories.)

Source: OCLC 15831501

☆ Zmijewsky, Steven, and Boris Zmijewsky

Elvis: Elvis Presley, Films et Carrière. [Montréal, Québec, Canada]: Librairie Beauchemin, 1977. 223 pp. ISBN: 00775004723.

Translation of *Elvis: The Films and Career of Elvis Presley.* Discography (pp. 216–[224]). (*See* The Music, The Movies/Filmography.)

Source: OCLC 15851795

Souvenir Magazines

☆ *À La Memoiré du King!* [Laval, Québec, Canada]: Ed. DuBoise, 1997. 58 pp. ISBN: 2980562602.

Covers the life and career of Elvis Presley, published on the twentieth anniversary of his death.

Source: OCLC 40534679

☆ *Elvis.* Laval, Québec, Canada: Les Editions Pop-Jeunesse Inc., [n.d.]. [46] pp. ISBN: none.

Life and career of Elvis Presley. Includes 16 pages of color photographs and four double-page posters.

Source: Compiler's collection

☆ *Elvis, 1935–1977 Album Souvenir. 1977.* Laval, Quebec, Canada: Les Editions Pop Jeunesse, 1977. 46 pp. ISBN: none.

Magazine published after Elvis Presley's death. Two hundred photographs.

Source: Compiler's collection

☆ *Elvis 1 an aprés.* Bio Mag series, Vol 1. No. 4. Laval, Québec, Canada: Éditions Pop Jeunesse, 1978. 46 pp. ISBN: none.

Biographical souvenir magazine. Approximately 200 color and black and white photographs, "jamais publices," (never before published). Four color posters.

Source: Compiler's collection

☆ *Elvis Superstars 1989/Album Souvenir 1989: Elvis Presley.* [Québec], Canada: [n.p.], 1989. 30 pp. ISBN: none.

Biographical souvenir magazine in French.

Source: Bibliotheque Nationale Quebec, Canada ML420.P7 E53

☆ Loubat, Bernard

Elvis: La Legende du King. [France]: Groupe International de Presse, 1977.

A magazine published after the death of Elvis Presley; a tribute to his life and career.

Source: Compiler's collection

☆ *Special Elvis*. Montreal, Québec, Canada: Magazine Vivre, [n.d.]. 46 pp. ISBN: none.

Life and career of Elvis Presley. Two double-page color posters.

Source: Compiler's collection

Unverified French Titles

☆ Delville, Jean-Pierre, *Elvis Presley*. (Source: Delessert, *Elvis, Mon Ami*.)

☆ *Elvis Presley Story*. (Source: Delessert, *Elvis, Mon Ami*.)

☆ Gendron, Jacques

Dans la Peau d'Elvis. Collection Célébrités. Montreal, Québec, Canada: Quebecor, 1983. 191 pp. ISBN: 2890891836.

A biography of David Scott. (No information about Scott's relationship to Elvis.)

Source: OCLC 15942532

☆ Tillinac, Denis

Elvis: Balade Sudiste; suivi de le tour des iles: balade polynesienne. Paris, France: Editions J'ai Lu, 1997. 88 pp. ISBN: 2277301868.

Source: Bibliotheque Nationale, France

CHAPTER 41

German and Greek

German

☆ Allen, William, David Gibbon, and Nicola Dent, editors

Elvis Presley. Translated by Almut Carstens. München, Germany: Orbis Verlag fur Puglizistik, 1992. 192 pp. ISBN: 3572006171.

A translation of *Elvis*. (*See* The Man/Biographies.) Bibliography, filmography, and discography (pp. 179–191).

Source: Osterreichische Nationalbibliothek (national library of Austria)

☆ Baumann, Peter, Norman Duncan, Peter Schittler, and Harald Trittner

Schittler is the co-author of another Bringin' It Back Special Edition relating to *Elvis, Unchained Melody*. (*See* The Movies, The Music/Concerts and Television Appearances.)

The Burbank Sessions and The Burbank Puzzle. Special Edition #1. [n.p.]: [n.p.], 1992. 96 pp. ISBN: none.

The story of the preparations for and the recording output of Elvis Presley's NBC-TV/ Singer Company *Elvis* special, which aired on December 3, 1968. (Note: this special is alternately known as "The '68 Special," and "The Comeback Special.")

Chart in English listing the special's "every known" audio and video recording, "every known mixing session," and "every known Master-Tape" (pp. 33–81). Also in English: "Songs from the Burbank Sessions and Where You Can Find Them" (pp. 82–84). Copies of the song list information sheets for the June 20, 1968, taping of the special's album at Western Recorders Inc. (pp. 85–86). "The Burbank Discography" (pp. 87–92) in German, listing titles and information about the singles, LPs, CDs, and bootleg LPs and CDs.

Source: Collection of Bill and Connie Burk, Memphis, TN

☆ Beggs, Karen, and Peter Beynon

Elvis Presley. Translated by Peter Budweg and Marie-Thérèse Schins. Stuttgart, Germany: Klett-Verl. Für Wissen und Bildung, 1994. 48 pp. ISBN: 3125547709.

Translation of *Elvis Presley.* (*See* The Academics/Educational Literature.)

Source: Die Deutsche Bibliothek (national library of Germany)

☆ Brown, Peter Harry, and Pat Broeske

Elvis: die Biographie. Translated by Karlheinz Durr. Stuttgart, Germany: Engelhorn-Verl., 1997. 543 pp. ISBN: 3872032429.

Translation of *Down at the End of Lonely Street.* (*See* The Man/Biographies.)

Source: Die Deutsche Bibliothek

☆ Burchill, Julie

Über Prince, Pop, Elvis. Translated by Clara Drechsler and Harald Hellmann. Koln, Germany: Kiepenheuer und Witsch, 1987. 206 pp. ISBN: 3462018353.

Source: Die Deutsche Bibliothek

☆ Burk, Heinrich

Elvis in der Wetterau: Der "King" in Deutschland, 1958 bis 1960. Frankfurt am Main, Germany: Eichborn, 1995. 123 pp. ISBN: 3821804769.

Story of Elvis Presley's tour of duty in Germany with the U.S. Army. Chronology of events during this time. Black and white photographs of Elvis during this period.

Source: New York Public Library JND 96-135
OCLC 36715952

☆ Carson, Lucas

Elvis Presley. Berlin, Germany: Taco Verlagsgesellschaft und Agentur mbH, 1989. 143 pp. ISBN: 3892680957. Berlin: Benedikt Taschen, 1990. 143 pp. ISBN: 3894501502.

A biography of Elvis Presley. Filmography in chronological order, including length of each film, the number of songs sung by Elvis, and the date of the film's premiere (p. 143). Black and white and color photographs that have been seen elsewhere.

Source: New York Public Library JNG 91-198
OCLC 23832998 (1989); 27180290 (1990)

☆ Cortez, Diego, editor

At the time of the book's publication, Diego Cortez was a filmmaker and performance artist.

Private Elvis. Stuttgart, Germany: FEY Verlags GmbH, 1978. 198 pp. ISBN: 3883611018.

Photographs taken by Rudolf Paulini of Elvis Presley during an evening at a Munich, Germany, nightclub in 1959. Text in German and English. Photographs are of Elvis, his friends, club guests and entertainers, and his romantic interest, actress Vera Tschechova. Additional black and white photographs of Elvis's 1958 arrival in and 1960 departure from Germany.

Short question and answer interviews with Cortez, as well as Tschechova and her friends. Essays on Elvis as a product, his biography, and his effect on the world. Reprints of *Stars and Stripes* newspaper articles written while Elvis was in Germany on active duty with the U.S. Army and the day after his death. Text in German and English. Photo index.

Source: Die Deutsche Bibliothek

✰ De Vecchi, Peter

Die Tonende Story: Elvis Presley. München, Germany: Sud-West Verlage, 1959. ISBN: none.

An early biography of Elvis Presley, written in German and published in paperback format. One in a series of books on various recording artists, such as Bill Haley and Tommy Steele. English translation of title: "The Sounding Story."

Source: Collection of Maria Columbus, Pacifica, CA

✰ Dunleavy, Steve, with Sonny West, Red West, and Dave Hebler

Elvis Wie Er Wirklich War. Trans. Bernhard Kramer-Dannhoff. Rocky Buch 1. Offenburg, Germany: A. Reiff, 1979. 223 pp. ISBN: none.

Translation of *Elvis, What Happened?.* (*See* The Man/Memoirs and Memories.)

Source: Die Deutsche Bibliothek DBF D 80/31469
The New York Public Library JNC 92-24
OCLC 27443165

✰ *Elvis. Facts und Platten.* [Germany]: Rastatt, 1988.

Source: Posener, Elvis Presley, *p. 151.*

✰ *Elvis Presley: Büch mit 30 Postkarten.* Stuttgart, Germany: Parkland, 1992. [64] pp. ISBN: 3880596832.

A booklet of 30 color postcards of Elvis Presley, 11 x 16 cm.

Source: Die Deutsche Bibliothek

✰ *Elvis Presley: Tutti Frutti Oder Die Allgemeine Erektion der Herzne: Photographen aus den Wunderbaren Jähren des Königs des Rock 'n' Roll 1954–1960.* München, Germany: Schirmer/Mosel, 1990. 119 pp. ISBN: 33888143586X.

Primarily photographs of Elvis during the 1954–1960 years: 64 duotone and color photographs; credited and captioned. Translation of "Where Were You When Elvis Died?" by Lester Bangs, (*See* The Man/Death, Conspiracy, Sightings.) Brief chronology of Elvis's life. Discography of Elvis's recorded song titles, 1954–1960, with composer attribution. Filmography, 1954–1960, with plots, stars, and discussion of songs in the films *Love Me Tender* (1956), *Loving You* (1957), *Jailhouse Rock* (1957), and *King Creole* (1958). Bibliography listing 13 Elvis titles.

Source: New York Public Library JNC 93-11
OCLC 28433010

☆ Ever, Harry S.

Das war Elvis Presley. München, Germany: W. Heyne, 1977; 1978; 1980; 1982. 127 pp. ISBN: 3453007751 (1977, 1978). ISBN: 3007743 (1980, 1982).

A biography published immediately after the death of Elvis Presley. Discography (pp. 118–127).

Source: Die Deutsche Bibliothek (1977, 1978, 1980, 1982)
OCLC 24870937 (1977)

☆ Fritz, Veronika

Elvis Presley, Verkauf der Träume. Leben, Werk, Wirkung series, #2819. Berneck, Germany: Schwengeler-Verlag, 1993. 119 pp. ISBN: 3856663029.

A biography of Elvis Presley that uses information from other cited Elvis biographies. Bibliographic references.

Sources: New York Public Library JNC 95-19
OCLC 33998963

☆ Geller, Larry, with Joel Spector and Patricia Romanowski

Elvis Presley: die Endgültige Biographie. Translated by Franz Josef Stupp. Munchen, Germany: Heyne, 1994. 427 pp. ISBN: 3453075935.

Translation of *If I Can Dream.* (*See* The Man/Memoirs and Memories.)

Source: Die Deutsche Bibliothek

☆ Goldman, Albert

Elvis, Die Letzten 24 Stunden: die Wahrheit uber den Tod des King of Rock 'n' Roll. Translated by Ekkehart Reinke. Bergisch Gladbach, Germany: Bastei Lubbe, 1993. ISBN: 3404612582.

Translation of Albert Goldman's *Elvis: The Last 24 Hours.* (*See* The Man/Biographies.)

Source: Die Deutsche Bibliothek

☆ *Graceland International Elvis Magazin.* Neumarkt, [West Germany]: Elvis Pres-
ley-Gesellschaft e.v., July 1979.

Souvenir magazine.

Source: Die Deutsche Bibliothek

☆ Graham, Robert

Elvis: ein Roman. Translated by Alexander Schmitz. Frankfurt am Main, Germany:
Fischer-Taschenbuch-Verlga, 1984. 313 pp. ISBN: 359628133.

Translation of *Elvis—The Novel.* (*See* Baty listing in The Phenomena/Fiction.)

Source: Die Deutsche Bibliothek

☆ Graves, Barry

Elvis, King der verlorenen Herzen: eine Biographie der ungewohnlichen Art. Berlin,
Germany: Albino, 1984; 1997. 148 pp. ISBN: 3888030145 (1984). ISBN:
3910079652 (1997).

Discography (pp. 133–139). Index.

Source: Bucher, German Books in Print, 1997/1998 (1997)
OCLC 35814542 (1984)

☆ Grust, Lothar F. W., and Jeremias Pommer

Elvis Presley Superstar. Bastei Lübbe: Sonderband series. Bergisch Gladback, Germany: G. Lübbe, 1978. 221 pp. ISBN: 3404007786.

A biography. Filmography (pp. 193–221). Discography, 1956-1977 (pp. 159–190). Bibliography (11 titles, p. 222). Black and white photographs; captioned and credited.

OCLC 5707094

☆ Hanna, David

Elvis: sein Leben, seine Filme, seine Musik. Translated by Margret von Eisenhart Rothe.
Bergisch-Gladbach, Germany: Bastei-Verlag. Lubbe, 1987. 50 pp. ISBN: none.

Translation of *Elvis: Lonely Star at the Top.* (*See* The Man/Biographies.)

Source: Die Deutsch Bibliothek

☆ Harper, Betty

Elvis: Erinnerungen an Elvis Presley. München, Germany: Heyne, 1980. [127] pp.
ISBN: 3453012283.

German edition of *Elvis: Newly Discovered Drawings of Elvis.* (*See* The Phenomena/ Art.)

Source: Die Deutsche Bibliothek

☆ Israel, Marvin

Elvis Presley 1956. Translated by Thomas Wollermann. München, Germany: Schirmer/Mosel, 1998. [91 pp.]. ISBN: 3888149061.

Translation of *Elvis Presley 1956* by Marvin Israel. (*See* The Man/Photographs.)

Source: Die Deutsche Bibliothek

☆ Kling, Bernd, and Heinz Plehn

Elvis. Rastatt, Germany: Moewig, 1988. 223 pp. ISBN: 281183357.

A biography.

Source: Die Deutsche Bibliothek

☆ Kling, Bernd, and Heinz Plehn, translators

Elvis Presley: eine. Illustrierte Dokumentation. "Melzer's Rock Edition." Dreieich: Abi Melzer Production, 1978. 117 pp. ISBN: 3820100059. Gutersloh, Germany: Bertelsmann, [1979]. 117 pp. ISBN: none.

Translations of Elvis Presley memorial articles printed in the September 22, 1977, edition of *Rolling Stone* and elsewhere. Among the authors included are Greil Marcus, Dave Marsh, Ben Fong-Torres, Caroline Kennedy, Lloyd Shearer, and Chet Flippo. Reproductions of Elvis-themed magazine covers, movie posters, and Elvis album covers. Discography (pp. 102–115). Filmography (pp. 90–98). Black and white photographs (some previously seen); captioned and credited. Reproductions of Elvis's motion picture posters. This book was also translated into Dutch. (*See* Foreign Language Titles/Dutch.)

Source: Die Deutsch Bibliothek
Library of Congress ML420.P96 E395 (1978)
OCLC 6921170 (1978)

☆ Koch, Reinhard

Elvis, Germany: ein Nachtrag zum Frühjahr 1964. Frankfurt am Main, Germany: Sauerlander, 1989. 160 pp. ISBN: 3794131746.

Source: Die Deutsche Bibliothek

☆ Kuhnel, Wolfgang, and Helmut Raderamcher

Elvis-Rillen-Revue Teil I: Singles. [Germany]: Bamberg, 1986. ISBN: none. *Elvis-Rillen-Revue Teil II: EPs, Schellacks, Werbeplatten und Singlnachtrag.* [Germany]: Bamberg, 1987. ISBN: none.

A discography. Teil I ("Volume I") reviews Elvis Presley's single recordings. Teil II ("Volume II") deals with Elvis's extended play records, "shellacs," commercial recordings, and additional single records.

Source: Posener, Elvis Presley, *p. 151.*

☆ Leinberger, Ursula

Elvis Forever: eine Hommage. Berlin, Germany: Frieling, 1995. 148 pp. ISBN: 389009872X.

Source: Die Deutsche Bibliothek

☆ Lohmeyer, Henno

Elvis-Presley-Report: Eine Dokumentation der Lugen und Legenden, Thesen und Theorien. Ullstein Buch series, #3426. Frankfurt am Main: Verlag Ullstein GmbH, 1978. 151 pp. ISBN: 3548034268.

Biography of Elvis Presley. Press and celebrity quotes about Elvis; undated. An interpretation of Elvis's horoscope (pp. 105–110). Filmography with German and English titles (pp. 141–[151]). Twenty-one previously seen black and white photographs; captioned and credited.

Source: New York Public Library JNC 79-11
OCLC 4488822

☆ Mansfield, Rex, and Elisabeth Mansfield

Rex Mansfield was inducted into the U.S. Army with Elvis. He went through basic training with him and served with him in Germany. Elisabeth Mansfield was Elvis's private secretary in Germany.

Elvis in Deutschland. Graceland Book series, #1. Bamburg, West Germany: Collectors Service GmbH, 1981. 163 pp. ISBN: 3922932002.

A memoir in which the authors—friends of Elvis—detail their experiences with him in the United States and in Germany during his military service. Color and black and white photographs of Elvis, Graceland, military locations, and individuals associated with him during this time. Many are candid shots taken by the authors and other Elvis friends. (Photographs are different in each version of the book.)

The book comes with a 33⅓, 8″ sound disc of a 1960 interview Elvis gave, in English, to the Armed Forces Network (AFN). In 1983 this book was translated into English and published as *Elvis the Soldier*, with the above-noted sound disc. (*See* The Man/Memoirs and Memories.)

Source: Die Deutsch Bibliothek

☆ Marcus, Greil

Dead Elvis: Meister, Mythos, Monster. Frankfurt am Main, Germany: Rogner and Bernhard bei Swietausendeins, 1993. 302 pp. ISBN: 3807702849.

Translation of *Dead Elvis.* (*See* The Man/The Impact of Elvis.)

Source: Die Deutsche Bibliothek

————.

Dead Elvis: Die Legende Lebt. Translation by Fritz Schneider. St. Andrä-Wördernf, Austria: W. Hannibal, 1997. 391 pp. ISBN: 385445144X.

Translation of *Dead Elvis*. (*See* The Man/The Impact of Elvis.) All illustrations are black and white. This edition also includes essays written by Marcus from 1992–1996, focusing on Elvis Presley and Bill Clinton. These were not included in the original edition.

Source: Greil Marcus
Die Deutsche Bibliothek

☆ Parker, John

Geheimakte Elvis; Die Mafia und das Rätsel um den Tod eines Idols. Translated by Aljoscha A. Schwarz and Ronald P. Schweppe. München, Germany: Droemer/Knaur, 1994. 383 pp. ISBN: 3426750619.

Translation of *Elvis: The Secret Files*. (*See* The Man/Death, Conspiracy, Sightings.)

Source: Die Deutsche Bibliothek

☆ Pearlman, Jill, and Wayne White

Elvis für Anfänger. Translated by Nikolaus Hansen. Reinbek bei Hamburg, Germany: Rowohlt, 1986. 145 pp. ISBN: 349917555X.

Translation of *Elvis for Beginners*. (*See* The Phenomena/Race.)

Source: Die Deutsche Bibliothek

☆ Posener, Alan, and Marie Posener

Posener has also authored books about John Lennon and President John F. Kennedy. The Poseners have been Elvis fans for more than 30 years. They reside in Berlin, Germany.

Elvis Presley: mit Selbstzeugnissen und Bilddokumenten. Rowohlts Monographien series, #495. Reinbek bei Hamburg, Germany: Rowohlt Taschenbuch Verlag GmbH, 1993; 1997. 160 pp. ISBN: 3499504952 (same for both editions).

A reference book on Elvis Presley. A chronology of his life. Quotes by American celebrities about Elvis; no sources or citations. Discography divided into sections: Sun recordings, greatest hits, studio LPs, soundtrack LPs, gospel recordings, and LPs (1968–1977) (pp. 143–[146]). Filmography including posthumous videos (pp. 147–[150]). Bibliography (pp. 151–[155]). Index. English translation of the title: "Elvis Presley: with self-portraits and photo documents."

Source: Die Deutsche Bibliothek
Library of Congress ML420.P96 P64 1993
OCLC 28945520 (1993)

☆ Presley, Priscilla, with Sandra Harmon

Elvis und Ich. Translated by Friedrich A. Hofschuster. Bergisch Gladbach: Lizenz des Lübbe-Verl., [1987]. 198 pp. ISBN: none.

Translation of *Elvis and Me.* (*See* The Man/Memoirs and Memories.)

Source: Die Deutsche Bibliothek

☆ Preute, Michael, and Renate Guldner

Elvis Presley. München, Germany: Goldmann, 1977. 207 pp. ISBN: 344203598X.

A biography published shortly after Elvis Presley's death.

Source: Die Deutsche Bibliothek

☆ Roberts, Dave

Elvis Presley. Translated by Gerald Jung. Rastatt, Germany: CD Books, 1994. 119 pp. ISBN: 3811839829.

Translation of *Elvis Presley.* (*See* The Man/Biographies.)

Source: Die Deutsche Bibliothek

☆ Schröer, Andreas

Elvis: seine Jahre in Deutschland (1958–1960). Konigswinter, Germany: Heel, 1994. 160 pp. ISBN: 3893653708.

Source: Die Deutsche Bibliothek

————.

Private Elvis. Weert, Germany: M en P, 1993. 160 pp. ISBN: 9065907343.

German-text version of *Private Presley: Elvis in Germany—The Missing Years.* Accompanied by one compact disc. (*See* The Man/Elvis in the Army.)

Source: Die Deutsche Bibliothek

☆ Seibel, Bernard, and Christian Unucka

Elvis Presley und Seine Filme: Ein Filmographischer Bildband. Herbertshausen, Germany: Vereinigte Verlagsgesellschaften Frank & Co. KG, 1988. 272 pp. ISBN: 388626002X.

A reference book on Elvis Presley written with the assistance of the Elvis Presley Society of Germany. Essay on Elvis Presley's Hollywood career. Chapter on Elvis's post-movie life and on posthumous Elvis films and documentaries. Filmography with U.S. and Germany release information as well as German press reviews of Elvis's films (pp. 71–152). Discography (pp. 154–255). Bibliography of German- and English-language Elvis books (pp. 268–269). Black and white photographs; captioned and credited. Color reproductions of Elvis movie posters.

Source: Library of Congress ML420.P96 S44
OCLC 24413316

☆ **Star Club Elvis.** [West Germany]: Star-Club-Seiten, Feb 1980. 46 pp. "Auf 48 munteren." ISBN: none.

Primarily color and black and white photographs.

Source: Die Deutsche Bibiolthek

☆ Streletz, Werner

Das Erste Erwachen Eines Elvis-Fans. Bottrop, Germany: Literar. Informationszentrum, 1979. 41 pp. ISBN: 3921821037.

Source: Die Deutsche Bibliothek

☆ Tilgner, Wolfgang

Elvis Presley. Berlin, Germany: Lied der Zeit Musikverlag, 1986; 1987; 1989. 254 pp. ISBN: 3733200004 (same for all editions).

A biography of Elvis Presley. Approximately 40 black and white photographs (candids, movie, and promotional stills); captioned, not all credited. Discography (pp. 245–249) consists of a chronology of singles, EPs, and LPs as issued by RCA, RCA International, and Billig-Label Camden bzw. ab 1976 Pickwick. Bibliography (pp. 249–254). This book was translated into Czech. (*See* Foreign Language Titles/Czech.)

Source: Die Deutsche Bibliothek (1989)
Osterreichische National Bibliothek (Austrian National Library)
OCLC 30157831 (1986); 27085895 (1987)

☆ Tosches, Nick

"Der Tote Elvis." *American Dreams.* Zurich, Switzerland: U. Bar Verlag, 1984.

Translation of one of the major essays on the obsession with Elvis Presley. (*See* The Man/The Impact of Elvis.)

Source: Die Deutsche Bibliothek

☆ Wallraf, Rainer, and Heinz Plehn

Elvis Presley: Eine Biographie. München, Germany: Verlag Monkia Nüchtern, 1977. 151 pp. ISBN: none.

A biography of Elvis Presley that includes a chronology of his life, a discography (p. 134) of 80 albums with record numbers, and a filmography (pp. 135–151) of Elvis's 31 films with cast and production information. Black and white photographs, some are candids; some captioned, none credited. This book was translated into English. (*See* The Man/Biographies.)

Source: Library of Congress ML 420.P96 W3
OCLC 4931333

☆ Wertheimer, Alfred, and Gregory Martinelli

Elvis '56: der Beginn. Hamburg, Germany: Rasch und Rohring, 1987. 147 pp. ISBN: 3891361424.

Translation of *Elvis '56: In the Beginning.* (*See* The Man/Photographs.)

Source: New York Public Library JNF 89-208
OCLC 244411541

Deceptive German Titles

☆ *Die Elvis-Tolle, die hatte ich mire unauffeallig wachsen lassen: Legensgeschichte und jugendliche Alltagskultur in den feunfziger Jahren.* Studien zur Jugend-forschung #3. Opladen, Germany: Leske + Budrich, 1985. 232 pp. ISBN: 3810005223.

An examination of the youth culture of the 1950s.

Source: Die Deutsche Bibliothek

☆ Kozicki, Norbert

"Als wenn Elvis nach Wanne käme . . ." Jugend zwischen Rock 'n' Roll, Jazz und Wirthschaftswunder: ein Bild der Fünfgziger Jahre im Revier. Herne [Germany]: Banana Press, 1988. 98 pp. ISBN: 3927063037.

English translation of title: "'It felt like Elvis came to Wanne' youth between Rock 'n' Roll, Jazz, and economic growth: a picture of the 50s in the coal mining area."

Source: Die Deutsche Bibliothek

Unverified German Titles

☆ Ekker, Ernst A.

Und Elvis in den Wolken. Munchen, Germany: Jugend und Volk, 1984. 94 pp. ISBN: 3224114266.

Source: Die Deutsche Bibliothek

☆ Konnecke, Ole

Elvis und der Mann mit dem roten Mantel. Hamburg, Germany: Carlsen, 1998. [32 pp.]. ISBN: 3551551588.

English translation of title: "Elvis and the Man in the Red Coat."

Source: Die Deutsche Bibliothek

☆ Kuhnel, Wolfgang, and Helmut Radermacher

Elvis-Rillen-Revue Teil I, Bamburg, 1986; Teil II, 1987.

Source: Posener, Elvis Presley p. 151.

☆ Schulz, Franz Joachim

Kein Elvis für Bayreuth: unwahrscheingliche Anekdoten und adnere respektlose.
Bayreuth, Germany: Ed. Schultz und Stellmacher, 1991. ISBN: none.

English translation of title: "No Elvis for Bayreuth: unlikely anecdotes and other disrespectful comments."

Source: Die Deutsche Bibliothek

See Also:

In The Man/Photographs:

Schittler, Peter, and Thomas Schreiber, *Unchained Melody.*

In The Music, The Movies/Discography:

Baumann, Peter, *Elvis on CD.*

Greek

☆ *Elbas, O Basilias.* [Greece]: Odos Panos. 1988. ISBN: 9607165128.

Greek translations of excerpts from other books, newspaper and magazine articles. Photographs. English translation of title: "Elvis, the King."

Source: David Neale, Elvis in Print, www.geocities.com/SunsetStrip/8200/books

☆ (*The Life and Songs of Elvis Presley.*) Athens, Greece. Post-1977. ISBN: none.

Greek translations for the lyrics to a number of Elvis Presley's recorded songs.

Source: The University of Memphis (TN)

☆ Marcus, Greil

Elvis: Presliad. Athens, Greece: Denise Harvey and Co., 1978. ISBN: none.

A Greek-language translation of Marcus's essay "Elvis: Presliad," published as a book. The essay originally appeared in Marcus's 1976 book, *Mystery Train.* (*See* The Man/The Impact of Elvis.)

Source: Greil Marcus

CHAPTER 42

Hungarian, Icelandic, Italian, Japanese, Korean, and Norwegian

Hungarian

☆ Dunleavy, Steve

Mi Történt, Elvis. Translation by Temesi Ferenc. Budapest, Hungary: Kozmosz, 1982. 350 pp. ISBN: 963211535X.

Translation of *Elvis, What Happened?* (*See* Red West *in* The Man/Memoirs and Memories.)

Source: Los Angeles Public Library HU 789.14 P93

☆ Du Sándor, Oszfolk, Dr., and Dr. Perlaky Árpád (lektorálta)

Selmeczy Attila: Elvis, (Emléktoredékek a rock and roll királyáról). Hungary: 1987. 128 pp. ISBN: 9630182165.

Measuring 1.5″ × 2″, this is possibly the smallest book ever published about Elvis. From cover: "Kepek az Elvis Mailés a szero gyujteményébōl." Black and white photographs. Brief chronology, biography, discography, and filmography. Index.

Source: Collection of Bill and Connie Burk, Memphis, TN

Icelandic

☆ Esposito, Joe, with Elena Oumano

Kóngurinn Elvis. Translated by Þórdís Lilja Gunnarsdóttir. [Reykjavík]: Spassia, 1995. 285 pp. ISBN: 9979921803.

Icelandic translation of *Good Rockin' Tonight.* (*See* The Man/Memoirs and Memories.)

Source: Landsbókasafn Islands (national library of Iceland) 927.8242 Pre

☆ Goldman, Albert

Elvis. Translated by Björn Jónsson. [Rekjavík, Iceland]: Almenna Bókafélagið, 1982. 411 pp. ISBN: none.

Icelandic translation of *Elvis* by Albert Goldman. (*See* The Man/Biographies.)

Source: Landsbókasafn Islands 927.8242 Pre

☆ Presley, Priscilla Beaulieu, with Sandra Harmon

Elsku Elvis! Translated by Ingibjörg Bergmundsdóttire. Reykjavik, Iceland: Fjölvi, 1990. 288 pp. ISBN: none.

Icelandic translation of *Elvis and Me.* (*See* The Man/Memoirs and Memories.)

Source: Landsbókasafn Islands 927.8242 Pre

☆ Sölvi, Sveinsson

Elvis Presley Hjá Tannlaekni: Bernskupankar Handa Vinum og Kunningjum Í Skammdeginu. Reykjavík: [hof.], 1997. 11 pp. ISBN: none.

Source: Landsbókasafn Islands 813 Sol

Italian

☆ *Elvis Presley: La Storia, Il Mito.* Manuali Rock, #19. [Italy]: Arcana, 1992. 190 pp. ISBN: 8885859844.

A catalog of Elvis Presley's songs and recordings. Compiled by L. Monari.

Source: Books in Print Italy. Vol. 2 (1997): 1894. (Library of Congress Z2341.A38a)

☆ Guralnick, Peter

Ultimo Treno per Memphis; L'Ascesa di Elvis Presley. Translated by S. Focacci. [Italy]: Tarab, 1996. 500 pp. ISBN: 8886675143.

Translation of *Last Train to Memphis.* (*See* The Man/Biographies.)

Source: Books in Print Italy. Vol. 2 (1997): 1894. (Library of Congress Z2341.A38a)

☆ Horrakh, Livio

Heartbreak Hotel/L'Hotel dei Cuori Spazzati. [Italy]: 1998. ISBN: none.

A story about the possibility of Elvis's existence in parallel universes. Homepage has an introduction in English.

Source: http://sunsite.unc.edu/elvis/italiam/italelv.html

☆ Presley, Priscilla Beaulieu, with Sandra Harmon

Elvis e Io. **Narra series, #60. Milano, (Italy): Sperling and Kupfer Editori, 1987. 276 pp. ISBN: 8820006766.**

Translation of *Elvis and Me.* (*See* The Man/Memoirs and Memories.)

Source: OCLC 16946513

☆ Ruggeri, Paolo

Elvis Presley: Vita, Canzoni, Dischi e Film. **Roma, (Italy): Lato Side, 1981. 157 pp. ISBN: none.**

A reference book covering Elvis's life, his recordings, and his motion pictures.

Source: Biblioteca Nazionale Centrale di Firenze, Italy

☆ Tatham, Dick

Elvis. **Milan, Italy: Edizione A.I.D. S.p.A., 1977. 30 pp. ISBN: none.**

Translation of *Elvis.* (*See* The Man/Biographies.)

Source: Compiler's collection

☆ *10 Propio 10.* **Italy. 16 pp.**

A magazine containing mostly color photographs of Elvis Presley.

Source: Cranor, Rosalind, Elvis Collectibles, p. 279.

☆ Zmijewsky, Boris, and Steve Zmijewsky

Elvis Presley. **(Italy): Gremese Editore, [n.d.]. 160 pp. ISBN: 870650507.**

Translation of *The Films and Career of Elvis Presley.* (*See* The Music, The Movies/ Filmography.)

Source: Books in Print Italy. Vol. 2 (1997): 1894. (Library of Congress Z2341.A38a)

Japanese

☆ Brewer-Giorgio, Gail

[Is Elvis Alive?] **1989.**

(*See* The Man/Death, Conspiracy, Sightings.)

Source: "Elvis World" Web site www.biwa.or.jp/~presley/book.htm

☆ de Barbin, Lucy, and Dary Matera

Eruvisu himitsuno ai. Translated by Kitai Ikuko (yaku). Tokyo, Japan: San'ichi Shobo, 1992. 382 pp. ISBN: none.

Translation of *Are You Lonesome Tonight?* (*See* The Man/Memoirs and Memories.)

Source: Los Angeles Public Library

Elvis Presley/Hawaii. [Japan]: Sono Journal, [1965].

Liner notes from a set of three picture disc recordings by Keibunsha Phono-Color.

Source: eBay auction item #39480259

☆ Flippo, Chet

[Graceland: The Living Legacy of Elvis Presley]. 1995. ISBN: none.

(*See* The Man/Graceland.)

Source: "Elvis World" Web site www.biwa.or.jp/~presley/book.htm

☆ *Gekido no Gendai: Henry Kissinger, Helen G. Brown and Hugh Hefner, Martin Luther King, Colonel Sanders, Muhammad Ali, Elvis Presley, Walter L. Cronkite, Andy Warhol.* People America Series, #8. Tokyo, Japan: Shueisha, 1984. 230 pp. ISBN: 4081860084.

A collection of the stories of Americans who overcame challenges to achieve success. Bibliography. Mitsuko Shimomura is listed on the OCLC entry for this book. No notation as to the role she played in its publication.

Source: OCLC 21305920

☆ Goldman, Albert

[Elvis]. 1985. ISBN: none.

(*See* The Man/Biographies.)

Source: "Elvis World" Web site www.biwa.or.jp/~presley/book/htm

☆ Guralnick, Peter

[Last Train to Memphis]. 1997. ISBN: none.

(*See* The Man/Biographies.)

Source: "Elvis World" Web site www.biwa.or.jp/~presley/book.htm

☆ Hayashi, Fuyuko

Erubisu Puresuri: nagareru ase no kirameki, kyonetsu no shinboru. Shine arubamu series, #53. Tokyo, Japan: Hoga Shoten, 1977. 192 pp. ISBN: none.

A biography published after Elvis Presley's death. English title on cover: "Elvis Presley."

Source: Los Angeles Public Library

☆ Hopkins, Jerry

[**Elvis: A Biography**]. [1973]. ISBN: 0397-7910160946.

(*See* The Man/Biographies.)

Source: Compiler's collection

☆ Hutchins, Chris, and Peter Thompson

[**Elvis Meets the Beatles**]. 1995.

(*See* The Man/Biographies.)

Source: "Elvis World" Web site www.biwa.or.jp/~presley/book.htm

☆ Koshitani, Mike M.

The Works of Elvis Presley. Japan, [1995]. 296 pp. ISBN: 4764103079.

A discography of Japanese Elvis Presley releases. Album titles are listed in Japanese and English. Color photographs and album cover reproductions.

Source: Jerry Osborne at www.jerryosborne.com.html

☆ Leviton, Jay B., and Ger J. Rijff

[**Elvis Close-Up**]. 1989. ISBN: none.

(*See* The Man/Photographs.)

Source: "Elvis World" Web site www.biwa.or.jp/~presley/book.htm

☆ Marcus, Greil

[**Dead Elvis**]. Tokyo, Japan: Kinema Junpo Sha, 1996. ISBN: none.

(*See* The Man/The Impact of Elvis.)

Source: Greil Marcus
"Elvis World" Web site www.biwa.or.jp/~presley/book.htm

☆ Marsh, Dave

[**Elvis**]. 1994.

(*See* The Man/Biographies.)

Source: "Elvis World" Web site www.biwa.or.jp/~presley/book.htm

☆ Misuhashi, Ikki

Elvis My Happiness. Japan, [1995]. ISBN: 4881696688.

A biography of Elvis as told through the sites associated with his life and career (i.e., Humes High School, Tupelo (Mississippi) fairgrounds, and Lauderdale Courts). Author's black and white photographs of these sites.

Source: Collection of Bill and Connie Burk, Memphis, TN

☆ Mohri, Yoshitsugu, and Takashi Kamata, editors

Elvis and Marilyn Immortal. Japan: Japan Art and Culture Association, 1997.

Catalog compiled for the Japanese exhibition of this show, the first visual arts examination of the societal, cultural, and religious influences of Marilyn Monroe and Elvis Presley. It ran in Japan from June 1997 to May 1998 in the cities of Hokkaido, Osaka, Takamatsu City, Sogo, and Fukuoka, and the Kumamoto Prefect. Selection and arrangement of photos is different than that of the catalog created for the American exhibitions of this show. (*See* de Paoli listing in The Phenomena/Art.)

Source: Compiler's collection

☆ Moody, Raymond A., Jr., M.D.

[Elvis After Life: Unusual Psychic Experiences Surrounding the Death of a Superstar.] 1991. ISBN: none.

(*See* The Phenomena/Psychic Elvis Experiences.)

Source: "Elvis World" Web site www.biwa.or.jp/~presley/book.htm

☆ Nakahara, Masagi

Guts Elvis. Tokyo, Japan: Eichi Shuppan, [1980]. 180 pp. ISBN: none.

The first Japanese-language biography of Elvis Presley. Black and white photographs.

Source: Los Angeles Public Library
OCLC 207025550

☆ Nash, Alanna, with Billy Smith, Marty Lacker, and Lamar Fike

[Elvis Aaron Presley: Revelations from the Memphis Mafia]. 1997. ISBN: none.

(*See* The Man/Memoirs and Memories.)

Source: "Elvis World" Web site www.biwa.or.jp/~presley/book.htm

☆ Parish, James Robert

[The Elvis Presley Scrapbook]. [Tokyo, Japan]: International Times Co., Ltd., 1977. 187 pp. ISBN: none.

Translation of *The Elvis Presley Scrapbook*. (*See* The Man/Biographies.)
Source: OCLC 6449978

☆ Presley, Priscilla Beaulieu
[**Elvis and Me**]. 1987.
(*See* The Man/Memoirs and Memories.)
Source: "Elvis World" Web site www.biwa.or.jp/~presley/book.htm

☆ Rijff, Ger
[**Faces and Stages: An Elvis Presley Time-Frame**]. 1987.
(*See* The Man/Biographies.)
Source: "Elvis World" Web site www.biwa.or.jp/~presley/book.htm

☆ Stearn, Jess, and Larry Geller
[**Elvis, His Spiritual Journey**]. 1991. ISBN: none.
Source: "Elvis World" Web site www.biwa.or.jp/~presley/book.htm

☆ Yagiu, Nozomu, and Seiko Yagiu
Eruvisu: Amerika no Seishun. Tokyo, Japan: Terebi Asahi, 1992. 237 pp. ISBN: 4881311794.

A biography of Elvis Presley for young adult readers. English translation of title, "Elvis: Symbol of Young America." Bibliographical references (p. 237).
Source: Los Angeles Public Library J 789.14 P394YA
OCLC 33787312

☆ Yancey, Becky, and Cliff Linedecker
My Life with Elvis. Tokyo, Japan: Tuttle-Mori, 1978. 315 pp. ISBN: none.
Translation of *My Life with Elvis*. (*See* The Man/Memoirs and Memories.)
Source: OCLC 7702913

Korean

☆ Yi, Hye-yong p'yonjo
Elvisu sut'ori: Rok'unrol ui Chewang. Seoul, Korea: Taewan toso, 1982. 150 pp. ISBN: none.

A biography of Elvis Presley. Photographs.
Source: Los Angeles Public Library Ko 791.43

Norwegian

☆ Canada, Lena

Til Elvis med Kjaerlig Hilsen. Translated by Finn B. Larsen. Sjoholt, Norway: Noril Forl., 1979. 160 pp. ISBN: 8272250276.

Translation of *To Elvis, with Love.* (*See* The Man/Memoirs and Memories.)

Source: Nasjonalbiblioteket (national library of Norway)

☆ Holm, Yngvar

Norway: Elvis på Kloss Hold. [Oslo, Norway]: [Forlagsentralen], 1974. 124 pp. ISBN: 8290135017.

Source: Nasjonalbiblioteket

———.

Elvis—Slik Jeg Motte Ham. Oslo, Norway: Ypsilon Fol., 1984. 112 pp. ISBN: 8299118301.

Photographs from the collection of Pal Granlunds.

Source: Nasjonalbiblioteket

☆ Lundby, Sven Erik

Elvis Presley. Gyldendals Biograhiserie for Barn og Ungdom, #11. Oslo, Norway: Gyldendal, 1985. 149 pp. ISBN: 8205148112.

A biography of Elvis Presley.

Source: Nasjonalbiblioteket

☆ Presley, Priscilla Beaulieu, with Sandra Harmon

Elvis og Jeg. Translated by Ragnar Aschim. Oslo, Norway: Mortensen, 1986. 317 pp. ISBN: 8252708498.

Translation of *Elvis and Me.* (*See* The Man/Memoirs and Memories.)

Source: Nasjonalbiblioteket

☆ Rolness, Kjetil

Elvis Presley. [Oslo, Norway]: Gyldendal, 1998. 236 pp. ISBN: 8205254370.

Source: Nasjonalbiblioteket

☆ Skar, Stein Erik

Elvis: The Concert Years, 1969–1977. Norway: The Official Elvis Presley Fan Club of Norway "Flaming Star," 1992. 192 pp. ISBN: 8299427800.

A documentary account of Elvis's concert tours from 1969 through 1977. Each concert is accompanied by press reviews, name of the jumpsuit worn by Elvis, attendance numbers, lists of musicians and backup singers, all songs performed—"including songs that he might have only sung one line of!" Final chapter covers statistical material related to Elvis and his career. "Over 200" color and black and white photographs of Elvis performing in these concerts; credited and captioned. Photographs also include more than 60 of Elvis's stage costumes. "Almost 200" press reviews. In 1997 this book was published in English. (*See* The Music, The Movies/Concerts and Television Appearances.)

Source: Nasjonalbiblioteket
Dewey Decimal 784.50092

☆ Søreide, Jan

Elvis: Død eller Levende? Bergen, Norway: Alma Mater, 1991. 131 pp. ISBN: 8241900813.

Title means "Elvis: Dead or Alive?"

Source: Nasjonalbiblioteket

☆ Thyboe, Kurt

Elvis: Myten-og Mannen. Translated by Petter Lønnebotn. [Oslo]: Føniks, [1977]. [141] pp. ISBN: 8290141998

A translation of *Elvis—Myten om Mannen.* (*See* Foreign Language Titles/Danish.)

☆ *Vi Møter Elvis: Alt om Hans Liv og Suksess.* [Fredrikstad, 1962]. 16 pp. ISBN: none.

The first Norwegian title about Elvis Presley; a biography.

Source: Nasjonalbiblioteket

☆ Wootton, Richard

Historien om Elvis Presley. Translated by Kari Gran. Elite-serien, #33. Oslo, Norway: Forlagshuset, [1982]. 189 pp. ISBN: 8251104394.

Translation of *Elvis Presley: King of Rock and Roll.* (*See* The Man/Biographies.)

Source: Nasjonalbiblioteket

☆ Yancey, Becky, and Cliff Linedecker

Mitt Liv med Elvis. Oslo, Norway: Fredhoi, [1977]. 249 pp. ISBN: 8204007051.

Translation of *My Life with Elvis.* (*See* The Man/Memoirs and Memories.)

Source: Nasjonalbiblioteket

CHAPTER 43

Polish, Portuguese, and Russian

Polish

☆ Eversz, Robert M.

Strzelilam do Elvisa. Translated by Katarzyna Kaliska. Posnan, Poland: REBIS, 1998. 220 pp. ISBN: 8371205295.

A deceptively titled Polish translation of a novel which does not relate to Elvis Presley. (*See* Eversz listing in The Rest/Deceptive Titles.)

Source: OCLC 39882853

☆ Plonski, Janusz

Elvis, Dlaczego Ja, Panir. Warszawa (Warsaw), Poland: Harp International, 1997. 196 pp. ISBN: 8390838907.

A biography of Elvis Presley emphasizing his musical roots, love for gospel music, and religious background. Also explores the possibility of an Elvis cult. Color photographs of Elvis fans and friends, as well as Elvis impersonators, taken by the author at the 1996 Elvis Tribute Week. Brief Bibliography of English-language books. The book is accompanied by the first original Polish-pressed Elvis CD.

English translation of title, "Why Me, Lord?," which is a title of one of Elvis's gospel recordings.

Source: Collection of Larry Geller, Los Angeles, CA

☆ Strzeszewski, Leszek C.

Elvis. Kontrapunkty series. Kraków, Poland: Polskie Wydawn, Muzyczne, 1986. 288 pp. ISBN: 8322402910.

A biography of Elvis Presley.

Source: OCLC 21352704

Portuguese

☆ Bruce, Mike

Elvis Presley, Um Rosto que Simboliza uma Epoca. Amadora, Portugal: Ibis, [D.L. 1962]. ISBN: none.

English-language translation of title, "Elvis Presley: A Face Which Symbolized an Epoch."

Source: Instituto de Biblioteca Nacional e do Livro (national library of Portugal)

☆ Camarinha, Isabel

Elvis. Coimbra, Portugal: Centelha, 1986. ISBN: none.

A biography of Elvis Presley.

Source: Instituto de Biblioteca Nacional e do Livro

☆ Campos, Cláudio

"Elvis Presley." *Por um Brasil Brasileiro.* São Paulo-SP, Brazil: Global Editora, 1985. ISBN: 8526000098. Pp. 97–98.

An article on the impact of Elvis Presley, reprinted from *Hora de Povo*, June 1983.

Source: Library of Congress HC187.C182 1985

☆ Carneiro, Antonio (Baelier)

Elvis Esotérico: (parte 1). Rio de Janeiro, Brazil: Achiame, 1983. 144 pp. ISBN: none.

Poetry about Elvis.

Source: Library of Congress ML420.P96 C32 1983
OCLC 1188003

———.

Epopéia Elvis: Canto 1. Rio de Janeiro, Brazil: Gráfica Sá Ltda., 1981. Unpaged. ISBN: none.

Poetry about Elvis.

Source: Yale University Library PQ9698.13 A747 E6
OCLC 38670517

☆ *Elvis. Colectivo Rock On.* Coimbra, Portugal: Fora do Texto, 1993.

A biography of Elvis Presley.

Source: Instituto de Biblioteca Nacional e do Livro

☆ *Elvis Por El Mesmo*. São Paulo, Brazil: Martin Claret, 1989. 154 pp. ISBN: none.

Black and white photographs with Portuguese text.

Source: Elvis Presley Enterprises, Inc.

☆ *Elvis Presley*. Lisboa, Portugal: Aguiar & Dias, [D.L. 1959]. ISBN: none.

The first Portuguese-language book about Elvis Presley. A biography.

Source: Instituto de Biblioteca Nacional e do Livro

☆ Roberts, Dave

Elvis Presley. Mania Club Show series. São Paulo, Brazil: Edipromo, 1995. 119 pp. ISBN: 9728068348.

Translation of *Elvis Presley*. (*See* The Man/Biographies.)

Source: Biblioteca Nazionale Centrale di Firenze, Italy

☆ Soares Júnior, José

A Morte de Elvis Presley. [Recife, Brazil]: [n.p.], 1977. 8 pp. ISBN: none.

A Brazilian chapbook of poetry relating to the death of Elvis Presley. (A "chapbook" is a small book containing ballads, poems, tales, or tracts.)

Source: OCLC 13913062

Russian

☆ Lyuty, A.

"Elvis the King—and the victim." Pravda (Special Monthly English Edition) (Dec 1987): 9.

An English-language article, from a Cold War Soviet point of view, on the tragedy of Elvis Presley's decline and what it says about American society.

Source: Compiler's collection

See Also:

In The Man/The Impact of Elvis:

Salisbury, Harrison, "Presley Records a Craze in Soviet."

In The Phenomena/Fans:

Hockstader, Lee, "Elvis Lives at Moscow Tribute."

CHAPTER 44
Spanish, Swedish, Thai, Welsh, and Yugoslavian

Spanish

☆ Ayala, Roberto Arturo

Muertes Misteriosas de la Farándula. México: Leo, 1994. 128 pp. ISBN: 96868011.

A discussion of well-known Americans and Mexicans whose deaths have resulted in controversies. Chapter on Elvis Presley.

Source: OCLC 32441899

☆ Brewer-Giorgio, Gail

Esta Vivo Elvis? Esplugues de Llobregat, Barcelona, Spain: Plaza and James, 1988. 288 pp. ISBN: 840137359X.

Translation of *Is Elvis Alive?* with audiocassette, *Grabacion Original de Elvis* (The Elvis Tape). (*See* The Man/Death, Conspiracy, Sightings.)

Source: OCLC 25528236 (book); 20972293 (sound cassette)

☆ *Canciónes: 40 Años de Rock and Roll/Elvis Presley.* Translated by Alberto Mansano. Espiral series. Madrid, Spain: Fundamentos, D.L., 1994. 127 pp. ISBN: none.

(Original title unknown. Compiler was unable to locate a copy of the original text.)

Source: Biblioteca Nacional (national library of Spain)

☆ Cuza-Malé, Belkis

Cuza-Male is the editor of *Linden Lane Magazine*, a quarterly literary journal published in Princeton, New Jersey.

Elvis: la Tumba Sin Sosiego o la Verdadera Historia de Jon Burrows. Ed. B.
   Padilla. Fort Worth, TX: Linden Lane Press, 1994. 235 pp. ISBN:
   0913827096.

A Cuban-American journalist's efforts to locate and become friends with Jon Burrows, the identity that some think was assumed by Elvis Presley after August 16, 1977. The author writes that she found him in Fort Worth, Texas, and that he agreed to tell her his story. Black and white photographs of the man she claims to be Jon Burrows. "Documents" section includes handwriting comparisons between Elvis and Jon Burrows. This book was translated into English. (*See* The Man/Death, Conspiracy, Sightings.)

Source: OCLC 31089348

☆ *El Hombre Senaldado—Historia de Elvis Presley.* Selecciónes del Reader's Digest
   series. Mexico, D.F., Mexico: Reader's Digest, 1983. 14 pp. ISBN: none.

A biographical overview article with a section on Elvis fan clubs in Britain. This article was originally published in 1975. Previously seen black and white and color photographs; captioned and credited.

Source: Compiler's collection

☆ Farren, Mick, compiler, and Pearce Marchbank

Elvis en Sus Propias Palabras. Translated by Pepa Lendínez. Madrid, Spain: Ediciones
   y Reproducciones Inernational, D.L., 1988. 123 pp. ISBN: none.

A translation of *Elvis in Quotes*. (*See* The Man/Elvis in Quotes.)

Source: Biblioteca Nacional, Spain

☆ Fraga, Gaspar

Elvis Presley. Colección Los Juglares series, #19. Madrid, Spain: Ediciones Júcar,
   1974; 1984. 168 pp. ISBN: 8433402137.

This is the first Spanish-language book about Elvis Presley. A collection of Spanish-language translations of the words to 20 of Elvis Presley's hit songs. Bibliography (pp. 167–168). Discography (pp. 163–165). Filmography (p. 166). Index.

Source: Biblioteca Nacional, Spain (1974; 1984)
Los Angeles Public Library (1974)
OCLC 6376265

☆ Godes, Patricia

Elvis Presley, Rock 'n' Roll. Todas las Músicas series. Valencia, Spain: La Máscara,
   1995. 239 pp. ISBN: 84797470949.

A biography of Elvis Presley. Bibliography (pp. 238–289).

Source: Biblioteca Nacional, Spain
OCLC 34075589

☆ Guralnick, Peter

Elvis Presley: Último Tren a Memphis. Translated by Angel Arino and Ivan Giesen. Colección Musica Zero, #6. Madrid, Spain: Celeste, 1998. 384 pp. ISBN: none.

A translation of *Last Train to Memphis.* (*See* The Man/Biographies.)

Source: Biblioteca Nacional, Spain
OCLC 40742818

☆ Jurado, Miguel

Elvis Presley. Video Rock Salvat series. Barcelona, Spain: Salvat, D.L., [1995]. 93 pp. ISBN: none.

A biography of Elvis Presley. Discography (pp. 64–93). Bibliography (p. 61).

Source: Biblioteca Nacional, Spain

☆ Labra, Victor Blanco

Blanco Labra is a Mexican journalist who has written numerous articles about Elvis Presley.

Elvis en El Bosque: (Pscicografía de Elvis Presley). México: Editorial Diana, 1989. 182 pp. ISBN: 9681306163.

An analysis of the impact of Elvis Presley. Author's candid photographs taken at Graceland, circa 1986–1987: Elvis fans at Graceland's wall and floral tributes at Elvis's grave, juxtaposed against photographs of offerings and displays at a 1986 celebration of El Dia de los Muertos (a religious holiday in the Catholic faith, relating to celebration of the dead [the Day of the Dead, November 1 and 2]). Bibliography (pp. 179–182). English translation of title, "Elvis in the Forest (Psychology of Elvis Presley)."

Source: New York Public Library JND 93-95
OCLC 9681306163

☆ Mann, Richard

Elvis. Translated by Eliseo Vila. Terrassa (Barcelona), Spain: Clie, D.L., 1980; 1984. 170 pp. ISBN: none.

Translation of *Elvis.* (*See* The Man/Biographies.)

Source: Biblioteca Nacional, Spain

☆ Martinez, Jorge, and Javier de Castro and Joaquín Luque

Elvis, El Rey en España: [Discografiá Espanola, 1956–1995). Lleida, Spain: Pages, 1996. Lieida, Spain: Milenio, 1996. 171 pp. ISBN: 8479353058.

A discography of Spanish releases of Elvis Presley's recordings from 1956 though 1995. Bibliography (p. 170).

Source: Biblioteca Nacional, Spain
OCLC 34841178

☆ Panter, Gary

Invasión de los Elvis Zombies. **Translation by Yoli and Pierre González. Colección Imposible, #6. Valencia, Spain: Arrebato Editorial, 1984. [32] pp. ISBN: 0915043017.**

Translation of *Invasion of the Elvis Zombies.* Includes English-language sound disc of the author's music. (*See* The Phenomena/Art.)

Source: Biblioteca Nacional, Spain
New York Public Library 07/31/91 CT

☆ Pérez, Adolfo

Elvis Presley. **Cinemania series, #1. Madrid, Spain: EDIMAT, [1998]. 186 pp. ISBN: none.**

A biography of Elvis Presley.

Source: Biblioteca Nacional, Spain

☆ Presley, Priscilla Beaulieu, with Sandra Harmon

Elvis y Yo. **Barcelona, Spain; Buenos Aires, Argentina: J. Vergara Editor, 1986. 294 pp. ISBN: 9501505812. México, D.F., Mexico: Lasser Press, 1986. 221 pp. ISBN: 9684583699 (Rústica).**

Translation of *Elvis and Me.* (*See* The Man/Memoirs and Memories.)

Source: Los Angeles Public Library (Lasser Press)
OCLC 15104402 (J. Vergara Editor); 15624422 (Lasser Press)

☆ Rios, Ruben Horacio

El Rey Elvis. **Buenos Aires, Argentina: Catalogos Editora, 1994. 126 pp. ISBN: 9509314986.**

A deceptively titled novel that does not relate to Elvis Presley.

Source: OCLC 32289576

☆ Sierra i Fabra, Jordi

Elvis Presley: la Historia del Rock and Roll. **Mitos Musicales series. Barcelona, Spain: Circulo de Lectores, D.L., 1986. 103 pp. ISBN: none.**

A biography of Elvis Presley.

Source: Biblioteca Nacional, Spain

☆ Tello, Antonio, and Gonzalo Otero Pizarro

Elvis, Elvis, Elvis: la Rebelión Domésticada. Bruguera Círculo series, #12. Barcelona, Spain: Bruguera, 1977. 125 pp. ISBN: 8402053254.

A biography of Elvis Presley published after his death. Incorporates United States history and music scene of the 1950s. Twenty black and white photographs; captioned. Discography (pp. 123–125). Filmography [p. 127].

Source: Los Angeles Public Library
OCLC 3841316 and 20200911

☆ Wallace, and Phillips Davis

Elvis Presley. Vidas de Cine series. Madrid, Spain: Edimat Libros: Nuevas Estructuras, 1998. 186 pp. ISBN: 8495002620.

Source: OCLC 40765075

Swedish

☆ Berglind, Sten

Elvis: Från Västerås till Memphis: En Bok Om Elvis Presley Och Det Svenska 50-talet. [Stockholm, Sweden]: Askild & Kärnekull, 1977. 185 pp. ISBN: 9170088799.

A biography of Elvis Presley, written after his death. Discography includes Swedish releases of Elvis's recordings (pp. 171–183).

Source: Swedish Union Catalog
Library of Congress ML420.P96 B5
The British Library X.439/4926
OCLC 405179

☆ Bruce, Caj (pseud.)

Boken om Elvis Presley. Stockholm, Sweden: Fröléen, 1958. 94 pp. ISBN: none.

An early Elvis Presley biography.

Source: Swedish Union Catalog

☆ Burk, Bill E.

Elvis: Tidernas Story. Translated by Bodil Svensson. Falun, Sweden: B. Wahlström, 1992. 223 pp. ISBN: 913231647X.

Translation of *Elvis Through My Eyes.* (*See* The Man/Memoirs and Memories.)

Source: Swedish Union Library L 0100 92/ 979
Memphis/Shelby County (TN) Public Library and Information Center 782.42166 P934xbu4
OCLC 26368450

☆ *Elvis! Allt om Rock-Kungen.* Stockholm, Sweden: Min Melodi, 1958. 34 pp. ISBN: none.

One of the earliest Swedish publications on Elvis. A biography with black and white photographs of Elvis and his family and friends.

Source: eBay auction item #27453757

☆ *Elvis Presley—En hyllning i ord och bild: [ett minnesalbum].* Stockholm, Sweden: Hemmets Journal, 1977. 127 pp. ISBN: none.

Translation of *Elvis Presley: A* Photoplay *Tribute.* (*See* The Rest/Souvenir Magazines.)

Source: Swedish Union Catalog

☆ Eriksson, Sven-Åke

Elvis International Tribute Week, '92, August 8–16. Falun, Sweden: [S.-A. Eriksson], 1993. 40 pp. ISBN: none.

Self-published memoir of the author's trip to Memphis, Tennessee, during the annual Elvis Tribute Week.

Source: Swedish Union Catalog

☆ Geller, Larry, and Joel Spector, with Patricia Romanowski

"If I Can Dream": Elvis egen berattelse. Translated by Solveig Rasmussen. Stockholm: B. Wahlstrom, 1990; 1991; 1997. 335 pp. ISBN: none.

Translation of *If I Can Dream.* (*See* The Man/Memoirs and Memories.)

Source: Swedish Union Catalog

☆ Goldman, Albert

Elvis. Translated by Sam J. Lundwall. Stockholm, Sweden: Norstedt, 1982. 480 pp. ISBN: none. Norstedts Faktapocket series. Stockholm: Norstedt, 1986. ISBN: none.

Translation of *Elvis.* (*See* The Man/Biographies.)

Source: Swedish Union Catalog

☆ Halegard, Roger

The EP Book—Swedish Rock and Pop Pressings, 1954–1969. [n.p.]: [n.p.], [n.d.]. ISBN: 9197189405.

Source: Kunliga Biblioteket (national library of Sweden)/Swedish Union Catalog

☆ Klinkmann, Sven-Erik

Elvis Presley: den karnevalistiske kungen. Abo, Norway: Abo Akademis Förlag, 1998. 433 pp. ISBN: 9517650086.

Library of Congress category heading: "Criticism and Interpretation." Filmography (pp. 373–374). Bibliography (pp. 371–390). Discography (pp. 391–393). Index.

Source: Kungliga Biblioteket

☆ Lundberg, Börje

Lundberg is a Swedish journalist who is also a longtime Elvis fan.

Elvis—Kung av Sverige: med illustrerad diskografi och värderingsguide. Stockholm, Sweden: Premium Publishing, 1997. 274 pp. ISBN: 919727141.

An exploration of the connections between Elvis Presley and Sweden. Discography of American, German, and Swedish releases. Filmography including Swedish press reviews. Color photographs and reproductions of record albums and movie posters, in Swedish.

Book is accompanied by an RCA/BMG compact disc of classic Sun Records hits, "Good Rockin' Tonight." This is a rare reproduction of a German release EP.

Source: Swedish Union Catalog
Kings Collectibles, Richland Hills, Ontario, Canada

☆ Presley, Priscilla Beaulieu, with Sandra Harmon

Elvis och Jag. Translated by Karin Coyet. Stockholm, Sweden: Viva, 1986. Stockholm: MånPocket, 1987. Stockholm: Wahlstrom and Widstrand, 1994. 250 pp. ISBN: none.

Translation of *Elvis and Me.* (*See* The Man/Memoirs and Memories.)

Source: Swedish Union Catalog

☆ Schöning, Ulf, compiler

Chocken: svenska fans berättar hur de upplevde Elvis död: en antologi. Söderhamn, Sweden: Gjutarbacken Information AB, 1991. [56] pp. ISBN: 9197173304.

An anthology of Swedish fans' memories of the death of Elvis Presley on August 17, 1977. Schoning was president of the Swedish Elvis fan club (Elvis Presley Svenska Beundrare Klubb) from 1969–1978. Black and white photographs of Elvis Presely record covers and magazines in Swedish.

Source: Swedish Union Library U Sv br 1992 450, X REF Tj. Biogr. G 92/523

☆ Stern, Jane, and Michael Stern

Elvis Värld. Translated by Magnus Gertten. Höganäs, Sweden: Wiken, 1988. 196 pp. ISBN: none.

Translation of *Elvis World.* (*See* The Man/Biographies.)

Source: Swedish Union Catalog

☆ Svedberg, Lennart, and Roger Ersson

Åren Med Elvis. Soderhamn, Sweden: AB Sandins Tryck. 73 pp. ISBN: none.

A year-by-year chronology of Elvis Presley's life. Never-before seen black and white photographs of Elvis in his army uniform in Paris. Filmography (p. 71). Maps of Tupelo, Mississippi, and Memphis, Tennessee, with Elvis-related sites marked.

Source: Collection of Bill and Connie Burk, Memphis, TN

☆ Tatham, Dick

Elvis: den fantastiska berattelsen om Elvis. Translated by Jeremy Pascall. [Sundbyberg], Sweden: Semic, 1977. 63 pp. ISBN: 9155216870.

Translation of *Elvis.* (*See* The Man/Biographies.)

Source: OCLC 13443393

☆ Taylor, John Alvarez

Elvis: The King Lives. Wigston, SE: Magna Books, 1990. 111 pp.

Translation of *Elvis: The King Lives.* (*See* The Man/Biographies.)

Source: Swedish Union Catalog

☆ Thyboe, Kurt

Elvis I Våra Hjärtan: [har har du hans liv]. Translated by Petter Lønnebotn. Stockholm, Sweden: Hson, [1977]. [28] pp. ISBN: none.

A biography of Elvis Presley. Translation of *Elvis: Myten On Manden.* (*See* Foreign Language Titles/Danish.)

Source: Swedish Union Catalog

Thai

☆ Kanchanawan, Nitaya, translator

[When Elvis Died]. Bangkok: National Research Council, 1987. ISBN: none.

Translation of *When Elvis Died.* (*See* The Man/Death, Conspiracy, Sightings.)

Source: Collection of Neal and Janice Gregory, Washington, D.C.

☆ Wongswang, Lek

Elvis Presley 1967. Thailand: [n.p.], [c.1967]. ISBN: none.

A hardcover songbook of Elvis Presley's music with text in English and Thai.

Source: Cranor, Rosalind, Elvis Collectibles, p. 280.

Welsh

☆ Wyn, Eirug

Elvis: Diwrnod I'r Brenin. Talybont, Wales, UK: Y Lolfa, 1996. 158 pp. ISBN: 0862433894.

A novel of Elvis Presley's life told in the form of fictionalized "interviews" with Elvis and people from his life.

Source: The British Library YK.1996.a.23473
OCLC 35665290

Yugoslavian

☆ *Fillmski Svet* (Feb 23, 1961): [24 pp.]. ISBN: none.

Cover color drawing of Elvis in his army uniform.

Source: eBay auction item #230082284

THE
REST
PART VI

CHAPTER 45
Deceptive Titles

JUST BECAUSE THE title says "Elvis," it is not necessarily so.

New York City ad agency wisdom knows that—along with "sex" and "free"—the word "Elvis" is a sure-fire interest-grabber. So it follows that authors and publishers seeking attention for their books will use "Elvis"—no matter how minor or non-existent a content role he plays. This has resulted in a confusing—and sometimes embarrassing—situation for researchers and readers.

In some instances the use of "Elvis" in the title is legitimate, even though there is no relation to the Presley one. Books by Maria Gripe of Sweden (i.e., *Elvis and His Friends*) are about the adventures of a little boy who is named Elvis by his fan mother. Her stories have nothing else to do with Elvis Presley, yet sometimes appear in Elvis bibliographies and on suggested Elvis reading lists.[1]

In other equally justifiable cases, the word "Elvis" in a title is used to conjure up an image that helps to convey the author's meaning. *Teenage Nervous Breakdown: Music and Politics in the Post-Elvis Age* by David Walley is an example.

Much of the rest smacks of shameless promotion—with content and writing that more than explain the need to flim-flam the book purchaser by luring them with the promise of an Elvis experience. Caveat Emptor!

☆　　☆　　☆　　☆

☆ Baucom, John Q., Ph.D.

The Elvis Syndrome: How to Avoid Death by Success. Minneapolis, MN: Fairview Press, 1995. 216 pp. ISBN: 0925190381.

Baucom uses Elvis Presley's name to describe a psychological syndrome in which high achievers sabotage themselves, or "Elvis" out. Elvis is not used as a case study in this book; his sole association is the syndrome's name. Baucom has written three self-help books on drugs. His degrees and accreditations are not mentioned.

Source: Los Angeles Public Library 157.3 B337

---

[1]See Opdyke listing in The Phenomena/Bibliographies; Hammontree listing in The Man/The Impact of Elvis; and Pierce, Sauers, and Torgoff listings in The Man/Reference.

☆ Caldwell, N. V., Jr.

Before Elvis. [U.S.]: J and P Publishers, 1996. ISBN: none.

The story of Elvis Presley's hometown of Tupelo, Mississippi, during the Great Depression, the tornado of 1936, and the Second World War—events that took place before Elvis became famous.

Source: Lee-Itawamba Library System, Tupelo, MS

☆ Clayton, D.

Comets: Beware the Elvis Man. [UK]: Collins Educational, 1996. ISBN: 0003230600.

In this supernatural thriller for children, a young girl is haunted by a vision of a strange man called Elvis Eyes. No other Elvis connection.

Source: www.amazon.com

☆ Darley-Doran, George

"Elvis the African." *Unesco Courier* (July–Aug 1994): 8–13; (Sept 1994): 47–49; (Oct 1994): 49–50.

A report on Elvis Johnson-Idan of Ghana, local chief of the Jukwaa.

Source: Smithsonian Institution Libraries Catalog q AS4.U8 A14X (Museum of African Art)

☆ Eversz, Robert M.

Shooting Elvis. New York: Grove Press, 1996. 217 pp. ISBN: 0802115829.

An action-thriller novel about a 1990s California young woman who unwittingly becomes involved in international terrorism. The only use of Elvis is two very minor non-plot-related mentions. This novel was translated into French, German, Hebrew, and Polish.

Source: OCLC 366968800

☆ Fagan, Kevin

Dad, I'm an Elvis Impersonator!: A Drabble Book. New York: Topper, 1991. Unpaged. ISBN: 0886876168.

Reprinted comic strips from the Drabble series (United Feature Syndicate, Inc.). None relate to Elvis Presley. The title comes from one strip in which an Elvis impersonator is used as a plot device.

Source: Library of Congress PN6728.D67 F28 1991

☆ Flinn, Mary, and George Garrett

Elvis in Oz: New Stories and Poems from the Hollins Creative Writing Program. Charlottesville, VA: University Press of Virginia, 1992. 29 pp. ISBN: 0813913810.

Short stories and poems from graduates of the Hollins (College) Creative Writing Program. The only Elvis Presley mention is a poem entitled "Elvis in Oz: Pondering Wild at Heart." It is a 38-line poem about violence and depravity, using Elvis's name three times.

Source: Library of Congress PS535.5.E45

☆ Force, John

John Force: I Saw Elvis at a Thousand Feet. Glendora, CA: National Hot Rod Association, 1995. 78 pp. ISBN: 0964911000.

Photographs and text relating to contemporary American car racing.

Source: OCLC 35018116

☆ Friedman, Kinky

Elvis, Jesus and Coca-Cola. New York: Simon and Schuster, 1993. 300 pp. ISBN: 0671869221. New York: Bantam Books, 1994, 1996. 256 pp. ISBN: 0553568914.

A detective novel in which an Elvis impersonator documentary assists in solving a murder. This is the story's sole relationship to Elvis Presley.

Source: Library of Congress PS3556.R527 E48

☆ Friesner, Esther M.

Alien Pregnant by Elvis. Daw Books, 1994. ISBN: 0886776104.

A fiction anthology featuring 36 tabloid stories written by science-fiction and fantasy writers. The story about Elvis is the title of this book.

Source: www.amazon.com

☆ Gordon, Karen Elizabeth, and Holly Johnson

My Dear Mother: Stormy, Boastful, and Tender Letters by Distinguished Sons—From Dostoevsky to Elvis. Chapel Hill, NC: Algonquin Books of Chapel Hill, 1997. 210 pp. ISBN: 156512121X.

A collection of 106 letters written by famous men to their mothers. The Elvis entry is a telegram he sent to his parents while he was performing in Houston, Texas, in the 1950s: "Hi Babies. Here's the money to pay the bills. Don't tell no one how much I sent. I will send more next week. There's a card in the mail. Love, Elvis." The authors sneeringly refer to Elvis as a "Southern Belle (with mascara) and an enfant terrible."

Source: Los Angeles Public Library NX90.M9 1997

☆ Gripe, Maria

Elvis Karlsson. (First English translation—1972); *Elvis and His Secret* (1972); *Elvis and His Friends* (1976); *Elvis! Elvis! Elvis!* (1976).

These are the English-language titles of Gripe's four books about Elvis Kaarlson—not Elvis Presley. Originally written in Swedish, they are children's stories about a fictional Swedish boy named Elvis by his Presley fan mother. Between 1972 and 1992, her "Elvis Karlsson" books were translated into Danish, English, German, and Spanish. Unfortunately, Gripe's Elvis titles are listed in a number of Elvis bibliographies and lists of Elvis suggested reading.

Source: OCLC (various numbers)

☆ Hill-Trevor, Caroline

Elvis's Experiment. Fireman Sam series, #7. London: Buzz Books, 1990. 32 pp. ISBN: 1855910322.

A children's novel. Plot: "Further adventures of Fireman Sam and his friends in Pontypandy, along with ace Firefighter Penny Morris from nearby Newton."

Source: www.amazon.com.
The British Library YK.1991.a.864

☆ Kirkman, Rick, and Jerry Scott

I Saw Elvis in My Ultrasound. Baby Blues Scrapbook, #7. Kansas City, MO: Andrew and McMeel, 1996. 127 pp. ISBN: 0836221303.

Cartoon from the comic series "Baby Blues." Only mention of Elvis Presley is in one cartoon frame in which Elvis appears on an ultrasound screen.

☆ Lee, Rob

Elvis's Big Day. Fireman Sam series, #18. London: Buzz Books, 1992. [29] pp. ISBN: 185591252X.

Children's novel about the character Fireman Sam.

Source: The British Library YK.1993.a.2526

☆ Livingston, Georgette

The Dog Named Elvis Caper. Jennifer Gray, Veterinarian, mystery series, #2. New York: Avalon Books, 1995. ISBN: 0803491492. [U.S.]: Thomas Bouregy and Co., 1996. 185 pp. ISBN: 0803491492.

Source: OCLC 33437104 (1995)

☆ Major, Andre

Hooked on Elvis. Translated by David Lobdell. Montreal, Quebec, Canada: Quadrant Editions, 1983. 90 pp. ISBN: 0864950276.

Translated from the French-language novella *La Folle d'Elvis: Nouvelles.* (*See* Foreign Language Titles/French.) The only Elvis Presley plot connection occurs when the protagonist has intercourse with a woman while Elvis recordings are played. There is a drawing of Elvis on the cover of the book.

Source: Library of Congress PQ3919.2.M282 F613 1983

☆ McEnroe, Colin

Lose Weight Through Great Sex with Celebrities (The Elvis Way). New York: Doubleday, 1989. 188 pp. ISBN: 0385248253.

A collection of the author's essays. In one, he ridicules Elvis Presley.

Source: OCLC 19723933

☆ McIngvale, Jim, with Dave White, Evin Thayer (photographer), and Pete Billac

Elvis Is on the Lot: Mattress Mac, The American Dream Lives On. Swan, TX: Swan Publishing Company, 1996. 248 pp. ISBN: 0943629209.

The secrets of how two men built the "most successful furniture store in America." (At the 1999 Guernsey Elvis Presley auction, the famous *Elvis Aloha Special* cape was purchased for display in McIngvale's store in Houston, Texas.)

Source: www.amazon.com

☆ Meyerowitz, Rick

Elvis the Bulldozer. New York: Random House, 1996. [32 pp.]. ISBN: 0679869581.

A children's story of an anthropomorphic bulldozer named Elvis.

Source: Library of Congress PZ7.M571554

☆ Nelkin, Dorothy, and M. Susan Lindee

"Elvis's DNA: The Gene as a Cultural Icon." *The Humanist* 55 (May/June 1995): 10–19.

An article adapted from the authors' book *The DNA Mystique: The Gene as a Cultural Icon*, in which they examine genetic predisposition. Elvis's genetic history, as defined by Elaine Dundy in *Elvis and Gladys* and Albert Goldman in *Elvis*, is used briefly in the introduction to this article. No other "Elvis" mention.

☆ *No More Diapers for Elvis!* [U.S.]: PPP Enterprises, 1999. ISBN: 0966439619.

A toilet-training kit that consists of a paperback book, cassette, and training chart. "Elvis" is the name of a large blue elephant that guides the child from diapers to the toilet.

Source: Jocelyn Yarbrough, Austin, TX

☆ Shankman, Sarah

The King Is Dead. ISBN: 0671734598.

A murder mystery set in the 1990s in Elvis Presley's birthplace, Tupelo, Mississippi. Elvis, his family, and Elvis-related events are mentioned in the story. The plot does not involve Elvis.

Source: Martin Luther King Library, Washington, D.C.

☆ Shepard, Steve

Elvis Hornbill: International Business Bird. New York: Henry Holt and Company, 1991. [32 pp.] ISBN: 0805016171.

A father bird pushes his bird son, Elvis Hornbill, toward a musical career, even though the little bird's interests are elsewhere. For young readers.

Source: Library of Congress PZ7.S54325 E1

☆ Sinclair, C. R.

Elvis A. Eagle: A Magical Adventure. San Francisco, CA: Scribe Press, 1996. 261 pp. ISBN: 1882833015.

Fiction for grades 6–8. The tale of an anthropomorphic bald eagle named Elvis.

Source: Library of Congress PZ7.S6114 E1 1996

☆ Spinner, Stephanie

Sing, Elvis, Sing! No. 2. in *The Weebie Zone* series. New York: Harpercrest, 1996. ISBN: 0060273372.

A children's novel about a dog named Elvis that wants to sing the national anthem at an Atlanta (Georgia) Braves baseball game.

Source: www.amazon.com

☆ Walley, David

Teenage Nervous Breakdown: Music and Politics in the Post-Elvis Age. Plenum Publishing Corp., 1998. 260 pp. ISBN: 0306458624.

The author defines the "Post-Elvis Age" as occurring after the "American Graffiti" culture of the 1950s and 1960s. He examines how this period was successfully transformed and commercially exploited. No specific mention of Elvis.

Source: Library of Congress ML3795.W19 1998

☆ Weiss, Hillary

The American Bandana: Culture on Cloth from George Washington to Elvis; History of Celebrity and Event Bandanas in America. San Francisco, CA: Chronicle Books, 1990. ISBN: 0877017832.

No mention of Elvis Presley in text. Only Elvis content: a small photograph of an Elvis scarf.

Source: Library of Congress GT605.W54 1990

☆ *Young Romance.* Feature Comics, Vol 13, #3. April–May 1960.

A romance comic book with a cover cartoon drawing of Elvis in army uniform with a young woman holding his arm, while another glowers in the background. Elvis is not identified. No article or mention about him in the text.

☆ Zolov, Eric

Refried Elvis: The Rise of the Mexican Counterculture. Berkeley, CA: University of California Press, 1999. ISBN: 0520208668/0520213141.

An examination of twentieth-century Mexican history, society, politics, government, and culture.

Source: Library of Congress F1235.Z65 1999

See Also:

In Foreign Language Titles/Spanish:

Rios, Ruben Horacio, *El Rey Elvis.*

CHAPTER 46
Elvis Impersonators

MEN AND WOMEN who impersonate Elvis Presley for fun and/or profit are an expanding, delightful segment of the world's population. The literature about them amply demonstrates this. But first, Elvis Impersonators 101.

Within the arena of those who re-create Elvis and his music, there are several distinct groupings. There are those who artistically, and eerily, reproduce the sound of Elvis's voice and music—professional recording artists such as Ronnie McDowell, Terry Mike Jeffries, and The Dempseys. They are known as "Elvis tribute artists." They do not dress and coif themselves as Elvis did and, thus, frequently entertain at Elvis Presley Enterprises, Inc.'s (EPE), events.

Other Tributarians—professionals and amateurs such as Trent Carlini—perform in Elvis costumes but stop short of referring to themselves as impersonators. The rest happily and unabashedly embrace their title of Elvis impersonator, or "E.I." Most E.I.s sanely maintain normal identities apart from Elvis—this is their hobby. But when enjoying their "E.I.-ness," they dress like Elvis, talk like Elvis, and have their own fan clubs. When discussing their impersonator passion, they refer to themselves as "doing Elvis"—as in "I have been doing Elvis for 10 years."

This merry band comes from around the world in a United Nations of races, ethnic groups, religions, ages, and nationalities. (Yes, there is the Sikh Elvis, a Navajo Elvis, and a Vietnamese Elvis.) They give The Elvis Presley Impersonators Association of America a membership rivaling that of the National Organization for Women (NOW). They hold numerous annual competitions as fierce and elaborate as Miss America and wear their winning titles with pride. (In 1999 one E.I. continued to bill himself as "Northern Virginia's Elvis Impersonator of the Year for 1994.") They are not acknowledged by EPE.

The literature about the Elvis impersonators and tribute artists, as does the literature about their idol, ranges widely: fiction to photography to biography to academic writing. Its growth and popularity indicates a strong possibility for a new sub-genre in the Elvis literature.

☆   ☆   ☆   ☆

☆ Barker, Kent, photographs, and Karin Pritikin, text

The King and I: A Little Gallery of Elvis Impersonators. San Francisco, CA: Chronicle Books, 1992. 95 pp. ISBN: 0811802442.

Photographs and brief "why I do this" statements from 42 Elvis impersonators, interviewed at the first convention of The Elvis Presley Impersonators Association of America, June 1989. Introductory essay explores the reasons behind the impersonators' interest in copying Elvis.

Source: Library of Congress ML88.P76B3 1992

☆ Bass, Holly

"Elvis Impersonator Uses Sequins and Spanish to 'Interpret' Original." *The Wall Street Journal* (Aug 16, 1994, Eastern Edition): B1.

A profile of "El Vez" (professional entertainer Robert Lopez), the Mexican-American Elvis, who considers himself an Elvis interpreter. El Vez performs full-time and records songs in which he changes the lyrics of popular Elvis songs to incorporate Mexican-American history and culture.

☆ Cabaj, Janice M. Schrantz

The Elvis Image. Smithtown, NY: Exposition Press, 1982. 184 pp. ISBN: 0682498378.

The odyssey of an Elvis fan searching for Elvis impersonators. Interviews with 27 Elvis impersonators. Interview with Lennie LaCour of Louisiana, the original "King Creole," upon whom Elvis's character in the movie *King Creole* was based. Thirty-six black and white photographs, mostly of Elvis impersonators.

Source: Library of Congress ML420.P96 C26 1982

☆ Gantos, Jack

Zip Six. Bridgehampton, NE: Bridge Works Publishing Co., 1996. 281 pp. ISBN: 1882593154.

A novel in which a young man is sent to prison where he meets an Elvis impersonator. The two team up and become an act within the prison system. The Elvis impersonating is used as a plot device to move the story forward.

Source: Library of Congress PS3557.A5297

☆ Hardy, Quentin

"This Elvis King's Royal Carriage Surely Ain't Nothin' But a Honda." *The Wall Street Journal* (Apr 20, 1993, Eastern Edition): B1.

Profile of Yasumasa Mori of Japan, the 1993 world-champion Elvis impersonator at The Sixth Annual International Elvis Impersonators Contest in Memphis, Tennessee.

☆ Henderson, William McCranor

William McCranor Henderson is a professor of English at North Carolina State University. He is also an Elvis impersonator.

I, Elvis: Confessions of a Counterfeit King. New York: Boulevard Books, 1997. 295 pp. ISBN: 1572972556.

The author's chronicle of his experiences as an Elvis impersonator, in which he reveals the culture of those who imitate Elvis.

Source: Library of Congress ML420.H372A3 1997

———.

Stark Raving Elvis. New York: Dutton, 1984. 217 pp. ISBN: 0525242643; New York: Simon and Schuster, 1987. 217 pp. ISBN: 067164081x; New York: Berkley Publishing Group, 1997. 272 pp. ISBN: 0425159353.

A novel about a factory worker and part-time Elvis impersonator who believes that Elvis has nominated him as heir apparent. He goes to Las Vegas to realize his dream.

Source: Library of Congress PS3558.E4946S7 1984; 1987

☆ Hudis, Mark A.

"Navajo Elvis Croons, KTNN Fans Swoon." *Mediaweek* 7.4 (Jan 27, 1997): 47.

Elvis impersonator Rex Redhair, known as "the Navajo Elvis."

☆ *I Am Elvis: A Guide to Elvis Impersonators.* New York: Pocket Books, 1991. 128 pp. ISBN: 0671731653.

Brief stories and photographs of 63 Elvis impersonators. Photo credits.

Source: Library of Congress ML400.I2 1991

☆ "Long Live the Kings." *People Weekly.* (July 27, 1992): 126–127.

Profile of Elvis impersonators Heimo Rock of Austria, Jacob Tobi of Israel, and others from outside of the United States.

☆ MacLeod, Joan

Toronto, Mississippi. In *Toronto, Mississippi and Jewel.* Ontario, Canada: Playwright's Canada Press, 1989. ISBN: 0887544746. Pp. 11–111.

A play about family dynamics in which the father makes his living as an Elvis impersonator. This play also appeared in *Modern Canadian Plays* (pp. 187–222). Vancouver, BC, Canada: Talonbooks, 1994. ISBN: 0889223408. OCLC 33030972.

Source: Library of Congress PS 8575.L46T67

☆ Miles, Cassie

Heartbreak Hotel. Harlequin Intrigue Edition, #237. Toronto; New York: Harlequin Books, 1993. 251 pp. ISBN: 0373222378.

A romance-mystery story in which an Elvis Presley impersonator dies in the arms of the young proprietor of a bed and breakfast nicknamed "Heartbreak Hotel." An admirer of the young woman, "armed with only sunglasses and a pink Cadillac," attempts to solve the murder in which the killer is an Elvis impersonator.

Source: Compiler's collection

☆ Pugh, Clifford

"The King Still Reigns." *Houston Chronicle* (Aug 29, 1999): F1+.

A profile of Vietnamese-American Elvis impersonator John Newinn, whose parents were Elvis fans in Vietnam in the 1950s and have carried that devotion throughout the years. (Newinn's father is president of the Asian Worldwide Elvis Fan Club.)

☆ Rubinkowski, Leslie

Impersonating Elvis. Boston: Faber and Faber, 1997. 256 pp. ISBN: 0571199119.

A well-researched study of Elvis impersonators with a variety of impersonator interviews and insights.

Source: Library of Congress ML400.R85 1997

☆ Spigel, Lynn

"Communicating with the Dead: Elvis as Medium." *Camera Obscura: A Journal of Feminism and Film Theory* 23. (May 1990): 177–204.

A scholarly study of the cultural impact and popularity of Elvis Presley impersonators. Spigel suggests that there is a need among Elvis fans to keep his memory alive because he "serves as means through which to reinvent their personal history and to participate in a community of shared cultural values." Commentary on Elvis impersonations' similarities to religious rites. Examination of impersonating and gender behaviors. Transcript of a dialogue between Elvis's first drummer, D.J. Fontana, and Elvis impersonator Dave Carlson about the media obsession with those who re-create Elvis. Notes with biographical references.

Source: Library of Congress PN 1993.9 W6C28

☆ Travis, Jessica

The Groom Wore Blue Suede Shoes. Silhouette Romance (1143). New York: Silhouette Books, 1996. 185 pp. ISBN: 037319143X.

A romance novel set in Memphis, Tennessee, telling of a single mother's romantic adventure with an Elvis Presley look-alike.

Source: OCLC 34104306

☆ Willard, Fred

Elvis and Juliet. 1994.

A comedy play about a soon-to-be married couple with interfering families. The young man's father is a professional Elvis impersonator in Las Vegas. Performed in Los Angeles, California, in May 1994.

Source: Los Angeles 39 (May 1994): 169.

CHAPTER 47
Souvenir Magazines

"I DON'T PAY any attention to movie magazines. I don't read 'em because they're all junk! . . . In my case, they make it up."
—Elvis, Las Vegas Hilton performance, September 2, 1974

Souvenir Magazines: The 1950s

1956

☆ *The Amazing Elvis Presley*. Fans' Star Library no. 2. New York: Renal, 1956. 46 pp. London: Amalgamated Press, 1958. 62 pp.

One of the earliest Elvis Presley biographies. Published in magazine format. Autobiographical articles. More than 100 black and white photos of Elvis, exclusive to this publication. Discography (p. [33]).

Source: University of California, Los Angeles ML420.P96 A489 1956
The British Library X.989/28378.(2.)
OCLC 1051685

☆ *Elvis and Jimmy*. 1956.

A double-feature magazine about the career of Elvis Presley and the death of actor James Dean.

Source: eBay auction item #51262451

☆ *Elvis Photo Album*. New York: The Girlfriend–The Boyfriend Publishing Corporation, 1956. 65 pp.

From the front cover: "Elvis's life story complete in 125 new photos." Eighteen articles on Elvis's life and career as of 1956. Black and white candid and publicity photographs.

Source: OCLC 12679216

☆ *Elvis Presley in Hollywood. Movieland Magazine.* New York: Gib Publishing Corporation, 1956. [64] pp.

Articles and approximately 70 photographs focusing on Elvis's first motion picture, *Love Me Tender.*

Source: OCLC 27637682

☆ *Official Elvis Presley Album.* New York: [A Centurion Publication], 1956.

Contents: "100 New Presley Pictures," "The Loves of Elvis Presley," "What Made Elvis Sing?," "The Real Elvis Presley," "Will Success Spoil Elvis?"

Source: eBay auction item #107076978

☆ *Rock 'n' Roll Battlers: Elvis Presley, Pat Boone, Bill Haley.* Ed. Marvin H. Adler. New York: Ideal Publishing Company, 1956. 65 pp.

Magazine devoted to the three entertainers in the title. Elvis Presley (33 pp.), Pat Boone (13 pp.), Bill Haley (9 pp.). Elvis section consists of 13 articles about his life and future. Black and white photographs.

Source: Library of Congress ML400.A3

☆ "Special Issue on Elvis Presley." *Hep Cat's Review* (Vol. 1, Issue No. 1) (Feb 1956). 66 pp.

The cover advertises "Exclusive Photos—Intimate Secrets." Black and white photographs of Elvis with family, fans, and friends.

Source: eBay auction item #64357486

1957

☆ *Elvis, His Loves and Marriage.* New York: The Girlfriend–The Boyfriend Corporation, 1957.

Biographical articles, as well as those speculating on who might become his wife. (He met Priscilla Beaulieu in 1959 and married her in 1967.) Black and white and color photos.

Source: Cranor, Rosalind, Elvis Collectibles, p. 224

☆ *Elvis Presley: The Intimate Story.* New York: Filoso Publications, 1957.

General biographical articles, Elvis statistics, and a comparison article discussing Elvis, Marlon Brando, and James Dean.

Source: David Neale, Elvis in Print, www.geocities.com/SunsetStrip/8200/books.html

☆ *Rock 'n' Roll Rivals.* New York: Ideal Publishing Corporation, 1957.

This magazine spotlights the biggest teenage celebrities of 1957: Elvis Presley, Tab Hunter, Pat Boone, and Tommy Sands.

Source: eBay auction item #652022275

☆ *16 Magazine* (July 1957).

Articles comparing Elvis Presley and Calypso recording artist Harry Belafonte.

Source: Cotten, The Elvis Catalog, p. 45.

☆ "Special Issue on Elvis Presley." *Cool* (Apr 1957).

"The bumps and grinds controversy from $40 to $10,000 per week" (cover). Singer Al Hibbler offers his tips for Elvis. Elvis-related articles on Pat Boone and disc jockey Alan Freed.

☆ *Tommy Sands vs. Belafonte and Elvis.* New York: The Girlfriend–The Boyfriend Corporation, 1957. 66 pp.

Speculation on "Will challenger Tommy Sands, new singing idol, knock off the crowns of the Calypso champion and the King of Rock 'n' roll?"

Source: OCLC 37564303

1958

☆ *Elvis in the Army.* Fan's Star Library No. 13. London: Amalgamated, 1959. New York: Ideal Corporation, 1959. 63 pp.

Ten articles and approximately 150 black and white photographs relating to Elvis Presley while he was in Germany, 1958–1960.

Source: OCLC 20702186

☆ *Elvis Presley Picture Parade Album.* London: Stanley Illkin, [1958]. 23 pp.

Source: The British Library 7902.c.16

See Also:

In The Man/Biographies:

Elvis Presley: His Complete Life Story in Words with More Than 100 Pictures.
Gehman, Richard, *Elvis Presley: Hero or Heel?*
Johnson, Robert, *Elvis Presley Speaks!*

In The Man/Photographs:

Concert Tour Albums/Folios.

Souvenir Magazines: The 1960s

1960:

☆ *Elvis: The King Returns.* New York: Edgar Publishing Corporation, 1960.

A magazine celebrating Elvis Presley's return from army service. Articles include speculation about his romantic life. Two Hundred "intimate" photographs, "many never seen before."

Source: eBay auction item #65198688

☆ [*Movie Teen's* Elvis Yearbook]. 1960.

"100 pages of photos and articles" about Elvis Presley.

Source: eBay auction item #31755143

☆ *The Music Reporter* (Mar 7,1960). 28 pp.

Issue devoted to Elvis Presley's return to the United States after his U.S. military service. Includes advertisements welcoming Elvis.

Source: eBay auction item #27469275

☆ *The Three Loves of Elvis Presley: The True Story Behind the Presley Legend.* Ed. Robert Holmes. London: Charles Buchon's Publications, 1960. 63 pp. ISBN: none.

Stories about Elvis Presley's parents, his romantic interests, fans, and life in the army. Published during the latter part of Elvis's military service.

Source: The British Library 10892.i.5
OCLC 3918520

☆ *TV Radio Mirror* (March 1960). 84 pp.

An issue with predominantly Elvis stories and pictures. Features a "Will Elvis still be King?" ballot for readers to express their opinion as to whether Elvis or one of nine others is the "King of Rock and Roll."

1961

☆ *Movie Teen Illustrated Special Elvis Issue* (Aug 1961). 50 pp.

Biographical articles and photographs. From the front cover: "Is Bobby Vee another Elvis?"

Source: eBay auction item #27499400

1965

☆ *Elvis vs. The Beatles.* Beatles Round the World No. 3. [US]: Summer 1965. 66 pp.

An examination of who is the most popular. More than 100 black and white and color photographs of Elvis and the Beatles.

Source: eBay auction item #43686594

1969

☆ *Elvis and Tom.* Ed. Micki Siegel. New York: Macfadden-Bartell/Bartell Media Corporation, 1969. 70 pp.

A magazine comparing Elvis Presley with Tom Jones. Nine articles on Tom Jones' life and career; eleven on Elvis's. All photographs are black and white.

Source: *Bowling Green State University ML420.P96 E48x*
OCLC 5797888

Souvenir Magazines: 1970–August 16, 1977

1970

☆ *TV Record Superstars: Glen Campbell and Elvis Presley.* 1970.

Biographical articles on Glen Campbell and Elvis Presley, and lyrics to some of their songs.

Source: *eBay auction item #26213790*

1971

☆ *Elvis: 1971 Presley Album.* A *Screen Stars* Special Edition. [U.S.]: Magazine Management Company, Inc., 1971. 74 pp.

Articles about Elvis and Priscilla, Elvis and a paternity suit, and anecdotes about his life "never told before." Photographs of his wedding, concerts, and scenes from all of his motion pictures.

Source: *eBay auction item #39490129*

1974

☆ *Elvis—21 Years a King.* New York: New English Library, 1974.

Source: *Cranor, Rosaliind, Elvis Collectibles, p. 273*

1975

☆ *The Elvis Years.* Ed. Nick Cohn. *Circus Magazine*'s Pinups No. 3. New York: Circus Enterprises, 1975. 69 pp.

From the cover: "Elvis: the idol revealed by words and photos." Color photograph centerfold.

Source: *Bowling Green State University, Ohio ML 420.P96 C6x*

☆ *Elvis Yesterday . . . Today: His Untold Life Story.* A Collector's Issue. No. 1. Ed. Seli Groves. New York: Ideal Publishing Corporation, 1975. 74 pp.

From the front cover: "Elvis talks about all his women; His life with Priscilla: what is still right with their love!; Inside Graceland's locked gates; On tour with Elvis; The miracle diet that keeps him alive; His favorite photos of daughter Lisa." Color pull-out centerfold. Biographical articles.

Source: *New York Public Library MFL + n.c. 2347 No. 10*

1976

☆ *Elvis: The Hollywood Years* #2. Ed. Seli Groves. New York: Ideal Publishing Corp., 1976. 74 pp.

Articles on scandals and anecdotes about Elvis in Hollywood.

Source: Book Baron, Anaheim, CA

Souvenir Magazines: August 17, 1977–1979

1977

☆ *Elvis Forever! A Salute to "The King."* Bronx, New York: RPM Sales Corp., 1977. 64 pp.

From the front cover: "Exclusive! 32 Full Color Pages of Never Before Seen Pictures of Elvis in Concert; Elvis's Life From a $35 a Week Truck Driver to The King of Rock!; His Fans Remember . . ." Photographs are from the collection of Elvis's friends Phil and Lenora Engledrum.

Source: Memphis/Shelby County (TN) Public Library and Information Center, Memphis, TN [MPHS RM] 784.80924 P93xe

☆ *Elvis the King.* Pasadena, CA: Wellington-Hall Publishers, Inc., 1977. 64 pp.

Thirteen articles, spanning his life, death, films, and music, as well as his charities, fan memoirs, and celebrity Elvis fans. Black and white photographs; most are not attributed. "Cover and some photographs" attributed to *Memphis Flash*, a Paul Lichter publication.

Source: The Margaret Herrick Library, Academy of Motion Picture Arts and Sciences

☆ *"Elvis the King Remembered." Country Music* (Dec 1977).

A special edition of *Country Music* magazine devoted to the memory of Elvis Presley.

☆ *Elvis Memories Forever.* New York: Lorelei Publishing Co., 1977. 90 pp.

From the front cover: "Book-length Life Story; All His Records; All His Movies; How Elvis Predicted His Own Death; The Two Fans Who Died with Him"; and "The Truth About His Drugs, the Guns, the Violence." Color fold-out poster.

Source: The Mississippi Valley Collection, The University of Memphis

☆ *Elvis Presley Memorial Edition.* (Collectors issue #3). Ed. Seli Groves. New York: Ideal Publishing Corporation, 1977. 82 pp.

Articles about Elvis's charity work, love interests, mother, as well as fan memoirs and a tribute to his mother, Gladys Love Presley. Presidential statement made by President Jimmy Carter upon the death of Elvis. Color and black and white photographs; some misidentified.

Source: Sarah Wilkinson, Cambridge, MA

☆ *Elvis Presley: A* Photoplay *Tribute.* Edited by the staff of *Photoplay.* New York: Cadrant Enterprises, Inc., 1977. 128 pp.

Published after Elvis Presley's death. Fifteen articles focusing on his life, from his marriage to Priscilla Presley to his death. Memoirs from fellow cast members, girlfriends, as well as a *Photoplay* reporter who knew him. Entertainers Jack Lord and Rick Nelson are interviewed about their Elvis memories. Black and white and color candid and publicity photographs; credited. Photograph of Elvis and Rudy Vallee singing a duet.

This souvenir magazine was translated into Swedish as *Elvis Presley—En hyllning i ord och bild: [ett minnesalbum]*; also translated into Finnish. (*See* Foreign Language Titles/Finnish, Swedish.) It was also published in English in hardcover. (*See* The Man/Biographies.)

Source: Los Angeles Public Library 789.14 P934 Ph 1977
Library of Congress ML420 P96

☆ *Elvis: A Tribute to the King of Rock 'n' Roll: Remembering You.* London: IPC Magazines, 1977. 62 pp.

Introduction by Todd Slaughter of the Official Elvis Presely Fan Club of Great Britain. Biographical articles. Album and 45-rpm discography. Chronological film listings. Black and white candid and publicity photographs and color motion picture stills; none credited.

(See also Remembering You, A Tribute to the King of Rock 'n' Roll in this section.)

Source: New York Public Library JNF 78-157
The British Library X.435/585
OCLC 3965888

☆ *The Life and Death of Elvis Presley.* Ed. Diane Masters Watson. New York: Manor Books, Inc, 1977. [78] pp.

Thirteen biographical articles, comprising a chronological overview of his life and career. Elvis commentary by five entertainers: Cher, Pat Boone, Carl Wilson, Frank Sinatra, and Roy Orbison. Black and white and color candids and publicity still photographs; captioned but not credited.

Source: The Margaret Herrick Library, Academy of Motion Picture Arts and Sciences

☆ *The Only Woman Elvis Ever Loved: Priscilla, Her Story.* Ed. Jennifer Davis. New York: Stories, Layouts and Press, Inc., 1977. 98 pp.

Articles covering Priscilla Presley's relationship with Elvis, from its beginning through the end of their marriage. One first-person article attributed to Priscilla Presley. Seven pull-out posters. Predominantly color photographs; some misidentified.

Source: Sarah Wilkinson, Cambridge, MA

☆ Osborne, Jerry, and Randall Jones

The Complete Elvis. New York: Funky Angel, 1977. 100 pp.

This magazine contains the lists—as of 1977—of Elvis's songs, albums, singles, interviews, movies, television appearances, concerts, illegal bootleg recordings, foreign releases, and unreleased songs. It also lists "Songs Others Sang About The King." Color reproductions of album covers, record labels, and "many never before published" photographs.

Magazine has a "King-Size" pull-out poster of Elvis.

(According to Osborne,[1] he selected the publishing company's name, Funky Angel, because it was Elvis-related. Elvis referred to the decorative angels on the walls of the Las Vegas Hilton Hotel Showroom, where he frequently performed, as "funky angels.")

This magazine was part of the Platinum Presents series, which issued eight magazines between 1978 and 1980. (*See* listings later in this chapter.)

Source: Memphis/Shelby County (TN) Public Library and Information Center

☆ *Remember Me, Elvis the King.* New York: Stories, Layouts & Press, Inc., 1977. 98 pp.

From the front cover: "Complete photos and stories of his life and career" and "The official Presley family personal story." Color and black and white photographs.

Source: Sarah Wilkinson, Cambridge, MA

☆ *Remembering You, A Tribute to the King of Rock 'n' Roll.*

See listing for Elvis: A Tribute to the King of Rock 'n' Roll: Remembering You earlier in this section.

Source: OCLC 20740382

☆ *Song Hits Magazine's Tribute to Elvis.* Derby, CT: Charlton Publications, 1977.

Words to more than 100 of Elvis Presley's hit songs. A biographical article. Elvis poems. From front cover: "How he changed music"; "Memories of the King in Concert"; "Photos from his Movies."

Source: Compiler's collection

☆ *A Tribute to the King, Elvis.* Ed. Harry Schreiner. New York: Cousins, 1977. 70 pp.

Black and white photographs. Biographical articles. Color centerfold. Color photographs on front and back. Pull-out color poster.

Source: The Margaret Herrick Library, Academy of Motion Picture Arts and Sciences OCLC 28120222

☆ *The World of Elvis.* Ed. John Thomas Church. New York: Kingsbridge Communications, Ltd., 1977. [64] pp.

"A photographic story of the idol of our times, Elvis Presley," published after Elvis's death. Biography of Elvis. Black and white photos, primarily previously seen. Color pull-out poster.

Source: Compiler's collection

[1]Interview, Feb 16, 1999.

See also:

In Appendix II:

Crawdaddy (Nov 1977).

1978

☆ *Always Elvis: Elvis's Father and the Colonel Present Official Reunion.* [Las Vegas, NV]: [n.p.], Sept 8, 1978. [20 pp.].

Official souvenir program from the "Always Elvis" celebration at the Las Vegas Hilton Pavilion, at which Carl Romanelli's Elvis statue was unveiled. Memorial poem to Elvis, bylined by Colonel Tom Parker.

Source: The Mississippi Valley Collection, The University of Memphis
OCLC 7702977

☆ *Elvis Anniversary Photo Album No. 1.* Ed. Sharon Gintzler. New York: Sterling Magazines, Inc., 1978. 66 pp.

Chiefly photographs, black and white and color of Elvis's life and career. Most not captioned. None are credited.

Source: Compiler's collection

☆ *Elvis Close-Up.* 1978.

More than 100 photographs from the private collection of a major Elvis fan club.

Source: eBay auction item #49474485

☆ *Elvis: Collector's Issue 1978.* Nashville, TN: Green Valley Record Store, 1978. 63 pp.

Biographical articles. "Hundreds of rare photographs." Black and white and color photographs. Comes with a 33⅓-rpm record, "Elvis Live," inserted in issue. Steve Goldstein, publisher.

Source: Bowling Green State University, Bowling Green, OH ML 420.P96 E46x
OCLC 3641452

☆ *Elvis: The Legend Lives On!* Ed. Todd Slaughter. Vol. 1, No. 1. New York: Marvel Comics Group, 1978. 50 pp.

The official memorial publication of the Official Elvis Presley Fan Club—worldwide (OEPFC). Five articles include a year-by-year summary of his career, 1956–1977, a discography of his music, and other articles about Elvis's army service and the Official Elvis Presley Fan Club. A message to European Elvis fans from his father, Vernon Presley. Black and white and color photographs from the Club's collection; captioned but not credited. (This is a separate publication from the Personality Parade Elvis: The Legend Lives On series.)

Source: Compiler's collection

☆ *Elvis: The Legend Still Lives On.* New York: Manor Books, Inc., 1978. 90 pp.

Articles include "Inside Graceland: The Changes, The Future." Others are biographical in nature, as well as a filmography, discography, and interviews with Elvis impersonators. Color and black and white photographs. One pull-out poster. (This is a separate publication from the Personality Parade Elvis: The Legend Lives On series.)

Source: eBay auction item #27908793

☆ *Elvis Lives! A Galaxy Special.* London: Galaxy Publications, Ltd., 1978. 49 pp.

Biographical articles. Chiefly black and white and color photographs.

Source: Dewey Decimal 784/.092/4 18
Trinity College, Dublin, Ireland PX-13-630
OCLC 16421435

☆ *Elvis: One Year Later.* Dell #041089. New York: Dell, 1978.

From the front cover: "Told for the first time: the mystery girl in Elvis's life." Never-before published color and black and white photographs of Elvis Presley. Color fold-out poster.

Source: eBay auction item #26262315

☆ *The Films of Elvis Presley.* New York: Platinum Publications, Inc., 1978.

A filmography of Elvis's 33 films, including cast lists, stories, and songs.

This magazine was part of the Platinum Presents series, which issued eight magazines between 1978 and 1980. (*See* listings later in this chapter.)

Source: eBay auction item #26709665

☆ Hit Parade *Presents The Immortal Elvis.* No. 102. Derby, CT: Charlton Publications, Summer 1978. 50 pp.

Mostly biographical articles. Others include the memoirs of Felton Jarvis, Elvis's record producer from 1966 to 1977. Words to more than 50 of Elvis Presley's recorded songs.

Source: Baron Books, Anaheim, CA

☆ *King Elvis.* Platinum Presents series. New York: Whizbang Publications, 1978.

A photographic tribute to Elvis Presley. Four fold-out color posters; four fold-out black and white posters. This magazine was part of the Platinum Presents series, which issued eight magazines between 1978 and 1980. (*See* listings later in this chapter.)

Source: Jerry Osborne, Port Townsend, WA

☆ Modern Screen *Presents Elvis Presley.* New York: Sterling Magazines, 1978. 66 pp.

This was the first of the Modern Screen Presents series. (*See* Souvenir Magazine Series section later in this chapter.)

Source: The University of Mississippi Archives

☆ 16 Magazine *Presents Elvis: August 16th, A Time to Remember*. Issue 1, No. 1. [U.S.]: Kia-Ora Publications, 1978. 84 pp.

From front cover: "His story from childhood to superstardom to tragedy."
    Color and black and white photographs; "rare photographs from the private archives of *16 Magazine*." Three-page color fold-out poster.

Source: The Margaret Herrick Library, Academy of Motion Picture Arts and Sciences

1979

☆ *The Elvis Years, 1956–1977*. The Elvis Years, Vol. 1. New York: Sterling Magazines, 1979.

Includes 42 stories from other magazines, mostly biographical in nature or memoirs of Elvis's friends, coworkers, and relatives. Color fold-out poster.

Source: eBay auction item #26862660

☆ *King Elvis Lives*. Ed. John Raffa. Scarsdale, NY: RPM Sales Corp., 1979. 72 pp.

Mostly black and white photographs covering Elvis's life and an article on fans grieving after his death. Color fold-out poster. Twenty-one pages of color photographs.

Source: Book Baron, Anaheim, CA

☆ *King Elvis*. Vol. II of Platinum Presents series. New York: Platinum Publications, 1979.

A pictorial history of Elvis Presley's life and career. Eight fold-out posters. (*See* Souvenir Magazine Series section later in this chapter.)

Source: Jerry Osborne, Port Townsend, WA

☆ *The Love of Elvis*. Platinum Presents series. New York: Platinum Publishing, Inc., 1979. 82 pp.

Magazine about Elvis memorabilia. Thirteen articles. Section of black and white candids. Q and A article with Elvis memorabilia collector Jean Brown of Houston, Texas. Elvis memorabilia expert Jerry Osborne served as consultant to this publication. (*See* Souvenir Magazine Series section later in this chapter.)

Source: The Margaret Herrick Library, Academy of Motion Pictures Arts and Sciences
OCLC 5304528

☆ Modern Screen *Presents: The Family Years*. 1979. 66 pp.

From the front cover: "Elvis's personal photographer shares his most intimate private pictures of The King"; "Guests at Elvis's wedding remember his happiest moment"; "Lisa Marie: She changed El's life forever." Twenty-five color photographs. This is magazine number 4 in the *Modern Screen* Section Presents Elvis: His Life Story series. (*See* Souvenir Magazine Series section later in this chapter.)

Source: eBay auction item #292278718

☆ Modern Screen *Presents: The Hollywood Years*. 1979. 66 pp.

From the front cover: "Memories of 'The King' by those who knew him best"; "Every movie Elvis ever made"; "The way Elvis lived at his fabulous Hollywood Hideaway"; "Starlets he dated." Twenty-eight color photographs. This is magazine number three in the *Modern Screen* Presents Elvis: His Life Story series. (*See* Souvenir Magazine Series section later in this chapter.)

Source: eBay auction item #29282878

☆ Teen Talk *Presents Elvis: The Memory Lingers On*. Ed. Harvey Godolphin. Van Nuys, CA: Calny Communication, 1979. 70 pp.

Mostly black and white photographs; none captioned or credited. Brief biography of Elvis Presley. Color pull-out poster.

Source: Compiler's collection

Souvenir Magazines: 1980–The Present

☆ *The Complete Elvis Almanac: The Legend That Will Never Die*. [U.S.]: Ideal Publishing, Co., 1981. 80 pp.

Color and black and white photographs, some "never before seen." Biographical articles.

Source: eBay auction item #57776937

☆ *Elvis*. Ed. David Hanna. New York: Mag Mania, 1987. 50 pp.

Biographical articles and photographs.

Source: The Margaret Herrick Library, Academy of Motion Picture Arts and Sciences

☆ *The Elvis Cover-Up*. Platinum Presents series. New York: Platinum Publications, Inc., 1980. 66 pp.

Fifteen articles relating to Elvis Presley's death and its controversy. From the front cover: "The true story of how Elvis Presley died—and the attempt to silence it"; "All the Facts about Elvis's life and death which couldn't be told until now!" Eight-page pull-out poster. Elvis memorabilia and discography experts and authors Jerry Osborne and Bruce Hamilton were consultants to this publication. (*See* Souvenir Magazines Series section later in this chapter.)

Source: Compiler's collection

☆ *Elvis Diary*. Platinum Presents series. New York: Platinum Presents, Inc., [1980].

The 25-year diary kept by an Elvis fan. From the front cover: "100s of photos and personal mementos."

Source: Jerry Osborne, Port Townsend, WA

☆ *Elvis: 15th Anniversary Collector's Edition*. Darwin Lamb, publisher. Thousand Oaks, CA: EIF Press, Aug 1992. Unpaged.

"A personal look back over the past with comments and memories by close friends, fellow musicians, singers, and fans." Quotes about Elvis, each with a black and white photo, from friends and fellow musicians. Eighteen candid fan photos. Quotes about Elvis from entertainers and celebrities, including President Ronald Reagan; not cited or sourced. Fan memorial essays and poems.

Source: Library of Congress ML420 P96 E373

☆ *Elvis: 50th Birthday Album.* (Superstar Special No. 14.) 1984. 83 pp.

From the front cover: "Relive the most intimate romantic moments in his life! Elvis . . . the loving father, tender lover, leading man, the man and his music." Forty color photographs and 27 "framed pinups."

Source: eBay auction item #27483083

☆ *Elvis, Just for You: A Special Goldmine Anthology.* Ed. Trey Foerster. Iola, WI: Krause Publications, 1987. 129 pp.

Includes Elvis Presley discographies and lists of Elvis's films. Bibliography [pp. 111–120]. Black and white and color photographs.

Source: Bowling Green State University Library ML420.P96 E465
OCLC 18568867

☆ *Elvis The King Lives On!* David Zentner, publisher. 1987. 96 pp.

From the front cover: "Complete guide to all his movies and records." Approximately 100 black and white and color photographs. Includes a biographical article and one on his charitable works. Two pull-out posters.

Source: eBay auction item #27924091

☆ *Elvis Lives On!* Ed. Jeff Dawson. New York: Proud Publishing Company, July 1992. 98 pp.

Eighteen articles, spanning Elvis's life and career, female co-stars, automobiles, airplanes, music, and films. Interview with Elvis's original drummer, D. J. Fontana. Approximately 200 photographs, black and white and color. Includes a pull-out color poster.

Source: Compiler's collection

☆ *Elvis: Luxury Lifestyles of the Rich and Fabulous.* Issue No. 8. Montreal, Canada: Globe International Inc., (Aug 27, 1997). 58 pp.

Sixteen articles, covering Elvis's love interests, relationship with his mother and stepmother, his death, the Memphis Mafia, two women who claim to be his "love children," and his genetic relationship with Oprah Winfrey. Articles also include Elvis collectibles and an Elvis word puzzle. "100s of rare photos"; mostly color.

Source: Compiler's collection

☆ *Elvis on His 60th Birthday: A Celebration in Pictures. Life* Collector's Edition. (Jan 1995). 96 pp.

Special-edition magazine from the publishers of *Life* magazine. A photographic biography with month-by-month description of Elvis's career and brief overview of his life before 1954. Interviews with Sam Phillips, Dr. George Nichopoulos, Red West, D. J. Fontana, Scotty Moore, Linda Thompson, and Mary Jenkins (Elvis's cook). Black and white and color photographs; captioned and credited.

Source: Compiler's collection
OCLC 32325932

☆ *Elvis Returns: His Life, Films and Music.* 1990.

Eight "giant" fold-out pin-ups.

Source: Compiler's collection

☆ *Elvis: A Saint or Sinner?* [U.S.]: *Photo Screen* magazine. Vol. 15. No. 3, (Sept 1980).

Interviews with Priscilla Presley, Dee Presley, Ginger Alden, Linda Thompson, and Red and Sonny West.

Source: eBay auction items #27018016 and #27022613.

☆ *Elvis: The Tenderest Lover.* New York: Sterling Magazines, 1982.

From the front cover: "25 beautiful love stories—reprinted for the first time"; and "Special photo scrapbook."

Source: eBay auction item #32284806

☆ *Elvis: 10th Anniversary Salute to the Greatest Entertainer of Them All.* Celebrity Spotlight Series No. 1. New York: Jack/Howard Publishing Company, Inc., 1987. 108 pp.

Articles on each of Elvis Presley's 31 Hollywood feature films. Discography list. An Elvis as-told-to story about his early years, "The Road to Growing Up." Articles on the beginning of his career, his army years, Graceland, and his family.

Source: Memphis/Shelby County (TN) Public Library and Information Center

☆ *Elvis 2000.* Ed. Claire Singer. [U.S.]: Starlog Group, Inc., 2000. ISBN: 0880130032.

A biography magazine, with previously told stories about Elvis, including the incorrect stories about the Mississippi/Alabama Dairy Fair second prize and the first record for his mother's birthday. Color and black and white photographs, some with captions.

Source: David Neale, Elvis in Print, www.geocities.com/SunsetStrip/8200/books

☆ *Exclusively Elvis.* Ed. JoAnn Sardo. Vol. 1, Nos. 1–4. Derby, CT: M L S Publications, Inc., 1987.

No. 1: Spring 1987. Includes a list of geographic sites associated with Elvis.

No. 2: Summer 1987, 82 pp. Nine articles on Elvis fan clubs, collectibles, wife and daughter, films, history of Graceland, and Elvis's relatives. Photos from the collections of Jim Curtin, Jerry Osborne, and Rogers and Cowan.

No. 3: Fall 1987. Focus on Elvis's concert years, with the words to his concert songs.

No. 4: Winter 1987. This issue was called *Song Hits Magazine Presents Elvis.* Special Collectors series. Christmas-related Elvis articles, including words to Elvis's Christmas songs.
Exclusively Elvis was published only four times. Its photographs came from the collection of Elvis author Jim Curtin.

Source: Vols. 1 and 2: Compiler's collection; Vols. 3 and 4: Jim Curtin

☆ *King Elvis.* Vol. III. Platinum Presents series. New York: Platinum Publications, [1980].

A pictorial tribute to Elvis Presley. Eight fold-out color and black and white posters. From the front cover: "Colorful Collection of Elvis's Greatest Close-Ups."

Source: Jerry Osborne, Port Townsend, WA

☆ *L.F.P. Presents Elvis an American Legend.* Beverly Hills, CA: L.F.P., 1995.

Pictures and text about Elvis Presley's life and career. Text by respected Elvis memorabilia dealer Jim Hannaford.

Source: Michael Ochs Archives, Venice, CA

☆ Modern Screen *Presents: Elvis Photo Album.* 1980. 66 pp.

Articles include "His Favorite Girl (Lisa Marie)" "A Devoted Son" "Elvis: In Concert." Mostly black and white photographs. This magazine is number five in the *Modern Screen* Presents Elvis: His Life Story series. (*See* Souvenir Magazine Series section later in this chapter.)

Source: The University of Mississippi

☆ Movie Mirror *Presents Elvis '97.* Ed. Michael Greenblatt. Vol. 39, No. 2. New York: Sterling/Macfadden Partnership, Inc., Fall 1997. 90 pp.

Interviews with Elvis's friends: Jerry Schilling, Janelle McComb, Ronnie McDowell, backup singers The Jordanaires, and Todd Morgan of Elvis Presley Enterprises, Inc. Reviews of 1997 CD releases. Six pull-out posters.

Source: Compiler's collection

☆ *Personality Parade* Elvis: The Legend Lives On series titles. (*See* Souvenir Magazine Series section later in this chapter.)

☆ *Song Hits Magazine Presents Elvis.* Derby, CT: Charlton Publications, 1985.

From front cover: "Words to over 100 of Elvis's greatest hits"; "Never before published Army photos"; "The Springsteen Connection"; "Priscilla: still a survivor"; "Elvis: win a date contest revisited"; "The last concert/1977"; "Album updates and video reviews."

Source: eBay auction item #30676225

☆ *Song Hits Magazine's Tribute to Elvis.* Derby, CT: Charlton Publications, 1977; 1982.

At least two magazines with this title were issued. 1977: Words to over 100 of Elvis Presley's hit songs. A biographical article. Elvis poems. From front cover: "How he changed music"; "Memories of the King in Concert"; "Photos from his Movies." 1982: Words to "over 100 of Elvis's greatest hits." "Up-to-the-Minute Look at His Women."

Source: Compiler's collection (1977); eBay auction item #31757358 (1982)

☆ Star Legend Magazine *Presents Elvis: 10th Anniversary Tribute.* Grace and Joseph Catalano, writers and designers. [U.S.]: Ultra Communications, 1987.

From front cover: "Hundreds of Never Before Seen Photos"; "Rare Elvis Collectibles"; "His Haunting Last Days"; "Elvis Says Goodbye to His Mother"; "Why Priscilla had to leave Elvis." Thirty-five color photographs.

Source: eBay auction item #268626600

☆ Teen Bag *Presents The Elvis Story.* "Produced by the editors of *Movieland,* and Peter Martin, editor of *The Elvis Yearbook.*" Adam Lopez, publisher. New York: Histrionic Publishing Company, 1981. 82 pp.

Reprints of 300 photographs and stories from the files of *Movieland* and *TV Time* magazines. Articles include "The Inside Story of Elvis's Wedding" and "Elvis and God." Two pull-out color posters.

Source: Once Upon a Book, Long Beach, CA

☆ *A Tribute to Elvis: 20th Anniversary Special.* [U.S.]: C To C Publishing, Inc., 1997. 98 pp.

"An unauthorized biography." Thirteen articles covering Elvis's life, Elvis Web sites, Elvis's love interests. Article on Elvis collectibles by Steve Templeton, Elvis memorabilia expert. Memories of Elvis's cousin Donna Presley Early. Seven pull-out posters.

Source: Compiler's collection

☆ *20th Anniversary of Elvis.* Ed. David Hanna. New York: Starlog Group, Inc., 1997. 70 pp. ISBN: 0934551200.

Fourteen articles covering Elvis's life. Mostly color photos. Eight pull-out posters.

Source: Compiler's collection

Souvenir Magazine Series

☆ *Elvis Yearbook.* [Tiburon, CA]: The Hound Dog News (1960-1977). 89pp. (1960)

A series published from 1960 to 1977. (Compiler was unable to verify the existence of issues other than those published in 1960, 1963, 1972, and 1977.) The 1960 issue was republished as a "Special Collectors Edition" after Elvis's death. Articles in the 1960 issue: "A Bride for Elvis"; "In Elvis's Arms"; "His Great Movies"; "The Great Elvis Records." Black and white photographs (candids and stills) and cartoons.

Source: Publisher's address: Box 375, Tiburon, CA 94920
Compiler's collection (1960)
Dallas (TX) Public Library 784.0924 P934 (1977)

Modern Screen Presents Elvis: His Life Story series.

☆ No. 1: Modern Screen *Presents Elvis Presley.* New York: Sterling Magazines, 1979. 66 pp.

Source: University of Mississippi Archives
OCLC 5393146

☆ No. 2: *The Romantic Years.* 1979. 66 pp.

☆ No. 3: *The Hollywood Years.* 1979. 66 pp.

From the front cover: "Memories of 'The King' by those who knew him best"; "Every movie Elvis ever made"; "The way Elvis lived at his fabulous Hollywood Hideaway"; "Starlets he dated"; "His private parties." Twenty-eight color photographs.

Source: eBay auction item #29282878

☆ No. 4: *The Family Years.* 1979. 66 pp.

From the front cover: "Elvis's personal photographer shares his most intimate private pictures of The King"; "Guests at Elvis's wedding remember his happiest moment"; "Lisa Marie—She changed El's life forever." Twenty-five color photographs.

Source: eBay auction item #292278718

☆ No. 5: *Elvis Photo Album.* 1980.

Articles include "His Favorite Girl (Lisa Marie); "A Devoted Son"; "Elvis: In Concert." Mostly black and white photographs.

Source: The University of Mississippi

☆ *Personality Parade* Elvis: The Legend Lives On series

At least six souvenir magazines were published by S. J. Publications in 1981 in the *Personality Parade* Elvis: The Legend Lives On series. The compiler located three of them. (Two unrelated souvenir magazines were published with similar titles: *Elvis: The Legend Lives*

On! [Marvel Comics Group, 1978] and *Elvis: The Legend Still Lives On* [Manor Books, Inc., 1978]. They are listed by title elsewhere in this section.)

☆ Personality Parade *Elvis: The Legend Lives On.* Vol. 2, No. 2. Ed. Kelly Doge. Fort Lee, NJ: S. J. Publications, Inc., Spring 1981. 66 pp.

Thirteen articles, most focusing on subjects such as Elvis Presley's alleged "secret marriage," a psychic's attempt to reach him postmortem, his romantic interests, "16-Year-Old Claims: Elvis Left Me $4 Million in a Secret Will," and "The Stories They Don't Want You to Know About Elvis." Publicity stills black and white photographs; none credited.

Source: Compiler's collection

☆ Personality Parade *Elvis: The Legend Lives On.* Vol. 2, No. 3. Ed. Kelly Doge. Fort Lee, NJ: S. J. Publications, Inc., May 1981. 66 pp.

Ten articles, including a comparative between Elvis and John Lennon. Others focus on Elvis's charitable works and impact, including "Elvis the Man Who Helped Bring Peace to the World"; "Helping the Terminally Ill to Live Again"; "Elvis: The Man Who Made Widows Forget"; "Used His Magic Power to Make the Poor Rich"; "Miners in Trouble: Elvis to the Rescue." Black and white photographs; none credited.

Source: Compiler's collection

☆ Personality Parade *Elvis: The Legend Lives On.* Vol. 2, No. 6. (Elvis's Lost Brother and His Family). Fort Lee, NJ: S. J. Publications, Inc., 1981. 64 pp.

A focus on Elvis Presley's alleged "lost brother," Dr. John Presley. Black and white photographs.

Source: Compiler's collection

Photoplay Presents a Tribute to Elvis Presley series. New York: Cadrant Enterprises, Inc., 1978–19??

1st Anniversary Memorial Edition. 1978.

2nd Anniversary Memorial Edition. 1979.

3rd Anniversary Memorial Edition. 1980.

4th Anniversary Memorial Edition. 1981.

From the front cover: "Over 200 pictures; over 50 color portraits." Diary article by an Elvis fan. Career and personal life milestones.

Source: eBay auction item #30289114

☆ Photoplay *Presents a Tribute to the Films of Elvis: 5th Anniversary Memorial Edition.* Eds. Amanda Murrah Matetsky and Rana Arons. New York: Cadrant Enterprises, Inc., 1982. 98 pp.

From the front cover: "Complete cast lists, stories and songs from every movie Elvis ever made." Background commentary on each film. Color reproductions of some movie posters, pin-ups, and lobby cards.

Source: eBay auction item #30288190

☆ *6th Anniversary Memorial Edition.* New York: Cadrant Enterprise, Inc., 1983. 98 pp.

From front cover: "100s of photos and color portraits; exclusive last interview; giant color fold-out."

Source: eBay auction item #30290278

Platinum Presents series. New York: Platinum Productions, 1978–1980

Eight magazines were issued in this series. Full details of each are available by individual title in this section. Elvis memorabilia and discography experts Jerry Osborne and Bruce Hamilton were consultants to this series.

No. 1: The Complete Elvis. 1978. (Listed in this chapter under Osborne, Jerry, and Randall Jones. It was published by Osborne's company, Funky Angel.)

No. 2: King Elvis. 1978.

No. 3: King Elvis. Vol. II, 1979.

No. 4: The Love of Elvis.

No. 5: The Films of Elvis Presley, 1978.

No. 6: Elvis Diary, 1979.

No. 7: *King Elvis.* Vol. III, 19??

No. 8: The Elvis Cover-Up. 1980.

Source: Jerry Osborne

CHAPTER 48
Unverified Titles

As WITH ANY large body of literature covering a significant period of time, the Elvis literature contains titles that are difficult to verify. Many are self-published or distributed by small publishers, limited attempts at books that were later expanded and republished, or were presold before publication, then never issued. Confusion reigns!

Thus, the compiler's rule for all entries in *Infinite Elvis* was to confirm a title's existence and contents through first-hand examination or a listing in a reputable library catalog. Even with these resources, the compiler was not always able to verify a title's reality, contents, and/or Elvis-relatedness. Therefore, these titles are listed separately. For a passionate and adventurous reader willing to track them to the ends of the earth, they may indeed turn out to be a treasure. Let us know when you strike gold.

☆　　☆　　☆　　☆

☆ Adler, Elizabeth

The Death of Elvis. New York: Dell Publishing Company, 1992. ISBN: 0440210488.

Source: www.amazon.com

☆ Baker, Cleo C.

No Hall of Fame. 1978. ISBN: none.

According to Elvis bibliographer Maria Columbus, this is a novel about football with minimal reference to Elvis Presley.

Source: Worth/Tamerius, Elvis: His Life From A to Z, *p. 140*

☆ Burns, C. L.

Elvis Aaron Presley. FL: Exposition Press of Florida, 1985. ISBN: 0682401854.

Source: www.amazon.com

☆ Culver, Eric

Journal of the Elvis Presley Tours, or How a Musician Came to Be Treated Like Royalty. Unpublished manuscript, 1976.

Source: Hammontree, Elvis Presley—A Bio-Biography, *1985*

☆ Danker, Frederick E.

Elvis Presley: The Sun Years. Boston: self-published, 1979. 14 leaves. ISBN: none.

Source: OCLC 5472843

☆ Fortas, Alan

My Friend Elvis. Nashville, TN: [n.p.], 1987. ISBN: none.

Source: Pierce, The Ultimate Elvis: Elvis Presley Day By Day, *p. 515. (See The Man/Reference.)*

☆ Gale, Pamela

Elvis in My Words. [UK]: Braunton Merlin, 1982. ISBN: none.

Poetry.

Source: The British Library X.439/11962

☆ Gilmore, Brian

Elvis Presley Is Alive and Well and Living in Harlem. Chicago: Third World Press, 1992. 78 pp. ISBN: 0883780046.

Poetry.

Source: New York Public Library
OCLC 27394110

☆ Hamilton, Gord, and Elvis Aaron Presley, Jr.

Elvis Jr. A Lost Son! 1996.

The story of an entertainer who claims to be the child of Elvis Presley and actress, now Mother Superior, Dolores Hart.

Source: www.island.net/~netsail/elvjr

☆ Hamm, Jim, and Steve Allely (illustrator)

Ishi and Elvis. Azle, TX: Bois D'Arc Press, 1997. 153 pp. ISBN: 0964574101.

Listed under Library of Congress subject heading: "Deer hunting—Texas." Hamm's previous titles include *Bows and Arrows of the Native Americans.*

Source: Smithsonian Institution, The National Museum of the American Indian, Suitland, MD; SK301.H19 1995

☆ Jones, Gwen

"I Was Elvis's Secret Woman" and Other Poems. Wire Poetry Booklet series, #10. Knaphill [UK]: Aramby, 1996. ISBN: 190046251.

Poetry.

Source: The British Library YK.1996.1.15040

☆ MacDougall, Carl

Elvis Is Dead. Glasgow, Scotland: Mariscat Press, 1986. 142 pp. ISBN: 0946588090.

Call numbers for this book at the University of Virginia library indicate that it is a work of fiction: PR6063.A177.

Source: OCLC 0946588090

☆ Matthews, Neal

Elvis: A Golden Tribute. Memphis, TN: 1985.

Possibly the work of Elvis's backup singer Neal Matthews.

Source: Worth, Elvis: His Life from A to Z, p. 53

☆ Pierson, Jean

Elvis, the Living Legend: and Other Heartwarming Poems. New York: Carlton Press, 1983. 31 pp. ISBN: 0806220031.

Poetry.

Source: OCLC 11040718

☆ Reed, Jeremy

The Sun King: Elvis—The Second Coming. Creation Books, 1997. ISBN: 1871592771.

Source: www.barnesandnoble.com

☆ Ridgway, Bill

Guitar Man: Elvis's Story. Blackwell Education, 1989. ISBN: 0631903658.

Listed under Library of Congress subject heading: "Fiction in English, 1945—Texts."

Source: The British Library

☆ Shamayyim-Nartoomid, Maia, with Simeon Nartoomid

Blue Star Love—From Elvis's Heart to Yours. ISBN: none.

A pre-publication announcement regarding this book was made on the Web site www.bluestarlove.org. This will be a depiction of "the good-hearted, religious, and spiritual nature of this soul [Elvis] who so graced the Earth with love during his life . . . ."

☆ Stanley, William Job, Jr.

Elvis: His Last Tour. ISBN: none. **(Author was unable to locate any information about this book other than as follows.)**

This book is listed in both Patricia Jobe Pierce's *Ultimate Elvis* (p. 374) and Steven Opdyke's *The Printed Elvis* (p. 7) as being authored by Billy Stanley. According to Stanley, he has not written a book with this title, and his name is "William Jabe Stanley, Jr."[1] The compiler was unable to find any evidence that this book exists.

☆ Tomlinson, Roger

Elvis Presley. Great Britain, 1973. ISBN: none.

Source: Pierce, The Ultimate Elvis, *p. 544*

☆ Vollmer, Karl

Dreams of Elvis: Poems and Songs. London: Adelphi, 1993. ISBN: 1856541061.

Source: The British Library

☆ Wesseler, Marlis

Elvis Unplugged. [Ottawa, Canada]: Oberon Press, 1998. 123 pp. ISBN: 0778010937.

Source: OCLC 40254449

---

[1]Correspondence, Nov 13, 1999.

APPENDIX I:
Elvis Literature Firsts

First Newspaper Interview—July 28, 1954

"Front Row: Overnight Sensation" by Edwin Howard, *Memphis Press-Scimitar.*

First Record Review—August 7, 1954

"That's All Right (Mama)." *Billboard.*

First Magazine Article—June 1955

"Sun's Newest Star." *Cowboy Song.*

First Elvis Songbook—1956

The Elvis Presley Album of Jukebox Favorites No. 1, Hill and Range.

First Mainstream Media Magazine—April 30, 1956

"A Howling Hillbilly Success." *Life.*

First Mainstream Newsmagazine Article(s)—May 14, 1956

"Hillbilly on a Pedestal." *Newsweek.*
"Teener's Hero." *Time.*

First Biography—1956

Elvis Speaks! by Robert Johnson.

First Dissertation/Thesis—1958

"The Symbolic Significance of the Elvis Presley Phenomenon to Teen-Age Females: A Study in Hero Worship Through the Media of Popular Singers and Song" by Ruth Pearl Granetz.

First Books About Elvis

De Vecchi, *Die Tonende Story: Elvis Presley*, 1959 (hardback).
Gregory, James, *The Elvis Presley Story*, 1960 (paperback).
Levy, *Operation Elvis*, 1960 (hardback).

First Congressional Record Statement—Jan 9, 1958

"Divinations, Soothsayings, and Young Mr. Tompkins." U.S. Senator Mike Monroney
(D-OK).

First Assessment of Elvis's Impact—1975

"Elvis: Presliad" by Greil Marcus (in *Mystery Train*).

First Discography—1974

Twenty Years of Elvis: The Elvis Session File by Martin Hawkins and Colin Escott.

First Filmography—1975

Elvis in Hollywood by Paul Lichter.

First Photograph Book—1974

Elvis . . . Through My Lens by Sean Shaver.

First Professional Journal Articles—1957, 1958

"Elvis Presley and Art" by Al Hurwitz.
"A Note on the Analysis of the 'Elvis Presley' Phenomenon" by Martin Reiser.

First Academic Assessment—1979

Elvis: Images and Fancies. Ed. Jac L. Tharpe. (Also published as the Fall 1979 issue of *The Southern Journal*.)

APPENDIX II:
Important Articles

The Man/Biographies

Booth, Stanley, "Hound Dog to the Manor Born." *Esquire.*
Brock, Van K., "Images of Elvis, the South and America." Ed. Jac L. Tharpe, *Elvis: Images and Fancies.*
Pratt, Linda Ray, "Elvis, or the Ironies of Southern Identity." Ed. Jac L. Tharpe, *Elvis: Images and Fancies.*

The Man/Death, Conspiracy, Sightings

Baker, Jackson, "Elvis: End of an Era." *City of Memphis.*
Bangs, Lester, "Where Were You When Elvis Died?" *Village Voice.*
Booth, Stanley, "The King Is Dead! Hang the Doctor!" Ed. Martin Torgoff, *The Complete Elvis.*

The Man/The Impact of Elvis

Sharnik, John, "The War of the Generations." *House and Garden.*
Tosches, Nick, "Elvis in Death." *Goldmine.*
Wilson, Charles Reagan, "The Iconography of Elvis." *Judgement and Grace in Dixie: Southern Faiths from Faulkner to Elvis.*

The Man/Major Articles

Blount, Roy, Jr., "Elvis!" *Esquire.*
Marcus, Greil, "Elvis: Presliad." *Mystery Train: Images of America in Rock 'n' Roll Music.*
Pleasants, Henry, "Elvis Presley." *The Great American Popular Singers.*
Wolfe, Charles, "Presley and the Gospel Tradition." Ed. Jac L. Tharpe, *Elvis: Images and Fancies.*

The Man/Memoirs and Memories
Presley, Vernon, "Elvis." *Good Housekeeping.*

Crawdaddy (Nov 1977)

The Elvis Presley memorial issue of this rock music magazine contains thoughtful and creative analyses of Elvis's impact. Important articles from this issue are listed below, along with *The Infinite Elvis* chapters in which they appear.

"Down at the End of Lonely Street," by Robert Ward. (The Phenomena/Fans)
"Front Page Blues: From Snap Shots to Cheap Shots. Watching the Media Cover the King," by Jerry Lazar. (The Man/Death, Conspiracy, Sightings)
"Too Soon the Hero," by Abbie Hoffman. (The Man/The Impact of Elvis)
"What Price Glory? Peddling the Relics of Royalty," by Fred Schruers. (The Phenomena/Collecting Elvis)
[*Crawdaddy* (Feb 1978): 6. Letters to the editor in response to the November 1997 issue. Writers are fans expressing their feelings about Elvis.]

Life Magazine
"A Howling Hillbilly Success," Apr 30, 1956. (The Phenomena/Fans)
"Elvis—A Different Kind of Idol," Aug 27, 1956. (The Man/Photographs)

Look Magazine
"He Can't Be . . . but He Is," Aug 7, 1956. (The Music, The Movies/Elvis's Influence on Music)
"The Great Elvis Presley Industry," Nov 13, 1956. (The Phenomena/Business and Finance)

Rolling Stone 248 (Sept 22, 1977): 38–84.

Some of the best writing about Elvis Presley and his impact are in this memorial section. The *Infinite Elvis* chapters in which entries for these articles appear are in parentheses.
"All the King's Splendor: A Performance," by Jon Landau. (The Music, The Movies/Concerts and Television Appearances)
"Big Boss Man: Working with the King," by Robert Palmer. (The Man/Memoirs and Memories)
"Blue Hawaii: Elvis Spirit and Flesh," by Greil Marcus. (The Man/Death, Conspiracy, Sightings)
"Broken Heart for Sale: Elvis's Bodyguards Talk About 'What Happened,' " by Ben Fong-Torres. (The Man/Memoirs and Memories)
"Echoes of Love: Elvis's Friends Remember," edited by Peter Herbst and Dave Marsh. (The Man/Memoirs and Memories)
"Fame and Fortune: The Life and Times of Colonel Tom Parker," by Jerry Hopkins. (The Man/Biographies)

"Funeral in Memphis: Love Me Tender," by Chet Flippo. (The Man/Death, Conspiracy, Sightings)

"Graceland: A Family Mourns," by Caroline Kennedy. (The Man/Death, Conspiracy, Sightings) (Note: Caroline Kennedy is the daughter of the late President and Mrs. John F. Kennedy. At the time of Elvis Presley's death, she was working as an intern at *Rolling Stone*.)

"How Great Thou Art: Elvis in the Promised Land," by Dave Marsh. (The Phenomena/Religion)

"Tupelo: From a Jack to a King," by Joe Klein. (The Man/Death, Conspiracy, Sightings)

TV Guide

The omnipresent television-schedule magazine that remains a staple of family rooms across America, *TV Guide* ran its first articles about Elvis Presley at the same time he was grabbing national attention on *The Ed Sullivan Show*. These were published as a three-part series in the fall of 1956, beginning the week of his initial *Ed Sullivan* appearance.

"Elvis Presley Part 1: The People Who Know Say He Does Have Talent," Sept 8–14, 1956. (The Man/Memoirs and Memories)

"Elvis Presley Part 2: The Folks He Left Behind Him," Sept 22–28, 1956. (The Man/Memoirs and Memories)

"Elvis Presley Part 3: He Tells How the Little Wiggle Grew," Sept 29–Oct 5, 1956. (The Man/Elvis in Quotes)

APPENDIX III:
Compiler's Sources

Academic Libraries

Bodleian Library Oxford University, UK; Bowling Green State University, OH; Brown University; Georgetown University; Harvard University; The University of California; The University of Memphis; The University of Mississippi; The University of Oxford, UK; The University of Southern California.

Bookstores and Others

(These are stores in which the compiler was allowed to conduct in-depth research.)
Baron Books, Anaheim, CA; Bluff Park Rare Books, Long Beach, CA; Booth Hardware Store, Tupelo, MS; Larry Edmunds Bookshop, Hollywood, CA; Loose Ends, Memphis, TN; Second Story Books, Washington, DC; Wooden Indian, Memphis, TN.

Catalogues of Books

Australian Books in Print
Bibliography of Discographies: Vol. 3 Popular Music (Bowker, 1983)
Bowker's Forthcoming in Print
Bowker's Books in Print
Catalogo dei Libri Italiani in Commercio
Les Livres Disponibles
Verzeichnis Lieferbarer Bucher
Whittaker's Books in Print

Databases

ATLA Religion Database; American History and Life; Arts and Humanities

Citation Index; ProQuest Abstracts.
FirstSearch (OCLC) databases: ArticleFirst, Book Review Digest, Books in Print, Business
and Industry, Contemporary Women's Issues, Dissertation Abstracts, Education Abstracts,
FactSearch, Facts on File, Humanities Abstracts, Newspaper Abstracts, PapersFirst, Period-
ical Abstracts, Reader's Guide Abstracts, RILM Abstracts of Music Literature, Social Sciences
Abstracts, Sociology Abstracts, World Cat.

Elvis Author Verification Interviews/Correspondence

Cathy Bei; Gail Brewer-Giorgio; Christopher Brown; Bill E. Burk; Jim Curtin; Susan Doll,
Ph.D.; Sara Erwin; Joe Esposito; D. J. Fontana; Larry Geller; Neal Gregory; Peter Guralnick; Betty Harper; Ira Jones; Nitaya Kanchanawan; Marty Lacker; Paul Lichter; Sue Manzu-
nak; Greil Marcus; Peter Nelson; Sean O'Neal; Jerry Osborne; Sean Shaver; Billy Stanley;
William Taylor, Ph.D.; Joe Tunzi; David Wall, Ph.D.; Sue Wiegert; Bill Yancey.

National Libraries

Austria; Belgium; Czech Republic; Denmark; Finland; France; Germany; Greece; Hungary;
Iceland; Ireland; Italy; Republic of Macedonia; The Netherlands; Norway; Poland; Portugal; Russia; Spain; Sweden; Switzerland; United Kingdom.

On-line Sources

"Elvis in Print" www.geocities.com/SunsetStrip/8200/books.html
"Elvis World/Elvis Presley Book List" (Japanese) www.biwa.or.jp/~presley/book.htm
"All the King's Things" (eBay) www.eBay.com/elvis.htm
www.amazon.com
www.arbooks.com/elvisp.html
www.barnesandnoble.com
www.bookpages.co.uk.html
www.bookshop.co.uk.html

Private Elvis Literature Collections

Bill E. and Connie Burk, TN; Maria Columbus, CA; Neal and Janice Gregory, DC; Paul
and Elvis Aaron MacLeod, MS; Paul Milliot, France; David Neale, Belgium; Richard Palmer,
England; Pam Presley-Wood, GA; Robin Rosaaen, CA; James Rubel, NY; Marilyn Tunstall,
CA; Marjorie Montgomery Wilkinson, CA; Sarah Wilkinson, MA.

Public, Corporate, and Foundation Libraries

American Film Institute; Atlanta Public Library, GA; Canterbury (UK) Public Library;
Cleveland Public Library, OH; Elvis Presley Enterprises, Inc.; The Margaret Herrick Library,
Academy of Motion Picture Arts and Sciences; Library of Congress; Long Beach Public
Library, CA; Los Angeles Public Library; Martin Luther King, Jr. Library, Washington, D.C.;
Memphis/Shelby County Public Library and Information Center, TN; Nashville Public
Library, TN; New York Public Library.

Acknowledgments

SEVERAL INDIVIDUALS FORMED the backbone of my effort. To them, I owe my deepest thanks for their unwavering support in bringing this book to completion. Few writers have been as fortunate as I to have sustainers such as these: my husband, Steve Hinds, my agent, Nina Graybill, my editor, Yuval Taylor, Dr. Hallie Lovett, and two of the truest friends with whom anyone could be blessed: Marjorie Montgomery Wilkinson and Bill E. Burk. And Greil Marcus, whose generous and gracious efforts on my behalf propelled this project to reality.

Then there are those whose kind words, suggestions, indulgences, and generosity added immeasurably to the richness and range of this compilation.

At the Library of Congress: Thomas Mann, Ph.D., and the Readers Services Reference Librarian staffs in the Main Reading Room and the Performing Arts Reading Room, without whose continuing support and professionalism this work could not have been completed.

At Elvis Presley Enterprises, Inc.: Jack Soden, Patsy Anderson, LaVonn Gaw, Angie Hadley, Greg Howell, Todd Morgan.

In California: Ross and Elizabeth Hancock, Tim and Diana Williams, Ted and Peter Gray, Louise Montgomery, Larry Geller, Helen Ashford, Michael Ochs, Robin Rosaaen, Joe Hix and Penny of Bluff Park Books, Maria Columbus, Joe Esposito, Marilyn Tunstall, Kristine Krueger, Sue Wiegert.

In Tennessee: Connie Burk, Patricia LaPointe of the Memphis/Shelby County Library and Information Center, Sharon Parker, Marty Lacker, Jimmy of Loose Ends Gift Shop, Roy and Linda Wells.

In Mississippi: George H. and C. L. Booth II of Tupelo's Booth Hardware Store, and Paul and Elvis Aaron MacLeod.

Elsewhere: Sarah Wilkinson, Arthur "Jack" Bullock, Pamela Presley-Wood, Jerry Osborne, Guy Sterling of the *Newark* [NJ] *Star-Ledger*, Silvia Adam, Jim Hannaford, William Ferris, Ph.D., of the National Endowment for the Humanities, the staff of Washington, DC's Second Story Books, Neal and Janice Gregory, and Thomas Ruehle, M.D., and Sabrina Mackey-Ruehle, "Uncle" David Neale, Paul Milliot, and Richard Palmer.

In Academia: Thomas Verich, Ph.D., and Naomi of The University of Mississippi Archives; The University of Memphis Special Collections, McWherter Library (Ed Frank, Sharon Banker, Jim Cole, Jim Montegue); Yura Ivanov, Massachusetts Institute of Technology; David Wall, Ph.D., University of Leeds, UK; Joel Williamson, Ph.D., University of North Carolina; Peter Nazareth, Ph.D., The University of Iowa; Charles Wolfe, Ph.D., East Tennessee State University; John Bakke, Ph.D., The University of Memphis; Vernon Chadwick, Ph.D., Oxford, MS.

Index